Astronomy, Calendar, and Science in Imperial China

Kang Lu

CONTENTS

LIST OF FIGURES

LIST OF TABLES

ABSTRACT

This dissertation is a series of textual case studies on nontraditional sources for *li* 曆 "calendro-astronomy" circa 250 B.C. – A.D. 250: (1) the silk manuscript guide to military planetary astronomy/astrology *Wuxing zhan* 五星占 (168 B.C.), (2) excavated calendars and state *li* manuals, and (3) the *Jin shu*'s 晉書 (A.D. 648) record of the debate surrounding a failed attempt at *li* reform in A.D. 226. This selection affords us a number of unique cross sections through the astral sciences. Balancing transmitted with excavated sources, I emphasize *realia* and their perspective on era technical knowledge, the formats in which it was produced and consumed, and its transmission and practice beyond an elite court-centered context. In addition to the three elements of *li*—calendrics, eclipses, and planetary astronomy—my selection draws together the broad array of astral sciences, exploring distinctions in genre, sociology, and epistemology between, for example, mathematical astronomy, hemerology, and omenology, and the (tortuous) processes by which knowledge moved between them. Each chapter also juxtaposes the normative descriptions of manual literature with products of practice—tables, calendars, and test results—to reflect upon the distance between them and, thus, the limitations of the former as historical testimony. Across these cross sections, my study focuses on the question of empiricism and progress. I foreground these topics *not* because they define twentieth-century notions of science but because, as I argue, they define early imperial notions of *li*—a point that our twenty-first-century aversion to positivism and Whig history tends to obscure. To this end, I catalog the conceptual vocabulary of observation and testing, submit empirical practices to mathematical and sociological analysis, and, most importantly, explore the formation and function of legend—the histories of science that early imperial actors wrote and recounted in their own day.

This study is divided into four chapters. Chapter 1 provides a history and sociology of the astral sciences in the Han, covering the sources, legend, and conceptual vocabulary of *li*, the history of Han *li* from the perspective of both ideas and institutional reforms, and a survey of participants' backgrounds, motivations, education, and epistemological contentions. Chapter

2 examines how the *Wuxing zhan* manuscript segregates and conflates distinct genres of planetary models, then sketches the subsequent history of these genres, showing how, despite seemingly opposite orientations to reality, actors gradually rewrote and reassessed (crude) hemerology-based omenological (*tianwen* 天文) models through the lens of progress made in mathematical (*li*) ones. Chapter 3 explores a similar gulf that opened between astronomy and calendrics in this period, as well as the gulf between imperial ideology—within which the calendar was the premier symbol of cosmo-ritual dominion—and the actualities of the production, distribution, and use of calendars in a manuscript culture. Lastly, Chapter 4 analyzes the two epistemic strategies at the center of (the *Jin shu*'s take on) the circa A.D. 226 court debate on *li*: the quantitative determination of "tightness" (accuracy) of lunisolar and planetary models through competitive testing, and the contestation of claims through the deployment of precedence from the history of the field.

INTRODUCTION

孟子曰：「天下之言性也，則故而已矣。故者以利為本。所惡於智者，為其鑿也。如智者若禹之行水也，則無惡於智矣。禹之行水也，行其所無事也。如智者亦行其所無事，則智亦大矣。天之高也，星辰之遠也，苟求其故，千歲之日至，可坐而致也。」

Mencius said, "The discussion of (human) nature in this world comes down to nothing more than [reasoning from] precedence (*gu* 故). The problem with precedent-reasoning (*gu*), however, is that it is so often rooted in ad hoc advantage, and what we detest most in wise men is their habit of chiseling their way through. If, by contrast, wise men could act as Yu did in guiding the flood waters, then there would be nothing to detest in them. Yu guided the water by imposing nothing on it that was against its natural tendency. If wise men too could just act without imposition, then great indeed would their wisdom be. Whatever the heights of the heavens and the distance of the stars, if one seeks out former instances (*gu*), one can calculate the solstices of a thousand years hence without stirring from one's seat" (*Mencius* IVB.26; tr. modified from D. C. Lau).

There is something special about astronomy. For Mencius (c. 382–300 B.C.) it was the perfect metaphor for knowledge—*scientia*—done right. The danger of philosophy, on the other hand, was its tendency to devolve into self-referential systems of meaning—*gu* 故 "phenomena," "precedence," "stories," and/or "reasons"—and come unmoored from human experience. After all, the betterment of the human condition was the prime directive of philosophy, and the exigencies of Mencius' day were no less dire than those that Yu the

Great 大禹 had braved. In Yu's day, humanity clung precariously to high ground, drowned, displaced, and ravaged to the brink of extinction by the hellish caprice of its rivers. And so too, like the failure of a dyke, did the fall of the Zhou 周 heartland in 771 B.C. unleash a catastrophic torrent across the land—a torrent of bloodshed that left Mencius' world a fetid wasteland of moral and cultural decay. Diligence and selflessness aside, it was by using the nature of water against it that Yu turned the tide, dredging, damming, and dyking its inexorable course to the sea; and so too (from his moral high ground) did Mencius labor to harness the nature of man, freeing it to follow *its* inexorable course to goodness. In the end, the difference between the philosopher and the world-mover, between the crackpot and the prophet, Mencius tells us, comes down to nothing more than their respective grasp of nature.

A decade after the Great War, amidst the rise of the National Socialist movement, humanity must have seemed to have been in no less of a state to German-born scientist Moritz Schlick (1882–1936). Schlick was a founding member of the Vienna Circle, a society of scientists and philosophers who, from 1925 to Schlick's assassination in 1936, met for weekly gatherings at the University of Vienna to discuss issues of the philosophy of science. They were dedicated, in the words of their manifesto, to a "scientific world-conception" characterized by two features: "*First* it is *empiricist and positivist*: there is knowledge only from experience, which rests on what is immediately given. This sets the limits for the content of legitimate science. *Second,* the scientific world-conception is marked by application of a certain method, namely *logical analysis*."[1] One of the aims of this self-described "logical positivist" or "logical empiricist" world-conception was to apply the scientific method to philosophical problems so as to solve *matters of truth* once and for all and to circumscribe self-referential *matters of meaning* as "metaphysics." An appeal to Enlightenment values, theirs was a losing battle fought against a culture of growing romanticism, mysticism, and

---

1. Otto Neurath, *Empiricism and Sociology*, ed. Marie Neurath and Robert S. Cohen, Vienna Circle Collection vol. 1 (Dordrecht: D. Reidel Pub. Co., 1973), 309. Emphasis is the author's.

nationalism and the Hegelian and Heideggerian philosophies—"idealism" or, they might say, "obscurantism"—that incubated it. In "The Future of Philosophy," a lecture delivered in Stockton, California in 1931, Schlick put his finger on, essentially, the same problem with which Mencius had grappled:

> Of course, the mere fact that thus far the great systems of philosophy have not been successful and have not been able to gain general acknowledgment is no sufficient reason why there should not be some philosophical system discovered in the future that would universally be regarded as the ultimate solution of the great problems. This might indeed be expected to happen if philosophy were a "science." For in science we continually find that unexpected satisfactory solutions for great problems are found, and when it is not possible to see clearly in any particular point on a scientific question we do not despair. We believe that future scientists will be more fortunate and discover what we have failed to discover. In this respect, however, the great difference between science and philosophy reveals itself. Science shows a gradual development. There is not the slightest doubt that science has advanced and continues to advance, although some people speak skeptically about science. It cannot be seriously doubted for an instant that we know very much more about nature, for example, than people living in former centuries knew. There is unquestionably some kind of advance shown in science, but if we are perfectly honest, a similar kind of advance cannot be discovered in philosophy.[2]

Mencius and Schlick were serious men born into serious times. Even so, twenty-first century scholars cannot help but look back on these episodes and laugh—a laugh of equal parts pity, amusement, and derision. "Oh, how terribly befuddled and self-certain, these men of old!"

Let's talk about solstices. We know nothing of the astronomy of Mencius' day; we begin to see the first rudimentary traces of that science only in the second and first centuries B.C.

---

2. "The Future of Philosophy," *College of the Pacific Publications in Philosophy* I (1932): 48.

Up to 104 B.C., Chinese experts had placed the winter solstice at the beginning of Ox.09 ($18^h20^m05.5^s$ right ascension at epoch), more than $-4°$ in error, and adopted a value for the tropical/sidereal year—which they had yet to distinguish—of $365\frac{1}{4}$ days, for an error of $+11^m26.3^s$ and $-9^m50.2^s$, respectively.[3] To make matters worse, the reform of 104 B.C. nudged the instant of winter solstice 28^h29^m forward to accommodate a neat coincidence of elements at SYSTEM ORIGIN (*li yuan* 曆元; see p. 113). Christopher Cullen explains:

> It is clear... that it was realized that the $365\frac{1}{4}$ day interval between solstices meant that the instant of solstice would not in general fall at noon, and that it would therefore take four solstitial cycles before the noon shadow length would, in theory, repeat exactly. Now, given the slow rate of change in solar north polar distance near the solstices, and the fact that the standard gnomon in use at this period was only 8 *chi* long (... 1840 mm high, or just over 6 feet), errors in the date of solstice were not likely to be obvious, compared to (say) errors in predicting the instant of new moon, which would reveal themselves plainly by a first or last crescent's being visible on the wrong day. What is more, the essence of setting up an astronomical system at this period was that one tried to find a date in the past when (on the basis of observations made now) it appeared that (typically) the winter solstice and new moon had coincided at midnight beginning a significant day of the sexagenary cycle. To achieve such a fit, it is obvious that the instant of winter solstice was the most 'tolerant' of the data to be adjusted.[4]

A thousand years hence from Mencius' day, in the early Tang 唐 (A.D. 618–907), these errors would have accumulated to immense proportions ($+7^d22^h38^m$ and $-6^d15^h17^m$, respectively) *on top of any systematic error in the position or instant of solstice at* SYSTEM ORIGIN. What hubris on Mencius' part! Of course, the advantage of reckoning unobservable phenomena for

---

3. On historical errors in the position and instant of winter solstice at SYSTEM ORIGIN, see Chen Meidong 陳美東, *Gu li xin tan* 古曆新探 (Shenyang: Liaoning jiaoyu chubanshe, 1995), 50–93.

4. "Huo Rong's Observation Programme of AD 102 and the *Han Li* Solar Table," *Journal for the History of Astronomy* 38, no. 1 (2007): 83.

an age beyond imagining—from the comfort of one's mat, no less—is that our philosopher-astronomer need never live to know how he was wrong or how his art might change in the prodigious span in between. In Mencius' time, the difference between astronomy and philosophy, we moderns might conclude, was less one of *truth* than of *certitude*.

Schlick's error cannot be so readily quantified. To do so would be gratuitous, of course, for we classicists and historians of science are, as a rule, more forgiving of our historical subjects than our predecessors: "Confucianism" is a legitimate field of study, "positivism," an invective. As with all things, though, this too has its history.

Logical positivism/empiricism found itself quickly embroiled with philosophical problems that would prove its undoing. The movement's first order of business was to establish a theory of confirmation from induction (the inference of generalizations from particular observations). This project faced skepticism—"there can be no *demonstrative* arguments to prove, *that those instances, of which we have had no experience, resemble those, of which we have had experience*" (David Hume)—but it also faced the adverse implications of its own logic: the problem of "black ravens" and the dependence of induction on (culturally-embedded) language and categories.[5] Stymied, (positivist) philosophers of science changed tack, Rudolf Carnap pursuing mathematical theories of probability, and Sir Karl Popper, falsificationism. Consumed by the problem of demarcation—separating "science" from "pseudo-science"—the latter conceded the issue of confirmation, arguing instead for an apophatic vision of science: that science proceeded by conjecture and attempted refutation, mankind inching ever backwards towards a truth at which, like Zeno's paradox, it would never fully arrive.[6] As popular as Popper's demarcation became among philosophers and scientists alike, it too

---

5. Hume, *A Treatise of Human Nature*, ed. L. A. Selby-Bigge, 2d ed. (1739 rpt.; Oxford: Clarendon Press, 1978), 89. Emphasis is the author's. "Black ravens" refers to Carl Hempel's problem of the logical equivalence of the statements "all ravens are black" and "all nonblack things are not ravens," which dictates that the confirmation of one—e.g. a white shoe—is a confirmation of the other—"all ravens are black." On this and the problem of the language and formal theory of induction in logical positivism/empiricism, see Nelson Goodman, *Fact, Fiction & Forecast* (Cambridge: Harvard University Press, 1955).

6. See Karl R. Popper, *Conjectures and Refutations: The Growth of Scientific Knowledge* (New York: Basic Books, 1962).

strained under further philosophical prodding. One problem was epistemological holism: theory guides the experiments we construct, the observations we make, and, ultimately, our *decision* whether or not to accept the results—whether or not "something went wrong." Without a theory of confirmation, furthermore falsificationism was at pains to explain why we tend to favor the tried and true over untested methods. Lastly, Popper's demarcation potentially excludes such scientific keystones as evolution, universal gravitation, and unified field theory and fails to distinguish between the *uses* to which theories are put, e.g. Freudianism as psychiatry and as literary theory.[7] The wheat, it seems, is not so easy to separate from the chaff.

These were conundrums, sure, but they were not the end of logical positivism/empiricism, for that came at different hands. One was Thomas Kuhn's 1962 *The Structure of Scientific Revolutions*, which presented the first compelling alternative to the incrementalist vision of science. Science, Kuhn argued, is marked by long periods of puzzle-solving ("normal science") within a given paradigm—that is, an *achievement* or *exemplar* and, in the broader sense, the collection of ideas and methods constituting the scientist's worldview and methodology—punctuated by crisis-induced revolutions, gestalt switches brought about by the sudden appearance and mass conversion to a *new* paradigm perceived to possess special problem-solving power. Ever broken down and reconstituted, the history of science is thus not *cumulative* but *cyclic*, each "revolution" placing people in different and incommensurable worlds of their own making.[8] The finishing blow to positivism was delivered by sociology, particularly the 1970s Edinburgh school's "strong programme" in the sociology of scientific knowledge. This blow was as elegant as it was fatal: it simply demanded that science done right is as deserving of explanation as science gone wrong. David Bloor enumerates the

---

7. For these criticisms of Popper's philosophy of science, see Hilary Putnam, "The 'Corroboration' of Theories," in *The Philosophy of Karl Popper*, ed. Paul Arthur Schlipp (La Salle, IL: Open Court, 1974), 221–240; Wesley C. Salmon, "Rational Prediction," *The British Journal for the Philosophy of Science* 32, no. 2 (1981): 115–125; W. H. Newton-Smith, *The Rationality of Science* (Boston: Routledge & Kegan Paul, 1981), 44–76.

8. *The Structure of Scientific Revolutions*, 3d ed. (Chicago: University of Chicago Press, 1996).

tenets of the strong programme as follows:

> (1) It would be causal, that is, concerned with the conditions which bring about belief or states of knowledge. Naturally there will be other types of causes apart from social ones which will cooperate in bringing about belief. (2) It would be impartial with respect to truth and falsity, rationality or irrationality, success or failure. Both sides of these dichotomies will require explanation. (3) It would be symmetrical in its style of explanation. The same types of cause would explain, say, true and false beliefs. (4) It would be reflexive. In principle its patterns of explanation would have to be applicable to sociology itself. Like the requirement of symmetry this is a response to the need to seek for general explanations. It is an obvious requirement of principle because otherwise sociology would be a standing refutation of its own theories.[9]

The effect was to *desacralize* science, to open it to sociological analysis and deconstruction like any other element of profane culture. A chaos ensued, a chaos we call "the science wars." As in all wars, there were atrocities committed by both sides that are better forgotten for the sake of healing, but war leaves us also with stirring tales of ardor.[10] Combatants turned to thick-description anthropology and ever sophisticated philosophies and *sciences* of epistemology to make their respective cases. The result, in monumental works like Steven Shapin and Simon Schaffer's *Leviathan and the Air-pump* and Bruno Latour and Steve Woolgar's *Laboratory Life*, was the proliferation of scientific agency among people, institutions, instruments, cultures, biological systems, and reality itself.[11] What remains for us today is largely

---

9. *Knowledge and Social Imagery* (London: Routledge & K. Paul, 1976), 4–5. For a more recent synthesis of the strong programme, see also Barry Barnes, David Bloor, and John Henry, *Scientific Knowledge: a Sociological Analysis* (Chicago: University of Chicago Press, 1996).

10. On the science wars, see Paul R. Gross and N. Levitt, *Higher Superstition: The Academic Left and Its Quarrels with Science* (Baltimore: Johns Hopkins University Press, 1994); Noretta Koertge, *A House Built on Sand Exposing Postmodernist Myths About Science* (New York: Oxford University Press, 1998).

11. Shapin and Schaffer, *Leviathan and the Air-pump: Hobbes, Boyle, and the Experimental Life* (Princeton: Princeton University Press, 1985); Latour and Woolgar, *Laboratory Life: The Social Construction of Scientific Facts*, 2d ed. (Princeton: Princeton University Press, 1986).

the legwork of mapping the intricate ways in which everything is tied together.

In the twenty-first century, our positivists would be sad to know, precedence is still betrayed by advantage, and wise men yet chisel their way through; philosophy lives on, positivism, not as such. As a concept, "positivism" has taken on a life—an *afterlife*—of its own. Unshackled from the corpse of the philosophical tradition that gave it name, it wanders the world restlessly, a specter and sum of all fears. "Positivism," through no fault of its own, has come to stand for everything that is stodgy, outmoded, and wrong-headed in the history and philosophy of science—everything, in other words, that is *bad*. It is the very sort of historiographic dogma against which Kuhn launched his revolution:

> History, if viewed as a repository for more than anecdote or chronology, could produce a decisive transformation in the image of science by which we are now possessed. That image has previously been drawn, even by scientists themselves, mainly from the study of finished scientific achievements as these are recorded in the classics and, more recently, in the textbooks from which each new scientific generation learns to practice its trade. Inevitably, however, the aim of such books is persuasive and pedagogic; a concept of science drawn from them is no more likely to fit the enterprise that produced them than an image of a national culture drawn from a tourist brochure or a language text. ...

> If science is the constellation of facts, theories, and methods collected in current texts, then scientists are the men who, successfully or not, have striven to contribute one or another element to that particular constellation. Scientific development becomes the piecemeal process by which these items have been added, singly and in combination, to the ever growing stockpile that constitutes scientific technique and knowledge. And history of science becomes the discipline that chronicles both these successive increments and the obstacles that have inhibited their accumulation. Concerned with scientific development, the historian then appears to have two main tasks. on the one hand, he must determine by

what man and at what point in time each contemporary scientific fact, law, and theory was discovered or invented. On the other, he must describe and explain the congeries of error, myth, and superstition that have inhibited the more rapid accumulation of the constituents of the modern science text.[12]

Kuhn's critique of the old ways of history writing rings as true in our day as in his own: to reduce the history of science (or indeed and human pursuit) to a *telos* and the accumulation of facts, dates, and names leading thereto is to do injustice to its complexity—its very *humanity*—and, an even greater sin, to tell a boring story. That said, there is at once a grand irony in this turn of events in the philosophy of science—"the social turn," as it is called—which, as I see it, is *our* ahistoric certitude about the erroneousness of such views. For to look back condescendingly at the past and chide it for its superstitions is, supposedly, the very thing that we most loathe.

It is not my intention in this study to solve profound philosophical questions about the nature and practice of science, nor to submit early Chinese materials to one systematic mode of analysis. If anything, I am shamefully promiscuous in my choice of theories. The advantage of *theory* for us historians of the ancient world, as I see it, lies also in apophasis: it helps us to do what we have always done—empty our minds of modern entanglements— to do what we will always do—the unenviable grunt work of philology, archaeology, and historiography. This is a mundane task indeed, but I wish to single out one entanglement in particular for the reader to empty his/her head of, and that is our postmodern certitude in the illegitimacy of "positivism." For the sake of honest historiography, I say, let Mencius and Schlick have their fetishes.

As a colleague once asked me: "So, you want to pursue a naive history of science?" In a way, that is precisely what I want to do. I came to the history of astronomy theory-laden and eager, searching ancient texts for traceries of how wiser minds have declared science to work—and I *saw* it, clear as day. What I *did not* see, then *chose not to* see, and only

---

12. *The Structure of Scientific Revolutions*, 1–2.

eventually *could not but* see entwining the literature that has been left to us was a worldview starkly simpler and more old-fashioned than our own. But how could this come as any surprise? The story of astronomy was woven, as we might expect, with mythology and classical learning, and the distinctions of magic, science, and religion are nowhere to be had; that said, ancient actors made distinctions—*vehement* distinctions—about right and wrong knowledge (and the right and wrong *context* for said knowledge) and tended to see history of astronomical knowledge as a triumphal process of accretion. The history of astronomy, all voices agree, was one of empiricism and progress. Whether or not this view is *naive* is beyond the point: it is theirs, and it deserves our sober consideration.

This is a history of science. That said, I refuse to encumber my history of science with the problem of what "science" is and is not (or should or should not be). Rather than banish the word, I have decided to repurpose it: "science" shall from here on denote knowledge (*scientia*), shall be used in the plural, and shall apply equally to "unscientific" knowledge, e.g. "mantic" and "ritual science." For better or for worse, "science" is an anachronism that we foist upon the ancient past; my true interest lies not there but in the ancient practice of *tianwen* 天文 "celestial patterns" and *li* 曆 "calendro-astronomy"—collectively, "the astral sciences." All that I ask the reader to concede of *tianwen* and *li* is that which we see expressed in *Mencius* IVB.26: that they are knowledge; that they are, in the popular imagination, *special* knowledge; and that what makes them special is their perceived realization of a certainty in foreknowledge grounded in observation (induction).

As to scope, this study focuses on the "early imperial period," by which I refer mainly to the Qin 秦 (221–207 B.C.), Han 漢 (206 B.C. – A.D. 220), and Cao-Wei 曹魏 (A.D. 220–265) empires, but which I also extend up to the Sui 隋 (A.D. 581–618). My selection is informed by two complementary circumstances. First, I wish to avoid neatly parceling the history of technical knowledge among regimes, for knowledge has a tendency to outlive power. Second, the early imperial period roughly coincides with a number of more natural divisions within the history of the astral sciences itself: the open, non-hereditary astronomical office (c. 2nd cent. B.C. – 8th cent. A.D.), the heyday of *tianwen* omen compendia (2nd–8th cent. A.D.), the transition from *liri* 曆日 "calendars" to *juzhu liri* 具注曆日 "almanacs" (7th cent. A.D.), and, in Qu Anjing's 曲安京 periodization of *li* mathematical astronomy, the period of "the settling of the basic framework."[13]

As to sources, this study highlights several, in my opinion, underrepresented sources for the history of astronomy in China, which I place in dialogue with more traditional ones (and one another) to better adumbrate the complex holism that I understand the astral sciences of this period to embody. First, I balance transmitted with excavated sources, emphasizing *realia* and the unique perspective that they afford on contemporary technical knowledge, the formats in which it was produced and consumed, and its transmission and practice beyond an elite court-centered context. Second, my selection devotes equal attention to the three constituent elements of *li* mathematical astronomy—calendrics, eclipses, and the planets—while at once exploring their interconnections with one another and an even broader array of astral, mantic, ritual, and political sciences. Third, each chapter juxtaposes the *prescriptions* of manual-literature with *descriptions* of practice as evidenced, in particular, by its products—tables, calendars, and test results. It is my hope that each of these three spreads may provide a unique cross section through which to contemplate the holism of the early imperial astral sciences from different angles.

As to the *explicanda*, this study is concerned first and foremost with the fine-grained detail of textual and historiographical questions. Each of the sources examined in this study is (in my opinion) underresearched, and we cannot even begin to theorize about the history and sociology of astral knowledge from them unless we can first determine, for example, what they say, what they intend to say, and in what sequence things were said. In so far

---

13. Qu divides the history of Chinese mathematical astronomy into five periods: (1) "the germination of traditional *li*," ?–5th cent. B.C.; (2) "the settling of the basic framework," 5th cent. B.C. – 6th cent. A.D.; (3) "the consummation of the theoretical system," 6th–13th cent. A.D.; (4) "the influence of foreign cultures," 13th–17th cent. A.D.; and (5) "replacement by modern astronomy," 17th cent. A.D. on. See Qu Anjing, *Zhongguo shuli tianwenxue* 中國數理天文學, Shuxue yu kexue shi congshu 4 (Beijing: Kexue chubanshe, 2008), 23–26.

as space allows us to move from basic questions such as these to broader ones of discourses and cultures, I exploit my cross sections to examine issues such as distinctions in genre, sociology, and epistemology between *sciences*, the flow of knowledge *between* said contexts, and the distance between normative and descriptive accounts. All of this, however, is tied together by one overarching theme: the conception of empiricism and progress in Chinese antiquity.

As to methodology, Chapters 2, 3, and 4 are textual case studies. Each begins with an in-depth textual and technical analysis of a particular text (or corpus of texts). The latter half of each chapter is then devoted to a discussion of said text's broader implications—some technical, most sociological and historiographical. Needless to say, these are the analyses which the outside reader may wish to skip to right away.

Chapter 1, "The Astral Sciences in and around the Han," lays a foundation for subsequent chapters in the history and sociology of the astral sciences in the Han—the central, best-documented, and most-researched span of the early imperial period. I begin with an overview of the sources, legend, and conceptual vocabulary, the aim being to flesh out the concepts of *tianwen* and *li* from the vantages of technical knowledge, philology, literary genre, and mythos. From there, I narrate the history of Han *li* in *two* threads, following the history of institutional reforms and ideas. Having established a historical framework—plural potential frameworks, to be exact—I move to sociology, surveying participants' backgrounds, motivations, education, and epistemological contentions. Finally, I conclude with a discussion of the problems in the history and philosophy of science that other scholars have raised of these materials as well as those that I intend to address in subsequent chapters.

Chapter 2, "A Second-Century B.C. Guide to the Planets," is a study of the the silk manuscript guide to military planetary astronomy/astrology *Wuxing zhan* 五星占 excavated from Mawangdui 馬王堆 tomb 3 (sealed in 168 B.C.). Following an introduction to early imperial planetary astronomy, my textual/technical analysis in Section 2.3 reveals how the *Wuxing zhan* manuscript segregates and conflates distinct genres of planetary models. From there, I sketch the subsequent history of these genres over the entire period, showing how, despite seemingly opposite orientations to reality, actors gradually rewrote and reassessed (crude) hemerology-based omenological models through the lens of progress made in mathematical ones. Then, in Section 2.6, I invite the reader to consider the *Wuxing zhan* as *manuscript*, discussing features of the use, transmission, and collection of technical literature in the age before print.

Chapter 3, "Calendars and Society," is a study of calendars, the majority of which are *realia* excavated from tombs and administrative dump sites. These materials are somewhat difficult to deal with, so I begin by dividing them into a four-fold typology—daily calendars, sexagenary calendar rounds, *shuo-run* 朔閏 tables, and handy tables—and discussing the noteworthy features of type and individual example. In Section 3.2, I gauge the extent to which calendars are the products and purpose of *li*, exploring a rift that appears to have *opened* between astronomy and calendrics over the same period as that discussed in Chapter 2. Then, in Section 3.3, I discuss the ritual and administrative science of the calendar, exposing another gulf between imperial ideology—within which the calendar was the premier symbol of cosmo-ritual dominion—and the actualities of the production, distribution, and use of calendars in a manuscript culture.

Chapter 4, "Testing, Debate, and the Institutional Framework for Astronomy," is a study of the *Jin shu*'s 晉書 (A.D. 648) record of the debate surrounding a failed attempt at *li* reform circa A.D. 226—the Yellow Inception debate. After a complete translation and excursus of the debate proceedings, I analyze the two epistemic strategies at the center of the debate: the quantitative determination of the *mi* 密 "tightness" (accuracy) of lunisolar and planetary models through competitive testing, and the contestation of claims through the deployment of precedence from the history of the field. As an extension of this last strategy, and the hermeneutical considerations we face when we read the dynastic histories' accounts of the astral sciences, I then discuss the nature of histories of science written *in* the early imperial period and how they reflect upon contemporary actors' conceptions of empiricism and progress.

Conventions

- Western-language scholarship on the history of science in China from the last half-century features no less than three different systems for romanizing the Chinese language (Wade-Giles, Joesph Needham's, and *pinyin* 拼音). This unfortunate (and unnecessary) fact makes the subject matter all the more inaccessible to the non-sinologist. In his monumental contributions to the field, Nathan Sivin has consistently advocated the use of Wade-Giles "because almost all previous literature on the history of Chinese astronomy employs it."[14] I must insist instead upon *pinyin*—whereby the title 保乾圖 is, for example, written *Baoqiantu* rather than *Pao-ch'ien-t'u*—due to its wide-spread acceptance within the academic, official, and popular cultures of our day (and the foreseeable future) as well as my personal aesthetic abhorrence to the alternative. Note, however, that I do preserve non-standard transliterations in direct quotes of secondary sources and in the names of East Asian colleagues as they have chosen to render them in Western-language publications, e.g. Huang Yi-long 黃一農 (Huang Yinong), Lai Swee Fo 賴瑞和 (Lai Ruihe), and Yabuuti Kiyosi 藪內清 (Yabuuchi Kiyoshi).

- As in any field of study, the Chinese astral sciences are possessed of their own technical vocabulary. In translation, this vocabulary requires special care because, on the one hand, it rarely overlaps with our own, and, on the other hand, it deploys common words to specialized ends, e.g. *chi-ji* 遲疾 "slow-fast," which refers in modern terms to both the inequality of apparent angular motion and the method—the equation of center—used to adjust therefor. In order to preserve the feel of astronomical jargon, I offer direct translations of key terms in SMALL CAPS. Historical actors are quite consistent in their usages, even over the centuries covered in this study; it is important

---

14. *Granting the Seasons: The Chinese Astronomical Reform of 1280, with a Study of Its Many Dimensions and a Translation of Its Records* (New York: Springer, 2009), 15.

to note, however, that *values* such as ORIGINS (*yuan* 元), ERAS (*ji* 紀), and DIPPER PARTS (*dou fen* 斗分) vary from system to system.

- Where I cite commentary y to a main text x, I delineate the two as such: $x \, |y|$.

- For old Chinese-style books, I cite *juan* 卷 (j) and page numbers (n) in the form $jj.nn$.

- The Chinese use denary—*tian gan* 天干 "heavenly stems" (S)—duodenary—*di zhi* 地支 "earthly branches" (B)—counts, which can also be combined into binomes for a sexagenary count, in order to enumerate hours, directions, days, years, etc. Throughout, I render these counters in *pinyin*, followed by the appropriate number in their respective sequences from Table 1, e.g. *ding*.$_{S04}$, *hai*.$_{B12}$, and *dinghai*.$_{24}$.

- The Chinese unit of angular measurement is the *du* 度 ("to measure/pass through"), which is defined as the angular distance traveled by the (mean) sun over the course of one day, such that, depending on the precise value for the solar year, $\approx 365\frac{1}{4} \, du = 360°$. I mark values given in *du* with a double degree sign—e.g. $15\frac{1}{2}^{°°}$—and those in *degrees* with a single degree sign. From time to time, however, I also translate *du* as "measure," "degree," etc. depending on the context.

- The Chinese had their own coordinates for locating points in space and time. For space, the predominate coordinate system was the twenty-eight lodges (*xiu* 宿), which Christopher Cullen aptly likens to orange slices dividing the celestial sphere pole-to-pole. It is here that analogy breaks down, however, since the slices are completely *asymmetrical*, being keyed each to the beginning of an established asterism.[15] Fig. 1 gives the widths and position of the lodges vis-à-vis the solstitial and equinoctial colures *according to the knowledge of the time covered in this study*. Likewise, fig. 2 gives the twenty-four *qi* 氣 fortnightly periods into which contemporary actors divided the

---

15. *Astronomy and Mathematics in Ancient China: The* Zhou Bi Suan Jing (Cambridge: Cambridge University Press, 1996), 17. On the lodges, see also Cullen, "Translating 宿 **sukh/xiu* and 舍 **lhah/she*—'Lunar Lodges', or Just Plain 'Lodges'?," *East Asian Science, Technology, and Medicine* no. 33 (2011): 76–88.

tropical year. Both lodges and *qi* are given in translation, followed by their appropriate number in their respective sequences, e.g. Dipper.$_{08}$ and Winter Solstice.$_{Q22}$.

- For Western/astronomical dates, I use the proleptic Julian calendar and, where it is important to be precise, the Julian day number (JD) counted from 4713 B.C. January 01, 12:00, e.g. 105 B.C. December 25 (JD 168 3430.2). The annotation x–y refers to the span of time between x and y, while x/y refers to an indeterminate point between x and y. Chinese dates are rendered in the order in which they read, each subsequent unit being separated by a hyphen, lunisolar months being counted in roman numerals, and intercalary months being marked by a "^{2}". Therefore, instead of translating the date 「建武廿二年閏正月廿六日癸巳」 as "Jianwu, year 22, intercalary month 1, day 26, day *guisi*.$_{30}$," I render it "Jianwu 22-I^2-26, *guisi*.$_{30}$."

- On Table 2, I provide a comprehensive list of *li* 曆 astronomical systems up through the Sui 隋 (A.D. 581–618). Following Sivin, Cullen, and others in the field, I refer to each system by its translation, to which I append a number that refers to the position of said system within Table 2, e.g. "the Epochal Excellence system (#22)."

Table 1: Heavenly branches (*tiangan* 天干), earthly stems (*dizhi* 地支), and sexagenary cycle

Stems	Branches	Binomes					
甲 *jia*.S01	子 *zi*.B01	甲子 *jiazi*.01	甲戌 *jiaxu*.11	甲申 *jiashen*.21	甲午 *jiawu*.31	甲辰 *jiachen*.41	甲寅 *jiayin*.51
乙 *yi*.S02	丑 *chou*.B02	乙丑 *yichou*.02	乙亥 *yihai*.12	乙酉 *yiyou*.22	乙未 *yiwei*.32	乙巳 *yisi*.42	乙卯 *yimao*.52
丙 *bing*.S03	寅 *yin*.B03	丙寅 *bingyin*.03	丙子 *bingzi*.13	丙戌 *bingxu*.23	丙申 *bingshen*.33	丙午 *bingwu*.43	丙辰 *bingchen*.53
丁 *ding*.S04	卯 *mao*.B04	丁卯 *dingmao*.04	丁丑 *dingchou*.14	丁亥 *dinghai*.24	丁酉 *dingyou*.34	丁未 *dingwei*.44	丁巳 *dingsi*.54
戊 *wu*.S05	辰 *chen*.B05	戊辰 *wuchen*.05	戊寅 *wuyin*.15	戊子 *wuzi*.25	戊戌 *wuxu*.35	戊申 *wushen*.45	戊午 *wuwu*.55
己 *ji*.S06	巳 *si*.B06	己巳 *jisi*.06	己卯 *jimao*.16	己丑 *jichou*.26	己亥 *jihai*.36	己酉 *jiyou*.46	己未 *jiwei*.56
庚 *geng*.S07	午 *wu*.B07	庚午 *gengwu*.07	庚辰 *gengchen*.17	庚寅 *gengyin*.27	庚子 *gengzi*.37	庚戌 *gengxu*.47	庚申 *gengshen*.57
辛 *xin*.S08	未 *wei*.B08	辛未 *xinwei*.08	辛巳 *xinsi*.18	辛卯 *xinmao*.28	辛丑 *xinchou*.38	辛亥 *xinhai*.48	辛酉 *xinyou*.58
壬 *ren*.S09	申 *shen*.B09	壬申 *renshen*.09	壬午 *renwu*.19	壬辰 *renchen*.29	壬寅 *renyin*.39	壬子 *renzi*.49	壬戌 *renxu*.59
癸 *gui*.S10	酉 *you*.B10	癸酉 *guiyou*.10	癸未 *guiwei*.20	癸巳 *guisi*.30	癸卯 *guimao*.40	癸丑 *guichou*.50	癸亥 *guihai*.60
	戌 *xu*.B11						
	亥 *hai*.B12						

Figure 1: The Han-era twenty-eight lodges polar-equatorial coordinate system

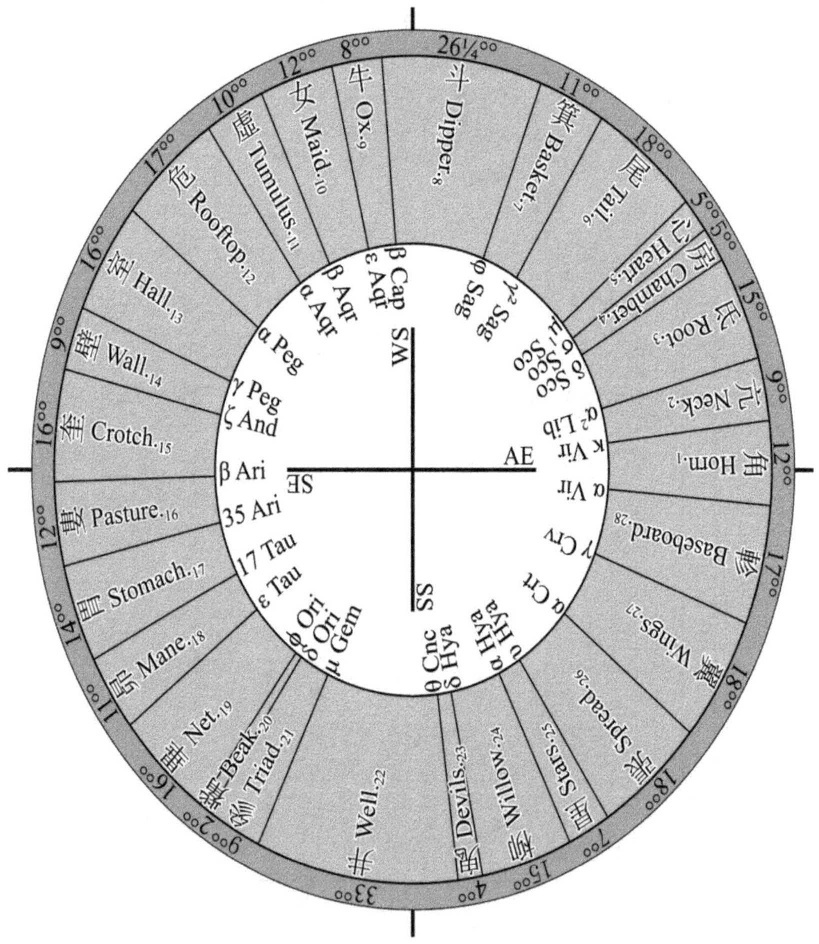

Figure 2: The twenty-four *qi* (epoch A.D. 5)

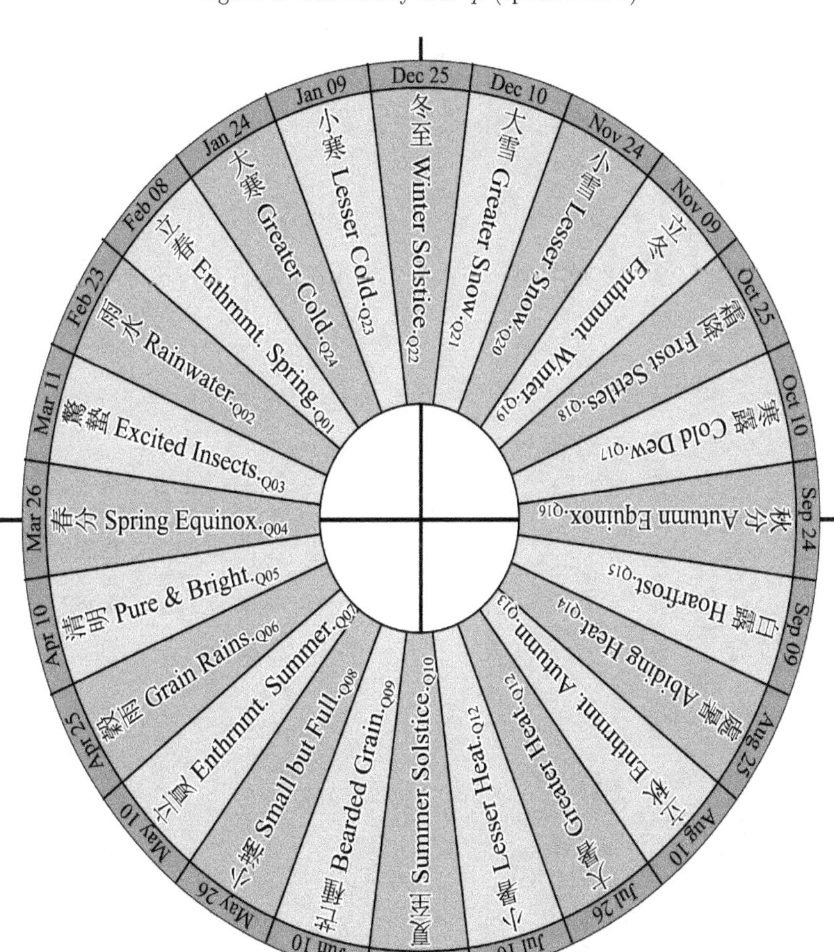

Table 2: Early imperial calendro-astronomical systems

no.	System	Lead Author	Dynasty	Creation	Implementation
1	黃帝調曆 Yel. Emp. Adjustment system	Yellow Emperor*	prehistory*	prehistory*	prehistory*
2	顓頊曆 Zhuanxu system	—	prehistory*		c. 221–104 B.C.
3	夏曆 Xia system	—	prehistory*		Xia Dynasty*
4	殷曆 Yin system	—	prehistory*		Shang Dynasty*
5	周曆 Zhou system	—	prehistory*		Zhou Dynasty*
6	魯曆 Lu system	—	prehistory*		Spring & Autumn period*
7	太初曆 Grand Inception system	鄧平 Deng Ping	W. Han	104 B.C.	104 B.C.
8	三統曆 Triple Concordance system	劉歆 Liu Xin	W. Han	c. A.D. 5	archaeoastronomy; mod. #7
9	四分曆 Quarter-remainder system	編訢 Bian Xin / 李梵 Li Fan	E. Han	85/86	Han: 85 / Cao-Wei: 221 / Shu Han: 221
10	乾象曆 Supernal Emblem system	劉洪 Liu Hong	E. Han	206	Sun-Wu: 223
11	黃初曆 Yellow Inception system	韓翊 Han Yi	Cao-Wei	c. 223	submitted & failed c. 226
12	太和曆 Grand Harmony system	高堂隆 Gaotang Long	Cao-Wei	c. 227	submitted & failed c. 227
13	景初曆 Luminous Inception system	楊偉 Yang Wei	Cao-Wei	237	Cao-Wei: 237 / N. Wei: ?
	泰始曆 Grand Beginning system				Jin: 265 (renamed)
	永初曆 Perpetual Inception system				Liu-Song: 420 (renamed)
14	正曆 Orthodox system	劉智 Liu Zhi	W. Jin	c. 274	?
15	【二元】乾度曆 [Dbl. Orig.] Supernal Standard	李修 Li Xiu / 卜顯 Bu Xian	W. Jin	275/280	submitted at court
16	春秋長曆 Spring and Autumn Long system	杜預 Du Yu	W. Jin	280/285	archaeoastronomy; tested
17	通曆 General system	王朔之 Wang Shuozhi	E. Jin	352	-
18	三紀甲子元曆 Triple-Era $Jiazi._{01}$-origin system	姜岌 Jiang Ji	L. Qin	384	-
19	壬辰元曆 $Renchen._{29}$-origin system	趙匪 Zhao Fei	N. Liang	?	-
20	玄始曆 Epochal Beginning system	趙匪 Zhao Fei	N. Liang	?	N. Liang: ?
	甲寅元曆 $Jiayin._{51}$-origin system				N. Wei: 452
21	既往七曜曆 Seven Luminaries Past system	徐廣 Xu Guang	Liu-Song	?	-

Table 2, continued

no.	System	Lead Author	Dynasty	Creation	Implementation
22	元嘉曆 Epochal Excellence system	何承天 He Chengtian	Liu-Song	445	Liu-Song: 445 Qi: 479 Liang: 502
23	五寅元曆 Five-$yin._{B03}$ origin system	崔浩 Cui Hao	N. Wei	449/451	n/a
24	延興曆 Protracted Ascendency system	龍宜弟 Long Yidi	N. Wei	471/476	-
25	己丑元曆 $Jichou._{26}$-origin system	張明豫 Zhang Mingyu	N. Wei	487	incomplete, abandoned
26	景明曆 Luminous Enlightenment system	公孫崇 Gongsun Chong 趙樊生 Zhao Fansheng	N. Wei	500–512	modification of #20 tested 507
27	甲午甲戌二元曆 $Jiawu._{31}$-$Jiaxu._{11}$ Dbl. Orig.	張洪 Zhang Hong	N. Wei	508/515	Collectively:
28	甲子己亥二元曆 $Jiazi._{01}$-$Jihai._{36}$ Dbl. Orig.	張洪 Zhang Hong	N. Wei	508/515	the "Three Experts'
29	甲子元曆 $Jiazi._{01}$-origin system	張龍祥 Zhang Longxiang	N. Wei	508/515	systems"; tested,
30	戊子元曆 $Wuzi._{25}$-origin system	李業興 Li Yexingg	N. Wei	508/515	not implemented
31	【李謐私曆】 [Li Mi's private system]	李謐 Li Mi	N. Wei	508/515	n/a
32	大明曆 Great Enlightenment system 甲子元曆 $Jiazi._{01}$-origin system	祖沖之 Zu Chongzhi	Liu-Song	462	Liu-Song: slated, failed 465 Liang: test. 509, impl. 510 Chen: impl. 557
33	神龜曆 Divine Tortoise system 正光曆 Orthodox Glory system	李業興 Li Yexing 張龍祥 Zhang Longxiang	N. Wei	518/520	N. Wei: 518/520
34	永安曆 Perpetual Peace system	孫僧化 Sun Senghua	N. Wei	528/530	-
35	靈憲曆 Numinous Pattern system	信都芳 Xindu Fang	N. Qi	?	n/a
36	興和曆 Ascendant Harmony system 甲子元曆 $Jiazi._{01}$-origin system	李業興 Li Yexing	E. Wei	539	E. Wei: 540
37	武定曆 Martial Stability system	anon.	E. Wei	543/550	-
38	大同曆 Great Unity system	虞廣	Liang	?	-
39	九宮行棋曆 Nine-grid Chess system	李業興 Li Yexing	E. Wei	547	-
40	天保曆 Celestial Preservation system	宋景業 Song Jingye	N. Qi	550	N. Qi: 550

Table 2, continued

no.	System	Lead Author	Dynasty	Creation	Implementation
41	甲寅元曆 *Jiayin*.51-origin system	董峻 Dong Jun	N. Qi	576	
		鄭元偉 Zheng Yuanwei			presented,
42	-	劉孝孫 Liu Xiaosun	N. Qi	576	tested in 576
43	-	張孟賓 Zhang Mengbin	N. Qi	576	
44	周曆 Zhou system	明克讓 Ming Kerang	N. Zhou	c. 557	N. Zhou: c. 557
45	天和曆 Celestial Harmony system	甄鸞 Zhen Luan	N. Zhou	566	-
46	武平曆 Martial Tranquility system	劉孝孫 Liu Xiaosun	N. Qi	570/576	-
47	甲寅元曆 *Jiayin*.51-origin system	馬顯 Ma Xian	N. Zhou	?	-
48	大象曆 Great Emblem system	馬顯 Ma Xian	N. Zhou	579	N. Zhou: 579
49	大象曆 Great Emblem system	王琛 Wang Chen	N. Zhou	579/581	-
50	開皇曆 Opening Sovereignty system	張賓 Zhang Bin	Sui	584	Sui: 584 (modified from #23
51	開皇曆 Opening Sovereignty system	李德林 Li Delin	Sui	?	-
52	大業曆 Great Patrimony system	張胄玄 Zhang Zhouxuan	Sui	597	Sui: 608
53	皇極曆 Sovereign Pole system	劉焯 Liu Zhuo	Sui	c. 605	Slated, failed in 608

22

CHAPTER 1

THE ASTRAL SCIENCES IN AND AROUND THE HAN

This chapter is a review of primary and secondary sources in which I shall lay out the context and questions informing subsequent chapters. I will begin in Section 1.1 by defining what I mean by "the astral sciences" in terms of actors' categories, textual genres, and the mythology of the field. In Section 1.2, I move from the mythology of pre-imperial times to a brief history of early imperial mathematical astronomy from the third century B.C. to the third century A.D., paying careful attention to narrate not only the traditional sequence of policy reforms but alternative historical threads unfolding concurrently. Then, in Section 1.3, I attempt an outline of the sociology of knowledge and practice that emerges from these sources, covering topics of institutions, individuals, education, employment, methodology, motivations, rhetoric, and epistemology. In conclusion, I present two topics in the history and philosophy of science that I will address throughout this study: empiricism and progress.

1.1 Text, Legend, and Terminology

Throughout this dissertation, I use the term "the astral sciences" to refer collectively to the actors' categories *tianwen* 天文 and *li* 曆.[1] While their practice is evident in, if not central to,

---

1. In this section and Chapter 2, I discuss the way that *tianwen* and *li* exist in dialogue at the level of text and practice, and show that history offers several examples of actors who practiced both. Sometimes sources combine the two terms in a way that seems to implicate a greater whole—my "astral sciences." For example, the *Hou Han shu* 後漢書 records that Zhi Yun 郅惲 (fl. 1st cent. A.D.) "was enlightened in *tianwen-lishu* (*tianwen* and *li* numbers)" 明天文歷數 as well as Zhang Heng's 張衡 (A.D. 87–140) plea that "*tianwen-lishu* and yin-yang divination are what we should be taking urgently" 天文歷數，陰陽占候，今 所宜急也 (*Hou Han shu* [Zhonghua shuju ed.], 29.1023, 30B.1085). For other examples of this pairing, see *Wei shu* 魏書 (Zhonghua shuju ed.), 48.1068; *Jiu Tang shu* 舊唐書 (Zhonghua shuju ed.), 36.1335, 79.2714, 191.5102. Note that I borrow the term "the astral sciences" from Assyriology, where it simply denotes plural forms of sky-related "knowledge" like astral omens, astral observation and record-keeping, and mathematical astronomy; for its usage there, see for example Hermann Hunger and David Edwin Pingree, *Astral Sciences in Mesopotamia* (Leiden: Brill, 1999).

23

the mythology and earliest written records of Chinese civilization, this study focuses on the period in which *tianwen* and *li* emerge as self-identified fields of knowledge within scholastic discourse.[2] The ways that historical actors deploy these categories reveal commonalities and distinctions between them that defy reduction. Scholars have described their relationship in three ways: that they are complimentary aspects of a single science, with *TIANWEN* : OBSERVATION :: *LI* : COMPUTATION ; that they are dichotomous approaches to a shared reality, with *TIANWEN* : "ASTROLOGY" : QUALITATIVE :: *LI* : "ASTRONOMY" : QUANTITATIVE ; and that (based somewhat on their modern definitions) they are distinctly spatial and temporal approaches to the cosmos, with *TIANWEN* : "ASTRONOMY" : SPACE :: *LI* : "CALENDRICS" : TIME.[3] In this section, I survey sources for the astral sciences in early imperial China. One goal of this is to familiarize the reader with the body of evidence from which this and other studies draw. Another is to expound upon actors' conceptual categories through their contents as textual genres. Doing so, I believe,

---

2. Judging from the sources currently available to us, *tianwen* and *li* only emerge as self-identified labels in the first few centuries B.C. Of course, evidence for the practice of calendrics and uranomancy are evident throughout the earliest written materials from the Yin-Shang 殷商 (?–1046 B.C.) and Western Zhou 西周 (1045–771 B.C.) eras; see for example David N. Keightley, *The Ancestral Landscape: Time, Space, and Community in Late Shang China, ca. 1200–1045 B.C.*, China Research Monograph 53 (Berkeley: Institute for East Asian Studies, University of California, Berkeley, 2000), 17–53; Adam Smith, "The Chinese Sexagenary Cycle and the Ritual Foundations of the Calendar," in *Calendars and Years II: Astronomy and Time in the Ancient and Medieval World*, ed. John M. Steele (Oxford: Oxbow Books, 2011), 1–37.

3. First, for the explicit identification of *TIANWEN* : OBSERVATION :: *LI* : COMPUTATION, see Zhang Wenyu 張聞玉, *Gudai tianwen lifa jiangzuo* 古代天文曆法講座 (Guilin: Guangxi shifan daxue chubanshe, 2008), 5–7. In most scholarship, this identification is implicit in the deployment of terms and primary sources under the rubric "astronomy," e.g. the deployment of *tianwen* texts to questions of observational astronomy and *li* texts to mathematical astronomy. Second, for the identification of *TIANWEN* : "ASTROLOGY" :: *LI* : "ASTRONOMY," see Chen Zungui 陳遵媯, *Zhongguo tianwenxue shi* 中國天文學史, 2d ed. (Shanghai: Shanghai renmin chubanshe, 2006), 1002; Nakayama Shigeru 中山茂, "Characteristics of Chinese Calendrical Science," *Japanese Studies in the History of Science*, no. 4 (1965): 124–131; "Characteristics of Chinese Astrology," *Isis* 57, no. 4 (1966): 442–454; Jiang Xiaoyuan 江曉原, *Tianxue zhen yuan* 天學真原, 2d ed. (Shenyang: Liaoning jiaoyu chubanshe, 2007), esp. 1–6, 109–115; Chen Meidong 陳美東, *Zhongguo gudai tianwenxue sixiang* 中國古代天文學思想 (Beijing: Zhongguo kexue jishu chubanshe, 2007), 1–16. Third, for the identification of *TIANWEN* : "ASTRONOMY" : SPACE :: *LI* : "CALENDRICS" : TIME , see Joseph Needham, *Science and Civilisation in China, Vol.3: Mathematics and the Sciences of the Heavens and the Earth* (Cambridge: Cambridge University Press, 1959), 390–408; Nakayama, "Characteristics of Chinese Calendrical Science"; Marc Kalinowski, "Astrologie calendaire et calcul de position dans la Chine ancienne: les mutations de l'hémérologie sexagésimale entre le IVe et le IIe siècles avant notre ère," *Extrême-orient, Extrême-occident* 18 (1996): 71–72; John B. Henderson, "Premodern Chinese Notions of Astronomical History and Calendrical Time," in *Notions of Time in Chinese Historical Thinking*, ed. Chun-chieh Huang and John B. Henderson (Hong Kong: Chinese University Press, 2006), 97.

will illustrate a complexity to these categories that neat heuristics fail to capture.

1.1.1 Sources for tianwen and li

Of foremost importance to the study of *tianwen* and *li* are the eponymous "treatises" (*zhi* 志) devoted to them in the dynastic histories. Together, these 30 treatises in 131 *juan* 卷 ("rolls") span a period of more than two thousand years—the most prolific and continuous record of the astral sciences in any pre-modern civilization. In addition, their contents and composition provide us valuable clues about scope, organization, and evolution of actors' conceptual categories.

Dynastic histories: *tianwen* treatises

The best introduction to the "*Tianwen* Treatise" genre is probably the *Jin shu* 晉書 "Tianwen zhi" 天文志. Compiled by the celebrated expert Li Chunfeng 李淳風 (A.D. 602–670) circa A.D. 648, this treatise represents the culmination of the genre's early imperial form. It is also the only such treatise to which a monograph-length translation and study have been devoted.[4] In modern terms, its contents include cosmology, instrumentation, the cataloging of stars as well as planetary, lunar, solar, and meteorological phenomena, omenology, and observational/divinatory records. The main organizational divide is that between the *catalog of facts* and the *record of phenomena*: both are lists, but one proceeds through space, and the other, time. To give the reader a sense of the contents and organization typical of these treatises, I have provided the *Jin shu* "Tianwen zhi" table of contents in Table 1.1.

This genre remained fairly stable up to the tenth century A.D. Its forerunner (and primary focus of scholarly attention) is the "Tianguan shu" 天官書 chapter of the *Shiji* 史記 (91 B.C.).[5] In terms of contents and organization, the "Tianguan shu" is identical to its

---

4. Ho Peng Yoke, *The Astronomical Chapters of the* Chin Shu (Paris: Mouton, 1967).

5. Seminal studies on the "Tianguan shu" include Zhu Wenxin 朱文鑫, *Shiji Tianguan shu hengxing tu kao* 史記天官書恒星圖考 (Shanghai: Shangwu yinshuguan, 1934) and Gao Pingzi 高平子, *Shiji Tianguan shu jinzhu* 史記天官書今註, Zhonghua congshu (Taibei: Zhonghua congshu bianshen weiyuanhui, 1965).

Table 1.1: *Jin shu* "Tianwen zhi" table of contents

天文上 Vol. I

— (**Introduction**): the history of the field

天體 "The Structure of Heaven": theories concerning the physical structure of the world and the cause of phenomena therein, i.e. "cosmology"

儀象 "Instruments": the invention, commission, and specifications of observational instruments

天文經星 "The Seminal Stars of *Tianwen*": a catalog of constellations describing their physical features, lore, and omenological significance, with special attention to the "zodiacal" divisions of the twenty-eight lodges (*xiu* 宿) and twelve stations (*ci* 次).

天文中 Vol. II

七曜 "The Seven Luminaries": a catalog of the seven moving bodies—the sun, moon, and five naked-eye planets—describing their physical characteristics, lore, five-agents and divine correlations, and omenological knowledge concerning their colors, potencies, configurations, and interactions.

雜星氣 "Sundry Stars and Vapors": a catalog of anomalies described in similarly empirical, mythic, and mystical terms.

> **星 "Stars"** (celestial objects) that we would identify as comets, supernovae, and meteors.

> **氣 "Vapors"** (atmospheric phenomena) that we would identify as aurorae, halos, parhelia (sun dogs), and clouds of peculiar color and/or shape.

史傳事驗 "Phenomena and Verifications Recorded in History": observational records for the period in question describing the time, location, and physical features of phenomena, some of which feature "prognostications" (*zhan* 占) and "verifications" (*yan* 驗):

> **天變 "Celestial disturbances"** (namely aurorae and loud sounds)

> **日蝕 "Solar eclipses"** (including also halos, sunspots, parhelia, and rainbows)

> **月變 "Lunar disturbances"** (halos, eclipses, etc.)

> **月奄犯五緯 "Lunar occultations and encroachments on the five woofs (planets)"** (various lunar-planetary configurations)

> **五星聚舍 "Five-star (planet) convergences on a single lodge"** (the coincidence of multiple planets in a single lodge)

天文下 Vol. III

(continued)

> **月五星犯列舍 "Lunar and planetary encroachments on the lodges"** (positions and interactions vis-à-vis asterisms, including also mentions of daylight appearances)

> **妖星客星 "Inauspicious stars and guest stars"** (comets, supernovae, etc.)

> **星流隕 "Meteor showers and meteorites"**

> **雲氣 "Clouds and vapors"**

eighth-century counterpart in all but four respects. First, after the "Tianguan shu," subsequent compilers do not share their their theories and sentiments about the field at the end of the treatise. Second, it is silent on cosmology and instrumentation—"*Tianwen* Treatise" topics that were first introduced in the *Song shu* 宋書 (A.D. 488).[6] Third, following the *Shiji* and *Han shu* 漢書 (A.D. 111), the number of stellar, solar, lunar, and planetary omens proliferate, while calendar divination (below) and peripheral areas of meteoromancy completely disappear. Fourth, observational records grow increasingly numerous and formulaic with each treatise. Marking this trend are two noteworthy transitions: the organization of records switches, beginning with the *Nan Qi shu* 南齊書 (c. A.D. 537), from chronological

---

6. "Cosmology," according to the *Oxford English Dictionary*, refers to "the science or theory of the universe as an ordered whole, and of the general laws which govern it." In sinology, the term "cosmology" is typically reserved for "correlative cosmology," that is the idea that all worldly phenomena are apportioned among numerical categories of cyclic cosmic forces (e.g. yin and yang, the five agents, and trigrams and hexagrams of the *Book of Changes*) through which they exert spontaneous influence upon one another over time and space. "Correlative cosmology" is a term that was coined in Western-language sinology of the twentieth century and for which there exists no word in Chinese except, by synecdoche, the ideas of *yinyang wuxing* 陰陽五行 "yin-yang and five agents," *tianren ganying* 天人感應 "stimulus and response between Heaven and man," etc. Because there is no room for "cosmology," in the traditional sense, in "correlative cosmology," scholars have tended to either deny cosmology, in the traditional sense, any legitimate role in Chinese thought or argue for a distinction between "cosmology" worldwide and "cosmology" particular to China, e.g. Nathan Sivin, "Cosmos and Computation in Early Chinese Mathematical Astronomy," *T'oung Pao* 2d ser., 55, no. 1/3 (1969): 3; Kalinowski, "Astrologie calendaire et calcul de position dans la Chine ancienne," 71. The "cosmography"/"cosmology" distinction was first introduced by Christopher Cullen:

> Cosmology covers the whole subject of the nature of the universe we inhabit in all its aspects and involves a wide range of essentially philosophical problems, such as those of causality and ontology. Cosmography I understand in a much more limited sense as including the discussion of the composition, size, shape, disposition and motion of the large-scale components of the physical universe (Christopher Cullen, "Cosmographical Discussions in China from Early Times up the T'ang Dynasty" [Ph.D. diss., University of London, 1977], 15; cf. *Astronomy and Mathematics in Ancient China: The* Zhou Bi Suan Jing [Cambridge: Cambridge University Press, 1996], xi n. 2).

I find this distinction problematic and prefer the terms "correlative thought" or "correlative philosophy" so as to avoid limiting the category "cosmology" to mystical thinking in the case of China. On "correlative cosmology," see John B. Henderson, *The Development and Decline of Chinese Cosmology* (New York: Columbia University Press, 1984); A. C. Graham, *Yin-yang and the Nature of Correlative Thinking* (Singapore: The Institute of East Asian Philosophies, National University of Singapore, 1986); Marc Kalinowski, *Cosmologie et divination dans la Chine ancienne: le compendium des cinq agents (Wuxing dayi, VIe siècle)* (Paris: Ecole française d'Extrême Orient, 1991); Michael Nylan, "Yin-yang, Five Phases, and Qi," in *China's Early Empires: a Re-appraisal*, ed. Michael Nylan and Michael Loewe (Cambridge: Cambridge University Press, 2010), 398–414. On cosmology/cosmography, see the works of Cullen mentioned above and Marc Kalinowski, "Le calcul du rayon céleste dans la cosmographie chinoise," *Revue d'histoire des sciences* 43, no. 1 (1990): 3–34; Chen Meidong, *Zhongguo gudai tianwenxue sixiang*, 128–532.

to typological; and the "*Tianwen* Treatise" becomes so bloated with observational records that, beginning with the *Jiu Tang shu* 舊唐書 (A.D. 945), they begin to exclude all other content. I discuss the evolution of the "*Tianwen* Treatise" in further detail in Chapter 2.

Up to the tenth century, the "*Tianwen* Treatise" genre had a strong divinatory bent. There is an ample body of secondary literature on this topic, for example, the syntheses of Nakayama Shigeru 中山茂, Jiang Xiaoyuan 江曉原, and Lu Yang 盧央.[7] Their level of detail cannot be reproduced here, however, a single paragraph drawn at random from the *Jin shu* "Tianwen zhi" is enough to sketch most of the genre's more noteworthy features (with numbered point inserted for the purposes of the following discussion):

日為太陽之精，主生養恩德，人君之象也。人君有瑕，必露其慝以告示焉。故日月行有道之國則光明，人君吉昌，百姓安寧。人君乘土而王，其政太平，則日五色無主。日變色，有軍，軍破；無軍，喪侯王。其君無德，其臣亂國，則日赤無光。日失色，所臨之國不昌。日晝昏，行人無影，到暮不止者，上刑急，下不聊生，不出一年有大水。日晝昏，烏鳥羣鳴，國失政。日中烏見，主不明，為政亂，國有白衣會，將軍出，旌旗舉。日中有黑子、黑氣、黑雲，乍三乍五，臣廢其主。日蝕，陰侵陽，臣掩君之象，有亡國。

The sun being the essence of Great Yang, governs all life, sustenance, benevolence and virtue, and is the symbol/simulacrum (*xiang*) of the Emperor [in Heaven]. ① If the lord of men has any imperfections, then [the latter] necessarily reveal their evil [in the sun] to serve as warning to him. ② Thus, if sun and moon travel through a state in possession of the Dao, then they are bright and lustrous, the lord of men meets good fortune, and the hundred surnames live in peace and security. ③ The lord of men rules by the virtue of Earth, and if he presides over a reign of great peace, then none of the five colors of the sun will predominate. ④

---

7. Nakayama, *Senseijutsu: sono kagaku shijō no ichi* 占星術：その科學史上の位置 (Tōkyō: Kinokuniya Shoten, 1964); "Characteristics of Chinese Astrology"; Jiang Xiaoyuan, *Xingzhanxue yu chuantong wenhua* 星占學與傳統文化 (Guilin: Guangxi shifan daxue chubanshe, 2004); *Zhongguo xingzhanxue leixing fenxi* 中國星占學類型分析 (Shanghai: Shanghai shudian chubanshe, 2009); Lu Yang 盧央, *Zhongguo gudai xingzhanxue* 中國古代星占學 (Beijing: Zhongguo kexue jishu chubanshe, 2007).

When the sun changes color, if it is in time of war, then [His] army will be broken; if in time of peace, then [He] will lose a marquis or king. ⑤ In the presence of either a lord lacking virtue or a minister disrupting the state, the sun is red and lusterless. ⑥ If the sun loses its color, then the state where it presides will not flourish. ⑦ If the sun is dusky during the day, pedestrians cast no shadows, and this continues unabated into the evening, then the superior [ranks] are quick to punishment, and the inferior [ranks] cannot make a living; within one year there will be a great flood. ⑧ If the sun is dusky during the day, and coincides with the chirping and flocking of crows and birds, then the state is misgoverned. ⑨ If the crow appears in the sun, then the ruler is unenlightened, governing [officials] are in turmoil, there is a grand funeral of state, generals set out, and standards (of war) are raised. ⑩ If in the sun there are black spots, black vapors, or black clouds, either in threes or fives, then ministers will abrogate their ruler. ⑪ If the sun is eclipsed, yin encroaches on yang, this is the symbol/simulacrum (*xiang*) of the minister usurping his lord, and the state will be lost.[8]

Omenology works on the principle of *xiang* 象 ("signs," "simulacra" or "doppelgängers"): the sky is a mirror of the human world, each and every entity therein reflecting the condition of its earthly counterpart.[9] Thus, for example, the sun is the illustriously virtuous emperor (: YANG), the moon the decorously loyal minister (: YIN), and any solar irregularity a sign of man's failure to fulfill his roles. Thus, furthermore, do the luminaries travel through and, in doing so, indicate the fortune of the states and regions of "the subcelestial realm" (*tianxia* 天下) via counterparts mapped to the ecliptic (items 2 & 6).[10] The science of

---

8. *Jin shu* 晉書 (Zhonghua shuju ed.), 12.317; translation modified from Ho Peng Yoke, *The Astronomical Chapters of the* Chin Shu, 121.

9. On *xiang*, see Edward H. Schafer, *Pacing the Void: T'ang Approaches to the Stars* (Berkeley: University of California Press, 1977), esp. 54–56. On the mapping of the offices and geography of empire onto the Chinese sky, see Sun Xiaochun 孫小淳 and Jacob Kistemaker, *The Chinese Sky During the Han: Constellating Stars and Society* (Leiden: Brill, 1997).

10. One of the pillars of *tianwen* omenology is "field allocation" (*fen ye* 分野), which divides the belt

omenology is a science of lists. Correspondence lists use simple equations to bridge different realms of experience, e.g. "[The asterisms] Crotch (Andromeda/Pisces), Pasture (Aries), and Stomach (Aries) are [the State of] Lu and [the Prefecture of] Xuzhou" 奎婁胃魯徐州.[11] Omen series, on the other hand, use protasis-apodosis ("if"–"then" clause) formulae to catalog actions across categories, e.g. "[If] the sun loses its color, [then] the state where it presides will not flourish" 日失色，所臨之國不昌 (item 6 above). Beneath whatever nebulous relations of causation or directionality may be distilled from classical syntax lies the idea that counterparts exist in a spontaneous continuum. Celestial phenomena are at once diagnostics of man's condition and prognostics of its consequences. Thus, for example, proper rule ensures the brilliance of the sun, and the latter's waning portends civil and military ruin—because, ultimately, ruin is wrought of misrule. In this continuum, distinctions between cosmic, political, and moral order collapse. *Tianwen* omenology is simply another means at the classicist's disposal to grasp the mysterious order of the universe and harness it to perfect both emperor and empire.

In his study of the *Jin shu* "Astronomical Chapters" ("Tianwen zhi"), Ho Peng Yoke 何丙郁 finds himself at odds to explain "the vast quantity of astrological matters in their contents."[12] Indeed, the "astronomy" (speculative cosmology, instrumentation, star catalogs, and observational records) is completely interlaced with "astrology" (omens). The utility of these labels breaks down even further, however, when we consider the rationale of omenology itself. The connections between protases and apodoses are sometimes informed by cultural

---

straddling the ecliptic through which the sun, moon, planets, and comets commonly pass into abstract zones, each of which corresponds with a geographic region of the known world, and which is further divisible to the level of prefecture, city, county, etc. This scheme allows celestial phenomena to speak to specific regions rather than the empire as a whole and is prevalent, for example, in military divination. On field allocation, see David W. Pankenier, "Applied Field-allocation Astrology in Zhou China: Duke Wen of Jin and the Battle of Chengpu (632 B.C.)," *Journal of the American Oriental Society* 119, no. 2 (1999): 261–279; "Characteristics of Field Allocation (*fenye* 分野) Astrology in Early China," in *Current Studies in Archaeoastronomy: Conversations Across Time and Space*, ed. J. W. Fountain and R. M. Sinclair (Durham: Carolina Academic Press, 2005), 499–513.

11. *Jin shu*, 11.311; cf. Ho Peng Yoke, *The Astronomical Chapters of the* Chin Shu, 118.

12. *The Astronomical Chapters of the* Chin Shu, 20.

and linguistic associations. We see, for example, *myths*—the three-legged crow in the sun (items 8 & 9 above)—*puns*—the "broom star" (*huixing* 彗星) comet, "its root resembles a star while its branches resemble a broom... it governs over sweeping, removing the old and spreading the new" 本類星，末類彗... 主掃除，除舊布新 —and *rhymes*—in regard to Saturn, "when it is ahead (*ljeŋ*), he who rules as king is ill at ease (*neŋ*); when it is behind (*srjuk*), he who commands an army does not return (*bjuks*)" 贏，為王不寧；其縮，有軍不復.[13]

Other omenological connections are found in the elaborations of coherent theories of correlative thought and numerology such as yin-yang and the five agents (wood, fire, earth, metal, water), which scholars have labeled "natural philosophy."[14] Above, for example, the entire dynamic of SUN : RULER : BRILLIANCE : ORDER :: MOON : MINISTER : DIMNESS : DISORDER is predicated upon the forces of yin and yang, as is the concern for threes and fives, since YANG : ODD :: YIN : EVEN; and the theme that the emperor's practice of earth-virtue maintains the proper color of the sun is likewise predicated on the five agents, wherein EARTH : CENTER : YELLOW :: WOOD : EAST : GREEN, etc. However, the basis of *tianwen* omen series are parameters of normal and anomalous phenomena clearly derived from experience. For example, the above *Jin shu* passage recognizes the normal state of the sun as being bright and yellow as well as the possibility, in order of anomalousness, that it may dim, change color (to red, white, black, or green), manifest the image of a crow or other black blemishes, or eclipse with the moon. Some possibilities—the crow and the green sun—we might explain as cultural imaginings or byproducts of theory, but others—sunspots—are clearly the product of empirical investigation. Rather than strive to delineate

---

13. The "broom star" quote is from *Jin shu*, 12.323. The Saturn quote is from *Shiji* 史記 (Zhonghua shuju ed.), 27.1320. A parallel phrase appears also in the *Jin shu*, but its prosody has been butchered (*Jin shu*, 12.319). All phonetic reconstructions are according to William Baxter's Minimal Old Chinese in *A Handbook of Old Chinese Phonology* (Berlin: Mouton de Gruyter, 1992).

14. Donald Harper, "Warring States Natural Philosophy and Occult Thought," in *The Cambridge History of Ancient China: From the Origins of Civilization to 221 B.C.*, ed. Michael Loewe and Edward L. Shaughnessy (Cambridge: Cambridge University Press, 1999), 813–84; G. E. R. Lloyd and Nathan Sivin, *The Way and the Word: Science and Medicine in Early China and Greece* (New Haven: Yale University Press, 2002), esp. 4–6.

the "astronomy" and "astrology" of these treatises, I suggest that we think of them simply as catalogs of "facts about Heaven."

Dynastic histories: *li* treatises

The typical counterpart to a "*Tianwen* Treatise" was a "*Li* Treatise" (Li zhi 曆志) or, less commonly, a "Harmonics and *Li* Treatise" (Lü li zhi 律曆志).[15] Fitful and unhappy, the marriage of *li* and harmonics was something of a historical accident. Having derived its "Treatise" from Liu Xin's 劉歆 (c. 50 B.C. – A.D. 23) work to synthesize the two, the *Han shu* was the first history to combine *li* and harmonics under a single chapter heading. Later, as the *Han shu* beat out the *Shiji* in terms of influence, this artifact of Western Han 西漢 (206 B.C. – A.D. 9) intellectual history became something of a generic convention. The joint heading is by no means universal nor, where it occurs, is it indicative of meaningful synthesis—it features in only six of fourteen subsequent treatises, and even there harmonics and *li* contents are segregated into discourses and textual units that are every bit as discrete as individual "treatises." With the exception of the *Han shu*, therefore, it is typical for historians of astronomy to set aside harmonics and treat only treatise sections relevant to *li*.[16] The *li*

---

15. Though the history of Chinese mathematical astronomy now enjoys a considerable body of secondary literature, only a handful of *li* treatises have been studied as integral texts in their own right. On the *Shiji* "Li shu," see Liu Caonan 劉操南, *Gudai tianwen lifa shizheng* 古代天文曆法釋證 (Hangzhou: Zhejiang daxue chubanshe, 2009), 3–64. On the *Han shu* "Lü li zhi," see Nōda Chūryō 能田忠亮 and Yabuuti Kiyosi 藪内清, *Kansho ritsurekishi no kenkyū* 漢書律曆志の研究, Tōhō bunka kenkyūjo kenkyū hōkoku 19 (Tōkyō: Zenkoku shobō, 1947); Liu Caonan, *Gudai tianwen lifa shizheng*, 76–271; Cullen, "The Birthday of the Old Man of Jiang County and Other Puzzles: Work in Progress on Liu Xin's *Canon of the Ages*," *Asia Major* 14, no. 2 (2001): 27–60. On the *Hou Han shu* 後漢書 (A.D. 445) "Lü li zhi," see Ōhashi Yukio, "Kōkan Sibunreki no seiritsu katei" 後漢四分曆の成立過程, *Sūgakushi kenkyū* 數學史研 93 (1982): 1–27; "Ka Ki no gekkō chishitsuron" 賈逵の月行遲疾論, *Sūgakushi kenkyū* 136 (1993): 29–41; Christopher Cullen, "Actors, Networks, and 'Disturbing Spectacles' in Institutional Science: 2nd Century Chinese Debates on Astronomy," *Antiqvorvm Philosophia* 1 (2007): 237–267; "Huo Rong's Observation Programme of AD 102 and the *Han Li* Solar Table," *Journal for the History of Astronomy* 38, no. 1 (2007): 75–98. On the *Yuan shi* 元史 (A.D. 1369) "Li zhi," see Yabuuti Kiyosi and Nakayama Shigeru, *Jujireki: yakuchū to kenkyū* 授時曆: 譯注と研究 (Kawasaki: I. K. Corporation, 2006); Nathan Sivin, *Granting the Seasons: The Chinese Astronomical Reform of 1280, with a Study of Its Many Dimensions and a Translation of Its Records* (New York: Springer, 2009).

16. On Liu Xin's astro-harmonic synthesis, see Kawahara Hideki 川原秀城, "The World-view of the *Santong-li*," *Historia Scientiarum* 42 (1991): 67–73; Hans Ulrich Vogel, "Aspects of Metrosophy and Metrology During the Han Period," *Extrême-Orient, Extrême-Occident* 16 (1994): 135–152. The other five histories

treatise (or *juan*) is organized chronologically and is essentially an annals of *li*-related events at court. This the compiler fleshes out with historical background and extended quotations from materials presumably drawn from, or were bases for, court records, e.g. memorials, edicts, debates, prefaces, and even complete technical works. In modern terms, its contents include mathematical astronomy, calendrics, instrumentation, observational programs and testing, and policy history and debate.[17]

Everything we know about mathematical astronomy in pre-modern China derives from the *li* "astronomical systems" or *fa* 法 "methods" excerpted in these treatises—i.e. manuals used for computing *li* "calendars" and *xingli* 星曆 "planetary tables." Liu Hong's 劉洪 (c. A.D. 135–210) Supernal Emblem system (#10) provides us with an excellent example of this genre's features (see Table 1.2). A system manual is comprised of discrete sections devoted to the *li* "the civil calendar, calendrics" and *li* "mathematical astronomy," each of which is comprised of *shu* 數 "numbers," *shu* 術 "techniques," *li* "tables," and/or *xingdu* 行度 "motion-degree models." The calendrical and astronomical aspects of *li* are quite distinct and not to be conflated. Calendrics provides astronomy with a temporal framework; and while astronomy supplies parameters to that framework, it is not its sole source, nor is this its sole function (Chapter 3). The Supernal Emblem system (#10), for example, fixes the calendar by the mean lunation, which in turn provides a framework for determining the instant and longitude of true lunar phenomena (adjusted by an equation of center) as well as lunar latitude (see below).

Sivin describes the system manual or "canon" as "a set of step-by-step instructions, worked out so that a minor functionary with limited mathematical skills could calculate the annual ephemeris."[18] In other words, these texts are not so much science as they are tech-

---

that feature a joint "Harmonics and *Li* Treatise" are the *Hou Han shu* (A.D. 445), *Song shu* 宋書 (A.D. 492/493), *Wei shu* 魏書 (A.D. 554), *Sui shu* 隋書 (A.D. 636), *Jin shu* 晉書 (A.D. 648), and *Song shi* 宋史 (A.D. 1346).

17. Note that the "Li shu" 曆書 chapter of the *Shiji* is an obvious exception to this rule both because of its brevity and its inclusion of a computed calendar in place of instructions. On the "Li shu" calendar, see Chapter 3.

18. *Granting the Seasons*, 21. In a similar vein, Cullen describes the astronomical system as "mathematical

Table 1.2: Supernal Emblem System (#10) table of contents (*Jin shu*, 17.504–531)

Section 1: [Lunisolar astronomy/calendrics]

Numbers: elements of mean solar year, mean synodic month, and eclipse month

Methods: (1) 推入紀 "Calculate entry into current era"; (2) 推朔 "Calculate dates of new moons"; (3) 推冬至 "Calculate date of winter solstice"; (4) 求二十四氣 "Find the dates of the 24 *qi*"; (5) 推閏月 "Calculate the intercalary month"; (6) 推弦望 "Calculate the dates of quarter and full moon"; (7) 推沒 "Calculate disappearances"; (8) 推日度 "Calculate the position of the sun (at midnight on any given day)"; (9) 推月度 "Calculate the position of the moon (at midnight on any given day)"; (10) 推合朔度 "Calculate the position of conjunction (and position of subsequent lunar phases)"; (11) 推月蝕 "Calculate month of lunar eclipse"; (12) 推卦用事日 "Calculate the management of affairs by the hexagrams"; (13) 推五行用事 "Calculate the management of affairs by the five agents"; (14) 推加時 "Calculate the hour (of any lunar phase)"; (15) 推漏刻 "Calculate the clepsydra marks (of any lunar phase)."

Section 2: 月行三道術 "Technique for the three roads of lunar motion"

Table: 遲疾曆 "Speed sequence" (daily lunar equation of center and interpolation)

Numbers: elements of the sidereal and anomalistic month

Methods: (1) 推合朔入曆 "Calculate entry of conjunction into sequence"; (2) 求弦望定大小餘 "Calculate fixed date of quarter and full moon"; (3) 求朔弦望加時定度 "Calculate fixed hour and position of new, quarter, and full moon"; (4) 推月行夜半入曆 "Calculate entry of lunar motion into sequence at midnight"; (5) 求月夜半定度 "Find fixed position of moon at midnight"; (6) 求變衰法 "Find interpolation method" ; (7) 求次曆 "Find subsequent sequence[-entries]"; (8) 求次日夜半定度 "Find the fixed position at midnight on subsequent day"; (9) 求次日夜半盈縮 "Find equation of center at midnight on subsequent day"; (10) 求昏明月度 "Find lunar position at dusk and dawn"; (11) 求月行遲疾 "Find speed of lunar motion."

Table: 陰陽曆 "Latitude sequence"

Numbers: elements of the nodical month

Methods: (1) 推朔入陰陽曆 "Calculate entry of new moon into latitude sequence"; (2) 求次月 "Find subsequent months"; (3) 求朔望定數 "Find fixed numbers for new and full moon"; (4) 推夜半入曆 "Calculate sequence-entry at midnight"; (5) 求夜半定日 "Find fixed date at midnight"; (6) 求昏明數 "Find dusk and dawn numbers"; (7) 求月去極度 "Find lunar latitude."

Section 3: 推五星 "Calculate the five stars (planets)"

Numbers: elements of the planets' mean synodic and visibility periods

Methods: (1) 推星合月 "Calculate month of planetary conjunction"; (2) 推入月日 "Calculate the date"; (3) 推星合度 "Calculate position of planetary conjunction"; (4) 求後合月 "Find month of next conjunction"; (5) 求後合朔日 "Find new-moon day of said month"; (6) 求後入月日術 "Find date of next conjunction"; (7) 求後度 "Find next position"; (8) 五星曆步術 "Method for planetary sequence-pacing."

Motion-degree models: (models of planetary behavior over one synodic period)

nology distilled therefrom. This presents us with a unique set of hermeneutical challenges: they are "black boxes" that efface the processes of their creation; they are tools that reveal neither how nor what they were used to create; and they are government property that tell us nothing of private practice. The manual-as-text also gives us a misleading impression of integrity. *Li* treatise chronicles suggest that a system's public lifespan was commonly marked by accretion and modification, dynamics for which our manuals provide but a single snapshot in time. The fact that what is recorded of some manuals is only their numbers or "essentials" (*yao* 要), furthermore, raises the question of less explicit abridgment.[19] For example, the Supernal Emblem system manual appears complete as it is preserved in one *juan* of the *Jin shu* "Lü li zhi" (A.D. 648), but the bibliographic treatise of the *Sui shu* 隋書 (A.D. 636) records editions in only three and five *juan*; moreover, the *Jin shu* attributes to it a method of solar inequality that is absent from the manual preserved in the selfsame *juan*.[20]

The relationship between *tianwen* and *li* was something of a one-way street. True, *li* "calendro-astronomy" functioned independent of speculative cosmology, like its counterparts in Mesopotamia and Mesoamerica, but *tianwen* star catalogs, instruments, or observational records fed into it in obvious and well-documented ways. It might seem equally obvious that

---

software" ("Actors, Networks, and 'Disturbing Spectacles' in Institutional Science," 244).

19. For example, the *Jin shu* "Lü li zhi" provides us with only basic numbers—mean lunisolar parameters—for the following systems: Han Yi's 韓翊 Yellow Inception system (#11; c. A.D. 223), Liu Zhi's 劉智 Orthodox system (#14; c. A.D. 274), Wang Shuozhi's 王朔之 General system (#17; A.D. 353), and Jiang Ji's 姜岌 Triple Era First-year Epoch system (#18; A.D. 384). See *Jin shu*, 17.498, 18.562–563, 565–570; cf. Liu Hongtao 劉洪濤, *Gudai lifa jisuanfa* 古代曆法計算法 (Tianjin: Nankai daxue chubanshe, 2003), 235–240. The *Sui shu* provides a similar treatment of Zhang Bin's 張賓 Opening Sovereignty system (#50; A.D. 584), which it introduces as "its essentials" 其要 (*Sui shu* [Zhonghua shuju ed.], 17.421–423).

20. The *Sui shu* "Jingji zhi" 經籍志 records a Supernal Emblem system in three *juan* as part of the Sui (A.D. 581–618) imperial holdings. It also notes that Liang (A.D. 502–557) bibliographers recorded a five-*juan* edition with commentary by Liu Hong, et al., a five-*juan* edition with commentary by Kan Ze 闞澤, and a *Supernal Emblem Planetary Magic* (*Qianxiang wuxing huanshu* 乾象五星幻術) in one *juan*, all of which were lost by the Sui (*Sui shu*, 34.1022). The *Xin Tang shu* 新唐書 confirms that a three-*juan* edition would have still been available to the *Jin shu*'s Tang compiler (*Xin Tang shu* [Zhonghua shuju ed.], 59.1546). The issue of the Supernal Emblem's *xiaoxi* 消息 model for solar inequality is addressed in Chapter 4. Note, however, that the *Jin shu*'s contradiction on this matter may not be the product of abridgment (at least not in the seventh century), since Yixing 一行 comments in the eighth century that "this technique has not been passed down" 術不傳 (ibid., 17B.622).

"*li fa* was in service of astrology" (Jiang Xiaoyuan), e.g. by predicting *tianwen* phenomena, but this does not really seem to be the case.[21] Generally speaking, *tianwen* omenology is the study of "anomaly" (*yi* 異), and thus the sort of "constancy" (*chang* 常) that is the purview of *li* is of little interest.[22] The majority of *tianwen* omen series are devoted to *purely observational* criteria like color, brightness, scintillation, altitude, strange celestial, meteorological, and optical phenomena, and precise configurations and interactions between bodies. Several series involve an object's failure to act the way that it "should" (*ying* 應, *dang* 當, etc.), but the normative models upon which such judgments are predicated are quite distinct from matters of contemporary *li*.[23] Lastly, *li* materials themselves intimate no such function, nor is there much evidence of them having been put to the purpose of predictive omenology.[24]

---

21. Jiang, *Tianxue zhen yuan*, 125. Cf. note 24.

22. The concept of *chang* in the astral sciences and the question of whether or not the recognized regularity of phenomena deprived them of significance are fascinating issues in Chinese omenology that have only just begun to be addressed. See Nakayama, "Characteristics of Chinese Astrology," 444–446.

23. For a typological study of *tianwen* omen series, see Jiang Xiaoyuan, *Zhongguo xingzhanxue leixing fenxi*. I specifically address the issue of omenological planetary models and their relationship with *li* mathematical astronomy In Chapter 2. On this topic, see also Christopher Cullen, "Understanding the Planets in Ancient China: Prediction and Divination in the *Wu Xing Zhan*," *Early Science and Medicine* 16 (2011): esp. 243–248.

24. The only omenological contents found in *li* literature is the instruction that "if it is the final 10 days of winter, and the moon is in Spread.$_{26}$ (Hydra) or Heart.$_{05}$ (Scorpius), then note it" 其冬下旬，月在張、心署之 in the calendar section of the Quarter-remainder system (#9), Supernal Emblem system (#10), and Luminous Inception system (#13; A.D. 237) (*Hou Han shu, zhi* 3, 3064; *Jin shu*, 17.507, 18.544; *Song shu* 宋書 [Zhonghua shuju ed.], 12.241). The reason is probably that, as the *Sui shu* "Xingfa zhi" 刑法志 ("Treatise on Punishments") states, "on the first and last day of the month, the eight seasonal nodes, and the six fasts, if the moon is in Spread.$_{26}$ or Heart.$_{05}$, then no punishments may be carried out" 晦朔、八節、六齊、月在張心日，並不得行刑 (*Sui shu*, 25.703). Common sense seems to dictate that *tianwen* omenology would have been central to the use and development of *li* mathematical astronomy. No one has presented the case for this more substantially or emphatically than Jiang Xiaoyuan, so his argument merits summary here (*Tianxue zhen yuan*, 124–137). First, he posits that eclipse and planetary theory in *li* mathematical astronomy must have developed in response to some need. That need is not *li* calendrics, since neither plays a discernible role there. Furthermore, one of the central assertions in Jiang's work is that "every type of ancient Chinese knowledge had an intensely practical nature" and that to pursue something like astronomy "purely out of curiosity for exploring the secrets of nature... this situation is extremely common in ancient Greek and modern science, but we have yet to discover a similar tradition in ancient China" (125). The only possibility left, he concludes, is that "*li fa* was in service of astrology" (125). In support of his conclusion, he offers a number of examples he describes as " 'passively' based on *already visible celestial* phenomena" (134; emphasis is the authors'). To this he adds two "active" examples. The first concerns Li Chunfeng, who warns the emperor that a *predicted* solar eclipse has been divined *ahead of time* as inauspicious, possibly due to its position among the lodges (*Taiping guangji* 太平廣記 [Zhonghua shuju ed.], 76.479). Eclipse prediction

This is not to imply that the distinction between *tianwen* and *li* is one of "magic" and "science." To the contrary, *tianwen* literature reminds us of the greater cultural meaning of the objects that *li* astronomy sets out to study and regulate. Also, more to the point is the fact that *li* calendrics is home to a *different* science of divination. As illustrated in Table 1.2, system manuals contain techniques (*shu*) for calculating the dates of *mo* 沒 "disappearance" and *mie* 滅 "extinction," and the ascendancy of the five agents and hexagrams—elements of calendar divination or "hemerology" that I will touch upon in Chapter 3.[25] Long ago, Nakayama astutely observed that "the Chinese art of fate calculation is not properly called 'astrology'."[26] *Tianwen* omenology is the science of "divining" (*zhan* 占) the fortune of state actors through the "observation" (*guan* 觀, *hou* 侯 or *wang* 望) of "signs" (*xiang*), "anomalies" (*yi*), "disturbances" (*bian* 變), "disasters" (*zai* 災), "tokens" (*fu* 符), etc. Hemerology, on the other hand, is the science of "selecting" (*ze* 擇) or "avoiding" (*bi* 避) fateful times

---

is the function of *li* mathematical astronomy that we see most often in historical sources; cases like this are extremely rare, however, as the majority concern the timing of imperial ceremonies. Jiang's second example concerns Cui Hao 崔浩 (d. A.D. 450), who predicts the reappearance of Mars in Well.$_{22}$ (Gemini) 80 days after it "suddenly disappeared one night" 一夜忽然亡失 in Gourd (56 Sgr), presaging the death of Latter Qin emperor Yao Xing 姚興 (r. A.D. 394–416) (*Wei shu*, 35.808–809). There are two problems with the latter story. First, the text describes Cui Hao as making this prediction on the basis of ganzhimancy rather than *li* mathematical astronomy. Second, *the story is clearly apocryphal.* A quick check via the computer program *Alcyone Ephemeris* v3.2 reveals that Mars entered Well.$_{22}$ around 414 Aug 30 (where it stayed until 415 Apr 18), some 235 days after it passed beneath (rather than through!) Gourd in 414 Jan 17—none of which occurred in the year prior to Yao Xing's death. While Jiang is right that it was completely within the power of contemporary actors to deploy *li* mathematical astronomy for the sake of *tianwen* omenology, there are simply not enough examples that I am aware of to support his secondary conclusion that "astrology requires *li fa*" (137).

25. Jean-Claude Martzloff discusses these concepts and techniques from the perspective of astronomical system manuals in *Le calendrier chinois: structure et calculs, 104 av. JC-1644: indétermination céleste et réforme permanente: la construction chinoise officielle du temps quotidien discret à partir d'un temps mathématique caché, linéaire et continu,* Sciences, techniques et civilisations du Moyen Âge à l'aube des Lumières 11 (Paris: Champion, 2009), esp. 68–69, 90–99, 221–240. As I will discuss in Chapter 3, these were integral more to the finished products of *li* calendrics—*li* calendars and *juzhu liri* 具注曆日 "almanacs"— than the science of *li* itself. *Li* texts themselves do not detail how to interpret this information the way that, for example, *tianwen* omen series do. In fact, most of what we know about early imperial calendar divination comes from excavated manuscripts; see Marc Kalinowski, "Les instruments astro-calendriques des Han et la méthode *liu ren*," *Bulletin de l'Ecole française d'Extrême-Orient* 72, no. 1 (1983): 309–419; "Les traités de Shuihudi et l'hémérologie chinoise a la fin des Royaumes-Combattants," *T'oung Pao* 2d ser., 72, no. 4/5 (1986): 175–228; Liu Lexian 劉樂賢, *Jianbo shushu wenxian tanlun* 簡帛數術文獻探論 (Wuhan: Hubei jiaoyu chubanshe, 2002); Ethan Richard Harkness, "Cosmology and the Quotidian: Day Books in Early China" (Ph.D. diss., University of Chicago, 2011).

26. "Characteristics of Chinese Astrology," 442.

and directions for quotidian affairs through the consultation of "prohibitions and taboos" (*jin ji* 禁忌), diagrams, or *shi* 式 divination boards in reference to a particular time or direction as counted in heavenly stems and earthly branches (*tiangan dizhi* 天干地支 or *ganzhi* 干支; see Table 1). Thus, if *tianwen*-divination is deserving of the title "astrology" or "uranomancy," this *li*-divination might be rightly called "calendérologie" (Mark Kalinowski) or "ganzhimancy."[27]

Dynastic histories: other sources

The dynastic histories are filled with other tangential sources for *tianwen* and *li*, such as the biographies of their practitioners and "Wuxing zhi" 五行志 (Five Agents Treatises), whose omen records sometimes overlap with "*Tianwen* Treatises." Perhaps the most significant resource for understanding these textual genres, however, are the bibliographies of imperial library holdings.[28] The *Han shu* "Yi wen zhi" 藝文志 is the earliest of these bibliographies still extant and a model for later treatises. It lists *tianwen* and *li* at the head of six categories of "Numbers and Techniques" (*shu shu* 數術):[29]

1. "*Tianwen*"

2. "*Li* and Chronologies" (*li pu* 曆譜)

3. "Five Agents" (*wu xing* 五行)

4. "Milfoil and Turtle [divination]" (*shi gui* 蓍龜)

5. "Miscellaneous Divination" (*za zhan* 雜占)

6. "Morphoscopy" (*xingfa* 形法)

---

27. Kalinowski proposes the term "calendérologie" in "Les instruments astro-calendriques des Han et la méthode *liu ren*," 311.

28. On the bibliographic treatises and early imperial libraries, see Jean Pierre Drège, *Les bibliothèques en Chine au temps des manuscrits: jusqu'au Xe siècle*, vol. 161, Publications de l'Ecole française d'Extrême-Orient (Paris: Ecole française d'Extrême-Orient, 1991).

29. *Han shu* (Zhonghua shuju ed.), 30.1763–1775.

All but one of the 190 works listed under "Numbers and Techniques" are now lost, but their titles provide further clues about the scopes of these genres. "*Tianwen*" titles appear to belong to one of three types of literature: descriptive catalogs of stars, objects, and phenomena; omen series (*zhan*); or omen records (*zhan yan* 占驗, lit. "prognostications and [their] verifications"). "*Li* and Chronologies" titles, on the other hand, fall into four very different categories: the systems and motion-degree models of *li* calendro-astronomy; gnomonics (*rigui* 日晷); royal chronologies (*pu* 譜); and mathematics (*suanshu* 算術). The later bibliographic treatises of the *Sui shu*, *Jiu Tang shu*, and *Xin Tang shu* 新唐書 (A.D. 1060) see the addition of several new varieties of titles: to "*Tianwen*" is added works on cosmology and Indian *tianwen*; and to the subsequent "*Li* and Mathematics" (*li shu* 曆數 or *li suan* 曆算) is added "seven luminaries *li*" (*qi yao li* 七曜曆), studies of ancient records and methods, and Indian mathematics.[30]

It it also worth noting what sky- and calendar-related knowledge bibliographers *do not* categorize as *tianwen* and *li*. First of all, titles related to calendar divination are consistently placed under the category "Five Agents." Celestial omens and meteoromancy are shared between "*Tianwen*," "Five Agents," and "Miscellaneous Divination." Ritual and festival calendars—most notably the "monthly ordinance" (*yue ling* 月令) genre—are organized under the "Ritual" (*li* 禮) subheading of "Classics" (*jing* 經). Lastly, techniques for absorbing celestial *qi* and traveling to the stars are found alongside works on bodily cultivation, alchemy, and other magico-religious practices under "Recipes and Skills" (*fang ji* 方技).[31] Scholars

---

30. *Sui shu*, 34.1018–1026; *Jiu Tang shu*, 47.2036–2039; *Xin Tang shu*, 59.1543–1549. On the "seven luminaries *li*," see Jiang Xiaoyuan, *Tianxue zhen yuan*, 266–293.

31. On monthly ordinance literature and the *Ming tang* 明堂, or Hall of Light ritual complex, see Henri Maspero, "Le *ming-t'ang* et la crise religieuse chinoise avant les Han," *Mélanges chinois et bouddhiques* 9 (1951): 1–71; William Edward Soothill, *The Hall of Light: a Study of Early Chinese Kingship* (London: Lutterworth Press, 1951); Lillian Lan-ying Tseng, *Picturing Heaven in Early China* (Cambridge: Harvard University Asia Center, 2011), 70–88. On religious practices involving space and time travel, see Schafer, *Pacing the Void*, 234–269; Kristofer Marinus Schipper and Wang Hsiu-huei, "Progressive and Regressive Time Cycles in Taoist Ritual," in *Time, Science, and Society in China and the West*, ed. Julius Thomas Fraser, Nathaniel Morris Lawrence, and Francis C. Haber (Amherst: University of Massachusetts Press, 1986), 185–205; Poul Andersen, "The Practice of Bugang," *Cahiers d'Extrême-Asie* 5 (1990): 15–53; Gil Raz, "Time Manipulation in Early Daoist Ritual: The East Well Chart and the Eight Archivists," *Asia Major* 18, no. 1 (2005): 67–102.

of excavated divination literature have in the last two decades spilled a considerable amount of ink about the significance of the bibliographic meta-category *shu shu*, as especially it concerns issues of "science" and "superstition." Lest it distract us from the topic at hand—*tianwen* and *li*—I would like to leave the problem of *shu shu* aside. For now, let us simply note that as far as "Numbers and Techniques" and its bibliographic subcategories go, we should neither presuppose their existence prior to the Western Han nor their conceptual stability or popular currency thereafter.[32]

Omen compendia

Outside of dynastic histories, the most voluminous (and poorly studied) sources for the astral sciences in early imperial China are omen compendia.[33] Of these, we posses six titles in 181 *juan*: the *Tongzhan daxiang lixing jing* 通占大象曆星經 (2 *juan*), Yu Jicai's 庾季才 (A.D. 516–603) *Lingtai miyuan* 靈臺秘苑 (c. A.D. 580; 15/120 *juan*), Li Chunfeng's *Yisi zhan* 乙巳占 (A.D. 656; 10 *juan*), Li Feng's 李鳳 *Tianwen yaolu* 天文要錄 (A.D. 664; 25/50 *juan*), Sa Shouzhen's 薩守真 *Tiandi ruixiang zhi* 天地瑞祥志 (A.D. 666; 9/20 *juan*), and Gautama Siddhārtha's 瞿曇悉達 *Kaiyuan zhanjing* (A.D. 729; 120 *juan*).[34] These works are explicitly

---

32. On "*shu shu*" and the bibliographic organization of technical literature in *Han shu* "Yi wen zhi" from the perspective of divination, see Li Ling 李零, *Zhongguo fangshu zheng kao* 中國方術正考 (Beijing: Zhonghua shuju, 2006), 1–24; Song Huiqun 宋會羣, *Zhongguo shushu wenhua shi* 中國術數文化史 (Kaifeng: Henan daxue chubanshe, 1999); Liu Lexian, *Jianbo shushu wenxian tanlun*, 3–52; Marc Kalinowski, "Technical Traditions in Ancient China and *Shushu* Culture in Chinese Religion," in *Religion and Chinese Society*, ed. John Lagerwey (Hong Kong: The Chinese University Press, 2004), 223–248. From the perspective of mathematical astronomy, see Jiang Xiaoyuan, *Tianxue zhen yuan*, 54; Christopher Cullen, "Numbers, Numeracy and the Cosmos," in *China's Early Empires: a Re-appraisal*, ed. Michael Nylan and Michael Loewe (Cambridge: Cambridge University Press, 2010), 323.

33. For the sake of clarity, by "omen" I refer to a single protasis-apodosis statement like those that I have enumerated in the citation from the *Jin shu* on p. 28. By "omen lists" I refer to lists of omens. By "omen series" I refer to groupings of omen statements, e.g. along a single topic or conceptual scheme. By "omen catalogs" I refer to texts comprised of multiple omen lists/series. Lastly, by "omen compendia" I refer to large multi-*juan* texts that collect and preserve omen lists/series.

34. Omen compendia are collected in vols. 4 & 5 of *Zhongguo kexue jishu dianji tonghui: tianwen juan* 中國科學技術典籍通彙・天文卷, ed. Bo Shuren 薄樹人, 8 vols. (Zhengzhou: Hebei jiaoyu chubanshe, 1993). The *Lingtai miyuan* (which for whatever reason is not included in this collection) and the *Kaiyuan zhanjing* are also found in the *Siku quanshu*, while the *Tongzhan daxiang lixing jing* can be found as fascicle 287 of the Daoist Canon (Kristofer Marinus Schipper and Franciscus Verellen, *The Taoist Canon: a Historical Companion to the Daozang* [Chicago: University of Chicago Press, 2004], 335–336). Higher-quality repro-

40

written in and identified with the *tianwen* genre.[35]

Other than volume, the major difference between omen compendia and "*Tianwen* Treatises" in terms of contents and organization is that the former does not pair catalogs of facts with records of phenomena. There are other minor differences: after 101 *juan* of *tianwen*, for example, the *Kaiyuan zhanjing* devotes several *juan* to *li*, mathematics, and terrestrial omens; similarly, the *Yisi zhan* supplements *tianwen* omen series with elements of *li* and ganzhimancy. All of this goes to show that *tianwen* and *li* genres are probably best likened to Venn diagrams in that they are defined by sets of core and peripheral elements rather than hard generic boundaries.

Where the two *are* utterly distinct is on the issue of attribution. *Tianwen* literature is in this regard a morass of ambiguity and pseudepigraphy. All six of these compendia have come down to us through harrowing circumstances, and while scholars agree that the *Kaiyuan zhanjing* and *Yisi zhan* are reliable and complete, the others are more problematic: the *Tongzhan daxiang lixing jing* is anonymous; the *Lingtai miyuan* underwent significant redaction in the eleventh century; and it is uncertain whether the *Tianwen yaolu* and *Tiandi ruixiang zhi* (both of which are missing half their contents) even originate in China.[36] What is more, these texts are catalogs of formulae drawn from a common pool of unqualified facts to which scholars only began to assign authorship at a relatively late date (and for relatively

---

ductions of twentieth-century manuscript copies of the *Tianwen yaolu* and *Tiandi ruixiang zhi* can also be found in Gao Keli 高柯立, *Xijian Tangdai tianwen shiliao san zhong* 稀見唐代天文史料三種, 3 vols. (Guojia tushuguan chubanshe, 2011). This list does not include five agents compendia like Xiao Ji's 蕭吉 (fl. A.D. 555-605) *Wuxing dayi* 五行大義 or the *Qiaozi wuxing zhi* 譙子五行志, whose contents occasionally wander into *tianwen* and *li*. On the *Wuxing dayi*, see the study and translation of Kalinowski, *Le compendium des cinq agents*. The *Qiaozi wuxing zhi* can be found in Gao Keli, *Xijian Tangdai tianwen shiliao san zhong*, vol. 3, 584–729.

35. The Xin Tang shu bibliographic treatise places *Lingtai miyuan*, *Yisi zhan*, and *Kaiyuan zhanjing* under the heading "*Tianwen*," as does the *Nihon-koku genzaisho mokuroku* 日本國見在書目錄 for *Tiandi ruixiang zhi* (*Xin Tang shu*, 59.1544–1545; *Guyi congshu* 古逸叢書 [Yiwen yinshuguan ed.], 19.30B). Though the *Tongzhan daxiang lixing jing* and *Tianwen yaolu* do not appear categorized in ancient bibliographies, their titles and contents show obvious affinities with this genre.

36. On the provenance of these sources, see their introductions in *Zhongguo kexue jishu dianji tonghui: tianwen juan; Xijian Tangdai tianwen shiliao san zhong*. On the *Lingtai miyuan*, see *Lingtai miyuan*, Zhongguo shida diwang cangshu 5 (Huhehaote: Nei Menggu renmin chubanshe, 2002), 1–2.

transparent rhetorical purposes). As a result, where facts are associated with names, they tend to be the names of deities, legends, and prophets. The distribution of attribution, in fact, creates the impression that the production of knowledge had ceased by the end of the second century A.D., when Han (206 B.C. – A.D. 220) scholars like Liu Rui 劉叡 began to compile the first compendia.[37] However, even sources that we may confidently attribute to the mid-Han, like weft texts, draw from a pool of common elements that goes back to at least the second century B.C.[38]

Other received sources

Of course, an upshot of the *tianwen* genre's piecemeal nature is that, like the "*Li* Treatises," it preserves whole and fragmentary texts that may otherwise have been lost to history. Without them, for example, we would not have access to the star canons of Shi Shen 石申, Gan De 甘德, and Wuxian 巫咸, Zhang Heng's 張衡 (A.D. 87–140) works on cosmology and the armillary sphere, the majority of weft-text fragments (which are replete with *tianwen* and *li* contents), earlier omen compendia like Liu Rui's *Jingzhou zhan* 荊州占, or the so-called "six ancient *li* calendar systems" (*gu liu li* 古六曆) of the pre-Qin.

Other than the omen compendia, however, the only work devoted to the astral sciences to have come down to us from this period both independently and intact is the *Zhou bi* 周

---

37. Liu Rui's *Jingzhou zhan* 荊州占 is the most comprehensive and synthetic of the sources cited throughout the *Kaiyuan zhanjing*. The *Jin shu* tells us that, "at the end of the [Eastern] Han Liu Biao was regional governor of Jingzhou and ordered the governor of Wuling, Liu Rui, to collect together the many *tianwen* omens, and this was named *Jingzhou zhan*" 及漢末劉表為荊州牧，命武陵太守劉叡集天文眾占，名『荊州占』 (*Jin shu*, 322). This is the first record of the sort of effort to collect, synthesize, and, ultimately, preserve a tradition that came to predominate post-Han omen literature—a sign, perhaps, of a shift away from the production of new knowledge.

38. Liu Lexian argues this point in two studies of the textual parallels between the River Chart weft *Di lan xi* 河圖・帝覽嬉 and the silk manuscript *Wuxing zhan* 五星占 found in Mawangdui 馬王堆 tomb 3 (sealed 168 B.C.); see his *Jianbo shushu wenxian tanlun*, 341–351; "Weishu zhong de tianwen ziliao—*Hetu Dilanxi* wei li" 緯書中的天文資料 —『河圖帝覽嬉』爲例, *Zhongguo shi yanjiu* 中國史研究 2007.2: 71–82. Liu fleshes out an even greater number of such parallels in his monograph on this and the other *tianwen* materials found at Mawangdui, *Mawangdui tianwen shu kaoshi* 馬王堆天文書考釋 (Guangzhou: Zhongshan daxue chubanshe, 2004). In Chapter 2, I show that the *li* astronomical contents of the *Wuxing zhan* are unmistakably Qin (221–207 B.C.) in origin. He Youqi 何幼琦 offers evidence that the text's *tianwen* contents date even earlier to the Warring States (480–222 B.C.) in "Shi lun *Wuxing zhan* de shidai he neirong" 試論『五星占』的時代和内容, *Xueshu yanjiu* 學術研究 1979.1: 80–83.

髀. Famous for its *gai tian* 蓋天 "Chariot-cover Heaven" theory of cosmology, the *Zhou bi* is primarily concerned with the question of how to measure Heaven and, thus, topics of cosmology and gnomonics. However, more so than other entries in the cosmology genre— *tian ti* 天體 "the substance of Heaven" or *tian lun* 天論 "the discourse on Heaven"—it goes into significant detail on related issues of mathematics and *li* calendrics.[39] In A.D. 656, Li Chunfeng included the *Zhou bi* among the ten "mathematical classics" (*suan jing* 算經) of the curriculum of the Tang 唐 (A.D. 618–907) State Academy, and the bibliographic treatise of the *Xin Tang shu* places Li's annotated edition under "*Li* and Mathematics." At the same time, however, the *Xin Tang shu, Jiu Tang shu,* and *Sui shu* list all other editions of the text under "*Tianwen,*" providing another example of ambiguity between genres.[40]

Finally, some of the most invaluable sources for the astral sciences are individual chapters of received works, e.g. the *Huainanzi* 淮南子 (139 B.C.), Ban Gu's 班固 (A.D. 32–92) *Baihu tong* 白虎通, Wang Chong's 王充 (A.D. 27 – c. 100) *Lun heng* 論衡, and Xu Gan's 徐幹 (A.D. 171–217/218) *Zhong lun* 中論. While each approaches the astral sciences as part of a larger project, and thus brings different questions and perspectives to bear on them, they do address the same range of topics, which they subsume under typical rubrics of *tianwen* and *li*.[41] The one exception—indeed, the most outstanding exception of the entire period—is the

---

39. Important studies of the *Zhou bi* include Qian Baocong 錢寶琮, "Zhoubi suanjing kao" 周髀算經考, in *Qian Baocong kexueshi lunwen xuanji* 錢寶琮科學史論文選集 (1924; rpt. Beijing: Kexue chubanshe, 1983), 119–136; Nōda Chūryō, *Shūhi sankei no kenkyū* 周髀算經の研究 (Kyōto: Tōhō bunka gakuin, 1933); Cullen, *Astronomy and Mathematics in Ancient China.* For comprehensive studies and translation of the greater discourse on cosmology in pre-modern China, see Cullen, "Cosmographical Discussions in China from Early Times up the T'ang Dynasty"; Chen Meidong, *Zhongguo gudai tianwenxue sixiang,* 128–532.

40. *Xin Tang shu,* 59.1534–1544, 1547; *Jiu Tang shu,* 47.2036; *Sui shu,* 34.1018.

41. Not included in this list is the outpour of Han scholarship on "correlative cosmology" or the "cosmological synthesis" surrounding the *Book of Changes,* for which I direct the reader to the larger studies of Wang Aihe and Richard Smith: Wang Aihe, *Cosmology and Political Culture in Early China* (Cambridge: Cambridge University Press, 2000); Richard J. Smith, *Fathoming the Cosmos and Ordering the World: The Yijing (*I Ching, *or* Classic of Changes*) and Its Evolution in China* (Charlottesville: University of Virginia Press, 2008), 31–88. Also not included in this list are sources for the "monthly ordinance" genre or Heaven-related magico-religious practices, see note 31. The *Baihu tong* subsections "San zheng" 三正 ("The Three First [Months]"), "Tian di" 天地 ("Heaven and Earth"), "Ri yue" 日月 ("The Sun and Moon"), and "Si shi" 四時 ("The Four Seasons"), which discuss basic *tianwen* objects and calendrical parameters in terms of their analogical meaning for proper government and with a strong bent towards yin-yang and five agents correlative thought. For a translation and study of the *Baihu tong,* see Tjan Tjoe Som 曾祖森, *Po Hu*

"Tianwen xun" 天文訓 chapter of the *Huainanzi*. While covering a range of typical *tianwen* contents—cosmogony, correlative thought, the geography of the sky, and planetary models and omens—the "Tianwen xun" devotes equal space to matters of *li* calendrics, harmonics, gnomonics, and, most importantly, ganzhimancy.[42] Whatever weight we decide to give this exception, it is important to note that it is also our earliest self-described source for *tianwen* and, thus, may not speak for enduring ambiguities between these genres.

Manuscript sources

My goal in this section is to survey the contents of *tianwen* and *li* as textual genres in prelude to a discussion of their meaning in myth and practice. I have begun with received sources for the simple reason that their authors and early biographers identify them with these genres. Equally important to the history of the astral sciences, however, is the growing corpus of excavated manuscripts from this period. Indeed, these are the sources to which this study is primarily devoted: in Chapter 2, I focus on the *Wuxing zhan* 五星占, a silk manuscript on planetary astronomy/astrology recovered from Mawangdui 馬王堆 tomb 3 (sealed 168 B.C.); and in Chapter 3, I examine calendars, more than fifty of which have

---

T'ung, the Comprehensive Discussions in the White Tiger Hall, 2 vols. (Leiden: Brill, 1952). Where the *Lun heng* addresses the astral sciences, it is to logically dismantle what its author identifies as scholastic and cultural fallacies: the chapters "Tan tian" 談天 ("Discussion of Heaven") and "Shuo ri" 說日 ("Explanation of the Sun") address problems at the core of cosmology, and the chapters "Lan shi" 讕時 ("False Charges against Time"), "Ji ri" 譏日 ("Slandering of Days"), and "Sui nan" 歲難 ("Difficulties with Taisui") present arguments against practices of calendar divination. For a translation and study of the *Lun heng*, see Alfred Forke, *Lun-hêng*, 2 vols. (1907; rpt. New York: Paragon Book Gallery, 1962); Marc Kalinowski, *Balance des discours: destin, providence et divination*, Bibliothèque Chinoise 5 (Paris: Les belles lettres, 2011). The *Zhong lun* chapter "Li shu" 曆數 ("*Li* Numbers") presents a standard explanation of the role of the ancient Sages Kings in establishing the science and methodology of *li* as the linchpin of cosmo-political harmony and narrates the history of *li* from their time to the end of the second century A.D. On the *Zhong lun*, see Michael Loewe, ed., *Early Chinese Texts: a Bibliographical Guide* (Berkeley: Institute of East Asian Studies, University of California, 1993), 88–93; John Makeham, *Balanced Discourses* (New Haven: Yale University Press, 2002).

42. John Major presents a complete translation and study of the "Tianwen xun" in *Heaven and Earth in Early Han Thought: Chapters Three, Four and Five of the* Huainanzi (Albany: State University of New York Press, 1993), 55–139. Equally important is Tao Lei's 陶磊 study of the ganzhimantic calendar divination that predominates the chapter's contents in Huainanzi Tianwen *yanjiu—cong shushu de jiaodu* 『淮南子・天文』研究 —從數術的角度 (Jinan: Qi Lu shushe, 2003). On the *Huainanzi*'s planetary models, which I discuss in passing in Chapter 2, see also Michel Teboul, *Les premières théories planétaires chinoises* (Paris: Collège de France, 1983), 145–148.

been recovered from the period between the third century B.C. to the seventh century A.D. Beyond the scope of the present study, there are a host of other relevant materials at our disposal as well: sources for calendar divination, such as the growing number of third and second-century B.C. daybook (*rishu* 日書) miscellanies; dozens of almanacs from the Tang and Song 宋 (A.D. 960–1279) found at Dunhuang; and further uranomantic texts recovered from Dunhuang and Mawangdui.[43]

The advantages of such materials are obvious. They are new. They are also a very different type of text: they are *realia* that inform us about the physical and textual format in which knowledge was produced and consumed; they were the property of non-specialists, who copied and crafted them for actual social uses rather than simply for posterity. Furthermore, the sources that I address are *products*, that is products of practice that illustrate how and why the knowledge that was manifested in system manuals, theoretical treatises, and debate records—sources that, for good reason, scholars tend to privilege—was actually put to use.

The question is not *if* we put these in communication with the received tradition but *how*. Donald Harper warns us against reading *shu shu* onto an age before its emergence as a bibliographic category in the *Han shu* or onto texts that were personal rather than public productions.[44] Is it then legitimate to talk about these manuscripts in terms of *tianwen* and *li*? In part, yes. Some of the practices and vocabulary surveyed here may be

---

43. For an overview of excavated sources related to calendar divination, see Liu Lexian, *Jianbo shushu wenxian tanlun*. Important studies of daybooks include Kalinowski, "Les traités de Shuihudi et l'hémérologie chinoise a la fin des Royaumes-Combattants"; Liu Lexian, "Shuihudi Qin jian rishu yanjiu" 睡虎地秦簡日書研究 (Ph.D. diss., Zhongguo shehui kexue yuan, 1993); Harkness, "Cosmology and the Quotidian." For a study of the non-daybook calendar divination materials found at Mawangdui, see Marc Kalinowski, "The *Xingde* 刑德 Texts from Mawangdui," trans. Phyllis Brooks, *Early China* 23–24 (1998–1999): 125–202. On the later almanacs found at Dunhuang, Deng Wenkuan 鄧文寬 has authored a prolific number of studies on individual almanacs, and Jean-Claude Martzloff analyzes the computations behind them; see Deng Wenkuan, *Dunhuang Tulufan tianwen lifa yanjiu* 敦煌吐魯番天文曆法研究 (Lanzhou: Gansu jiaoyu chubanshe, 2002); Martzloff, *Le calendrier chinois*, esp. 267–302. For the standard translation and study of the *Wuxing zhan* and the other uranomantic materials from Mawangdui, see Liu Lexian, *Mawangdui tianwen shu kaoshi*. Lastly, for an overview of the almanacs and the texts on calendar divination and uranomancy recovered from Dunhuang, see Marc Kalinowski, ed., *Divination et société dans la Chine médiévale: étude des manuscrits de Dunhuang de la Bibliothèque nationale de France et de la British Library* (Paris: Bibliothèque nationale de France, 2003).

44. "Zhoujiatai de shushu jian" 周家臺的數術簡, trans. Liu Jing 劉淨 and Yan Changgui 晏昌貴, *Jianbo 簡帛* 2 (2007): 398.

unambiguously traced back to pre-Qin times. And while we have yet to find manuscripts from the period in question that bear the titles *tianwen* or *li*, the contents of excavated sources manifest unambiguous ties with their transmitted counterparts.[45] At the same time, however, one of the points that I underscore in Chapters 2 and 3 is that excavated sources also reveal important clues about the fluidity, evolution, and interplay between genres that is less evident in elite traditions.

1.1.2 Sages and the legend of the astral sciences

Now that we have a sense of *tianwen* and *li*'s contents as textual genres, let us turn to the meaning and conceptual vocabulary of practice. To this end, there is no better place to begin than the wellspring of legend from which actors traced the practices of their day.

One of the earliest and most influential formulations of *tianwen* is found in the *Book of Changes*. The "Xi ci zhuan" 繫辭傳 commentary juxtaposes *tianwen* "celestial patterns" with *dili* "terrestrial forms" as manifestations of a cosmic order or *Dao* 道 —an occult order apprehended by the Sages and distilled into the *Changes*.

> 易與天地準，故能彌綸天地之道。仰以觀於天文，俯以察於地理，是故知幽明之故。原始反終，故知死生之說。精氣為物，遊魂為變，是故知鬼神之情狀。與天地相似，故不違。知周乎萬物，而道濟天下，故不過。

The *Changes* is congruent with Heaven and Earth, thus it is able to tie together the Dao of Heaven and Earth. Looking up, [the Sage] contemplates (*guan*) the celestial patterns (*tianwen*); looking down, [he] investigates the terrestrial forms (*dili*)—thus does [he] know the principles of darkness and light. [He] traces things to their beginnings and follows them to their ends—thus does [he] know the lessons of death and life. Seminal *qi* produces [living] things, and the wandering of souls produces change—thus does [he] know the true conditions of ghosts and

---

45. The problem is that the majority of excavated technical literature is untitled. The title *liri* 曆日 does appear on excavated calendars, but only from the fifth century A.D. (see Chapter 3).

spirits. [He] is similar to Heaven and Earth—thus does [he] never turn against them. [He] has complete knowledge of the myriad things and by [his] Dao brings salvation to the subcelestial realm—thus does [he] commit no transgression.[46]

古者包犧氏之王天下也，仰則觀象於天，俯則觀法於地，觀鳥獸之文，與地之宜，近取諸身，遠取諸物，於是始作八卦，以通神明之德，以類萬物之情。

When in early antiquity Baoxi (i.e. Fuxi 伏羲) reigned over the subcelestial realm as king, he looked up and contemplated (*guan*) the signs (*xiang*) in Heaven; he looked down and contemplated the patterns on Earth. He contemplated the markings (*wen*) of birds and beasts and their suitabilities to the land. He gathered near at hand from himself and far away from things, and from this he created (*zuo*) the eight trigrams in order to enter into connection with the virtue of the light of the spirits and to categorize the conditions of the myriad things.[47]

From here, the "Xi ci zhuan" goes on to narrate how all of human civilization unfolds from this single act of *tianwen*, as later sages like the Divine Husbandman, the Yellow Emperor, Yao, and Shun extrapolate key technologies and practices from the trigrams—fishing, agriculture, markets, boats, carts, city defenses, archery, shelter, and writing. In so doing the *Changes* also runs through the semantic range of *wen* 文: *wen* is at once the "patterns" manifest in nature, the "cultural patterns" that the Sages distilled therefrom, the Sages' project of "civilization," and the key component of that project—"writing."[48] It is important to remember, therefore, that embedded in "celestial patterns" is more than just the idea of constellations and periodicities but the germ and blueprint of civilization.

Li is the subject of similar legend. Its core is drawn from the Sagetime stories of pre-

---

46. *Zhouyi zhushu* 周易注疏 (Siku quanshu 四庫全書 ed.), 11.12a; cf. Richard Wilhelm, *The I Ching or, Book of Changes*, tr. Cary F. Baynes, 3d ed., Bollingen Series XIX (Princeton: Princeton University Press, 1967), 293–294.

47. *Zhouyi zhushu*, 12.6a; cf. Wilhelm, *The I Ching*, 328–329.

48. For more on *wen*, see David Schaberg, *A Patterned Past: Form and Thought in Early Chinese Historiography* (Cambridge: Harvard University Asia Center, 2001), esp. 57–95.

imperial classics, such as the *Book of Documents*, the *Analects*, *Guo yu* 國語, and the *Shan hai jing* 山海經.[49] Typical of the early imperial synthesis of these sources is the following account from the *Han shu* "Lü li zhi:"

曆數之起上矣。傳述顓頊命南正重司天，火正黎司地，其後三苗亂德，二官咸廢，而閏餘乖次，孟陬殄滅，攝提失方。堯復育重、黎之後，使纂其業，故書曰：「乃命羲、和，欽若昊天，曆象日月星辰，敬授民時。」「歲三百有六旬有六日，以閏月定四時成歲，允釐百官，衆功皆美。」其後以授舜曰：「咨爾舜，天之曆數在爾躬。」「舜亦以命禹。」

The rise of *li* numbers was [in the past] above. Tradition states that Zhuanxu commanded Chong, the Rector of the South, to administer Heaven and Li, the Rector of Fire, to administer Earth. Later, the San Miao disrupted their virtue, and both offices were abolished. The intercalary remainder perverted the stations, the *meng-zou* [correspondence] was destroyed, and the Regulators slipped from their proper direction. Yao reeducated the descendants of Chong and Li, making them carry on their patrimony. Thus the *Documents* says:

> And then he charged Xi and He, in reverent accordance with august Heaven, to *li* and *xiang* the sun, moon, and stars and respectfully grant the people the seasons... The year has three hundred, sixty, and six days, by means of an intercalary month do you fix the four seasons and complete the agricultural year. If you earnestly control all the functionaries, the achievements will all be resplendent.[50]

Afterward, he transferred this to Shun, saying "Oh, Shun, the *li* numbers of

---

49. For more substantial studies of the mythology of *li* calendro-astronomy, see Jiang Xiaoyuan, *Tianxue zhen yuan*, 9–108; Anne Birrell, *Chinese Mythology: An Introduction* (Baltimore: Johns Hopkins University Press, 1993), esp. 91–95.

50. *Shangshu zhushu* 尚書注疏 (Siku quanshu ed.), 1.8b; tr. modified from Bernhard Karlgren, "The Book of Documents," *Bulletin of the Museum of Far Eastern Antiquities* 22 (1950): 3.

Heaven have fallen to thy person," and "Shun commanded Yu in like manner."[51]

至周武王訪箕子，箕子言大法九章，而五紀明曆法。故自殷周，皆創業改制，咸正曆紀，服色從之，順其時氣，以應天道。

When King Wu of Zhou (r. 1049/45–1043 B.C.) called on Jizi, Jizi spoke of the great method in nine chapters and illuminated calendric method (*li fa*) by means of the five regulators (*ji*).[52] Thus, of all those since the Yin (?–1045 B.C.) and Zhou (1045–256 B.C.) who have founded patrimony and initiated reform, all correct the calendric rules (*li ji*) and follow this in the color of court costume so as to obey the *qi* of its season and respond to the Dao of Heaven.

三代既沒，五伯之末，史官喪紀，疇人子弟分散，或在夷狄，故其所記，有黃帝、顓頊、夏、殷、周及魯曆。戰國擾攘，秦兼天下，未皇暇也，亦頗推五勝，而自以為獲水德，乃以十月為正，色上黑。

After the Three Dynasties had disappeared and at the end of [the period of] the Five Earls (the Spring and Autumn period, 770–481 B.C.), the Clerk's Office lost its [calendrical] rules (*ji*), and its hereditary practitioners and their disciples dispersed, some to the Yi and Di (peripheral peoples). This is why their records include the Yellow Emperor (#1), Zhuanxu (#2), Xia (#3), Yin (#4), Zhou

---

51. *Analects* XX.1; tr. modified from D. C. Lau, *Confucius: The Analects* (Hong Kong: The Chinese University Press, 2000), 201. Here the "Dayu mo" 大禹謨 chapter of the *Book of Documents* reads: "I luxuriate in your virtue and esteem your great achievements; the *li* numbers of Heaven rests on your person, eventually you will ascend [to the throne] of the great sovereign" 予懋乃德，嘉乃丕績，天之曆數在汝躬汝，汝終陟元后 (*Shangshu zhushu*, 3.12a).

52. According to the commentary of Yan Shigu 顏師古 (A.D. 581–645), "the 'great method in nine chapters' is the nine divisions of the 'Hong fan' ('The Great Plan'). The fourth of which is the coordination of the five regulators" 大法九章即洪範九疇也。其四曰協用五紀也 (*Han shu*, 21A.973 [commentary]). Preserved in the *Book of Documents*, the "Hong fan" is supposedly the manifesto for good government that Jizi, a virtuous minister of the Yin-Shang, passed to King Wu of Zhou. It states, "as to the five regulators, the first is the agricultural year; the second is the moon; the third is the sun; the fourth is the stars; and the fifth is the *li* numbers" 五紀：一曰歲，二曰月，三曰日，四曰星辰，五曰歷數 (*Shangshu zhushu*, 11.13b). The term *ji* 紀 is a term that defies direct translation. In calendro-astronomical discourse, *ji* refers variously to: ① an era or other period of time; ② a point of coincidence marking the beginning of such a period; ③ a cycle returning to such a point at a regular interval of time; ④ even subdivisions of such a cycle; ⑤ the act of demarcation that produces any of the above; ⑥ an agent of demarcation, such as the sun, moon, planets (e.g. Jupiter, the "*ji* star" 紀星), or fixed stars; and thus ⑦ an overarching order of regularities/regulations governing Heaven and man.

(#5), and Lu (#6) calendar systems (*li*).[53] In the tumult of the Warring States (480–221 B.C.), Qin was able to consolidate the subcelestial realm but not yet pacify it. The Qin, for its part, eagerly promoted the five conquests [theory], and took itself to have obtained the virtue of water, and so took month X as the first [month of its civil calendar] and promoted the color black.[54]

The text attributes Sage King Zhuanxu and his ministers Chong and Li with the invention of "*li* numbers" (*li shu*) as an instrument of order. At one level, "*li* numbers" refers to the civil calendar. A lunisolar calendar like that used by the early Chinese is comprised of three elements: a roughly $354\frac{1}{2}$-day lunar/civil year (*nian* 年) comprised of 12 roughly $29\frac{1}{2}$-day lunations/months (*yue* 月) beginning at new moon; a $365\frac{1}{4}$-day solar/agricultural year (*sui* 歲) comprised of 4 seasons (*shi* 時), 12 medial *qi* (*zhong qi* 中氣), and/or 24 *qi*; and a sexagenary day-count of *ganzhi* binomes. Due to the roughly 11-day lag between civil and solar years—the "intercalary remainder" (*run yu* 閏餘)—it is necessary every few years to insert a thirteenth intercalary month (*run yue* 閏月) into the civil calendar to keep the two aligned and "fix the four seasons and complete the agricultural year."

Intercalation requires a determination of solar/seasonal progress, something much less obvious than, say, the phase of the moon. To this end one relies on seasonal indications of fixed stars like the Northern Dipper (Bei dou 北斗, i.e. Ursa Major) or, lying on a straight line off its handle, the Regulators (Sheti 攝提, i.e. Boötes). Each night at dusk, the Dipper's handle shifts slightly "leftward" (clockwise) in relation to the horizon; and as it moves through the twelve branch-directions it marks twelve seasonal months—the first (*meng* 孟),

---

53. Together, these are known as "the six ancient calendar systems" (*gu liu li* 古六曆). Sources like the *Zuo Tradition of the Spring and Autumn Annals* confirm that after the fall of the Western Zhou various states implemented calendar systems appropriate to the ruling clans from which they had descended; see Zhang Peiyu 張培瑜 et al., Zhongguo gudai lifa 中國古代曆法 (Beijing: Zhongguo kexue jishu chubanshe, 2008), 251–327; Hirase Takao 平勢隆郎, *Chūgoku kodai kinen no kenkyū: tenmon to koyomi no kentō kara* 中國古代紀年の研究 : 天文と曆の檢討から (Tōkyō: Kyūko Shoin, 1996); Robert H. Gassmann, *Antikchinesisches Kalenderwesen: die Rekonstruktion der chunqiu-zeitlichen Kalender des Fürstentums Lu und der Zhou-Könige* (Bern: Peter Lang, 2002). This became a topic of scholarly interest in the Han, though the six ancient systems then extant were generally considered to be apocryphal. For early imperial scholarship on the six ancient systems, see Zhang Peiyu et al., *Zhongguo gudai lifa*, 327–390.

54. *Han shu*, 21A.973.

middle (*zhong* 仲), and last (*ji* 季) months of each season—"established" (*jian* 建) in said directions.[55] On one hand, what is at stake for the Sages was the maintenance of proper intercalation. Disruption, like that provoked by the San Miao, results in misalignment: the sun and moon slide from their proper zodiacal stations (*ci* 次); the first month of the civil year (*zou* 陬) no longer corresponds to the first month of the season (*meng*); and the Regulators drift from their proper direction.[56] On the other hand, the Sages were also committed to reform. They heralded the founding of a dynasty by changing regalia like the first month (*zheng* 正) of the civil calendar and the color of court costume to suit the cosmic cycle that brought them to power. At first, it was the "three concordances" (*san tong* 三統) of the Xia, Yin-Shang, and Zhou, which the Qin in turn argued to replace with the conquest sequence of the "five virtues" (*wu de* 五德).

So central are *li* numbers to the project of kingship that Yao and Shun transferred them to symbolize their abdication. The function of the Sage King, as stated more concisely in later tradition, is to "contemplate the signs and grant the seasons" 觀象授時 —to deploy his penetrating knowledge of the cosmic order to choreograph the world of man to the rhythms of nature and the spirits. Of course, it is the Sage himself who is distinctly suited to the task, but he delegates this his most solemn responsibility to officials. The classics, for their part, record not only the names and deeds of the noteworthy among them but the day-to-day minutiae of their offices. In its blueprint of the Zhou bureaucratic apparatus, the *Rites of Zhou* divvies the astral sciences among the Great Clerk (*dashi* 大史) and his subordinates, the Minor Clerk (*xiaoshi* 小史), Observer (*fengxiang shi* 馮相氏), and Guardian of the Rule (*baozhang shi* 保章氏). A precursor to the Clerk's Office (*shi guan* 史官) of early imperial times, they work together to observe Heaven, warn the throne of anomalies, maintain a

---

55. On the elements of the Chinese civil calendar, see Martzloff, *Le calendrier chinois*, esp. 23–106. On the Northern Dipper as seasonal indicator, see Chen Jiujin 陳久金, "Beidouxing doubing zhixiang kao" 北斗星斗柄指向考, *Ziran kexue shi yanjiu* 自然科學史研究 13, no. 3 (1994): 209–214.

56. *Zou* is the first of the twelve months of the civil year as enumerated in the *Erya* 爾雅 and the Chu Silk Manuscript from Zidanku 子彈庫, Changsha; see Wang Zhiping 王志平, "Chu boshu yueming xintan" 楚帛書月名新探, *Huaxue* 華學 3 (1998): 181–188.

Table 1.3: The Dipper directions, first months, three concordances, and five virtues

Date	Medial-*qi*	Solar Station	Dipper Direction		Month	Three Concordances			Five Virtues		
						con.	dyn.	col.	vir.	dyn.	col.
Dec 24	Winter Solstice.Q22	Dipper $21\frac{8}{32}^{oo}$	*zi.*B01	N	win II	man	Zhou	red	fire	Zhou	red
Jan 24	Greater Cold.Q24	Tumulus $5\frac{18}{32}^{oo}$	*chou.*B02	NNE	win III	heaven	Yin	white	metal	Yin	white
Feb 23	Rain Water.Q02	Hall $8\frac{28}{32}^{oo}$	*yin.*B03	ENE	spr I	earth	Xia	black	wood	Xia	green
Mar 26	Spring Equinox.Q04	Crotch $14\frac{10}{32}^{oo}$	*mao.*B04	E	spr II				earth	Y. Emp.	yellow
Apr 25	Grain Rains.Q06	Mane $2\frac{24}{32}^{oo}$	*chen.*B05	ESE	spr III						
May 25	Grain Small but Full.Q08	Triad $4\frac{6}{32}^{oo}$	*si.*B06	SSE	sum I						
Jun 25	Summer Solstice.Q10	Well $25\frac{20}{32}^{oo}$	*wu.*B07	S	sum II						
Jul 25	Greater Heat.Q12	Stars $4\frac{2}{32}^{oo}$	*wei.*B08	SSW	sum III		↑			↑	
Aug 25	Abiding Heat.Q14	Wings $9\frac{16}{32}^{oo}$	*shen.*B09	WSW	aut I						
Sep 24	Autumn Equinox.Q16	Horn $4\frac{30}{32}^{oo}$	*you.*B10	W	aut II						
Oct 25	Frost Settles.Q18	Root $14\frac{12}{32}^{oo}$	*xu.*B11	WNW	aut III						
Nov 24	Lesser Snow.Q20	Basket $1\frac{26}{32}^{oo}$	*hai.*B12	NNW	win I				water	Qin	black

NOTE: The Date column is meant only for reference; these dates have been calculated for the year A.D. 111 (the *Han shu*'s date of completion) according to the Han Quarter-remainder system (#9). The Solar Station column is also taken from the Quarter-remainder system; for more on these stations, see Chapter 2. Note that the progression of the concordances and virtues is contrary to that of the earthly branches. Note also that this is not the only scheme for either; for more on the three concordances and five virtues, see Chapter 4.

lunisolar civil calendar, and select auspicious days for ceremonies of state.[57]

Certainly, the legend of the astral sciences is informed just as much by later imagination as by historical memory, *but that is precisely why it is valuable.* What is at issue in this study (esp. Chapter 4) is not the historicity of pre-imperial events, institutions, and knowledge, or the provenance of testimony thereto, but how legend shaped the meaning of early imperial practice.[58] The role of legend cannot be overstated. Repeated *ad nauseam* through the received tradition, it is at the core of actors' every attempt to frame a discussion about the astral sciences.[59] An excellent case in point is the description that Cai Yong 蔡邕 (A.D. 133–192) and Liu Hong give their field in the *Hou Han shu*:

夫曆有聖人之德六焉：以本氣者尚其體，以綜數者尚其文，以考類者尚其象，以作事者尚其時，以占往者尚其源，以知來者尚其流。大業載之，吉凶生焉，是以君子將有興焉，咨焉而以從事，受命而莫之違也。若夫用天因地，揆時施教，頒諸明堂，以為民極者，莫大乎月令。帝王之大司備矣，天下之能事畢矣。過此而往，羣忌苟禁，君子未之或知也。

[The practice of] *li* has to it six virtues of the Sage: (1) one venerates [Heaven's] substance (*ti*) through the comprehension of *qi*; (2) one venerates its patterns (*wen*) through the aggregation of numbers; (3) one venerates its signs (*xiang*) through the investigation of categories; (4) one venerates its seasons through the initiation of affairs (agriculture and sacrifice); (5) one venerates its source

---

57. *Zhouli zhushu* 周禮注疏 (Siku quanshu ed.), 17.19a–20a, 26.15b–34b. For a summary of their individual functions, see Hucker, *A Dictionary of Official Titles in Imperial China* (Stanford: Stanford University Press, 1985), entries 1981, 4453, 6018.

58. The the authenticity and historicity of the pre-Qin classics is a problem that has engaged generations of scholars and, with the excavation of period manuscripts, continues to evolve today. For an introduction to the issues and scholarship surrounding each text, see Loewe, *Early Chinese Texts*.

59. In regard to the early imperial period, one finds this legend repeated in the prefaces to every "*Li* Treatise": *Shiji*, 26.1255–1260; *Hou Han shu, zhi* 3, 3055–3058; *Song shu*, 12.227–228; *Wei shu*, 107A.2659; *Jin shu*, 17.497–498; *Sui shu*, 17.415–416. One finds it in the prefaces and memorials introducing the Luminous Inception system (#13; A.D. 237), the Epochal Excellence system (#22: A.D. 445), and the Orthodox Glory system (#33; A.D. 523): *Song shu*, 12.232–233, 260–262; *Wei shu*, 107A.2662–2663; *Jin shu*, 18.535–536. One finds it strewn through debate, as I will examine in the case of the *Jin shu* in Chapter 4. One also finds it in the chapter "Li shu" in *Zhong lun* 中論 (Siku quanshu ed.), A.11a–12b.

through the divination of things past; and (6) one venerates its course through the knowledge of things to come. It (*li*) is conveyed in the great patrimony [of the Sages], and blessing and blight are born of it. This is why the gentleman rises by it, why he consults it in the pursuance of affairs, and why he accepts his Mandate (fate) and never violates it. [The Sage] conforms to Heaven and accords with Earth, in his survey of seasons and bestowal of teachings, and he promulgates this at the Hall of Light, acting as the polestar of the people—and for this there there is nothing greater than the monthly ordinances. When the Emperor's great affair is replete, [his] competence [toward] the subcelestial realm is complete. Beyond this, the gentleman need know nothing of the teeming taboos and negligent prohibitions (of calendar divination).[60]

To the second-century expert, to practice *li* is to do the work of Sages: to apprehend the substance, principle, past, and future of the cosmos, and to deploy that knowledge in the context of state ritual to establish a utopian society. This is the paradigm for the astral sciences in the imperial period, and it is a paradigm for which tradition offers no alternative. That said, thinkers engaged with and reinterpreted this paradigm in their own ways. A salient example of this, which I discuss in Chapter 4, is how the Sage Kings were transformed by the brush of the calendro-astronomer from inaccessible paragons of spontaneous gnosis to meticulous technicians and proponents of the sound technologies and methods of the day. According to Xu Gan's *Zhong lun*, for example:

昔者聖王之造厤數也，察紀律之行，觀運機之動，原星辰之逆中，窬暑景之長短，於是營儀以准之，立表以測之，下漏以考之，布筭以追之；然後元首齊乎上，中朔正乎下，寒暑順序，四時不忒。夫厤數者，先王以憲殺生之期，而詔作事之節也，使萬國之民不失其業者也。

---

60. *Hou Han shu, zhi* 3, 3057. I attribute this passage to Cai Yong and Liu Hong because Sima Biao's 司馬彪 (A.D. 243–306) "Lü li zhi" in the current *Hou Han shu* is based on a similar treatise (now lost) written by Cai and Liu at the end of the second century; see B. J. Mansvelt Beck, *The Treatises of Later Han: Their Author, Sources, Contents, and Place in Chinese Historiography* (Leiden: E.J. Brill, 1990), 56–63.

As to the Sage Kings' creation of *li* numbers in the ancient past, they inspected the operation of periods and harmonies, observed the movement of the rotating mechanism, plumbed the consecutive culminations of the stars, and apprehended the varying lengths of light and shadow.[61] Thereupon, they constructed instruments to square them, erected gnomons to measure them, issued clepsydrae to investigate them, and distributed counting rods to pursue them. Thereafter, the origin and [cycle] heads were aligned [in the past] above, and the medial [*qi*] and new moons were straightened [in the present] below; cold and hot proceeded in proper order, and the four seasons did not err.[62] These *li* numbers are that by which former kings announced the periods of taking life and ordered the rhythms of the initiation of affairs—that which ensures that the people of the myriad states are not remiss in their patrimonies.[63]

1.1.3   The terminology of li

As introduced in the previous section, *tianwen*'s range of associations as "celestial patterns" fits nicely with its scope as textual genre. *Tianwen* is the study of the physical objects and patterns of Heaven both in themselves—cosmology, the cataloging of fixed and moving objects, and observational records—and as manifestations of a cosmic order imperative to the project of civilization. *Li,* on the other hand, is a term that is so polyvalent that it

---

61. The term *ji lü* 紀律 is somewhat polyvalent, referring at once to the idea of "regulations and rules" and to "periods and harmonics"; on the term *ji,* see note 52. The term *yun ji* 運機 "rotating mechanism" clearly refers to the *xuanji* 璿璣. The "Yao dian" chapter of the *Book of Documents* records that Yao "attended to the *xuanji* and jade transverse so as to order the seven matters of government" 在璿璣玉衡以齊七政 (*Shangshu zhushu,* 2.6a). This term is archaic and highly ambiguous. Commentators have glossed it to mean something like "rotating mechanism," referring to the Northern Dipper or an instrument or abstract principle of some kind. See Christopher Cullen and Anne S. L. Farrer, "On the Term *Hsuan Chi* and the Three-lobed Jade Discs," *Bulletin of the School of Oriental and African Studies* 46, no. 1 (1983): 53–76.

62. This sentence describes elements of calendrics contemporary to the Han. An ORIGIN (*yuan* 元) is the point in time and space where all sequences coincide, and a HEAD (*shou* 首) is the beginning point of such sequences. MEDIAL QI (*zhong qi* 中氣) are twelve equal divisions of the solar year beginning at winter solstice, which in later intercalation practices are linked to specific months or "new moons" of the calendar year.

63. *Zhong lun,* B.11a–b.

is impossible to settle on a single translation. In *li* literature, we see the term refer to any number of things: a/the "calendar" or "astronomical table"; a/the "system manual" from which these are generated; "tables" and "sequences" within such a manual; a/the "astronomical system" from which a manual is distilled; and the study of any or all of the above.[64] The only thing it does not seem to include is, oddly, calendar divination. Furthermore, we have seen the classics use *li* as a verb and *li shu* as a symbol of dynastic transition.

The etymology of the word *li* (**c-rek*), written variously as 曆, 歷, 歴, and 秝, derives from a root meaning of "sequence." The *Shuowen jiezi* 說文解字 (2nd cent. A.D.) glosses its phonophoric 秝 as "sparse and regular" 稀疏適 and 秝 as "to put in order" 治也; and since 秝 (OBI 𝕏) is a pictograph of millet plants side-by-side, one imagines that the underlying metaphor is that of planting grain in orderly rows and spaced intervals.[65] The most common member of this family is 歷, which is derived from the semantic classifier 止 (foot) and means "to pass (sequentially) through" units of time or space. Our 曆, which is derived from the semantic classifier 日 (sun/star), is simply the extension of this metaphor to Heaven—in fact, one is even said to "pace out" (*bu* 步) the five naked-eye planets. Lastly, the *Erya* 爾雅 also identifies 秝 with "calculation" (*suan*) and "numbers" (*shu*), a logical correlate to the idea of putting things in ordered rows.[66] In this vein, Sima Tan 司馬談 (165–110 B.C.) translates the phrase "to *li* and *xiang* the sun, moon, and stars" 歷象日月星辰 from the *Book of Documents* as "to number (*shu*) and model (*fa*) the sun, moon, and stars" 數法日月星辰.[67] *Li shu* ("*li* numbers") usually refers to the numerical constructs of the calendar

----

64. For a typology of *li*, see Sivin, *Granting the Seasons*, 38–40; cf. Martzloff, *Le calendrier chinois*, esp. 367–372.

65. *Shuowen jiezi zhu* 說文解字注 (Shanghai guji 上海古籍 ed.), 7A.55b, 9B.20b.

66. *Erya zhushu* 爾雅注疏 (Siku quanshu ed.), 1.45a.

67. *Shangshu zhushu*, 1.8b; *Shiji*, 1.16. On the etymology of *li*, see Bernhard Karlgren, *Grammata Serica Recensa* (Stockholm: Museum of Far Eastern Antiquities, 1957), 227; Axel Schuessler, *ABC Etymological Dictionary of Old Chinese* (Honolulu: University of Hawai'i Press, 2007), 353. Variants of 秝 occur in oracle bone and bronze vessel inscriptions from the Yin-Shang and Western Zhou. It appears most often in the formula *mie li* 蔑曆, which scholars understand to mean "to encourage, reward" a subordinate, though there is debate about how to understand *li*, e.g. as 歷 "experience, merits" or as 勵 (**c-rjats*) "encourage, efforts."

system. For example, when the "Hong fan" 洪範 chapter of the *Book of Documents* lists it as one of the "five regulators," behind the agricultural year, moon, sun, and stars, Kong Yingda 孔穎達 (A.D. 574–648) glosses "*li* numbers" as "the numbers of the timing of the *li*-accounted *qi* and new moons that come from the calculation of the sun and moon's travel of their paths—that which comprises the *li* calendar of one year" 算日月行道所歷計氣朔早晚之數，所以為一歲之歷.[68] However, later thinkers understood Yao's declaration to Shun that "the *li* numbers of Heaven have fallen to thy person" 天之歷數在汝躬 to refer to more than just the transfer of a calendar system. Kong Anguo 孔安國 glosses "*li* numbers" as "the Dao of Heaven" 天道, and He Yan 何晏 (d. A.D. 249) glosses it as "sequence" 列次, implying a celestially preordained sequence of ruling houses like that of the three concordances or five dynastic virtues.[69] In other words, if *tian ming* 天命 is the "Mandate of Heaven," then *li shu* is its term limit.

This leads us to one final point: like *wen* "patterns," our *li* "sequences" and *shu* "numbers" are themselves inherent in the cosmic order. As such, it is not always possible to determine from context whether we are dealing with *tianwen* and *li shu* as the cosmic order or the work of humans to model that order.

The early imperial vocabulary of *li* is in large part built upon that of the classics. Over time, however, a variety of compounds evolved to distribute its semantic load and designate

---

For a recent study and summary of past scholarship on the word *mie li*, see Chao Fulin 晁福林, "Jinwen 'mie li' yu Xizhou mianli zhidu" 金文「蔑曆」與西周勉勵制度, *Lishi yanjiu* 歷史研究 2008.1: 33–42. The graph does appears on its own in the 43rd year Lai *ding* 四十三年逨鼎, where Li Xueqin 李學勤 glosses it as "to count and select" officers ("Meixian Yangjiacun xinchu qingtongqi yanjiu" 眉縣楊家村新出青銅器研究, *Wenwu* 文物 2003.6: 69). Though the word does occur in received literature originating from the Warring States, Qin, and Han, it is relatively rare in excavated sources from the same period. One Qin-era government document from Liye 里耶, for example, does use the term *li* in a mathematical sense in a "count (*li*) and investigation of the black-haired people (commoners)" 黔首曆課 (fragment BIII 8-483 in Zhang Chunlong 張春龍, ed., *Hunan Liye Qin jian* 湖南里耶秦簡 [Chongqing: Chongqing chubanshe, 2010]). I would like to thank Professors Edward Shaughnessy and He Youzu 何有祖, respectively, for pointing these two examples out to me.

68. *Shangshu zhushu*, 11.13b–14a. Kong Yingda is elaborating Kong Anguo's 孔安國 gloss that " '*li* numbers' are the measures of the nodal *qi* used to produce the *li* calendar to 'respectfully grant the people the seasons' " 歷數，節氣之度，以為歷，敬授民時.

69. Ibid., 3.12a; *Lunyu zhushu* 論語注疏 (Siku quanshu ed.), 20.1a.

new concepts as they appeared. I have enumerated vocabulary in dictionary-entry fashion in Table 1.4.

After this survey of the generic contents, legend, and vocabulary of *tianwen* and *li*, the limitations of the characterizations listed at the beginning of this section should be apparent. We cannot equate *tianwen* to space and *li* to time, because each are possessed of their own spatial and temporal dimensions. We cannot equate *tianwen* to "astrology" and *li* to "astronomy," both because rigorous *tianwen* observation feeds into *li* and because each are possessed of their own qualitative and quantitative dimensions. The most we can say in this regard is that, in general, the two devote different levels of emphasis to divination and calculation. Lastly, we cannot exactly equate the two with observational and computational facets of "astronomy" because of what this label excludes and because of the presence of distinct *li*-like elements within *tianwen* (see Chapter 2).

Modern distinctions like "science," "magic," and "religion" fall even further short. As I hope the example above (p. 28) has sufficiently demonstrated, if we were to apply such categories to *tianwen* texts, we would have to do so sentence-by-sentence. The case of *li* is similarly ambiguous: the dry mathematics of astronomical system manuals incorporate elements of numerology and calendar divination but relegate them to superficial functions; and accounts like Cai Yong and Liu Hong's describe the practice of *li* as an experience of spiritual communion with the universe and the Sages while at once rejecting calendar divination and prophecy texts. This is not so say that "science," "magic," and "religion" were as one in the ancient mind, but that these anachronisms distract us from the equally emphatic (and culturally-embedded) distinctions that actors themselves were making.

If we must essentialize, I would like to suggest a different characterization: that the difference between *tianwen* and *li* is that between the *observational* and *textual* sciences. Be it quantitative or qualitative, *tianwen* is all about observation. The whole project of *li* depends just as much on observation; however, where observation feeds into *li* is generally through *texts*, e.g. historical records, "the observation notes of the Clerk's Office" 史官候

Table 1.4: The vocabulary of *li* (origins to 8th cent. A.D.)

曆/歷/厤/厤 *li*: ①* a celestial "sequence" (*Documents*, 11.13b); ②* a/the "calendar" or "astronomical table" (*Zuo Tradition*, Xiang 27; Ai 12); ③ a/the "system manual" from which these are generated; ④ "tables" and "sequences" within such a manual (Supernal Emblem system [#10], in *Jin shu, j.* 17); ⑤ a/the "calendro-astronomical system" from which a manual is distilled; ⑥ to "calculate" or "sequence" any of the above (*Documents*, 1.8b); ⑦ the study of any of the above.

曆數 *li shu*: **"calendro-astronomical numbers"** ①* numbers inherent in Heaven and reproduced by man (*Documents*, 11.13b); ②* the term limit of the Mandate of Heaven (*Documents*, 3.12a, *Analects* XX.1); ③ the numbers forming the body of a calendro-astronomical system/manual; ④ by synecdoche, a calendro-astronomical system/manual (*Han shu*, 6.212); ⑤ the study of calendro-astronomy (*Han shu*, 58.2634); ⑥ "calendro-astronomy and mathematics" (*Sui shu*, 34.1026).

天曆 *tian li*: **"celestial *li*"** ① the state astronomical system (*Shiji*, 130.3285; uncommon); ② abbreviation of "the *li* numbers of Heaven" 天之曆數, i.e. the term limit of the Mandate of Heaven (*Taiping jing hejiao*, 137.707).

天數 *tian shu*: **"celestial numbers"** ① the numbers inherent in Heaven and their study (*Shiji*, 27.1343; uncommon).

曆術 *li shu*: **"calendro-astronomical technique(s)"** ① a calendro-astronomical system/manual (*Shiji, j.* 26); ② a "sequence technique" for computing lunar latitude or equation of center (Luminous Inception and Epochal Excellence systems, in *Song shu, j.* 12 & 13); ③ the study of calendro-astronomy (*Wei shu*, 48.1068).

曆法 *li fa*: **"calendro-astronomical method(s)"** ① calendro-astronomical system/manual (*Song shu*, 12.230).

曆算 *li suan*: **"calendro-astronomical calculation"** ① the study of calendro-astronomy (*Han shu*, 12.258); ② to perform calendro-astronomical calculations (*Sui shu*, 18.479); ③ "calendro-astronomy and mathematics" (*Jiu Tang shu*, 47.2039).

星曆 *xing li*: **"star/planet *li*"** ① stellar/planetary sequences inherent in nature (*Guanzi*, 41.703); ② an undefined responsibility of the Prefect Grand Clerk (*Han shu*, 99.4170); ③ undefined mysterious knowledge (*Han shu*, 62.2732; common); ③ the study of calendro-astronomy (*Jiu Tang shu*, 66.2463).

年曆 *nian li*: **"annual calendar"** ① a/the civil calendar (Zhong lun, B.13a); ② an annals (*Jiu Tang shu*, 149.4030).

曆日 *li ri*: ① "sequence day," i.e. the number of days entered into the lunar speed or latitude sequence (Supernal Emblem system (#10), in *Jin shu, j.* 17); ② a civil calendar (*Wu li lun* 物理論, in *Yiwen leiju*, 5.97; uncommon).

日曆 *ri li*: a civil calendar (*Lun heng*, 70.994).

曆書 *li shu*: ① a treatise on calendro-astronomy (*Shiji, j.* 26; uncommon); ② an/the almanac (Song and later).

具注曆 *ju zhu li*: **"annotated calendar"** ① a/the almanac (excavated examples from Dunhuang; see Deng, *Dunhuang tianwen lifa wenxian jijiao*).

NOTE: Appended to each usage is a citation of its earliest unambiguous instance and a note concerning its subsequent ubiquity. Usages evident in the pre-Qin classics are marked with an asterisk.

注, or results from observation programs at the state observatory.[70] In Latourian terms, *li* depends on *tianwen*'s task of "inscription," that is the "transformations through which an entity becomes materialized into a sign, an archive, a document, a piece of paper, a trace."[71] All the calendro-astronomer needs is data, but he need not collect his own where there are state resources devoted to this task and ample records of the past at his disposal. Thus, the distinction between *tianwen* and *li* may come down to the sort division of labor that we see at the Clerk's Office itself between, if I may, "outdoor astronomers" chosen for their eyesight and talent with instruments and "indoor astronomers" chosen for their ability with numbers.[72]

If we are to write a history of astronomy in ancient China it is crucial that we recognize the conceptual categories that actors brought to bear; to make sense of it, however, it is equally important that we not lose ourselves in their ambiguities. The problem with

---

70. The dynastic histories are replete with examples of actors utilizing to such materials. For example, Sima Qian 司馬遷 (145/135–86 B.C.) reports that "I have contemplated the historical records and investigated 'past events', and in 100 years there has never been a case when the five [planets] have not gone into retrograde" 余觀史記，考行事，百年之中，五星無出而不反逆行 (*Shiji*, 27.1350). For examples of actors making use of the Clerk's Office's *xingshi* 行事 "past events," *houzhu* 候注 "observation notes," *zhu* 注 "notes," *zhuji* 注記 "note records," or *jizhu* 記注 "record notes" observational records, see *Hou Han shu, zhi* 2, 3027, 3029, 3030, 3034, 3039, 3041, 3042; *Jin shu*, 17.498, 18.564; *Song shu*, 12.290, 13.309, 311, 312, 315; *Sui shu*, 18.460. The most important resource in terms of historical records was the *Spring and Autumn Annals* and its commentaries, which record eclipses and sporadic positions of Jupiter between 722 and 481 B.C. On Liu Xin's famous study of these records, the *Shi jing* 世經, see Cullen, "The Birthday of the Old Man of Jiang County and Other Puzzles." For other examples of actors utilizing *Spring and Autumn Annals* records, see *Jin shu*, 18.563–565, 565–567; *Song shu*, 13.308, 314; *Sui shu*, 17.418, 424–426, 430. An excellent example of the last type of record are the results of the an eclipse and solstice shadow observation program carried out by the Liu-Song (A.D. 420–479) Clerk's Office between A.D. 435 to 443 at the command of Wendi (r. A.D. 424–453). These results were incorporated into He Chengtian's 何成天 (c. A.D. 370-447) Epochal Excellence system (#22), and became important data points for later calendro-astronomy; see *Song shu*, 12.262–264, 13.309–310; *Sui shu*, 17.426–428.

71. Bruno Latour, *Pandora's Hope: Essays on the Reality of Science Studies* (Cambridge: Harvard University Press, 1999), 203.

72. Of course, this characterization has its own limitations. First, this "division of labor" was in no way absolute, since innovative figures in *li* calendro-astronomy like Liu Hong, Xu Guang 徐廣 (A.D. 351/352–425), He Chengtian, and Zhang Zixin 張子信 (fl. A.D. 526–576) are known to have carried out their own long-term observation programs (*Jin shu*, 17.499; *Song shu*, 12.261; *Sui shu*, 20.561). Second, *tianwen* literature was just as often used for textual hermeneutics or symbolic communication; see Wu Hung, *The Wu Liang Shrine: The Ideology of Early Chinese Pictorial Art* (Stanford: Stanford University Press, 1989), 73–107; Donald Harper, "Communication by Design: Two Silk Manuscripts of Diagrams (*tu*) from Mawangdui Tomb Three," in *Graphics and Text in the Production of Technical Knowledge in China: The Warp and the Weft*, ed. Francesca Bray, Vera Dorofeeva-Lichtmann, and Georges Métailie (Leiden: Brill, 2007), 169–189.

relying on romanization or direct translation is twofold. First, it fails to highlight well-attested context-sensitive meanings. There is no good reason to conflate a calendar and a system manual, for example, just because they are both entitled "*li*"; nor is it helpful to insist on a cumbersome all-inclusive translation for both, e.g. "calendro-astronomical text." Second, it fails to highlight connections with pan-cultural practices and real-world phenomena. For example, the linguistic and cultural background of a term like Yinghuo 熒惑 ("the Sparkling Deluder") is interesting, but this is not a term that fails to refer: Yinghuo is simply another name for Mars, and descriptions of its behavior and periodicity accord with those of other modern and pre-modern civilizations alike.[73] Therefore, throughout this study I will employ a combination of actors' and observers' categories carefully chosen to highlight the ambiguities or specifics relevant in the contexts we encounter.

1.2   A Brief History of People and Events

Let us now pick up where legend leaves off and consider how the history of early calendro-astronomy is told. Whether it be in primary or secondary literature, the standard unit for narrating this history is the state calendro-astronomical system and the reforms that it underwent. This is a good place to begin, but it is imperative that we work our way out from there to pursue alternative historical threads. My intent here is not to present a comprehensive survey of the period, for which the reader would be well advised to turn to the classic studies of Yabuuti Kiyosi 藪內清, Ōhashi Yukio 大橋由紀夫, Chen Meidong, or Zhang Peiyu, for example; it is instead to outline traditional historical frameworks within which to situate the topics of subsequent chapters and, at once, to remind us of the diversity of historical perspectives at our disposal.[74]

---

73. For non-Chinese approaches to Mars, see for example Otto Neugebauer, *A History of Ancient Mathematical Astronomy*, 3 vols. (Berlin; New York: Springer-Verlag, 1975), 170–206, 454–460, passim. On the cultural symbolism of Mars in China, see Schafer, *Pacing the Void*, 511–519.

74. For the period covered here, see Yabuuti, *Chūgoku no temmon rekihō* 中國の天文曆法 (Tōkyō: Heibonsha, 1969), 21–45; Chen Meidong, *Zhongguo kexue jishu shi: tianwenxue juan* 中國科學技術史：天文學卷 (Beijing: Kexue chubanshe, 2003), 103–217; Zhang Peiyu et al., *Zhongguo gudai lifa*, 375–597. Ōhashi goes

1.2.1 A history of policy reforms

The first reform for which we have any evidence was that initiated by Ying Zheng 嬴政, the King (r. 246–222 B.C.) and then First Emperor (Shihuang 始皇; r. 221–210 B.C.) of Qin. Prior to this, the kingdom of Qin had operated on a "Xia calendar," which "establishes" month I at $yin._{B03}$, i.e. the first month of spring, i.e. the month containing the medial qi Rainwater.$_{Q02}$ and thus sliding between January and February of the proleptic Julian calendar (see Table 1.3). In the wake of the total dissolution of the Eastern Zhou 東周 (770–256 B.C.), Ying Zheng sought to project the immanence of Qin rule by invoking the "five virtues"—the concept that ruling houses inevitably succeed one another in an order determined by the virtues that they embody, either metal, fire, water, earth, or wood. To evoke a transition from the Zhou (: FIRE) to the Qin, his court changed the theme of regalia such as uniforms, flags, measurements, and vehicles to black and sixes (five-agents correlates to water, which conquers fire), renamed the Yellow River "the Virtue Waters" (De shui 德水), and moved the beginning of the civil year to month X, the first month of winter (another correlate of water). Although calendars and administrative documents unearthed in recent years have begun to fill in the gaps, we still know very little about the *substance* of the so-called "Zhuanxu system" (#2) introduced by this reform. What we do know is that the new civil calendar beginning on month X was introduced by 246 B.C.[75]

---

into significant depth on the topics covered in this section in "Kōkan Sibunreki no seiritsu katei"; "Ka Ki no gekkō chishitsuron"; and "Ka Ki no temmon teisūkan ni tsuite" 賈逵の天文定數觀について, *Sūgakushi kenkyū* 153 (1997): 1–17.

75. The main source for this reform is *Shiji*, 6.237–238; cf. Christopher Cullen, "Motivations for Scientific Change in Ancient China: Emperor Wu and the Grand Inception Astronomical Reforms of 104 BC," *Journal for the History of Astronomy* 24, no. 3 (1991): 188–190. The *Shiji* places the reform of all regalia together in 221 B.C., upon Ying Zheng's unification of the Warring States and adoption of the title Emperor. However, clues from excavated sources indicate that the change in the civil calendar went back to at least his first year as king in 246 B.C.: there are (as of 2013) three full dates prior to his reign of king falling in months X and XII wherein the binome day works only if said month falls *prior* to month I of said year, rather than after. Furthermore, we know that this "Zhuanxu system" replaced a "Xia system" because month I of the Qin calendar is actually still "established" at $yin._{B03}$ around January and February, it is just that the civil year now begins on month X rather than month I, the same way that our *December* is no longer the tenth month. For important studies of these problems, see Huang Yi-long 黃一農, "Qin wangzheng shiqi lifa xinkao" 秦王政時期曆法新考, *Huaxue* 5 (2001): 143–149; Zhang Peiyu and Zhang Chunlong 張春龍, "Qindai lifa he Zhuanxu li" 秦代曆法和顓頊曆, in *Liye fa jue bao gao* 里耶發掘報告, ed. Hunan Sheng

The second landmark reform took place in 104 B.C. under Han Wudi 漢武帝 (r. 140–87 B.C.). The Qin Zhuanxu system (#2) appears to have undergone minor adjustment in the first few decades of the Han, amid calls for the adoption of new regalia, but it was not until Wudi's reign that proposals for reform found their political footing. Proponents variously cited three reasons for reform:

1. The current system was "behind heaven" in terms of lunar phenomena;

2. For the sake of legitimacy, it was appropriate that the Han associate itself with the virtue earth (earth conquers water) in its regalia and readopt the "Xia calendar" according to the "three concordances," by which the rule of Zhou (skipping the Qin) reverts to the Xia (see Table 1.3);

3. The propitious discovery in 113 B.C. of an ancient tripod buried beneath the altar to the Sovereign of Earth and the culmination, according to the calendar of the time, of winter solstice, new moon, and day $jiazi._{01}$ on midnight, 105 B.C. December 25 (JD 168 3430.2) would reproduce for Wudi the conditions permitting the mythic Yellow Emperor (:: EARTH) to achieve transcendence, and this new beginning merited just such a reform.

Finally convinced by a petition from Grand Palace Grandee Gongsun Qing 公孫卿 (the mastermind of reason 3), Hu Sui 壺遂, and Grand Clerk Sima Qian 司馬遷, Wudi initiated and presided over a complex sequence of events that unfolded over the first seven months of that year. After seeking a second opinion from Grandee Secretary Ni Kuan 兒寬, he issued an edict expressing his aspirations for immortality and inaugurating the Grand Inception reign period (104–101 B.C.). He then ordered Gongsun Qing, Hu Sui, and Sima Qian to deliberate with a Gentleman-in-Attendance Zun 尊 and Great Director of Stars She Xing 射姓 about the creation of a Han calendro-astronomical system. They carried out a number of observations to determine the basic elements of that system but ultimately declined for the

wenwu kaogu yanjiusuo 湖南省文物考古研究所 (Changsha: Yuelu shushe, 2006), 735–747.

reason that they "couldn't do the math" 不能爲算. Instead, they recommended that the emperor recruit calendarists more up to the challenge of creating a Grand Inception system (#7).

For this the emperor assembled a team of more than 20 people led by Calendarist Deng Ping 鄧平, Sima Ke 司馬可 of Changle 長樂, Marquis Yi Jun 宜君 of Jiuquan 酒泉, *fangshi* 方士 ("man of methods") Tang Du 唐都 (Sima Tan and Qian's calendro-astronomy teacher), Luoxia Hong 落下閎 of Ba Commandery 巴郡, and "calendarists from among the populace" 民間治曆者. Luoxia Hong and Deng Ping arrived at the same method, in which they claim to have derived lunar parameters from harmonics and *Book of Changes* numerology. These were verified by various forms of observational and computational testing, then handed to Sima Qian to eliminate seventeen inaccurate competitors and submitted to a further round of testing. Eunuch Chunyu Lingqu 淳于陵渠 then reviewed Deng Ping's Grand Inception system (#7), confirmed its accuracy, and submitted it to the throne. Finally, in month V of that year, the emperor instituted the system, promoted Deng Ping to Assistant to the Grand Clerk, and changed the first month of the civil year to month I.[76]

Like the Qin system before it, the Grand Inception system (#7) underwent modification over its lifetime. In 78 B.C., Prefect Grand Clerk Zhang Shouwang 張壽王 memorialized that the Han should address a maladjustment of yin-yang by switching to the Yellow Emperor Adjustment system (#1), which he claimed had been in use since the inaugural year of the Han. Zhaodi 昭帝 (r. 86–74 B.C.) ordered Zhang's subordinate Xianyu Wangren 鮮于妄人, a manager of *li* functionaries, to interrogate him and, after Zhang refused to cooperate, for Xianyu to go ahead with observations of lunar and seasonal phenomena at the Shanglin Pure Terrace 上林清臺 observatory to rank the accuracy of eleven competing systems. Xianyu

---

76. The preceding is a summary of the account preserved in *Han shu*, 21A.974–978. Cullen provides a richer description of events and their context in Han politics, state ritual, and the religious aspirations of Wudi in "Motivations for Scientific Change in Ancient China." Zhang Peiyu brings up-to-date excavated sources to bear on the question of the Qin calendar system, the early Western Han adoption and modification of it, and the tenuity of either's connection to the Zhuanxu system (#2) as known from received sources in "Genju xinchu liri jiandu shilun Qin he Han chu de lifa" 根据新出歷日簡牘試論秦和漢初的曆法, *Zhongyuan wenwu* 中原文物 2007.5: 62–77.

ran this program from 78–74 B.C. with the help of a recently constructed armillary sphere and a staff of more than twenty people, including Calendarist and Assistant to the Grand Minister of Agriculture Ma Guang 麻光, a Chancellor, a secretary, a General-in-chief, and a clerk of the General of the Right. The result was that "the Grand Inception system was number one, the Grand Inception system made by Xu Wanju of Jimo and Xu Yu of Chang'an was also number one" 太初曆第一，即墨徐萬且、長安徐禹治太初曆亦第一, and Zhang's team was thoroughly discredited. Another result of this program appears to be that Xianyu produced more accurate measurements of the lodges that were incorporated into the work of the Clerk's Office and *Mr. Shi's Star Canon (Shishi xingjing* 石氏星經).[77]

Then, sometime during the reign of Pingdi 平帝 (r. 1 B.C. – A.D. 5), Liu Xin produced the Triple Concordance system (#8). From what we can gather, Liu Xin's work seems to have been to elaborate the basic framework of the Grand Inception system with numerology and planetary models. Early sources agree that his goal in doing so was to "explain the *Spring and Autumn Annals*" 說春秋 rather than initiate policy reform, and the only evidence that his system ever saw state service is circumstantial: the *Han shu* tells us that Liu Xin composed his Triple Concordance system after his transfer to the post of Xi-He 羲和, under the Grand Clerk.[78] We also know that all of this took place amid the sweeping reforms of state ritual and regalia surrounding the regent Wang Mang's 王莽 (c. 45 B.C. – A.D. 23) final consolidation of imperial authority.[79]

---

77. *Han shu*, 21A.978; *Song shu*, 12.228; cf. Cullen, *Astronomy and Mathematics in Ancient China*, 30–31. For evidence of Xianyu's use of a *hun tian* 渾天 armillary sphere, see *Yangzi Fa yan* 揚子法言 (Siku quanshu ed.), 7.2a–b; *Jin shu*, 11.284; see also Cullen, *Astronomy and Mathematics in Ancient China*, 59–66. Sun Xiaochun and Jacob Kistemaker summarize previous scholarship on this issue and present the case that angular measurements of *Mr. Shi's Star Canon* (as preserved in later sources) originate from this observation program in *The Chinese Sky During the Han*, esp. 37–69.

78. *Han shu*, 36.1972. Named after the Xi-He brothers, which Sage King Yao set in charge of calendro astronomy (see p. 48), Pingdi established the office of Xi-He in spring of 1 B.C. to "promulgate indoctrination, prohibit excessive sacrifices, and to banish [lascivious music]" 班教化，禁淫祀，放鄭聲 (ibid., 12.351). On the contents and history of this short-lived office, see Yoshino Ken'ichi 吉野賢一, "Zenkan matsu ni okeru gika no setchi ni tsuite" 前漢末における羲和の設置について, *Kyūshū daigaku Tōyōshi ronshū* 九州大學東洋史論 31 (2003): 44–66. For the organization of the Clerk's Office, see Table 1.5.

79. *Han shu*, 21A.979. Much of the sequence of events here is speculative. On the life and work of Liu Xin, see Xu Xingwu 徐興無, *Liu Xiang pingzhuan: fu Liu Xin pingzhuan* 劉向評傳：附劉歆評傳, Zhongguo

Whatever its connection to the Triple Concordance system (#8), Wang Mang inaugurated his Xin 新 "New" Dynasty (A.D. 9–23) with a change of first month from $yin._{B03}$ (Xia; c. February) to $chou._{B02}$ (Yin; c. January). As a result, the calendar skipped in A.D. 9 from Inaugural Beginning 3-**XI** to Establishment of the State 1-**I**, only to be reset in A.D. 24 with the insertion of an extra month XII. Two things are particularly remarkable about this reform. The first is the complete silence of received literature on the subject. As both the *earliest* and *longest-running* instance of three-concordance-inspired calendar reform in Chinese history, this should have set an epoch-making precedent on the matter. Instead, later generations seem to have actively purged it from cultural memory—they purged it to the point, in fact, that we only know of it through archaeological evidence.[80] It is also remarkable for the incoherence and contentiousness that it reveals in imperial ideology. Having established earth as the dynastic virtue of the Han only in 104 B.C., the following century saw a protracted debate about the five virtues that resulted in a shift from the conquest to production sequence and the identification of Han with fire. This once again left the emblems of earth the coveted prize of the aspiring dynast (fire produces earth); however, the fact that the Han continued to operate a Xia calendar (: $YIN._{B03}$: WOOD : GREEN, etc.)

---

sixiangjia pingzhuan congshu 21 (Nanjing: Nanjing daxue chubanshe, 2005).

80. For example, an inscription on the Xin tong *zhang* 新銅丈 bronze measure records the following proclamation:

> 黃帝初祖，德帀于虞，虞帝始祖，德帀于新。歲在大梁，龍集戊辰，戊辰直定，天命有民，據土德受，正號即真，改正建丑，長壽隆崇，同律度量衡，稽當前人。龍在己巳，歲次實沈，初班天下，萬國永遵，子子孫孫，享傳億年。

> First ancestor Yellow Emperor, His virtue passed full circle to Yu. First ancestor Emperor Yu, His virtue passed full circle to the Xin. Jupiter was in the Great Bridge.$_{JS5}$ (Aries) and the dragon (Taisui) alighted on $wuchen._{05}$, and in that year $wuchen._{05}$ (A.D. 8) Heaven's mandate to possess the people was bestowed in accordance with the virtue earth. And so was there a rectification of titles that [Wang Mang] may take true [control of the throne], and there was a change of first month to that established at $chou._{B02}$ that [the emperor] may be long-lived and lofty, but the pitches and measures were kept the same in accordance the standards of our predecessors. When the dragon was at $jisi._{06}$ and Jupiter stationed itself at Shi Chen.$_{JS6}$ (Taurus) (A.D. 9), these were first promulgated throughout the subcelestial realm that the myriad states may eternally obey them, and that son's sons and grandson's grandsons may enjoy and transmit them for 100,000 years (*Qin Han jinwen huibian* 秦漢金文匯編 [Shanghai: Shanghai guji chubanshe, 1997], 198).

Similar testimony can be found on the Xin heng *gan* 新衡杆 and Xin jia *liang* 新嘉量 in ibid., 201, 208.

left Wang Mang to move to an Yin one (because Xia → Yin, despite the fact that YIN :
CHOU.$_{B02}$: METAL : WHITE ≠ EARTH).[81]

With the unseemly events of the Wang Mang interregnum safely out of mind, the next
landmark reform took place in A.D. 85–86 at the order of Han Zhangdi 漢章帝 (r. A.D.
76–88). After more than a century of use, the Grand Inception system (#7) was perceived
to have fallen out of sync with Heaven, sliding behind the observed position of the moon and
ahead that of the sun. In A.D. 32, Grand Coachman Zhu Fu 朱浮, Grand Palace Grandee
Xu Shu 許淑, et al. petitioned without effect that the official system was incorrect and
should be changed. Expectant Appointee Yang Cen 楊岑 finally caught the attention of
the throne in A.D. 64 when he correctly predicted a lunar eclipse a full day prior to the full
moon of the civil calendar.[82] In response, Mingdi 明帝 (r. A.D. 58–75) ordered the Clerk's
Office to conduct further testing of the lunar phases. After five months, Yang's system
was found to be consistently on the mark, so the emperor ordered Expectant Appointees
Zhang Sheng 張盛, Jing Fang 景防, Bao Ye 鮑鄴, et al. to conduct further tests against
a "quarter-remainder method" 四分法, which Yang's system again outperformed over the
course of more than one year. After Expectant Appointee to the Grand Clerk Dong Meng
董萌 submitted another petition for reform in A.D. 66, deliberation was held between the
Three Excellencies and "those who understood *li*" (*zhi li zhe* 知曆者) in the office of the
Grand Master of Ceremonies (to which the Clerk's Office belonged), but this dragged on
into the next year without result.[83] In the winter of A.D. 69, the emperor then ordered the

---

81. For an excellent study of the debate concerning the three concordances, five virtues, the legitimacy
of the Han imperial clan, and the rise of Wang Mang amid the political and intellectual background of the
late-Western Han, see Gopal Sukhu, "Yao, Shun, and Prefiguration: The Origins and Ideology of the Han
Imperial Genealogy," *Early China* 30 (2005–2006): 91–151.

82. According to the *Hou Han shu*, the "official calendar" (*guan li* 官曆) placed the moment of full moon on
Eternal Tranquility 5-VII-16 (A.D. 62 September 8), but the lunar eclipse (which happens at true opposition
or full moon) occurred as predicted by Yang Cen on 5-VII-15 (September 7) (*Hou Han shu, zhi* 2, 3035).
There was indeed a penumbral eclipse that occurred on September 7 at 20:44 local apparent time (LAT)
according to Fred Espenak and Jean Meeus, *Five Millennium Canon of Lunar Eclipses: −1999 to +3000*
(NASA/TP-2009-214172, 2009), A–83.

83. In a paragraph describing the reform of Eternal Harmony year 2 (A.D. 85), the *Hou Han shu* mentions
these events as occurring in "year 9," referring apparently to Mingdi's Eternal Tranquility reign (A.D. 58–75).

replacement of Yang Cen's method with that of Zhang, Jing, Bao, et al., neither of which appears to have been a full-fledged astronomical system.[84]

Finally, in A.D. 85 both the systematic error of the official system—described as 1 day and 5°° for lunar phases—and the helplessness of the Grand Clerks to do anything about it had become such an embarrassment that Zhangdi issued a direct order to their subordinates, Calendarists Bian Xin 編訢, Li Fan 李梵, et al., to come up with a solution. Bian and Li submitted Han Quarter-remainder system (#9) that very year, and Zhangdi ordered its immediate implementation, citing the following reasons in his edict:

1. According to the classics and the weft and prophecy texts, the Sage Kings effected sagacious rule by upholding the cosmic rhythm of Heaven. Thus, the disastrous state of the world in his own time must be the consequence of Zhangdi allowing the *li* (and its schedule of precisely timed rituals) to fall out of sync with Heaven. It therefore behooved the emperor to solve this problem in the manner laid out by the Sages.

2. Sages knew Heaven through repeated experiential investigation of it. It is through such investigation that they formulated the rule recorded in the *Spring and Autumn Annals* weft *Bao qian tu* 保乾圖 that "every 300 years there must be a reform of the Dipper *li*" 三百年斗曆改憲 to keep up with the times, and A.D. 85 was obviously such a time.

3. Technical features of the Quarter-remainder system, such as its DAY FACTOR and ORIGIN, had scriptural precedent in the weft texts.[85]

Though the matter was settled, Zhangdi began to plow through the classics and prophecy literature in response to a detail of the new system involving the arrangement of large and

---

84. For a translation and study of this episode, see Cullen, "Actors, Networks, and 'Disturbing Spectacles' in Institutional Science," 245–247.

85. For a comprehensive study of the calendro-astronomy contained in Han weft and prophecy literature, see Takeda Tokimasa 武田時昌, "Isho rekihō kō: Zenkan matsu no keigaku to kagaku no kōryū" 緯書曆法考: 前漢末の經學と科學の交流, in *Chugoku kodai kagakushi ron* 中國古代科學史論, ed. Yamada Keiji 山田慶兒 (Kyōto: Kyōto daigaku jinbun kagaku kenkyūjo, 1989), 55–120. For an excellent study of how weft texts erupt into Eastern Han calendro-astronomy debate, see Cullen, "Actors, Networks, and 'Disturbing Spectacles' in Institutional Science."

small months that conflicted with the intercalation RULE (19 years = 235 months = $19\times12+7$ months). Unsatisfied with this innovation's classical precedence, he ordered General of the Gentlemen-of-the-Household Jia Kui 賈逵 (A.D. 30–101) to talk the matter over with Calendarists Wei Cheng 衛承 and Li Chong 李崇, subordinate to the Grand Commandant Liang Wei 梁鮪, Clerk to the Minister over the Masses Yan Xu 嚴勗, Member of the Suite of the Heir-apparent Xu Zhen 徐震, Grandee of the Eighth Order Su Tong 蘇統 of Julu 鉅鹿, Bian Xin, and Li Fan. Expert advice in hand, Zhangdi ordered the Clerk's Office in A.D. 86 to correct this detail over the protests of its creators.[86]

Again, like its predecessors before it, the Quarter-remainder system (#9) underwent several modifications over its lifetime. One came in A.D. 102, when Expectant Appointee to the Grand Clerk Huo Rong 霍融 successfully petitioned to reform the standard by which government clepsydrae were adjusted for seasonal daylight hours, changing it from a function of time to a function of solar declination. Another came in A.D. 173, when a gnomonics program culminated in the solar table now appended to the received version of the Quarter-remainder system manual.[87]

The next two landmark reforms took place in the state of Sun-Wu 孫吳 (A.D. 220–280) in A.D. 222 and Cao-Wei 曹魏 (A.D. 220–265) in A.D. 237. However, since these are the subject of Chapter 4, let us return for now to the Han and consider how else we might present the history of its astral sciences.

---

86. The preceding is a summary of the account preserved in *Hou Han shu, zhi* 2, 3025–3027.

87. On Huo Rong's reform, see ibid., *zhi* 2, 3032–3033. According to Zu Chongzhi 祖沖之 (A.D. 429–500), "as to the Quarter-remainder system (#9) method, though its division of RULES and establishment of OBSCURATIONS (its basic calendrical contents) was created in Epochal Harmony (A.D. 84–87), all the shadow and instrument numbers (of its solar table) were fixed in Illustrious Tranquility year 3 (A.D. 173)" 四分曆法，雖分章設籥創自元和，而晷儀眾數定於熹平三年 (*Song shu*, 13.312). Some 88 years after the institution of the Quarter-remainder system, the date Illustrious Tranquility year 3 appears in said table as appended to the Quarter-remainder system manual in *Hou Han shu, zhi* 3, 3081. For a study of both, see Cullen, "Huo Rong's Observation Programme."

1.2.2 A history of knowledge in practice

It is tempting to read the history of pre-modern Chinese astronomy as a sequence of government policies, especially when all that we possess of its technical literature are state manuals. We moderns are not alone in this habit; neither is it without its merits. When we begin to read through the "*Li* Treatises" at even a cursory level of detail, however, it becomes immediately apparent that our system reforms are themselves open-ended and evolving entities, and that calendro-astronomy is *a field of knowledge* that thrives unpunctuated by state policies, and whose fruits cannot always be divvied between them. While I have hinted at these points in Section 1.2.1, the case of Han lunar theory speaks to them more substantially.

At its earliest stage, Chinese calendro-astronomy posited a moon that travels at an even clip around the celestial equator, which the real moon does not do. In 52 B.C., Grand Minister of Agriculture and Palace Assistant Secretary Geng Shouchang 耿壽昌 memorialized that by use of a *tuyi* 圖儀 "diagram instrument" (?) that he had fashioned for himself, he found that the sun and moon move faster along the Red Road (*chi dao* 赤道; i.e. equator) at Ox.$_{09}$ (Capricorn) and Well.$_{22}$ (Gemini)—the solstices—than at Pasture.$_{16}$ (Aries) and Horn.$_{01}$ (Virgo)—the equinoxes. The reason for this, he offered, is that the sun and moon travel obliquely to the Red Road along the Yellow Road (*huang dao* 黃道; i.e. ecliptic), and one could eliminate the one-day discrepancy common to predicted and observed phenomena by switching to Yellow Road coordinates.[88]

This solution lead to another problem: while the moon does essentially travel along the ecliptic, it does not do so at an even rate there either due to the eccentricity of its orbit. In the following decades we see the concept of the Nine Roads (*jiu dao* 九道) emerge to deal with *this* variability in the work of Liu Xiang 劉向 (79–8 B.C.) and the weft texts. These describe the Nine Roads variously as a nine-year cycle of lunar motion or nine colored paths in space along which the moon travels. One such description appears in the manual for Liu Xin's Triple Concordance system (#8) preserved in the *Han shu*, but it appears at the very

---

88. *Hou Han shu, zhi* 2, 3029.

end, where it is neither integrated into the system itself nor explained in sufficient detail for independent use.[89] The only thing we know for certain about its relationship with the state's Grand Inception system (#7) is that first- and second-century A.D. actors toyed with it to compensate for the aging system's increasing lag.[90] According to Jia Kui's discourse on calendrics (memorialized in A.D. 92), the Nine Roads posit that the variability of lunar motion along the Yellow Road is due to the moon's changing distance from Earth, and that the "speedy place" (*ji chu* 疾處; i.e. perigee) precesses $3^{\circ\circ}$ per month, circuiting Heaven once every nine years (i.e. the 8.85-year precession of the line of apsides). Jia tells us that it was Li Fan and Su Tong who worked out some of the details of this though, again, it did not feature in the reform for which they were responsible. Neither, Jia Kui bemoaned, had the Clerk's Office adopted Yellow Road coordinates or instrumentation in the 143 years since Geng Shouchang's petition.[91]

In his very first year on the throne it was apparent that Hedi 和帝 (r. A.D. 89–105) had inherited something of a mess. First, a lunar eclipse occurred one lunation earlier than predicted by the new Quarter-remainder system (#9) on Eternal Origin 1-VII^2-16 (A.D. 89 September 9) and once again on 2-I-16 (A.D. 90 March 5), the latter of which Grandee of the Eighth Order Zong Gan 宗紺 of Meng had predicted and memorialized four days in advance.[92] After the obligatory round of testing, Zong was appointed to the staff of the Grand Clerk, where Hedi ordered the implementation of his method, establishing an eclipse program independent of the astronomical system. Zong's solution proved adequate until

---

89. *Han shu*, 21B.1007.

90. *Hou Han shu*, zhi 2, 3035. I would like to thank Christopher Cullen and Yin Shoufu 殷守甫 for kindly sharing their notes on the Nine Roads with me. While their insights were formative to my understanding of this concept, particularly as they led me to Chen Jiujin and Wang Shengli's 王勝利 scholarship on the topic: Chen Jiujin, "Jiudaoshu jie" 九道術解, *Ziran kexue shi yanjiu* 1, no. 2 (1982): 131–135; Wang Shengli, " 'Jiudao' gaishuo" 「九道」該說, *Lishi yanjiu* 歷史研究 2 (1982): 91–101. For more on the Nine Roads, see also p. 305, n. 58.

91. *Hou Han shu*, zhi 2, 3027–3030.

92. These correspond to lunar eclipses that we know to have occurred on A.D. 89 September 9 at 00:56 LAT and on A.D. 90 March 5 at 00:26 LAT; see Espenak and Meeus, *Five Millennium Canon of Lunar Eclipses*, A–85.

A.D. 145, when it too became off by one lunation, sparking a frenzy of competition amongst Zong's grandchildren and officials inside and outside the Clerk's Office in the A.D. 170s. Second, after reading Jia Kui's discourse in A.D. 92, Hedi ordered the Clerk's Office to run observational tests on the Nine Roads method and, in A.D. 103, commissioned a "Grand Clerk's Yellow Road bronze instrument" 太史黃道銅儀 for them. Though both held up excellently to testing, nothing ultimately came of this: the Clerk's Office "abandoned and did not work on" 廢而不修 the technique and barely used the instrument because they found it "difficult to make observations with" 難以候.[93]

While the Clerk's Office had long since given up, interest in the Nine Roads continued unabated into the second century. At the Protracted Glory debate of A.D. 123, Gentleman of the Masters of Writing Zhang Heng 張衡 and Zhou Xing 周興, who the *Hou Han shu* describe as "capable at *li*" 能曆, emphasized again that the Nine Roads method was the most accurate of any when compared against observational records.[94] Erudit Huang Guang 黃廣 and Prefect Grand Usher Ren Qian 任僉 chimed in on their behalf, but forty officials led by Yin Zhi 尹祉 of Henan and Member of the Suite of the Heir-apparent Li Hong 李泓 disputed its accuracy on account that "if you use the Nine Roads for new moons, there will be three big months and two little ones in a row" 用九道為朔，月有比三大二小. This is to say that the application of the "fixed" (*ding* 定) lunation—the true lunation, adjusted for the inequality of lunar motion—would upset the calendar's neat alternation of 30- and 29-day "big" and "small" months, which are based on a mean lunation of roughly $29\frac{1}{2}$-days. At the Peaceful Han debate of A.D. 143, there was further mention of Grand Inception system (#7)

---

93. *Hou Han shu, zhi* 2, 3029–3030, 3040–3043.

94. Zhang Heng is perhaps the most famous astronomer from this period. Important studies of his work include Chen Jiujin, "Zhang Heng de tianwenxue sixiang" 張衡的天文學思想, *Keji shi wenji* 科技史文集 6 (1980): 23–31; Christopher Cullen, "Seeing the Appearances: Ecliptic and Equator in the Eastern Han," *Ziran kexue shi yanjiu* 2000.4: 352–382; Bo Shuren, "Zhang Heng" 張衡, in *Bo Shuren wenji* 薄樹人文集 (Hefei: Zhongguo kexue jishu daxue chubanshe, 2003), 525–538; Y. Edmund Lien, "Zhang Heng's *Huntian Yi Zhu* Revisited," *T'oung Pao* 98, no. 1–3 (2012): 31–64. On his life, times, and other intellectual pursuits, see Xu Jie 許結, *Zhang Heng pingzhuan* 張衡評傳, Zhongguo sixiangjia pingzhuan congshu 26 (Nanjing: Nanjing daxue chubanshe, 1999); Lien, "Zhang Heng, Eastern Han Polymath, His Life and Works" (Ph.D. diss., University of Washington, 2011).

revivalists working on the Nine Roads, and in the Illustrious Tranquility reign (A.D. 172–178), former Calendarist Gentleman Liang Guozong 梁國宗 submitted yet another version to the emperor, who sent it to the Grand Clerk for testing. Again, neither attempt proved successful.[95]

It is around this time that Liu Hong emerged on the scene. A member of the royal clan of the King of Lu, Liu Hong hailed from Mengyin 蒙陰, Taishan 泰山, where he began his career as a Colonel. In the Protracted Illustriousness reign (A.D. 158–167) he was recruited by the Grand Clerk and began his career in *li* amid the learned circles of the capital. He continued with his own research through his subsequent transferal to Gentleman-of-the-Palace, then Chief Clerk of Changshan 常山, on the Shandong Peninsula, from where he submitted two works to the throne in A.D. 174 as part of an effort at the Clerk's Office to replace Zong Gan's failing method for eclipse prediction.[96] After a leave of office to mourn for his father, Liu Hong returned to the capital as Official Who Hands up Accounts and, again, Gentleman-of-the-Palace.

Liu Hong's second stint in the capital lasted between three to seven years (A.D. 177/178–180/184). In A.D. 178 Cai Yong recommended him to the Eastern Observatory to assist with the *li* and mathematics of compiling a "*Li* and Harmonics Treatise" for the current dynasty.[97] By A.D. 179 he had been reassigned within the palace as Internuncio and enfeoffed as Marquis

---

95. *Hou Han shu, zhi* 2, 3030, 3034–3037. At the Peaceful Han debate, Prefect Grand Clerk Yu Gong 虞恭 and Calendarist Zong Xin 宗訢 acknowledge the merits of the Nine Roads, but successfully argue that these are insufficient allow the old Grand Inception system (#7) to compete with the Quarter-remainder (#9). Liang Guozong's proposal was picked up by the Clerk's Office, who tried different variations, all of which placed the moon ahead or behind Heaven by as far as 10°°.

96. These works, now lost, were the *Qi yao shu* 七曜術 (Seven Luminaries Method) and *Ba yuan shu* 八元術 (Eight Origins Method). For supposition about the relationship between Liu's *Qi yao shu* and Indian astronomy, see Jiang Xiaoyuan, *Tianxue zhen yuan*, 266–269. Chen Meidong argues that the coincidence of these activities with the compilation of the Quarter-remainder solar table in A.D. 173 (see note 87) suggests that Liu may also have been part of that project ("Liu Hong de shengping, tianwenxue chengjiu he sixiang" 劉洪的生平、天文學成就和思想, *Ziran kexue shi yanjiu* 5, no. 2 [1986]: 129). All that the *Hou Han shu* says about his activities this year is that he authored these works and "sent them up" (*shang* 上) (*Hou Han shu, zhi* 2, 3040). It is thus unclear whether he was actually in the capital when the solar table project was settled.

97. This treatise formed the basis of the *Hou Han shu* "Lü li zhi"; see note 60.

of Guchengmen 穀城門 (near Taishan). However, in this and the following year the court called upon his expertise in no less than three important matters of *li*, which suggests that he remained in Luoyang. Not long after, Liu was deployed to the eastern seaboard as Chief Commandant of the Kuaiji 會稽 Eastern Regiment.

It was in his time in the provinces that Liu Hong finished his Supernal Emblem system (#10), on which he had been working for some ten or twenty years. In the late spring of A.D. 189, Liu journeyed to the capital to present his system to Lingdi 靈帝 (r. A.D. 168–189) but had to turn back before he had arrived due to the emperor's death and the turmoil resulting from Dong Zhuo's 董卓 (d. A.D. 192) military occupation of the capital. Soon after he was transferred to serve as Minister to the Marquis of Qucheng 曲城, then the Governor of Shanyang 山陽. Back on the Shandong Peninsula, Liu continued to work on his Supernal Emblem system (#10) until at least A.D. 206. In the meantime, Liu taught his method to Zheng Xuan 鄭玄 (A.D. 126–200) in A.D. 196, who later wrote a commentary and explanation to it (now lost), as well as Xu Yue 徐岳 of Donglai 東萊, an important player in the Cao-Wei Yellow Inception debate discussed in Chapter 4. Xu, in turn, taught it to Kan Ze 闞澤, who also wrote a commentary to it (now lost), and who would become the Palace Prefect Writer of the state of Sun-Wu. There in A.D. 222, well after Liu Hong's death in office, the Supernal Emblem was finally instituted at a state level.[98]

The Supernal Emblem system is best known for its lunar theory: its SPEED SEQUENCE (*chiji li* 遲疾曆) for lunar anomaly, LATITUDE SEQUENCE (*yinyang li* 陰陽曆) for the moon as it travels on its White Road (*bai dao* 白道), itself slightly oblique to the Yellow Road,

---

98. There is no extant biography for Liu Hong from the period; what we know about his life and work must be pieced together from fragmentary sources. Chen Meidong collects these and weaves them into a coherent biography in Chen Meidong, "Liu Hong de shengping, tianwenxue chengjiu he sixiang," 129–132. The only place where my understanding of events differs from Chen's is in the order of his two final posts. The problem comes down to how to reconcile the *Bowu ji*'s 博物記 claim that he served as the Minister of the Marquis of Qucheng with the *Yuanshan songshu*'s 袁山松書 account that in A.D. 189 "he was sequestered back to the capital but before arriving he was named the Governor of Shanyang, where he died in office" 徵還，未至，領山陽太守，卒官 (*Hou Han shu*, *zhi* 2, 3043 [commentary]). Chen notes that Shanyang's proximity to Xuzhou 徐州, where Zheng Xuan was known to be when he "received his method" in A.D. 196, suggests that Liu Hong began there before dying in office in Qucheng circa A.D. 210.

its implementation of the eclipse limit, and something called *xiao xi* 消息, which I will discuss in Chapter 4.[99] It is the SPEED SEQUENCE that interests us here. In brief, the SPEED SEQUENCE is a period of 164466/5969 days or, to six significant figures, 27.5534 days—the anomalistic month (to the same precision, the modern value is 27.5546 days)— and a table of lunar velocity for adjusting the true moon's displacement in time and space from the mean moon. We do not know enough about Nine Roads methods to assess to what degree Liu Hong improved upon their parameters; however, the concept is clearly the same, since the Supernal Emblem system produces a 3.10°° precession of Jia Kui's "speedy place" each sidereal month, which returns to its initial position in 8.89 years.[100] What we do know is that the Supernal Emblem system (#10) outdid its predecessors on three important points. First, it successfully integrated a period for the anomalistic month into the numerical superstructure of a coherent and adequate system.[101] Second, it effectively segregated astronomy and the calendar, retaining the mean moon for the latter to avoid the "three big months... in a row" problem while reaping the benefits of lunar anomaly for eclipse prediction. Third, it won state approval and was transmitted to posterity.

---

99. On Liu Hong's lunar theory, see Christopher Cullen, "The First Complete Chinese Theory of the Moon: The Innovations of Liu Hong c. A.D. 200," *Journal for the History of Astronomy* 33 (2002): 21–39.

100. Jia's is the most detailed extant description of a Nine Roads method, but its parameters appear to be either rounded or numerically inconsistent. The fact that brilliant minds like Jia Kui, Zhang Heng, etc. describe having used it to predict and retrodict phenomena suggests to me that we do not have the full picture, let alone an understanding of how the method evolved over the span of two centuries. Liu Hong does not directly discuss the speedy place, but its precession can be derived from the parameters of his system.

101. In the materials covered by the *Han shu* and *Hou Han shu* covered above, discussion of the Nine Roads invariably occurs in the context of the Grand Inception/Triple Concordance system. Their numerical superstructure is based on factors of nine, which allows for the perfect integration of a nine-year cycle. However, the systematic error in lunar and solar phenomena that was evident by the beginning of the Eastern Han 東漢 (A.D. 25–220) left its proponents struggling with stopgap measures that actors and the authorial voice of the *Hou Han shu* "Lü li zhi" treat as inadequate. On the other hand, the numerical superstructure of the Quarter-remainder system (#9), as its name suggests, is based on factors of four, which precludes its integration with the Nine Roads.

1.3 A Sociology of *Li* Calendro-astronomy

1.3.1 The cast of participants

As we have touched upon above, the classics describe the role of the Sage King as "contemplating the signs and granting the seasons"—that is, promoting cosmo-political harmony by delegating to capable officials the duties of inspecting Heaven for signs of discord and disseminating a calendar that brings agricultural and sacrificial affairs into sync with its rhythms. The precedence of Sage-time legend had a lasting impact on the organization of the imperial bureaucracy. As per the *Rites of Zhou* and the institutions of its immediate predecessors, the Han court delegated the work of *tianwen* and *li* to the [Prefect] Grand Clerk and his *shi guan* ("Clerk's Officials/Office"), a subsidiary of the Ministry of Rites. The *Hou Han shu* provides the following description of his office, which reflects its dual task of "contemplating" and "granting":

掌天時、星曆。凡歲將終，奏新年曆。凡國祭祀、喪、娶之事，掌奏良日及時節禁忌。凡國有瑞應、災異，掌記之。

He is charged with the seasons/time of Heaven and the sequence of the stars (*xing li*). Near the end of each year, he memorializes the new yearly calendar. For all state matters of sacrifices, funerals, and weddings, he is charged with memorializing auspicious dates and seasonal prohibitions. For every time that the state experiences an auspicious response (omen) or calamitous anomaly, he is charged with recording it.[102]

The history of the Clerk's Office is extremely complex, so I will focus here on the Eastern Han office as documented by the *Hou Han shu* and extant fragments of "Han Office" (*Han guan*

---

102. *Hou Han shu, zhi* 25, 3572. The *Rites of Zhou* attributes the Great Clerk (*dashi* 大史) with additional legal, administrative, archival, and ritual responsibilities of state (*Zhouli zhushu*, 26.18a). For the history and responsibilities of this office in the Han, see Hans Bielenstein, *The Bureaucracy of Han Times* (Cambridge: Cambridge University Press, 1980), 22–23.

漢官) literature (Table 1.5).[103] Under the Grand Clerk were three officers. The first was his Assistant, who supervises thirty-seven Expectant Appointees in areas of calendro-astronomy, divination, and ritual supplication.[104] The second is the Assistant for the Hall of Light, the ritual complex where the emperor "acts as the polestar of the people" by promulgating the calendar and performing monthly rituals.[105] The third is the Assistant for the Numinous Terrace observatory, who supervises forty-two Expectant Appointees responsible for observing astronomical, meteorological, and harmonic phenomena.[106] Despite their unique access to Heaven and the emperor, none of these offices ranked particularly high in the civil service. There are signs of upward mobility within the Clerk's Office, as I have laid out in Table 1.6, but only the Grand Clerk himself ever seems to move on to higher office.[107]

---

103. *Hou Han shu, zhi* 25, 3572; *Han guan liu zhong* 漢官六種 (Zhonghua shuju ed.). For studies of these sources, see Mansvelt Beck, *The Treatises of Later Han*, 196–226; Bielenstein, The Bureaucracy of Han Times, esp. 1–4. For a complete history of the state astronomical office, see Thatcher Elliot Deane, "The Chinese Imperial Astronomical Bureau: Form and Function of the Ming Dynasty Qintianjian from 1365 to 1627" (Ph.D. diss., University of Washington, 1989); Chen Xiaozhong 陳曉中 and Zhang Shuli 張淑莉, *Zhongguo gudai tianwen jigou yu tianwen jiaoyu* 中國古代天文機構與天文教育, Zhongguo tianwenxueshi daxi (Beijing: Zhongguo kexue jishu chubanshe, 2008). Note that the name and affiliation of the office itself change over the centuries; however, given the currency of the term *shi guan* over the period covered in this study, I shall refer to this agency throughout as "the Clerk's Office" or "the Office of the Grand Clerk."

104. The *daizhao* 待詔 "Expectant Appointee" is a complex title in the Han designating someone who has been singled out for office by a higher authority (usually the emperor) due to particular talents. In some cases, this means that the person so-designated is in line for an official post; however, Sugimoto Kenji 杉本憲司 and Yang Hongnian 楊鴻年 point out that in the context of the Clerk's Office, *daizhao* appear to be specialist functionaries *not* awaiting further appointment; see Sugimoto, "Kandai no taishō ni tsuite" 漢代の待詔について, *Shakai kagaku ronshū* 社會科學論集 4, no. 5 (1973): 86–87; Yang Hongnian, *Han Wei zhidu congkao* 漢魏制度叢考 (Wuhan: Wuhan daxue chubanshe, 1985), 109, 124–125.

105. On the Hall of Light, see note 31.

106. On the Numinous Terrace and observatories of the Han, see Chen Xiaozhong and Zhang Shuli, *Zhongguo gudai tianwen jigou yu tianwen jiaoyu*, 38–41. For a site report of the Eastern Han Numinous Terrace complex unearthed in 1974-1975, see Zhongguo shehui kexue yuan kaogu yanjiusuo Luoyang gongzuo shi 中國社會科學院考古研究所洛陽工作隊, "Han-Wei Luoyang cheng nanjiao de lingtai yizhi" 漢魏洛陽城南郊的靈台遺址, *Kaogu* 考古 1977.1: 54–57.

107. The one exception in this period and on Table 1.6 is Bao Ye, who appears as Expectant Appointee to the Grand Clerk in A.D. 64, then in A.D. 77 as Assistant for Music, having been promoted to a different technocratic position within the Ministry of Rites. It makes a certain sense that technicians that excelled at their jobs would be retained in them rather than bounced around the bureaucracy the way that administrators were. However, the reason that we do not see more cases like Bao's might have more to do with their lowly position and minuscule impact on the sort of grand, high-level events that interest the compilers of dynastic histories.

The turnover rate in the administrative-level offices was quite high and, with the sole exception of Sima Tan and Qian, there is no evidence of the sort of hereditary transmission of office that is more typical of the Tang and later periods.[108] Rather, we see actors hired into the Clerk's Office for one of two reasons. The first type of hire (rare) are "king makers" like Liu Xin, Gaotang Long, and Xu Zhi—figures central to a founding emperors' legitimacy-building project through their expertise in yin-yang, the occult arts, *tianwen* omenology, and/or classical state ritual.[109] The second type of hire (common) are experts like Deng Ping and Zong Gan, who are appointed in response to some demonstrated faculty with or marked contribution to the field of *li*.[110] Whatever on-the-job training the Clerk's Office may have provided its functionaries, it was just as much in the business of collecting talent from elsewhere as it was in cultivating its own.[111]

Twentieth-century histories of science often describe the "official character of Chinese astronomy" as a double-edged sword: "from early times Chinese astronomy had benefited

108. Sima Qian inherited the office of Prefect Grand Clerk from his father Tan. On the hereditary office-holders of the Tang, see Lai Swee Fo 賴瑞和, "Tangdai de Hanlin daizhao he Sitiantai" 唐代的翰林待詔和司天臺, *Tang yanjiu* 唐研究 9 (2003): 315–342; Jiang Xiaoyuan, "Liuchao Sui Tang chuanru zhongtu zhi Yindu tianxue" 六朝隋唐傳入中土之印度天學, *Hanxue yanjiu* 漢學研究 10, no. 2 (1992): 253–277.

109. On Liu Xin's role in legitimizing Wang Mang's rise to power, see Xu Xingwu, *Liu Xiang pingzhuan*, 432–478. On Gaotang Long and Xu Zhi, see Chapter 4. Jiang Xiaoyuan and Nathan Sivin give special emphasis to the role of this criterion in later periods, see Jiang, *Tianxue zhen yuan*, 50–52; Sivin, *Granting the Seasons*, 1–33, 133–150.

110. In A.D. 174, Zong Gan's grandson Cheng 誠 is also hired on as Member of the Suite in a similar situation involving a petition on eclipse prediction (*Hou Han shu, zhi* 2, 3040–3041). We may also add to this list three figures from Table 1.6. First, Yin Xian's expertise is suggested by the fact that he worked with Liu Xin on the *Zuo Tradition of the Spring and Autumn Annals* and was responsible for collating the "Numbers and Techniques" literature of the imperial library (*Han shu*, 30.1701, 36.1976). Second, Andi 安帝 (r. A.D. 106–125) assigned Zhang Heng Prefect Grand Clerk because he "heard that Heng was adept at technical studies" 聞衡善術學 (*Hou Han shu*, 59.1897). Third, Shan Yang was promoted to this post due to his moral standing and the fact that he "was adept and enlightened in the celestial offices (constellations) and mathematics" 善明天官、筭術 (ibid., 82B.2733). Here we might also note that Zhang Shouwang (above) was removed from the office of Prefect Grand Clerk due to his crackpot ideas (*Han shu*, 21A.978).

111. The Clerk's Office did not take on an explicitly educational function until the Sui, when its staff began to include Erudits and Students in *li*, *tianwen*, the clepsydra, and omenology (*Sui shu*, 28.775; *Tang liu dian* 唐六典 [Siku quanshu ed.], 10.13a–16a [commentary]; cf. Chen Xiaozhong and Zhang Shuli, *Zhongguo gudai tianwen jigou yu tianwen jiaoyu*, 297–304). Given the fact that soldiers, scribes, and other functionaries received on-the-job literacy training, it is conceivable that the Clerk's Office would have provided similar training in "science" literacy. On education in the astral sciences, see Section 1.3.1. Note that the bans of later times often went hand-in-hand with nationwide searches and conscription of talent; see Chen Meidong, *Zhongguo gudai tianwenxue sixiang*, 17–32.

Table 1.5: The organization of the Eastern Han Clerk's Office)

no.	Office	Salary
1	皇帝 Emperor	∞
2	三公 Three Excellencies	10,000 shi
3	九卿 Nine Ministers	2,000 shi
4	太常 Grand Master of Ceremonies	2,000 shi
5	太史令 Prefect Grand Clerk	600 shi
6	太史丞 Assistant to the Grand Clerk	200 shi
7	待詔 Expectant Appointees (37)	-
8	治曆 Calendarists (6)	-
9	龜卜 Diviners by Tortoise Shell (3)	-
10	廬宅 Directors of Buildings (3)	-
11	日時 Experts in the Phases of the Sun (4)	-
12	易筮 Directors of Sacrifices to Expel Evil Influences (3)	-
13	典禳 Directors of Sacrifices to Expel Evil Influences (2)	-
14	典星 Director of Stars*	-
15	籍氏 Experts in the Tradition of Master Ji (3)	-
16	許氏 Experts in the Tradition of Master Xu (3)	-
17	典昌氏 Experts in the Tradition of Masters Dian and Chang (3)	-
18	嘉法 Specialists of Methods (2)	-
19	請雨 Supplicants for Rain (2)	-
20	解事 Elucidators (2)	-
21	醫 Physicians (2)	-
22	明堂丞 Assistant for the Hall of Light (calendro-ritual complex)	200 shi
23	靈台丞 Assistant for the Numinous Terrace (observatory)	200 shi
24	待詔 Expectant Appointees (42)	-
25	候星 Watchers of the Stars (14)	-
26	候日 Watchers of the Sun (2)	-
27	候風 Watchers of the Wind (3)	-
28	候氣 Watchers of the Qi (12)	-
29	候晷景 Watchers of the Sun's Shadow (3)	-
30	候鍾律 Watchers of the Zhong Pitch Pipes (7)	-
31	舍人 Member of the Suite	-

NOTE: This table is based on the *Hou Han shu* "Baiguan zhi" and fragments of the *Han guan yi* 漢官儀. While we do not posses a similar list for the Western Han, we know from historical records that it saw the following changes: (4) 太常 renamed 奉常 in 144 B.C., then reverted; (5) 太史 renamed 太史公 in 140/110 B.C., then 太史令 in 86 B.C., lastly, the short-lived office Xi-He 羲和 (and his four *zi* 子 "masters") was added in 1 B.C., his pay-grade and responsibilities being identical to the Grand Clerk's; (23) 靈台 observatory established in 78 B.C., prior observatory named 清台 "Clear Terrace." The following offices also appear in Western Han sources: 1-8, 14, 26. *Note that office 26 "Director of Stars" appears in the Eastern Han but goes unmentioned in the "Baiguan zhi" or *Han guan yi*. The Three Kingdoms and Western Jin inherited the Eastern Han model basically unchanged, however, there sometimes appear to have been multiple Grand Clerks at one time (see p. 297 n. 44).

Table 1.6: Career paths in the Clerk's Office (Han – Three Kingdoms)

Office	Shi	Office	Shi
司馬談 Sima Tan (d. 110 B.C.)		**劉洪 Liu Hong** (c. A.D. 135–210)	
Ass't to the Grand Clerk	200	Colonel	=2,000
Prefect Grand Clerk	600	Clerk's Office, post unknown	–
鄧平 Deng Ping (fl. 104 B.C.)		Gentleman-of-the-Palace	=300
Calendarist	<200	Chief Clerk of Changshan	600
Ass't to the Grand Clerk	200	Official in Charge of Accounts	600
劉歆 Liu Xin (c. 50 B.C. – A.D. 23)		Gentleman-of-the-Palace	=300
Colonel of the Capital Rampart	2000	Eastern Observatory, comp."Lü li zhi"	
Grand Administrator of Henei	2000	Internuncio	=600
Grand Palace Grandee	=1000	Marquis of Guchengmen	
Colonel of the Capital Rampart	2000	Chief Cmdt. of Kuaiji E. Regiment	=2000
Xi-He	2000	Minister to the Marq. of Qucheng	?
Marquis of Hongxiu		Grand Administrator of Shanyang	2000
尹咸 Yin Xian (fl. 26 B.C. – A.D. 5)		**許芝 Xu Zhi** (fl. A.D. 220–230)	
Prefect Grand Clerk	600	Recommended Filially Pious and Incorrupt	
Chancellor	10000	Ass't to the Grand Clerk	200
Grand Minister of Agriculture	2000	Prefect Grand Clerk	600
鮑鄴 Bao Ye (fl. A.D. 64–77)		**高堂隆 Gaotang Long** (fl. A.D. 213–240)	
Expectant Appt. to the Gr. Clerk	<200	Chancellery Consultant Div. [Head]	400?
Ass't for Music of the Grand M.C.	200	Tutor to the Marq. of Licheng	?
宗紺 Zong Gan (fl. A.D. 89)		Minister to the Marquis of Licheng	?
Grandee of the Eighth Order		Chief of Tangyang	300-400
Expectant Appt. to the Gr. Clerk	<200	Tutor to the King of Pingyuan	2000
張衡 Zhang Heng (A.D. 78-139)		Serving within the Palace	
Gentleman-of-the-Palace	=300	Erudit	=600
Prefect Grand Clerk	600	Chief CMDT of Attendant Calvary	=2000
Pft. of Majors of Ofcl. Carriages	600	Grand Administrator of Chenliu	2000
Prefect Grand Clerk	600	Accounts Division [Head]	400?
Master of Writing	?	Gentleman-of-the-Palace	=300
單颺 Shan Yang (fl. A.D. 170)		Regular Mounted Attendant	
Prefect Grand Clerk	600	Marquis within the Passes	
Palace Attendant	=2000	Prefect Grand Clerk	600
Grand Administrator of Hanzhong	2000	Palace Attendant	=2000
Master of Writing	?	Supt. of the Imperial Household	2000
劉固 Liu Gu (fl. A.D. 173-175)			
Clerk's Office's Gent.-of-the-Palace	=300		
Calendarist	<200		

NOTE: Offices and titles (SMALL CAPS) are in chronological order. Sima Tan: *Shiji*, 130.3288 (comm.). Deng Ping: HS 21A.975-978. Liu Xin: Xu, *Liu Xiang pingzhuan*, 480-511. Yin Xian: HS 30.1701, 36.1967, 19B.856. Bao Ye: HHS *zhi* 3, 3025; *zhi* 2, 3015 (comm.); *Sui shu*, 15.352. Zong Gan: HHS *zhi* 2, 3040. Zhang Heng: HHS *j.* 59. Shan Yang: HHS 60B.1990, 82B.2733. Liu Gu: HHS *zhi* 2, 3037, 3040. Liu Hong: Section 1.2.2. Xu Zhi: SGZ, 2.62 (comm.); *Song shu*, 34.1011; *Jin shu*, 12.338, 17.499. Gaotang Long: SGZ, *j.* 25.

from State support, but the semi-secrecy which it involved was to some extent a disadvan-tage."[112] However, scholars have since moved from this understanding to one wherein "much of the technical novelty came from outsiders."[113] Why? The key is the recognition that *the duty of the Clerk's Office was not to advance knowledge but to produce and disseminate inscriptions*—calendars, astronomical tables, observational records, and divinatory reports. Its duties were in fact so mechanical that, as we saw in the previous section, any decision whatsoever seems to have been passed immediately up the chain of command.

Ultimate authority rested with the emperor. He and only he was in the position to dictate reform and commission instruments, but the emperor also micromanaged observa-tion, testing, and prediction programs, personnel, and sometimes the minutiae of technical protocol. While not every emperor could be a Fuxi or a Yao, his secretariat ensured that decrees on these matters were commensurately well-informed. In fact, his secretariat was so well-informed on matters of *li* that it was often the Masters of Writing who were at the

---

112. Needham, *Science and Civilisation in China, Vol.3*, 186, 193. To be fair, Needham's description *is* more appropriate to the Song and Ming (A.D. 1368–1644), which he is discussing, and he notes the possession and manufacture of high-tech armillary instruments by private individuals as a counterexample. In his early work, Sivin refers to this idea somewhat facetiously as "the blighting hand of bureaucracy" but upholds many of its assumptions, e.g. the secret and inviolable nature of astronomical systems ("Cosmos and Computation in Early Chinese Mathematical Astronomy," esp. 4).

113. For Cullen and Chen Meidong's enlightening studies on the openness of the early imperial astral sciences and Clerk's Office, see Cullen, "Actors, Networks, and 'Disturbing Spectacles' in Institutional Science"; Chen Meidong, *Zhongguo gudai tianwenxue sixiang*, esp. 17–32. Sivin's description of the Season Granting system reform (from which the above quote is taken) is particularly insightful:

> The majority of officials who staffed the various astronomical organizations in most periods of history were hereditary practitioners better at trivially adjusting step-by-step computational protocols than breaking through to new techniques. Grand Astrologers were generally an exception, but they were seldom chosen because of their desire for change or their propensity to innovate. Most were non-specialist appointees, expected to run a large organization engaged in routine work, and to minimize unsettling surprises.
>
> Not surprisingly, much of the technical novelty came from outsiders who discovered serious weaknesses in the current system and proposed not minimal adjustments but a new system. Some who did so were officials; others were commoners. But to know astronomy in the first place they were necessarily well educated, and that usually implied a family history of civil service.
>
> The researches of private practitioners kept astronomy vital, but were also a potential threat. A better computational schema could be a priceless symbol of legitimacy in the hands of a potential rebel. It was tempting for rulers to forbid the private study of astronomy, as happened in a few periods of history (*Granting the Seasons*, 58–59).

forefront of the field, even those who had not themselves served in the Clerk's Office (as did Zhang Heng and Shan Yang).[114]

The emperor's first order of business was almost always to order the Clerk's Office to conduct testing, i.e. theoretical analysis, comparing the results of retrodiction to observational records, and/or running a predictive competition. *This* was his office's primary function in regard to innovation. And other than in cases of internal dissent, the inscriptions and determinations that they produced were generally accepted as unbiased fact—Latourian "black boxes" that are sometimes questioned but rarely reopened.[115] If the stakes were high or the results unclear, then the emperor passed the matter on for *yi* 議 deliberation, usually at the level of the Three Excellencies and "the hundred officials" (all Officialdom).

---

114. On the composition and role of the imperial secretariat, see Bielenstein, *The Bureaucracy of Han Times*, 48–49. Both Zhang Heng and Shan Yang went from Prefect Grand Clerk to Master of Writing; see 1.6. In A.D. 123, we see Gentlemen of the Masters of Writing Zhang Heng, Zhou Xing, and a Prefect Master of Writing Zhong 忠 repudiate and convince the emperor to table a reform proposal (p. 72; *Hou Han shu*, *zhi* 2, 3034–3035). For more on Zhang Heng and Zhou Xing's petition, see p. 231 ff. In A.D. 143 we see Gentleman-in-Attendance of the Masters of Writing Bian Shao 邊韶 propose a return to the Grand Inception system (#7) that results in a large debate (ibid., *zhi* 2, 3035–3037). Then, in the early third century A.D. we see Sun-Wu Prefect of the Palace Writers Kan Ze receive the Supernal Emblem system (#10) from Liu Hong's disciple Xu Yue and author a commentary to it (Page 74; *Song shu*, 12.259). In the Cao-Wei Yellow Inception debate of circa A.D. 223/226, two of the major figures are Prefect Master of Writing Chen Qun 陳羣 and Gentleman of the Master of Writing Yang Wei 楊偉 —the latter of which goes on to create the Luminous Inception system (#13), which Mingdi 明帝 (r. A.D. 226–239) implemented without debate in A.D. 237. Lastly, of the thirteen officials who voted on Prefect Grand Clerk Gaotang Long's proposal to reform the civil calendar in A.D. 227, five of them were officials of the Masters of Writing and the Palace Writers. On the last two points, see Chapter 4.

115. First, whatever the predictive accuracy of the calendars or astronomical tables that they produce, actors generally treat the Clerk's observational records and test results as hard facts when arguing for or against some mathematical model. The most noteworthy example of skepticism expressed towards such materials is an anecdote in which Gao Yun 高允 (A.D. 390–478) declared before an audience of historians that the [*Han shu*'s apocryphal] record of a five-planet convergence in Eastern Well.$_{22}$ (Gemini) on the first month of the inaugural year of the Han (207 B.C. Nov 14 – Dec 14) is "empty discourse" (*konglun* 空論), "conceit" (*qian* 淺), and an "absurdity" (*miu* 謬) (*Wei shu*, 48.1068). Such a convergence actually occurred around May of 205 B.C. but was re-imagined to have coincided *exactly* with the founding of the Han (*Shiji*, 27.1348, 89.2581; *Han shu*, 26.1301, 100A.4212). It is worth noting that Gao simply dismisses the event, and that his proof is based not on calculation but a sound rule of thumb that the inferior planets cannot be anywhere near Eastern Well.$_{22}$ in winter. Second, the Clerk's Office sometimes failed to reach decisive conclusions from testing programs because the responsible parties had come to loggerheads. For example, in A.D. 227/233 Wei Mingdi ordered Gaotang Long to work with Master of Writing Yang Wei and Prefect Grand Clerk Luo Lu 駱祿 to run competitive testing *on the calendro-astronomical system that Gaotang himself had submitted.* The result was that Gaotang, Luo, and Yang ended up quarreling and reporting each other to the throne for several years, each ultimately championing their own system over that of the others, leaving the emperor to arbitrate in favor of the Grand Clerk due, it seems, to reputation (*Sanguo zhi* 三國 志 [Zhonghua shuju ed.], 35.708 [commentary]).

Cullen's study of the debates of A.D. 62–69, A.D. 92–103, and A.D. 175 illustrates important features of the debate process and the "culture of rational and evidence based public argument about natural knowledge" (265) that it embodied. Cullen affirms that the state was perfectly open to public disagreement and criticism in matters of *li*, given its vested interest in the timing of state cosmo-ritual. Astronomical expertise was critical to this end, but it came from unlikely corners—not Office leadership but lowly Expectant Appointees and outside officials—and had to assert itself through persuasion, navigating a network of "human beings... observational instruments... systems of official rank, databanks of observations... sacred texts... rules of official procedure, and even seating plans for the buildings in which debates take place" (244). A cornerstone of the imperial decision-making process, "the institution of the *yi* [is] an arena for orally delivered persuasion before a mass audience" (254) where on matters of *li* the insider, outsider, expert, and laymen meet and contend. All more-or-less accepted the experts' emphasis on predictive accuracy achieved through *shifa* 師法 "master methods" ("a coherent and methodical schema, possibly validated by authoritative transmission" [247]); however, each brought to the table distinct interests, assumptions, and level of understanding with which the expert would need to negotiate to build consensus.[116]

The reason that I have chosen to speak of "actors" rather than "astronomers" is to at once accommodate and differentiate participants in the field of *li*. Participating in the advancement of knowledge and policy were people of various spectra: the professional and the enthusiast; the official and the private citizen; the man of the capital and the man of the provinces; the expert and the novice; the cognoscente and the crackpot; and, last but not least, the emperor. To further confuse matters, these categories are in constant flux as actors move from office to office and place to place. The texts themselves tend to introduce actors by their office, noble title, place of origin, and cultural status, but also their level of

---

116. "Actors, Networks, and 'Disturbing Spectacles' in Institutional Science." On the institution of the Expectant Appointee, see also Lai Swee Fo, "Tangdai daizhao kaoshi" 唐代待詔考釋, *Zhongguo wenhua yanjiusuo xuebao* 中國文化研究所學報 12 (2003): 69–105.

engagement with *li*: "*li* lineage-expert," "technique expert," "person who knows *li*," "person adept at *li*," "person who creates *li* systems," "person who works on *li*," "transmitter of Heaven's numbers," or "gentleman of *li* calculation."[117] To simply label someone like Liu Hong an "astronomer" tells us very little about his ability, his reputation, or the military and administrative matters that occupied his career.

To recognize the complexity of individual actors we might simply locate them along these spectra as they appear. Wherever that may be, such "astronomers" are not specialists like their modern counterparts but polymaths devoted to a common elite culture.[118] Sivin and Sir Geoffrey Lloyd provide an excellent summary of this situation. The greatest social divide at this time, they state, was between those eligible for office and those not. The *shi* 士 were wellborn, literate, and had access to education in sacred and philosophical texts that, more than anything, inculcated in them "a nostalgia for an imagined hierarchy... that has already slipped away" (the world order of the Sage Kings) and a belief in "an unending governmental quest to control society from the top down" (19). The extent of their actual achievement of these ends, however, was simply to indoctrinate the small elite in a common cultural idiom of myth, values, ritual practices, hierarchical etiquette, personal deportment, and literary tradition. Thus, they argue that:

> Those whose livelihood comes from being able to predict the future or to deter-

---

117. *Li jia* 曆家 "*li* lineage-expert" can refer to masters of calendar divination but mostly refers to calendro-astronomers; for examples, see *Shiji*, 127.3222; *Hou Han shu, zhi* 18, 3357 (commentary); *Song shu*, 13.306; *Sui shu*, 17.418, 18.461, 20.555; *Tang liu dian*, 10.12a (commentary). *Shu jia* 術家 "technique expert" can refer to masters of calendar divination, harmonics, or calendro-astronomy, depending on context; for examples, see *Hou Han shu, zhi* 2, 3038, 3043; *zhi* 18, 3368 (commentary); *Song shu*, 13.306, 13.315, 23.675; *Sui shu*, 19.523. For *zhi li zhe* 知曆者 "person who knows *li*," see *Hou Han shu, zhi* 2, 3025. For *shan li zhe* 善曆者 "person adept at *li*," see *Song shu*, 12.231; *Nan Qi shu* 南齊書 (Zhonghua shuju ed.), 52.905; *Sui shu*, 17.424. For *zao li zhe* 造曆者 "person who creates *li* systems," see *Wei shu*, 35.825, 107B.2698–2699. For *zhi li zhe* 治曆者 "person who works on *li*" as distinct from the office *zhi li* 治曆 "Calendarist," see *Hou Han shu, zhi* 2, 3027, 3028; *Song shu*, 12.228. For *chuan tian shu zhe* 傳天數者 "transmitter of Heaven's numbers," see *Shiji*, 27.1343; *Sui shu*, 19.504. For *li suan zhi shi* 曆算之士 "gentleman of *li* calculation," see ibid., 18.459.

118. Goodman has begun to tackle the issue of the polymathy of the early imperial cultural elite in two recent studies, see his "Chinese Polymaths, 100–300 AD: The Tung-kuan, Taoist Dissent, and Technical Skills," *Asia Major* 3d ser., 18, no. 1 (2005): 101–174; *Xun Xu and the Politics of Precision in Third-century AD China* (Leiden: Brill, 2010).

mine what has gone wrong in the human body must satisfy their clients that they have access to special knowledge not open to everyone else. Chinese diviners and physicians did not generally stake their authority on the metaphysical foundations of what they knew, nor on the formal rigor with which they presented it... Their qualifications tended to be social. Because expertise was not inherently problematic, it was initiation that separated insiders and outsiders, and gentlemanly behavior that marked the superior insider.[119]

While this holds somewhat true for the astral sciences, it is again important not to overstate their "secret" or "official character" in this period. This impression is largely based on the later history of government bans. Beginning in A.D. 267, each successive dynasty issued bans on the private ownership of *tianwen* and prophecy literature, which the Tang expanded to include instruments and calendar printing, and which the Ming expanded to a blanket ban of the astral sciences. The scope and effectiveness of these bans is a question of some debate, but two important points are clear. First, there was no ban on *li* prior to the second millennium A.D. Second, it is senseless to read the desire to ban *li* or *tianwen* technical literature back any further than the third century A.D., since the Qin banned everything *except* technical literature in 213 B.C., and since the A.D. 267 ban was a reaction to the *tianwen* contents of the weft and prophecy literature *that enjoyed state sponsorship under the Han.*[120]

Where the astral sciences *were* "special knowledge not open to everyone else" was in the sense that they existed in networks of education and textual transmission to which not everyone may have been privy in a pre-print culture. Of course, like omen and prophecy

---

119. Lloyd and Sivin, *The Way and the Word*, 205. Also helpful to think with in this regard is Steven Shapin's meticulous sociological analysis of the role of gentlemanly culture in the development of European science: Shapin, *A Social History of Truth: Civility and Science in Seventeenth-century England.* Chicago: University of Chicago Press, 1994.

120. For discussion of the history of state bans in the astral sciences, see Jiang Xiaoyuan, *Tianxue zhen yuan,* 52–57; Chen Meidong, *Zhongguo gudai tianwenxue sixiang,* 23–32. For the history of bans on the private printing of calendars, see Susan Whitfield, "Under the Censor's Eye: Printed Almanacs and Censorship in Ninth-century China," *British Library Journal* 24, no. 1 (1998): 4–22.

literature, Cullen points out that *mathematics* too was an integral element of the education of our *shi* elite; and while the reason seems to be its obvious applications in the running of a paperwork empire, he notes, mathematics was not at the time a field wholly independent of harmonics or *li*.[121] But how specifically did actors come to learn *li* in this period? Some like Sima Qian, Liu Xin, Zheng Zhong 鄭眾 (d. A.D. 83), and Zong Gan's grandsons Cheng 誠 and Zheng 整 (fl. A.D. 174–180) clearly carried forward family traditions.[122] *Li* and calculation were also taught at schools. Zhang Heng and Zheng Xuan learned them at the Imperial Academy, and it was from Liu Xin's private lectures that Zheng Zhong's father Xing 興 (fl. A.D. 14–33) learned them—the latter a model of private education that we know in the provinces to have attracted hundreds of pupils to the subject.[123] There are also those who learned from social inferiors, suggesting relationships of private tutelage. Empress Dowager Deng Sui 鄧綏 (A.D. 81–121), for example, learned them from the female literatus Ban Zhao 班昭 (c. A.D. 45 – c. 117), and Sima Qian learned his *tian guan* 天官 "celestial offices" from

---

121. "People and Numbers in Early Imperial China: Locating 'Mathematics' and 'Mathematicians' in Chinese Space," in *Oxford Handbook of the History of Mathematics* (Oxford: Oxford University Press, 2009), 591–618. For an example of the centrality of omen literature to government discourse in the Han, see Wolfram Eberhard, "The Political Function of Astronomy and Astronomers in Han China," in *Chinese Thought and Institutions*, ed. John Fairbank, Comparative Studies of Cultures and Civilizations (Chicago: University of Chicago Press, 1957), 37–70. On the role of mathematics in harmonics and imperial ritual music, see Howard L. Goodman, *Xun Xu and the Politics of Precision in Third-century AD China* (Leiden: Brill, 2010), 215–277.

122. Both Sima Qian's and Liu Xin's fathers were involved in *li*, and Qian inherited the post of Prefect Grand Clerk from his father. As the son of Zheng Xing 鄭興, Zhong "received the *Zuo Tradition of the Spring and Autumn Annals* from his father, was vigorous in his studies, and understood the Triple Concordance system (#8)" that his father had learned from Liu Xin; see note 123 and *Hou Han shu*, 36.1224. Zong Cheng and Zheng appear in A.D. 174–180 as experts on eclipse prediction like their grandfather before them; see note 110 and ibid., *zhi* 2, 3040–3041.

123. For Zhang Heng, see *Hou Han shu*, 59.1897. For Zheng Xuan, see ibid., 35.1207. While learning from Liu Xin, "Xin praised [Zheng] Xing's talents, making him compose 'regulation' and 'sentence and verse' commentarial exegesis as well as collate the Triple Concordance system (#8)" 歆美興才，使撰條例、章句、傳詁，及校三統歷 (ibid., 36.1217). Liao Fu and Fan Ying were provincial wonder-workers from the *Hou Han shu* "Fang shu liezhuan" 方術列傳 who, among other things, are associated with *tianwen* and *xing suan* 星筭 "star calculation," respectively, and were known to have taught large numbers of disciples (ibid., 82A.2719–2721). It seems that it is under these circumstances, for example, that Yang Tong 楊統 (fl. A.D. 76) is said to have learned "the techniques of *tianwen* and [astronomical] calculation" 天文推步之術 from a "Zheng Boshan of his same commandery" 同郡鄭伯山, i.e. Xindu 新都, near Chengdu 成都 (ibid., 30A.1074).

the *fangshi* Tang Du.[124] Actors of similar standing also seem to have shared knowledge with one another, as is clearly the case with Liu Hong's transmission to Zheng Xuan.[125] Lastly, as the case of Sima Qian and Liu Xin should remind us, it is important to recognize that none of these avenues were exclusive of one another.[126]

It is not strange to think that knowledge and texts would have circulated in this manner when we consider that the Clerk's Office was merely the auditor (and beneficiary) of what was an independent field of inquiry. What *is* somewhat strange to think about is how actors advanced this knowledge outside of an institutional setting, both in terms of means and time. First of all, I suggested above that the availability of inscriptions produced by the Clerk's Office may have enabled actors to practice "indoors" or "textual astronomy" at the same leisure and level of investment by which one might, say, commentate the classics.[127] Of course, the fabrication of observational instruments does not seem to have been prohibitively difficult or expensive for private citizens either, but one wonders where they might have found the time to carry out their own observation programs.[128] For the upper-level official, one

---

124. The daughter of historian Ban Biao 班彪 (A.D. 3-54) and the sister of General Ban Gu, Ban Zhao was a prominent literatus, and in A.D. 108 Empress Dowager Deng sought her out to learn "the classics as well as *tianwen* and mathematics" 經書，兼天文、筭數 (*Hou Han shu*, 10A.424). Tang Du was one of the outside experts called in to participate in the Grand Inception reform project, his responsibility being *li* numbers, stars, and the division of Heaven (*Shiji*, 26.1260, 27.1349, 112.2965). For his role educating Sima Qian, see ibid., 130.3288.

125. Zheng Xuan was already 69 years old and quite accomplished by the point that the similarly mature and accomplished Liu Hong transmitted his Supernal Emblem method to him in A.D. 196. Similarly, around 26 B.C. Chancellor Zhai Fangjin 翟方進 (d. 7 B.C.) taught the *Zuo Tradition* to Liu Xin (who would bind this classic inextricably to the astral sciences) and stellar/planetary *li* to the Mayor of Chang'an, Tian Zhongshu 田終術 (*Han shu*, 36.1967, 84.3421).

126. On the history of astronomy education in pre-modern China, see Thomas H. C. Lee, *Education in Traditional China: a History*, Handbuch Der Orientalistik. Vierte Abteilung, China 13 (Leiden: Brill, 2000), 512–541; Chen Xiaozhong and Zhang Shuli, *Zhongguo gudai tianwen jigou yu tianwen jiaoyu*, 249–352.

127. The accessibility of such records is suggested by the fact that figures not on the staff of the Clerk's Office frequently cite them. For example, General of the Gentlemen-of-the-Household Jia Kui cites them in his discourse on *li* (*Hou Han shu*, *zhi* 2, 3027, 3030); Gentleman Consultant Cai Yong cites them in his argument against the proposed reform of A.D. 175 (ibid., *zhi* 2, 3039); the Ministry of Rites invites Palace Attendant Han Yue 韓說, Erudit Cai Jiao 蔡較, Marquis of Guchengmen Liu Hong, and Gentleman-of-the-Palace of the Right Chen Tiao 陳調 to check them to determine the merit of competing eclipse models in A.D. 179 (ibid., *zhi* 2, 3041); and Attendant Clerk Zu Chongzhi of Southern Xuzhou cites Han and Jin observational records in A.D. 462 (*Song shu*, 12.290, 13.311). See also note 70.

128. The history of observational instruments in early imperial China is one driven by private innovation and fabrication, e.g. private citizen Luoxia Hong of Ba Commandery and Grand Minister of Agriculture

obvious answer is "at night," although we really have no idea how consuming his duties may have been or whether, like Tycho Brahe (A.D. 1546–1601), he might have retained a coterie of family members, students, and/or servants to aid him in observation.[129] One option was to go into seclusion like Zhang Zixin 張子信 (fl. A.D. 526–576) who, in another parallel to Brahe, "went into hiding on an island on the sea and devoted himself for more than thirty years to the observation by means of armillary sphere of data on the differences and changes in the sun, moon, and five stars (planets)" 隱於海島中，積三十許年，專以渾儀測候日月五星差變之數.[130] However, there are just as many cases where actors managed to conduct their own multi-decade research programs while serving important and totally unrelated offices.[131]

Since the last century, historians of Chinese astronomy have tended to focus on the court history of system reforms, which is a natural choice given that it is what preoccupies received sources. In the following chapters of this dissertation, however, I intend to build out from this in two directions. The first is that, as in Section 1.2.2 above, I will explore knowledge

Geng Shouchang's Western Han innovations that fed into the observational program of 78 B.C. and Geng's discovery of the constancy of lunar motion along the ecliptic, as well as the instrument presumably behind Fu An's 傅安 work on the ecliptic which inspired the emperor to commission the Grand Clerk's Yellow Road bronze instrument in A.D. 103. On the history of observational instruments, see Pan Nai 潘鼐, ed., *Zhongguo gu tianwen yiqi shi* 中國古天文儀器史, color print ed. (Taiyuan: Shanxi jiaoyu chubanshe, 2005); Wu Shouxian 吳守賢 and Quan Hejun 全和鈞, *Zhongguo gudai tianti celiangxue ji tianwen yiqi* 中國古代天體測量學及天文儀器, Zhongguo tianwenxueshi daxi (Beijing: Zhongguo kexue jishu chubanshe, 2008); Sivin, *Granting the Seasons*, 561–572. On private ownership, see Needham, *Science and Civilisation in China, Vol.3*, 193–194.

129. Though I have no evidence for this, it strikes me that the retainership culture of local courts like King of Huainan Liu An's 劉安 (c. 179–122 B.C.) and the culture of enormous live-in schools operated out of master's homes seen in Han China might well have produced in the astral sciences some sort of analog to the ad hoc, semi-feudal, semi-familial, and semi-educational institutional organization of Brahe's Uraniborg as described in J. R. Christianson, *On Tycho's Island: Tycho Brahe and His Assistants, 1570–1601* (Cambridge: Cambridge University Press, 2000). On patronage and retainer culture, see Lloyd and Sivin, *The Way and the Word*, 28–34. On the organization of private schools, see Yu Shulin 余書鱗, "Lianghan sixue yanjiu" 兩漢私學研究, *Shida xuebao* 師大學報 11 (1966): 109–148; Lee, *Education in Traditional China*, 54–57.

130. *Sui shu*, 20.561. On Zhang Zixin, see Chen Meidong, *Zhongguo kexue jishu shi: tianwenxue juan*, 298–303.

131. For example, Liu Hong is said to done his own observations as part of his more than twenty-year Supernal Emblem project, while He Chengtian (Director of the Watches for the Heir Apparent and Palace Assistant Secretary) and his uncle Xu Guang (Retainer of the Western Section, Gentleman of the Imperial Library, Gentleman of the Ministry of Sacrifices, Grand Minister of Agriculture, and Inspector of the Imperial Library) each conducted forty-year observation programs; see note 72 and *Jin shu*, 17.499; *Song shu*, 12.261.

and practices that exist beyond a neat sequence of official systems to underscore what I see as an important divide between the history of *policy* and the history of *practice*. The second is that through excavated manuscripts I attempt to shift some of the focus away from the production and advancement of calendro-astronomical knowledge, about which we learn chiefly as it erupts at court, and instead move toward its transmission and consumption in non-governmental contexts.

1.3.2 *Motivations*

The state practiced calendro-astronomy because it was in its primal and sacred constitution. To do otherwise would be to violate the natural order of things and to invite disaster and regime change upon the subcelestial realm. One object of its attention was the symbolism of the civil calendar, but the other was astronomical accuracy in the obvious sense. Jiang Xiaoyuan has debunked the assumption common to early histories of science that the latter somehow allowed the state to more scientifically regulate agricultural production.[132] Jiang is almost certainly correct, but it is important to recognize that this *is* more or less what the early imperial state *thought* it was doing. This—and the greater project of cosmo-social harmony—it solemnly went about through the standardization of civil time and the scheduling of sacrifices carefully timed to the agricultural year. Cullen raises Zhangdi's edict of A.D. 85 as an example of the perceived need for accuracy in this endeavor:

先立春一日，則四分數之立春也，而以折獄斷大刑，於氣已迕，用望平和，蓋亦遠矣。

The Quarter-remainder reckons the [real] Enthronement of Spring.$_{Q01}$ to fall one day prior to the [official] Enthronement of Spring.$_{Q01}$, so if one were to open prisons and end great punishments by [the latter], one would violate the *qi* (cosmic energies) and distance oneself from any prospect of peace or harmony.[133]

---

132. *Tianxue zhen yuan*, 115–118.

133. *Hou Han shu, zhi* 2, 3026; tr. modified from Cullen, "Actors, Networks, and 'Disturbing Spectacles' in

This example is interesting because it is a tautology. The Enthronement of Spring.Q01 is an arbitrary calendrical construct three *qi* ($\approx$ 45.7 days) after winter solstice. However, because the only means available at the time to *test* when this occurs—gnomon shadows and meridian stars (*zhong xing* 中星)—were not precise down to the day, the only thing one had to go by were the predictions of mathematical models.[134] So, if such *models* conflicted, how was one to choose between them? Solar eclipses are a different matter all together, but the state had a clever way around the limitations of contemporary predictive models there: it made sacrificial preparations in anticipation of an eclipse from the last to second day of *every month*.[135] In the end, however, questions of *belief* or the circularity of ritual reasoning are not what matters; what matters is that from the emperor and the Three Excellencies all the way down to the hundred officials, it was simply *expected* that the state pursue matters of astronomical accuracy in the name of good rule.

The interesting question, therefore, is not why the state practiced *li*, but why the individual chose to do so. Advanced calendro-astronomy was not compulsory to elite education, and while there were certainly those who were born into it, for most it was a choice. While it is possible that pragmatic considerations informed this choice, the Clerk's Office does not seem to have offered anything special in terms of salary or opportunities for career advancement. A more obvious reason then might be curiosity—that someone might have been, as He Chengtian 何承天 (c. A.D. 370–447) describes himself, "quite fond of *li* numbers ever since childhood" 自昔幼年，頗好曆數.[136] Of course, Jiang Xiaoyuan reminds us that there is no simple curiosity for curiosity's sake in the context of a field framed as the work of the Sages and the linchpin of human destiny. Instead, we might think of *li* as an equally religious experience wherein, like the Renaissance astronomer, the study of nature is at once

---

Institutional Science," 241; cf. "People and Numbers in Early Imperial China," 597–598.

134. For a sense of the complexity of determining solstitial and equinoctial points from gnomon shadows, see Zu Chongzhi's fifth-century A.D. method as explained in Sivin, *Granting the Seasons*, 259–262.

135. This is at least the case in the Han, Jin 晉 (A.D. 265-420), and Liu-Song; see *Hou Han shu, zhi* 4, 3101; *Jin shu*, 19.594; *Song shu*, 14.351.

136. *Song shu*, 12.260.

the study of God's design.[137]

1.3.3 Epistemologies

When someone proposes institutional change, his innovation is typically judged by a combination of four demands: (1) that it prove more accurate in trial; (2) that it have precedent—either in scripture or a "master's method"—; (3) that it manifest a superior knowledge of numerology/correlative thought; and (4) that it serve as an appropriate symbol of the ruling house's cosmic legitimacy. While the relative emphasis that each of these demands receives differs case by case, the perfect system is really one that meets all four. Simply put, *li* is the study of an order inherent in nature, part of which is manifest (e.g. numbers of periodicities), part of which is occult (e.g. their greater numerological meaning), and all of which has conspired to bring the current regime to power.

When the matter at hand is selection of the first month of the civil calendar, the criterion of accuracy is irrelevant. The question, rather, is the scriptural precedent for or against reform and the correlative theory informing the choice of symbols. In Chapter 4, I outline a debate about this issue at the opening of the Cao-Wei dynasty and argue the importance of recognizing, as do our sources, the distinction between this and the following type of reform.

When the matter at hand is that, for example, eclipses and lunar phases are occurring at the wrong times, then the criterion of accuracy takes the lead, and the criterion of symbolism is distributed among the other three. What do I mean by "accuracy"? In Hashimoto Keizō's 橋本敬造 study of the rhetoric of accuracy, he identifies a vocabulary organized around the concepts of striking (*zhong* 中 "to hit the mark" vs. *shi* 失 "to miss the mark"), accordance (*he* 合 "to match" vs. *cha* 差 "to differ"), distance (*jin* 近 "close" vs. *yuan* 遠 "far, off"), grouping (*mi* 密 "tight" vs. *shu* 疏 "loose"), and quality (*jing* 精 "fine" vs. *cu* 粗 "course").[138]

---

137. For a nuanced study of the role of religion in pre-modern European scientific inquiry, see John H. Brooke, *Science and Religion: Some Historical Perspectives*, Cambridge History of Science, (Cambridge: Cambridge University Press, 1991).

138. "Seidō no shisō to dentō Chūgoku no tenmongaku" 精度の思想と傳統中國天文學, *Kansai daigaku*

The last pair has also to do with the issue of *precision*, which is discussed further in terms of *xi* 細 "fine," *xiang* 詳 "detailed," *shen* 審 "meticulous," and *lüe* 略 "cursory." Of course, it is not enough to claim that something is TIGHT, one must verify it through examination:

以是言之，則術不差不改，不驗不用。天道精微，度數難定，術法多端，曆紀非一，未驗無以知其是，未差無以知其失。失然後改之，是然後用之，此謂允執其中。

If a technique (*shu*) isn't off then don't revise it, and if it isn't verified (*yan*) then don't use it. The way of Heaven is perfect and subtle, and its degrees and numbers are hard to fix; techniques and models are multifarious, and there is no singular program for calendro-astronomy. If something has not been proven, then there is no way to know if it is correct, and if it has not [been shown to] err then there is no way to know if it is amiss. If it is amiss, then you revise it; if it is correct, then you use it. This is called "holding truly to the middle way" (*Analects* XX.1).[139]

Examination can involve "observation" (*guan* or *hou*) and "measurement" (*ce* 測), but it just as often involves observational records. Whether its object is experiential or textual, the vocabulary of examination is the same (Table 1.7). Each word shares the same core meaning of "examine/test/inspect/study," while several have more specific connotations concerning comparison, modeling, verification, and ranking. Whatever the metaphors behind the language of accuracy and examination, actors tend not to qualify them when they assert that "examination" reveals that this or that is "loose," which is why in Chapter 4 I myself examine a set of test results to understand the sort of procedure and conclusions that are hinted about throughout *li* literature.

"Tight" results are, however, not all that matter in such situations. A new idea is more credible when it is associated with a known quantity—be it an established name or

shakai gakubu kiyō 關西大學社會學部紀要 11, no. 1 (1979): 93–114.

139. *Hou Han shu, zhi* 2, 3041.

Table 1.7: The vocabulary of examination

		Examine	Calculate	Compare	Match	Model	Verify	Rank
稽	*ji*	x	x		x	x		
考	*kao*	x						
校	*jiao*	x	x	x				
效効	*xiao*	x		x		x	x	
檢	*jian*	x				x		
驗	*yan*	x					x	
察	*cha*	x						
審	*shen*	x						
參	*can*	x						
課	*kc*	x		x			x	x

scripture—especially to those unqualified to judge it on its technical merits. Thus it is that we find the rhetoric of *li* woven around quotations of the *Analects* and appeals to "master methods"; but experts also remind us that "though alternative ORIGINS are disclosed in the charts and prophecies, each stands in its own right as the technique of one school and must have had validity in its own time" 他元雖不明於圖讖，各自一家之術，皆當有效於當時，and that sometimes "though he has a master method, it is the same as if he had none at all" 雖有師法，與無同.[140] Furthermore, a new system better resonates with an audience when it seems to capture the correlative order of the universe. What made Liu Hong truly awesome, the *Jin shu* explains, was that he "set up his numbers according with the *Changes*, such that fleeting motions called out to one another, and hidden places sought one another out" 依易立數，遁行相號，潛處相求.[141] All the same, very few actually engaged in this sort of synthesis, and those who did were not necessarily recognized for their efforts.[142] Jia Kui, for example, gives us the following assessment of one Zhang Long 張隆:

---

140. Ibid., *zhi* 2, 3038, 3043; tr. modified from Cullen, "Actors, Networks, and 'Disturbing Spectacles' in Institutional Science," 247, 259.

141. *Jin shu*, 17.498.

142. On the limited role of numerology in calendro-astronomy, p. 163 ff.

永平中，詔書令故太史待詔張隆以四分法署弦、望、月食加時。隆言能用易九、

六、七、八爻知月行多少。今案隆所署多失。臣使隆逆推前手所署，不應，或

異日，不中天乃益遠，至十餘度。

During the Eternal Tranquility reign (A.D. 57–75), there was an edict ordering former Expectant Appointee to the Grand Clerk Zhang Long to note (predict) the [future] hour of lunar phases and eclipses according to the Quarter-remainder method. Long said that he was able to use the nine, six, seven, and eight lines from the *Changes* to know the extent of lunar motion. We now know Long's notes to have missed the mark (*shi*) in most cases. Your subject has made Long retrodict those [hours] noted by former hands, and they did not match, sometimes even falling on different days; he was even further off (*yuan*) in failing to hit the mark (*zhong*) in Heaven, by up to a matter of more than $10^{\circ\circ}$.[143]

The difference between a Liu Hong and a Zhang Long is not in the Kuhnian sense that they live in different worlds or incommensurate paradigms. Both commit themselves to the language and goals of a common *épisteme*, addressing questions of SYSTEM ORIGINS, lunar lag and inequality, *as well as* scripture, correlative philosophy, and politics; and both recognize the proper hierarchy of priority that these elements take in different contexts. The difference, rather, is that *one is able to deliver*, while the other fails common expectations of TIGHTNESS due either to inexperience or concessions made in a rigid application of epistemologies (2)–(4).[144]

---

143. *Hou Han shu, zhi* 2, 3030. The "nine, six, seven, and eight lines from the *Changes*" refer to the combinatorial results of each line of the hexagram as arrived at through the counting of yarrow sticks; for an explanation of the divinatory procedure of the Changes, see Richard Rutt, *The Book of Changes (*Zhouyi*): a Bronze Age Document Translated with Introduction and Notes*, Durham East-Asia Series 1 (Richmond, Surrey: Curzon, 1996), 151–201.

144. For Thomas Kuhn's theories on the incommensurability between paradigms and the result of scientific practitioners living in "different worlds" because of it, see his *The Structure of Scientific Revolutions*, 3d ed. (Chicago: University of Chicago Press, 1996). I use the term "*épisteme*" rather than "science" here in the sense intended by Michel Foucault:

I would define the episteme retrospectively as the strategic apparatus which permits of separating out from among all the statements which are possible those that will be acceptable

1.4 Problems in the History and Philosophy of Science

By now it should be abundantly clear how a modern label like "science" fails to capture the complexities of *tianwen* and *li* in early imperial China. My goal in this dissertation is not to privilege these as "science"—at least not to claim that they are "science" in anything more than the sense of "knowledge," as in my "astral sciences"—but to highlight how, in certain contexts, ancient actors themselves differentiated and privileged certain forms of knowledge over others. To this end, I turn to two topics of perennial interest in the history and philosophy of science: empiricism and progress. I choose these topics not because they define twentieth-century notions of "science" but because they define *early imperial ones.*

Historians of science are keenly sensitive to the danger of reading onto the past modern ideas of empiricism and progress that have been problematized even for their own time— the danger, that is, of anachronism and "positivism." For their part, sinologists have long since abandoned questions of "why China failed to..." and the vision of history as a march of progress.[145] In the history of astronomy, no one has presented a stronger case against these notions than Nathan Sivin. Amid grandiose claims for the viability of their own projects, early imperial astronomers often discuss the failings of their predecessors in terms of imperceptible subtitles and discrepancies in Heaven. Sivin argues that while the former may be safely dismissed as rhetoric, the latter reveals an underlying belief "that the scale

within, I won't say a scientific theory, but a field of scientificity, and which it is possible to say are true or false. The episteme is the 'apparatus' which makes possible the separation, not of the true from the false, but of what may from what may not be characterised as scientific (*Power/knowledge: Selected Interviews and Other Writings,* 1972–1977, ed. Colin Gordon [New York: Pantheon Books, 1980], 197).

Scholars in other fields note the ways in which, rather than operating in incommensurate *épistemes,* "magic" appeals to the paradigm of "science" to establish its legitimacy. For example, Lloyd shows how this to be the case for ancient Greek medical science and temple medicine, as does Tanya Luhrmann for practitioners of witchcraft in 1980s London; see G. E. R. Lloyd, *Magic, Reason, and Experience: Studies in the Origin and Development of Greek Science* (Cambridge: Cambridge University Press, 1979), 37–49; Tanya Luhrmann, *Persuasions of the Witch's Craft: Ritual Magic in Contemporary England* (Cambridge: Harvard University Press, 1989), esp. 115–143.

145. For example, see Nathan Sivin, "Why the Scientific Revolution Did Not Take Place in China—or Didn't It?," *Chinese Science* 5 (1982): 45–66; Roger Hart, "Beyond Science and Civilization: a post-Needham Critique," *East Asian Science, Technology, and Medicine* 16 (1999): 88–114.

95

of the cosmos is too large, and the texture of nature is too fine, too subtle, too closely intermeshed... for phenomena to be fully predictable."[146] Furthermore, to temper the idea of linear progress in astronomy he contextualizes its course within the politics of system reform:

> If astronomical reform were a straightforward technical task, new systems would have come into being only to resolve crises or to introduce major innovations, and each would have generated significantly more accurate ephemerides than its predecessor. The reality was quite different. Some systems were not significantly new... Some systems were noticeably inferior in predictive accuracy to those they replaced... More than one excellent system was denied official status due to friction between factions or powerful individuals... It is impossible to understand the historical distribution of astronomical treatises without attending to their political circumstances.... An emperor often ordered up a reform as a gesture, even when he did not make any substantive changes in his policies... Over the centuries instituting a new astronomical system became the norm for each dynasty, and sometimes for each newly enthroned emperor. At such times of transition, it became easy to introduce astronomical novelties in a reform; a very long reign often meant no reform, and no opportunity to innovate.[147]

Recently, John Henderson has somewhat complicated this picture by insisting that "astronomical triumphalism" was as serious an intellectual commitment as "astronomical fatalism." In fact, because "astronomy was one of the few fields of knowledge in pre-modern China in which progress was so evident as to override the more deeply ingrained regressive and cyclical models of time," he shows how intellectuals struggled for centuries to reconcile this with more

---

146. "On the Limits of Empirical Knowledge in the Traditional Chinese Sciences," in *Time, Science, and Society in China and the West,* ed. Julius Thomas Fraser, Nathaniel Morris Lawrence, and Francis C. Haber (Amherst: University of Massachusetts Press, 1986), 155.

147. *Granting the Seasons,* 56–58.

traditional views of history.[148] To this I would add several points. First, the recognition of "limits" is neither an argument against empirical knowledge nor a disavowal of its improvement over time; in fact, several of the thinkers that Sivin cites express similar ambivalence towards other modes of knowing as well.[149] Second, because "astronomical fatalism" and "astronomical triumphalism" often occur hand-in-hand in the context of political persuasion, I suspect that these are not as much coherent intellectual positions as they are rhetorical strategies.[150] Lastly, if we follow our historical actors and insist upon a distinction between matters of the calendar and matters of astronomy, matters of public policy and matters of private practice, then we find that Sivin's caveats about progress do not hold for the whole picture.[151]

Whether and how we should read modern ideas of empiricism and progress onto the ancient past is a matter of considerable dispute. Coming out of the Science Wars, most philosophers of science now concede the basic tenets of realism, e.g. Sokal and Bricmont's "modest realism," "which insists that the goal of science is to find out how things really are and which asserts we are making progress in that direction, but which recognizes that this goal will always be incompletely achieved and which is aware of the principal obstacles."[152] Steven Shapin, Simon Schaffer, Latour, and Steve Woolgar have raised philosophically profound questions about the role of instruments in the construction of facts and ontologies,

---

148. "Premodern Chinese Notions of Astronomical History and Calendrical Time."

149. See especially Shen Gua's 沈括 (A.D. 1031–1095) statement that "the uninitiated say that, mathematical knowledge of the heavenly bodies being difficult to be sure of, only correlations between the Five Phases and time periods are reliable, but this is also untrue" (Sivin, "On the Limits of Empirical Knowledge in the Traditional Chinese Sciences," 160).

150. For example, see Li Yexing's defense of the Ascendant Harmony system (#36) in Section 2.5.1.

151. Sivin offers sound caveats concerning empiricism and progress but does not dismiss the value of these concepts out of hand: "On the other hand, since ancient astronomers valued and sought to improve both accuracy and precision, no historical analysis that ignores them can be adequate. What I am trying to reconstruct is the complex of social, political, intellectual, and technical relations and meanings within which individual astronomers did their own work" (*Granting the Seasons*, 552).

152. Alan D. Sokal and Jean Bricmont, "Defense of a Modest Scientific Realism," in *Knowledge and the World: Challenges Beyond the Science Wars*, ed. Martin Carrier et al., The Frontiers Collection (Berlin: Springer, 2004), 17–54.

and while the early Chinese astronomer's observations were also mediated by instrumentation and theory, there is to my mind something inherently less problematic about, say, apparent lunar motion in a world of naked-eye observation than theoretical unobservables like phlogiston or TRF(H).[153] It is true that we are still learning about the moon—about the effects, for example, of tidal friction and secular deceleration—but our current knowledge of celestial mechanics is sufficient to retrodict and match ancient eclipse records to within a standard deviation of several minutes.[154] Whatever the philosophical underpinnings of such an argument, to dismiss modern knowledge such as this as an under-determined cultural construct would deny the historian an important tool for understanding the descriptions and theorizations of ancient actors and render the latter into nonsense.[155]

Lastly, whether or not science experiences "progress" is a matter of definition. Typical of Kuhn's idea of "normal science," for example, we see in *li* literature empirically derived values that, as a general historical trend, get nearer and nearer to our own.[156] As in the case of lunar motion presented in Section 1.2.2, however, we also see actors make "erotetic progress," in Philip Kitcher's terms, "by asking better questions, and, if the questions recapitulate old themes, they do so in more adequate ways, discarding faulty presuppositions, identifying points on which all disputants concur, and circumscribing more precisely what remains unknown or undecided."[157]

All of these are interesting problems, but my primary concern in this study is *emic* ideas

---

153. Shapin and Schaffer, *Leviathan and the Air-pump: Hobbes, Boyle, and the Experimental Life* (Princeton: Princeton University Press, 1985); Latour and Woolgar, *Laboratory Life: The Social Construction of Scientific Facts*, 2d ed. (Princeton: Princeton University Press, 1986).

154. See F. Richard Stephenson's magnum opus, *Historical Eclipses and Earth's Rotation* (Cambridge: Cambridge University Press, 1997).

155. For a considerably more nuanced argument to this end in the context of ancient Rome, see Daryn Lehoux, *What Did the Romans Know? An Inquiry into Science and Worldmaking* (Chicago: University of Chicago Press, 2012), 200–242.

156. Chen Meidong provides a comprehensive study of the historical change of such values in *Gu li xin tan* 古曆新探 (Shenyang: Liaoning jiaoyu chubanshe, 1995).

157. *The Advancement of Science: Science Without Legend, Objectivity Without Illusions* (New York: Oxford University Press, 1993), 57.

of empiricism and progress. One would be right to point out that there is no *word* for these in classical Chinese—that *jingyanzhuyi* 經驗主義 and *qianjin* 前進 are late European concepts that arrived through Japanese—but my contention is that analogous *concepts* clearly shaped the practice, discussion, and historical trajectory of *tianwen* and *li*. Again, I use these terms as helpful analogies rather than cognates. By "empiricism" I simply refer to the observe-model-test epistemology that we see throughout *li* discourse and that actors often sum up with that quote from the *Book of Documents*: to be "in reverent accordance with august Heaven" 欽若昊天. As I will explore in subsequent chapters, this empiricism is something imperfect, something cultural, and something that appears in strange places, but it is something nonetheless that is at the very core of the astral sciences and how contemporary actors insisted that they be practiced. "Progress" is something of an obviously much more limited scope in antiquity than modernity, but pre-modern peoples did recognize it in specific arenas of culture like the astral sciences.[158] Thus we are told, for example, that with Liu Hong "there was finally a turn from the previous methods towards the FINE and TIGHT" 方於前法，轉為精密矣 and that "because Liu [Xin] and Jia [Kui] were able to relate [lunar inequality], we can pursue TIGHTNESS through the accumulation of achievements" 劉、賈能述，則可累功以求密矣.[159] But as I hope to illustrate in the chapters that follow, nowhere are these concepts more evident than in the way that our ancient astronomers write their own histories of science.

---

158. On this point, see Henderson, "Premodern Chinese Notions of Astronomical History and Calendrical Time." For the idea of progress in Greek culture and history of science, see Ludwig Edelstein, *The Idea of Progress in Classical Antiquity* (Baltimore: John Hopkins Press, 1967); Leonid Zhmud, *The Origin of the History of Science in Classical Antiquity*, Peripatoi 19 (Berlin: de Gruyter, 2006), esp. 1–22. On philosophical ideas concerning cultural progress in early China, see Michael J. Puett, "Humans, Spirits, and Sages in Chinese Late Antiquity: Ge Hong's 葛洪 Master Who Embraces Simplicity (*Baopuzi*) 抱朴子," *Extrême-Orient, Extrême-Occident* 29, no. 29 (2007): 95–119; "The Temptations of Sagehood, or: The Rise and Decline of Sagely Writing in Early China," in *Books in Numbers: Seventy-fifth Anniversary of the Harvard-Yenching Library*, ed. Wilt L. Idema (Cambridge: Harvard-Yenching Library, 2007), 23–47.

159. *Jin shu*, 17.498; *Song shu*, 12.231, 13.315.

CHAPTER 2

A SECOND-CENTURY B.C. GUIDE TO THE PLANETS

In this chapter I focus on the *Wuxing zhan* 五星占, a second century B.C. manuscript on planetary omenology and astronomy recovered from Mawangdui 馬王堆 tomb 3. From the vantage of the history of astronomy, the *Wuxing zhan* is at once an important and difficult text. Its contents are incomplete, corrupt, contradictory, and often curiously irreconcilable with astronomical reality as we (and later Chinese texts) know it. After introducing the basics of early Chinese planetary astronomy through Liu Xin's 劉歆 (c. 50 B.C. – A.D. 23) Triple Concordance system (#8; c. A.D. 5) in Section 2.2, I offer an extended textual study of the *Wuxing zhan*'s astronomical contents in Section 2.3. While the text's treatment of Venus looks more-or-less like an incipient version of later planetary models, I attempt to explain the more incongruous features of its treatment of Jupiter, Saturn, and Mercury in the context of divination culture, both in terms of their indebtedness in form to hemerology and the logic of their function in celestial omen literature. Though we may be able to rationalize their features in this way, the fact remains that these are not particularly realistic models of planetary behavior, which leaves us in Section 2.4 to ask if they represent the formative stage of planetary astronomy in China or something else entirely.

After introducing what I perceive to be a generic distinction between planetary models in mathematical and omenological texts, in Section 2.5 I explore the relationship between observation and practice in both fields. On the surface, the two genres appear to have opposite orientations to observed reality—the one (mathematics), seeking to capture the regularity of celestial phenomena, finds fault with the model, while the other (omenology) holds reality to its standard, looking for meaning in aberration. However, an analysis of changes that occur in theory and practice over the course of the following centuries shows this relationship to be considerably more complicated. Having established the possibility that the *Wuxing zhan*'s planetary models belong in part to different genres of knowledge, in Section 2.6 I return to the question of its incongruity as a text, which I attempt to explain in the context of early manuscript culture and the information that we can glean about its makers and owner.

2.1 Introduction

The *Wuxing zhan* is a unique document. It is at once the earliest extant Chinese treatise on the astral sciences and the only treatise *in manuscript form* to survive from the first millennium of the history of astronomy in China.[1] As a period "book" belonging to a private collector, *Wuxing zhan* is a wholly different category of text than those that later generations of imperial scholars selected to transmit through the ages—different not only in the knowledge that it preserves, but in its focus, format, textual features and history.

In 1973, archaeologists discovered the Wuxing zhan in the manuscript horde sealed in Mawangdui tomb 3 in Changsha, Hunan—the tomb of a Western Han 西漢 (206 B.C. - A.D. 9) noble, Li Xi 利豨, the second marquis of Dai 軑, closed in 168 B.C.[2] As with other Mawangdui materials, publication has been somewhat disorganized. Early photographs and transcriptions were incomplete, unclear, and inaccurate, and the divinatory portion of the text languished unpublished for more than a decade. Scholars have since redressed these

---

1. This statement requires two qualifications. First, fragments of works attested to famous Pre-Qin figures—in particular, Wuxian 巫咸, Shi Shen 石申, and Gan De 甘德 —that exist in later quotation do purport to date even earlier, but their provenance is the subject of long debate (note 65). Second, archaeologists supposedly discovered other materials related to planetary astronomy in 1977 at Shuanggudui 雙古堆 tomb 1 (closed in 165 B.C.) in Fuyang, Anhui; these were, however, badly damaged and never published; see Hu Pingsheng 胡平生, "Fuyang Shuanggudui Han jian shushu shu jianlun" 阜陽雙古堆漢簡 數術書簡論, *Chutu wenxian yanjiu* 出土文獻研究 4 (1998): 12–30.

2. For the site report, see Hunan sheng bowuguan 湖南省博物館 and Zhongguo kexueyuan kaogu yan-jiusuo 中國科學院考古研究所, "Changsha Mawangdui er, san hao Han mu fajue jianbao" 長沙馬王堆二、 三號漢墓發掘簡報, *Wenwu* 文物 1974.7: 39–48, 63. A wooden placard in the tomb records the date of interment as [Wendi] 12-II-*wuchen*.05 (168 B.C. April 3). Since its discovery, scholars have disagreed about whether the tomb occupant is indeed Li Xi or a close male relative of his, but new evidence brought to light by Chen Songchang 陳松長 seems to support the former identification. See "Mawangdui san hao mu de zai renshi" 馬王堆三號墓的再認識, *Wenwu* 2003.8: 56–59, 66.

Figure 2.1: Reconstruction of *Wuxing zhan* manuscript folds

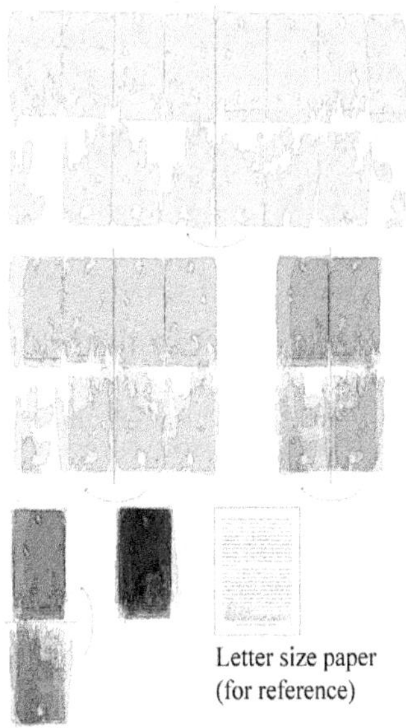

issues: in 1996, Chen Songchang 陳松長 published a complete and detailed photographic reproduction of the manuscript, and in 2004, Liu Lexian 劉樂賢 produced a superior annotated transcription of the entire text that has become the new standard.[3]

The *Wuxing zhan* is written in typical Clerical Script on a piece of silk approximately 104 cm wide by 48 cm (two Han *chi* 尺) tall, with a margin of 1.6 cm at the top and bottom. The silk is ruled in red ink, and the text's 8,000+ characters fill 144 lines. There is a one-line margin at the beginning and nineteen blanklines at the end of the text. This manuscript was stored with others in a rectangular partition of a lacquer box, and judging from reverse impressions and the coincidence of holes and other damage, the silk appears to have been folded in half lengthwise three times, then height-wise, forming a 13 cm x 28 cm rectangle six layers deep, as depicted in Figure 2.1.

As is common in the early period, the manuscript itself is untitled, leaving the editors

---

3. Chen Songchang, ed., *Mawangdui boshu yishu* 馬王堆帛書藝術 (Shanghai: Shanghai shudian, 1996), 8–9, 175–188; Liu Lexian, *Mawangdui tianwen shu kaoshi* 馬王堆天文書考釋 (Guangzhou: Zhongshan daxue chubanshe, 2004), 29–194. Unless otherwise noted, I adopt Liu's transcription and line numbers throughout.

assign it a title descriptive of its contents—*Wuxing zhan* ("Prognostications on the Five Stars [Planets]").[4] As one can see in Figure 2.2, the text is divided into eight coherent textual units, each of which begins on a new line.[5] Reminding us that we are in a world in which all "natural" phenomena are potentially portentous, the first five units (lines 1–74) are devoted to the omenology of the five naked-eye planets—Suixing 歲星 ("Year Star," i.e. Jupiter), Yinghuo 熒惑 ("Sparkling Deluder," i.e. Mars), Zhenxing 填星 ("Garrison Star," i.e. Saturn), Chenxing 晨星 ("Morning Star," i.e. Mercury), and Taibai 太白 ("Great White," i.e. Venus), respectively.[6] Each section is prefaced with an introduction to the correlative and divine associations of said planet and a description of its normal behavior, after which follows omen series in terse protasis-apodosis clauses, which are typical of, and in most cases parallel to, transmitted omen literature. The last three sections (lines 75–144), on the other hand, provide for Jupiter, Saturn, and Venus, respectively, tables recording the dates and positions of visibility phenomena for the 70 years between 246–177 B.C. and models describing their periodicities and normal motions over the course of their synodic periods. It is worth noting that equal space is devoted to the divinatory and computational sections of the text (74 and 70 lines, respectively) and that Venus' omenology constitutes exactly half of the former.

The text of the *Wuxing zhan* appears to have a complex history typical of what we

---

4. The ancient Chinese conceived of the planets as stars—"moving stars" (*xingxing* 行星) as distinct from the "fixed stars" (*hengxing* 恒星). This conception deserves emphasis; however, since my intent in this chapter is not to explore this issue, and since I find the terms "star," "moving star," and "the five stars" to be either too ambiguous or too ungainly, I prefer to use "planet." I find the title *Wuxing zhan* apt; in fact, there are five works with that title, all attributed to different authors, recorded in the Sui imperial bibliography (*Sui shu* 隋書 [Zhonghua shuju ed.], 34.1018–1019).

5. Preservation workers glued the fragments of the original manuscript onto a board according to the textual reconstruction of contemporary scholars. Since then, however, it has become evident that one large block of text has been misplaced; see Liu Lexian, *Mawangdui tianwen shu kaoshi*, 205–210. I have taken the liberty of correcting this in Figures 2.1 and 2.2.

6. It is worth noting that the *Wuxing zhan* gives the name of Mercury as the "Morning" *chen* 晨 Star rather than the "Chronogram" *chen* 辰 Star, as is the standard in later texts. As the "Morning Star" is a perfectly reasonable name for Mercury, I refrain from treating this as a mistake or character variant. In the case of Saturn, on the other hand, Zhen 填 is a common variant of Zhen 鎮 "Queller," the former seemingly playing off of the planet's association with Earth (*tu* 土).

Figure 2.2: *Wuxing zhan* dimensions and textual units

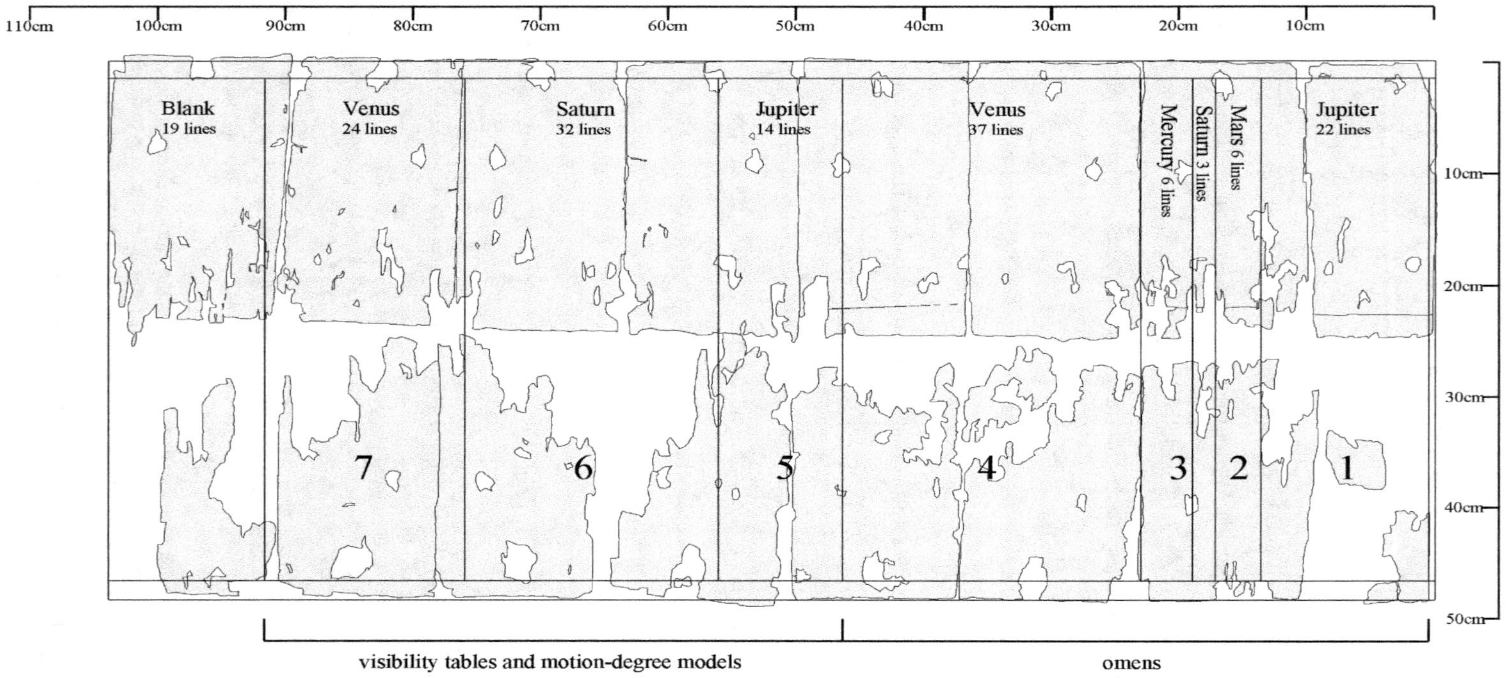

know about the unfixity of texts in the manuscript age. The sealing of the tomb provides a *terminus ante quem* of 168 B.C., and while its visibility tables are filled out in reign years to Wendi year 3 (177 B.C.), it avoids the personal name of Emperor Gaozu 高祖 (r. 202–194 B.C.), Bang 邦, but not that of Wendi 文帝 (r. 179–157 B.C.), Heng 恆. Assuming the rigorous application of such taboos, we might conclude that the manuscript was produced sometime between 202 and 180 B.C., and that its owner continued to add to its tables into Wendi's reign. Aside from the tables, however, the the text's astronomical contents are unmistakably Qin in origin, while the prevalence of numerical corruption suggests that the Mawangdui manuscript is at some remove from this portion's Qin authors (below).

Upon its discovery, the astronomical contents of the *Wuxing zhan* received immediate attention. Early inquiries focused primarily on the explanation of basic terms and principles, struggling to make sense of the the unclear photographs and transcriptions so as to fill out damaged text and introduce its contents to readers.[7] Later scholarship has gravitated towards Jupiter and the details of the Jovian year-count.[8] Several recent studies deserve

7. Liu Yunyou 劉雲友 (Xi Zezong 席澤宗), "Zhongguo tianwen shi shang de yi ge zhongyao faxian—Mawangdui Han mu boshu zhong de *Wuxing zhan*" 中國天文史上的一個重要發現 —馬王堆漢墓帛書中的『五星占』, *Wenwu* 1974.11: 28–36; modified and reprinted as Xi Zezong, "Mawangdui Han mu boshu zhong de *Wuxing zhan*" 馬王堆漢墓帛書中的『五星占』, in *Zhongguo gudai tianwen wenwu lunji* 中國古代天文文物論集, ed. Zhongguo shehui kexue yuan kaogu yanjiusuo 中國社會科學院考古研究所, Kaoguxue zhuankan A.21 (Beijing: Wenwu chubanshe, 1989), 46–58; He Youqi 何幼琦, "Shi lun *Wuxing zhan* de shidai he neirong" 試論『五星占』的時代和內容, *Xueshu yanjiu* 學術研究 1979.1: 79–87; "Guanyu *Wuxing zhan* wenti da ke nan" 關於『五星占』問題答客難, *Xueshu yanjiu* 1981.3: 97–103; Hashimoto Keizō 橋本敬造, "Senshin jidai no seiza to temmon kansoku" 先秦時代の星座と天文觀測, *Tōhō gakuhō* 東方學報 53 (1981): 189–232; Yabuuti Kiyosi 藪內清, "Baōtai san go bo shutsudo no *Gosei sen* ni tsuite" 馬王堆三號墓出土の「五星占」について, in *Tōhōgaku ronshū: Ono Katsutoshi Hakushi shōju kinen* 東方學論集 : 小野勝年博士頌壽記念, ed. Ono Katsutoshi 小野勝年 (Kyōto: Ryūkoku daigaku tōyō shigaku kenkyūkai, 1982), 1–12; Michel Teboul, *Les premières théories planétaires chinoises* (Paris: Collège de France, 1983), 161–168; Chen Meidong 陳美東, *Zhongguo kexue jishu shi: tianwenxue juan* 中國科學技術史：天文學卷 (Beijing: Kexue chubanshe, 2003), 98–101. In general, these early studies were brief, introductory, and often mired in assumptions concerning especially the dichotomy between "science" and "superstition" and how the text reflects positively or negatively the "scientific advancement" of the Chinese state. Particularly noteworthy in this regard is an article by Xu Zhentao 徐振韜 in which he argues that the size of the denominator used throughout the text (240) is proof that the invention of the armillary sphere occurred in Pre-Qin China, earlier than it had in the West ("Cong boshu *Wuxing zhan* kan 'Xianqin hunyi' de chuangzhi" 從帛書『五星占』看「先秦渾儀」的創製, *Kaogu* 考古 1976.2: 89–94, 84). Of these, the studies of He Youqi (1979) and Yabuuti are the most valuable.

8. In brief, the Jovian year-count is an antecedent to the sexagenary year-count based on the heavenly stem and earthly branch (*tiangan dizhi* 天干地支) binomes current in the third to first centuries B.C. It relies on the fact that Jupiter's nearly 12-year sidereal period means that it moves basically one of twelve

special mention. Around the same time, Takeda Tokimasa 武田時昌 and I produced studies
working out a number of the more detailed technical issues underlying the text's mathematical astronomy.[9] Takeda's article focuses on the evolution of Venus models through the Han,
exploring the the role of numerology apparently at play, using the *Wuxing zhan* to address
curious features of early models, which he attributes to textual corruption, and explaining
how subsequent modifications augmented their predictive accuracy. In my study, I explore
the interconnectedness between early astronomy and hemerology, attempting to root features of early planetary models in the idealized mechanics of mantic diagrams and calendar
deities. In another recent article, Christopher Cullen takes a sweepingly innovative approach
to the text, attempting to undermine basic assumptions about the nature of the tables, the
phenomena they describe, and the purport of the planetary models, and arguing that the
text's astronomy must be read in the context of omenology, where it functions less as an
accurate description of celestial motion than as a yardstick for gauging the ominousness of
observed phenomena.[10] On the omenological side, Liu Lexian has mapped out the network

---

"stations" (*ci* 次) per year, allowing a universal year count independent of the political reign of any one
state. For scholarship on Jupiter and the Jovian year-count in the *Wuxing zhan*, see Chen Jiujin 陳久金,
"Cong Mawangdui boshu *Wuxing zhan* de chutu shitan woguo gudai de Suixing jinian wenti" 從馬王堆帛
書『五星占』的出土試探我國古代的歲星紀年問題, in *Zhongguo tianwenxue shi wenji* 中國天文學史文集,
ed. Zhongguo tianwenxue shi wenji bianji zu 中國天文學史文集編輯組, vol. 1 (Beijing: Kexue chubanshe,
1978), 48–65; "Guanyu Suixing jinian ruogan wenti" 關於歲星紀年若干問題, *Xueshu yanjiu* 1980.6: 82–86;
Chen Jiujin and Chen Meidong, "Cong Yuanguang lipu ji Mawangdui boshu *Wuxing zhan* de chutu zai tan
Zhuanxu-li wenti" 從元光曆譜及馬王堆帛書『五星占』的出土再談顓頊曆問題, in *Zhongguo tianwenxue
shi wenji*, ed. Zhongguo tianwenxue shi wenji bianji zu, vol. 1 (Beijing: Kexue chubanshe, 1978), 95–117;
Hashimoto Keizō, "Sengyoku rekigen to Saisei kinenhō" 顓頊曆元と歲星紀念法, *Tōhō gakuhō*, no. 59 (1987):
323–343; Wang Shengli 王勝利, "Xingsui jinian guanjian" 星歲紀年管見, in *Zhongguo tianwenxue shi wenji*,
ed. Zhongguo tianwenxue shi wenji bianji zu, vol. 5 (Beijing: Kexue chubanshe, 1989), 239–245; Liu Binhui
劉彬徽, "Mawangdui Han mu boshu *Wuxing zhan* yanjiu" 馬王堆漢墓帛書『五星占』研究, in Mawangdui
Han mu yanjiu wenji 馬王堆漢墓研究文集, ed. Hunan Sheng bowuguan 湖南省博物館 (Changsha: Hunan
chubanshe, 1994), 69–79; Mo Shaokui 莫紹揆, "Cong *Wuxing zhan* kan woguo de ganzhi jinian de yanbian"
從『五星占』看我國的干支紀年的演變, *Ziran kexue shi yanjiu* 自然科學史研究 17, no. 1 (1998): 31–37;
Marc Kalinowski, "The Xingde 刑德 Texts from Mawangdui," trans. Phyllis Brooks, *Early China* 23-24
(1998-1999): 23–24; Tao Lei 陶磊, *Huainanzi* Tianwen *yanjiu—cong shushu de jiaodu* 『淮南子・天文』研究
—從數術的角度 (Jinan: Qi Lu shushe, 2003), 73–97; Liu Lexian, *Mawangdui tianwen shu kaoshi*, 219–229.

9. Takeda, "Taihaku kōdo kō: Chūgoku kodai no wakusei undōron" 太白行度考 —中国古代の惑星運動
論, *Tōhō gakuhō* 85 (2010): 1–44; Mo Zihan 墨子涵 (Daniel Morgan), "Cong Zhoujiatai Rishu yu Mawangdui
Wuxing zhan tan rishu yu Qin Han tianwenxue de huxiang yingxiang" 從周家臺『日書』與馬王堆『五星占』
談日書與秦漢天文學的互相影響, *Jianbo* 簡帛 6 (2011): 113–137.

10. Christopher Cullen, "Understanding the Planets in Ancient China: Prediction and Divination in the

of parallels between the *Wuxing zhan* and other omen literature and explored the relationship between Qin-Han divinatory manuscripts and the weft texts of the Eastern Han 東漢 (A.D. 25–220).[11] Lastly, in addition to Liu Lexian's annotated transcription, Kawahara Hideki 川原秀城 and Miyajima Kazuhiko 宮島一彥, Zheng Huisheng 鄭慧生, Chen Jiujin, and Christopher Cullen have produced full translations and studies of the text in their respective languages.[12]

2.2 The Basics of Chinese Planetary Astronomy

2.2.1 The explananda

Since the aim of Chinese planetary astronomy is to model the motions of the planets, it behooves us to begin with a description of those motions. For the sake of simplicity, I will attempt to describe phenomena as they were more-or-less perceived, adding to the complexity of these descriptions as we see contemporary actors struggle with new problems.

First of all, not all planets are alike: Mars, Jupiter, and Saturn—the superior planets— behave differently than do Mercury and Venus—the inferior planets. When a superior planet is opposite the Sun in **conjunction** (*he* 合) it is invisible, but when the Sun, which is faster, leaves it far enough behind, the planet is able to "emerge in the morning in the east" (*chen chu dongfang* 晨出東方)—i.e. **first morning rising** (FMR)—before the brightness of the rising Sun drowns it out. It rises earlier and earlier each morning, traveling prograde (*shun* 順) through the stars, all the while gradually slowing until it comes to a stop (*liu* 留)—

<hr>

Wu Xing Zhan," *Early Science and Medicine* 16 (2011): 218–251.

11. *Jianbo shushu wenxian tanlun* 簡帛數術文獻探論 (Wuhan: Hubei jiaoyu chubanshe, 2002), 341–351; "Weishu zhong de tianwen ziliao—*Hetu Dilanxi* wei li" 緯書中的天文資料 —『河圖帝覽嬉』爲例, *Zhongguo shi yanjiu* 中國史研究 2007.2: 71–82.

12. Kawahara and Miyajima, "Go sei sen" 五星占, in *Shinhatsugen Chūgoku kagakushi shiryō no kenkyū* 新發見中國科學史史料の研究, ed. Yamada Keiji 山田慶兒 (Kyōto: Kyōto daigaku jinbun kagaku kenkyūjo, 1985), 1–44; Zheng Huisheng, *Gudai tianwen lifa yanjiu* 古代天文曆法研究 (Kaifeng: Henan daxue chubanshe, 1995), 181–217; Chen Jiujin, *Boshu ji gudian tianwen shiliao zhu xi yu yanjiu* 帛書及古典天文史料注析與研究 (Taibei: Wan juan lou, 2001), 102–147; Christopher Cullen, "*Wu Xing Zhan* 五星占 'Prognostics of the Five Planets'," *SCIAMVS* 12 (2011): 193–249.

Figure 2.3: Synodic period of superior (left) and inferior (right) planets

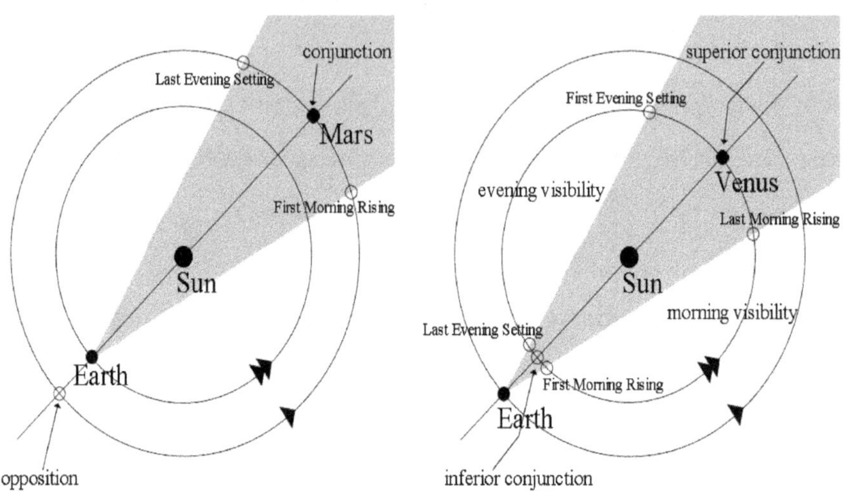

first station. It then begins to accelerate backwards in retrograde (*ni* 逆) until it reaches **opposition** (*chong* 沖). The superior planet then slows and comes to another stop—**second station**—before again moving forward. It gradually accelerates while the Sun catches back up with it, setting earlier and earlier each night until, for the last time, it "enters in the evening in the west" (*xi ru xifang* 夕入西方)—i.e. **last evening setting** (LES).

An inferior planet travels faster than the Sun, so after **superior conjunction** it speeds past it until it is far enough away to "emerge in the evening in the west" (*xi chu xifang* 夕出西方)—i.e. **first evening setting** (FES). It appears higher and higher in the sky each evening, traveling prograde through the stars, all the while slowing until the Sun begins to catch up. It comes to a stop—**evening station**—and begins to go retrograde before "entering in the evening in the west"—i.e. **last evening setting**. Going backwards, it quickly goes into **inferior conjunction** and moves far enough from the Sun to "emerge in the morning in the east"—i.e. **FMR**. It rises earlier and earlier while it slows, goes into **morning station**, and accelerates forward again. After a while it begins to close the gap with the Sun, eventually "entering in the morning in the east" (*chen ru dongfang* 晨入東方)—i.e. **last morning**

rising (LMR).

The length of time it takes each planet to complete these actions and return to the same position vis-à-vis the Sun is its **synodic period**. This is distinct from, though proportionally related to, its **sidereal period**—the amount of time it takes to return to the same point among the stars.

2.2.2 *The approach of later mathematical astronomy*

Before turning to the *Wuxing zhan*, it is important to consider the approach that later, more coherent texts take towards these phenomena so as to shed light on the places where the *Wuxing zhan* manuscript is defective. The first systematic mathematical approach to planetary astronomy to have come down to us in China is Liu Xin's Triple Concordance system (#8) of circa A.D. 5, which established a model in terms of methodology, terminology, and even style and formatting that astronomers continued to adopt and build upon until the introduction of Islamic and European astronomy. For the purposes of introduction and comparison, it is an adequate representative of the later mature tradition of planetary astronomy preserved in the "Lüli zhi" 律曆志 (Harmonics and *Li* Treatise) of the dynastic histories.[13]

The planetary astronomy of Liu Xin's and subsequent systems is comprised of four components. The first component is the "numbers" (*shu* 數), which come down to two elements: the lunar and solar parameters of the calendar and the planets' synodic periods. The former is essential since the calendar provides the basic temporal structure onto which one maps

---

13. On the Triple Concordance system (#8) and its planetary astronomy, see Nōda Chūryō 能田忠亮 and Yabuuti Kiyosi, *Kansho ritsurekishi no kenkyū* 漢書律曆志の研究, Tōhō bunka kenkyūjo kenkyū hōkoku 19 (Tōkyō: Zenkoku shobō, 1947); Teboul, *Les premières théories planétaires chinoises*. On the life and work of Liu Xin, see Xu Xingwu 徐興無, *Liu Xiang pingzhuan: fu Liu Xin pingzhuan* 劉向評傳：附劉歆評傳, Zhongguo sixiangjia pingzhuan congshu 21 (Nanjing: Nanjing daxue chubanshe, 2005). Later writers treat Liu Xin's work as a revision of the Grand Inception system (#7; 104 B.C.) rather than a standalone system; his basis in its lunar and solar parameters is clear, but there is no evidence concerning what if any planetary knowledge it contained, leaving us to assume that the Triple Concordance system's (#8) planetary astronomy is Liu Xin's innovation. On planetary astronomy in later systems, see Qu Anjing 曲安京, *Zhongguo shuli tianwenxue* 中國數理天文學, Shuxue yu kexue shi congshu 4 (Beijing: Kexue chubanshe, 2008), 532–628.

all other phenomena, but also because, in Chinese astronomy, the position of the Sun is necessary for calculating the position of a planet. At the core of the synodic period is a resonance period expressed in a ratio of appearances to years. For example, Liu Xin gives Venus a ratio of 2161 appearances—the APPEARANCE MEDIAL QI FACTOR (*xian zhong fa* 見中法)—in 3456 years—the YEAR NUMBER (*sui shu* 歲數). The planet's other numbers are all derived from these two elements and consist of the dividends and divisors of the ratio of the synodic period as expressed in different units of time—medial *qi* (i.e. solar months), months, and days.[14]

The second component is the "motion-degree" (*xingdu* 行度) model, a formulaic description of the planet's motion over the course of one synodic period. Liu Xin's motion-degree model for Venus, for example, reads:

金，晨始見，去日半次。**逆**，日行二分度一，六日。**始留**，八日而旋。**始順**，日行四十六分度三十三，四十六日。**順疾**，日行一度九十二分度十五，百八十四日而伏。凡見二百四十四日，除逆，定行星二百四十四度。**伏**，日行一度九十二分度三十三有奇。伏八十三日，行星百一十三度四百三十六萬五千二百二十分。凡晨見、伏三百二十七日，行星三百五十七度四百三十六萬五千二百二十分。

Metal (Venus): First morning visibility at half a STATION from the Sun. **Retrograde:** travels $\frac{1}{2}$ *du* per day, 6 days. **First station:** 8 days, then circles back. **Beginning prograde:** travels $\frac{33}{46}$ *du* per day, 46 days. **Prograde fast:** travels $1\frac{15}{92}$ *du* per day, 184 days, then hides (LMR). Visible for a total of 244 days, and, retrograde aside, travels a fixed 244 *du* through the stars. **Hidden:** travels $1\frac{33}{92}$ plus *du* per day, hiding 83 days and traveling $113\frac{4\ 365\ 220}{9\ 977\ 337}$ *du* through the stars. Visible in the morning and hidden for a total of 327 days, traveling $357\frac{4\ 365\ 220}{9\ 977\ 337}$

---

14. For the representation, derivation, and development of lunar, solar, and planetary periodicities in Chinese astronomy, see Chen Meidong, *Gu li xin tan* 古曆新探 (Shenyang: Liaoning jiaoyu chubanshe, 1995), 211–277, 385–405. The Chinese divide the solar year into 24 equal stages, which alternate between "nodal" (*jie* 節) and "medial" (*zhong* 中) *qi*. Liu Xin uses the unit "medial *qi*" to refer to the time elapsed between two medial *qi*, i.e. one twelfth of a year or one "solar month."

du through the stars.

夕始見，去日半次。**順**，日行一度九十二分度十五，百八十一日百七分日四十
五。**順遲**，日行四十六分度三十三，四十六日。**始留**，七日百七分日六十二分
而旋。**逆**，日行二分度一，六日而伏。凡見二百四十一日，除逆，定行星二百
四十一度。**伏逆**，日行八分度七有奇。伏十六日百二十九萬五千三百五十二分，
行星十四度三百六萬九千八百六十八分。一凡夕見伏，二百五十七日百二十九
萬五千三百五十二分，行星二百二十六度六百九十萬七千四百六十九分。

First evening visibility at half a STATION from the Sun. **Prograde**: travels $1\frac{15}{92}$ *du* per day, $181\frac{45}{107}$ days. **Prograde slow**: travels $\frac{33}{46}$ *du* per day, 46 days. **First station**: $7\frac{62}{107}$ days, then circles back. **Retrograde**: travels $\frac{1}{2}$ *du* per day, 6 days, then hides. Visible for a total of 241 days, and, retrograde aside, it travels a fixed 241 *du* through the stars. **Hidden in retrograde**: travels $\frac{7}{8}$ plus *du* per day, hiding $16\frac{1\,295\,352}{9\,977\,337}$ days and traveling $14\frac{3\,069\,868}{9\,977\,337}$ *du* through the stars. Visible in the evening and hidden for a total of $257\frac{1\,295\,352}{9\,977\,337}$ days, traveling $226\frac{6\,907\,469}{9\,977\,337}$ *du* through the stars.

一復，五百八十四日百二十九萬五千三百五十二分。行星亦如之，故曰日行一
度。

One cycle: $584\frac{1\,295\,352}{9\,977\,337}$ days. Travel through the stars [in *du*] is also as much, thus we say it travels (on average) 1 *du* per day.[15]

Motion-degree models work on two principles: symmetry and, for lack of a better word, an "angle of invisibility." All motion models that come before and after the Triple Concordance system (#8) exhibit symmetry between each grade of the two halves of the planet's synodic period (that is, beginning half-way through "hidden" at conjunction). For whatever reason, Liu Xin makes each of his models asymmetrical, and in a way that only complicates calcula-

---

15. *Han shu* 漢書 (Zhonghua shuju ed.), 21B.998–999.

Table 2.1: Triple Concordance System (#8) motion-degree model for Venus

Grade		Du per day	Days	Arc
	MORNING			
1	Retrograde (at FMR)	$-\frac{1}{2}$°°	6d	[−3°°]
2	Station	−	8d	−
3	Prograde slow	$\frac{33}{46}$°°	46d	[33°°]
4	Prograde fast	$1\frac{15}{92}$°°	184d	214°°
	(SUBTOTAL	1°°	244d	244°°)
5	Hidden (at LMR)	$1\frac{33}{92}$°°	83d	$113\frac{4\,365\,220}{9\,977\,337}$°°
	EVENING			
6	Prograde fast (at FES)	$1\frac{15}{92}$°°	$181\frac{45}{107}$d	[211°°]
7	Prograde slow	$\frac{33}{46}$°°	46d	[33°°]
8	Station	−	$7\frac{62}{107}$d	−
9	Retrograde	$-\frac{1}{2}$°°	6d	[−3°°]
	(SUBTOTAL	1°°	241d	241°°)
10	Hidden in retrograde (at LES)	$-\frac{7}{8}$°°	$16\frac{1\,295\,352}{9\,977\,337}$d	$-14\frac{3\,069\,868}{9\,977\,337}$°°
	TOTAL	1°°	$584\frac{1\,295\,352}{9\,977\,337}$d	$584\frac{1\,295\,352}{9\,977\,337}$°°

NOTE: the subtotals are for the planet's two visible arcs. The total and subtotals for "Du per day" are derived by averaging the angular velocity over the entire period, i.e. from the total or subtotal of "Days" and "Arc" that follow. Bracketed "Arc" values are calculated from rate and time.

tion.[16] In this regard, the Triple Concordance system (#8) is a bad example; however, the slightness of its asymmetry, as one can see in 2.1, is still a good indication of the primacy of this principle.

Motion-degree models also hinge upon the assumption that first and last appearances occur at a fixed distance from the Sun—my "angle of invisibility." Liu Xin adopts a universal value of half a STATION (*ci* 次) or 15° (the sky being divided into 12 STATIONS). Because the inferior planets are moving constantly in the vicinity of the Sun, one consequence of this assumption is that their net speed over one synodic period and between first and last appearances is the same as the Sun (1 *du* per day); and since the *du* is defined as the motion

---

16. Other models tend to distribute the fractional remainder of the planet's synodic period and arc to grades of invisibility, which, since "methods" do not require one to compute the position of the planet when invisible, greatly reduces the complexity of calculation.

of the (mean) Sun in one day, this makes the number of *du* traveled equal the number of days traveled in that period. Thus, Liu Xin has Venus travel 244 *du* in the 244 days between FMR and LMR, 241 *du* in the 241 days between FES and LES, and over its $584\frac{1295352}{9977337}$-day synodic period "travel through the stars [in *du*] is also as much" 行星亦如之.[17]

The third component is the SYSTEM ORIGIN (*liyuan* 曆元), a point in recent history at which a number of calendrical and astronomical cycles coincide. Liu Xin, for example, follows the Grand Inception system's (#7; 104 B.C.) origin of midnight at Winter Solstice.$_{Q22}$ with the Sun at the beginning of Ox.$_{09}$ (β Cap) on the first day of month XI of the inaugural year of the Grand Inception reign on day *jiazi*.$_{01}$, i.e. 105 B.C. December 25 (JD 168 3430.2). From the SYSTEM ORIGIN, one then extrapolates a HIGH ORIGIN (*shangyuan* 上元), a point in distant history (prehistory, to be precise) at which *all* cycles coincide and from which one counts their subsequent iterations.

A SYSTEM ORIGIN need not be perfectly accurate so long as it functions within an astronomical system to produce accurate results for the intended age, which is often decades or centuries later.[18] The Triple Concordance system (#8) is an excellent case in point. Working a full century after SYSTEM ORIGIN, Liu Xin created the Triple Concordance system (#8) for the purpose, according to later scholars, of retrodicting the planetary phenomena of the Spring and Autumn period (770–481 B.C.)—a goal for which he adopts an older value for the position of the Sun at Winter Solstice.$_{Q22}$ (the Sun was actually 19½ *du* into Dipper.$_{08}$ at SYSTEM ORIGIN, 6¾ *du* behind Ox.$_{09}$).[19] Furthermore, the SYSTEM ORIGIN itself is not a result of precise observation but an artifact of the inaccurate civil calendar that the Grand

---

17. For a more detailed explanation of the principles of symmetry and the "angle of invisibility" with diagrams, see Teboul, *Les premières théories planétaires chinoises*, 51–79.

18. Nathan Sivin, "Cosmos and Computation in Early Chinese Mathematical Astronomy," *T'oung Pao* 2d ser., 55, no. 1/3 (1969): 1–73. Cullen demonstrates the complexity of the derivation, function, and accuracy of the SYSTEM ORIGIN in Christopher Cullen, "Huo Rong's Observation Programme of AD 102 and the *Han Li* Solar Table," *Journal for the History of Astronomy* 38, no. 1 (2007): 75–98.

19. On the relationship between Liu Xin's astronomy and his work on the *Zuo Tradition*, see Christopher Cullen, "The Birthday of the Old Man of Jiang County and Other Puzzles: Work in Progress on Liu Xin's *Canon of the Ages*," *Asia Major* 14, no. 2 (2001): 27–60.

Inception system (#7) was instituted to replace: 105 B.C. December 25 is a *jiazi*.$_{01}$ day, but new moon and winter solstice actually occurred about $15^{\text{h}}40^{\text{m}}$ and $28^{\text{h}}29^{\text{m}}$ prior to midnight, respectively.[20] The fourth component of early planetary astronomy are the "methods" (*shu* 術) used to compute planetary phenomena from the aforementioned data. These are very deliberate, detailing each and every step of calculation. These are so deliberate, in fact, that Nathan Sivin characterizes the astronomical texts preserved in the "Treatises on Harmonics and Calendrics" as manuals for unskilled functionaries responsible for calculating annual ephemerides.[21]

There are essentially two sets of procedures: THE ERA METHOD (*ji shu* 紀術) and the prediction of THE FIVE PACES (*tui wubu* 推五步), in Liu Xin's terminology. The first consists of counting off from high origin to determine when and where a recent synodic period begins. This should be a simple matter but it consists of more than two dozen steps. One reason for this is that the complexity of the lunisolar civil calendar requires one to essentially compute a calendar as one goes. Another reason is that the Triple Concordance system (#8) performs parallel procedures in solar and lunar time using different sets of numbers.[22]

---

20. Zhang Peiyu 張培瑜 et al., *Zhongguo gudai lifa* 中國古代曆法 (Beijing: Zhongguo kexue jishu chubanshe, 2008), 257–258. Note that my values, derived from *Alcyone Ephemeris* v3.2, vary slightly from Zhang Peiyu's, which are based on his *Sanqianwubai nian liri tianxiang* 三千五百年曆日天象 (Zhengzhou: Daxiang chubanshe, 1997).

21. *Granting the Seasons: The Chinese Astronomical Reform of 1280, with a Study of its Many Dimensions and a Translation of its Records* (New York: Springer, 2009), 58–59.

22. In brief, the procedure is as follows. (1.☉) "Extrapolate planetary appearances and returns" 推五星見復: count off the number of appearances since high origin to the year in question using the synodic period in years. (2.☉) "Extrapolate the medial *qi* and STATION of planetary appearance" 推星所見中次: convert the time elapsed from high origin to the previous appearance into medial *qi* and cast out completed years to find the medial *qi* in the year in question, which corresponds also to the STATION of the Sun. (3.☾) "Extrapolate the month of planetary appearance" 推星見月: perform the same procedure with the synodic period in months to get the month of first appearance. (4.☉) "Extrapolate the day of the solstice" 推至日: convert the number of medial *qi* elapsed from ORIGIN HEAD to days and cast out complete sexagenary cycles to find the sexagenary day of the first day of the medial *qi* of appearance. (5.☾) "Extrapolate the new moon day" 推朔日: perform the same procedure for months to find the first day of the month of appearance. (6.☉) "Extrapolate the number of days and degrees entered into said medial *qi* and STATION" 推入中次日度數: convert the remainder of elapsed medial *qi* to days/*du* to find both the sexagenary day and the position of the Sun within its STATION, adding or subtracting half a STATION gives the position of the planet. (7.☾) "Extrapolate the number of days entered into said month" 推入月日數: perform the same procedure for months to find the day of the month and the same sexagenary day extrapolated in the previous procedure. Steps (8-11) repeat the previous steps to extrapolate the next appearance, and step

2.3 The Planetary Astronomy of the *Wuxing zhan*

2.3.1 The motion-degree model for Venus

The *Wuxing zhan* provides the following motion-degree model for Venus:

秦始皇帝元年正月，大白出東方，【日】行百廿分，百日。行益【疾，日行一度，
六】十日。行有（又）益疾，日行一度百八十七半 [分] 以從日，六十四日而復
遝日，晨入東方，凡二百廿四日。浸行百廿日，夕出西方。太白出西【方，日
行一度百八十七半分，百日】。行益徐，日行一度以侍（待）之，六十日。行有
（又）益徐，日行卅分，六十四日而入西方，凡二百廿四日。伏十六日九十六分。

In the first month of the first year of Emperor Qin Shihuang (r. 246–210 B.C.)
Great White (Venus) rises in the east (FMR), traveling 120 parts[23] [per day], 100
days. Movement increases in [speed: travels 1 *du* per day, 6]0 days. Movement
again increases in speed: travels 1 *du* and 187 and a half (parts) per day following
the Sun, 64 days, then catches up again with the Sun and sets in the morning in
the east (LMR). This comes to a total of 224 days. It travels submerged for 120
days, then rises in the west (LMR).

Great White rises in the west, [traveling 1 *du* and 187 and a half parts per day,
100 days.] Movement slows: travels 1 *du* per day waiting for it (the Sun), 60
days. Movement again slows: travels 40 parts per day, 64 days, then sets in the
west (LES). This comes to a total of 224 days. It hides for 16 days and 96 parts.

【太白一復】爲日五【百八十四日九十六分日。凡出入東方各五，復】與營室晨
出東方，爲八歲。

---

(12) concerns the differentiation of morning and evening appearances for the inferior planets. Subsequent
systems simplify this procedure by eliminating the redundant solar procedures. The second set of procedures
is considerably simpler. One uses it to determine the position of a planet at any given time by counting off
the number of *du* a planet travels from the point of its first visibility— the position of the Sun ± the "angle
of invisibility"—according to its motion-degree model, then casting out complete lodges.

23. *Wuxing zhan* divides the day and *du* into 240 parts throughout, as is particularly evident in the
motion-degree models for Jupiter and Saturn (see p. 127).

[One return of Great White] takes 5[84 days and 96 parts of days. In total it rises and sets in the east and west each five times, then again] rises in the morning with Hall.$_{13}$ in the east, constituting 8 years (lines 143–146).

This model clearly belongs to the same tradition or genre as the Triple Concordance system (#8): it is similarly formulaic in its description and it takes the same approach to planetary phenomena, including its assumptions of symmetry and an angle of invisibility. The manuscript is damaged in areas, but these principles allow us to reconstruct its text with confidence.

In addition to filling in the damaged text we must deal with two numerical errors. First, in grade 7 (see 2.2) the text gives a speed of "40" 卌 parts per day, which appears to be a copy error for "120" 百卄, as we have in the parallel grade 1. Second, the text inverts the order of angular velocities in grades 5-7 but not, as we would expect, the number of days (compare with 2.1). It appears that in copying from another manuscript, the copyist grasped that there is some symmetry at play in the array of data, but confused the proper order, either because he skipped to the wrong line, or set out to correct the master copy with a weak understanding of the principles of the mathematical model.[24] Corrected, the *Wuxing zhan*'s motion-degree model falls short of the Triple Concordance system (#8) in a number of important ways. Scholars have touted the accuracy of its synodic period, but this is the felicitous product of the simple ratio of 8 appearances : 5 years, whereas the later "Harmonics and *Li* Treatise" tradition uses much more complex ratios to achieve a different order of accuracy (2.3). The *Wuxing zhan*'s motion-degree model also exaggerates the amount of time that the planet is invisible near superior conjunction and omits any description of station or retrograde. In addition, *Wuxing zhan* does not mention an angle of

---

24. The period between FMR and LMR clearly reflects the principle of the "angle of invisibility," since the planet travels as 224 *du* in as many days (see p. 112); furthermore, the speeds are clearly derived from an integer number *du* that the planet is to traverse in each grade. A speed of 40 parts/day is asymmetrical and produces a non-integer arc $\left(\frac{40}{240}^{\circ\circ}/\mathrm{d} \times 100\mathrm{d} = 16\frac{160}{240}^{\circ\circ}\right.$ and $\left.\frac{40}{240}^{\circ\circ}/\mathrm{d} \times 64\mathrm{d} = 26\frac{160}{240}^{\circ\circ}\right)$ as does a duration of 100 days for grade 5 $\left(1\frac{187.5}{240}^{\circ\circ}/\mathrm{d} \times 100\mathrm{d} = 178\frac{30}{240}^{\circ\circ}\right)$. Moreover, with these durations the planet is unable to travel exactly 224 *du* in as many days to return to the same position vis-à-vis the Sun where it began.

Table 2.2: *Wuxing zhan* motion-degree model for Venus

	Grade	*Du* per day	Days	Arc
	MORNING			
1	Prograde slow (at FMR)	$-\frac{120}{240}^{\circ\circ}$	100d	[50$^{\circ\circ}$]
2	Prograde medium	1$^{\circ\circ}$	64d	[114$^{\circ\circ}$]
3	Prograde fast	$1\frac{187.5}{240}^{\circ\circ}$	64d	[114$^{\circ\circ}$]
	(SUBTOTAL	1$^{\circ\circ}$	224d	224$^{\circ\circ}$)
4	Submerged (at LMR)	–	120d]	–
	EVENING			
5	Prograde fast (at FES)	$[1\frac{187.5}{240}^{\circ\circ}]$	[100(64)d]	[114$^{\circ\circ}$]
6	Prograde medium	1$^{\circ\circ}$	60d	[60$^{\circ\circ}$]
7	Prograde slow	$\frac{40(120)}{240}^{\circ\circ}$	64(100d)	[50$^{\circ\circ}$]
	(SUBTOTAL	1$^{\circ\circ}$	224d	224$^{\circ\circ}$)
8	Hidden (at LES)	–	$16\frac{96}{240}$d	–
	TOTAL	1$^{\circ\circ}$	$584\frac{96}{240}$d	$[584\frac{96}{240}^{\circ\circ}]$

NOTE: the subtotals are for the planet's two visible arcs. The total and subtotals for "*Du* per day" are derived by averaging the angular velocity over the entire period, i.e. from the total or subtotal of "Days" and "Arc" that follow. Bracketed "Arc" values are calculated from rate and time. Note also that this table corrects the manuscript's reversal of grades 5, 6, and 7.

invisibility. Takeda argues that the model implies a non-angle of 0 *du*, otherwise it would give the planet an absurdly large greatest elongation (an inferior planet's maximum angular distance from the Sun). In reality, the planet's greatest elongation varies between 45–47°. The Triple Concordance system (#8) produces one of 44.6°, while the *Wuxing zhan* would give 49.3°—both of which are conceivable estimates—assuming a 0° angle of invisibility. On the other hand, were we to suppose an angle of invisibility on the order of the Triple Concordance's half-STATION, the *Wuxing zhan* would result in a greatest elongation for Venus of 64.3°, which is one third larger than its actual value. The only problem is that Takeda's solution replaces one absurdity with another: under this condition the planet would remain visible until the precise moment it reaches the Sun.[25]

---

25. "Taihaku kōdo kō," 9–12, 32. Note that such an absurdly large greatest elongation is not unprecedented: Sima Qian's Venus model generates a greatest elongation of $\approx$ 59.1° plus whatever angle of invisibility one assumes (*Shiji* 史記 [Zhonghua shuju ed.], 27.1323).

Table 2.3: Mean synodic periods for Venus

Astronomical system	appear. : years	*Sui*-length	Synodic period	Error
Wuxing zhan	8 : 5	365.25d	584.4d	+698.2 min
Triple Concordance (c. A.D. 5)	3 456 : 2 161	365.25016d	584.12983d	+300.2 min
Quarter-remainder (A.D. 85)	9 322 : 5 830	365.25d	584.02410d	+147.9 min
Supernal Emblem (A.D. 206)	14 426 : 9 022	365.24618d	584.02146d	+144.1 min
TRUE MEAN VALUE		.	583.92138d	

Whichever assumption is actually at play, it is difficult to imagine that it was derived from direct observation. Instead, I suspect that what we see here is the product of extrapolation, e.g. from observations of the planet's elongation and daily motion at various points in its progress, as well as a principle of symmetry. Whatever the limitations of its own assumptions and predictive accuracy, the Triple Concordance system (#8) is by contrast a complete and internally coherent model. It not only avoids the sort of flagrant contradictions with observational reality that we see in the *Wuxing zhan*, it sees beyond it, hypothesizing a planet's motions even when invisible. Its simplistic and incomplete likeness to later models gives one the impression that the *Wuxing zhan*'s Venus model is something inchoate—a rudimentary attempt to model the visible arcs of the planet's movements cobbled together with a set of durations.

The *Wuxing zhan*'s SYSTEM ORIGIN also presents us with an interesting problem. The text describes Jupiter, Saturn, and Venus as all "rising in the morning with Hall.$_{13}$ in the east" on the first day of "the first month of the first year of Emperor Qin Shihuang (246 B.C.)."[26] The term "rise with x" (*yu* x *chu* 與某出) has been the subject of some controversy, but I take it to mean a planet's position at first visibility (FMR or FES).[27] This description

---

26. Lines 1, 18, 89–90, 121–122, 143–146. For the determination that this occurs on the first, see note 40.

27. In relation to horizonal phenomena, *chu* 出 and *ru* 入 are used to describe rising and setting; however, in the context of planetary astronomy they describe first and last visibility. In the first article ever written on the *Wuxing zhan*, Xi Zezong takes *chu* to mean *any* rising to provide enough latitude to argue that its origin is correct and that its tables are accurate astronomical records ("Zhongguo tianwen shi shang de yi ge zhongyao faxian"). This interpretation contravenes standard usage and the usage that is evident in the organization of the text's motion-degree models. The meaning of *yu* 與 is a more complicated matter. On the face of it, *yu* ("with") seems uncontroversial: a planet rises "with" a particular lodge when it is

118

bears an obvious relationship with the high origin of the Qin Zhuanxu 顓項 system (#2) as recalled by later scholars:[28]

曆記始於顓項，上元太始閼蒙攝提格之歲，畢陬之月，朔日己巳立春，七曜俱在營室五度。

Calendrical records began with Zhuanxu, his high origin being the year Yanmeng-Shetige (year *jiayin*.01), month Bi-Zou (month I), the day of the new moon, *jisi*.06, the Enthronement of Spring, with the seven luminaries all at the fifth *du* of Hall.13.[29]

---

in said lodge. However, the lodges that the planets are "with" at origin and at in the Jupiter and Venus tables are in each case the lodges occupied by the Sun at the same time—that is, the mean Sun according to contemporary *richan* 日躔 (note 50). If we assume normal angles of invisibility for the planets this is a problem; furthermore, for Venus, an angle of invisibility greater than 8.2°° would require it to move *backwards* in the 16.4 days between LES and FMR, while the "with" lodges on Venus' visibility table move *forward*. One solution to this conundrum, as I have previously argued for, is to read *yu* as a technical term indicating the position of the Sun as distinct from the planet's (Yabuuti, "Baōtai san go bo shutsudo no *Gosei sen* ni tsuite," 2; Mo Zihan, "Cong Zhoujiatai rishu yu Mawangdui *Wuxing zhan* tan rishu yu Qin Han tianwenxue de huxiang yingxiang," 124, note 1). There are several problems with this reading: first, it is forced and unprecedented; second, the text at one points states that after 24 years the periods of Jupiter and Venus coincide and they "go into conjunction in Hall.13" 合營室 (line 90), which seems to corroborate that it is indeed the *planets* that begin in Hall.13; third, Liu Xiang 劉向 (79–8 B.C.), Cai Yong 蔡邕 (A.D. 133–192), and Dong Ba's 董巴 (3rd cent. A.D.) description of the Qin Zhuanxu 顓項 (#2) SYSTEM ORIGIN alternate between *yu, yu* 於 "at", and *zai* 在 "at," and place the Sun, Moon, and planets together (see p. 120); lastly, I have discovered that the term is used in a small number of astronomical records from the Han where, upon consulting an ephemeris program, I have confirmed that it is used to mean "at" or "in." The other solution is to accept Takeda's argument concerning the 0°° angle of invisibility, which (counterintuitively) places the planet and Sun at the same position during invisibility and at first and last visibility.

28. High origin often features a different sexagenary date than SYSTEM ORIGIN, but it is unclear to me how a *jisi*.06 high origin is compatible with the *Wuxing zhan*'s SYSTEM ORIGIN of Qin Shihuang 1-I-1,*wuyin*.15. The *Wuxing zhan* attributes the planets with the following periods: Jupiter-12y, Saturn-30y, Mercury-1y, Venus-8y, Mars-n/a. As such, their periods coincide in $10 \times 12y = 4 \times 30y = 15 \times 8y = 120y$. This would coincide with the 19y RULE (*zhang* 章) intercalation cycle in 2280y, over which time planetary phenomena would reoccur exactly at the same times each year. However, in 2280y the sexagenary day at New Year day would shift by 30 positions: $2,280y \times 365.25d \mod 60 = 30$. This would thus seem to imply two ERAS (*ji* 紀) beginning at *jisi*.06 and *jihai*.36, excluding the possibility of the FMR of Jupiter, Saturn and Venus coinciding with New Year day and the Enthronement of Spring on any other day.

29. Liu Xiang, *Hongfan zhuan* 洪範傳, cited in *Xin Tang shu* 新唐書 (Zhonghua shuju ed.), 27A.602. According to the *Erya* 爾雅, "when Taisui is in *jia*.S01 it is called Yanfeng (alternatively Yanfeng 焉逢 or Yanmeng 閼蒙)... when Taisui is in *yin*.B03 it is called Shetige...when the month is in *jia*.S01 it is called Bi 畢. ... Month I is Zou (alternatively Ju 聚)" 大歲在甲曰閼逢... 大歲在寅曰攝提格... 月在甲曰畢... 正月為陬 (*Erya zhushu* 爾雅注疏 [Siku quanshu 四庫全書 ed.], 5.17b–20b). *Qiyao* 七曜 ("the seven luminaries") is a term that appears becomes popular under later Buddhist influence. Jiang Xiaoyuan 江曉原 suggests that its earliest presence in astronomy, in the title of a work by Liu Hong 劉洪 (c. A.D. 135–210), is evidence of Buddhist influence (*Tianxue zhen yuan* 天學真原, 2d ed. [Shenyang: Liaoning jiaoyu chubanshe, 2007], 266–

顓頊曆術曰：「天元正月己巳朔旦立春，俱以日月起於天廟營室五度。」今月令
孟春之月，日在營室。

The Zhuanxu system method states: "The celestial origin is the first month, day
jisi.06, new moon, Enthronement of Spring.Q04, when the Sun and Moon begin
together in the fifth *du* of the Celestial Temple, Hall.13." This is the first month
of spring according to modern monthly ordinances, when the Sun is in Hall.13.[30]

According to the reconstructions of Zhang Peiyu 張培瑜 and Li Zhonglin 李忠林, the
Qin calendar for Qin Shihuang 1-I-1 (counting from his reign as king), fell on *wuyin*.15,
246 B.C. February 3.[31] This coincides roughly with new moon (*dingchou*.14, February 2,
07:48 local apparent time) and the Enthronement of Spring (*renwu*.19, February 7), the
precise dates of *qi* being more flexible than new moons. However, any semblance with
reality ends there: at SYSTEM ORIGIN, Mars was on the other side of the sky; the other
planets were within 30° of one another and Hall.13 but spread out over four different lodges;
and their FMR would have occurred weeks apart (see Figure 2.3.1 and Table and 2.4).
The accuracy of a SYSTEM ORIGIN is immaterial, as we mentioned above, so long as it
functions to produce accurate results for the period for which it is intended. The problem
here is that the period of intended use—246–177 B.C., the range of its planetary tables—
begins at SYSTEM ORIGIN. This guarantees that whatever errors built therein would cascade
through subsequent iterations of planetary phenomena without the hypothetical time needed

---

293). This term, however, does appear in other early texts like the *Huangdi neijing* 黃帝內經 and *Taiping jing* 太平經 (*Huangdi neijing suwen* 黃帝內經素問 [Siku quanshu ed.], 19.4b, 13b; *Taiping jing hejiao* 太平經合校 [Zhonghua shuju ed.], 1.3).

30. Cai Yong, cited in Li Xian's 李賢 (A.D. 654–684) commentary, *Hou Han shu* 後漢書 (Zhonghua shuju ed.), *zhi* 1, 3038 (commentary). See also the descriptions of Liu Hong and Dong Ba in, respectively, Ibid., *zhi* 2, 3042–3043; *Jin shu* 晉書 (Zhonghua shuju ed.), 17.502.

31. The common reference for historical calendars and the dates of lunar and solar events in China is Zhang Peiyu, *Sanqianwubai nian liri tianxiang*. In 1997, when Zhang Peiyu published this work little was known about the calendar of the Qin and early Western Han; since then, the discovery of calendars from this period has filled in a number of gaps in our knowledge. For reconstructions based on these materials, see Zhang Peiyu, "Genju xinchu liri jiandu shilun Qin he Han chu de lifa" 根据新出歷日簡牘試論秦和漢初的曆法, *Zhongyuan wenwu* 中原文物 2007.5: 62–77; Li Zhonglin 李忠林, "Zhoujiatai Qin jian lipu xinian yu Qin shiqi lifa" 周家臺秦簡曆譜係年與秦時期曆法, *Lishi yanjiu* 歷史研究 2010.6: 36–53.

Figure 2.4: Eastern horizon at *Wuxing zhan* SYSTEM ORIGIN

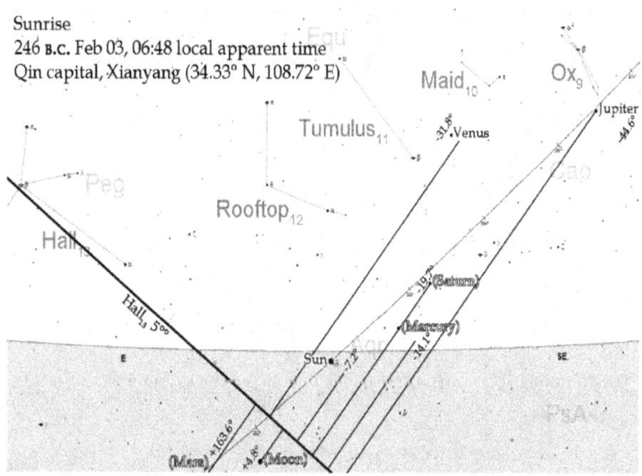

NOTE: Figure produced by *Alcyone Ephemeris* v3.2 for the Qin capital Xianyang and using the guide stars of the "ancient degree" system as reconstructed in Pan Nai, *Zhongguo hengxing guance shi*, 29. Distances from Hall.13 5°° (taking η Pegasi as Hall.13 0°°) are given in degrees of right ascension (RA). Parentheses indicate bodies not yet visible at dawn as calculated by *Planetary, Lunar, and Solar Visibility* v3.1.

Table 2.4: FMR in vicinity of *Wuxing zhan* SYSTEM ORIGIN

Planet	Date	RA	Lodge	
Mars	247 May 03	–	–	
Mercury	247 Dec 12	239.9°	Basket.07	0.4°°
Jupiter	246 Jan 04	268.1°	Dipper.08	18.5°°
Venus	246 Jan 20	294.8°	Tumulus.11	4.3°°
Saturn	246 Feb 13	301.7°	Tumulus.11	11.3°°

to synchronize with reality. What is the rationale of this construct then if not to align models with observation? The key, it seems, is the most prominent coincidence of the bunch: the inauguration of Qin Shihuang. In omen literature, five-planet convergences mark global disruptions in cosmo-political order, and where they coincide with the founding of a dynasty they mark a clear transferal of Heaven's Mandate thereto. What makes this convergence an even bolder affirmation of Qin sovereignty is its purported occurrence in Hall.$_{13}$, the Celestial Temple, in the northern quadrant of the sky, which is associated with water—the dynastic symbol of the Qin. According to the *Hetu* 河圖 as preserved in the *Kaiyuan zhanjing* 開元占經 (A.D. 729), for example:

辰精帥五精聚于北方七宿，黑帝以清平、靜潔、通明起。

If the chronogram essence (: MERCURY : WATER : BLACK) commands the five essences (planets) to converge in the seven lodges of the north, then the Black Emperor (: WATER : QIN) will arise by virtue of clear peace, quiet purity, and penetrating perspicacity.[32]

The political significance of this SYSTEM ORIGIN, He Youqi 何幼琦 argues, is evidence that symbolic considerations outweighed empirical ones in its selection.[33] Huang Yi-long 黃一農 has shown that there is a long history of reimagining and fabricating celestial omens in China, especially five-planet convergences. The *Shiji* 史記 and *Han shu* 漢書, for example, both record a five-planet convergence in Eastern Well.$_{22}$ heralding the reign of Han Gaozu (r. 206/202–195 B.C.) upon his entry into the Qin capital in the winter of 207 B.C., though the actual convergence (< 30°) occurred *around* Eastern Well.$_{22}$ in the summer of 205 B.C.[34]

Moreover, ours is also not the only instance where political symbolism has obtruded a SYSTEM ORIGIN upon astronomy. In 105 B.C., amid proposals for reform and a rare

---

32. *Kaiyuan zhanjing* 開元占經 (Siku quanshu ed.), 19.3b.

33. He Youqi, "Shi lun *Wuxing zhan* de shidai he neirong," 85.

34. Huang Yi-long, *Shehui tianwenxue shi shi jiang* 社會天文學史十講 (Shanghai: Fudan daxue chubanshe, 2004), 1–71. For this specific event, see ibid., 63–65; *Shiji*, 89.2581; *Han shu*, 26.1301.

calendrical coincidence, Han Wudi 漢武帝 (r. 141–87 B.C.) issued an edict declaring:

十一月甲子朔旦冬至已詹，其更以七年為太初元年。年名「焉逢攝提格」，月名「畢聚」，日得甲子，夜半朔旦冬至。

The coincidence in the eleventh month of *jiazi*.$_{01}$, new moon, and Winter Solstice.$_{Q22}$ is already here. May that we change [Original Enfeoffment] year 7 to the inaugural year of the Grand Inception reign. The year is named Yanfeng-Shetige (*jiayin*.$_{51}$), the month, Bi-Ju (month I), and for the day we obtain *jiazi*.$_{01}$, with the new moon and Winter Solstice.$_{Q22}$ at midnight.[35]

The problem was that the inaugural year of the Grand Inception reign was, by the established year-count, not a *jiayin*.$_{51}$ but a *dingchou*.$_{14}$ year. In response, the men in charge of the reform petitioned the emperor to report that, "they were unable to do the calculations and desired that calendar-makers be enlisted... to create the Han Grand Inception system (#7)" 不能為算，顧募治曆者... 以造漢太初曆, after which the problem was solved with a little creative numerology. To further complicate matters, however, the coincidence of day *jiazi*.$_{01}$, Winter Solstice.$_{Q22}$, and New Year's Day was nothing more than an artifact of the civil calendar—the very calendar that the emperor set out to reform amid protests of its inaccuracy (see Section 2.2). In reality, the three events occurred spread out over three different days: day *jiazi*.$_{01}$ on December 25 00:00, new moon on December 24 08:00, and winter solstice on December 23 19:31. The establishment of a Grand Inception Epoch on midnight, 105 B.C. December 25, left subsequent astronomers in the position of having to compensate for the discrepancy between new moon and SYSTEM ORIGIN by such means as the "insert half a day method" (*jie ban ri fa* 借半日法).[36]

---

35. *Shiji*, 26.1261–1262.

36. *Hou Han shu*, 28A.975. On this problem and the history of the Grand Inception reform, see Zhang Peiyu et al., *Zhongguo gudai lifa*, 250–258. The *Wuxing zhan* similarly places the Jovian year Shetige—implying an *yin*.$_{B03}$ year in the first year of Qin Shihuang's reign when the *Xingde* 刑德, another manuscript found at Mawangdui, correctly identifies that that year as *yimao*.$_{52}$. For problems with the *Wuxing zhan* Jovian year-count, see note 8.

Table 2.5: *Wuxing zhan* visibility table for Venus (lines 123–142)

Mo.	Phen.	Lodge	Days	±	Years								
I	FMR	Hall.$_{13}$	224		246	238	230	222	214	206	198	190	182
VIII	LMR	Horn.$_{01}$	120										
XII	FES	Tumulus.$_{11}$	224	−21	245	237	229	221	213	205	197	189	181
VIII†	LES	Wings.$_{27}$	16.4				始			高		呂	惠
VIII	FMR	Baseboard.$_{28}$	224				皇			祖		后	帝
III	LMR	Mane.$_{18}$	120	+78	244	236	228	220	212	204	196	188	180
VIII†	LES	Wings.$_{27}$	224										
II	LES	Pasture.$_{16}$	16.4	+57	243	235	227	219	211	203	195	187	179
III	FMR	Mane.$_{18}$	224										文
XI†	LMR	Basket.$_{07}$	120										帝
III†	FES	Pasture.$_{16}$	224	+52	242	234	226	218	210	202	194	186	178
X	LES	Heart.$_{05}$	16.4										
XI†	FMR	Basket.$_{07}$	224	−73	241	233	225	217	209	201	193	185	177
VI†	LMR	Willow.$_{24}$	120										
IX	FES	Heart.$_{05}$	224	−94	240	232	224	216	208	200	192	184	
V	LES	Well.$_{22}$	16.4										
VI†	FMR	Devils.$_{23}$	224										
I	LMR	Hall.$_{13}$	120	+5	239	231	223	215	207	199	191	183	
V	FES	Well.$_{22}$	224										
XII	LES	Tumulus.$_{11}$	16.4										

2.3.2 The visibility table for Venus

Above the motion-degree model for Venus is a 70-year visibility table calculated therefrom. Each line describes the month of a visibility phenomenon, the lodge with which the planet/sun rise, and the period between this and the next phenomenon. Appended thereto in a staggered fashion are numbers marked with "remainder" (*yu* 余) and "take" (*qu* 取) (marked "+" and "–," respectively) and the year in which said phenomenon occurs. The years run down several columns, each column representing five synodic periods in eight years, such that the planet's visibility phenomena are shown to repeat exactly in each subsequent eight-year period. For the sake of convenience, I have distilled this information into Table 2.5, rendering the years into the Julian calendar and smoothing over two copy errors.[37] We might assume that the table has arranged Venus' first and last appearances onto the civil

---

37. Row 7: LMR is given as month IX in line 128 but VIII in line 129, the latter of which is preferable. Row 17: FMR is given as month IX in line 138 but VI in line 139, the latter of which is preferable.

calendar, but it is not that simple. The Chinese civil year of 12 or 13 lunar months (around 354 and 384 days, respectively), regulated as it was in period calendars by a 19-year intercalation scheme, is incompatible with this neat pattern of repetition; furthermore, the number of days elapsed between phenomena are sometimes incompatible with the respective month-dates.[38] Instead of the civil calendar, it appears that the compiler has arranged the phenomena around a purely solar year of 365¼ days divided evenly into twelve $30\frac{7}{16}$-day "months" to facilitate repetition.[39] The key is in the "remainder" and "take" numbers, which mark phenomena occurring immediately before or after each subsequent year, indicating the gap between them in days. Inspection shows that the planet's periods of visibility and invisibility are counted from the first day of each eight-year period and that the length of each year amounts to between 365 and 365.4 days—i.e. a solar year.[40]

This is unlike any calendar seen in this period. Unsatisfied with the precedence for purely solar timekeeping, Cullen reads the table as a civil calendar and attempts to experiment with intercalation schemes to explain the dates for one template period, ultimately concluding that the features of the table are "idealized and distant from likely observation."[41] I am more confident about the tables' status as solar calendars for three reasons: the indication of

---

38. On these points, see Cullen, "Understanding the Planets in Ancient China," 231–243. For intercalation practices in the Qin and early Western Han, see Li Zhonglin, "Shilun Qin-Han chu lifa de zhirun guize" 試論秦漢初曆法的置閏規則, *Sichuan daxue xuebao* 四川大學學報 2009.6: 5–11; "Zhoujiatai Qin jian lipu xinian yu Qin shiqi lifa."

39. Yabuuti, "Baōtai san go bo shutsudo no *Gosei sen* ni tsuite," 6.

40. In the first year: $224 + 120 = 344 = 365 - 21$. In the second year: $344 + (224 + 16.4 + 224) = 808.4 = (365 + 365.4) + 78$. In the third year: $808.4 + (120 + 224) = 1152.4 = (2 \times 365 + 365.4) + 57$. In the fourth year: $1152.4 + (16.4 + 224 + 120) = 1512.8 = (2 \times 365 + 2 \times 365.4) + 52$. In the fifth year: $1512.8 + (224 + 16.4) = 1753.2 = (2 \times 365 + 3 \times 365.4) - 73$. In the sixth year: $1753.2 + (224 + 120) = 2097.2 = (3 \times 365 + 3 \times 365.4) - 94$. In the seventh year: $2097.2 + (224 + 16.4 + 224) = 2561.6 = (3 \times 365 + 4 \times 365.4) + 5$. In the eighth year: $2561.6 + (120 + 224 + 16.4) = 2922 = (3 \times 365 + 5 \times 365.4) = 8 \times 365.25$. The average year-length is 365¼ days. Counting backwards from the first remainder places SYSTEM ORIGIN on 246-I-1.

41. Cullen, "Understanding the Planets in Ancient China," 248. Two of the month-dates are impossible to reconcile, but Cullen points out that one 8-year period in which intercalary months fall at the end of the third and sixth years would basically work to produce 15 of the 20 month-dates with two more being very close. Unfortunately, none of the eight-year periods in the *Wuxing zhan* visibility table for Venus coincide with such a pattern according to the calendar of the period as reconstructed in Zhang Peiyu, "Genju xinchu liri jiandu shilun Qin he Han chu de lifa," 72–76; Li Zhonglin, "Zhoujiatai Qin jian lipu xinian yu Qin shiqi lifa," 52–53.

internal textual evidence here and in the Jupiter table (below); the fact that all the relevant concepts—the solar year (*sui* 歲) and its duodenary divisions, the 12 or 24 *qi* and the 12 solar steps (*richan* 日躔)—are in place by the time of the *Wuxing zhan*; and the centrality of solar time to the planetary astronomy of the Triple Concordance system (#8) and earlier texts.[42] Even so, the allotment of phenomena to "months" is still off in seven of twenty cases (marked with †).[43] Regardless of whether it is intended as a civil or solar calendar, it seems as if the table is either corrupt or its compiler did not entirely understand what he was doing. Moreover, it is difficult to know what use a purely solar timescale would be beyond the initial steps of calculation or how aware the user may have been of any of these issues.

Before passing judgment on the compiler, we should note that he does an impeccable job computing the lodges. Assuming that he indeed begins five *du* into Hall.$_{13}$, he correctly extrapolates the position of every single phenomena according to the number of days elapsed and the "ancient degree" (*gudu* 古度) system of lodge-widths as it has come down to us in

---

42. The concept of the solar year is evident in intercalation practices centuries before the Qin, and several presumably Warring States texts even define *sui* in apparent contradistinction with *nian* 年 (the civil year). For example, in the "Yao dian" 堯典 chapter of the *Book of Documents*, Yao commands the Xi-He 羲和 brothers, "a period of 366 days, use intercalary months to fix the four seasons and complete the *sui*" 朞 三百有六旬有六日，以閏月定四時成歲; and the *Rites of Zhou* describes that it is the duty of the Grand Clerk to "set straight the *sui* and the *nian* to order affairs" 正歲年以序事, to which Zheng Xuan 鄭玄 (A.D. 127–200) comments, "the number of medial *qi* is called '*sui*,' and the number of new moons is called '*nian*'" 中數曰歲，朔數曰年 (Shangshu zhushu 尚書注疏 [Siku quanshu ed.], 2.21b; *Zhouli zhushu* 周禮注疏, [Siku quanshu ed.], 26.401b). There are exceptions and ambiguities to this usage in other genres, e.g. the *Jiuzhang suanshu* 九章算術, which at one point gives a *sui* as 354 days long (*Huijiao Jiuzhang suanshu* 匯校九章算術 [Shenyang: Liaoning jiaoyu chubanshe, 2004], 115). However, astronomical texts consistently use *sui* to denote the solar year; see Qu Anjing, *Zhongguo shuli tianwenxue*, 66–67. The concept of the 24 *qi* is well attested by the time of the *Wuxing zhan*. Most of the important terms occur in the *Zuo Tradition* (c. 4th–3rd cent. B.C.) and the *Lü shi chunqiu* 呂氏春秋 (239 B.C.), while complete lists occur in the "Zhou yue" 周月 and "Shi xun" 試訓 chapters of the *Yi Zhou shu* 逸周書 (c. 4th–2nd cent. B.C.) and, 20 years after the sealing of Mawangdui tomb 3, in the "Tianwen xun" 天文訓 chapter of the *Huainanzi* 淮南子. The *Wuxing zhan*'s "solar months" would be the functional equivalent of Liu Xin's "medial *qi*;" the difference being that the Zhuanxu system's (#2) high origin (and, it appears, the *Wuxing zhan*'s SYSTEM ORIGIN) begins on a nodal *qi*, the Enthronement of Spring. As we will see below, the *Wuxing zhan* and its parallels with early planetary models resort exclusively to solar units of time: *sui*, solar months (Jupiter), solstices and equinoxes (Mercury), and days. Lastly, the "solar steps" (*richan*) in Warring States, Qin, and Western Han texts are also predicated upon the concept of the solar year and its duodenary division (note 50).

43. The "month" is in each case one too large. According to my calculations, using the 19-year intercalary scheme of the Qin and early Western Han produces around eight or nine errors a year in each iteration of the 8-year cycle.

the Qin daybook B from Fangmatan 放馬灘 tomb 1 and in the later work of Liu Xiang 劉
向 (79–8 B.C.).[44]

2.3.3 *The superior planets*

The *Wuxing zhan* offers much simpler descriptions of the remaining planets. The simplest
by far is reserved for Mars, whose motions have always been the most challenging for astronomers to master. According to the *Wuxing zhan*, "[its advancing and retreating] are
without constancy and cannot be taken as a [standard]" 【進退】無恒，不可為【極】 (line
45).[45] The text does provide motion-degree models for Jupiter and Saturn, but they are
markedly simpler than the Venus model: they provide only rough sidereal and synodic peri
ods, the latter of which is divided into only visible and invisible periods, and a constant mean
velocity averaged from the planets' sidereal periods without consideration for the variability
of their motions.

秦始皇帝元年正月，歲星日行廿分，十二日而行一度，終【歲行卅】度百五分，
見三【百六十五日而夕入西方】，伏卅日，三百九十五日而復出東方。【十二】
歲一周天，廿四歲一與大【白】合營室。

In the first month of the first year of Emperor Qin Shihuang, Year Star (Jupiter)
[rose in Hall.$_{13}$][46], traveling 20 parts per day, traveling 1 *du* in 12 days and
[traveling 30] *du* and 105 parts [in a complete year]. It is visible for 3[65 days
before setting in the evening in the west], where it hides for 30 days. In [a total
of] 395 days it rises again in the east. [In 12] years it makes one circuit through
Heaven, and every 24 years it goes into conjunction with Great [White] in Hall.$_{13}$

---

44. For a table showing at how I arrived at this conclusion, Mo Zihan, "Cong Zhoujiatai rishu yu Mawangdui
Wuxing zhan tan rishu yu Qin Han tianwenxue de huxiang yingxiang," 132–134. On the "ancient degree"
lodge system, see Pan Nai 潘鼐, *Zhongguo hengxing guance shi* 中國恆星觀測史, 2d ed. (Shanghai: Xuelin
chubanshe, 2009), 26–31.

45. The missing characters in this line can be filled in from a citation by Han Yang 韓楊 (Jin Dynasty) in
Kaiyuan zhanjing, 30.3a.

46. The copyist appears to have omitted several characters concerning the planet's FMR here.

(lines 89–90).

秦始皇帝元年正月，填星在營室，日行八分，卅日而行一度，終歲行【十二度
卅二分，見三百四十五】日，伏卅二日，凡見三百七十七日而復出東方，卅歲
一周于天，廿歲與歲星合爲大陰之紀。

In the first month of the first year of Emperor Qin Shihuang, Queller Star (Saturn) was in Hall.₁₃, traveling 8 parts per day, traveling 1 *du* in 30 days and traveling [12 *du* and 2 parts] in a complete year. [It is visible for 345] and hides 30 days. In a total of 377 days it rises again in the east. In 30 years it makes one circuit through Heaven, and every 20 years it goes into conjunction with Year Star making a Taiyin era. (lines 121–122).

In the omenological section on Jupiter, the *Wuxing zhan* also includes a list of Jupiter's positions in each of the twelve Jovian years (Table 2.6) followed by another description of the parameters of the planet's synodic period that is slightly at odds with that found in the computational section:

皆出三百六十五日而夕入西方，伏卅日而晨出東方，凡三百九十五日百 [六十]
五分【日而復出東方】。

In all, it rises and in 365 days it sets in the evening in the west and hides for 30 days before rising in the morning in the east. In a total of 395 days and 1[6]5 parts [of a day it rises again in the east] (line 5).

The visibility tables for Jupiter and Saturn are also considerably simpler than that for Venus. One reason is that superior planets experience half as many first and last risings in one synodic period than inferior planets; however, their tables also omit LES, days, "remainder" and "take" numbers, and the months of FMR.

Here, and in parallels in other early texts, there are a number of features that do not make astronomical sense but, I believe, can only be understood in the context of Warring

Table 2.6: *Wuxing zhan* Jovian year list (lines 1–5)

Year	Month	FMR Lodge	Year name
1	I	Hall.13	[Shetige] 攝提格
2	[II]	[Wall.14]	Shanyan 單閼
3	III	Stomach.17	Zhixu 執徐
4	IV	Net.19	Dahuang[luo] 大荒落
5	[V]	[Well.22]	Dunzang 敦牂
6	[VI]	[Willow.24]	Zhiji 汁給
7	VII	Strung Bow.26	Ruijian 芮蓳
8	VIII	Baseboard.28	[Zuoe] 作噩
9	[IX]	[Neck.02]	[Yanmao] 閹茂
10	X	Heart.05	Dayuanxian 大淵獻
11	XI	Dipper.08	Kundun 困敦
12	XII	Tumulus.11	[Chifenruo] 赤奮若
13	I	Hall.13	Sheti[ge] 攝提格

Table 2.7: *Wuxing zhan* visibility table for Jupiter (lines 77–88)

FMR lodge	Years					
Hall.13	246	234	222	210	198	186
Wall.14	245	233	221	209	197	185
Pasture.16	244	232	220	208	196	184
Net.19	243	231	219	207	195	183
Well.22	242	230	218	206	194	182
Willow.24	241	229	始	高	呂	惠
Strung Bow.26	240	228	皇	祖	后	帝
Baseboard.28	239	227	215	203	191	文
Neck.02	238	226	214	202	190	帝
Heart.05	237	225	213	201	189	177
Dipper.08	236	224	212	200	188	
Tumulus.11	235	223	211	199	187	

Table 2.8: *Wuxing zhan* visibility table for Saturn (lines 91–120)

FMR lodge	Years		
Hall.13	246	216	186
Hall.13	始	215	惠
Wall.14	皇	214	帝
Crotch.15	243	213	183
Pasture.16	242	212	182
Stomach.17	241	211	181
Mane.18	240	210	180
Net.19	239	209	文
Beak.20	238	208	帝
Triad.21	237	207	177
Well.22	236	206	
Well.22	235	高	
Devils.23	234	祖	
Willow.24	233	203	
Seven Stars.25	232	202	
Strung Bow.26	231	201	
Wings.27	230	200	
Baseboard.28	229	199	
Horn.01	228	198	
Neck.02	227	197	
Root.03	226	196	
Chamber.04	225	195	
Heart.05	224	194	
Tail.06	223	呂	
Basket.07	222	后	
Dipper.08	221	191	
Ox.09	220	190	
Maid.10	219	189	
Tumulus.11	218	188	
Rooftop.12	217	187	

States and Qin-Han divination culture.[47] As we now know from numerous manuscript finds, a particular form of hemerology (calendar divination) thrived in this period, largely in the form of occult miscellanies called "daybooks" (*rishu* 日書). Daybook hemerology features a wide variety of schemes, simple and complex, for determining the auspiciousness of various times and directions for performing everyday activities, e.g. sacrifice, marriage, business, travel, construction, and agriculture. The majority of divinatory schemes are based on the correlative relationships of the ten heavenly stems and twelve earthly branches, which are used to count the years, months, days, and hours of civil time as well as directions. The more complex systems involve calendar spirits, stars, and mantic functions moving in simple repetitive patterns through diagrams arranged around the stems and branches, like the "day court" (*riting* 日廷) or "chord-hook diagram" (Figure 2.5).[48]

One famous example of the coalescence of hemerology and planetary astronomy is Taisui 太歲, also known as Taiyin 太陰. Taisui is a terrestrial mantic function that contemporary texts describe as moving left (clockwise) through the earthly branches at the rate of one per year for twelve years in counterpoint to Jupiter, which travels right (counterclockwise) in Heaven, making one circuit through the lodges in the same period. In the past, scholars translated Taisui as "counter-Jupiter," treating it as if it were an invisible planet akin to Philolaus' counter-Earth, however, divinatory texts never linger on the ontological status of these mantic functions, and what little we can glean about Taisui indicates that it is a dragon that operates on earth.[49] The term "counter-Jupiter" is misleading also in the

---

47. The following argument is presented more fully in Mo Zihan, "Cong Zhoujiatai rishu yu Mawangdui *Wuxing zhan* tan rishu yu Qin Han tianwenxue de huxiang yingxiang."

48. On hemerology, see Marc Kalinowski, "Les traités de Shuihudi et l'hémérologie chinoise a la fin des Royaumes-Combattants," *T'oung Pao* 2d ser., 72, no. 4/5 (1986): 175–228; "The *Xingde* Texts from Mawangdui"; John S. Major, *Heaven and Earth in Early Han Thought: Chapters Three, Four and Five of the Huainanzi* (Albany: State University of New York Press, 1993); Liu Lexian, "Shuihudi Qin jian rishu yanjiu" 睡虎地秦簡日書研究 (Ph.D. diss., Zhongguo shehui kexue yuan, 1993); Jianbo shushu wenxian tanlun; Ethan Richard Harkness, "Cosmology and the Quotidian: Day Books in Early China" (Ph.D. diss., University of Chicago, 2011).

49. On the hemerology of Taisui and its terrestrial movements, see Hu Wenhui 胡文輝, "Shi 'Sui'—yi Shuihudi Rishu wei zhongxin" 釋「歲」—以睡虎地『日書』為中心, in *Zhongguo zaoqi fangshu yu wenxian congkao* 中國早期方術與文獻叢考 (Guangzhou: Zhongshan daxue chubanshe, 2000), 88–134; Tao Lei,

131

sense of subordination it infers: in all descriptions, it is Jupiter (the "Year Star") that is the counterpart of Taisui ("Great Year"), such that it is Taisui's annual position determines the sidereal and synodic progress of the planet. The *Wuxing zhan* explains the relationship thus:

歲星與大陰相應也，大陰居維辰一，歲星居維宿星二，大陰居中辰一，歲星居中宿星【三】。□□□□□□□□□□□□□□□□□□ 【歲】星居尾箕，大陰左徙，會於陰陽之界，皆十二歲而周於天地。

The Year Star and Taiyin correspond. When Taiyin occupies a corner ("hook") chronogram (earthly branch), Year Star occupies the two corner lodges, and when Taiyin occupies a center ("chord") chronogram, Year Star occupies the three center lodges.... [Year Star] occupies Tail.$_{06}$ and Basket.$_{07}$. Taiyin shifts left (clockwise) and they meet at the boundaries of *yin* and *yang*, circling Heaven and Earth, respectively, in 12 years (lines 42–43).

The planet Jupiter does not behave so simply, and considerable revisions were necessary over the centuries to maintain a correspondence between the two. One problem is that Jupiter's actual sidereal period of 11.86 years is too short, making it "exceed a chronogram" (*chao chen* 超辰) every 144 years. Another problem is that the Taiyin/Taisui model treats the lodges as counters on a diagram akin to the earthly branches, when in actuality they are uneven zones demarcated by specific asterisms (see Figure 2.5).

The Taiyin model is inconsistent with the other descriptions, but features of the *Wuxing zhan*'s "astronomical" treatment of Jupiter are still reminiscent of Taiyin hemerology. The text provides two lists of the time and place of Jupiter's FMR over a twelve-year period

---

Huainanzi Tianwen *yanjiu*, 73–97. According to the *Huainanzi*, "of all the venerable spirits of Heaven none is more venerable than the Green Dragon, which is also called Heavenly Monad or Taiyin" 天神之貴者，莫貴於青龍，或曰天一，或曰太陰 (*Huainan honglie jijie* 淮南鴻烈集解 [Zhonghua shuju ed.], 3.126). According to Li Ling 李零, the "Bing bi Taisui" 兵避太歲 ("Weapon to Avoid Taisui") *ge* 戈 dagger-ax discovered in 1960 in a Warring States tomb in Jingmen, Hubei, and the Mawangdui "Taiyi bibing tu" 太一避兵圖 both depict Taisui/Taiyin as a (or all three) dragon assistant(s) to the north pole deity Grand Monad (Taiyi 太一) ("'Taiyi' chongbai de kaogu yanjiu" 「太一」崇拜的考古研究, in *Zhongguo fangshu xu kao* 中國方術續考 [Beijing: Zhonghua shuju, 2006], 158–181). On Taisui's later incarnations as a wriggly lump of meat and a fungus, see Song Huiqun 宋會羣, *Zhongguo shushu wenhua shi* 中國術數文化史 (Kaifeng: Henan daxue chubanshe, 1999), 173–176.

Figure 2.5: The twenty-eight lodges: a comparison

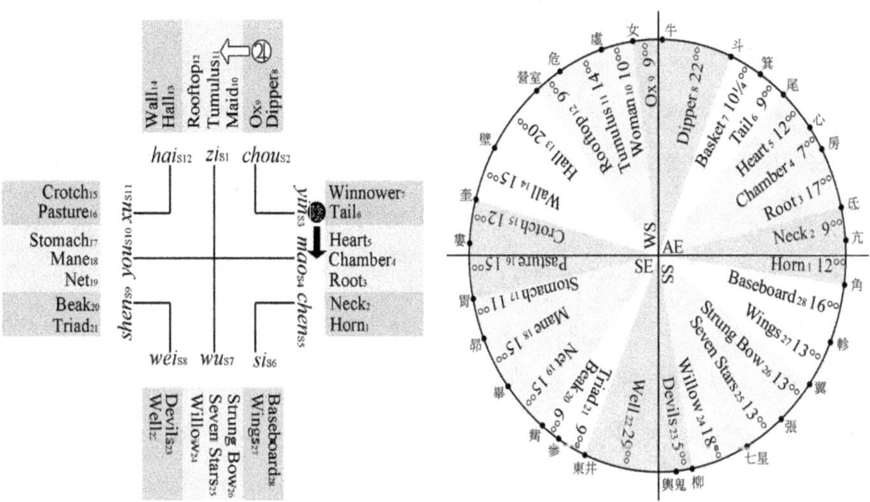

LEFT: Jupiter (white) and Taisui (black) move in opposite directions through two- and three-lodge zones assigned to the twelve earthly branches. RIGHT: the lodge widths according to the "ancient degree" system.

in its description of the Jovian-year count (2.6) and in the planet's visibility table (2.7). These two lists are somewhat at odds, but they bear a striking resemblance to the twelve "ancient degree" solar steps as preserved in the *Lü shi chunqiu* 呂氏春秋 (c. 239 B.C.) and era daybooks (Table 2.9)—i.e. the position of the Sun at twelve equal intervals through the solar year counting, in this case, from the Enthronement of Spring with the Sun five *du* into Hall.13.[50] For the first twelve years it makes sense that the two would overlap since

---

50. The "ancient-degree" solar steps appear in the the 12 *ji* 紀 of the *Lüshi chunqiu* and the daybooks from the late Warring States Chu tomb at Jiudian 九店 M56 (s. 78-80), the Qin tomb at Zhoujiatai 周家臺 M30 (s. 1a-154b) and Shuihudi 睡虎地 M11 (RSA s. 1-13a *recto*, 47-58a *recto*, RSB s. 80-107a); see Hubei sheng wenwu kaogu yanjiusuo 湖北省文物考古研究所 and Beijing daxue zhongwen xi 北京大學中文系, eds., *Jiudian Chu jian* 九店楚簡 (Beijing: Zhonghua shuju, 2000); Hubei sheng Jingzhou shi Zhouliang yuqiao yizhi bowuguan 湖北省荊州市周梁玉橋遺址博物館, ed., *Guanju Qin-Han mu jiandu* 關沮秦漢墓簡牘 (Beijing: Zhonghua shuju, 2001); Shuihudi Qin mu zhujian zhengli xiaozu 睡虎地秦墓竹簡整理小組, ed., *Shuihudi Qin mu zhujian* 睡虎地秦墓竹簡, 2d ed. (Beijing: Wenwu chubanshe, 1990). Wu Jiabi 武家壁 analyzes their discrepancies and archaeoastronomical basis in "Cong chutu wenwu kan Zhanguo shiqi de tianwen lifa chenjiu" 從出土文物看戰國時期的天文曆法成就, in *Gudai wenming* 古代文明, ed. Beijing daxue Zhongguo kaoguxue yanjiu zhongxin 北京大學中國考古學研究中心 and Beijing daxue gudai wenming yanjiu zhongxin 北京大學古代文明研究中心, vol. 2 (Beijing: Wenwu chubanshe, 2003), 265–272. All sources agree that in month VIII (the mid-autumn month) the Sun should be at Horn.01, while Wu shows that it would have been instead at the end of Baseboard.28; Wu argues that the former was chosen over the latter due to

133

the *Wuxing zhan* places the Sun and planet together at first visibility and gives Jupiter's synodic period in terms of solar months: a total of $395\frac{1[6]5}{240}$ days (13 solar months) divided into 365 days (12 solar months) of visibility and 30 days (1 solar month) of invisibility (line 5).[51] However, we would expect the cycle to repeat in the fourteenth year, 13 solar months after a FMR in "month" XII of year 12, not one "month" later at the beginning of the thirteenth year, as the text indicates. From the perspective of astronomy this appears like an amateurish mistake, but as counterintuitive as it is, it is an ingrained feature of the Jovian year-count as it is recorded here and in the *Huainanzi* 淮南子, *Shiji*, *Han shu*, and other early sources.[52] Though the *Wuxing zhan* does not make the relationship explicit, the Jovian year-count is based on the aforementioned idealized relationship between Jupiter and Taiyin, and thus treats the month of FMR like a calendar spirit, which cycles forward one unit per year for twelve years and then repeats, irrespective of how this cuts the last synodic period short by 12 solar months. It is interesting that while this pattern is repeated uncritically in Jupiter's visibility table, the sequence of lodges from the Jovian year list in lines 1–5 is not.

The case of Saturn is more stark. The lodges of its FMR over the course of the 30 years of its sidereal period simply cycle one-by-one through the 28 lodges, repeating twice at Well.$_{22}$ and Hall.$_{13}$. The sequence makes no concession to the unequal lengths of the lodges—except that it spends two years in the first and third largest ones—nor to the fact that there are likewise whole years in which no FMR occurs. The compiler is clearly working off the rule,

---

its premier position among the lodges, and I have modified my table accordingly. Note also that the second ancient-degree solar step begins at the intersection between Wall.$_{14}$ and Crotch.$_{15}$, which might explain the *Wuxing zhan*'s choice of the former.

51. In the omenological section on Jupiter, the planet's synodic period is given as "395 days and 105 parts [of a day]" 凡三百九十五日百五分【日】 (line 5), and in the computational section, as simply "395 days" 三百九十五日 (line 89). I believe that the remainder in the first quote should not be overlooked. The correspondence between the lodges of Jupiter's FMR and the "ancient degree" solar steps hints that the text is counting Jupiter's periodicity in terms of solar months of $365\frac{1}{4} \div 12 = 30\frac{21}{48} = 30\frac{105}{240}$ days, thirteen of which constitute $395\frac{165}{240}$ days. I believe that these numbers are too close to be a coincidence, and that either the copyist omitted the two graphs *liu shi* 六十 "60" or the writer forgot to add the quarter day (60 parts) at the end of the solar year. Furthermore, I surmise that the solar month, with its denominator of 48, might be the origin of the denominator 240 (= 48 × 5) used throughout the text.

52. *Huainan honglie jijie*, 3.117–120; *Shiji*, 27.1313–1316; *Han shu*, 26.1289–1291; *Kaiyuan zhanjing*, 23.4a–10a.

Table 2.9: Comparison of *Wuxing zhan* Jupiter FMR with "ancient degree" solar steps

| | | *Wuxing zhan* FMR | | "Ancient" solar steps | |
year	month	lines 1–5	table	month	lodge
1	I	Hall.13	Hall.13	I	Hall.13
2	II	...	Wall.14	II	Crotch.15
3	III	Stomach.17	Pasture.16	III	Stomach.17
4	IV	Net.19	Net.19	IV	Net.19
5	V	...	Well.22	V	Well.22
6	VI	...	Willow.24	VI	Willow.24
7	VII	Strung Bow.26	Strung Bow.26	VII	Strung Bow.26
8	VIII	Baseboard.28	Baseboard.28	VIII	Baseboard.28
9	IX	...	Neck.02	IX	Root.03
10	X	Heart.05	Heart.05	X	Heart.05
11	XI	Dipper.08	Dipper.08	XI	Dipper.08
12	XII	Tumulus.11	Maid.10	XII	Maid.10
13	I	Hall.13	Hall.13		

like that given in the *Shiji*, that "each year Queller moves one lodge, and the state that it occupies is fortuned" 歲填一宿，其所居國吉.[53]

However, unlike its parallels in the Shiji and other early texts, the *Wuxing zhan* attributes Saturn a sidereal period not of 28—one for each lodge—but 30 years.[54] Scholars have generally taken this as a sign of improved accuracy, since Saturn's actual sidereal period is 29.46 years. This may be, but the motivation may also be to create a simpler set of nested cycles, such that "every 20 years it goes into conjunction with Year Star making a Taiyin era" 廿歲與歲星合爲大陰之紀 (lines 121–122), and every 60 years it coincides again with Jupiter, the sexagenary cycle, Taiyin, and all the calendar spirits. The Jupiter passage also attempts to reconcile these two planets' periods—"every 24 years it goes into conjunction with Great [White] in Hall.13 廿四歲一與大【白】合營室 (lines 89–90)—though all the

---

53. *Shiji*, 27.1319. The omenological section on Saturn in the *Wuxing zhan* is corrupt at the point where we would expect it to describe Saturn's behavior, but Liu Lexian and his predecessors have reconstructed line 51 based on the *Shiji* to read: "Verily is it the star that quells lands: each year [Queller moves one lodge, where the state that it occupies is fortuned and obtains land" 實填州星，歲【填一宿】，【其所居國吉，得地】 (*Mawangdui tianwen shu kaoshi*, 48–49).

54. *Huainan honglie jijie*, 3.90; *Shiji*, 27.1319–1320; *Kaiyuan zhanjing*, 38.2b–5b.

planets' cycles coincide only every two sexagenary cycles (120 years).[55]

2.3.4 Mercury

Mercury, like Mars, appears only in the first half of the *Wuxing zhan*, in a short section
devoted to its omenology. In contrast to the succinct agnosticism shown towards Mars,
however, the text expounds a simple and specific description of Mercury—a planet equally
unpredictable but considerably more difficult to see.

主正四時，春分效【婁】，夏至【效鬼，秋分】效亢，冬至效牽牛… 其出四中
（仲），以正四時，經也；其上出四孟，王者出；其下出四季，大耗敗。凡是星
出廿日而入，經也。□□ 廿日不入 □□。

It rules and rectifies the four seasons: at Spring Equinox.$_{Q04}$ (SE) it appears in
[Pasture.$_{16}$], at Summer Solstice.$_{Q10}$ (SS) [it appears in Devils.$_{23}$, at Autumn
Equinox.$_{16}$ (AE)] it appears in Neck.$_{02}$, and at Winter Solstice.$_{Q22}$ (WS) it appears in Led Ox.$_{09}$… If it rises in the four middle months, it does so to set
straight the four seasons—this is normal—; if it rises up in the four first months,
a [new] true king emerges; if it rises down in the four final months, there is great
depletion and defeat. In general, this star (planet) sets 20 days after rising—this
is normal—while… not setting in twenty days… (lines 54–56).

The medieval omen literature compendium *Kaiyuan zhanjing* preserves numerous variations
on this scheme, which I detail in Section 5.2. Suffice it to say here that it attributes a
description that exactly parallels the *Wuxing zhan*'s to Gan De 甘德, a legendary founding
father of the astral sciences in the Warring States.[56] To his counterpart Shi Shen 石申, on
the other hand, it attributes the following:

---

55. The 20-year "Taiyin era" is the amount of time, given their respective speeds, that it takes Jupiter to
make one circuit through Heaven and go back into conjunction with Saturn. 24 years is the time it takes
Jupiter and Venus to complete two and three cycles, respectively

56. For Gan De's model, see *Kaiyuan zhanjing*, 53.4a. For more variations of this scheme, see Section 5.2.

辰星仲春春分，暮出奎、胃東五舍，為齊；仲夏夏至，暮出東井、輿鬼、柳東七舍，為楚；仲秋秋分，暮出角、亢、氐、房東四舍，為漢中。仲冬冬至，晨出東方，與尾、箕、斗、牛俱出西方為中國。

The Chronogram Star (Mercury): in the mid-spring month on the Spring Equinox.$_{Q04}$, it rises in the evening (FES) in Crotch.$_{15}$, Stomach.$_{17}$, and the five lodges to the east [of the Sun], where it acts upon the State of Qi; in the mid-summer month on the Summer Solstice, it rises in the evening (FES) in Eastern Well.$_{22}$, Cartbourne Devils.$_{23}$, Willow.$_{24}$, and the five lodges to the east [of the Sun], where it acts upon the state of Chu; in the mid-autumn month on Autumn Equinox.$_{Q10}$, it rises in the evening (FES) in the four lodges Horn.$_{01}$, Neck.$_{02}$, Root.$_{03}$, and Chamber.$_{04}$ to the east [of the Sun], where it acts upon the Han Valley; in the mid-winter month on Winter Solstice.$_{Q22}$, it rises from the east in the morning (FMR), emerging with Tail.$_{06}$, Basket.$_{07}$, Dipper.$_{08}$, and Ox.$_{09}$ to the west [of the Sun], where it acts upon the central states.[57]

In considering these two descriptions—indeed, whether even to read them against one another—we encounter a number of difficulties. To help visualize the issues involved I have provided a diagram of Mercury's visibility phenomena in 203 B.C.—a year that best illustrates what I understand these sources to describe—calculated by *Planetary, Lunar, and Stellar Visibility* v3.1 (PLSV) (Figure 2.6).[58]

One difficulty is vocabulary. Like the Gan De attribution, the *Wuxing zhan* describes Mercury's behavior with the verb *xiao* 效 ("to render service" or "to appear") as distinct

---

57. Ibid.

58. Such diagrams can only approximate what may have been observed at that time and place. The precise moment that a planet becomes or ceases to be visible from a particular point on the Earth is determined by several factors that are beyond our ability to retrodict, e.g. weather, atmospheric conditions at the horizon, and the acuity of the observer's eyesight. Furthermore, seeing and reporting a planet's visibility can be rather subjective enterprises with any number of personal and social factors at play. For these and other caveats about the uncritical use of software to solve these sorts of problems in the history of astronomy, see Cullen, "Understanding the Planets in Ancient China," 234–235. That said, I find such diagrams helpful here for the purpose of illustration and highlighting *impossibilities*.

from *chu* 出 ("to emerge"), the latter of which it consistently uses to denotes first visibility. In other contexts the two seem to be interchangeable, but we should attend to the possibility that this distinction in word choice might just as well reflect a distinction in meaning, e.g. that *xiao* might refer not to *first* visibility but *any* visibility.[59] Whatever it is that is happening—be it *xiao* or *chu*—it happens quarterly on the solstices and equinoxes or, as the *Wuxing zhan* also states, in the "four mid-season months" (*si zhong* 四仲), i.e. the months that contain them.

Another difficulty is time frame. First of all, Mercury does not experience first visibility only four times a year. Mercury's mean synodic period is 115.88 days (cf. 115.91 days in the Triple Concordance system [#8]). Thus, the planet goes through three full synodic periods in just under the span of one year. To be precise, three mean periods fall 17½ days short of a solar year, 6 days short of a 12-month civil year, and 36 days short of an intercalary civil year. Given that the synodic period of an inferior planet cycles between periods of morning and evening visibility, we might expect six or seven first visibilities each year. In reality, there are fewer than this because the eccentricity of Mercury's orbit sometimes prevents it from moving far enough from the Sun to be visible (e.g. months VI-VIII in 203 B.C.).[60]

A broader interpretation would be that these schemes posit that four of the planet's six or seven potential first visibilities occur on the days of, or the months containing, the solstices and equinoxes. This does not work either for two reasons. The first is that the the planet's potential first visibilities are staggered between uneven periods of invisibility around superior/inferior conjunction in a pattern (e.g. the Triple Concordance system [#8] gives 28/37.9/26/24 days of visibility to invisibility, respectively) incompatible with solstitial/equinoctial points (the long horizontal white lines) or any feasible scheme of lunar

---

59. Note that different versions of this seasonal scheme for Mercury seem to freely interchange *chu, xiao* (alternatively *xiao* 効 or *jiao* 効), and *xian* 見 "appear;" see p. 167.

60. For a detailed description of this problem and how Zhang Zixin 張子信 first addressed it in China, see Jiang Xiaoyuan and Niu Weixing 鈕衛星, "Zhang Zixin zhi Shuixing 'ying xian bu xian' shu jiqi keneng laiyuan" 張子信之水星「應見不見」術及其可能來源, in *Ouzhou tianwenxue dongjian fawei* 歐洲天文學東漸發微 (Shanghai: Shanghai shudian chubanshe, 2009), 223–239.

Figure 2.6: Rise times and visibility phenomena for Mercury (203 B.C.)

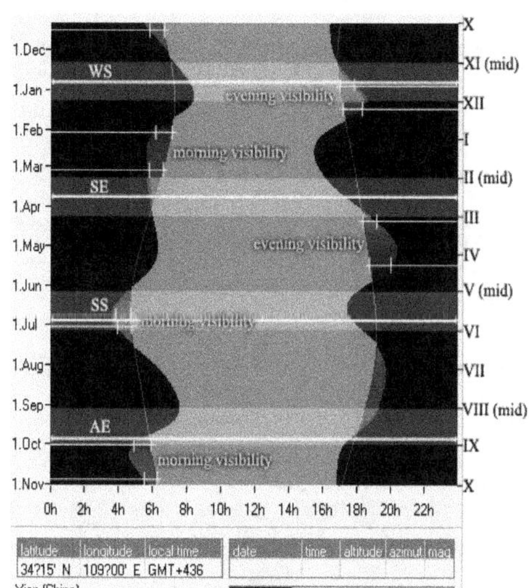

NOTE: Image modified from PLSV. The Y-axis indicates date, the Roman numerals on the left-hand side indicating the months of the lunisolar civil calendar, and "mid" indicating mid-season months. The X-axis indicates time of day. The two gray lines running vertically through the diagram indicate the hour of sunrise and sunset as it changes throughout the year. The wobbly area at the center of the diagram represents the time that the planet is above the horizon—the light gray area being time that it is above the horizon with the sun, and thus invisible, and the dark gray area beyond the vertical lines being the time that it is above the horizon in the absence of the sun, and thus potentially visible. The short horizontal lines running from the edges of the diagram to the vertical lines of sunset/sunrise indicate the dates of first and last visibilities, as calculated by PLSV. The long, white horizontal lines indicate the solstices and equinoxes (WS, SE, SS, & AE). The lighter horizontal bars indicate the span of the mid-season months. For example, this diagram tells us that in 203 B.C. FES and FMR might have almost coincided with Winter Solstice.$_{Q22}$ and Autumn Equinox.$_{Q16}$, respectively, and that the planet was likely visible in the mid-winter and mid-summer months and near the tail end of the mid-autumn month, but not in mid-spring.

months containing them (the white bars). The second is that any conceivable coincidence would be ephemeral due to the discrepancy between the planet's synodic period and the solar year, which causes any pattern of visibility phenomena to slide around through the seasons. The variability of a lunisolar civil year, of course, only exacerbates things further. The broadest possible interpretation is that these schemes posit that Mercury experiences *any* visibility (*xiao*) at *any* point within each mid-season month. This *can* happen on occasion—203 B.C. is about as close as we normally get before sliding back through the seasons—but this interpretation fails to capture anything of the planet's regularity and looks unlike anything we might call a planetary model.

Yet another difficulty is the choice of lodges. At solstice and equinox, Shi Shen's scheme places visibility phenomena somewhere along an array of four to seven lodges beginning from the setting/rising Sun and spreading in the direction opposite (east/west) the horizon. This would be sufficiently broad to work were Mercury to rise like clockwork in the mid-season months (which, again, it does not). So, while his choice of lodges may well have some basis in observation, one suspects that they were the product of extrapolation, e.g. from a diagram. The *Wuxing zhan* and Gan De's scheme, on the other hand, is much more specific. They place visibility phenomena in the four lodges to the immediate east of the Sun at the solstitial and equinoctial points in the "ancient degree" system (see Figure 2.5). Their choice of lodges east of the sun implies four periods of *evening* visibility, which in turn implies four full synodic periods per year (which, again, cannot be). Shi Shen's scheme, on the other hand, implies an alternation between evening and morning visibilities more befitting the planet's behavior (see Figure 2.6).

Given Mercury's eccentricity and proximity to the sun, we might not expect the same level of coherence from early descriptions of its behavior as we do of, for example, Venus. However, unlike the case of Venus, it is extremely difficult to understand these descriptions from the perspective of modern or even first-century A.D. astronomy.[61] Again, I would like

---

61. For an attempt, see Teboul, *Les premières théories planétaires chinoises*, 134–137, 143–145.

to argue that there are principles other than empiricism at play here—principles deriving from hemerology. One is schematic symmetry: irrespective of lodge-widths, the *Wuxing zhan* allots visibility phenomena to lodges neatly to the east of each solstitial/equinoctial point, i.e. the second lodge of each of the Four Palaces (*sigong* 四宮).[62] Another principle is calendrical harmony: a one-season synodic period folds Mercury neatly into the 60-year cycle of Jupiter, Saturn, and Taisui. Yet another principle is hemerological symbolism: in counterpart to Taisui (the ruler of the year) and Saturn (the ruler of the lodges), who travel sequentially through their domains, Mercury "rules and rectifies the four seasons" 主正四時 (line 54) by hopping between solstices and equinoxes. In this light, it is the planet's *a posteriori* synodic period that requires explanation and accommodation.

2.4 The Nature of the Text and its Place in the History of Astronomy

The planetary knowledge contained in the *Wuxing zhan* is heterogeneous, ranging within a spectrum between idealized hemerological schemes to purely mathematical models. At one end of this spectrum is Mercury. The *Wuxing zhan* attributes to Mercury a one-year cycle at odds with its actual periodicity, in which it plays the role of calendar spirit, appearing at the solstices and equinoxes in corresponding quadrants of the sky—the sky, that is, as represented in the idealized space of a hemerological diagram. The text provides similar schemes for Jupiter and Saturn *in conjunction with* mathematical models incompatible with their hemerological duties. At the other end of the spectrum is Venus. Though Venus' omenology accounts for one quarter of the text, the *Wuxing zhan*'s description of the planet's behavior is consistently quantitative and mathematically sophisticated.

Because of its incongruity, it is difficult to compare the *Wuxing zhan* to the Triple Con-

---

62. The Four Palaces—East, West, South, North—also known as the Four Emblems (*si xiang* 四象)—Green Dragon, White Tiger, Vermilion Sparrow, and Dark Warrior (a turtle and a snake)—are the seasonal divisions of the night sky—spring, autumn, summer, winter—each of which is comprised of seven lodges.

Figure 2.7: *Wuxing zhan* planetary hemerology (year 1 of 60)

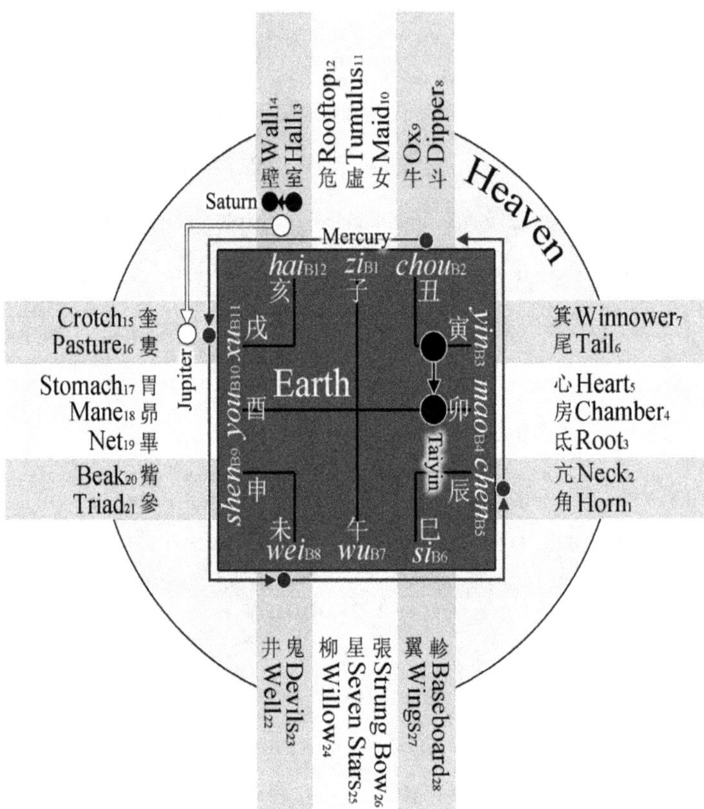

cordance system (#8). In terms of coherence and the ability to accurately model celestial phenomena, hemerological schemes are incommensurable with motion-degree models. The motion-degree models that the *Wuxing zhan* does provide are comparatively crude: they count synodic and sidereal periods in simple numbers of years and solar months and confuse the relationship between the two; they do not account for station or retrogradation; and they have the planets appear and disappear at no distance from the Sun.[63] Lastly, while

---

63. Not only do the hemerological models and the visibility tables confuse the relationship between synodic and sidereal periods by restarting the former period at the end of the latter, the periods given do not evidence the knowledge of the proportional relationship between them. In modern terms, the planet's sidereal period P, synodic period S, and the Earth's sidereal period E have the relationship:

$$\text{inferior planets: } \frac{1}{P} = \frac{1}{E} + \frac{1}{S} \qquad \text{superior planets: } \frac{1}{P} = \frac{1}{E} - \frac{1}{S}$$

both are anchored to problematic SYSTEM ORIGINs determined for ideological reasons, the *Wuxing zhan*'s introduces dramatically larger systematic errors for its period of operation.

What can we speculate about their relationship? One possibility, as has been advanced in the past, is that the *Wuxing zhan* is ancestral to the Triple Concordance system (#8). This might explain the seemingly inchoate nature of its mathematical models as well as the way that incompatible schemes from hemerology surround and bleed into them—that these reflect formative attempts to integrate astronomical observation with *li* theory, before the "numbers and methods" (*shushu* 數術) of the two had fully parted ways. Positing such a developmental relationship is fraught with danger—the danger, for example, that we imply a ladder of progress connecting hemerological "magic" with astronomical "science," or what is defective in 168 B.C. to what is coherent two centuries later. That said, let us not dismiss the possibility out of hand in this case.

Hemerology and mathematical astronomy are, or came to be, distinct bodies of knowledge with different goals, methods, and social contexts that have coexisted until modern times. It is true that numerous intellectuals over the course of history expressed disdain over hemerology and the integrity of diviners, but no one before the twentieth century would have thought to categorically juxtapose it with mathematical astronomy.[64] "Science," "magic,"

The Chinese took the sidereal periods of the inferior planets to be 1 year (see p. 112). However, beginning with the Triple Concordance system (#8), the knowledge of their proportional relationship in the superior planets is evident in the way that astronomers derived their synodic arcs $\Delta\alpha$—the angular distance traveled in one synodic period—from the length of the year (also the circumference of Heaven) E and the synodic period expressed in terms of appearances A : years Y:

$$\Delta\alpha = \frac{Y - A}{A} \times E$$

In the case of the *Wuxing zhan*, the superior planets' angular velocities are averaged from their crude sidereal periods and are incompatible with their synodic periods. For example, Saturn is given an angular velocity of $\frac{8}{240}$ *du* per day, which over its 377-day synodic period results in a synodic arc of $12\frac{136}{240}$ *du*; however, using its synodic period and the text's 365¼-day year, we derive from the above formula a synodic arc of 11.75 *du*.

64. Wang Chong's critiques of hemerological practices in his *Lunheng* 論衡 are particularly famous; see Kalinowski's translation of its chapters on fate and divination in *Balance des discours: destin, providence et divination*, Bibliothèque Chinoise 5 (Paris: Les belles lettres, 2011), 3216–3217, 3289. For concerns about the integrity of popular diviners, see for example *Shiji*, 127.3216–3217, 130.3289; *Yanshi jiaxun* 顏氏家訓 (Siku quanshu ed.), B.43a–44b. Joseph Needham gathers together sources exemplifying what he frames as a skeptical tradition opposed to the "pseudo-sciences" in *Science and Civilisation in China, Vol.2: History of Scientific Thought* (Cambridge: Cambridge University Press, 1956), 365–395.

and the antagonism between them are late European concepts. In the absence of perceived tension between the two, therefore, it makes sense that the regular motions of the spiritual entities of the calendar may well have informed calendricists' first attempts to quantify the regular motions of the spiritual entities that they perceived the planets to be.

The astronomical contents of the *Wuxing zhan* are, furthermore, *earlier* than Liu Xin's Triple Concordance system (A.D. 5/9) by at least 210 years. It is also safe to say that the *Wuxing zhan* is representative of planetary knowledge in this period since it features abundant parallels with models in the *Huainanzi*, *Shiji*, and quotations attributed to the purported Warring States founders of planetary astronomy, Shi Shen and Gan De.[65] Considering the similarity of approach and style in their motion-degree models, we might surmise that Liu Xin improves upon, or perhaps revolutionizes, a centuries-old tradition.[66]

Another possibility is that the *Wuxing zhan* and the Triple Concordance system (#8) represent different genres of knowledge. Cullen argues that the *Wuxing zhan*'s planetary models must be read in the context of its omenology. These models, while not wholly ungrounded in observation, are numerically simple ideals, which function somewhat like Babylonian "goal-year texts" in establishing parameters by which to judge whether a planet's motion is normal or ominous.

It would be a mistake to see the constructors of these simple predictive schemes as having done their work in the consciousness that they had only succeeded to a

---

65. For a study of the parallels between the planetary models of the *Wuxing zhan, Huainanzi, Shiji*, and quotations attributed to the Pre-Qin figures Shi Shen, Gan De, and Wuxian 巫咸, see Teboul, *Les premières théories planétaires chinoises*, 110–170; Takeda, "Taihaku kōdo kō." Pseudepigraphy is rampant in the *tianwen* 天文 celestial omen genre and there are clear indications that quotations attributed to them in works like the *Han shu* and *Kaiyuan zhanjing* were added to or written by later people, especially in the case of Wuxian, supposedly a minister of the Shang (?–1045 B.C.) whose work appears only after the Han. Thus far, scholarship has focused primarily on the date of their star catalogs. For a recent study dealing with the date and history of the texts attributed to them, see Sun Xiaochun 孫小淳 and Jacob Kistemaker, *The Chinese Sky During the Han: Constellating Stars and Society* (Leiden: Brill, 1997), esp. 25–27, 37–39, 75–88.

66. As for direct evidence of Liu Xin's knowledge of Qin planetary astronomy in specific, the *Han shu* "Yiwen zhi" 藝文志 bibliography of the imperial library, which Liu Xiang and his father helped organize, records a *Zhuanxu li* 顓項曆 (Zhuanxu astronomical system) in 21 *juan* 卷 and a *Zhuanxu wuxing li* 顓項 五星曆 (Zhuanxu Five-Star astronomical system) in 14 *juan* (*Han shu*, 30.1765). Liu Xiang's description of the Zhuanxu SYSTEM ORIGIN in *Hongfan zhuan* also matches the text of the *Wuxing zhan* (see p. 119).

moderate degree in representing planetary motions as they actually are. We need to recall what David Brown has written in the context of ancient Mesopotamian astronomy: one of the advantages of schematic depictions of celestial motions is that they automatically generate portents through their divergence from what is actually observed. A celestial diviner who had constructed something like the Venus table in the *Wu xing zhan* may well have felt a double satisfaction: [on] the one hand he had uncovered the ideal reality of what Venus *ought* to do, but on the other hand he also had the ability to interpret for his clients what it meant when Venus did not act as it should have done. Regard (and reward) for his professional competence was thus assured on two fronts.[67]

The majority of planetary omens in the first half of the *Wuxing zhan* involve observed phenomena like a planet's color or emanation of "beards" (*mang* 芒), "horns" (*jiao* 角) or comets, its position in the sky, and its interactions with lodges and other moving bodies. However, a number of omens concern planets "missing the mark" (*shi* 失), as we see in the case of Mercury:

北方水，其帝端玉（顓項），其丞玄冥，【其】神上為晨（辰）星。

The north is the agent water; its thearch is Zhuanxu, its minister is Xuanming, and [its] spirit above is the Morning Star (Mercury).

主正四時，春分效【婁】，夏至【效鬼，秋分】效亢，冬至效牽牛。

It is master and rectifier of the four seasons: at Spring Equinox.$_{Q04}$ it appears in [Pasture.$_{16}$], at Summer Solstice.$_{Q10}$ [it appears in Devils.$_{23}$, at Autumn Equinox.$_{Q16}$] it appears in Neck.$_{02}$, and at Winter Solstice.$_{Q22}$ it appears in Led Ox.$_{09}$.

一時不出，其時不利；四時不出，天下大飢。

---

67. Cullen, "Understanding the Planets in Ancient China," 248–249." For David Brown's research on the Babylon celestial omen tradition, see his *Mesopotamian Planetary Astronomy-astrology* (Groningen: Styx, 2000).

If it does not rise in one season, that season is disadvantageous; if it does not rise in four seasons, there is a world-wide famine.

其出蚤（早）於時為月蝕，其出免（晚）於時為天夭【及彗】星。

If it rises earlier than its proper season, it occasions lunar eclipses; while if it rises later, it occasions demonic celestial portents and comets.

其出不當其效，其時當旱反雨，當雨反旱，【當溫反寒】,【當】寒反溫。

If it rises when it is not supposed to appear, that season experiences rain when there should be drought and drought when there should be rain, warmth when it should be cold and cold when it should be warm.

其出房、心之間，地盼動。

If it rises between Chamber.$_{04}$ and Heart.$_{05}$, there is an earthquake.

其出四中（仲），以正四時，經也；其上出四孟，王者出；其下出四季，大耗敗。凡是星出廿日而入，經也。□□ 廿日不入 □□。

If it rises in the four mid-season months, it does so to set straight the four seasons—this is normal—; if it rises up in the four first months of the seasons, a [new] true king emerges; if it rises down in the four last months of the seasons, there is great depletion and defeat. In general, this star (planet) sets 20 days after rising—this is normal—while... not setting in twenty days... (lines 54–56).

The text's Mercury model makes better sense in this context. It is not a motion-degree model but a simple rule of thumb for divination grounded in the mysterious workings of the calendar and open to creative elaboration. It is not a problem that *the planet* Mercury does not behave this way; to the contrary, it is in "missing the mark" that it is made to speak in endlessly shifting configurations of meaning.

Cullen's article focuses only on the *Wuxing zhan*, but I believe that we can extend his conclusion to its close parallels in other period texts and identify distinct genres of planetary models. Contemporary actors themselves maintained a distinction between two bodies of knowledge in the astral sciences: *tianwen* 天文 ("Heavenly patterns/writing") and *li* 曆 ("calendro-astronomy"). *Tianwen* texts consist of what we might classify as observational astronomy, uranography and uranomancy, while *li* texts concern the mathematical modeling of celestial phenomena for the purpose of prediction and the standardization of civil time (see Chapter 1). It just so happens that seasonal schemes for Mercury like those of Shi Shen and the *Wuxing zhan* are invariably embedded in omenology and often occur in texts with the words "*tianwen*" or "prognostication" (*zhan* 占) in their titles—texts, furthermore, that are consistently categorized as *tianwen* in bibliographies and contemporary descriptions.[68] Thus, the *Wuxing zhan* and Triple Concordance system (#8) might simply represent incommensurate approaches to the planets, each with its own function and rationale.

This solution leaves two important questions unanswered. First, at what point, if any, do such normative *a priori* models become so distant from reality and contemporary knowledge about calendro-astronomy that people begin to alter or abandon them? In other words, when and why do people begin to suspect that it is not the planet but *the model* that is "missing the mark"? Second, the text's planetary hemerology clearly belongs to a different genre of knowledge than the Triple Concordance system (#8), but how do we account for the incongruity of the *Wuxing zhan* itself?

2.5 Developments in the Astral Sciences

To gauge how actors modified *li* and *tianwen* planetary knowledge—in response to both reality and one another—it behooves us to compare how these fields developed over time. It is not unreasonable to expect that real observed astronomical phenomena would have played

---

68. This is the case, for example, for the models found in the "Tianwen xun" chapter of the *Huainanzi*, the "Tianguan shu" 天官書 chapter of the *Shiji* (as opposed to the following chapter, "Li shu" 曆書), and the "Tianwen zhi" 天文志 chapters of subsequent dynastic histories. The sources of Shi Shen, Gan De, and Wuxian quotations is unclear, but these figures are attributed with the following works: Shi Shen, *Tianwen*; Gan De, *Tianwen* and *Tianwen xing zhan* 天文星占 ("Heavenly Pattern Star Divination"); Wuxian, *Wuxian Wuxing zhan* 巫咸五星占 ("Wuxian's Five-Star [planet] Divination"). See *Shiji*, 27.1343; *Sui shu*, 19.541, 34.1018. For more examples, see Table 2.10.

a role in the history of *tianwen* and *li, since both were practices grounded in observation.*[69] At the same time, the astral sciences employed observation to such different ends that it seems inevitable that they would have developed along divergent trajectories. One might say that *li* looks to expose the underlying regularity of phenomena. Extolling empiricism, its proponents claim to better capture that regularity with the expedients of ever-new numbers and methods. On the other hand, *tianwen* omenology is often the study of aberration. Confident in the knowledge of how celestial bodies *should* act, the diviner interprets anomalies as signs of Heaven's will and man's moral influence upon it.[70] As antithetical as these approaches seem, when we examine the changes that occurred in *tianwen* and *li* planetary knowledge over the course of the early imperial period, we find that the relationship between them—and between reality and practice—is much more complex than that suggested by such characterizations.

2.5.1   Why it is relevant to discuss "progress"

Beyond the *Wuxing zhan*, everything we know about the mathematical astronomy of the early imperial period we know from the eponymous treatises of the dynastic histories. Of course, these sources have their own perspective on things: they record the history of *li* only as it intersects the people and practices of the upper echelons of government; they abridge the contents of practice to manuals for low-end users; and they obscure the processes by which knowledge was produced and disseminated. The picture of practice that the dynastic histories present in petitions, debates, and biographies is often brief, formulaic, and, one suspects, normative. That said, they furnish us with a record of the history of astronomy

---

69. For a statement of my Realist commitments and belief in the utility of modern astronomical knowledge of simple observables like the existence and periodicities of large celestial objects, see Section 1.4

70. I say "often" because there are other equally important areas of Chinese celestial omen literature devoted to the interpretation of regular phenomena, e.g. the "field allocation" (*fen ye* 分野) system, which identifies correspondences between asterisms or artificial celestial demarcations and geographical territories, upon which the Sun, Moon, planets, and other bodies exert their influences as they move about in a regular fashion. See David W. Pankenier, "Applied Field-allocation Astrology in Zhou China: Duke Wen of Jin and the Battle of Chengpu (632 B.C.)," *Journal of the American Oriental Society* 119, no. 2 (1999): 261–279. Furthermore, as I will discuss below, omen literature and omen reports concentrate more and more on regular phenomena of the Sun, Moon, and planets as time goes on.

that is more abundant and contiguous than that offered by any other pre-modern civilization. Furthermore, however normative we might suspect these accounts to be, they do at least give us a clear sense of actors' values. In matters of astronomy, the one value that actors reliably exalt above all others is that of accuracy—"accordance," "proximity," "tightness," "fineness," etc.—as verified through third-party testing. This, contemporary actors believed, was how the Sages had gone about it; it was also something that they believed themselves in a better position to realize than like-minded men of previous generations.[71]

My contention is that planetary calendro-astronomy experienced "progress" over this period. How are we moderns to measure this progress? As a community, we now consider it immodest to narrate "scientific progress" as being towards our own textbook-knowledge; even so, there has yet to emerge a viable alternative to the sort of sweeping progressive histories offered by Joesph Needham, Yabuuti Kiyosi 藪內清, Chen Zungui 陳遵媯, Chen Meidong 陳美東, and Zhang Peiyu 張培瑜.[72] One hurdle is the fact that, in the broadest possible terms, *li* knowledge *does* look and function more like modern astronomical knowledge over time. The fact that it also looks and functions more and more like the knowledge of other pre-modern civilizations, furthermore, is probably a good indication of the independent reality of celestial objects and the reliability of humanity's experiential access to them.[73]

---

71. The claims of this this paragraph are substantiated in Chapters 1 & 4.

72. Joseph Needham, *Science and Civilisation in China, Vol.3: Mathematics and the Sciences of the Heavens and the Earth* (Cambridge: Cambridge University Press, 1959); Yabuuti Kiyosi, *Chūgoku no temmon rekihō* 中國の天文曆法 (Tōkyō: Heibonsha, 1969); Chen Zungui, *Zhongguo tianwenxue shi* 中國天文學史, 2d ed. (Shanghai: Shanghai renmin chubanshe, 2006); Chen Meidong, *Zhongguo kexue jishu shi: tianwenxue juan*; Zhang Peiyu et al., *Zhongguo gudai lifa*. For an extended critical appraisal of twentieth-century modes of historiography of science, see Joseph Agassi, *Science and Its History* (Dordrecht: Springer, 2008). For a careful recent assessment of the accuracy of the Chinese tradition of li from the perspective of modern astronomical knowledge, see John M. Steele, *Observations and Predictions of Eclipse Times by Early Astronomers*, Archimedes: New Studies in the History and Philosophy of Science and Technology (Dordrecht: Kluwer Academic Publishers, 2000), 161–216.

73. For example, compare the Venus model in the fourth-century B.C. Cuneiform tablet B.M. 33552 with the motion-degree models presented here and post-sixth century A.D. algorithms for seasonal variations in visibility phenomena; see J. P. Britton and C. B. F. Walker, "A 4th Century Babylonian Model for Venus: B.M. 33552," *Centaurus* 34 (1991): 97–118; Liu Hongtao 劉洪濤, *Gudai lifa jisuanfa* 古代曆法計算法 (Tianjin: Nankai daxue chubanshe, 2003), esp. 414–429. Striking parallels between astronomical traditions inspired previous generations of scholars to speculate about the possibility of a Eurasian transmission—be it in one direction or the other. However, because the only evidence of transmission is both late and limited

However, let us set aside all that is simply self-evident to the modern and consider instead *emic* measures of progress. What were early imperial actors trying to achieve? The arithmetic planetary models of *li* literature were designed to predict two things: the dates and positions (RA/longitude) of visibility phenomena and position/disposition of a planet at any point in between. Were sixth-century A.D. experts able to produce quantitatively "tighter" results with their predictions than their second-century B.C. counterparts? Absolutely: the *Wuxing zhan* Jupiter table produces an average error in daily position at midnight of 33.3° RA over the 70-year period of its tables; by contrast, in the first six years of its implementation the Quarter-remainder system (#9) of A.D. 85/86 produces an average error of 6.7° RA (Figure 2.8). It was quantitative measures of error such as these that preoccupied experts in their centuries-long quest to outdo one another.

One of the clearest examples of the progress of planetary astronomy over this period—and actors' perception of that progress—is an exchange between Xindu Fang 信都芳 and Li Yexing 李業興 recorded in the *Wei shu* 魏書. In A.D. 523, Li Yexing authored the Orthodox Glory *Renzi*.$_{49}$-origin system (#33) for the Northern Wei (A.D. 386–535) court, which in the following decade would be rent apart in an east-west schism. Upon his ascension to the throne, the founding emperor of the Eastern Wei (A.D. 534–550) solicited Li to create another new system to mark his receipt of Heaven's mandate. In A.D. 539, Li and his team submitted the Ascendant Harmony *Jiazi*.$_{01}$-origin system (#36) to the throne, but it met with resistance:

芳關通曆術，駁業興曰：「今年十二月二十日，新曆歲星在營室十三度，順，疾；天上歲星在營室十一度。今月二十日，新曆鎮星在角十一度，留；天上鎮

---

in scope, the question has made little headway since the eighteenth century. For a collection of recent and substantial studies on early transmissions, see Jiang Xiaoyuan and Niu Weixing, *Ouzhou tianwenxue dongjian fawei* 歐洲天文學東漸發微 (Shanghai: Shanghai shudian chubanshe, 2009). It is my contention that if we can agree on the independent origins of, for example, the Mesopotamian and Chinese traditions, we might instead take the parallels between them to be an exemplar cases of perspectival realism—that there is a reality and that it is accessible to humans, if only in piecemeal form through limited and idiosyncratic perspectives. On perspectival realism, see Ronald N. Giere, *Scientific Perspectivism* (Chicago: University of Chicago Press, 2006).

Figure 2.8: Jupiter predictions: a comparison

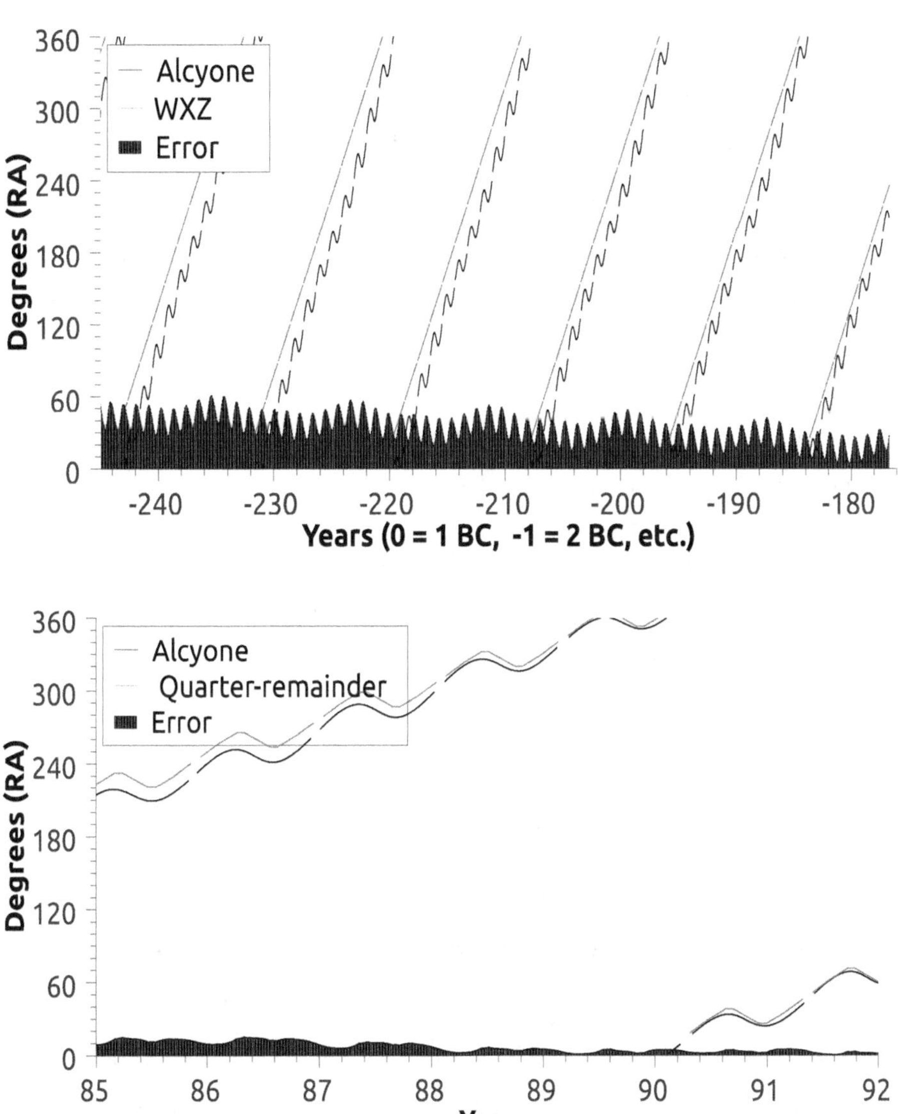

NOTE: these graphs compare the daily position of Jupiter at midnight as retrodicted by the *Wuxing zhan* table (above) and Quarter-remainder system (below) against *Alcyone Ephemeris* v3.2. The *Wuxing zhan* table is treated as a solar calendar beginning on 246 B.C. February 3. Breaks represent periods of invisibility. RA is calculated from one guide-star specific to ancient- and modern-degree systems, respectively: Hall.$_{13}$ $0^{\circ\circ} = \eta$ Peg (*Wuxing zhan*); Ox.$_{09}$ $0^{\circ\circ} = \beta$ Cap (Quarter-remainder).

星在亢四度，留。今月二十日，新曆太白在斗二十五度，晨見，逆行；天上太
白在斗二十一度，逆行。便為差殊。」

[Xindu] Fang was an expert in *li* techniques and denounced Yexing thusly: "On
XII-20 of this year (A.D. 540 Jan 15), the new system has Jupiter in prograde-
slow at Hall.$_{13}$ 13°°; up in Heaven it was at Hall.$_{13}$ 11°°. On the 20th, the new
system has Saturn in station at Horn.$_{01}$ 11°°; up in Heaven it was in station at
Neck.$_{02}$ 4°°. On the 20th, the new system has Venus make its first morning rising,
traveling in retrograde at Dipper.$_{08}$ 25°°; up in Heaven, it was in retrograde at
Dipper.$_{08}$ 21°°. These are egregious errors."[74]

Li's response to these charges is prolix, but it bears repeating for what it reveals about how
planetary astronomy had changed:

歲星行天，伺候以來八九餘年，恒不及二度。今新曆加二度。至於夕伏晨見，
纖毫無爽。今日仰看，如覺二度，及其出沒，還應如術。鎮星，自造壬子元以
來，歲常不及，故加壬子七度，亦知猶不及五度，適欲并加，恐出沒頓校十度、
十日，將來永用，不合處多。太白之行，頓疾頓遲，取其會歸而已。近十二月
二十日，晨見東方，新舊二曆推之，分寸不異。行星三日，頓校四度。如此之
事，無年不有，至其伏見，還依術法。

Observation over the last eight or nine-odd years has revealed that the [pre-
dicted] celestial motions of Jupiter have experienced a constant lag of 2°°. The
new *li* system has added [a] 2°°[-compensation]. As to evening hidings (LES)
and morning appearances (FMR), [however,] there is not a hair's breadth of
a discrepancy. You might perceive [a] 2°°[-error] if you took a look up today,
but first and last visibilities should still be in accordance with the technique.
[The predicted position of] Saturn has normally been behind every year since
the creation of the *Renzi*.$_{49}$-origin [system] (#33), which is why we have added

---

74. *Wei shu* 魏書, 107B.2697.

[a] 7°°[-compensation] to the *Renzi*.[49]; we do know that it still falls 5°° behind, [however,] which is why we wanted to add another, but we were afraid that its first and last visibilities might suddenly reveal [an error of] 10 days and 10°°. [So for Saturn,] if [our system] is used in perpetuity there will be many places where it does not accord. The motion of Venus is suddenly fast and suddenly slow, so it is important only to take up [into consideration] its returns. As to its [FMR] last XII-20, the predictions of the new and old *li* systems both agree down to the fraction of the inch. After three days' travel through the stars, [however,] it was suddenly off by 4°°. This sort of thing happens every single year, but [what is important is that] its first and last visibilities were still according to the technique-method!

又芳唯嫌十二月二十日星有前却。業興推步已來，三十餘載，上算千載之日月星辰有見經史者，與涼州趙㪤、劉義隆廷尉卿何承天、劉駿南徐州從事史祖沖之參校，業 2698 興甲子元曆長於三曆一倍。考洛京已來四十餘歲，五星出沒，歲星、鎮星、太白，業興曆首尾恒中，及有差處，不過一日二日、一度兩度；三曆之失，動校十日十度。熒惑一星，伏見體自無常，或不應度。祖沖之曆多甲子曆十日六度，何承天曆不及三十日二十九度；今曆還與壬子同，不有加增。辰星一星，沒多見少，及其見時，與曆無舛，今此亦依壬子元不改...

What is more, Fang's only aversion is to the stars' (planets') displacement on XII-20. In the 30 years that Yexing has been calculating, Yexing has checked Zhao Fei of Liangzhou, Liu Yilong's (Song Wudi; r. A.D. 424–453) Chief Minister of Justice, He Chengtian (c. A.D. 370–447), and Liu Jun's (Song Xiaowudi; r. A.D. 454-464) Attendant Clerk of Southern Xuzhou, Zu Chongzhi (A.D. 429-501) against one another in their ability to retrodict the thousand years' solar, lunar, and stellar(/planetary) [phenomena] appearing in the classics and histories. Yexing's *Jiazi*.[01]-origin system (#36) runs longer than the other three by a factor of two. After investigating the first and last visibilities of the Five Stars (planets) in Luoyang over the last forty-odd years, it has been found that Yexing's system is, from head to tail, consistently on the mark for **Jupiter**, **Saturn**, and **Venus**, and where there are discrepancies they do not exceed 1 or 2 days or *du*, whereas the other three systems miss the mark by 10 days and 10°°. The star (planet) **Mars** does sometimes fail to accord with its [predicted] *du* since the essence of its appearance/disappearance is inherently inconstant. Zu Chongzhi's [Great Enlightenment] system (#32) was 10 days and 6°° in excess of the *Jiazi*$_{01}$-origin system (#36); He Chengtian's [Epochal Excellence] system (#22) fell 30 days and 29°° short; and our current system was the same as the *Renzi*$_{49}$ here, without addition or subtraction either way. The star (planet) **Mercury** is invisible longer than it is visible, but when it does appear, it does not disagree with [Yexing's] *li*—this too is unchanged from the *Renzi*$_{49}$-origin system (#33)...

業興以天道高遠，測步難精，五行伏留，推考不易，人目仰窺，未能盡密，但取其見伏大歸，略其中間小謬，如此曆便可行。若專據所見之驗，不取出沒之效，則曆數之道其幾廢矣。夫造曆者，節之與朔貫穿於千年之間，閏餘斗分推之於毫釐之內。必使盈縮得衷，間限數合... 如芳所言，信亦不謬，但一合之裏星度不驗者，至若合終必還。依術，鎮星前年十二月二十日見差五度，今日差三度；太白前差四度，今全無差... 將來永用，大體無失...

Yexing recognizes that the Dao of Heaven is lofty and distant; that it is difficult to be precise in the pacing thereof; that it is not easy to calculate and investigate of the last visibilities and stations of the Five Agents (planets); and that the upward glances of the human eye cannot be completely tight (accurate); but if you take the main points of their visibilities/invisibilities and overlook the little errors between them, that is the only way for *li* to proceed. If you only go by the proof of what you see but neglect the evidence of [visibility phenomena], then you might as well abolish the Dao of *li* numbers! The creators of *li* run the nodal [*qi*] and syzygy through the space of a thousand years while calculating the INTERCALARY REMAINDER and DIPPER PARTS to within a fraction of a hair. They must make progress/retreat achieve moderation that their intervals be limited and their numbers accord. ... We may take Fang at his word that he is not mistaken; it is just that even if a [planet's] *du* between conjunctions is not verified, it invariably returns upon terminating at conjunction. By our technique, Saturn manifests [a] 5°°[-error] on XII-20 of last year and an error of 3°° today; Venus was formerly 4°° in error, but today it is completely without error. ... If [our system] is used in perpetuity, it will generally not miss the mark. ...

校於壬子舊曆，鎮星差天五度，太白歲星亦各有差，是舊曆差天為多，新曆差天為少。凡造曆者，皆須積年累日，依法候天，知其疏密，然後審其近者，用作曆術。不可一月兩月之間，能正是非。若如熒惑行天七百七十九日，一遲、一疾、一留、一逆、一順、一伏、一見之法，七頭一終；太白行天五百八十三日，晨夕之法，七頭一終；歲星行天三百九十八日，七頭一終；鎮星行天三百七十八日，七頭一終；辰星行天一百一十五日，晨夕之法，七頭一終。造曆者必須測知七頭，然後作術。得七頭者造曆為近，不得頭者其曆甚疏，皆非一二日能知是非。自五帝三代以來及秦、漢、魏、晉，造曆者皆積年久測，術乃可觀。其倉卒造者，當時或近，不可久行。若三四年作者，初雖近天，多載恐失。今甲子新曆，業興潛構積年，雖有少差，校於壬子元曆，近天者多。若久而驗天，十年二十年間，比壬子元曆，三星行天，其差為密。

If we check [Fang's specific accusations of error] against the old *Renzi.*49 system (#33), we find that Saturn is [indeed] 5°° in error and that Venus and Jupiter each [indeed] have their own errors—but this is because the old system frequently errs from Heaven, and the new system [does not]. Creators of *li* must accumulate years and days of experience observing Heaven according to the method and get to know its looseness/tightness (accuracy), and only then can they investigate the near at hand for use in making *li* techniques. You can't determine its correctness in the space of one or two months! For example, Mars travels through Heaven for 779 days, and its slow-fast-station-retrograde-prograde-hide-appear method terminates in seven heads (its motion-degree model divides its synodic period into seven grades), [and so too for the other superior planets and the morning and evening halves of the inferior planets' synodic periods]. Creators of *li* must measure and know the seven heads before they can produce techniques. He who gets the seven heads has created a *li* that is CLOSE, while the *li* that does not get the heads is quite LOOSE—you simply can't determine its correctness in one or two days! From the time of the Five Emperors to the Qin, Han, [Cao-]Wei, and Jin, the creators of *li* were only able [to produce] impressive techniques after sustained measurement accumulated over many years. Those created in a hurry were sometimes close in their own time but could not work over any sustained period. ... As for the new *Jiazi*.$_{01}$ system (#36), Yexing has plotted about it for many years, and though it has slight errors, comparison with the *Renzi*.$_{49}$-origin system (#33) shows that it is more often close to Heaven (accurate). If you test it against Heaven over a longer period, like ten or twenty years, then the errors in the celestial motions of the three stars (planets) will be tighter (more accurate) in comparison to the *Renzi*.$_{49}$-origin system (#33).[75]

Whatever may be going on behind the scenes, the explicit point of contention here is quantitative predictive accuracy, pure and simple. Li Yexing defends the functionality of his model by reinterpreting Xindu's observational data to put it in proper perspective. First, Li questions the relevance (rather than the reliability) of his opponent's testimony: minor errors are to be expected, especially with a difficult planet like Mars; Xindu's examples were extreme and unrepresentative of the system's average performance; but never mind this, since the modeling of daily progress counts for less than the prediction of visibility phenomena; also, the new system outperforms its predecessors on both counts anyways. Second, Li accuses his opponent of shortsightedness: the study of *li* is to grapple with cosmic patterns of inhuman

75. Ibid., 107B.2697–2699.

scale; to create new and better knowledge in this arena is a prodigious task requiring decades of observation, comparison, and research; and to knit-pick trivialities once all is said and done is to demean the endeavor.

Whether or not these errors are representative of the Ascendant Harmony system's overall predictive accuracy, Xindu Fang and Li Yexing's expectations are telling. What to Xindu's mind constituted an "egregious error" in the sixth century A.D. (2°°- to 5°°-displacements in RA) was considerably smaller than the average error of his ancient predecessors (smaller, in the case of the *Wuxing zhan* Jupiter table, by a factor of almost 20). Furthermore, Li Yexing's description makes it clear that the object of all this "creation" (*zao* 造) and "novelty" (*xin* 新) is *improvement*. Improvement is so central to the rhetoric of *li* that, like many others, Li Yexing is compelled to quantify his improvement over both the luminaries of the field and his own former self. Lastly, as I take up in detail later, active engagement with tradition made experts keenly aware that they were participating in a greater historical trend of improvement—what I hazard to call "progress."

2.5.2 The planets in li mathematical astronomy

Having settled on a definition of progress suitable to the present task, let us briefly examine the progress that occurred in *li* planetary astronomy over the early imperial period. Given our current sensitivity to this term, it seems necessary here to affirm the axiom that progress was embedded in a social context and unfolded in a manner much more complex than that envisioned by early twentieth-century—and, as I emphasize throughout this study, even early imperial Chinese—historiographies of science. My intent here is to connect the dots between the *Wuxing zhan* and Li Yexing with as much attention to this embeddedness and complexity as is possible.

To begin with, actors produced increasingly accurate values for astronomical constants. Though progress here was by no means linear, total, or even meaningful beyond a certain point, graphs of historical values for solar, lunar, and planetary periodicities all show unequivocal general trends leading towards their respective modern values.[76] Backslides did occur, due sometimes to "externalist" factors—losses ensuing from social and institutional changes—and sometimes to "internalist" ones—e.g. Yang Wei's 楊偉 Luminous Inception system (#13; A.D. 237) adopted a set of planetary constants that proved so inferior to the Supernal Emblem system's (#10; A.D. 206) that the Jin (A.D. 265-420) court scrapped them in favor of the latter after A.D. 317. Qu Anjing 曲安京 posits that this latter type of back-slide was a consequence of the nested nature of *li* number systems, wherein the alteration of any one constant necessarily cascades into the others.[77] A planet's synodic period is a fine-tuned thing, and any error there creates an inversely proportionate error in its sidereal period. The Supernal Emblem and Luminous Inception systems give Jupiter a synodic period of 398.880 days (error: –5.7 min) and 398.942 days (error: +84.0 min), respectively. In astronomy, small errors add up quickly: Over 100 years the Supernal Emblem system (#10) exhibits a systematic error of –0.4 day and +0.7°, and the Luminous Inception system (#13), one of +5.3 day and +5.8°, which would severely limit the latter's long-term feasibility and accordance with past astronomical records.

The variability of visibility phenomena was another recalcitrant problem for the calendro-astronomer. FMR and FES occur when a planet rises/sets far enough from the sun that it is first visible against the illuminated background of the dawn/dusk horizon. The time that it takes from conjunction for this to happen is determined by a number of factors. Some are beyond anyone's ability to predict: weather, atmospheric conditions at the horizon, as well as the observer's eyesight and confidence. Some factors are fairly constant: each planet's magnitude (luminosity) varies within different ranges, being the product of the planet's reflectivity (determined by its geology and the chemical composition of its atmosphere), its proximity to the Sun and the observer, and its phase (area of illumination). Still other factors vary seasonally: it is the planet's distance from the Sun in *altitude* that is critical,

---

76. Nowhere is this laid out more clearly than in Chen Meidong, *Gu li xin tan*.

77. "Dong Han dao Liu Song shiqi lifa wuxing huihe zhouqi shuyuan" 東漢到劉宋時期歷法五星會合周期數源, *Tianwen xuebao* 天文學報 33, no. 1 (1992): 109–112.

and this is a product of the planet's longitude, latitude, and the seasonal fluctuation in the angle at which the ecliptic intersects the horizon at sunrise or sunset.

The Triple Concordance system (#8) does not compensate for this variability at all. Its motion-degree models fix all the planets' first and last visibilities at a set "angle of invisibility" from the sun—half a STATION (15°) in right ascension—and a set number of days appropriate to each planet's angular velocity near conjunction. While this works surprisingly well for Jupiter, it fails to capture the more capricious nature of "the Bright Star" (Mingxing 明星, i.e. Venus) which, depending on the season and the direction of its retrograde arc away from the ecliptic, can experience FMR anywhere from 4 to 22 days after LES at a distance from the Sun of 3°° to 14°° in right ascension when viewed from Chang'an. The Quarter-remainder system (#9; A.D. 85) introduced an elementary solution to this problem, assigning distinct angles of invisibility to each planet: Jupiter-13°°, Mars-16°°, Saturn-15°°, Venus-9°°, and Mercury-16°°.[78] Subsequent systems adjusted these values back and forth and, presumably, began applying them to the ecliptic, but it was not until Li Yexing's time in the sixth century A.D. that we see a change in conceptual approach to this problem.

Zhang Zixin 張子信 is one of the more interesting characters in the history of Chinese astronomy. An accomplished literatus, astronomer, doctor, and diviner, Zhang escaped from Ge Rong's 葛榮 uprising (A.D. 526–528) by fleeing to an island where he spent more than thirty years observing the inequalities of solar, lunar, and planetary motion with an armillary sphere. Zhang's introduction of solar and planetary equations of center was nothing less than a paradigm shift: the sun—the symbol of all that is perfect in the world—was made imperfect; the du—the angular distance traveled by the (mean) sun in 1 day ($365\frac{1}{4}^{\circ\circ} = 360°$)—was made arbitrary; and all celestial motion was hereafter subject to periodic inequalities. That said, all Zhang really did was extend elements of lunar theory to the other luminaries (Section 1.2.2). He was not even the first to do this for the sun: Liu Hong 劉洪 (c. A.D. 135–210) appears to have beat him to it by three and a half centuries with his $xiaoxi$ 消息 technique,

---

78. *Hou Han shu, zhi* 3, 3091–3072.

which inexplicably vanished thereafter (see Section 4.3.1). Zhang's true innovation—if that indeed matters—was his introduction of *qi*-based algorithmic corrections to the mean dates of visibility phenomena to compensate for seasonal variation. Combined, Zhang Zixin's novel methods represented an epoch-making advancement for planetary *li*, that is in terms of the specific goals that actors had set for it.

For Zhang Zixin, *li* was not an *entrée* into politics but an escape. He made no known attempt to initiate policy reform, and Li Yexing's triumph of A.D. 540—which he boasts might be "used in perpetuity, and generally not miss the mark" 將來永用，大體無失 —shows no sign of the new paradigm brewing offshore. In fact, nothing survives of Zhang's methods except what has been filtered through the work of his disciples. Two of his students—Zhang Mengbin 張孟賓 and Liu Xiaosun 劉孝孫 (d. A.D. 632)—*were* politically engaged, and in A.D. 576 they petitioned the Northern Qi 北齊 (A.D. 550–577) court to adopt their respective *li*. The very next year, before anything had come of their requests, the capital fell to the Northern Zhou 北周 (A.D. 557-581). Adding insult to injury, the occupiers then adopted their own Grand Clerk, Ma Xian's 馬顯, Great Emblem system (#48; A.D. 579)—a conservative throwback to the fifth century. Yang Jian 楊堅 (b. A.D. 541; r. 581–604 as Wendi 文帝) dethroned the Zhou emperor only two years later but ordered the Sui 隋 (A.D. 581–618) court to retain Daoist Zhang Bin's 張賓 revision of the Great Emblem system. Successive courts may have promoted the Great Emblem system (#48), but Zhang's disciples were winning the ground war, converting a new generation of experts to the Zhangian paradigm. Figures like Liu Xiaosun, Liu Zhuo 劉焯 (A.D. 544–610), and Zhang Zhouxuan 張胄玄 (d. c. A.D. 613) actively challenged the court's conservatism, but it was not until the latter's Great Patrimony system (#52) of A.D. 597—some 70 years after Zhang Zixin had begun his work—that they finally prevailed upon the court.[79]

These examples serve to show us how progress was neither linear nor incremental but a

---

79. On Zhang Zixin and Sui astronomy, see Chen Meidong, *Zhongguo kexue jishu shi: tianwenxue juan*, 298–303; Chen Jiujin, ed., *Zhongguo gudai tianwenxuejia* 中國古代天文學家, Zhongguo tianwenxueshi daxi (Beijing: Zhongguo kexue jishu chubanshe, 2008), 186–196; Zhang Peiyu et al., *Zhongguo gudai lifa*, 425–457.

tortuous process subject to the complexities of individuals, social settings, and the culture of specific knowledge-systems. Individual calendro-astronomers focused on problems that they perceived to be important—they spent more effort as a whole, for example, on eclipses and visibility phenomena than daily planetary positions or latitude. Given minute errors in assumed correlations and the nested nature of early *li* number systems, one might also have to sacrifice one goal for another—the Luminous Inception system (#13), for example, sacrificed planetary astronomy for eclipse prediction. Sometimes, actors even promoted slipshod systems, be it because they were under-prepared or because they were full-fledged crackpots.[80] For the most part though, people went with what worked best, and failed experiments were forgotten.

These examples also reveal problems inherent in measuring progress—and indeed narrating the history of Chinese astronomy—from the lone vantage of government policy. Emperors and ministerial committees entertained the idea of reform for a variety of reasons, many having nothing to do with the current state of knowledge.[81] More importantly, the voice for progress was almost never the state astronomical office but figures like Liu Xin, Liu Hong, Yang Wei, Zhang Zixin, Zhang Mengbin, Liu Xiaosun, and Liu Zhuo—actors who existed in textual and educational networks independent of the state astronomical office, who pursued their research on their own time while serving in unrelated posts, possibly for reasons

---

80. Noteworthy examples of crackpots in this period include Zhang Long 張隆 (fl. A.D. 57/85) and Zhang Shouwang 張壽王 (fl. 78 B.C.); see p. 93 and Christopher Cullen, *Astronomy and Mathematics in Ancient China: The* Zhou Bi Suan Jing (Cambridge: Cambridge University Press, 1996), 30–31. Of course, this type of trial and error is perfectly in accord with, for example, Karl Popper's definition of "science" as a process of conjecture and falsification that brings human knowledge progressively closer to reality (*Conjectures and Refutations: The Growth of Scientific Knowledge* [New York: Basic Books, 1962]).

81. For example, see Cullen's detailed study of the political and ideological context of the Grand Inception reform of 104 B.C. and his sociological analysis of the astronomical debates in the *Hou Han shu*: "Motivations for Scientific Change in Ancient China: Emperor Wu and the Grand Inception Astronomical Reforms of 104 BC," *Journal for the History of Astronomy* 24, no. 3 (1991): 185–203; "Actors, Networks, and 'Disturbing Spectacles' in Institutional Science: 2nd Century Chinese Debates on Astronomy," *Antiqvorvm Philosophia* 1 (2007): 237–267. For an overview of reasons cited for astronomical reform—empirical, cultural, and political—over the course of Chinese history, see Niu Weixing, "Han Tang zhi ji lifa gaige zhong de zuoyong yinsu zhi fenxi" 漢唐之際曆法改革中各作用因素之分析, *Shanghai jiaotong daxue xuebao (zhexue shehui kexue ban)* 上海交通大學學報（哲學社會科學版）12, no. 5 (2004): 33–38, 54; Chen Meidong, *Zhongguo gudai tianwenxue sixiang* 中國古代天文學思想 (Beijing: Zhongguo kexue jishu chubanshe, 2007), 581–619.

other than influencing state policy, and whose contributions were only later presented for government approval with varying degrees of success.[82]

That said, since our calendro-astronomers were products of classical education and citizens and servants of bureaucratic empires, the state was there, in everything they did. To successfully enter one's work into state service was not only an honor, it was a divine imperative with solemn consequences for human destiny. The coveted nature of this prize meant that political incidents, infighting, and the disbandment of working groups could work to slow or stifle individual efforts.[83] As I discuss in Chapter 4, furthermore, the future of new ideas

---

82. Liu Xin publicized his Triple Concordance system (#8) after he was named Xihe 羲和 in the Office of the Grand Clerk in A.D. 5 by Wang Mang 王莽 (c. 45 B.C. – A.D. 23); however, like his father he had made his career in the Imperial Secretariat and other posts, and his interest in astronomy appears to have been archaeoastronomical, relating to his work on the Zuo zhuan. On Liu Xin, see note 13. Liu Hong frequently shifted posts, and while he was assigned to the Office of the Grand Clerk and the Eastern Observatory (Dongguan 東觀) at different points in his life, his observation program and completion of the Supernal Emblem system (#10) date after this to his time as an administrator in Kuaiji and Shanyang Commanderies. Some two decades after his death, Liu Hong's disciples saw its successful adoption by the Sun-Wu state (229-280). On Liu Hong, see Section 1.2.2. Yang Wei was a Gentleman of the Masters of Writing when he participated in the astronomical debate of A.D. 226 and created his Luminous Inception system (#13) of A.D. 237 (*Jin shu*, 17.503, 18.531). It is unclear what Zhang Zixin was doing on his island other than astronomy, but he was given the position of Physician of the Director of Palace Medications and Grand Palace Grandee sometime between A.D. 561/576. On Zhang Zixin, see note 79. Nothing is known about Zhang Mengbin except that he was a student of Zhang Zixin's (*Sui shu*, 17.418). Both Liu Xiaosun and Liu Zhuo pursued astronomy over the course of complex careers that did not intersect with the state astronomical office (*Jiu Tang shu* 舊唐書 [Zhonghua shuju ed.], 72.2583; *Sui shu*, 75.1718–1719). The one exception in the figures surveyed in this section is Zhang Zhouxuan, who was an acting grand clerk when he produced and publicized his astronomical system (ibid., 78.1779–1783). For other clear examples of the importance of bureau outsiders in the history of Chinese astronomy, see Cullen, "Actors, Networks, and 'Disturbing Spectacles' in Institutional Science," esp. 246; Sivin, *Granting the Seasons*, 58–59, 121–124, 133–170. Beginning in the Jin Dynasty successive regimes issued dozens of bans against the private possession of texts on the divinatory aspects of the astral sciences, e.g. "charts and books on *tianwen*." Based on this and the fact that the government ran an astronomical office, a number have scholars have argued that astronomy was a secretive government affair, e.g. Needham, *Science and Civilisation in China*, *Vol.3*, 186–194; Lai Swee fo 賴瑞和, "Tangdai de Hanlin daizhao he Sitiantai" 唐代的翰林待詔和司天臺, *Tang yanjiu* 唐研究 9 (2003): esp. 332–335; Martzloff, *Le calendrier chinois*, 28–30. There are three problems with this position: it ignores overwhelming evidence about real astronomers; it is overconfident about the effectiveness of bans; and, most importantly, it conflates *tianwen* with "astronomy" in the modern sense, when this was actually quite distinct from *li* mathematical astronomy. For an excellent case against this position, see Chen Meidong, *Zhongguo gudai tianwenxue sixiang*, 17–32. The exception to this is the Ming, when bans extended to *li* and seem to have been effective, see Chen Meidong, *Zhongguo kexue jishu shi: tianwenxue juan*, 555–558.

83. For example, Han Yi 韓翊 disappears from the history of astronomy after A.D. 226 when his proposal for reform meets with heavy criticism and the emperor dies before any decision is made (*Jin shu*, 17.493–503). In another example, the Northern Wei court appoints an astronomical reform commission under Grand Clerk Zhao Fansheng 趙樊生 in A.D. 500, after which, one after another, its members die, are replaced, or are transferred to posts outside the capital, causing the project languish for more than twenty years before eventually culminating in to Orthodox Glory system (#33) (*Wei shu*, 107A.2660–2663).

very much depended on the methodology, rigor, and impartiality of the state observatory, with whom the role of arbitrating accuracy was entrusted.

As embedded and complex as this process was, it did produce measurable, qualitative change. The *Jin shu*, for example, tells us that with Liu Hong "there was finally a turn from the previous methods towards the fine and tight" 方於前法，轉為精密矣.[84] On the same page, however, it also extols him for having "established his numbers according to the Changes" 依易立數, reminding us that quantitative progress might be expected to go hand-in-hand with *qualitative* progress.[85] Liu Xin purports to derive his synodic periods for Jupiter, Venus, and Saturn thus:

> 木金相乘為十二，是為歲星小周。小周乘乾策，為千七百二十八，是為歲星歲數。

Wood (: 3) and Metal (: 4) (Metal conquers Wood) multiplied by one another make 12, this is the Year Star's LESSER CYCLE (i.e. Jupiter's roughly 12-year sidereal period). Its LESSER CYCLE multiplied by the Qian [1] ☰ sticks (i.e. the 216 yarrow sticks that remain after arriving at Qian [1] ☰ through the "Great Expansion" [*dayan* 大衍] counting rule) makes 1728, and this is the Year Star's YEAR NUMBER (which divided by its APPEARANCE MEDIAL QI FACTOR, 1583, makes a synodic period of 1.09 years or 398.71 days).

> 金火相乘為八，又以火乘之為十六而小復。小復乘乾策，為三千四百五十六，是為太白歲數。

Metal (: 4) and Fire (: 2) multiplied by one another make 8, multiply it again

---

84. *Jin shu*, 17.498.

85. Ibid. Liu Xin's interest in numerology is the most famous; see Nōda and Yabuuti, *Kansho ritsurekishi no kenkyū*; Lü Zifang 呂子方, "*Santong li* liyi jiqi shu yuan" 『三統曆』曆意及其數源, in *Zhongguo kexue jishu shi lunwen ji* 中國科學技術史論文集, vol. 1 (Chengdu: Sichuan renmin chubanshe, 1983), 20–127; Teboul, *Les premières théories planétaires chinoises*; Kawahara Hideki, "The World-view of the *Santong-li*," *Historia Scientiarum* 42 (1991): 67–73; Bo Shuren 薄樹人, "*Santong li* he *Taichu li*" 『三統曆』和『太初曆』, in *Bo Shuren wenji* 薄樹人文集 (Hefei: Zhongguo kexue jishu daxue chubanshe, 2003), 329–368; Hans Ulrich Vogel, "Aspects of Metrosophy and Metrology During the Han Period," *Extrême-Orient, Extrême-Occident* 16 (1994): 135–152.

by Fire (: 2) making 16, its LESSER RETURN (i.e. twice Venus' roughly 8-year :
5-synodic period cycle). Its LESSER RETURN multiplied by the Qian [1] ☰ sticks
(216) makes 3456, and this is Great White's YEAR NUMBER (which divided by
its APPEARANCE MEDIAL QI FACTOR, 2161, makes a synodic period of 1.60 years
or 584.13 days).

土木相乘而合經緯為三十，是為鎮星小周。小周乘坤策，為四千三百二十，是
為鎮星歲數。

Earth (: 5) and Wood (: 3) multiplied by one another and combined warp-
and-weft (doubled) make 30 (i.e. its roughly 30-year sidereal period), this is the
Queller Star's LESSER CYCLE. Its LESSER CYCLE multiplied by the Kun [2] ☷
sticks (144) makes 4320, and this is the Queller Star's YEAR NUMBER (which
divided by its APPEARANCE MEDIAL QI FACTOR, 4175, makes a synodic period
of 1.03 years or 377.93 days).[86]

The difference between Liu Xin's Triple Concordance system (#8) and the planetary hemerology of the *Wuxing zhan* is thus not a matter of "science" vs. "magic" but the elegance with
which each synthesized form and function. Liu Xin flaunts a mastery of occult forces, *but he
can model the visible ones well enough too.* This qualitative ideal continued to resonate with
later generations, especially as it relates Han luminaries and ancient Sages. All the same, it
is important to note that *in practice* numerology essentially disappeared from *li* literature
by the third century A.D.[87]

---

86. *Han shu*, 21B.992–995; see also Teboul, *Les premières théories planétaires chinoises*, 8–19. I omit
Mars and Mercury for the sake of space. It is worth noting that Liu Xin's manipulation of each planet's
corresponding five-agents and Qian-Kun numbers are different. It is also worth noting that each planet's
LESSER CYCLE or LESSER RETURN hearkens back to the simple ratios of the *Wuxing zhan* but shows itself
expanding upon them into much larger numbers for more accurate periodicities.

87. For an overview of numerology in the history of Chinese mathematical astronomy, see Chen Meidong,
Zhongguo gudai tianwenxue sixiang, 551–565. Chen concludes that numerology played an ancillary role to
empiricism, imbuing constants that had been derived through empirical work with mystical potency. For
a similar conclusion, see Martzloff, *Le calendrier chinois*, 38–44. The largest exception to this was the
astronomy in Han weft texts, see Takeda Tokimasa, "Isho rekihō kō: Zenkanmatsu no keigaku to kagaku no
kōryū" 緯書曆法考：前漢末の經學と科學の交流, in *Chūgoku kodai kagakushi ron* 中國古代科學史論, ed.
Yamada Keiji (Kyōto: Kyōto daigaku jinbun kagaku kenkyūjo, 1989), 55–120.

2.5.3   The planets in tianwen omen literature

We might expect planetary models in *tianwen* omen literature to have changed very little or on a different trajectory than those of *li* mathematical astronomy. They exist, after all, in self-contained interpretative systems seemingly free from the danger of falsification, and they are distinct in form and function.[88] This incommensurability is most evident in the seasonal schemes for Mercury introduced in Section 3.4, which, as we saw, do not look like models of the planet's synodic period but divinatory rules of thumb informed by its perceived function as master and regulator of the seasons. Other schemes are clearly embedded in the distinct idiom of observational astronomy, dealing with a planet's altitude (*gao* 高) or linear measures like *zhang* 丈, *chi* 尺, and *cun* 寸 (concepts absent from *li* mathematical astronomy).[89] For example, the *Kaiyuan zhanjing* attributes the following omen series to Gan De and to Liu Biao 劉表 and Liu Rui's 劉叡 late Eastern Han *Jingzhou zhan* 荊州占:

甘氏曰：「熒惑之東行也：急則一日一夜行七寸半，其益此則行疾。疾。行疾則兵聚於東方… 熒惑法東方，修緯及常十六舍而止，逆行西運動以成章，舍一舍半。」

Mr. Gan says, "in regards to the eastward (prograde) motion of Sparkling Deluder (Mars), when it is in a hurry it travels 7½ *cun* in the course of one day and one night; more than this and its motion is fast. If its motion is fast then armies group in the east... Sparkling Deluder submits (moves) to the east, cultivating the weft for usually 16 lodges before stopping, it then travels retrograde to the

---

88. This section attempts to address the interesting topic raised by Nakayama Shigeru 中山茂 some a half a century ago— the empirical development of portent astrology—in "Characteristics of Chinese Astrology." *Isis* 57, no. 4 (1966): 442–454. In the same vein, for scholarship on the change of attitude towards omenology in the Tang and Song, see Tiziana Lippiello, *Auspicious Omens and Miracles in Ancient China: Han, Three Kingdoms and Six Dynasties*, Monumenta Serica Monograph Series 39 (Sankt Augustin: Monumenta Serica Institute, 2001), 122–127; Wu Yiyi, "Auspicious Omens and Their Consequences: Zhen-Ren (1006–1066) Literati's Perception of Astral Anomalies" (Ph.D. diss., Princeton University, 1990), esp. 171–261.

89. On the use of linear measures in observational astronomy, see Wang Yumin 王玉民, *Yi chi liang tian— Zhongguo gudai mushi chidu tianxiang jilu de lianghua yu guisuan* 以尺量天 —中國古代目視尺度天象記錄的量化與歸算 (Jinan: Shandong jiaoyu chubanshe, 2008).

west, its movement coming to completion in 1 or 1½ lodges."[90]

荊州占曰：「熒惑日行一尺以上，期五月至十五月而廢；五寸以上，期十五月至二十五月而廢；三寸以上，期二十五月至三十月而廢；一寸以上，期三十月至五十月廢。諸廢期，月或皆為日。」

Jingzhou zhan says, "if Sparkling Deluder travels more than 1 *chi* (= 10 *cun*) per day, then in a period of 5 to 15 months there is abrogation; more than 5 *cun*, then in a period of 15 to 25 months there is abrogation; more than 3 *cun*, then in a period of 25 to 30 months there is abrogation; more than 1 *cun*, then in a period of 30 to 50 months there is abrogation. For the various abrogation periods, the number of months are sometimes all given instead as the number of days."[91]

The context of observation (rather than computation) might also explain the preference for simpler numbers and cruder measures like "lodges."

Unlike *li* mathematical astronomy, provenance is a constant problem in omen literature. Anonymity and pseudepigraphy are rampant, and most texts survive in fragments or in manuscripts of questionable origin, or both. Though it is difficult to establish even the roughest of chronological frameworks for these materials, I believe that focused comparison may yet reveal meaningful traces of historical change. Seasonal schemes for Mercury are particularly informative since they are an extreme example of the difference between genres. These may well represent some formative stage of Chinese planetary knowledge, but they did not simply disappear after the motion-degree models of *li* literature highlighted their, in Gautama Siddhārtha's 瞿曇悉達 (fl. A.D. 729) words, "absurdities" (below) and

---

90. *Kaiyuan zhanjing*, 30.4a–b.

91. Ibid., 30.4b. According to the *Jin shu*, "at the end of the [Eastern] Han Liu Biao was regional governor of Jingzhou and ordered the governor of Wuling, Liu Rui, to collect together the many *tianwen* omens, and this was named *Jingzhou zhan*" 及漢末劉表為荊州牧，命武陵太守劉叡集天文眾占，名『荊州占』 (*Jin shu*, 12.322). Other sources disagree on its authorship: the *Sui shu* bibliography says it was written by Liu Yan 劉嚴, and the *Xin Tang shu* lists two different *Jingzhou xingzhan* 荊州星占 of 2 and 20 *juan* written by Biao and Rui, respectively (*Sui shu*, 34.1020; *Xin Tang shu*, 59.1544).

surpassed them in predictive accuracy. Ranging over a thousand-year period from the Qin to the Tang, I have discovered 26 sources for this seasonal scheme, which I have arranged in rough chronological order in Table 2.10. No two descriptions are exactly alike. Each source appears to be drawing from a common set of building blocks, which it arranges into different configurations, elaborating freely upon the basic themes and patterns thereof:[92]

- Verb: ① sources 2, 4, 5 & 19 have *xiao* "appear;" ② sources 1, 3, 10, 18 & 23 have *chu* "emerge;" ③ sources 7 & 12 have *xian* 見 "appear;" and ④ source 6 has *chu xiao* "emerge and appear."

- Time: ① sources 2, 4 & 10 have the solstices and equinoxes; ① sources 7 & 12 have the second day of the solstices and equinoxes; ③ sources 1, 8, 9, 15, 16, 18 & 25 have the mid-season months; ④ sources 3, 5, 6, 19, 20 & 23 have the mid-season months plus the solstices and equinoxes; and ⑤ sources 11, 13, 14, 17, 21 & 22 have the four seasons.

- Visibility sequence: ① sources 1, 2, 4, and 18 have morning-morning-morning-morning; ② sources 3, 6, 10, 19 & 23 have evening-evening-evening-morning; and ③ sources 7 & 11 have morning-morning-evening-evening.

- Lodges: ① sources 1, 2, 4 & 18 have Pasture.16 → Devils.23 → Neck.02 → Ox.09; ② sources 7 & 11 have Crotch.15 → Well.22 → Root.03 → Maid.10; ③ sources 5 & 19 have Crotch.15 and Pasture.16 → Well.22 and Devils.23 → Horn.01 and Root.03 → Dipper.08 and Ox.09; and ④ sources 3, 6 & 23 have a range of lodges east and west of the Sun.

---

92. For studies of Chinese celestial omen literature, see Ho Peng Yoke, *The Astronomical Chapters of the* Chin Shu (Paris: Mouton, 1967); David Pankenier, "Characteristics of Field Allocation (*fenye* 分野) Astrology in Early China," in *Current Studies in Archaeoastronomy: Conversations Across Time and Space,* ed. J. W. Fountain and R. M. Sinclair (Durham: Carolina Academic Press, 2005), 499–513; Lu Yang 盧 央, *Zhongguo gudai xingzhanxue* 中國古代星占學 (Beijing: Zhongguo kexue jishu chubanshe, 2007); Jiang Xiaoyuan, *Zhongguo xingzhanxue leixing fenxi* 中國星占學類型分析 (Shanghai: Shanghai shudian chubanshe, 2009).

Table 2.10: Seasonal schemes for Mercury in *tianwen* omen literature

no.	Author	Text	Date	Extant/Cite
1	Wuxian 巫咸?	anon.	?	KYZJ 53.4,8–9,10
2	Gan De 甘德?	anon.	?	KYZJ 53.4,8
3	Shi Shen 石申?	anon.	?	KYZJ 53.4,8
4	anon.	*Wuxing zhan* 五星占	168 B.C.	MS
5	Liu An 劉安 et al.	*Huainanzi* "Tianwen xun" 淮南子 · 天文訓	139	extant
6	Sima Qian 司馬遷	*Shiji* "Tianguan shu" 史記 · 天官書	91	extant
7	Li Shuo 李朔?	*Wuling ji* 五靈紀	W. Han?	TWYL 10.1b–2a
8	Liu Xiang 劉向	*Hongfan zhuan* 洪範傳	1st cent.	KYZJ 53.2–3,9
9	Li Xun 李尋	petition	c. 6	*Han shu*, 75.3187
10	anon.	*Chunqiu* weft 春秋緯	1st cent. A.D.	KYZJ 53.3,8
11	anon.	*Kaolingyao* 考靈曜	1st cent.	KYZJ 53.8
12	anon.	*Luo shu* 洛書	1st cent.	KYZJ 53.3
13	anon.	*Shangshu* weft 尚書緯	1st cent.	KYZJ 53.4
14	anon.	*Yuanmingbao* 元命包	1st cent.	KYZJ 53.8
15	anon.	*Yuanshenqi* 元神契	1st cent.	KYZJ 53.4
16	anon.	*Haizhong zhan* 海中占	1st cent.?	KYZJ 53.9
17	Ban Zhao 班昭	*Han shu* "Tianwen zhi" 漢書 · 天文志	111	extant
18	Liu Biao 劉表 & Liu Rui 劉叡	*Jingzhou zhan* 荊州占	2nd cent.	KYZJ 53.2,9–10
19	Huangfu Mi 皇甫謐	*Nian li* 年歷	3rd cent.	KYZJ 53.4
20	Jin Zhuo 晉灼	commentary	4th cent.?	*Shiji*, 27.1372
21	Li Chunfeng 李淳風	*Sui shu* "Tianwen zhi" 隋書 · 天文志	636	extant
22	Li Chunfeng	*Jin shu* "Tianwen zhi" 晉書 · 天文志	648	extant
23	anon.	P.2811	Tang?	MS
24	Li Feng 李鳳?	*Tianwen yaolu* 天文要錄 (TWYL)	664	extant
25	Puyang Xia 濮陽夏?	*Qiaozi wuxing zhi* 譙子五行志	Tang	extant
26	Gautama Siddhārtha 瞿曇悉達	*Kaiyuan zhanjing* 開元占經 (KYZJ)	729	extant

The omens built around this scheme are similarly diverse. For example, the *Kaiyuan zhanjing* attributes Shi Shen with three omens, which we can summarize as:

1. **If** it does not rise when it ought to, **then** armies arise (cf. sources 17, 21 & 22; variant in source 6).

2. **If** it does not rise in the four mid-season months, **then** there are disasters, famine, crop failure, tumult between yin and yang, state collapse, seasonal disturbances, injury to the people, and disharmony between lord and minister (cf. source 8).

3. **If** it rises early in the four first months of the seasons, **then** there is regime change. (cf. source 1, 4, 8, 9, 18 & 25; variant in sources 4, 6, & 16).

Wuxian's omenology overlaps with Shi Shen only at Point (3), which he and other sources develop into an early/late dichotomy:

4. **If** it rises late in the four last months of the seasons, **then** there is a comet, demonic celestial portents, and the collapse of the state (cf. sources 4, 6, 9, 16 & 18).

    (a) And/or the marquis do not report in (no parallels).

Wuxian then proceeds to enumerate a number of much more complex schemes involving Mercury's failure to rise correctly in specific seasons and locations:

5. **If** it does not rise for one season, **then** it will be disharmonious and armies will arise; **if** for two seasons, **then** a flood; **if** for three, **then** a big military uprising; and **if** for four, **then** a dam breach and a flood that kills the populace and/or a comet in the east (cf. sources 10, 18 & 25).

6. **If** it does not appear in a specific season: **if** in spring, **then** 100 days of wind and rain, harming the sprouts; **if** in summer, **then** drought, famine, and 90 days of population displacement; **if** in autumn, **then** 60 days of floods; and **if** in winter, **then** empty storehouses and death and displacement of the populace. **If** it rises in no season, **then** there are river and sea waves and a comet (cf. source 18).

(a) **If**, furthermore, it does not appear in the appropriate lodge each time, **then** the crops will be damaged (no parallels).

All 26 sources agree on one basic scheme: under normal circumstances, Mercury rises around the solstices and equinoxes, where it regulates the agricultural seasons; if it fails to do so, it is disastrous for agriculture, the populace, and the government; furthermore, Mercury's timeliness is affected by the propriety of government action. Each source presents that scheme in its own language and with different levels of specificity, often elaborating in new directions.[93]

I believe that this variability is evidence that the seasonal scheme for Mercury was still living knowledge in these centuries. This was no mere theoretical abstraction; in fact, the dynastic histories record no less than six instances where this scheme was applied to contemporary events.

1. The reign of Qin Ershi 秦二世 (209–207 B.C.): in the late first century B.C., Liu Xiang recounts a number of heavenly and earthly signs presaging the fall of the Qin, one of which is that "the Chronogram Star emerged in the four first months of the seasons" 辰星出於四孟.[94]

2. The inaugural year of Han Gaozu (204 B.C.): the *Han shu* astronomical records again state that "the Chronogram Star emerged in the four first months of the seasons," "a sign of a change of rulers" 易王之表 presaging the conquest of Chu two years later.[95]

3. Han Xuandi 宣帝, Foundational Beginning 1-IV-*renxu*.59, *jia*.S01 [watch] at night (the first month of summer; 73 B.C. May 9, 18:36/20:46 local apparent time): the *Han shu* astronomical records state that Mercury emerged in the west with Triad.21 (FES) and again on the evening of 2-VII-*xinhai*.48 (the first month of autumn; 72 B.C. Aug 16

---

93. In a similar vein, Huang Yi-Long argues that omens surrounding Mars "garrisoning" Heart.05 evolved over time in response to historical outcomes in *Shehui tianwenxue shi shi jiang*, 43–47.

94. *Han shu*, 36.1965; *Shuoyuan* 說苑 (Siku quanshu ed.), 18.3a–b.

95. *Han shu*, 26.1302.

?) in Wings.$_{27}$. Both times Mercury was early, presaging the execution of a great minister.[96]

4. Nanyang rebellion (A.D. 30): Su Jing 蘇竟, writing to convince a friend not to participate in the rebellion, states that "the Chronogram Star has not appeared for a long time" 辰星久而不効 and that "Great White and the Chronogram Star have since the time of the fall of the Xin (A.D. 23) missed the mark of their calculated positions" 太白、辰星自亡新之末，失行筭度.[97]

5. Han Guangwudi 光武帝, 30-IV^2-*jiawu*.$_{31}$ (A.D. 54 June 09): the *Hou Han shu* astronomical records state that Mercury was in the 20th *du* of Well.$_{22}$ when it emitted a white *qi* that turned into a comet. Because it "appeared before it ought to appear" 未當見而見 in Well.$_{22}$ in intercalary month IV rather than month V (the mid-summer month), it presaged a devastating flood. Its comet, which entered the Purple Palace, also presaged the death of Guangwudi three years later.[98]

6. Song Shundi 順帝, Rising Enlightenment 3-I-18 (A.D. 479 February 24): the *Nan Qi shu* 南齊書 astronomical records state that "the Chronogram Star appeared in the west in the first month of the season. The prognosis: 'the world under Heaven will change kings' " 辰星孟効西方。占曰「天下更王」. This presaged the establishment of the Qi 齊 Dynasty (A.D. 479–502) that very year.[99]

There is little to say about Records (1) and (4), which are vague, retrospective, and occur in the context of political rhetoric. Comparing the astronomical records to visibility phenomena

---

96. Ibid., 26.1308. 2-VII began on *jiayin*.$_{51}$ (72 B.C. August 24), placing *xinhai*.$_{48}$ at the end of month VI, meaning that either the month or the sexagenary day is incorrect. PLSV confirms that Mercury, which was setting around 50 min after the Sun, could have conceivably been visible around this time. Since the text describes this emergence as "early" (*zao* 早)—i.e. in the first month of autumn (month VII) rather than the last month of summer (month VI)—I suspect that it is the sexagenary day that is incorrect.

97. *Hou Han shu*, 30A.1043–1044.

98. Ibid., *zhi* 10, 3223.

99. *Nan Qi shu* (Zhonghua shuju ed.), 12.204.

calculated by PLSV for the appropriate years, Records (2), (3) and (6) appear plausible, it is, however, difficult for the modern mind to comprehend what is happening in Record (5).[100] Given the frequency with which Mercury would have violated its seasonal scheme over this period, the fact that there are only six such records hints that the art of astral divination and/or of compiling a dynastic history is a highly selective process. Regardless of how selective, biased, or even possibly disingenuous these records may be, they are evidence that people continued to use the seasonal model for Mercury as living knowledge through this period.[101]

At the same time that omenological planetary models continued to flourish, their reception underwent a number of significant changes. The first is that intellectuals began to *quote* them. Whereas the *Wuxing zhan* and weft texts, for example, simply state them as facts, intellectuals began to treat them as *opinions* belonging to *books* with *authors*, effectively distinguishing them from contemporary observational and computational facts and transforming them into subjects of academic and historical curiosity. For example, Sima Qian

---

100. In the case of Record (2), PLSV predicts that first visibilities would have occurred in one first month of the season (month I), two last months of the season (months III and IX), and two mid-season months (months XI and V), though it may also have been visible between months VII and VIII. It is possible that the planet was simply *visible* in each of the first months of the season, though this contradicts the usual sense of *chu* ("first visibility") and it is difficult to see what might have been considered special about the way that Mercury's periodicity overlapped with the civil calendar this year. In the case of Record (3), everything checks out other than the problem with the second date (see note 96). In the case of Record (6), the prognosis of regime change usually requires that Mercury appear in *all four* of the first months of the seasons. In A.D. 479, PLSV indeed predicts FES in months I and IV and FMR in months VII and X, warranting the prognosis so long as one is not bothered by the additional FMR in month III or the possible FES in month IX. In the case of record (5), *Alcyone Ephemeris* predicts that Mercury would have been only about 5.8° or 5.9°° into Well.$_{22}$ (μ Gem) on A.D. 54 June 6; furthermore, the planet could not possibly have been visible until late June. I suspect that the observer is either describing the comet or has mistaken another object for Mercury.

101. On the selective nature of early imperial celestial omenology and its use in political discourse, see Hans Bielenstein, "An Interpretation of the Portents in the *Ts'ien-Han-Shu*," *Bulletin of the Museum of Far Eastern Antiquities* 22 (1950): 127–143; Wolfram Eberhard, "The Political Function of Astronomy and Astronomers in Han China," in *Chinese Thought and Institutions*, ed. John Fairbank, Comparative Studies of Cultures and Civilizations (Chicago: University of Chicago Press, 1957), 37–70; Rafe De Crespigny, *Portents of Protest in the Later Han Dynasty: The Memorials of Hsiang Kai to Emperor Huan in 166 A.D.* (Canberra: Australian National University Press in association with the Faculty of Asian Studies, Australian National University, 1976); Martin Kern, "Religious Anxiety and Political Interest in Western Han Omen Interpretation: The Case of the Han Wudi Period (141–87 B.C.)," *Chūgoku shigaku* 中國史學 10 (2000): 1–31; Huang Yi-long, *Shehui tianwenxue shi shi jiang*, 1–92.

offers the following criticism of his predecessors:

故甘、石曆五星法，唯獨熒惑有反逆行；逆行所守，及他星逆行，日月薄蝕，皆以為占。

In the old Gan [De] and Shi [Shen] methods for calendrically computing the Five Stars only Sparkling Deluder had retrogradation. They took the [asterisms] it guards in retrograde, the retrogradation of other stars (planets), and the veilings and eclipses of the Sun and Moon all as the objects of prognostication.

余觀史記，考行事，百年之中，五星無出而不反逆行，反逆行，嘗盛大而變色... 此其大度也。... 水、火、金、木、填星，此五星者，天之五佐，為（經）緯，見伏有時，所過行贏縮有度。... 凡天變，過度乃占。

I have looked at the historical records and investigated phenomena as they happen, and in 100 years the Five Stars have never emerged without going into retrograde; and when they retrograde they invariably become grand and change color... this is their great rule. Water, Fire, Metal, Wood, and the Queller Star—these five stars are the five assistants of Heaven. As for their actions in warp and weft (declination and right ascension), their appearance and hiding have their times, and the gain and retreat by which they exceed their [expected] travels have their rules... With celestial incidents, one only prognosticates when they have exceeded their rules.[102]

In the *Han shu* "*Tianwen* treatise," Ban Zhao 班昭 (c. A.D. 45–c. 117) attempts instead to rationalize this historical curiosity. She posits that early models do not account for retrogradation because it "has never been correct behavior" 皆非正行也 and because it only began to occur rather late in history in response to the political and moral decline of the Eastern Zhou 東周 (770–256 B.C.).[103] Furthermore, instead of simply explaining the facts of

---

102. *Shiji*, 27.1349–1350.

103. *Han shu*, 26.1290–1291.

the Jovian year-count, she juxtaposes conflicting quotations, presenting different historical opinions about the matter:

太歲在寅曰攝提格。歲星正月晨出東方，石氏曰「名監德，在斗、牽牛。失次、杓，早水，晚旱。」甘氏在建星、婺女。太初曆在營室、東壁…

When Taisui is in *yin*.$_{B03}$ it is called Shetige. The Year Star emerges in the morning in the east in month I. Mr. Shi says, "it is named 'Overseeing Virtue' and is at Dipper.$_{08}$ and Led Ox.$_{09}$. If it misses its station or the [direction of the Northern Dipper (UMa)] handle, then if it is early there is flooding, and if it is late there is drought." Mr. Gan has it in Establishment Star.$_{08}$ and Maid.$_{10}$. The Grand Inception system (#7) has it at Hall.$_{13}$ and Eastern Wall.$_{14}$…[104]

In the Sui and Tang, intellectuals begin further to catalog and *preserve* this knowledge in large compendia like the *Yisi zhan* 乙巳占 (A.D. 656), *Tianwen yaolu* 天文要錄 (A.D. 664), and *Kaiyuan zhanjing* (A.D. 729), and were it not for their efforts we would know next to nothing about Chinese omen literature.[105] In the *Kaiyuan zhanjing* the final stage of disassociation is complete. Its compiler, Gautama Siddhārtha, feels the need to insert commentary after the first instance of each such model to judge it by the standard of *li*. For example:

『洪範五行傳』曰：「辰星… 右行迅疾，常與日月相隨，見於四仲以正四時，歲一周天。」

---

104. Ibid., 26.1289–1290. The Establishment Star (Jianxing 建星) is the equivalent of Dipper.$_{08}$ in Gan De's nomenclature.

105. For example, in his preface to the *Yisi zhan*, Li Chunfeng 李淳風 states his purpose and method thus:
余不揆末學，集某所記，以類相聚，編而次之。採摭英華，刪除繁偽，小大之間，折衷而已。
I do not consider superficial/later work, I collect what is recorded by so-and-so, group it according to category, then edit and order it. All I do is collect the cream of the crop, excise the prolix and the false, and take the middle road between small and large (*Yisi zhan*, vi.a, in *Zhongguo kexue jishu dianji tonghui: tianwen juan* 中國科學技術典籍通彙・天文卷 [Zhengzhou: Hebei jiaoyu chubanshe, 1993], v. 4, p. 457).

Li Feng 李鳳 expresses a similar design in his preface, *Tianwen yaolu*, 1.2b, in ibid., v. 4, p. 27.

The *Hongfan wuxing zhuan* says: "The Chronogram Star... travels swiftly to the right, constantly accompanying the Sun and the Moon, and it appears in the four mid-season months to set straight the four seasons, making one circuit through Heaven in one year."

| 案歷法，辰星夕見西方三十日而伏二十二日而晨見東方而伏，伏入三十三日一千五百四十分日之一千一百六十八奇六十六復夕見西方如初。一終凡一百一十五日一千一百七十八奇六十六，星行度數亦如之。是七十七年而二百四十九終也。星平行日一度，一年周天。舊説皆云「辰星效四仲」以為謬矣。|

COMMENTARY: |According to *lifa*, the Chronogram Star appears in the evening in the west for 30 days before hiding, 22 days before appearing in the morning in the east and then hiding, it hides and enters for $33\frac{1168\frac{66}{x}}{1540}$ days and appears again in the evening like the first time. From start to finish it takes a total of $115\frac{1168\frac{66}{x}}{1540}$ days, and the *du* traveled are also as much. This makes 249 complete cycles in 77 years. The star's mean motion is one *du* per day, making a circuit of Heaven in one year. The old doctrines all say that "the Chronogram Star appears in the four mid-season months," which is absurd.|>[106]

Intellectuals had actually begun to eschew *tianwen* planetary models early on. In the *Han shu* "*Tianwen* Treatise," Ban Zhao omits reference to Saturn traveling one lodge per year and treats the Jovian year-count as an object of historical interest. Then, beginning with the *Hou Han shu* (c. A.D. 445), normative models of planetary behavior at odds with contemporary *li* begin to disappear—with the sole exception, that is, of Mercury. With the *Jiu Tang shu* 舊唐書 (A.D. 941), practical/theoretical contents are finally phased out of the "*Tianwen* Treatise" all together. The rationale for this seems to be twofold: these contents had become redundant with other previous entries in the genre; and they were a logical concession to the burgeoning number of observational/divinatory records. In other words, it was as if there

---

106. *Kaiyuan zhanjing*, 53.2b–3a.

was a conscious effort at specialization in the fifth and sixth centuries A.D. that segregated historical records and practical knowledge between histories and reference works, respectively.

This was not the only demand that the proliferation of observational/divinatory records placed on generic structure. Beginning with Xiao Zixian's 蕭子顯 (A.D. 489–537) *Nan Qi shu*, the "*Tianwen* Treatise" shifts from a chronological to typological organization, subsuming planetary phenomena under the categories "encroachments" (*fan* 犯), "occultations" (*yan* 掩), "guarding in station" (*liu shou* 留守), "convergences" (*heju* 合聚), and "daylight appearances" (*zhou xian* 晝見). What is noteworthy about this typology is that *it is built around the parameters of actual planetary behavior* with no room for the fantastic or *a priori*—A.D. 479 is, for example, the last time our seasonal scheme for Mercury appears in such records. It is tempting to read this as evidence of *demystification*, especially since the number of "divinations" (*zhan* 占) in these texts dramatically tapers out over time, disappearing completely by the *Song shi* 宋史 (A.D. 1343). It is probably better to think of it, however, as evidence of a fundamental reorientation or "paradigm shift" within the field—the manic detail with which "encroachments" were recorded, for example, assuages our suspicion that people simply stopped believing in omenology. That this indeed reflects a reorientation of observational/divinatory practice is further suggested by a parallel trend unfolding in period omen compendia. In the *Lingtai miyuan* 靈臺秘苑 (c. A.D. 580), Yu Jicai 庾季才 (A.D. 516–603) significantly streamlines planetary omen series, focusing on encroachments upon asterisms and other moving bodies (again, normal planetary behavior); more to the point, he also substitutes traditional *tianwen* schemes with proper motion-degree models. Half a century later, Li Chunfeng 李淳風 (A.D. 602–670) does the very same in his in his *Yisi zhan*. Of course, it is worth noting that the models that Yu and Li provide are still much simpler than contemporary *li* ones, which might suggest that they were catering to *tianwen*-specific needs.[107]

---

107. *Lingtai miyuan* 靈臺秘苑 (Siku quanshu ed.), *juan* 9; *Yisi zhan*, *juan* 4-6, in *Zhongguo kexue jishu dianji tonghui: tianwen juan*, 505–534. The *Lingtai miyuan* evidently uses a very small denominator for the fractional parts of different grades' duration and distance, however, the numbers are so corrupt that it is difficult to reconstruct. The *Yisi zhan* uses larger denominators befitting contemporary motion-degree

2.5.4   Conclusion

Having determined a generic distinction between *tianwen* and *li* planetary models, I set out in this section to explore the relationship between reality and practice in each. Over the span of early imperial Chinese history, *li* planetary astronomy improved in the areas that counted to contemporary actors—the accuracy with which it could predict the date and position of visibility phenomena and a planet's subsequent position/disposition. This improvement took place in a complex social context. On the one hand, it was this context that inculcated actors with the shared values of empiricism, critical thinking, and innovation, that, despite their limitations in practice, allowed them to discover new problems, proffer new solutions, and outdo their ancestors, teachers, and social superiors. On the other hand, this social context also shaped their goals, methodologies, questions (i.e. the theory-ladenness of observation), the relative emphasis that they gave to those questions, and the success or failure of their projects. Astronomers set out to master the regularity of astronomical reality and, in their own way, they were much closer by the Sui.

On the face of it, *tianwen* omen literature took an antithetical stance towards observation, treating reality as a malleable medium for the encoding of divine will. This instilled a degree of confidence in *a priori* correlative and/or textual claims that allowed "facts" like the seasonal scheme for Mercury to carry on down the ages into Tang *tianwen* literature like the Dunhuang manuscript P.2881 and the *Qiaozi wuxing zhi* 譙子五行志. That said, reality *did* eventually impinge upon these "facts" at at least the level of renowned intellectuals and astral scientists, who began to question, historicize, ignore, and replace them in their contributions to the field. In my opinion, this contradiction hints at a growing divide in this period between

---

models as well as a seasonal algorithm for adjusting the predicted dates of mean visibility phenomena; however, unlike contemporary models, it does not include procedures for calculating the equation of center. It is also worth noting that the planetary astronomy of the *Yisi zhan* is completely distinct from that of Li Chunfeng's Chimera Virtue system (*Linde li* 麟德曆) instituted the year prior to his completion of the *Yisi zhan* (*Jiu Tang shu*, 33.1175–1219). Note that Wang Anli 王安禮 (A.D. 1034–1095) et al. redacted the *Lingtai miyuan* from 120 or 115 *juan* to 15 and added contemporary observational data to it in the Song. The fact, however, that the planetary models are corrupt and look very much like seventh-century ones leads me to believe that they are original.

both expert and popular literature and between practice and tradition. If the "*Tianwen* Treatise*" and omen compendium are any reliable indication, the omenology practiced at the state astronomical office might be said to have experienced its own form of progress— a progress in the practitioner's expectations towards reality as informed by observational experience and parallel advancements in *li*. However we define it, omen experts stopped accusing Mercury of misbehavior and turned their attention to the meaning of phenomena as they simply are.

What does this tell us about the hemerologically inspired planetary schemes of the *Wuxing zhan* and their parallels prior to the Triple Concordance system (#8)? Can we extend a generic distinction between *tianwen* and *li* models back to the second or third centuries B.C., or does hemerology represent a formative stage in Chinese planetary astronomy? This brings us to the second problem raised in Section 2.4: the *Wuxing zhan*'s incongruity as a text.

2.6   The *Wuxing zhan* as Manuscript

As a manuscript, the *Wuxing zhan* is a very different type of text from the other sources surveyed in this chapter. Texts like the *Huainanzi* come down to us because scholars in later centuries selected them for preservation, while texts that ceased to resonate with later generations—e.g. the *Jingzhou zhan*—all but disappear. Of course, preservation is not only selective, it requires redaction and adaptation to new formats.[108] The *Wuxing zhan*, on the other hand, is a real second-century B.C. text reflecting second-century B.C. interests and is written in the material and format in which second-century B.C. people wrote and consumed such texts.

The *Wuxing zhan* also belonged to someone—presumably the occupant of Mawangdui

---

108. On the *Huainanzi*, see Harold D. Roth, *The Textual History of the* Huai-nan Tzu, Monographs of the Association for Asian Studies 46 (Ann Arbor: Association for Asian Studies, 1992). On the other hand, of the 68 titles in 560 *juan* with obvious uranomantic contents recorded in the *Sui shu* imperial bibliography only one is extant: Yu Jicai's *Lingtai miyuan*, though this was edited down to one tenth its original size in the Song.

tomb 3, Li Xi, marquis of Dai. Li Xi appears to have been a wide reader considering that the *Wuxing zhan* was stored with more than twenty other manuscripts on topics ranging from political philosophy, history, divination, medicine, and macrobiotic hygiene, to celestial omens. The corruption of the mathematical portions of the *Wuxing zhan* manuscript suggests that its creator and owner were not expert astronomers. Rather, the owner may have simply collected it as an act of dilettantism, for its omenological contents, or perhaps, as Donald Harper has suggested, for the perceived numinousness of occult knowledge.[109]

Having no title, no author, and no authorial voice, the *Wuxing zhan* is not a "book" in the same sense as the *Huainanzi* or the *Shiji*. As Harper and Marc Kalinowski have argued at length, manuscripts on "numbers and techniques" in this and later periods tend to be personal creations of a highly variable and miscellaneous nature tailored to individual practical ends.[110] In the context of this manuscript culture, there is no reason to assume that the constituent elements of the *Wuxing zhan*—its omens, tables, and motion-degree models—were copied from a single source, nor that the copyist would synthesize these sources into one coherent theoretical system.

Its status vis-à-vis transmitted sources affords us a unique perspective on the astral sciences in early imperial China. At the most basic level, it preserves knowledge that is otherwise lost to us, e.g. details of Qin astronomical knowledge and the only extant example of planetary visibility tables. However, it also gives us clues about the way that people

---

109. "Warring States, Qin, and Han Manuscripts Related to Natural Philosophy and the Occult," in *New Sources of Early Chinese History: An Introduction to the Reading of Inscriptions and Manuscripts*, ed. Edward L. Shaughnessy (Berkeley: Society for the study of Early China and the Institute of East Asian Studies, University of California, Berkeley, 1997), 227. Several other manuscripts found at Mawangdui suggest that the tomb occupant had an interest in uranomancy: the *Huixing tu* 彗星圖 ("Comet Diagrams"), *Tianwen qixiang zazhan* 天文氣象雜占 ("Miscellaneous Celestial and Meteorological Prognostications"), and *Ri yue feng yu yun qi zhan* 日月風雨雲氣占 ("Sun, Moon, Wind, Rain, Clouds, and *Qi* Prognostications").

110. See especially Xia Dean 夏德安 (Donald Harper), "Zhoujiatai de shushu jian" 周家臺的數術簡, trans. Liu Jing 劉淨 and Yan Changgui 晏昌貴, *Jianbo* 2 (2007): 397–407; Donald Harper, "The Textual Form of Knowledge: Occult Miscellanies in Ancient and Medieval Chinese Manuscripts, Fourth Century B.C. to Tenth Century A.D.," in *Looking at It from Asia: The Processes That Shaped the Sources of History of Science*, ed. Robert S. Cohen, Jürgen Renn, and Kostas Gavroglu (Dordrecht: Springer, 2010), 37–80; Marc Kalinowski, "Les livres des jours (*rishu*) des Qin et des Han: la logique éditoriale du recueil A de Shuihudi (217 avant notre ère)," *T'oung Pao* 94, no. 1 (2008): 1–48.

transmitted and interacted with technical texts. For example, the numerical corruption and inversion is clear evidence that this text was copied visually from another source or sources. It also appears that the owner added to the text, filling out the tables several years after having produced the manuscript (see p. 105). The archaeological context of this manuscript furthermore confirms a number of facts gleaned from transmitted sources: that access to astronomical and omenological knowledge was relatively free, and that Qin knowledge and institutions carried on uninterrupted into the Han.

Lastly, the *Wuxing zhan* highlights another overlooked aspect of "science literacy" in the age of manuscripts. As is clearly the case with the proliferation of daybooks—and as Harper has shown also to be true of medicine and macrobiotic hygiene—nobles and intellectuals became connoisseurs of the technical knowledge of experts.[111] The *Wuxing zhan* reminds us, however, that before the age of printing, the transmission of technical knowledge relied upon a very selective and imperfect human process that, when texts circulated independent of experts, was particularly liable to corruption and the profusion of outmoded knowledge.

The planetary knowledge contained in the *Wuxing zhan* is heterogeneous and incongruous. It defies the generic distinction that we see elsewhere between *tianwen* an *li* in the way that it devotes equal halves of the text to both. The motion-degree models are corrupt, but even if they were not, the inaccuracy of the SYSTEM ORIGIN—Qin propaganda in a Han text— would skew results calculated therefrom. Lastly, the visibility tables are compiled using an incompatible mixture of hemerological and mathematical knowledge and plotted onto solar rather than civil time. All in all, it is not a particularly functional text from the vantage of astronomy. This is a consequence, I believe, not of genre but of the context of manuscript culture. I suspect that the *Wuxing zhan* does not come together as a coherent whole because it is has been pieced together from different texts and added to by someone who might not have entirely understood its contents. This, I believe, is particularly evident in the case of the

---

111. Donald Harper, *Early Chinese Medical Literature: The Mawangdui Medical Manuscripts* (London: Kegan Paul International, 1998), 55–67; cf. "Warring States, Qin, and Han Manuscripts Related to Natural Philosophy and the Occult."

visibility tables, where the compiler is able to correctly calculate the subsequent positions of Venus, but opts for the easier hemerological models for Jupiter and Saturn seemingly unaware of, or unbothered by, their contradictions with the motion-degree models which he appends to the tables. The fact that the tables are incompatible with the civil calendar and are oriented *to the past* rather than to the future also leads me to believe that they are there more objects of intellectual curiosity than of practical use.

2.7   Conclusion

It is difficult to know where to place the *Wuxing zhan* in the history of the astral sciences due to the text's incongruous nature. In this chapter, I have attempted to explain its incongruities in terms of genre and provenance. I argue that many of its planetary models are at odds with reality as a product of the formal influence of hemerological schemes and their function in omenology to produce meaning out of incongruity. The fact that they are also inconsistent with one another, furthermore, I suspect to be related to the personalized and miscellaneous nature in which period technical knowledge was transmitted through manuscripts. Likewise, I suspect that the textual corruption and the inconsistent application of knowledge in the compilation of the visibility tables is a product of the inexpertise of the compiler, copyist, and/or owner, whatever their relationship may be.

In this chapter, I also broach the question of the relationship between reality and practice in the Chinese astral sciences. The case of planetary knowledge is more complex than we might have expected. In *li* calendro-astronomy, actors shared a common set of values emphasizing empiricism and critical thinking. These and a variety of complex motives allowed them to effect real progress over time—progress, at least, in terms of the goals that they set for themselves and within the limits of the methodologies they employed. Other individual and social complexities, however, acted to determine the focus, inertia, and recognition of actors' projects in ways that made this progress less linear and more human. In omenology, *a priori* planetary knowledge continued to thrive in certain types of literature;

however, experts began to hold them up to contemporary observational and mathematical knowledge, transforming them from facts to objects of historical curiosity, marginalizing, omitting, replacing, and eventually *preserving* this knowledge in their contributions to the genre.

One question remains: do the incongruous models of the *Wuxing zhan* and their parallels in other early texts represent the formative stage of planetary astronomy in China or can we extend the generic distinction between *tianwen* and *li* planetary models to them as well? Setting aside the problematic claims of precedence for Pre-Qin figures like Shi Shen and Gan De, the *Wuxing zhan* is the earliest extant source on planetary astronomy in China by several decades. It is thus telling that we see already in the *Wuxing zhan* two distinct types of model—one, a clear parallel with later *tianwen* models, that uses measures like months and lodges, and the other, a clear antecedent to the *li* motion-degree model, that uses measures like days and *du* down, in each case, to a precision of 240 parts. These model-types, furthermore, are *segregated* in the first and second halves of the text in implied acknowledgment of their difference and, perhaps, incommensurability. Therefore, instead of looking at the *Wuxing zhan* as a whole, we might look at it as the sum of different parts— parts through which distinct types of knowledge filter down to us, including a crucial clue about the beginnings of mathematical planetary astronomy in the Qin.

CHAPTER 3

CALENDARS AND SOCIETY

In this chapter I turn from the *Wu xing zhan* 五星占 to a very different excavated source for the astral sciences: early imperial calendars. Be it between astronomy and calendrics, professional and quotidian product, or expert and public knowledge, calendars sit at the opposite end of the spectrum from the other materials treated in this study. Legend tells us that the prime directive of *li* 曆 is the betterment of everyday life, the coordination of social and natural rhythms to ensure bounteous harvests, harmonious relations, and the appeasement of the spirits. Given this soteriological outlook, it is crucial for any history of Chinese astronomy to take up the *realia* through which the state insinuated its presence *and its science* into the daily lives of its citizenry. Considering the end products of *li* sheds invaluable light on the networks of knowledge and textual production that linked the intellectual labors of the "great men" of the history of science to the more mundane labors of the early imperial everyman, addressing the common themes of empiricism, progress, and plurality. It also allows us to flesh out the ceremonial and administrative logistics of this production to understand how real historical actors went about the sacred task of "reverently granting the people the seasons" 敬授人時. [1]

In Section 3.1, I offer a survey of extant calendars, discussing the codicology, layout, contents, and organizational principles of four types of early imperial *li*: daily calendars, sexagenary calendar rounds, *shuo-run* 朔閏 tables, and handy tables. As in the previous chapter, my analysis of primary sources places particular emphasis on questions of functionality and textual corruption. In Section 3.2, I examine what these sources reveal about the relationship between astronomy and calendrics within the field of *li* "calendro-astronomy,"

---

1. *Shangshu zhushu* 尚書注疏 (Siku quanshu ed.), 1.8b. On the legend of *li*, see Section 1.1.2

asking how much *li* goes into the typical calendar, and how much of the typical calendar comes from *li*. I argue that, while not unrelated, we see a schism between calendrics and astronomy reminiscent of that between the *tianwen* 天文 and *li* planetary models explored in Chapter 2. In Section 3.3, I then address the logistics of the state's production, ritualization, and dissemination of civil time. From an overview of classical precedence in Section 3.3.1, I move in Section 3.3.2 to the question of how early imperial courts interpreted and implemented classical patterns. What I find is that there existed manifest incongruities between ritual scholarship and ritual practice, and that, perhaps surprisingly, the state seems to have mastered the administrative logistics of time-control long before the ceremonies. Lastly, in the conclusion, I briefly discuss the hybridity of public and private space inherent in "the calendar" of the manuscript age.

3.1 Survey of Extant Calendars

Scholars break the history of calendars in China into two periods along an absolute divide circa A.D. 630–658: the period of *liri* 曆日 "calendars" and the period of *juzhu liri* 具注曆日 "annotated calendars," or "almanacs." For whatever reason, self-titled *juzhi liri* at once wholly replaced their "calendar" forerunners in the archaeological record between these dates. Other than title, era, and medium (bamboo & wood vs. paper), the difference, according to Jiang Xiaoyuan 江曉原, is that while *liri* might offer hemerological annotations, *juzhu liri* give direct hemerological advice about the auspiciousness of each day for various quotidian activities.[2] The latter is beyond the scope of this dissertation; everything else is just "calendars." Being defined as what it's not, the term "calendars" rings somewhat

---

2. "Lishu qiyuan kao" 曆書起源考, *Zhongguo wenhua* 中國文化 1992.6: 150–159. On the transition between "calendars" and 'annotated calendars," see also Deng Wenkuan 鄧文寬, "Cong 'liri' dao 'juzhu liri' de zhuanbian" 從「曆日」到「具注曆日」的轉變, in *Dunhuang Tulufan tianwen lifa yanjiu* 敦煌吐魯番 天文曆法研究 (Lanzhou: Gansu jiaoyu chubanshe, 2002), 134–144. For the "annotated calendars" of the Dunhuang 敦煌 cave library, see Deng Wenkuan ed., *Dunhuang tianwen lifa wenxian jijiao* 敦煌天文曆法文 獻輯校 (Nanjing: Jiangsu guji chubanshe, 1996); Marc Kalinowski ed., *Divination et société dans la Chine médiévale: étude des manuscrits de Dunhuang de la Bibliothèque nationale de France et de la British Library* (Paris: Bibliothèque nationale de France, 2003), 85–211.

hollow when we deprive it of its foil. So-called *liri* feature a variety of media, layouts, and, importantly, *titles*, unbound by any single actors' category except, perhaps, *li*—"sequence," "table," "calendar," "calendro-astronomy," etc. (see Section 1.1.3).[3] Whatever they should be called, there are dozens of calendar-like texts extant from the early imperial period, most of which are manuscripts excavated from tombs and administrative dump sites. The corpus is extremely fragmentary; fortunately, Bo Shuren 薄樹人 and Yoshimura Masayuki 吉村昌之 have produced authoritative catalogs that give us easy access to relevant photographs and transcriptions.[4]

Be they ancient or modern, calendars do not make particularly good reading. The majority of scholarship on the topic is devoted to the reconstruction of the civil calendar and the mathematical algorithms behind it. This is a labor of love shared by only a very few, the polished veneer of reference works like Zhang Peiyu's 張培瑜 *Sanqianwubai nian liri tianxiang* 三千五百年曆日天象 being the threshold beyond which the average historian does not pass. He is wise in this, for beyond this threshold lies vertiginous uncertainty. What we know about calendrics prior to Qin Shihuang's 秦始皇 reign (246–221 B.C. as king; 221–210 B.C. as emperor) is incomplete, contentious, and unlikely to see satisfactory resolution.[5] After 246 B.C., the archaeological record begins to provide us with clearly dated documents and honest-to-goodness calendars, but the more we find, the more they disagree with contemporary accounts *and one another*, leaving experts like Zhang Peiyu and Li Zhonglin 李

---

3. The locus classicus for the term *liri* as "calendar" is Wang Chong's 王充 *Lunheng* 論衡 of circa A.D. 70/80 (*Lunheng jiaoshi* 論衡校釋 [Zhonghua shuju ed.], 17.757), and it features as the title of only a single excavated calendar from A.D. 450/451 (see p. 213).

4. Bo Shuren 薄樹人 ed., "Han jian lipu" 漢簡曆譜, in *Zhongguo kexue jishu dianji tonghui: tianwen juan* 中國科學技術典籍通彙 · 天文卷, 1:221–261 (Zhengzhou: Hebei jiaoyu chubanshe, 1993); Yoshimura Masayuki 吉村昌之, "Shutsudo kandoku shiryō ni mirareru rekihu no shūsei" 出土簡牘資料にはみれる曆譜の集成, in *Henkyō shutsudo mokkan no kenkyū* 邊疆出土木簡の研究, ed. Tomiya Itaru 冨谷至, 459–516 (Kyōto: Hōyū shoten, 2003). Unless otherwise noted, all manuscript materials discussed in this chapter are derived from these sources.

5. For recent attempts to address the uncertainties of pre-Qin calendrics, see Hirase Takao 平勢隆郎, *Chūgoku kodai kinen no kenkyū: tenmon to koyomi no kentō kara* 中國古代紀年の研究 : 天文と曆の檢討から (Tōkyō: Kyūko Shoin, 1996); Robert H. Gassmann, *Antikchinesisches Kalenderwesen: die Rekonstruktion der chunqiu-zeitlichen Kalender des Fürstentums Lu und der Zhou-Könige* (Bern: Peter Lang, 2002).

忠林 no choice but to produce new tables after every significant find. As of 2007, for example, Zhang Peiyu has concluded that, over the period when all sources agree that the Qin Zhuanxu system (#2) was in effect—?–103 B.C.—there were no less than two different systems in operation, neither of which accord with its parameters as recorded in transmitted literature.[6] After the Grand Inception *li* reform of 104 B.C., we begin to find a glut of calendars, which, overall, better accord with what we know about period calendrics. Even so, modern scholars are caught in something of an epistemic loop, dating calendar fragments based on numerical tables and, on the other hand, correcting the self-same tables by means of the self-same fragments.[7] Even more unsettling is the evidence that Huang Yi-long 黄一農 has brought to light about arbitrary human intervention in calendrical algorithms, which I discuss in Section 3.2.1.

Second to the project of reconstruction is the study of annotation. Annotations on extant calendars invariably fall into one of three categories: holidays, hemerologies (elements of calendar divination), and personal/official journal entries. These do make for better reading than the rows and columns of *ganzhi* 干支 dates within which they are woven, but they are so formulaic and laconic as to tell stories only in the aggregate. There is a growing body of scholarship concerned with glossing such annotations and connecting them with relevant fields of knowledge, particularly the daybook (*rishu* 日書) hemerological miscellanies excavated from the third and second centuries B.C.[8] Particularly interesting in this regard

---

6. Entries in this genre are too numerous to list here. For recent works, see Zhang Peiyu, "Genju xinchu liri jiandu shilun Qin he Han chu de lifa" 根据新出歷日簡牘試論秦和漢初的曆法, *Zhongyuan wenwu* 中原文物 2007.5: 62–77; Li Zhonglin, "Zhoujiatai Qin jian lipu xinian yu Qin shiqi lifa" 周家臺秦簡曆譜係年與秦時期曆法, *Lishi yanjiu* 歷史研究 2010.6: 36–53. Note that Huang Yi-long 黄一農 posits an even more complex situation for the Qin-Han period in "Qin wangzheng shiqi lifa xinkao" 秦王政時期曆法新考, *Huaxue* 華學 5 (2001): 143–149.

7. See the methodological remarks in Luo Jianjin 羅見今 and Guan Shouyi 關守義, "Dunhuang, Juyan Hanjian zhong yu shuorunbiao bu he zhu jian kaoshi" 敦煌、居延漢簡中與朔閏表不合諸簡考釋, *Wenshi* 文史 no. 1 (2000): 57–72, esp. 58.

8. For example, see Wang Su 王素, "Qushi Gaochang lifa chutan" 麴氏高昌曆法初探, in *Chutu wenxian yanjiu xuji* 出土文獻研究續集, ed. Zhang Qingling 張慶玲 and Guojia wenwu ju gu wenxian yanjiu shi 國家文物局古文獻研究室 (Beijing: Wenwu chubanshe, 1989), 148–180; Zhang Peiyu, "Chutu Han jian boshu shang de lizhu" 出土漢簡帛書上的曆注, in ibid., 135–147; Liu Lexian 劉樂賢, "Yinwan Han mu chutu lipu jiqi xiangguan wenti" 尹灣漢墓出土曆譜及其相關問題, *Huaxue* 3 (1998): 247–257; Deng Wenkuan,

is Huang Yi-long's study of the Yinwan 尹灣 M6 calendars, wherein he compares the tomb occupant's diary entries concerning official travels with travel-related hemerologies found in the same tomb, concluding that, in practice, hemerology was much more flexible and open to interpretation than it appears in theory.[9] There is always more work to be done on this topic, but one cannot escape the feeling that most of what can be said has been said already.

It is not my intent to move either of these discourses forward; if anything, this chapter does not resolve confusion surrounding the civil calendar but embrace it. My intent, rather, is to make these calendars tell a story that is relevant to the central themes of this dissertation, i.e. the diversity of practices within the astral sciences, incongruities between theory and practice, ideal and reality, features of technical knowledge in a manuscript culture, and, of course, questions of empiricism and progress. To this end, I have deemed it more important to provide scale reproductions of the text and physical support of manuscript calendars than to translate them in full, because their dimensions, layout, and other codicological features tell just as much of that story as their textual contents. Guided as I am by different questions, my selection of primary sources and organization of those sources into typological categories differ from previous surveys: I have divided early imperial calendars (and calendar-related *li*) into four types based on their underlying organizational principle, subordinate to which I place textual/material layout.[10] Irrespective of whether or not a calendar is titled (or what

---

"Dunhuang guli congshi" 敦煌古曆叢識, in *Dunhuang Tulufan tianwen lifa yanjiu*, 105–122; "Yinwan Han mu chutu lipu bushuo" 尹灣漢墓出土曆譜補說, in ibid., 296–303; Alain Arrault, "Les premiers calendriers chinois du IIe siècle avant notre ère au Xe siècle," in *Les Calendriers: Leurs enjeux dans l'espace et dans le temps: colloque de Cerisy, du 1er au 8 juillet 2000*, ed. Jacques Le Goff, Jean Lefort, and Perrine Mane, 169–191 (Paris: Somogy, 2002).

9. "Cong Yinwan Han mu jiandu kan Zhongguo shehui de zeri chuantong" 從尹灣漢簡牘看中國社會的擇日傳統, *Guoli zhongyang yanjiuyuan lishi yuyan yanjiusuo jikan* 國立中央研究院歷史語言研究所集刊 70, no. 3 (1999): 589–625.

10. For other typologies, see Michael Loewe, "Some Notes on Han-time Documents from Chüyen," *T'oung Pao*, 2d ser., 47, no. 3/5 (1959): 294–322; Arrault, "Les premiers calendriers chinois du IIe siècle avant notre ère au Xe siècle"; Yoshimura, "Shutsudo kandoku shiryō ni mirareru rekihu no shūsei"; Cai Wanjin 蔡萬進, "Yinwan Han jian Yuanyan er nian riji wenshu yuanyuan tansuo" 尹灣漢簡『元延二年日記』文書淵源探索, *Zhengzhou daxue xuebao (zhexue shehui kexue ban)* 鄭州大學學報（哲學社會科學版） 37, no. 1 (2004): 22–26; Li Ling 李零, "Shiri, rishu he yeshu—san zhong jianbo wenxian de qubie he dingming" 視日、日書书和葉書 —三種簡帛文獻的區別和定名, *Wenwu* 文物 2008.12: 73–80; Su Junlin 蘇俊林, "Guanyu 'zhiri' jian de mingcheng yu xingzhi" 關於「質日」簡的名稱與性質, *Hunan daxue xuebao (shehui kexue ban)* 湖南大學

187

that title might be), Chinese-language scholarship has tended to identify excavated calendars by reign, regnal year, and either *lipu* 曆譜 or *liri* 曆日 ("calendar"), with the archaeological source being optional.[11] To avoid confusion, albeit at the danger of prolixity, I have decided instead to identify titled calendars by their titles and untitled calendars by their source, (transliterated) reign, regnal year, Julian year, and type.

3.1.1 Daily calendars

As of 2013, the earliest form of excavated calendar in our possession is the "daily calendar." We have no less than six examples of daily calendars from between 220 B.C. and 142 B.C., five of which bear the title *zhiri* 質日, preceded by the year of the assumed reign period.[12] Early examples are typically divided into six registers, each of which runs through two consecutive months. Found at the beginning and middle of each register, the month is written either above or before the *ganzhi* 干支 date of its inception (below) and is often highlighted by means of conspicuous ink blocks (the one exception to this rule is intercalary month IX^2, which one finds appended to the end of such calendars, running across multiple registers like

---

學報 (社會科學版) 24, no. 4 (2010): 17–22.

11. There are a number of problems inherent in this practice. First, the date of any one calendar is arguable, and thus different chronologies propagate different names for the same objects. Second, there are in some cases multiple calendars belonging to the same year, placing multiple objects under the same name. Third, this practice fails to distinguish between titled and untitled manuscripts, obfuscating actors' categories for said objects. Fourth, it sometimes results in the renaming of titled manuscripts, such as the Yinqueshan 銀雀山 M2 *Qi nian shiri* 七年視日, which earlier scholars renamed the *Yuanguang yuan nian lipu* 『元光元年曆譜』 because Jianyuan 7 (134 B.C.), to which said calendar belonged, was later changed by imperial order to Yuanguang 1. The scholarship mentioned in note 10 has already begun to address these problems.

12. In addition to the (1) Zhoujiatai 周家臺 and (2) Yuelu Academy Shihuang 34 (213 B.C.) calendars discussed below, there are also the Yuelu (3) *X-qi nian zhiri* □ 七年質日 (220 B.C.) and (4) *Sawu nian si zhiri* 卅五年私質日 (212 B.C.) calendars, and the currently unpublished (5) *Qi nian zhiri* 七年質日 (179 B.C.) from Zhangjiashan 張家山 M136 and (6) *Zhiri* from Shuihudi 睡虎地 M77 (Chen Songchang 陳松長 ed., *Yuelu Qin jian* 嶽麓秦簡 [Shanghai: Shanghai cishu chubanshe, 2010], 3–9, 19–24, 47–65, 91–106; Jingzhou diqu bowuguan 荊州地區博物館, "Jiangling Zhangjiashan liang zuo Han mu chutu dapi zhujian" 江陵張家山兩座漢墓出土大批竹簡, *Wenwu* 1992.9: 1–11; Hubei sheng wenwu kaogu yanjiusuo 湖北省文物考古研究所, and Yunmeng xian bowuguan 雲夢縣博物館, "Hubei Yunmeng Shuihudi M77 fajue jianbao" 湖北雲夢睡虎地 M77 發掘簡報, *Jiang Han kaogu* 江漢考古 2008.4: 31–37). To this list one might also add (7) the Edsen-gol (Juyan 居延), Mu-durbeljin (Pochengzi 破城子) A14 (111 • 6) Benshi 4 (13 B.C.) calendar fragment.

an afterthought). Counted in sexagenary *ganzhi* binomes, the days are arrayed one-by-one from the start of each month, which necessitates at least 59–60 columns per register and, thus, the capacious medium of the bamboo or wood bookmat (excavated examples run just shy of a half a meter in length).

Let us begin with the Yuelu Academy *Sasi nian zhiri* 卅四年質日 Shihuang 34 calendar (fig. 3.1) and the untitled Zhoujiatai 周家臺 M30 Shihuang 34 calendar (fig. 3.2)—*zhiri* from the same year (213 B.C.) but different sites.[13] In terms of form, the two are as close to carbon copies as one gets in early manuscript culture, especially between separate finds. Their differences come down to only a few points: (1) the Yuelu manuscript is titled; (2) the Zhoujiatai slips (≈ 29.5 cm by 0.6 cm) are 2.5 cm longer than the Yuelu slips (≈ 27 cm by 0.6 cm); (3) the Zhoujiatai manuscript ends with four blank slips; (4) the Yuelu manuscript omits block-highlighting along the center binding; and (5) the Zhoujiatai manuscript marks the rows of intercalary month dates off from the rest of the calendar with dots. Furthermore, the two were put to the same use, recording the travels and activities of local-level administrators in the Chu 楚 region (Table 3.1).

The formal and functional congruity between these and other other manuscripts suggest that the *zhiri* was a standardized bureaucratic document. In 2008, Li Ling 李零 argued to read *zhi* 質 (**tśit*) as "compare" or "check" (*shi* 視 [**gi*]), explaining *zhiri* as a "date-lookup" archival record of official business.[14] Two years later, the publication of the Yuelu Academy calendars somewhat complicated this reading, particularly the *Sawu nian si zhiri* 卅五年私質日 (212 B.C.). This "private *zhiri*" bears an identical repertoire of annotations—"lodging" (*su* 宿), "management" (*zhi* 治), and so on—from which Su Junlin 蘇俊林 argues that *zhiri* manuscripts were personal *aide-mémoires* rather than official documents. Su's argument is

---

13. For original photographs and transcriptions, see *Yuelu Qin jian*, 10–18, 67–89; *Guanju Qin-Han mu jiandu* 關沮秦漢墓簡牘, ed. Hubei sheng Jingzhou shi Zhouliang yuqiao yizhi bowuguan 湖北省荊州市周梁玉橋遺址博物館 (Beijing: Zhonghua shuju, 2001), 11–17, 93–99.

14. "Shiri, rishu he yeshu—san zhong jianbo wenxian de qubie he dingming." Phonetic reconstructions according to Axel Schuessler's Later Han Chinese in his *ABC Etymological Dictionary of Old Chinese* (Honolulu: University of Hawai'i Press, 2007).

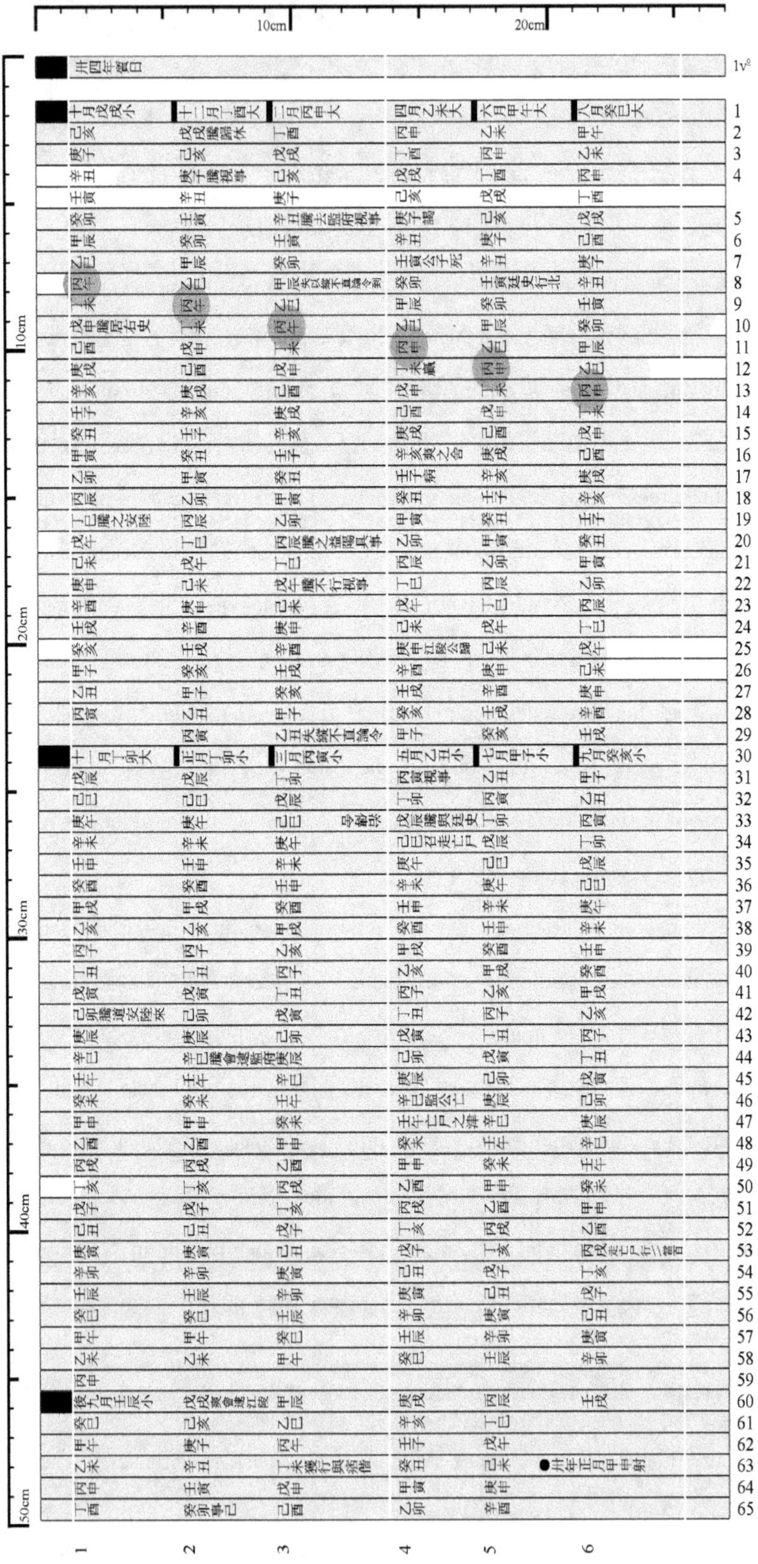

Figure 3.1: Yuelu Academy *Sasi nian zhiri* 卅四年質日 Shihuang 34 (213 B.C.) calendar

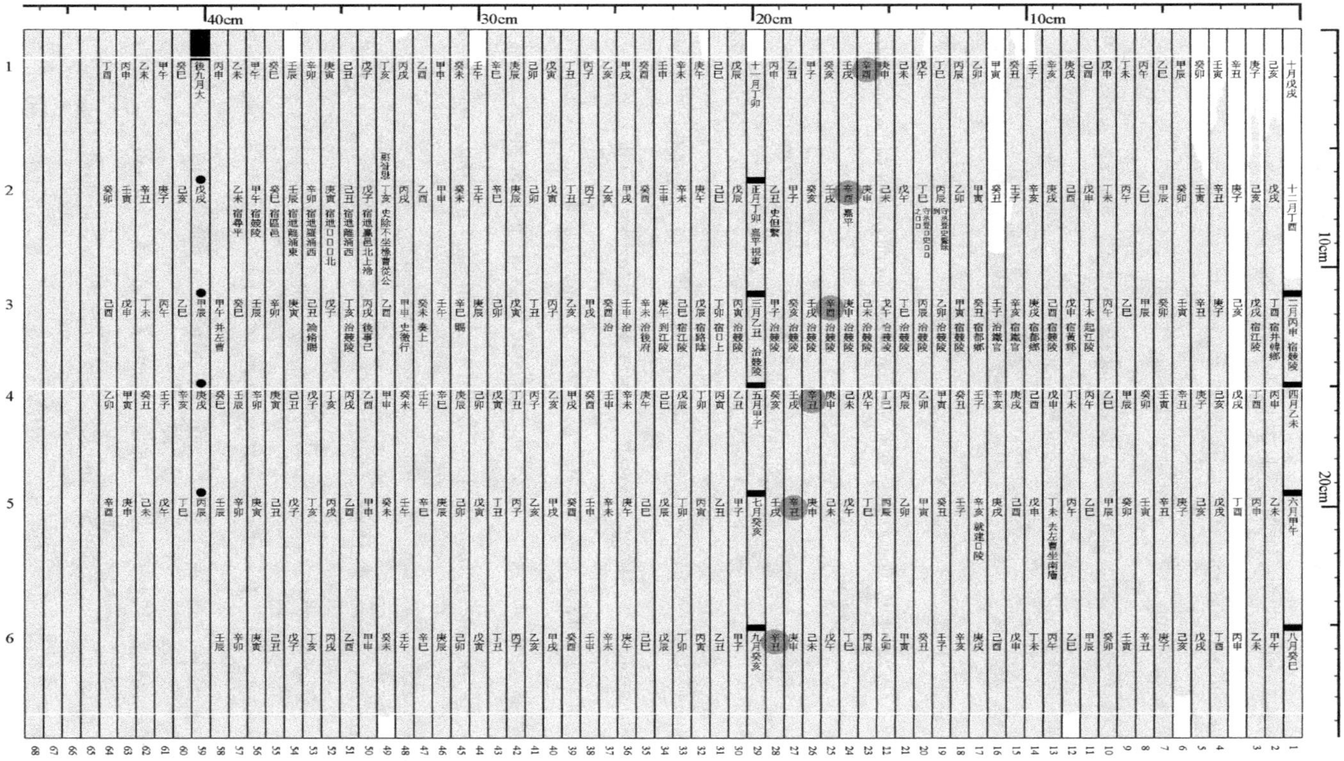

Figure 3.2: Zhoujiatai 周家臺 M30 Shihuang 34 (213 B.C.) calendar

twofold: first, the archaeological context—tombs—and notational style—e.g. the omission of the subject—are inconsistent with archival materials; second, the fact that literate tomb occupants were almost invariably government office workers necessarily confounds distinctions of public and private spheres.[15] Given our current understanding of Qin-Han bureaucratic procedure and tomb culture, this question is unlikely to see swift resolution.

Where these calendars *do* bear the unambiguous mark of the personal is in their production. In a manuscript culture, even highly standardized documents such as these are liable to idiosyncrasies and human imperfections. In the Yuelu and Zhoujiatai Shihuang 34 calendars, for example, the second character of a number of *ganzhi* dates is clearly miswritten: Yuelu register 6, slips 5–7 read *wuxu*.35 → *jiyou*.46 → *gengzi*.37, and Zhoujiatai register 1, slips 27–29 read *yichou*.02 → *bingshen*.33 → *dingmao*.04. Sometimes these mistakes cascade down through subsequent registers. As I have used circles to indicate in figs. 3.1 & 3.2, for example, the aforementioned errors occur on register 4 of both the Yuelu and Zhoujiatai manuscripts and are repeated in registers 5 & 6. The Zhoujiatai Shihuang 34 calendar exhibits yet another idiosyncrasy: in register 1, it skips the blank that the Yuelu calendar (slip 29) leaves between the last day of month X (small) and the first day of month XI such that, by the new moons on slip 29, subsequent registers fall one space short of the 30 days spanned by the large months II, IV, VI, and VIII. In register 2, the compiler skips *bingyin*.03, placing the new moon on *dingmao*.04, as we would expect; in registers 3–5, however, he continues the sexagenary count uninterrupted, shifting months III, V, and VII one day forward; then, apparently aware of his mistake, he skips *renyin*.39 in register 6, returning month IX to the correct date. Given that *ganzhi* were common and basic knowledge covered at the beginning of one's elementary education, it likely that these mistakes were the products of careless copying (after all, the compiler of the Zhoujiatai Shihuang 34 calendar was able to correct himself). Furthermore, the fact that errors cascade down through subsequent registers suggests that calendar copying was preformed visually rather than, say, by memory,

---

15. "Guanyu 'zhiri' jian de mingcheng yu xingzhi."

Table 3.1: Yuelu and Zhoujiatai Shihuang 34 (213 B.C.) calendar annotations

Date		Event	
Chinese	Julian	Yuelu	Zhoujiatai
Month I, Shihuang 30 (217 B.C.)			
jiashen.21	Mar 08	射 Archery [ritual]	
...			
Month X, Shihuang 34 (212–213 B.C.)			
wushen.45	Nov 12	騰居右史 Teng occupied Clerk of the Right	
bingchen.53	Nov 20	騰之安陸 Teng went to Anlu	
Month XI			
jimao.16	Dec 13	騰道安陸來 Teng came to Anlu (?)	
Month XII			
wuxu.35	Jan 01	騰歸休 Teng returned, rested	
gengzi.37	Jan 03	騰視事 Teng assumed office	
bingchen.53	Jan 19		守丞登史豎除 Follow Assistant Deng; Clerk Shu transferred
dingsi.54	Jan 20		守丞登 □ 史 □□ 之 □□ Follow Assistant Deng; Clerk ... arrived ...
xinyou.58	Jan 24		嘉平 Jiaping [festival]
yichou.02	Jan 28		史但擊 Scribe Dan arrested
Month I			
dingmao.04	Jan 30		嘉平視事 Jiaping [festival], assumed office
xinsi.18	Feb 13	騰會逮監府 Teng taken into custody by supervisory office	
dinghai.24	Feb 19		史除不坐橡曹從公宿長道 Scribe transferred; not sitting in at clerk's office, following his Excellency; lodged in Changdao
wuzi.25	Feb 20		宿迣贏邑北上淛 Lodged in Shangdi, north of Ying Settlement, Zhi
jichou.26	Feb 21		宿迣離涌西 Lodged west of Liyong, Zhi
gengyin.27	Feb 22		宿迣 □□ 北 Lodged north of ... Zhi
xinsi.28	Feb 23		宿 迣 羅 涌 西 Lodged west of [Li]yong, Zhi
renchen.29	Feb 24		宿迣離涌東 Lodged east of Liyong, Zhi
guisi.30	Feb 25		宿區邑 Lodged in Qu Settlement
jiawu.31	Feb 26		宿競陵 Lodged in Jingling
yiwei.32	Feb 27		宿尋平 Lodged in Xunping

Table 3.1, continued

| Date | | Event | |
Chinese	Julian	Yuelu	Zhoujiatai
		Month II	
*bingshen.*33	Feb 28		宿競陵 Lodged in Jingling
*dingyou.*34	Feb 29		宿井韓鄉 Lodged in Jinghan District
*wuxu.*35	Mar 01		宿江陵 Lodged in Jiangling
*xinchou.*38	Mar 04	騰去監府視事 Teng left supervisory office and assumed office	
*jiachen.*41	Mar 07	失縱不直論令到 AWOL ordinance arrived	
*dingwei.*44	Mar 10		起江陵 Departed Jiangling
*wushen.*45	Mar 11		宿黃郵 Lodged in Huang postal station
*jiyou.*46	Mar 12		宿競陵 Lodged in Jingling
*gengxu.*47	Mar 13		宿都鄉 Lodged in Du District
*xinhai.*48	Mar 14		治鐵官
*renzi.*49	Mar 15		治鐵官 Managed iron office
*guichou.*50	Mar 16		治鐵官 Managed iron office
*jiayin.*51	Mar 17		宿都鄉 Lodged in Du District
*yimao.*52	Mar 18		宿競陵 Lodged in Jingling
*bingchen.*53	Mar 19	騰之益陽具事 Teng went to Yiyang on business	治競陵 Managed Jingling
*dingsi.*54	Mar 20		治競陵 Managed Jingling
*wuwu.*55	Mar 21	騰不行視事 Teng did not travel, assumed office	治競陵 Managed Jingling
*jiwei.*56	Mar 22		治競陵 Managed Jingling
*gengshen.*57	Mar 23		治競陵 Managed Jingling
*xinyou.*58	Mar 24		治競陵 Managed Jingling
*renxu.*59	Mar 25		治競陵 Managed Jingling
*guihai.*60	Mar 26		治競陵 Managed Jingling
*jiazi.*01	Mar 27	失縱不直論令 AWOL ordinance	治競陵 Managed Jingling
*yichou.*02	Mar 28		治競陵 Managed Jingling
		Month III	
*bingyin.*03	Mar 29		治競陵 Managed Jingling
*dingmao.*04	Mar 30		宿 □ 上 Lodged upon ...
*wuchen.*05	Mar 31		宿路陰 Lodged in Luyin
*jisi.*06	Apr 01		宿江陵 Lodged in Jiangling
*gengwu.*07	Apr 02		到江陵 Arrived in Jiangling
*xinwei.*08	Apr 03		治後府 Managed back office
*renshen.*09	Apr 04		治 Managed
*guiyou.*10	Apr 05		治 Managed
*xinsi.*18	Apr 13		賜 Ci
*guiwei.*20	Apr 15		奏上 Petition superior

Table 3.1, continued

| Date | | Event | |
Chinese	Julian	Yuelu	Zhoujiatai
jiashen.21	Apr 16		史徹行 Scribe Che traveled
bingxu.23	Apr 18		後事已 Back [office] matters finished
dinghai.24	Apr 19		治競陵 Managed Jingling
jichou.26	Apr 21		論脩賜 Tried Xiu & Ci
jiawu.31	Apr 26		并左曹 Merged with Office of the Left
Month IV			
gengzi.37	May 02	謁 Paid respects	
renyin.39	May 04	公子死 His Excellency died	
dingwei.44	May 09	嬴 Ying	
xinhai.48	May 13	爽之舍 Shuang went to [his] lodge	
renzi.49	May 14	病 Sick	
gengshen.57	May 22	江陵公歸 Excellency of Jiangling returned	
Month V			
bingyin.03	May 28	視事 Assumed office	
wuchen.05	May 30	騰與廷史治傳舍 Teng and court scribe managed the inn	
jisi.06	May 31	召走亡尸 Summoned escaped corpse (?)	
xinsi.18	Jun 12	監公亡 Supervisor Excellency AWOL	
renwu.19	Jun 13	亡尸之津 Lost corpse (?) went to Jin	
guisi.30	Jun 24	廷史行＝南 Court scribe traveled, traveled south	
Month VI			
renyin.39	Jul 03	廷史行北 Court scribe traveled north	
dingwei.44	Jul 08		去左曹坐南廥 Departed Office of the Left, sat in at barn
xinhai.48	Jul 10		就建口陵 Went to Jian...ling
Month VII			
		—	
Month VIII			
		—	
Month IX			
bingxu.23	Oct 15	走亡尸行＝當百 Escaped corpse traveled, traveled about 100 (?)	

Table 3.1, continued

Date		Event	
Chinese	Julian	Yuelu	Zhoujiatai
		Month IX[2]	
wuxu.35	Oct 27	爽會逮江陵 Shuang taken into custody in Jiangling	
guimao.40	Nov 01	事已 Matter finished	
dingwei.44	Nov 05	獲行與痁偕 Apprehended Xing and Pi together	

which makes intuitive sense given how the *ganzhi* of each register tend to repeat one slip to the left (below).

In addition to the early self-styled *zhiri*, we have recovered a second corpus of daily calendars from administrative dump sites along the Gansu Corridor and, secondarily, Eastern Seaboard tombs (i.e. Yinqueshan 銀雀山 M2 in Linyi 臨沂 and Yinwan M6 in Lianyungang 連雲港). Not only is this corpus distinct in terms of geographic location and archaeological context, it spans a different historical period—134 B.C. – A.D. 90—and is dominated by a different medium—wood. It also features slight variations on the *zhiri* layout: sexagenary dates are written horizontally, each month is given its own register, and each slip/column is labeled with an ordinal date counted from new moon. This last point coincides with a shift from sexagenary to ordinal date notation that Loewe has identified as occurring in Eastern Han 東漢 (A.D. 25–220) official documents—a shift, Lao Gan 勞榦 suggests, from a traditional to a more utile and popular form.[16] Whatever the popular status of ordinal dating, it is important to note that it was implicit in the *zhiri* layout from the very start—the first slip/column is the first day of each month, the second the second, and so on, and, as we saw above, compilers interrupt the sexagenary cycle to maintain the integrity of this ordinal

---

16. Loewe, "Some Notes on Han-time Documents from Chüyen," 308–314; Lao Gan, "Shangsi kao" 上巳考, *Minzuxue yanjiusuo jikan* 民族學研究所集刊 29, no. 1 (1970): 243–262, esp. 248. It is important to note that Loewe and Lao identify this as a gradual shift between existing conventions, since there is precedence for ordinal date notation as early as Han Wudi's 漢武帝 reign (140–87 B.C.). On this point, see Yu Zhongxin 俞忠鑫, *Han jian kao li* 漢簡考曆 (Taipei: Wenjin chubanshe, 1994), esp. 15 ff. I would like to thank Ian Chapman for drawing my attention to Lao Gan's article.

196

scheme. The difference is simply one of labeling; were calendar compilers beholden only to the sexagenary cycle, we might expect the calendar round layout (Section 3.1.2) to be the dominant form.

The *Qi nian shiri* 七年視日 (134 B.C.) from Yinqueshan M2 (fig. 3.3) is the only calendar from this second corpus that bears a title.[17] Originally transcribed as *liri* 觀（曆）日 "calendar," visual inspection has revealed to Liu Lexian 劉樂賢 that the title is actually *shiri* 視日 "date-lookup," which, as already noted, scholars have identified as phonologically, semantically, and orthographically proximate with the label *zhiri*.[18] The sparse annotations are of a decidedly public nature: "reversal" 反 days, a staple hemerology; holidays, e.g. La 臘/Jiaping 嘉平 (the last $xu._{B11}$ day of the year), Fu 伏 (the three $geng._{S07}$ days following Summer Solstice.$_{Q10}$), and "selecting seeds" 出（潼）【種】; as well as *qi* 氣 tropical fortnights, i.e. Enthronement of Spring.$_{Q01}$ (*lichun* 立春), Summer Solstice.$_{Q10}$ (*Xiarizhi* 夏日至), Enthronement of Autumn.$_{Q13}$ (*liqiu* 立秋), and Winter Solstice.$_{Q22}$ (*dongrizhi* 冬日至). Of course, it is important to note that while the *Qi nian shiri* (≈ 2070 cm^2) is almost twice as large as the Zhoujiatai M30 Shihuang 34 *zhiri* (≈ 1069 cm^2 and ≈ 1221 cm^2, respectively), its characters are written so large that each day accommodates an annotation of only 2–3 characters in length (compare this to the 8-character annotation on slip 49, register 2 of the Zhoujiatai manuscript).[19] Thus, though they essentially bear the same title, the two seem to be suited to different purposes: the Yinqueshan M2 *Qi nian shiri*, for display, and the Zhoujiatai M30 Shihuang 34 *zhiri*, for note-taking.

The untitled Shenjue 3 (59 B.C.) calendar from Dunhuang 敦煌 T6b is identical to the *Qi nian shiri* in almost every regard but its dimensions (fig. 3.4). At two-thirds the length,

---

17. For original photographs and transcriptions, see *Yinqueshan Han mu zhujian* 銀雀山漢墓竹簡, ed. Yinqueshan Han mu zhujian zhengli xiaozu 銀雀山漢墓竹簡整理小組 (Beijing: Wenwu chubanshe, 1975).

18. *Jianbo shushu wenxian tanlun* 簡帛數術文獻探論 (Wuhan: Hubei jiaoyu chubanshe, 2002), 25. On the equation of *shi* and *zhi*, see p. 189.

19. Note that these surface areas, calculated from average slip dimensions, assume a number of missing slips necessary to bring each month up to a full 30 days and omit the surface area of the gaps between slips that would have existed in their original bound state.

Figure 3.3: Yinqueshan 銀雀山 M2 *Qi nian shiri* 七年視日 (134 B.C.) calendar

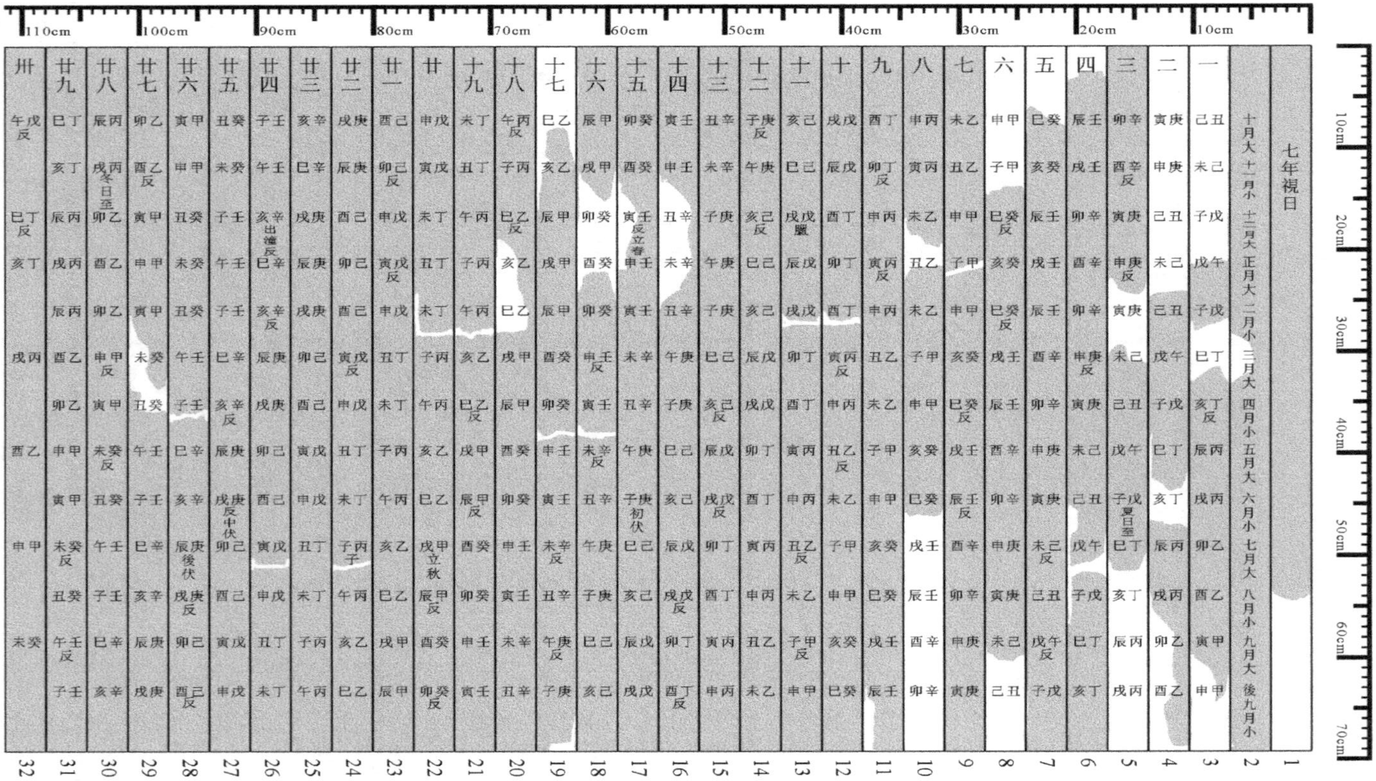

七年視日

日	十月大	十一月小	十二月大	正月大	二月小	三月大	四月小	五月大	六月小	七月大	八月小	九月大	後九月小
一	己丑	己未	戊子	戊午	戊子	丁巳	丁亥	丙辰	丙戌	乙卯	乙酉	甲寅	甲申
二	庚寅	庚申	己丑	己未	己丑	戊午	戊子	丁巳	丁亥	丙辰	丙戌	乙卯	乙酉
三	辛卯	辛酉	庚寅	庚申	庚寅	己未	己丑	戊午	戊子 夏日至	丁巳	丁亥	丙辰	丙戌
四	壬辰	壬戌	辛卯	辛酉	辛卯	庚申	庚寅	己未	己丑	戊午	戊子	丁巳	丁亥
五	癸巳	癸亥	壬辰	壬戌	壬辰	辛酉	辛卯	庚申	庚寅	己未	己丑	戊午	戊子
六	甲午	甲子	癸巳	癸亥	癸巳	壬戌	壬辰	辛酉	辛卯	庚申	庚寅	己未	己丑
七	乙未	乙丑	甲午	甲子	甲午	癸亥	癸巳	壬戌	壬辰 反	辛酉	辛卯	庚申	庚寅
八	丙申	丙寅	乙未	乙丑	乙未	甲子	甲午	癸亥 反	癸巳	壬戌	壬辰	辛酉	辛卯
九	丁酉	丁卯	丙申	丙寅	丙申	乙丑	乙未	甲子	甲午	癸亥	癸巳	壬戌	壬辰
十	戊戌	戊辰	丁酉	丁卯	丁酉	丙寅	丙申	乙丑 反	乙未	甲子	甲午	癸亥	癸巳
十一	己亥	己巳	戊戌	戊辰	戊戌	丁卯	丁酉	丙寅	丙申	乙丑	乙未	甲子	甲午
十二	庚子	庚午	己亥	己巳	己亥	戊辰	戊戌	丁卯	丁酉	丙寅	丙申	乙丑	乙未
十三	辛丑	辛未	庚子	庚午	庚子	己巳	己亥	戊辰 反	戊戌	丁卯	丁酉	丙寅	丙申
十四	壬寅	壬申	辛丑	辛未	辛丑	庚午	庚子	己巳	己亥	戊辰	戊戌	丁卯	丁酉
十五	癸卯	癸酉	壬寅 立春 反	壬申	壬寅	辛未	辛丑	庚午	庚子 初伏	己巳	己亥	戊辰	戊戌
十六	甲辰	甲戌	癸卯	癸酉	癸卯	壬申	壬寅	辛未	辛丑	庚午	庚子	己巳	己亥
十七	乙巳	乙亥	甲辰	甲戌	甲辰	癸酉	癸卯	壬申	壬寅	辛未	辛丑	庚午	庚子
十八	丙午	丙子	乙巳	乙亥	乙巳	甲戌	甲辰	癸酉	癸卯	壬申	壬寅	辛未	辛丑
十九	丁未	丁丑	丙午	丙子	丙午	乙亥	乙巳	甲戌	甲辰	癸酉	癸卯	壬申	壬寅
廿	戊申	戊寅	丁未	丁丑	丁未	丙子	丙午	乙亥	乙巳	甲戌 立秋	甲辰 反	癸酉	癸卯 反
廿一	己酉	己卯	戊申	戊寅	戊申	丁丑	丁未	丙子	丙午	乙亥	乙巳	甲戌	甲辰
廿二	庚戌	庚辰	己酉	己卯	己酉	戊寅	戊申	丁丑	丁未	丙子	丙午	乙亥	乙巳
廿三	辛亥	辛巳	庚戌	庚辰	庚戌	己卯	己酉	戊寅	戊申	丁丑	丁未	丙子	丙午
廿四	壬子	壬午	辛亥 出種 反	辛巳	辛亥 反	庚辰	庚戌	己卯	己酉	戊寅	戊申	丁丑	丁未
廿五	癸丑	癸未	壬子	壬午	壬子	辛巳	辛亥 反	庚辰	庚戌 中伏 反	己卯	己酉	戊寅	戊申
廿六	甲寅	甲申	癸丑	癸未	癸丑	壬午	壬子	辛巳	辛亥	庚辰 後伏	庚戌 反	己卯	己酉 反
廿七	乙卯	乙酉 反	甲寅	甲申	甲寅	癸未 反	癸丑	壬午	壬子	辛巳	辛亥	庚辰	庚戌
廿八	丙辰	丙戌 冬日至	乙卯	乙酉	乙卯	甲申 反	甲寅	癸未 反	癸丑	壬午	壬子	辛巳	辛亥
廿九	丁巳	丁亥	丙辰	丙戌	丙辰	乙酉	乙卯	甲申	甲寅	癸未 反	癸丑	壬午 反	壬子
卅	戊午 反		丁巳 反	丁亥		丙戌		乙酉		甲申		癸未	

Note: many cells carry a small "反" notation and the seasonal notes (夏日至, 立春, 初伏, 中伏, 後伏, 立秋, 冬日至, 出種) transcribed above; the figure is reproduced with a scale bar (10 cm–70 cm across the top, 10 cm–110 cm down the left).

Figure 3.4: Dunhuang 敦煌 T6b Shenjue 3 (59 B.C.) calendar

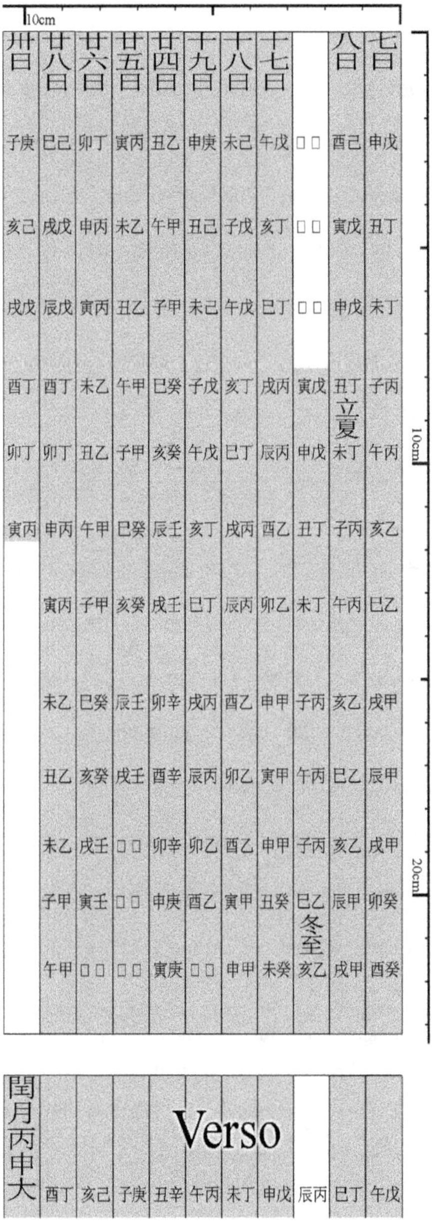

10cm

卅日	廿八日	廿六日	廿五日	廿四日	十九日	十八日	十七日		八日	七日
子庚	巳己	卯丁	寅丙	丑乙	申庚	未己	午戊	□□	酉己	申戊
亥己	戌戊	申丙	未乙	午甲	丑己	子戊	亥丁	□□	寅戊	丑丁
戌戊	辰戊	寅丙	丑乙	子甲	未己	午戊	巳丁	□□	申戊	未丁
酉丁	酉丁	未乙	午甲	巳癸	子戊	亥丁	戌丙	寅戊	丑丁 立夏	子丙
卯丁	卯丁	丑乙	子甲	亥癸	午戊	巳丁	辰丙	申戊	未丁	午丙
寅丙	申丙	午甲	巳癸	辰壬	亥丁	戌丙	酉乙	丑丁	子丙	亥乙
	寅丙	子甲	亥癸	戌壬	巳丁	辰丙	卯乙	未丁	午丙	巳乙
	未乙	巳癸	辰壬	卯辛	戌丙	酉乙	申甲	子丙	亥乙	戌甲
	丑乙	亥癸	戌壬	酉辛	辰丙	卯乙	寅甲	午丙	巳乙	辰甲
	未乙	戌壬	□□	卯辛	卯乙	酉乙	申甲	子丙	亥乙	戌甲
	子甲	寅壬	□□	申庚	酉乙	寅甲	丑癸	巳乙 冬至	辰甲	卯癸
	午甲	□□	□□	寅庚	□□	申甲	未癸	亥乙	戌甲	酉癸

10cm

20cm

Verso

閏月丙申大										
	酉丁	亥己	子庚	丑辛	午丙	未丁	申戊	辰丙	巳丁	午戊

its surface is more crowded, allowing only for two-character annotations—Enthronement of Summer.$_{Q07}$ (*lixia* 立夏) and Winter Solstice.$_{Q22}$ (*dongzhi* 冬至)—and forcing the compiler to move intercalary month XII^2 to the verso. Given the 75 years and some 1800 km separating them, the congruity in form between the Yinqueshan M2 *Qi nian shiri* (134 B.C.) and the Dunhuang Shenjue 3 (59 B.C.)—as well as the dozens of other such calendars from the Northwest—is suggestive of standardization.[20] It is uncertain whether the differences between the *zhiri* and a *shiri* layout are due to time, as Loewe and Lao Gan might argue, or factors such as medium, function, regional administrative culture, and/or archaeological context. However documentation may have changed over the decades, certain copyist errors remained persistent. The Shenjue 3 (59 B.C.) calendar, for example, places Winter Solstice.$_{Q22}$ on XI-*yisi*.$_{42}$ (Dec 05) rather than XI-*yichou*.$_{02}$ (Dec 25), two *tiangan* 天干 cycles earlier than the date posited by the Grand Inception system (#7)—yet another example of a compiler mixing up his *dizhi* 地支.[21]

While majority of daily calendars from this period are of the *Qi nian shiri* (134 B.C.) and Shenjue 3 (59 B.C.) type, two exceptions merit mention. The first is the Yanshou 7 (A.D. 630) paper calendar fragment from the state of Gaochang 高昌 (A.D. 460–640) excavated from Asitana 阿斯塔那 M387, Turpan (fig. 3.5).[22] That the latest and furthest-flung calendar that we possess is also a daily calendar attests to the prevalence of this form. Going one step beyond the *zhiri* and *shiri*, however, this fragment leaves *no* space for annotation beyond the *jian-chu* 建除 hemerology sequence and the 24 *qi*, which we find nestled between the tightly packed *ganzhi*. This, it appears, is was not intended to be a blank slate for record keeping

---

20. By my accounting, there are more than two dozen fragmentary examples of this type of calendar from administrative dump sites at Dunhuang and Edsen-gol, for which I refer the reader to Yoshimura, "Shutsudo kandoku shiryō ni mirareru rekihu no shūsei" and Bo Shuren ed., "Han jian lipu."

21. Luo Jianjin 羅見今, "Dunhuang Han jian zhong lipu niandai zhi zai yanjiu" 敦煌漢簡中曆譜年代之再研究, *Dunhuang yanjiu* 敦煌研究 61, no. 3 (1999): 98. My own calculations with the Triple Concordance system (#8), which possess the same lunisolar elements as the Grand Inception system, confirm Luo's correction. Note that the true astronomical solstice occurred at the Western Han capital Chang'an 長安 on Dec 23, 23:33:30 local apparent time (LAT).

22. See Deng Wenkuan, "Tulufan xinchu Gaochang Yanshou qi nian liri kao" 吐魯番新出「高昌延壽七年曆日」考, *Wenwu* 1996.2: 34–40.

Figure 3.5: Asitana 阿斯塔那 M387 Yanshou 7 (A.D. 630) calendar from Gaochang 高昌

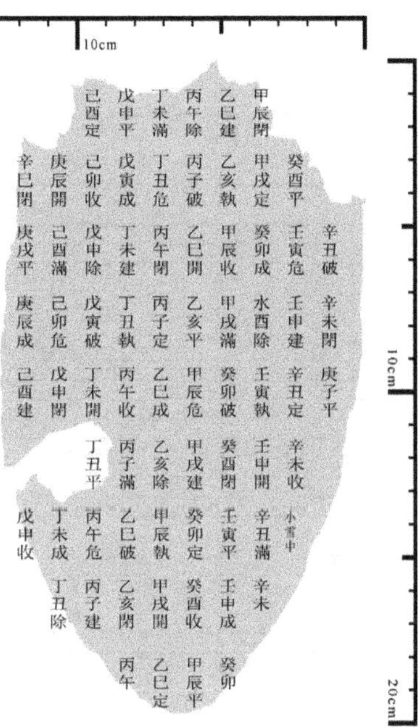

but a hemerological lookup table. The second exception is the the Yinwan M6 *Yuanyan er nian* 元延二年 (11 B.C.) calendar (fig. 3.6).[23] What is noteworthy about this manuscript is the way that it synthesizes the features of the *zhiri* and *shiri* forms. Written on bamboo slips, this calendar affords ample room for annotation—by now familiar matters of travel, lodging, and business, as well as weather—by resorting to six two-month registers. On the other hand, the *ganzhi* dates are presented horizontally, and each slip/column is labeled "no. #" (*di* # 第幾), a curious variation on the more typical formula, "day #" (# *ri* 幾日).

Lastly, there are also a handful of daily calendars that cover only single months.[24] Typically given in ordinal, then sexagenary, notation, the one-month daily calendar arranges

---

23. For original photographs and transcriptions, see *Yinwan Han mu jiandu* 尹灣漢墓簡牘, ed. Lianyungang shi bowuguan 連雲港市博物館 (Beijing: Zhonghua shuju, 1997), 61–67, 139–144.

24. Note that the Dunhuang T15A (D1968) Yongyuan 6-XII (A.D. 94) calendar introduced in this paragraph also contains dates for a month VII in its third register. However, Luo Jianjin argues that this belongs to a different year from the month XII calendar ("Dunhuang Han jian zhong lipu niandai zhi zai yanjiu," 94–95).

201

Figure 3.6: Yinwan 尹灣 M6 *Yuanyan er nian* 元延二年 (11 B.C.) calendar

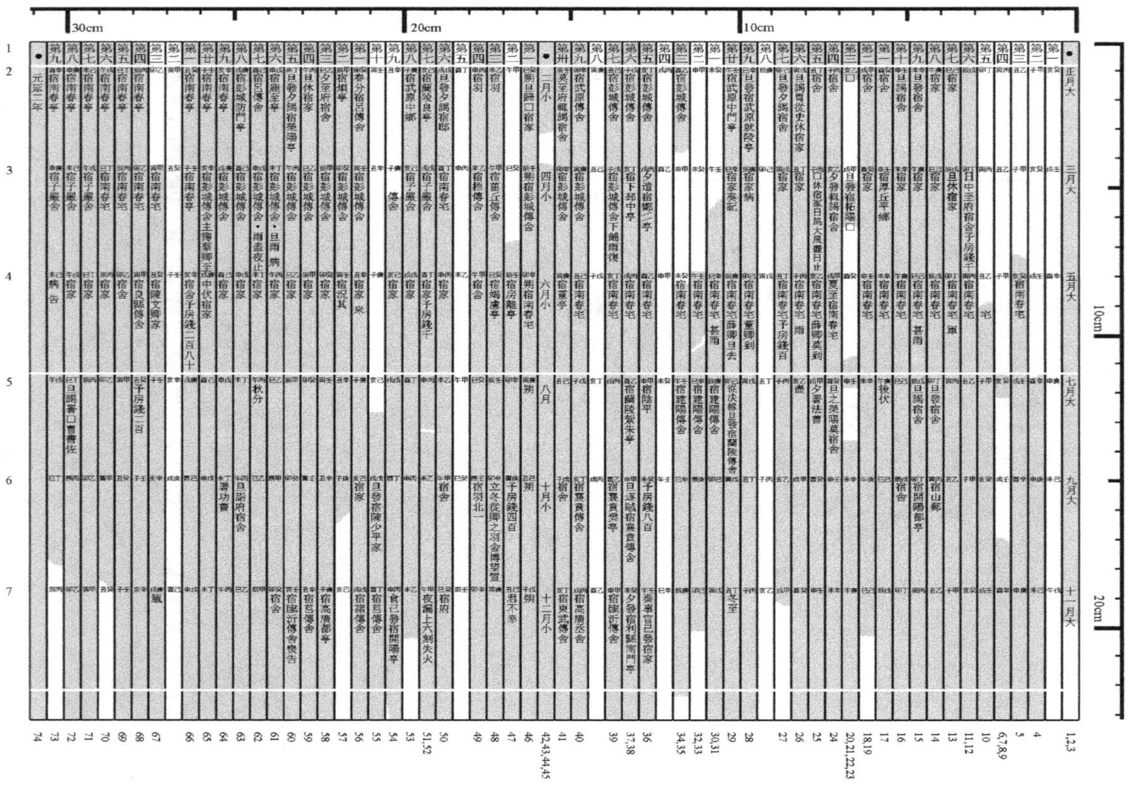

Figure 3.7: The Yinwan Yuanyan 3-V (10 B.C.) and Dunhuang Yongyuan 6-XII (A.D. 94) calendars

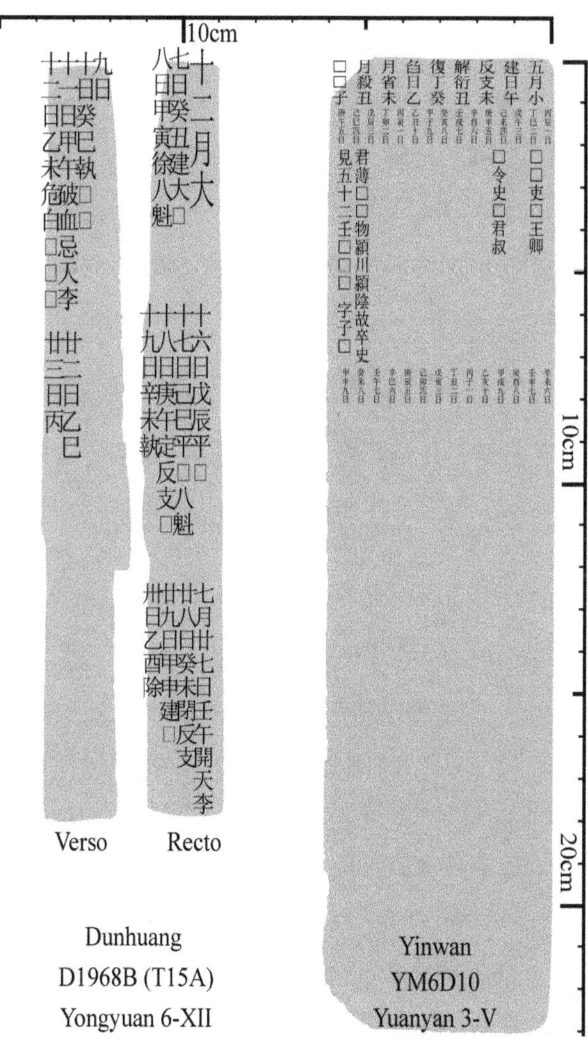

dates into multiple registers, allowing the entire document to fit on a single wooden board. Some, like the Yinwan M6 Yuanyan 3-V (10 B.C.) calendar, leave ample room for annotation, while others, like the Dunhuang D1968 (T15A) Yongyuan 6-XII (A.D. 94) calendar, are too compact (fig. 3.7). Both of these examples devote considerably more space to hemerology than other calendar forms. The former, for example, lists *ganzhi* dates relevant to eight distinct mantic items across the top of the manuscript—*jian* 建 "establish" and *fan* "reverse," with which we are already familiar, as well as *jieyan* 解衍 "release & expansion," *fu* 復 "return," *xian* 臽 "pitfall," *yuexing* 月省 "month examination" (?), *yuesha* 月殺 "month kill," and one last item where the board is defective.[25] These examples show how well-suited the scope of the monthly calendar is to the needs of hemerology, which concerns itself with dozens if not hundreds of mantic items beyond "reverse" days and the *jian-chu* sequence. Of course, form does not necessarily dictate function, since there are just as many monthly calendars without any hemerological annotation whatsoever.[26]

3.1.2 Sexagenary calendar rounds

Day-by-day calendars come in various forms. Those that I have placed under the rubric "daily calendars" I have grouped together based on their grounding in the ordinal day-count. For its part, the "sexagenary calendar round" is also "daily," but it embodies a different organizational principle—the arrangement of months around the sexagenary cycle rather than vice versa. With only four extant examples as of 2013, the calendar round appears to have been relatively rare. Furthermore, in these four examples we see two strikingly different forms—horizontal and circular—suited to different mediums—bamboo bookmats and wood boards—and, it would appear, crafted for different purposes.

The earliest of these forms is the horizontal calendar round, which we see in the Zhoujiatai

---

25. For an explanation of the Yuanyan 3-V (10 B.C.) calendar hemerologies, see Liu Lexian 劉樂賢. "Yinwan Han mu chutu lipu jiqi xiangguan wenti."

26. See, for example, the Edsen-gol, Mu-durbeljin P9 (457 • 19) Benshi 2 (72 B.C.), Edsen-gol, Jinguan 金關 A33 (179 • 10) Shenjue 1 (61 B.C.), and Edsen-gol, Mu-durbeljin A21 (290 • 11A) Jushe 1 (A.D. 6) calendars in Yoshimura, "Shutsudo kandoku shiryō ni mirareru rekihu no shūsei," 500–507.

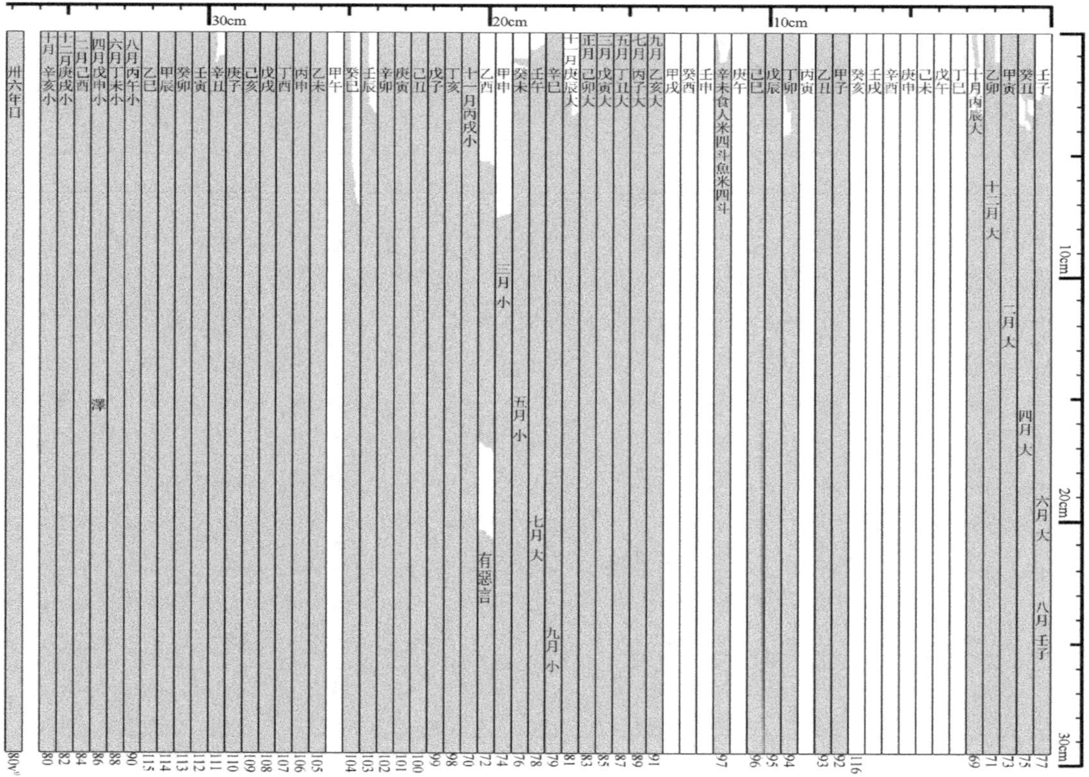

Figure 3.8: Zhoujiatai M30 Shihuang 36–37 (211–210 B.C.) calendar

M30 *Saliu nian ri* 卅六年日 (211 B.C.) and Kongjiapo 孔家坡 M8 Jingdi Houyuan 2 (142 B.C.) calendars.[27] On fig. 3.8, we see how the sexagenary cycles runs once across the top of the bookmat, with the months placed in separate registers beneath the sexagenary dates of their respective new moons, running up and to the left like stairs with even and odd months 29–30 days apart. The months (and the ordinal day count) are subordinate to the sexagenary cycle in all but one regard: since the first (even) sequence of months (X, XII, II, IV, VI, and VIII) comes at the beginning of the manuscript, the sexagenary count starts from *renzi*$_{49}$ rather than *jiazi*$_{01}$. The surface of the horizontal calendar round is mostly blank, affording considerable space for annotation, and though the Zhoujiatai and Kongjiapo examples leave this space blank, we might none-the-less surmise that their intended function was similar to the *zhiri*. In fact, this layout offers so much space that, together with the subordination of the month to the sexagenary cycle, it allows the user/compiler to add the months of additional years, as in the case of the *Saliu nian ri*, where the new moon days of Shihuang 37 (210 B.C.) are written in along the top margin. For all its versatility, however, the horizontal calendar round does have its limitations: without ruling, it might be difficult to ensure that annotations are neatly ordered and easy to look up, and the nesting of several years within a single sexagenary cycle might well exacerbate that confusion.

I focus here on the *Saliu nian ri* (211 B.C.) because it is both the earliest and the more interesting of the two horizontal calendar rounds. It is the only calendar round that bears a title, though it is doubtful that this nondescript title—"36th Year Days"—refers to a specific genre of document like the *zhiri*. It is also one of the only calendars in our possession to have (apparently) been written or bound together with another text.[28] Based

---

27. For original photographs and transcriptions, see *Guanju Qin-Han mu jiandu*, 18–24, 99–102; Hubei sheng wenwu kaogu yanjiusuo 湖北省文物考古研究所 and Suizhou shi kaogu dui 隨州市考古隊 eds., *Suizhou Kongjiapo Han mu jiandu* 隨州孔家坡漢墓簡牘 (Beijing: Wenwu chubanshe, 2006), 117–122, 191–194. Note that scholars have offered a number of rearrangements of the Zhoujiatai Shihuang 36–37 (211–210 B.C.) manuscript slips and that mine follows that of Liu Guosheng 劉國勝, which is based in part on the position of the slips upon excavation, in "Guanyu Zhoujiatai Qin jian 69–130 hao de jianxu bianpai wenti" 關於周家臺秦簡 69–130 號的簡序編排問題, *Jianbo* 簡帛 4 (2009): 27–35.

28. The one other example is the the Northern Wei 北魏 (A.D. 386–535) *Taiping zhenjun shiyi nian liri* 太平真君十一年曆日 (A.D. 450) and *Taiping zhenjun shier nian liri* 太平真君十二年曆日 (A.D. 451) paper

Figure 3.9: Jinguan 金關 Wufeng 3 (55 B.C.) calendar

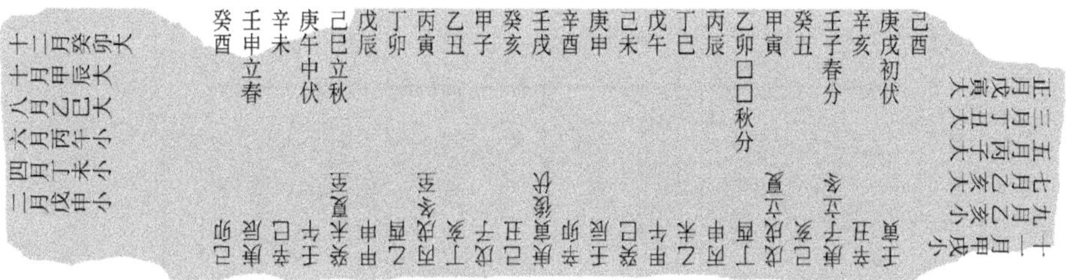

on archaeological diagrams and contents of the Zhoujiatai daybook (*rishu* 日書) tailored to Shihuang 36 (211 B.C.), Donald Harper has argued that the two were likely bound together into a single manuscript and that, even if the one was simply *rolled* inside the other, the two were clearly meant to be used together.[29] This is not particularly surprising, since daybook hemerology is essentially the mantic assessment of civil time, and since such annotations are typical of period calendars. What *is* perhaps surprising then is that a calendar dedicated to this purpose would itself bear no trace of such annotation but only unrelated matters of personal/official business—"marsh" 澤 (slip 88), "there were vicious remarks" 有惡言 (slip 72), and "ate four *dou* of others' rice, four *dou* of fish rice" 食人米四斗，魚米四斗 (slip 97). This should serve as a reminder that, whatever the contents or intended function of a given calendar, it may well have been put to a variety of different uses in its lifetime.

Written each on a single wooden board, the Edsen-gol Wufeng 3 (55 B.C.) and the Yinwan M6 *Yuanyan yuan nian* 元延元年 (12 B.C.) calendars present us with a very different form of calendar round (figs. 3.9 & 3.10).[30] Here, the sexagenary cycle winds around the edges of the board forming a closed loop, with the months placed neatly on opposite ends. The

---

calendars from Dunhuang discussed on p. 213 ff., which are written on the back of the "Zhouyu xia" 周語 下 chapter of the *Guoyu* 國語, a pre-Qin collection of historical anecdotes. Other than the shared physical support, however, there does not appear to be any meaningful relationship between these texts.

29. Xia Dean 夏德安 (Donald Harper), "Zhoujiatai de shushu jian" 周家臺的數術簡, tr. Liu Jing 劉淨 and Yan Changgui 晏昌貴, *Jianbo* 2 (2007): 397–407.

30. For the the Edsen-gol Wufeng 3 (55 B.C.) calendar round, see Zhongguo shehui kexue yuan kaogu yanjiusuo 中國社會科學院考古研究所, ed. *Zhongguo gudai tianwen wenwu tuji* 中國古代天文文物圖集, Kaoguxue zhuankan 考古學專刊 17 (Beijing: Wenwu chubanshe, 1980), 38, plate 36.

Figure 3.10: Yinwan M6 *Yuanyan yuan nian* 元延元年 (12 B.C.) calendar

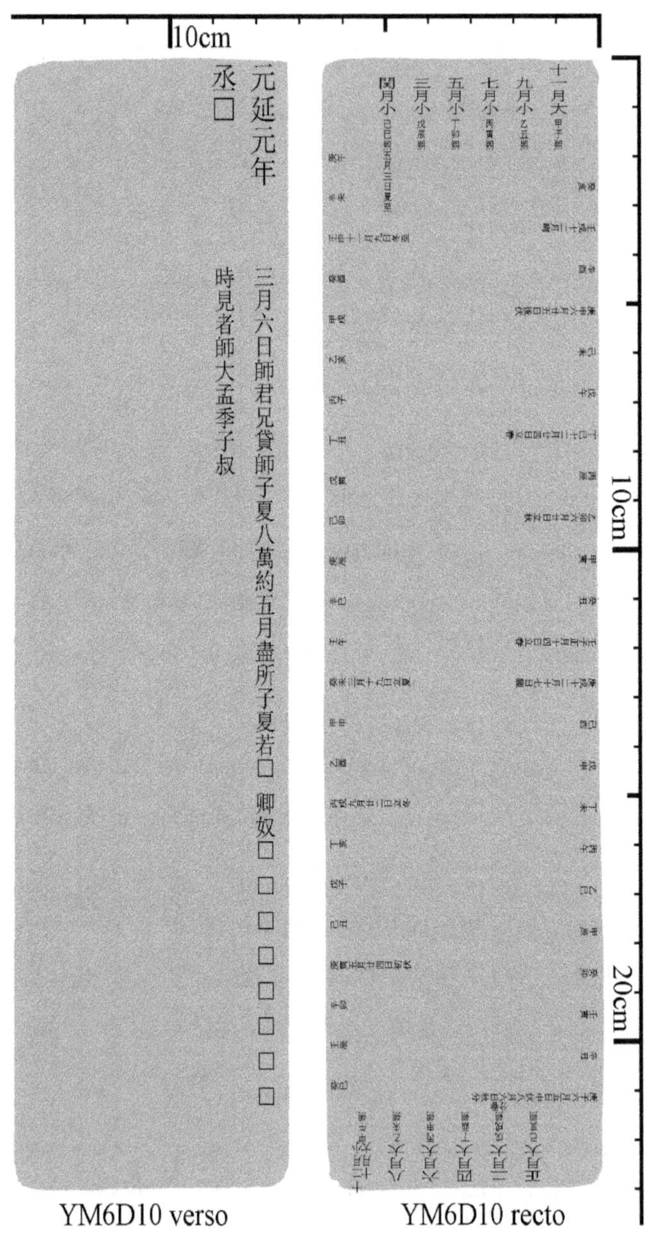

circular calendar round is extremely compact, using almost one tenth the surface area of the horizontal form (compare the *Yuanyan yuan nian*'s 149.5 cm^2 to the *Saliu nian ri*'s 1060.2 cm^2). Given the surface area and the way that annotations run inward toward the center of the board (potentially cutting off those running from different directions), it is understandable that our two examples feature only the typical selection of *qi* and holidays. Of course, the *Yuanyan yuan nian* reminds us that, while the calendar side of such objects might have left no room for interaction, their *versos* provided convenient, uninterrupted surfaces for note-taking or, in this case, bookkeeping (the *Yuanyan yuan nian*'s verso records a money-lending transaction).

3.1.3 Shuo-run 朔閏 *tables*

Even more compact than the circular calendar round is the *shuo-run* ("new & intercalary moon") table. In terms of prevalence, the *shuo-run* table falls somewhere between the daily calendar and calendar round, there being seven extant examples from 209 B.C. to A.D. 451.[31] *Shuo-run* tables are simple lists of the size and new moon date of each month, which proceeds month-by-month rather than day-by-day. To these, the basic building blocks of the civil calendar, are sometimes added the ordinal dates of *qi* and holidays, but the user is rarely provided more information than could fit on a modern business card. For the sake of comparison, I have reproduced three rather distinct examples of *shuo-run* table on fig. 3.11.

The Zhoujiatai M30 Ershi 1 (209 B.C.) board presents us with only the basics—size and new moon date—which fill less than one half of the recto. Like the Yinwan M6 *Yuanyan yuan nian* (12 B.C.), the verso has been used as a notepad. Register 1 reads:

---

31. In addition to those examined below, see also the Dunhuang D38 (81.D38:59–61) Yuanfeng 3 (78 B.C.), Dunhuang D21 (D565) Yangshuo 1 (24 B.C.), and Huaguoshan 花果山 LHM1 Yuanshou 2–3 (1 B.C. – A.D. 1) calendars in Dunhuang xian wenhuaguan 敦煌縣文化館, "Dunhuang Suyoutu Handai fengsui yizhi chutu de mujian" 敦煌酥油土漢代烽燧遺址出土的木簡," in *Han Jian Yanjiu Wenji* 漢簡研究文集, eds. Gansu sheng wenwu gongzuodui 甘肅省文物工作隊 and Gansu sheng bowuguan 甘肅省博物館, 1–14 (Lanzhou: Gansu renmin chubanshe, 1984); Yoshimura, "Shutsudo kandoku shiryō ni mirareru rekihu no shūsei," 464–466; Li Hongfu 李洪甫, "Jiangsu Lianyungang shi Huaguoshan chutu de Handai jiandu" 江蘇連雲港市花果山出土 的漢代簡牘, *Kaogu* 考古 1982.5: 476–480.

Figure 3.11: *Shuo-run* 朔閏 tables

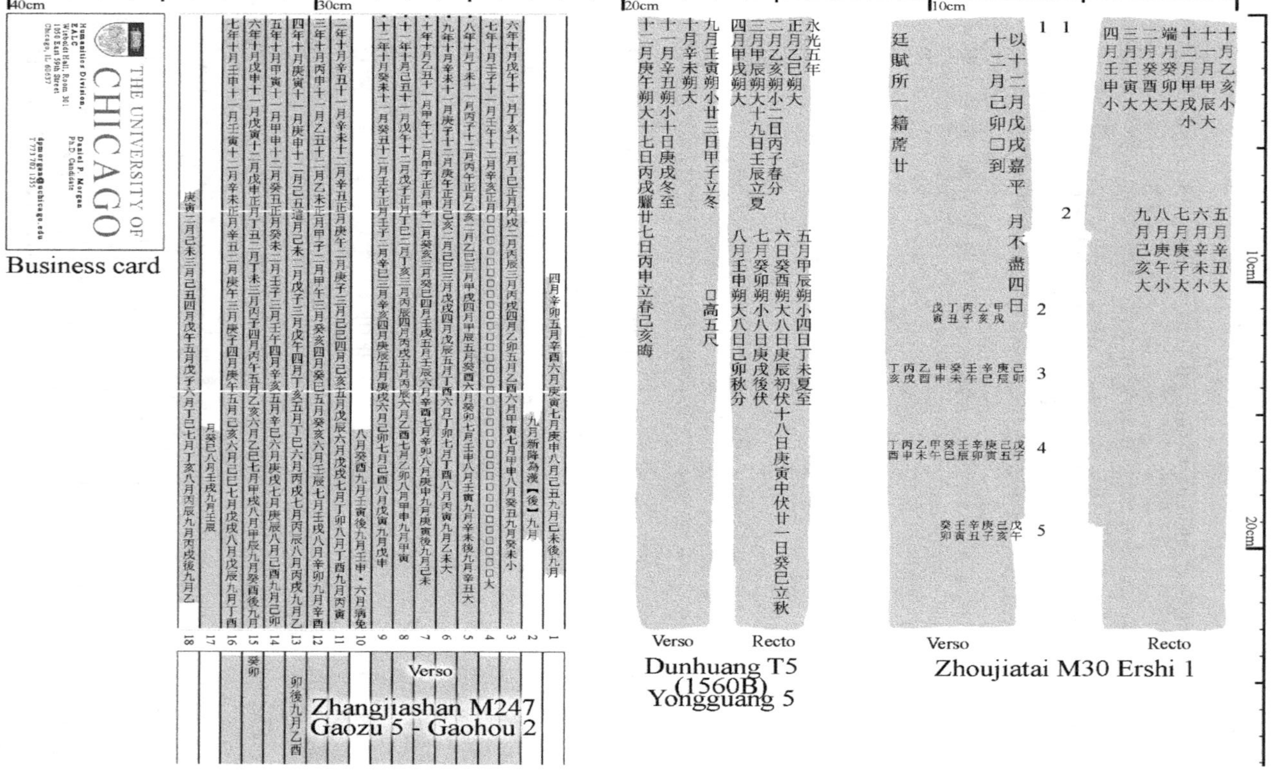

以十二月戊戌嘉平月不盡四日

Jiaping [Festival] on XII-*wuxu*.35 (209 B.C. Feb 09), four days out from the end of the month.

十二月己卯 □ 到

XII-*yimao*.52 (209 B.C. Jan 21), ... arrived at

廷賦所一籍薦廿

court tax office a total of 20 mat cushions.

In much smaller characters, registers 2–5 list 30 *ganzhi* dates evidently beginning from XII-1 and ending on I-1, covering the period mentioned in register 1. It appears as if the manuscript's user wrote out these dates to clarify where the Jiaping Festival and the transfer of the cushion mats fell between months XII and I (and vis-à-vis one another). This brings up an interesting point: used as a calendar, the *shuo-run* table requires the user to visualize dates in terms of *ganzhi*, and just as the modern reader must sometimes resort to a checking or writing out a *ganzhi* table (e.g. Table 1 on p. 17), so too might some ancient readers.

The Zhangjiashan 張家山 M247 Gaozu 5 – Gaohou 2 (202–186 B.C.) *shuo-run* table is even more compact, compressing the new moon days of 17 civil years into as many bamboo slips. Its layout is not as neatly tabular as the others on fig. 3.11. Each slip records the new moon dates of a single year, but they do so without any spaces; furthermore, the unevenly sized graphs result in columns of different lengths, two of which run onto the verso for lack of space (slips 13 & 15). There is clearly no room for annotation or note-keeping here, which suggests that this "table" was solely for reference, but it is unclear to what end. The one- and two-year calendars introduced up to this point were conceivably for use during said year(s), especially the Zhoujiatai M30 *Saliu nian ri* (211 B.C.), which has clearly been altered for use in the subsequent year (see p. 206). However, because this *shuo-run* table enumerates years through multiple reigns—[Gaozu] 5–12, [Huidi] 1–7, and [Gaohou] 1–2—we might conclude that it was a *historical* table for some purpose other than marking present or future time.

Figure 3.12: Dunhuang Northern Wei Taiping zhenjun 11–12 (A.D. 450–451) *shuo-run* table

太平真君十一年曆日
歲在庚寅
大陰大將軍在子
廿七日社

正月大一日壬戌收
二月小一日壬辰滿
三月大一日辛酉破
四月小一日辛卯閉
五月大一日庚申平
六月小一日庚寅成
七月大一日己未建
閏月小一日己丑執
八月大一日戊午收社
九月小一日戊子滿
十月大一日丁巳破
十一月小一日丁亥閉
十二月大一日丙辰平

九日立春正月節
十一日驚蟄二月節
十一日清明三月節
十二日立夏四月節
十三日望種五月節
十四日小暑六月節
十五日立秋七月節
十五日白露八月節

廿五日雨水
廿五日春分
廿六日穀雨
廿七日小滿
廿八日夏至
廿九日大暑
卅日處暑
十七日寒露九月節
十七日立冬十月節
十九日大雪十一月節
十九日小寒十二月節
十日臘

大將軍在卯大歲在丑
廿一日立春正月節

太平真君十二年曆日
其年改為正平元年
太歲在辛卯

正月小一日丙戌成
二月大一日乙卯建
三月大一日乙酉執
四月小一日乙卯閉
五月大一日甲申滿
六月小一日甲寅危
七月大一日水未閉
八月小一日水丑定
九月大一日壬午成
十月小一日壬子除
十一月大一日辛巳執
十二月小一日辛亥閉

二日始耕
四日社
八日穀雨
八日小滿
十日夏至
十一日大暑
十日處暑
十一日秋分
十二日霜降
十三日小雪
十四日冬至
十五日大寒
十八日臘

六日雨水
七日春分
廿三日立夏四月節
廿三日望種五月節
廿五日小暑六月節
廿五日立秋七月節
廿七日白露八月節
廿六日春分
七日春分
廿九日立冬十月節
廿九日大雪十一月節
卅日大寒十二月節
十六日立春正月節

廿一日驚蟄二月節
十六日月食
廿二日清明

廿七日寒露九月節

The *shuo-run* table is able to compress the fundamental data of the civil calendar into a minimalist form factor, but it is equally amenable to the typical array of public annotations. Written below each month on the Dunhuang T5 (1560B) Yongguang 5 (39 B.C.) board (fig. 3.11), for example, we find the ordinal and sexagenary dates of principal *qi* (Spring Equinox.$_{Q04}$ [*chunfen* 春分], Enthronement of Summer.$_{Q07}$, Summer Solstice.$_{Q10}$, Enthronement of Autumn.$_{Q13}$, Autumn Equinox.$_{Q16}$ [*qiufen* 秋分], Enthronement of Winter.$_{Q19}$ [*lidong* 立冬], and Winter Solstice.$_{Q22}$) and holidays (Fu and La.[32] The Northern Wei *Taiping zhenjun shiyi nian liri* 太平真君十一年曆日 (A.D. 450) and *Taiping zhenjun shier nian liri* 太平真君十二年曆日 (A.D. 451) take this one step further (fig. 3.12).[33] Written on the same piece of paper—on the back of the "Zhouyu xia" 周語下 chapter of the *Guoyu* 國語 —the Taiping zhenjun 11 & 12 *liri* "calendars" are delineated by title columns indicating the year, the position of hemerological entities—Taisui 太歲, Taiyin 太陰, and Dajiangjun 大將軍 —and the change of reign periods—" 'Taiping zhenjun 12 Calendar', this year was changed to Zhengping 1" 太平真君十二年曆日，其年改爲正平元年. Each month is provided with its size and *ganzhi* date and also the position of new moon day within the *jian-chu* sequence. Beneath each month is then listed the ordinal dates of holidays—La and She 社 —as well as *all* of the 24 *qi,* which are divided into "nodal" (*jie* 節) and, by implication, medial *qi.* Lastly, unlike any early imperial calendar currently extant, the Taiping zhenjun 11 & 12 *liri* also mark the dates of two lunar eclipses: 12-II-16 (A.D. 451 Apr 02) and 12-VII-16 (A.D. 451 Sep 27). Both correspond to historical eclipses, but since the former

---

32. For photographs and transcriptions, see Bo Shuren ed., "Han jian lipu," 227, 238.

33. The Taiping zhenjun 11–12 *shuo-run* table manuscript managed to make its way from the Dunhuang cave library to the hands of a private Japanese collector, who in 1997 anonymously donated it back to China. The manuscript is currently held in the Dunhuang Academy under the accession number 0368V; see Deng Wenkuan, "Dunhuang ben Beiwei lishu yu Zhongguo gudai yueshi yubao" 敦煌本北魏曆書與中國古代月食預報, in *Dunhuang-Tulufanxue yanjiu lunji* 敦煌吐魯番學研究論集, eds. Beijing tushuguan Dunhuang-Tulufanxue ziliao zhongxin 北京圖書館敦煌吐魯番學资料中心 and Taibei Nanhai zazhishe 臺北《南海》雜誌社, 360–372 (Beijing: Shumu wenxian chubanshe, 1996); "Guanyu Dunhuang liri yanjiu de ji dian yijian" 關於敦煌曆日研究的幾點意見, in *Dunhuang Tulufan tianwen lifa yanjiu* 敦煌吐魯番天文曆法研究, 182–188 (Lanzhou: Gansu jiaoyu chubanshe, 2002), 188. As a result of the manuscript's tortuous history, no photographs of it have been published to date. The transcription in fig. 3.12 is based on *Dunhuang tianwen lifa wenxian jijiao*, 101–110.

would not have been visible in East Asia, these annotations must be *predictions* rather than observations, and experts have shown how the Luminous Inception system (#13), by which the Taiping zhenjun 11 & 12 *liri* were calculated, indeed successfully predicts these dates.[34]

3.1.4 Handy tables

Under this last heading I break away from my organization-based typology, placing together two organizationally distinct *li* "calendars/tables" based instead on their level of astronomical specialization: the Mawangdui 馬王隊 M3 *Wuxing zhan* planetary tables and the *Shiji* 史記 "Lishu jiazi pian" 曆術甲子篇. Surveys of early imperial calendars tend to omit these sources from consideration, and for good reason. The *Wuxing zhan* tables are not "calendars" per se, at least not like anything covered thus far, and the exact nature of their time frame has been the topic of considerable debate. The "Lishu jiazi pian," for its part, stands out as a transmitted source—the only of its kind considered here—and is even more condensed than a *shuo-run* table, making the label "calendar" seem similarly inappropriate. Whatever we choose to call them, these texts are equally concerned with the measurement of time, befitting the rather more vague actors' category *li*. Their principles, contents, and functions may be completely different from the excavated calendars surveyed above, but that is precisely why they deserve equal attention.

As the *Wuxing zhan* tables are the topic of Chapter 2, we need not go into additional detail here. To recapitulate, the *Wuxing zhan* features 70-year planetary visibility tables for Jupiter, Saturn, and Venus, the years of which cycle through the respective periodicities of each planet. The tables for Jupiter and Saturn (superior planets) list the lodge of first morning rising for each year of the planets' respective sidereal periods—12 and 30 years—in individual columns, through which calendar years cycle in multiple rows. The table for Venus

---

34. See Deng Wenkuan, "Dunhuang ben Beiwei lishu yu Zhongguo gudai yueshi yubao"; Jean-Claude Martzloff, *Le calendrier chinois: structure et calculs, 104 av. JC-1644: indétermination céleste et réforme permanente: la construction chinoise officielle du temps quotidien discret à partir d'un temps mathématique caché, linéaire et continu*, Sciences, techniques et civilisations du Moyen Âge à l'aube des Lumières 11 (Paris: Champion, 2009), 267–279.

(an inferior planet) is more complex, listing the "month" (*yue* 月) and lodge of four different visibility phenomena (first and last morning rising, first and last evening setting) at different intervals through each year; like the previous tables, the years cycle through these (uneven) columns in multiple rows organized around the planet's 8-year resonance period (5 synodic periods : 8 years). Were we to extend the organization-based typology from above, we might call these "planetary resonance period tables." In the context of calendrics, the single most important fact about these tables is that, while they give date in regnal years and *yue*, the very nature of the resonance-period-based table requires that they operate on purely solar time—$365\frac{1}{4}$-day *sui* 歲 divided into 12 solar "months"—as distinct from the lunisolar civil calendar.

The "Lishu jiazi pian" section of the *Shiji* "Li shu" 曆書 is a different beast.[35] Beginning from the Grand Inception system origin, it counts out 76 years between 104 and 29 B.C., providing a number of formulaic computational data for each year (see Table 3.2). The fact that this range of dates stretches beyond the closing of the *Shiji* in 91 B.C. and the death of its author, Sima Qian 司馬遷, in 86 B.C. suggests that this section was either inserted or added to at a later date.[36] Either way, it is at the very least still a production of the early imperial period.

The text itself leaves the origins and purpose of the data unexplained, so we must turn instead to later scholarship like Sima Zhen's 司馬貞 (A.D. 679–732) *Suoyin* 索隱 commentary. First, the 76-year period is divided into four 19-year periods, each of which begins with a cardinal direction—north, west, south, then east. The combination of a 76-year OBSCU-RATION (*bu* 蔀) with a 19-year RULE (*zhang* 章), it should be noted, is a feature of the early quarter-remainder systems (e.g. #1–6 & #9), *not the Grand Inception system* (#7). Sima Zhen points out that these mark the cardinal positions of the hour of Winter Solstice.[Q22]

---

35. For the "Lishu jiazi pian," see *Shiji* 史記 (Zhonghua shuju 中華書局 ed.), 28.1262–1287.

36. Like the Zhangjiashan M247 Gaozu 5 – Gaohou 2 (202–186 B.C.) *shuo-run* table (p. 211 and the *Wuxing zhan* planetary tables, the fact that the "Lishu jiazi pian" counts out years in reign periods is clear proof that it too is backward- rather than forward-looking.

Table 3.2: Shiji 史記 "Lishu jiazi pian" 曆術甲子篇

太初元年，歲名「焉逢攝提格」，月名「畢聚」，日得甲子，夜半朔旦冬至。

Grand Inception 1 (104 B.C.), the *sui* is named Yanfeng-Shetige, the month is named Bi-ju, the day is *jiazi*.$_{01}$, and Winter Solstice.$_{\mathrm{Q22}}$ is on midnight, New Year's Day (105 B.C. Dec 25 00:00).

正北

Due north

十二

12

無大餘，無小餘；

No GREATER REMAINDER, no LESSER REMAINDER;

無大餘，無小餘；

No GREATER REMAINDER, no LESSER REMAINDER;

焉逢攝提格太初元年。

Yanfeng-Shetige, Grand Inception 1 (104 B.C.).

十二

12

大餘五十四，小餘三百四十八；

GREATER REMAINDER 54, LESSER REMAINDER 348;

大餘五，小餘八；

GREATER REMAINDER 5, LESSER REMAINDER 8;

端蒙單閼二年。

Duanmeng-Chanye 2 (103 B.C.).

閏十三

Intercalary, 13

大餘四十八，小餘六百九十六；

GREATER REMAINDER 48, LESSER REMAINDER 696;

大餘十，小餘十六；

GREATER REMAINDER 10, LESSER REMAINDER 16;

游兆執徐三年。

Youzhao-Zhixu 3 (102 B.C.).

...

正西 Due west

...

正南 Due south

...

正東 Due east

...

閏十三

Intercalary, 13

大餘十五，小餘九十三；

GREATER REMAINDER 15, LESSER REMAINDER 93;

大餘三十三，小餘二十四；

GREATER REMAINDER 33, LESSER REMAINDER 24;

祝犁大荒落四年。

Zhuli-Dahuangluo [Jianshi] 4 (29 B.C.)

at the end of each RULE—*zi.*$_{B01}$ (00:00) : north :: *you.*$_{B10}$ (18:00) : west :: *wu.*$_{B07}$ (12:00) : south :: *mao.*$_{B04}$ (06:00) : east.[37] The next line, which reads either "12" or "intercalary, 13" is the number of months in said year. Next, the two sets of GREATER and LESSER REMAINDERS indicate the progress of the astronomical first month (*tianzheng* 天正; month XI) and Winter Solstice.$_{Q22}$ through the sexagenary cycle. With the coincidence of the astronomical first month, Winter Solstice.$_{Q22}$, and day *jiazi.*$_{01}$, the system origin provides a base point where all REMAINDERS are 0. After 12 months, however, the date of astronomical first month falls $54\frac{348}{940}$ days after *jiazi.*$_{01}$ 00:00, on *wuwu.*$_{55}$ 08:53; and after one *sui*, the date of Winter Solstice.$_{Q22}$ falls $5\frac{8}{32}$ days later, on *jisi.*$_{06}$ 06:00. Under 103 B.C., therefore, the *Shiji* notes a GREATER REMAINDER of 54 with a LESSER REMAINDER of 348[/940]—the lunar remainder—followed by a GREATER REMAINDER of 5 with a LESSER REMAINDER 8—the solar remainder (see Table 3.2). After this, the "Lishu jiazi pian" gives the year-count both in the sexagenary cycle, for which it uses archaic equivalents to *ganzhi* binomes (Table 3.3), and in ordinal years counted from the beginning of each *named* reign period.[38]

The *Wuxing zhan* and "Lishu jiazi pian" tables are not "calendars" in any traditional sense of the word. Without providing the *ganzhi* dates of each month, they cannot be used to directly count civil time in even the manner of the *shuo-run* tables. Rather, it is the one trait that unites them that reveals their function—expandability.

The way the *Wuxing zhan* tables wrap solar time around planetary periodicities allows for infinite expansion into the future. With the manuscript the way it is, for example, there is enough room to expand the Saturn table all the way to A.D. 84. True, the use of regnal years does limit the scope of expansion into the future at any one time, and the *Wuxing zhan*'s

---

37. In the Grand Inception (#7) and Triple Concordance (#8) systems, which posit a solar year of $365\frac{385}{1539}$ days, the next cycle up from the RULE is the CONCORDANCE (*tong* 統), which is 1539 years, or 81 RULES (81 × 19 = 1539). Starting from *zi.*$_{B01}$ (00:00) in a Quarter-remainder system, which posit a solar year of $365\frac{1}{4}$ days, Winter Solstice.$_{Q22}$ will fall exactly at *you.*$_{B10}$ (18:00) after one 19-year RULE, since $(365\frac{1}{4} × 19)$ mod 1 = $\frac{3}{4}$, and since $\frac{3}{4}$ of a day is 9 double-hours. Sima Zhen refers to the four cardinal directions here as *zhang shou* 章首 "RULE HEADS" (*Shiji*, 28.1263, commentary).

38. For an explanation of the "Lishu jiazi pian" data, see also Liu Hongtao 劉洪濤, *Gudai lifa jisuanfa* 古代曆法計算法 (Tianjin: Nankai daxue chubanshe, 2003), 1–11.

Table 3.3: Year-count names

Tiangan 天干			_Dizhi_ 地支		
焉逢 Yānféng	_jia._S01		攝提格 Shètígé	_zi._B01	
端蒙 Duānméng	_yi._S02		單閼 Chányè	_chou._B02	
游兆 Yóuzhào	_bing._S03		執徐 Zhíxú	_yin._B03	
彊梧 Qiángwú	_ding._S04		大荒落 Dàhuāngluò	_mao._B04	
徒維 Túwéi	_wu._S05		敦牂 Dūnzāng	_chen._B05	
祝犂 Zhùlí	_ji._S06		協洽 Xiéqià	_si._B06	
商橫 Shānghéng	_geng._S07		涒灘 Tūntān	_wu._B07	
昭陽 Zhāoyáng	_xin._S08		作鄂 Zuòè	_wei._B08	
橫艾 Héng'ài	_ren._S09		淹茂 Yānmào	_shen._B09	
尚章 Shàngzhāng	_gui._S10		大淵獻 Dàyuānxiàn	_you._B10	
			困敦 Kùndūn	_xu._B11	
			赤奮若 Chìfènruò	_hai._B12	

owner/compiler stopped adding to its tables nine years prior to its interment in Mawangdui M3, but the _Qiyao rangzai jue_ 七曜攘災決 demonstrates the possibilities of this layout. Preserved in the Japanese Taishō 大正 Buddhist canon, the _Qiyao rangzai jue_ (_T_ no. 1308) purports to have been "written and collated by the Brahmin monk of west India, Koṅta" 西天竺國婆羅門僧金俱吒撰集之 (_T_ no. 1308, 426:b22) in the ninth century A.D., before it was taken to Japan. Its tables cover the lodge-position as well as the date and lodge-position of all the five naked-eye planets' characteristic phenomena—first and last rising and settings, station, and retrograde—on a month-by-month basis. The months are arranged into twelve rows, and the years of each planet's resonance period are arranged into as many columns, each column being marked with several _ganzhi_ as many years apart, thus allowing the years to cycle through the planets' periodicities in the same fashion as the _Wuxing zhan_ tables. To ensure regular repetition, the _Qiyao rangzai jue_ resorts to the same solar time scheme as the _Wuxing zhan_—a solar year (_sui_) beginning at Enthronement of Spring.Q01 and divided into 12 solar "months" corresponding to the nodal _qi_—the difference being that the _Qiyao rangzai jue_ explains itself, providing instruction for converting between solar and civil time:

每年十二月皆以月節為正。其伏見入月日數各從節數之。假令三月十日者。當
數清明後十日是也... 推之考驗。往古及今。年所留宿度。若應符契分毫無差也。

218

The 12 months (*yue*) of every year are all based on the nodal *qi* of the [civil]
months. The number of days into each month of hiding, appearance, etc. are
each counted from the nodal *qi*. Suppose that we have III-10: one should count
10 days after Pure and Bright.$_{Q05}$ (the nodal *qi* of month III). ... Calculate it and
examine the results: back to antiquity and up to today the lodge-degrees where
[the planets] linger each year, like matching tallies, do not differ by a fraction of
a hair's breadth.[39]

In addition to the *ganzhi* year-count, the columns note the beginning of reign periods—
Japanese reign periods running between Kantoku 寬德 (A.D. 1044–1046) and Tenji 天治
(A.D. 1124–1126). Niu Weixing 鈕衛星 and Jiang Xiaoyuan 江曉原 note that the Jupiter
table begins on Chōkyū 長久 4 (A.D. 1043), exactly three 83-year Jupiter resonance periods
(83 years : 76 synodic periods : 7 sidereal periods) after the text's given system origin
in Zhenyuan 10 (A.D. 794), which suggests that these tables were indeed being filled out
centuries after their inception.[40]

The "Lishu jiazi pian" evidently provides a similar function vis-à-vis the lunisolar calendar. In *li* system manual literature, e.g. the Triple Concordance system manual (#8), the
calculation of the calendar begins with fixing the *ganzhi* date and remainder of the astronomical first month and Winter Solstice.$_{Q22}$, which serve as anchor points for extrapolating
subsequent lunisolar phenomena.[41] The "Lishu jiazi pian" GREATER and LESSER REMAIN-
DER numbers provide these very anchor points, which would allow the user to skip several
steps of calculation when compiling a calendar for said year. Furthermore, since the 76-year

---

39. *T* no. 1308, 448: b7–c4.

40. "*Qiyao rangzai jue* Muxing libiao yanjiu" 『七曜攘災訣』木星曆表研究, *Zhongguo kexueyuan Shanghai tianwentai niankan* 中國科學院上海天文台年刊 18 (1997): 241–249.

41. The Triple Concordance system (#8) is as good a point as entry as any, since it is the earliest extant system manual, and since its procedures (*shu* 術) are typical of the early imperial tradition. After counting out the cycles elapsed between system origin and the year sought, the Triple Concordance system manual instructs its user to "calculate the syzygy of the astronomical first month" 推正月朔 and "calculate Winter Solstice.$_{Q22}$" 推冬至, from which the user counts of subsequent months and *qi* using mean values, $29\frac{43}{81}$ and $15\frac{1010}{4617}$ days, respectively. For the Triple Concordance system manual, see *Han shu* 漢書 (Zhonghua shuju ed.), 21B.991–1011, esp. 1001.

OBSCURATION represents the time necessary for the astronomical first month and Winter Solstice.$_{Q22}$ to coincide once again at 00:00, the GREATER and LESSER REMAINDER numbers repeat every year with an offset of 39 *ganzhi* days, allowing once again for infinite expansion into the future.[42]

Their expandability would seem to make the *Wuxing zhan* and "Lishu jiazi pian" tables time-saving reference tools—"handy tables"—for anyone wishing to perform lunisolar (calendrical) or planetary calculations. Their functionality thus implies a very different sort of readership than the calendars surveyed above: experts versed and interested in the *production* of *li* rather than its workaday consumers. The one exception to this distinction is perhaps the highly-condensed *shuo-run* tables, which, as we saw with the Zhoujiatai M30 Ershi 1 (209 B.C.) board (fig. 3.11), might require the user to extrapolate them into a more accessible layout. The difference, however, is that the *shuo-run* table is only good for said year(s); and while *shuo-run* tables require only that the user be versed in the sexagenary cycle, the "Lishu jiazi pian" requires him to perform more complex mathematical operations using a number of implicit values and rules.

3.2 Calendrics, Astronomy, and *Li*

In the twentieth century, it was common among Western-language historians of science to render the term *li* as "calendrics," "calendrical science," or "calendrical astronomy." While early scholars like Joseph Needham were clear in insisting that this rubric embraced what we might now call "astronomy" or, more specifically, "mathematical astronomy," twenty-first-century works tend to favor these latter content-specific labels.[43] Both have their merits: the

---

42. With the RULE ratio of 235 months : 19 years and a *sui* of $365\frac{1}{4}$ days, 76 years corresponds to exactly 940 lunations and 27759 days. At the end of one OBSCURATION, however, the *ganzhi* day of the coincidence of the astronomical first month, Winter Solstice.$_{Q22}$, and midnight slides 39 places forward, since 27759 mod 60 = 39. In quarter-remainder systems like the "Lishu jiazi pian," all four coincide only after one 1520-year ERA (*ji* 紀), which corresponds to 18800 months and 555180 days, the latter number being evenly divisible by 60.

43. For "calendrics," etc., see Joseph Needham, *Science and Civilisation in China, Vol.3: Mathematics and the Sciences of the Heavens and the Earth* (Cambridge: Cambridge University Press, 1959), 390–409;

latter, a modern concession, allows us to speak across time and culture, while the former stays relatively true to the actors' own terminology. "Calendrics" is appropriate, it is important to note, *not* because the calendar is *li*'s earliest or primary referent—this, as we have seen in Sections 1.1.3 & 3.1, is simply not the case—but because the classics and early imperial legend frame its practice around the civil calendar. To practice *li*, the slogan goes, is to "contemplate the signs and grant the seasons" 觀象授時 (see Section 1.1.2). In other words, *the calendar is both its product and raison d'être.*

We see this claim repeated throughout early imperial sources and the majority of modern scholarship on the topic, and it is easy to understand why. By the time of most of the events discussed in this dissertation, the astronomers and governments of Egypt and Rome had actively abandoned traditional lunisolar calendars. The coordination of lunar and solar time was a lot of trouble: it took a considerable amount of math to, in Needham's words, "reconcile the irreconcilable," and the fast-paced and manifest nature of lunar phenomena guaranteed that any flaw therein became embarrassingly apparent embarrassingly soon; the use of lunisolar calendars also made time-accounting extraordinarily convoluted, as each year and each subsequent month was different from the next in terms of beginning and duration (let alone the variation that ensues when calculated by the dozens of methods that saw historical use). The natural alternative was a simple 365-day affair modeled on the solar/sidereal/agricultural year divided into regular month-sized (but lunation-independent) periods. United as it was by sailing, dependent as it was on tides, and skilled as it was in astronomy, the Mediterranean world decided that the moon was simply too much trouble for calendrics.[44]

Nakayama Shigeru 中山茂, "Characteristics of Chinese Calendrical Science," *Japanese Studies in the History of Science* no. 4 (1965): 124–131; Nathan Sivin, "Cosmos and Computation in Early Chinese Mathematical Astronomy," *T'oung Pao* 2d ser., 55, no. 1/3 (1969): 1–73. Starting in the 1990s, one finds a strong push towards the vocabulary of "astronomy" driven primarily by Christopher Cullen; for example, see "Motivations for Scientific Change in Ancient China: Emperor Wu and the Grand Inception Astronomical Reforms of 104 BC," *Journal for the History of Astronomy* 24, no. 3 (1991): 185–203.

44. See Otto Neugebauer, "The Origin of the Egyptian Calendar," *Journal of Near Eastern Studies* 1, no. 4 (1942): 396–403.

The Chinese persevered. One might, like Shen Gua 沈括 (A.D. 1031–1095), point to reasons of tradition or culture—i.e. "non-scientific" reasons—but the average expert would have surely insisted that it was their unfailing devotion to empiricism that kept them going.[45] Neither would have been wrong. The operation of a rigorous lunisolar calendar is where "calendrics" and "astronomy" truly coalesce, unlike in the West, the latter might complain, which substituted precise astronomical periods with 28-, 30- & 31-day "months" and 365-day "years." That said, the Chinese calendar was by no means free from arbitrary convention. These are obvious points—*any* calendar is by definition an amalgam of astronomical reality and cultural convention—my interest, rather, is in the tensions that existed between ideological claims and the situation on the ground to which such claims were responding.

3.2.1   Calendars as products of li

The dynastic histories present the history of *li* as a succession of systems which various courts saw fit to *yong* 用 "use," *shi* 施 "implement," *xing* 行 "put into action," or *gai* 改 "reform" for the sake of regulating civil time. What we know of the technical contents of *li* we know from only two sources—system manuals and calendar/tables—and since the former instructs the user how to compile the latter, scholars generally treat the history of the civil calendar as a mathematical puzzle to be solved with the *shu* 數 "numbers" and *shu* 術 "techniques" of the former.

The "numbers" and "techniques" of the calendar inevitably occupy the first section of any system manual. The computational procedures involved are rather stable over time, making any one early imperial example an adequate reflection of the others. For step-by-step details, the reader is advised to turn to Liu Hongtao 劉洪濤 and Jean-Claude Martzloff's compendious studies on the topic.[46] In addition to Table 1.2 (p. 34), in which I provide the reader an itemized catalog of typical contents, I offer here a brief sketch of how the basic

---

45. On Shen Gua's advocacy of a solar civil calendar, see *Mengxi bitan jiaozheng* 夢溪筆談校證 (Zhonghua shuju ed.), entry 545.

46. Liu Hongtao, *Gudai lifa jisuanfa*; Martzloff, *Le calendrier chinois*.

procedures work.

Let us take for our example the Quarter-remainder system (#9; A.D. 85/86) and the year Xiping 3 (A.D. 174), when we know it to have still been in use. Winter Solstice.$_{Q22}$, Xiping 3 falls 335 years after SYSTEM ORIGIN (*li yuan* 曆元)—Winter Solstice.$_{Q22}$, Gaozu 45-X-1 *jiazi*.$_{01}$ 00:00 (162 B.C. December 25 00:00 local apparent time [LAT]). First, "the technique for calculating OBSCURATION entry" 推入蔀術 has us count off the relevant cycles elapsed since SYSTEM ORIGIN, by which we find that Xiping 3 is year 335 of the current ORIGIN (*yuan* 元, 4560 years) and ERA (*ji* 紀, 1520 years), year 31 of the current OBSCURATION (*bu* 蔀, 76 years), and year 12 of the current RULE (*zhang* 章, 19 years). Next, "the technique for calculating the astronomical first month" 推天正術 has us convert the time elapsed since OBSCURATION HEAD (*bu shou* 蔀首) from years into months using the RULE ratio (19 years : 235 months), $371\frac{1}{19}$ months in this case. The fractional remainder, $\frac{1}{19}$, is the INTERCALATION SURPLUS (*runyu* 閏餘), which means an intercalary month that year if greater than or equal to $\frac{12}{19}$. Next, "the technique for calculating the date of new moon for the astronomical first month" 推天正朔日 has us convert the integer number of months elapsed since OBSCURATION HEAD into days using the ratio OBSCURATION DAYS (27759) : OBSCURATION MONTHS (940) (i.e. the moon's synodic period, $\frac{27759}{940} = 29\frac{499}{940} = 29.53085...$ days). From the result, $10955\frac{889}{940}$ days, we cast out complete sexagenary cycles, to find how far we have moved through the sexagenary cycle since OBSCURATION HEAD: in this case, we have moved $10955\frac{889}{940}$ mod 60 = $35\frac{889}{940}$ days through the sexagenary cycle from OBSCURATION HEAD, which began on *gengzi*.$_{37}$, thus placing syzygy $\frac{889}{940}$ of a day past midnight, day *yihai*.$_{12}$ (A.D. 173 December 22, 22:41).[47] If the LESSER REMAINDER—the $\frac{889}{940}$ day here—is greater than or equal to $\frac{441}{940}$, the month is *da* 大 "big," otherwise, it is *xiao* 小 "small." Then, counting off from the astronomical first month by the moon's synodic period, we produce something like Table 3.4.

---

47. One finds the *ganzhi* date of OBSCURATION HEAD from a table via the number of OBSCURATIONS elapsed.

Table 3.4: *Shuo-run* table calculated by the Quarter-remainder system (#9) for A.D. 174

Ast. mo.	New Moon	L. RMNDR	Size	Civ. mo.	Julian Date
I	*yihai*.12	889/940	big	XI	Dec 22
II	*yisi*.42	448/940	big	XII	Jan 21
III	*yihai*.12	7/940	small	I	Feb 20
IV	*jiachen*.41	506/940	big	II	Mar 21
V	*jiaxu*.11	65/940	small	III	Apr 20
VI	*guimao*.40	564/940	big	IV	May 19
VII	*guiyou*.10	123/940	small	V	Jun 18
VIII	*renyin*.39	622/940	big	VI	Jul 17
IX	*renshen*.09	181/940	small	VII	Aug 16
X	*xinchou*.38	680/940	big	VIII	Sep 14
XI	*xinwei*.08	239/940	small	IX	Oct 14
XII	*gengzi*.37	738/940	big	X	Nov 12
I	*gengwu*.07	297/940	small	XI	Dec 12
II	*jihai*.36	796/940	big	XII	Jan 10

The product of these initial steps is a *shuo-run* table not unlike the excavated ones presented in Section 3.1.3, the difference being that the data in Table 3.4 require conversion from astronomical to civil time. First comes the figuring of "big" & "small" months, which itself has no mathematical function, then the "calculation of the position of the intercalary month" 推閏月所在 (I have omitted this step since A.D. 174 is a normal year). With the exception of "the technique for calculating the 24 *qi*" 推二十四氣術, the rest of what follows in the average system manual's opening section—lunar phases, lunisolar positions on various dates and times of day, and hemerologies—does not make it into calendars as such.

The *shuo-run* tables of formidable reference works like Wang Yuezhen's 汪曰楨 (1813–1881) *Lidai changshu jiyao* 歷代長術輯要 and Zhang Peiyu's *Sanqianwubai nian liri tianxiang* are invariably compiled in this manner, treating the dates of the civil calendar as a mathematical problem solvable with period *li* manuals. Zhang Peiyu, for example, describes his methodology thus: "the almanacs in this book are calculated from the *lifa* astronomical systems that saw actual use through successive dynasties and are, to the extent that is possible, checked against sources both from these new [archaeological] discoveries and transmitted almanacs and calendars."[48] Indeed, if you compare the two, you will find that my *shuo-run*

calculations in Table 3.4, based on the Quarter-remainder system (#9) as preserved in *Hou*

Han shu 後漢書, match exactly those of Zhang Peiyu's tables.[49] There are, however, two

serious problems with this approach.

The first problem is determining what systems to use and when. To this end, historians

of astronomy have since the early twentieth century compiled a number of master lists that

enumerate official *li* systems and their precise dates of implementation. What is frustrating

about these lists is that no two of them are the same, and none of them explain their criteria

for selecting start and end dates.[50] From my own efforts to compile such a master list, I

have concluded that other scholars' criteria are as follows: in the absence of clear evidence,

a system was in effect from the year that historical records note that it was first *yong*, *shi*,

xing, or *gai wei* 改爲 "reformed to" up to the year that the next such system is mentioned

in these terms.

The problem, as I have attempted to show in Chapter 1, is the ambiguity of "reform"

history. Sometimes, sources use the terms *yong* or *gai* at the private rather than official level.

For example, the *Jin shu* 晉書 tells us that "in the Xiping period (A.D. 172–178), Liu Hong

劉洪 reformed to (*gai wei*) the Supernal Emblem [system] (#10)" 至熹平中，劉洪改為乾象，

though we know from other sources that his system was first submitted to the court circa

A.D. 189 and first officially "reformed to" only in A.D. 222 (see Section 1.2.2). Sometimes, we

---

48. *Sanqianwubai nian liri tianxiang* 三千五百年曆日天象 (Zhengzhou: Daxiang chubanshe, 1997), 2.

49. Ibid., 124. For the Quarter-remainder system manual, see *Hou Han shu* (Zhonghua shuju ed.), *zhi* 3, 3057–3054.

50. For master lists, see Zhu Wenxin 朱文鑫, *Tianwen kaogu lu* 天文考古錄 (Shanghai: Shangwu yin-shuguan, 1933), 49–53, Table 2; Chen Zungui 陳遵嬀, *Zhongguo tianwenxue shi* 中國天文學史, 2d ed. (Shanghai: Shanghai renmin chubanshe, 2006), 1005–1019, Table 50; Yabuuti Kiyosi 藪內清, "Astronomical Tables in China, from the Han to the T'ang Dynasties," in *Chūgoku chūsei kagaku gijutsushi no kenkyū* 中國中世科學技術史の研究, ed. Yabuuti Kiyosi (Tōkyō: Kadokawa shoten, 1963), 445–492. "Astronomical Tables in China—from the Wutai to the Ch'ing Dynasties," *Japanese Studies in the History of Science* no. 2 (1963): 94–100; Chen Meidong 陳美東, *Gu li xin tan* 古曆新探 (Shenyang: Liaoning jiaoyu chubanshe, 1995), 215–223, Table 8-1; Nathan Sivin, *Granting the Seasons: The Chinese Astronomical Reform of 1280, with a Study of Its Many Dimensions and a Translation of Its Records* (New York: Springer, 2009), 43–53, Table 2.1.

have evidence of actual calendars calculated according to systems that were not supposed to have been in use. For example, scholars have shown that the Northern Wei *shuo-run* tables of A.D. 450 & 451 were products of the Luminous Inception system (#13), even though the *Wei shu* 魏書 clearly states, "when Shizu 世祖 (r. 423–452) pacified Liang 涼 soil (A.D. 439), he obtained the Epochal Beginning system (#20) devised by Zhao Fei 趙歐, and since the latter was TIGHTER, it was used to replace the Luminous Inception [system]" 世祖平涼土，得趙歐所修玄始曆，後謂為密，以代景初.[51] Sometimes there is also evidence that the use and/or contents of official system manuals underwent modification (see Section 1.2).

This brings us to the second problem with the mathematical approach: the history of human intervention. In an important 1992 article, Huang Yi-long takes up the question of how evidence of the actual civil calendar from excavated and transmitted sources matches up against the calendar produced by Li Chunfeng's 李淳風 Chimera Virtue system (*Linde li* 麟德曆), as preserved in the *Jiu Tang shu* 舊唐書, over the period of its official tenure (A.D. 666–728). What he finds is that there are a large number of discrepancies in both the dates of new moon and the placement of intercalary months. Some of these were due to overt manipulation, such as Gaozong's 高宗 (r. A.D. 650–683) A.D. 683-VII edict to change the upcoming New Year's Day from *guiwei*.$_{20}$ (Jan 22) to *jiashen*.$_{21}$ (Jan 23)— a *jia*.$_{S01}$ day being a more befitting beginning. Others, Huang deduces from mathematical analysis, appear to have have resulted from no less than two changes to the rules for counting new moon *in practice*, on which the system manual itself is silent.[52] For their part, Zhang Peiyu and other scholars of pre-104 B.C. Qin-Han calendrics have introduced similar solutions to address inconsistencies between early Qin-Han calendars.[53]

My own tentative exploration of this question has confirmed that the period between

---

51. *Wei shu* (Zhonghua shuju ed.), 107A.2659. On the calculation of the Dunhuang cave library *Taiping zhenjun shiyi nian liri* (A.D. 450) and *Taiping zhenjun shier nian liri* (A.D. 451) *shuo-run* tables, see Martzloff, *Le calendrier chinois*, 267–279.

52. "Zhongguo shi libiao shuorun dingzheng juyu" 中國史曆表朔閏訂正舉隅, *Hanxue yanjiu* 漢學研究 10, no. 2 (1992): 279–306.

53. See note 6.

104 B.C. and A.D. 666 is not without its own idiosyncrasies. First, there is of course the common (non-calendrical) problem of textual corruption whereby *ganzhi* dates have become confused. In two different places, for example, the *Han shu* 漢書 records a solar eclipse as occurring on *hui* 晦 "the last day of the month," Yuanfeng 1-VII-*yihai*.$_{12}$ and *jihai*.$_{36}$; since the former does not work as a date, and the latter corresponds to an actual eclipse that would have been visible in Chang'an 長安 on 80 B.C. September 20, it seems that, as commonly happens, someone somewhere along the way confused one *ganzhi* component of the binome with another.[54]

More relevant to the topic at hand are cases where seemingly reliable sources offer contradictory *ganzhi* dates one day apart. In 198 B.C., for example, the Zhangjiashan M247 Gaozu 5 – Gaohou 2 (202–186 B.C.) *shuo-run* table lists month VII as beginning on *dingyou*.$_{34}$ (August 09), while the *Han shu* records a total solar eclipse on *last day of the month*, VI-*yiwei*.$_{32}$, that indeed matches an eclipse visible in Chang'an on August 07.[55] Similarly, we find the following dates written on two administrative documents found both at Edsen-gol: "Shenjue 1-IV-new moon *renzi*.$_{49}$-day *jiyou*.$_{46}$" 神爵元年四月壬子朔己酉 (A615 [109 • 7]) and "Shenjue 1-IV-new moon *guiwei*.$_{48}$-day *yiyou*.$_{22}$" 神爵元年四月癸未朔乙酉 (A1618A–B [306 • 4A–B]).

We also find inconsistencies in intercalation. In 18 B.C., for example, Edsen-gol 32.17 records the date "Hongjia 3-[VIII]^2.-new moon *gengwu*.$_{07}$" 鴻嘉三年閏月庚午朔 (Sep 26) where the Grand Inception system (#7) has a IX-new moon *gengwu*.$_{07}$ (Sep 26) followed by a IX^2-new moon *gengzi*.$_{37}$ (Oct 26).[56] Likewise, in A.D. 54 the *Hou Han shu* tells us that "on [Jianwu] 30-[IV]^2-*jiawu*.$_{31}$ (Jun 09), Mercury was at Eastern Well.$_{22}$ 20$^{\circ\circ}$... and disappeared

---

54. According to the *Han shu*, "Yuanfeng... year 1... autumn, VII-*yihai*.$_{12}$, last day of the month: there was an eclipse of the sun and it was total" 元鳳⋯元年⋯秋七月乙亥晦，日有蝕之，既 (*Han shu*, 7.226) and "Yuanfeng 1-VII-*jihai*.$_{36}$, last day of the month: there was an eclipse of the sun, it was almost total, and it was at Spread.$_{26}$ 12$^{\circ\circ}$" 元鳳元年七月己亥晦，日有食之，幾盡，在張十二度 (ibid., 27B.1503). Note that the former does not work as a date because Yuanfeng 1-VII began on *bingshen*.$_{33}$ (Aug 22), which would place day *yihai*.$_{12}$ either 21 days prior or 39 days after new moon and, thus, in a different month.

55. Ibid., 27B.1500.

56. See Yu Zhongxin, *Han jian kao li*, 116.

on V-*jiazi*.$_{01}$ (Jul 09), being visible for a total of 31 days... the intercalary month was on month IV[2]" 三十年閏月甲午，水在東井二十度... 五月甲子不見，凡見三十一日... 閏月在四月, while the Triple Concordance system (#8) produces an intercalary month III[2].[57]

Lastly, on the topic of calendars as the product of *li*, let us consider the copyist and user's perspective on calendar-making. In the process of researching this chapter, producing the numerous figures found herein, and entering almost a thousand years of *shuo-run* tables into a spreadsheet for an upcoming date conversion tool, I have spent at least two weeks of my life copying calendars and *shuo-run* tables. During that process, I found myself quickly falling back upon a number of rote procedures based on simple patterns inherent to the material. My modern experience entering *ganzhi* into Photoshop and LibreOffice is obviously different from that of the early imperial scribe, for whom "copy & paste" was a more literal and time-consuming affair, but it seems to me sufficiently relevant to warrant a brief description.

First, new moon *ganzhi* are the *sine qua non* of calendrics, and daily calendars and calendar rounds are but extrapolations of *shuo-run* tables. Like the verso of the Zhoujiatai M30 Ershi 1 (209 B.C.) *shuo-run* board (p. 209), the latter do nothing more than enumerate the dates between new moons, and thus require nothing more from their compilers than that they know how to count. Second, *shuo-run* tables are comprised of binome pairs. A pair share the same *tiangan*, but their *dizhi* are diametrically opposed (6 places apart), and to move between pairs one counts backwards by one binome. For example, a typical sequence would be: 甲子 *jia*$_{S01}$*zi*$_{B01}$(01) & 甲午 *jia*$_{S01}$*wu*$_{B07}$(31) → 癸亥 *gui*$_{S10}$*hai*$_{B12}$(60) & 癸巳 *gui*$_{S10}$*si*$_{B06}$(30) → 壬戌 *ren*$_{S09}$*xu*$_{B11}$(59) & 壬辰 *ren*$_{S09}$*chen*$_{B05}$(29), etc. Binome pairs result from the sequence of "big" (30-day) and "small" (29-day) months required to approximate the moon's 29.5306-day synodic period. These sequences are occasionally interrupted by the occurrence of two "bigs" in a row, the result of which, in terms of *ganzhi*, is a set of three wherein the first and last *ganzhi* are the same, e.g. 壬戌 *ren*$_{S09}$*xu*$_{B11}$(59) → 壬辰 *ren*$_{S09}$*chen*$_{B05}$(29) → 壬戌 *ren*$_{S09}$*xu*$_{B11}$(59). Third, on a *zhiri* which places two months on

---

57. *Hou Han shu, zhi* 10, 3223.

every register, the *ganzhi* of each subsequent register will repeat exactly one place to the left so long as the "big-small" sequence proceeds uninterrupted (see figs. 3.1 & 3.2). Fourth, on a *shiri* which gives every month its own register, the *ganzhi* dates of *every other* register likewise repeat one place to the left. The last two points allow one to copy daily calendars with relative ease, and, for this reason, it is not surprising that we find textual errors cascade down subsequent registers in excavated calendars of this type.

3.2.2 *Calendars as the purpose of li*

Very little of what is in a *li* system manual actually goes into a calendar. As we recall from Chapter 1, a system manual is as a rule organized into three primary divisions: lunisolar astronomy/calendrics, eclipse prediction, and planetary astronomy. Of these, it is only the first (and, indeed, only the first few lines thereof) that enters into the sort of calendars that we see from the early imperial period.

This impression, of course, may well be the product of selection bias. *All* of our calendars and *shuo-run* tables were, after all, recovered from low- to mid-level local administrative contexts, be it dump sites or the humble tombs of middle management and scribes. For their part, the two handy tables in Section 3.1.4 hint at products that may have existed at the opposite end of the spectrum, in the context of practicing experts. Transmitted sources offer further clues about the diversity of the tabular products of *li* that may have been available at the time. The *Hou Han shu* "Harmonics and *Li* Treatise," for example, mentions expert access to a *guan li* 官曆 "official *li*" that *shu* 署 "notes" lunar eclipses:

> 至永平五年，官曆署七月十六月食。待詔楊岑見時月食多先曆，即縮用筭上為日，因上言「月當十五日食，官曆不中」。詔書令岑普候，與官曆課。起七月，盡十一月，弦望凡五，官曆皆失，岑皆中。

In Yongping 5 (A.D. 62), the official *li* (*guan li*) noted a lunar eclipse on VII-16 (Sep 08). Expectant Appointee Yang Cen 楊岑 had seen that the majority of lunar eclipses were ahead of the *li* at the time, so he closed the gap by using an *inclusive* day count and memorialized accordingly, saying "the moon ought to be eclipsed on the 15th (Sep 07), the official *li* is off the mark." Cen was ordered by imperial edict to perform comprehensive observations with which to rank the official *li*. From month VII all the way to month XI, out of a total of five [lunations], the official *li* consistently missed the mark, and Cen consistently hit it.[58]

Since system manuals use the term *shu* to instruct the user to "note" lunar phenomena—e.g. "if the moon is in Spread.$_{26}$ or Heart.$_{05}$ in the last decade of winter, then note (*shu*) it" 其冬下旬月在張、心署之 —it is safe to assume that the *guan li* here is some sort of computed ephemeris rather than computational manual.[59] As important as eclipse prediction and prophylaxis was to imperial ideology, the rarity of such annotations in extant calendars is interesting: of the dozens of manuscripts from between 220 B.C. and A.D. 630, it is only on the Northern Wei *Taiping zhenjun shiyi nian liri* (A.D. 450) and *Taiping zhenjun shier nian liri* (A.D. 451) that we find them. Again, this might be a matter of selection bias, but it might also indicate the level of access that certain sectors of society were granted to such foreknowledge (in writing, at least).

In the absence of an extant *guan li*, we can speak only to administrative calendars, which, given their prevalence in the archaeological record, we might suppose represent popular forms. Very little of the astronomy of calendro-astronomy went into these forms. Certainly, lunar phases, right ascension, and the like would have been irrelevant for the purposes of ceremony and civil administration, but the true schism between calendrics and astronomy comes to the fore with Liu Hong's introduction of the SPEED SEQUENCE (*chiji li* 遲疾曆) model of lunar inequality. Described in Section 1.2.2, the SPEED SEQUENCE allows the user to *ding* 定 "fix" the time and position of true lunar phenomena via application of an

---

58. *Hou Han shu, zhi* 2, 3025. According to *Alcyone Ephemeris* v3.2, a penumbral eclipse indeed occurred A.D. 62 September 07, moonrise, 18:23 and 21:20 LAT.

59. *Hou Han shu, zhi* 3, 3064; *Jin shu*, 17.507, 18.544; *Song shu*, 12.241.On the significance of this annotation, see p. 36, n. 24.

equation of center to mean phenomena. In Liu Hong's SPEED SEQUENCE, "fixed" syzygy can occur up to $7^\text{h}15^\text{m}$ before, and $10^\text{h}35^\text{m}$ after, mean syzygy such that "fixed" and mean new moons sometimes fall on different days. Under the rubric "Nine Roads" (*jiu dao* 九道), experimentation with lunar inequality can be traced back to at least the first century B.C., but it was not until the seventh century A.D. that it was finally ported from astronomy to civil calendrics.

There was a long history of resistance against the "fixing" of civil months. In A.D. 123, Gentleman of the Masters of Writing Zhang Heng 張衡 (A.D. 87–140) and Zhou Xing 周興 weighed in on a recent spate of memorials advising the throne to switch to either the *Jiayin*.51-origin (?) or (back) to the Grand Inception system (#7). To this end, they "consulted the [Clerk's Office's] instrument notes (observational records) and, examining the past and testing the present, concluded that the Nine Roads method was the TIGHTEST" 參案儀注，考往校今，以為九道法最密.[60] After some debate back-and-forth, forty people led by Yin Zhi 尹祉 of Henan 河南 and Member of the Suite of the Heir-apparent Li Hong 李泓 issued the following *yi* 議 "opinion":

即用甲寅元，當除『元命苞』天地開闢獲麟中百一十四歲，推閏月，【不】直其【月】，或朔、晦、弦、望，二十四氣宿度不相應者非一。用九道為朔，月有比三大二小，皆疏遠。元和變曆，以應『保乾圖』「三百歲斗曆改憲」之文。四分曆本起圖讖，最得其正，不宜易。

Were we to use the *Jiayin*.51-origin [system], we must remove 114 years from the elapsed time between the [*Spring and Autumn Annals* weft] *Yuanmingbao*'s 元命苞 separation of Heaven and Earth and the capture of the unicorn; when you calculate the intercalary month, you [do not] get the (correct) [month], and sometimes the lodge-degrees of [lunar phases] and the 24 *qi* do not accord—and not just once![61] If you use the Nine Roads for new moons, there will be three

---

60. *Hou Han shu, zhi* 2, 3034.

61. My revision of the original phrase *tui runyue liu zhi qi ri* 推閏月六直其日 "calculate the intercalary

231

big months and two little ones in a row, which is completely LOOSE and OFF (inaccurate). The Yuanhe (A.D. 84–87) change of *li* (to the Quarter-remainder system [#9]) was in response to the line "every three-hundred years there must be a reform of the Dipper *li*" from the [*Spring and Autumn Annals* weft] *Baoqiantu* 保乾圖. The Quarter-remainder system (#9) arose out of diagrams and prophecies, and it gets the closest to the truth, so change would be inadvisable.[62]

Nothing came of this debate, and subsequent system manuals like Liu Hong's opted to segregate the mean and true moon between calendrics and eclipse theory, respectively.

In A.D. 443, He Chengtian 何承天 (c. A.D. 370–447) actively lobbied to introduce the "fixed" new moon into civil calendrics. Upon careful review, Prefect Grand Clerk Qian Lezhi 錢樂之 (fl. fifth cent. A.D.) and his assistant Yan Can 嚴粲 wrote a positive recommendation of He's Epochal Excellence system (#22) to the throne with but one modest proviso:

又承天法，每月朔望及弦，皆定大小餘，於推交會時刻雖審，皆用盈縮，則月有頻三大、頻二小，比舊法殊為異。舊日蝕不唯在朔，亦有在晦及二日。公羊傳所謂「或失之前，或失之後」。愚謂此一條自宜仍舊。

One further point on Chengtian's method: it "fixes" the GREATER and LESSER REMAINDER of the [lunar phases] of each and every month. While this is prudent for calculating the moment of CROSSING COINCIDENCE (*jiaohui* 交會) [for eclipse prediction]—for which everyone uses SURPLUS/SHRINKAGE (*yingsuo* 盈縮; i.e. equation of center)—[*in civil calendrics,*] it results in there being three big, and two little, months in a row, which is markedly different from the old method. In the old [way], solar eclipses do not occur on new moon alone but also on last and second days, which is what the *Gongyang Tradition* refers to as "some miss

---

month, and be on duty six times" (?) is based on the Zhonghua shuju edition's suggestion to read said phrase as I have given it in the transcription. On the problems afflicting the the *Jiayin.*$_{51}$-origin system discussed here, see Christopher Cullen, "Actors, Networks, and 'Disturbing Spectacles' in Institutional Science: 2nd Century Chinese Debates on Astronomy," *Antiqvorvm Philosophia* 1 (2007): 237–267, esp. 259–261.

62. Ibid.

ahead of the mark, some miss behind." In our humble opinion, it is advisable that we persist in the old [way of doing things] on this one point.[63]

Then, Supernumerary Gentleman of the Cavalier Attendants Pi Yanzong 皮延宗 added a second charge against He Chengtian's proposition:

若晦朔定大小餘，紀首值盈，則退一日，便應以故歲之晦，為新紀之首。

If the fixed GREATER and LESSER REMAINDER of the last and first day of the month coincide with a SURPLUS (a positive equation of center) at ERA HEAD, then you move back one day, and must take the last day of the previous year as the HEAD of the new ERA.[64]

Faced with these objections, He Chengtian quickly gave up. He "thereupon amended his new method according to the old techniques without resort to the fixed GREATER and LESSER REMAINDERS for each month, as per Yanzong's objection and the Grand Clerk's memorial" 改新法依舊術，不復每月定大小餘，如延宗所難，太史所上.[65]

Exactly one century later, the tide seems to have shifted. In A.D. 544, the Liang 梁 (A.D. 502–557) court "issued an edict calling for the creation of a new *li*... that fixed the LESSER REMAINDER of new moon by means of a SPEED SEQUENCE, such that there would be 'three-big-two-small' " 制詔更造新曆... 月朔以遲疾定其小餘，有三大二小.[66] The matter was tabled four years later amid the Hou Jing 侯景 turmoil, before anything had come of this edict. It is not until midway through the Sui 隋 (A.D. 581–618) that we see the advocates of 'fixing' the civil month actually go on the offensive. In A.D. 608, Liu Xiaosun 劉孝孫 and Cultivated Talent Liu Zhuo 劉焯 of Yizhou 冀州 denounced Zhang Bin's 張賓 Opening Sovereignty system (#50; impl. A.D. 584), one of their criticisms being that "Bin et al. only knew to sequentially add the GREATER REMAINDER 29 to find [subsequent] (mean)

---

63. *Song shu* 宋書 (Zhonghua shuju ed.), 12.264.

64. Ibid.

65. Ibid.

66. *Sui shu* 隋書 (Zhonghua shuju ed.), 17.417.

new moons, and did not understand to take the CONJUNCTION-COINCIDENCE of sun and moon as the standard for fixing [them]" 賓等唯識轉加大餘二十九以為朔，不解取日月合會準以為定.[67] Then, in a long memorial, Liu Xiaosun and Liu Zhuo go on to recount the history of such lunar models and their importance in eclipse prediction, as developed by luminaries like Yang Wei 楊偉 (fl. third cent. A.D.), He Chengtian, and Long Yidi 龍宜弟 (fl. fifth cent. A.D.), concluding:

此三人者，前代善曆，皆有其意，未正其書。但曆數所重，唯在朔氣。朔為朝會之首，氣為生長之端，朔有告餼之文，氣有郊迎之典，故孔子命曆而定朔旦冬至，以為將來之範。今孝孫曆法，並按明文，以月行遲疾定其合朔，欲令食必在朔，不在晦、二之日也。縱使頻月一小、三大，得天之統。

These three men, the *li* experts of previous dynasties, were all of the intention (to pursue fixing the civil month) but had yet to correct their writings. The only thing that matters in *li* numbers are new moons and *qi*. The [first] new moon is the crown of the court audiences, and the [first] *qi* is the beginning of the growth of life; the new moon is possessed of the cultural pattern (*wen* 文) of declaration and food sacrifice, and the *qi* is is possessed of the ceremonies of suburban sacrifice and reception—thus it was that Confucius mandated *li* and fixed (*ding*) the new moon and winter solstice as a model for the future [in the *Spring and Autumn Annals*]. Today, Xiaosun's *li* method accords with both the manifest and cultural patterns: it fixes (*ding*) the syzygy by means of a lunar SPEED SEQUENCE, desiring to make it such that [solar] eclipse necessarily occurs on new moon, not on the last or second day of the month. Even if it concatenates the months "one small, three big," [it does so to] get at the integrity (*tong* 統) of Heaven.[68]

____

67. Ibid., 17.424.

68. Ibid., 17.424. Note that the authors of this memorial seem to be punning on technical and colloquial meanings of the word *ding*, using it in the first case to describe Confucius' "correction" of ritual and moral travesties such as this in recension of the *Spring and Autumn Annals.*

Their forceful plea succeeded only in "confusing" (*huo* 惑) the Sui emperor, and the civil moon went "unfixed" until the Tang, some six centuries after Zhang Heng and Zhou Xing had first endorsed it. Like the problem of planetary models explored in Chapter 2, this lag points to another near insuperable divide in the astral sciences—one, this time, within *li* calendro-astronomy itself. Finally, lest we mistake these as exceptional circumstances, it is important to remember that the "fixing" of civil *qi* was introduced only in Johann Adam Schall von Bell's (A.D. 1592–1666) Sino-Jesuit Temporal Pattern system (*Shixian li* 時憲曆) of A.D. 1645, more than one thousand years after Zhang Zixin's 張子信 (fl. A.D. 526–576) first model of solar inequality.[69]

In the past, scholars have been quick to judge the history of resistance to the "fixing" of civil time. In He Chengtian's defense, for example, Chen Meidong 陳美東 pleads, "this is an unreasonable reason, all we've done is adapt the calendar to Heaven, there is nothing wrong with 'fixing' New Year's day to correspond with Heaven; in an age when the apparent mean lunation was canonical, however, people considered this a major problem for 'fixed' lunations."[70] Chen's indignation mirrors that of Liu Xiaosun, Liu Zhuo, and other medieval experts, who, for example, dismiss Pi Yanzong's concerns with qualifications like "raising objection by glossing over his own faults" 飾非致難 and "had no idea in the first place" 本來不知.[71] Modern and ancient alike, experts in Chinese *li* generally agree that the purpose of *li* is to create an astronomically accurate civil calendar, and that anyone questioning that aim stood in the way of progress. In regards to the calendar, Martzloff tells us, "l'idée

---

69. On Zhang Zixin, see p. 159 ff.

70. *Zhongguo kexue jishu shi: tianwenxue juan* 中國科學技術史：天文學卷 (Beijing: Kexue chubanshe, 2003), 262.

71. In the aforementioned memorial, Liu Xiaosun and Liu Zhuo frame the episode thus: "It was Chengtian's original intention to establish a [new] technique for syzygy, but he met with Pi Yanzong's raising objection by glossing over his own faults, and was thus unable to carry it through" 然承天本意，欲立合朔之術，遭皮延宗飾非致難，故事不得行 (*Sui shu*, 17.424). After explaining the approach in his own day, which included "always selecting [SYSTEM ORIGIN] to accommodate the fixed new moon" 常取定朔之宜, Fu Renjun 傅仁均 (fl. seventh cent. A.D.) comments that, "Pi Yanzong had no idea in the first place, and even He Chengtian himself had not yet come to this realization" 皮延宗本來不知，何承天亦自未悟 (*Jiu Tang shu* 舊唐書 [Zhonghua shuju ed.], 79.2714.)

fondamentale et sans cesse répétée, est que les calculs doivent tendre à se conformer aux apparences célestes."[72]

What does it mean to have an astronomically accurate calendar? To us moderns, who have unmoored the flow of time from the revolutions of an increasingly opaque sky, the pre-modern quest for "calendrical empiricism" is likely to seem fanatical, if not fatuous. As Nathan Sivin puts it:

> There was no need for Chinese to be as demanding as they were. In one sense, by the reform of A.D. 85 (the Quarter-remainder system [#9]), they had met the needs of agriculture and government for accurate predictions. In another, no single ephemeris could predict seasonal phenomena for the whole of an empire larger than Europe. Encompassing that climatic diversity was something no official almanac even tried to do. Doing so would have compromised the official picture of one government ruling over a single, cosmically unified empire.[73]

In a masterful exercise of argumentum ad absurdum, Jiang Xiaoyuan 江曉原 has debunked the claim that "*li* was in the service of agriculture"—a claim common among both modern and pre-modern scholarship. It is only the sun, he points out, that matters in agriculture, and yet Chinese solar theory was the slowest to develop among the great Eurasian civilizations. Precise divisions of the tropical year did not appear until *after* the great agricultural advances of the Warring States 戰國 (480–222 B.C.); conversely, neither did the publication of solar terms in calendars and almanacs coincide with any subsequent agricultural revolution. As is evident with the eventual adoption of "fixed" *qi*, which might differ from mean *qi* by a matter of minutes, the level of precision with which *li* was concerned was so fine as to preclude any practical meaning for agriculture.[74]

Of course, the issue at stake is not how *we* understand the benefits of calendrical empiri-

---

72. *Le calendrier chinois*, 41.

73. *Granting the Seasons*, 41.

74. *Tianxue zhen yuan* 天學真原, 2d ed. (Shenyang: Liaoning jiaoyu chubanshe, 2007), esp. 115–123.

cism, but how early imperial scholars and ideologues did. To them, as already discussed in Section 1.3.2, the point was not so much the micromanagement of peasant farmers as it was the alignment of the state's ritual schedule with the rhythms of nature and the spirits—less agricultural science than ritual science. The sort of anxiety with which *li* experts grappled, Cullen invites us to imagine, was probably along the lines that "given that a small shift in the timing of a predicted astronomical event near midnight can move the date of a ceremony from one day into the next, the potential demand for accuracy was unlimited."[75] In an age in which all agreed that mistiming meant misgovernment, and misgovernment meant misfortune, the ritual sciences encouraged a gravity and rigor in the astral sciences that we must take every bit as seriously as we do, say, the convictions informing the Time Service Dept. of the U.S. Naval Observatory.

Taking actors' convictions seriously, however, does not mean that we need to take them at face value, for the idea of calendrical empiricism is itself something of a paradox. "The only thing that matters in *li* numbers," Liu Xiaosun and Liu Zhuo remind us, "are new moons and *qi*," neither of which can be directly observed or precisely timed, save for in the rare event of an eclipse. So, how is anyone to judge the TIGHTNESS of the civil calendar? The *Hou Han shu* gives us a number of examples that contemporary intellectuals and *li* experts considered *the wrong way* to go about this. One might, for example, appeal to the authority of one's office or the calculated results of a different (perhaps more self-evidently trustworthy) astronomical system, as did Member of the Suite Zong Cheng's 宗誠 enemies within the Clerk's Office in A.D. 175:

光和二年歲在己未，三月、五月皆陰，太史令修、部舍人張恂等推計行度，以為三月近，四月遠。誠以四月。奏廢誠術，施用恂術。其三年，誠兄整前後上書言：「去年三月不食，當以四月。史官廢誠正術，用恂不正術。」整所上正屬太史，太史主者終不自言三月近，四月遠。食當以見為正，無遠近。詔書下太常：「其詳案注記，平議術之要，效驗虛實。」太常就耽上選侍中韓說、博士蔡

---

75. "Actors, Networks, and 'Disturbing Spectacles' in Institutional Science," 241.

較、穀城門候劉洪、右郎中陳調於太常府，覆校注記，平議難問。恂、誠各對。

Guanghe 2 *jiwei.*56 (A.D. 179), months III and V were both overcast. Prefect Grand Clerk Xiu 修 and Divisional Member of the Suite Zhang Xun 張恂 et al. calculated the motion-degrees [of eclipse], concluding that month III was CLOSE and month IV was FAR OFF. [Zong] Cheng predicted month IV, so they petitioned to scrap his technique in favor of implementing [Zhang] Xun's. In year 3 (A.D. 180), [Zong] Cheng's older brother [Zong] Zheng 宗整 sent a number of memorials to the throne, saying:

> Last year there was no eclipse on month III, it should have been on month IV. The Clerk's Office wants to scrap [Zong] Cheng's correct technique and use [Zhang] Xun's incorrect technique.

Those that [Zong] Zheng memorialized about were direct subordinates of the Grand Clerk, but the head of the Grand Clerk['s Office] maintained that [his office] never said that that month III was CLOSE and month IV was OFF, and that, furthermore, with eclipses one must go by what has [actually] been seen, and that there is no "FAR OFF" or "CLOSE." [At this,] an edict was sent down to the Grand Master of Ceremonies:

> May that you meticulously research the records and notes and fairly discuss the essentials of technique so as to effectively verify what is empty and what is full (of truth).

The Grand Master of Ceremonies took it upon himself to handpick Palace Attendant Han Yue 韓說, Erudit Cai Jiao 蔡較, Marquis of Guchengmen 穀城門候 Liu Hong, and Gentleman-of-the-Palace of the Right Chen Tiao 陳調 to proceed to the Ministry of the Grand Master of Ceremonies, where they reviewed and collated the notes and records, and put the matter to fair debate and difficult questions, to which [Zhang] Xun and [Zong] Cheng each responded.[76]

So, the petitioners were called out for their fallacious, if not disingenuous, tautology, but such was not always the case, especially when the offending document was an imperial edict. We have seen, for example, how Han Wudi 漢武帝 (r. 140–87 B.C.) ordered the Grand Inception system (#7) SYSTEM ORIGIN begin at a coincidence of the astronomical first month, Winter Solstice.$_{Q22}$, and midnight *as determined by the failing astronomical system that it was commissioned to replace*; we have also seen Han Zhangdi 漢章帝 (r. A.D. 76–88) opine on the potential consequences of the one-day difference in the date of Enthronement of Spring.$_{Q01}$ as predicted by the Grand Inception/Triple Concordance (#7/8) and Quarter-remainder (#9) systems.[77]

Another wrong way to go about calendrical empiricism is to argue for or against the TIGHTNESS of a particular system based on its perceived cosmo-political effects—since good *li* is one of the *sine quibus non* of good government, good government must be a sign of good *li* (and vice versa). This appears to have been one of the leading contentions of the Grand Inception system (#7) revivalist movement of the Eastern Han. In a memorial of A.D. 123, for example, Prefect Master of Writing Zhong 忠 offered the following assessment of this movement's claims:

諸從太初者，皆無他效驗，徒以世宗攘夷廓境，享國久長為辭。或云孝章改四分，災異卒甚，未有善應。臣伏惟聖王興起，各異正朔，以通三統。... 昔仲尼順假馬之名，以崇君之義。況天之曆數，不可任疑從虛，以非易是。

Those who follow the Grand Inception [system] have no other proof of its effectiveness [but this]: followers talk about how Shizong 世宗 (Wudi) pushed out the *yi* 夷 (barbarians) and expanded our territory, and how he enjoyed a long and drawn out reign; some say that since [Zhangdi] reformed to the Quarter-remainder disasters and anomalies have been sudden and severe, and there has

---

76. *Hou Han shu, zhi* 2, 3041.

77. For these edicts, see pp. 122 & 89, respectively.

yet to be any positive response. [I,] your humble servant lying prostrate on the ground, [hold that] when sage kings arise, each is different in their first month (i.e. civil calendar), in accordance with the three concordances. ... In the past, [Confucius] smoothed out the term "to borrow a horse" so as to revere the meaning of lordship—and how much more so the case for the *li* numbers of Heaven?! One cannot rely on what is suspect and abide by what is empty, trading right for wrong.[78]

In the end, the only effective way to determine *calendrical* accuracy is through *astronomical* testing, specifically eclipse observation. The problem with this approach, however, is the calendar's admixture of astral science and civil convention. A lunar eclipse, for example, might occur on the right night but the wrong "day" based solely on the choice of hour for the beginning of the new day.[79] What is more, once the inequality of lunar motion had been recognized, modeled, and barred from calendrics (as happened very early on), astronomical testing essentially loses all meaning: the mean moon—the "month"—is but a mathematical construct and is nowhere to be observed.

Having somewhat complicated the position of calendrical empiricism, let us return to Qian Lezhi, Yan Can, and Pi Yanzong's case against it. To be clear, it was the "fixing" of the civil month that is at issue, not the SPEED SEQUENCE per se or its by then well-proven application to eclipse prediction—this no one argued to abandon. The dilemma, rather, was whether or not to adjust the civil calendar's current balance of astral science and convention. Doing so would mean improved astronomical accuracy (and the perceived benefits that that entails for ritual science), but that accuracy would come at a cost. For as long as anyone could remember, and as long as the written record takes us back, the calendar had always been a well-ordered sequence of *ganzhi* pairs and big & small months regulated by a short

---

78. *Hou Han shu, zhi* 2, 3034. "To borrow a horse" is a reference to the following anecdote from the *Han Shi waizhuan* 韓詩外傳, wherein Confucius walks a member of Lu's ruling Jisun 季孫 clan through a "rectification of names," insisting that lords do not *jia* 假 "borrow" horses from their subjects, they *qu* 取 "take" them (*Han Shi waizhuan* (Siku quanshu ed.), 5.16a–b.

79. On the variable definition of the "day" for the purposes of counting lunar phenomena, see p. 320 ff.

and simple procedure—and an ERA HEAD had always begun on the day for which it was named—but the "fixing" of civil time was poised to change all of that.

Lest the inertia of such conventions fail to impress themselves upon the reader, let us consider an example of "scientific" calendar reform more close at hand: the French Republican Calendar. In a drive to replace the trappings of the *ancien régime* with institutions founded on transnational scientific principles, the French Republic introduced a host of social, legal, and metrological reforms. The latter, which would go on to become the metric system, sought to replace a confusing array of anthropometric weights and measures that varied from locale to locale with a single universal standard—a *decimal* standard, based on the circumference of the earth, that would at once facilitate easy conversion between units and transcend both the body and the body politic. Taking decimalization one step further, Charles Gilbert Romme (1750–1795) formed a commission to create a new calendar on these same principles. The result—the French Republican calendar—was a calendar of twelve 30-day months (plus 5 or 6 days placed at the end of the year) beginning on the day of the spring equinox. Each month was divided into three 10-day weeks, each day, into 10 hours, each hour, into 100 minutes, and each hour, into 100 seconds. Instituted in 1793, the French Republic disseminated its new calendar via printed almanacs and conversion guides. Though the state promoted calendar reform with all the vigor that it had the metric system, it abandoned the former a mere fourteen years later in 1806 amid religious resistance and popular confusion.[80]

"How 'scientific' does the civil calendar need to be?"—we ask ourselves this question time and again in human history, vacillating along a narrow spectrum arbitrarily drawn between nature and convention. The dilemma is of our own making, and so too is its solution. Sometimes precision beats convention, and sometimes simplicity outweighs science, but since calendrics have no practical effect on agriculture or navigation, we can go back

---

80. For a recent study of the French Republican Calendar, see Matthew John Shaw, *Time and the French Revolution: The Republican Calendar, 1789–year XIV*, Royal Historical Society Studies in History (Woodbridge: Royal Historical Society/Boydell Press, 2011).

and forth without consequence. Calendrics, after all, is not eclipse prediction, where the second-century A.D. Clerk's Office reminds us that "there is no 'FAR OFF' or 'CLOSE' " but only right and wrong. It is better to think of the civil calendar as an arena—the most prominent and symbolic of arenas—in which tensions between competing values are allowed to play out. From one time to another, and from one empire to another, the game never plays out the same way, *but it always takes two to play.* Driven by the ideal of *li* empiricism, a handful of astral and ritual scientists pushed to close the Chinese astronomy-calendrics gap. Over time, they were ultimately successful; theirs, however, was a long uphill struggle against cultural forces *and other experts* with cogent reasons of their own for supporting the "old ways."

3.3   State, Society, and Time

Calendars speak to the issues at the heart of this dissertation—empiricism, progress, and diversity—but they are all the more valuable as testimony to the interface between astronomy and society. In theory, the very point of *li* was to coordinate human and celestial rhythms to ensure productivity, harmony, and fealty, but how was this to work *in practice*? As always, one turns first to the classics, where one is exhorted of its urgency and given nothing of its details. As always, this left centuries of ritual scholars to bicker ineffectually about the ancient ways while, in the real world, presiding over complex and evolving canons of rites addressing the exigencies of their day. It is the *realia* that we find plastered on public walls and forgotten in office dumps and private tombs that give us our first honest glimpse into how the state actually deployed the astral sciences and how it "reverently granted the people the seasons" on the ground.

3.3.1 The classical precedent

Legend attributes the invention of *li* to the sage king Zhuanxu 顓頊, who delegated the task of "managing Heaven" 司天 to Rector of the South Chong 重. Later, after an unfortunate interruption of this office, the sage king Yao 堯 delegated that task to the Xi-He 羲和 brothers, who he dispatched to the far corners of the world to observe the behavior of the sun up close. It is here that the contents of *li* are explicitly described for the first time: the empirical determination of a lunisolar calendar/astronomy for the purpose of "reverently granting the people the seasons." In the time of the great human kings of the Three Dynasties, this timeless and sacred task devolved upon the office of the Great Clerk (*da shi* 大史). Among his many functions, for example, the *Rites of Zhou* lists the following: "he rectifies the agricultural and civil years so as to put (sacrificial) affairs in order, disseminating this among the officers and offices and around the capital and peripheries, disseminating the announcement of new moons to the states" 正歲年以序事，頒之于官府及都鄙，頒告朔于邦國.[81]

What did this look like? The classics mention four rituals concerning the ruler and his role vis-à-vis civil time: "sighting the new moon" (*shi shuo* 視朔), "hearing the new moon" (*ting shuo* 聽朔), "announcing the new moon" (*gao shuo* 告朔), and "announcing the moon/month" (*gao yue* 告月). One of the more detailed accounts is that found in the *Zuo Tradition* of the *Spring and Autumn Annals*:

五年，春，王正月，辛亥朔，日南至，公既視朔，遂登觀臺以望，而書，禮也。凡分，至，啟，閉，必書雲物，為備故也。

Year 5, spring, royal month I, [day] *xinhai*.48, new moon, the sun reached its southern limit (winter solstice): upon sighting the new moon, the duke ascended the observation terrace to look upon it and write it down—this is what is ritually appropriate. At every equinox, solstice, opening (Enthronement of Spring.Q01

81. *Zhouli zhushu* 周禮注疏 (Siku quanshu ed.), 26.19b.

& Enthronement of Summer.$_{Q07}$), and closing (Enthronement of Autumn.$_{Q31}$ & Enthronement of Winter.$_{Q19}$), one must take note of clouds and (prodigious) things for the sake of preparedness (Xi 5 [655 B.C.]).[82]

The term *shi* 視 "to see" and its correlation with the "observation terrace" suggests a scene reminiscent of the Islamic calendar, whereby the month is announced to begin at the first sighting of the crescent moon. Of course, while there is debate about whether the civil calendars of the early historical period counted lunations from new moon (syzygy) or, like the Islamic calendar, from first sighting, all agree that *shuo* 朔 refers to new moon, which means that Chinese dukes were tasked with "sighting" the invisible.[83] The *Guliang Tradition* suggests that they were probably aided in this task by some sort of report:

夏，五月，公四不視朔。天子告朔于諸侯，諸侯受乎禰廟，禮也。

> Summer, month V: four times the duke did not sight the new moon. The Son of Heaven announces the new moons to the marquises, and the marquises receive them at the temples to their fathers—this is what is ritually appropriate (Wen 16 [611 B.C.]).[84]

Local rulers were meant to be passive agents of the Son of Heaven in this regard. Of course, when the Son of Heaven announced the new moons, he too was simply conveying information that had been relayed to him. The passivity of the Son of Heaven's role is made abundantly clear in the "Yu zao" 玉藻 chapter of the *Record of Rites*:

玄端而朝日於東門之外，聽朔於南門之外，閏月則闔門左扉，立於其中。皮弁以日視朝，遂以食，日中而餕，奏而食。日少牢，朔月大牢；五飲：上水、漿、酒、醴、酏… 年不順成，則天子素服，乘素車，食無樂。

---

82. *Chunqiu Zuo zhuan zhushu* 春秋左傳注疏 (Siku quanshu ed.), 11.27a–b.

83. On the case *for* the use of an observational calendar in early times, see Chang Yuzhi 常玉芝, *Yin-Shang lifa yanjiu* 殷商曆法研究 (Changchun: Jilin wenshi chubanshe, 1998), 318–340. I would like to thank Adam Smith for directing me to her presentation of what I understand to be a minority position among early China scholars.

84. *Chunqiu Guliang zhuan zhushu* 春秋穀梁傳注疏 (Siku quanshu ed.), 11.18b.

He wears his dark cap robes to hold court with the sun outside the eastern gate and hear the new moon outside the southern gate—in the case of an intercalary month, he has the left leaf of the gate closed and stands in at the center [of the opening]. He wears his skin cap for his daily court audience, after which he proceeds to take his [morning] meal, the leftover from which he eats at midday. He eats to music. Every day it is a "lesser pen" (sheep and pig), and every new moon it is a "greater pen" (ox, sheep, and pig) [that are butchered/sacrificed]. There are five beverages: water, to which the first place is given, syrup, spirits, sweet wine, and millet wine. ... If the year has not been a smooth and successful one, then the Son of Heaven wears plain clothes, rides a plain carriage, and eats without music.[85]

Like its ducal counterpart, "sighting," the royal "hearing" ceremony was meant to have been held on a monthly basis.[86] This, the terminological distinction of the *Guliang Tradition* and *Record of Rites* suggest, was distinct from the "announcement" ceremony. Though the classics are silent on this point, the logistics of interstate communication would seem to necessitate some distinction: for the announcement of new moons to be of any practical use in coordinating regional lords, it would have had to reach them in time and, thus, been made in significant advance of hearing and sighting. The logical solution (and indeed the only solution for which there is historical precedent) would be to announce them all at once before/at the beginning of the calendar year. He Xiu 何休 (A.D. 129–182), for one, reads this practice onto the pre-imperial age in his commentary to the *Gongyang Tradition*:

閏月不告月，猶朝于廟。不告月者何？不告朔也。曷為不告朔？天無是月也。
閏月矣，何以謂之天無是月？是月非常月也。

---

85. *Liji zhushu* 禮記注疏 (Siku quanshu ed.), 29.1b–7a. For an alternate interpretation of this passage, see p. 258.

86. First, the previous quote from the *Guliang Tradition* marks the duke's failure to sight the new moon *on month V* and mentions a total of four such failures (presumably in that one year). Second, the quote from the "Yu zao" chapter of the *Record of Rites* offers provisions for intercalary months, which, as a rule, never fall at the beginning of the civil year.

On the intercalary month, [the Duke of Lu] did not announce the month because he was still holding court at the temple. Q: What does it mean to "not announce the month"? A: It means not announcing the new moon. Q: Why not announce the new moon? A: Because there is no such month in Heaven. Q: As to the intercalary month, why is it said that there is so such month in Heaven? A: Because this month is not a common month (Wen 6 [621 B.C.]).

| 禮，諸侯受十二月朔政於天子，藏于大祖廟，每月朔朝廟。使大夫南面，奉天子命；君北面而受之，比時，使有司先告朔，謹之至也。受於廟者，孝子歸美先君，不敢自專也。|

COMMENTARY: |Ritual [dictates] that the marquises receive the new moons and policies of the twelve months [of the civil year] from the Son of Heaven, store them in their great ancestral temples, and hold court at temple on the new moon day of every month. The grandees are made to face south to present the Son of Heaven's mandate, and the lord faces north to accept it. In times past, officers were made to first announce the new moon. This is the apogee of solemnity! The reason for accepting it at temple is that the filially pious son renders the glory unto the former lord(s), not daring to monopolize it for himself.|[87]

Whatever the basis of He Xiu's reading, it points to an expectation common among early commentators that the classics endorsed the issuance of something like a yearly calendar by the beginning of the year. According to the *Rites of Zhou*, it was the Great Clerk who was responsible for both preparing such a calendar for approval by the Son of Heaven and disseminating his official announcement thereof throughout the subcelestial realm. The classics are, again, silent on the logistics of this, but the *Spring and Autumn Annals* suggests that transmission was to occur first horizontally, from the Clerk's Office to a handful of agencies and local administrative centers, then vertically, down the latter's respective chains

---

87. *Chunqiu Gongyang zhuan zhushu* 春秋公羊傳注疏 (Siku quanshu ed.), 13.20a–b.

of command. In sum, the Son of Heaven and regional lords alike were passive relay points along a network of transmission, each responsible for both receiving and announcing the new moons.

Of course, regional courts were not only meant to be in communication with the royal court, they were meant to be scale replicas of it operating at the local level. The ceremonial duties of regional lords were mirrored upon, and synchronized with, those of the Son of Heaven. The king announced the new moon to his subjects, and so too did his dukes. For the king, this entailed the sacrifice of an ox, sheep, and pig, and for a duke, a sheep. Confucius himself would have had it no other way:

子貢欲去告朔之餼羊。子曰：「賜也，爾愛其羊，我愛其禮。」

Tzu-kung wanted to do away with the sacrificial sheep at the [Duke of Lu's] announcement of the new moon. The Master said, "Ssu, you are loath to part with the price of the sheep, but I am loath to see the disappearance of the rite."[88]

Lastly, the *Zuo Tradition* indicates that both royal and regional courts were also responsible for holding prophylactic rites in the event of a solar eclipse occurring that day:

日有食之，天子不舉，伐鼓于社，諸侯用幣于社，伐鼓于朝，以昭事神，訓民事君，示有等威，古之道也。

When there is an eclipse of the sun, the Son of Heaven does not sacrifice, but has drums beaten at the soil altar, while the marquises sacrifice offering cloth at the soil altar and have drums beaten at [their] courts. [They do this] to illustriously serve the spirits, train the commoners to serve their lords, and show that there are distinct ranks of authority, for this is the *dao* of antiquity (Wen 15 [612 B.C.]).[89]

---

88. *Analects* III.17; tr. D. C. Lau, *Confucius: The Analects* (Hong Kong: The Chinese University Press, 2000), 25.

89. *Chunqiu Zuo zhuan zhushu*, 19.34b–35b.

3.3.2 Interpretation and implementation

Whatever bearing these descriptions may have had on pre-imperial reality (for we need not assume any at all), they were to early imperial classicists vestiges of hallowed knowledge raised to glory, and lost to history, centuries before living memory. Underlying the hodgepodge of off-hand comments on new moons and *li* was assumed to be an intellectually coherent vision for civilization—tools of social engineering with the potential, if properly tapped, to consummate a second golden age.

The devil is in the details, of course, and *no one* agreed on the details. And how could they have? In the third and second centuries B.C., when the political reality of empire had only just began to dawn, there was nothing like this in practice. Textual archaeologists, ritual scholars dug through the classics, piecing together orthodox canons of state ritual from a patchwork of clues and, where there were none to be had, from assumptions based on the knowledge, practices, and exigencies under which they worked in their respective times. The discourse on calendar-related ritual science deserves its own monograph; my interest in this section, however, is not the history of scholarship, per se, but the situation on the ground that it in large part informed. To that end, I limit myself to a superficial treatment of several key points such as we encounter in dynastic history treatises and late ceremonial compendia and place these in dialog with excavated *realia*. To fill as many gaps in our knowledge as possible, I shall work backwards from better-documented periods, convinced as I am that Song 宋 (A.D. 960–1279), Yuan 元 (A.D. 1271–1368), and even Ming 明 (A.D. 1368–1644) practices are probably better indicators of early imperial ones than the products of my modern intuition.

Calendar distribution

The *Tang liu dian* 唐六典, a compendium of state regulations compiled in A.D. 738 by Zhang Yue 張說, Zhang Jiuling 張九齡, et al., describes the duty of the Bureau of the Grand Clerk (*Taishi ju* 太史局) vis-à-vis *li* as such: "to each year fabricate in advance a *li* of the upcoming year and promulgate it through the subcelestial realm" 每年預造來歲曆，頒于天下.[90] This is consistent with the *Rites of Zhou* (see p. 243). Unfortunately, entries in the "Hundred Officials" genre between the two are silent on the exact duties of this office, but it is safe to assume that they accorded with this same basic directive.

How was a single office to distribute a time-sensitive document throughout the known world? The Yuan astronomical office housed its own printer and printing staff for this purpose.[91] It is unclear what sort of text-reproduction facilities earlier Clerk's Offices may have enjoyed, but we do know that calendar printing caught on very early. Mentioned in Feng Su's 馮宿 "Jin banyin shixianshu zou" 禁版印時憲書奏 (Memorial on the Banning of the Woodblock Printing of Almanacs) of A.D. 835, in fact, the first printing ordinance in human history seems to have been aimed at excesses in the Chinese calendar industry:

準敕禁斷印歷日版。劍南兩川及淮南道，皆以版印歷日鬻於市。每歲司天臺未奏頒下新歷，其印歷已滿天下。有乖敬授之道。

We have by imperial decree prohibited the woodblock printing of calendars. Throughout the markets of Jiannan's 劍南 Two Rivers [region] (Sichuan) and Huainan 淮南 Circuit there are woodblock-print calendars for sale. Every year, before the [Clerk's Office] has even submitted the new calendar (*li*) for approval and promulgated it [around], these printed calendars have already flooded the subcelestial realm. This is a perversion of the *dao* of [the court] "reverently granting" [the seasons].[92]

According to the *Tang yulin* 唐語林, the problem seems to have persisted for decades, especially in the provinces and in times of political turmoil:

---

90. *Tang liu dian* (Siku quanshu ed.), 10.13a.

91. Sivin, *Granting the Seasons*, 169.

92. *Quan Tang wen* 全唐文 (Zhonghua shuju ed.), 624.6301a. For more on censorship and early printed calendars, see Susan Whitfield, "Under the Censor's Eye: Printed Almanacs and Censorship in Ninth-century China," *British Library Journal* 24, no. 1 (1998): 4–22.

僖宗入蜀。太史曆本不及江東，而市有印貨者，每差互朔晦，貨者各徵節候，因爭執。里人拘而送公，執政曰：「爾非爭月之大小盡乎？同行經紀，一日半日，殊是小事。」遂叱去而不知陰陽之曆，吉凶是擇，所誤於眾多矣。

[Amidst the Huang Chao 黃巢 Rebellion in A.D. 881,] when Xizong 僖宗 (r. A.D. 862–888) entered Shu 蜀 (Sichuan), the Grand Clerk's edition calendar was not reaching River East (south of the Yangtze). There were prints for sale at market, but they invariably confused the last and first days of the month. Each merchant maintained the veracity of his [calendars'] solar cycle and, thus, wrangled with one another. They were detained by the men of the quarter and delivered to the authorities. The functionary in charge responded: "You're fighting over [nothing more than the arrangement of] the big & small months? If concurrent orders are [off by] a day or a half a day, then it is really no big deal." He then shouted [in exasperation] and walked out, ignorant of the fact that the yin-yang *li*, from which auspicious and inauspicious [days] are chosen, had introduced numerous errors to the masses.[93]

The introduction of printing presented the imperial court with a powerful tool for standardizing the construction, branding, and consumption of civil time. That said, its potential was not realized overnight, nor was calendar production ever really wrested from local hands. From these ninth-century A.D. sources, we can ascertain that the holdup was not one of technology per se but of pre-industrial limitations on the scale of production and the logistics of distribution. There was no "revolution" marking a clean break between print and pre-print cultures in calendrics; instead printing operated on a cultural model much closer to—and still fully intertwined with—manuscript production than, say, our twenty-first-century pub-

---

93. *Tang yulin jiaozheng* 唐語林校證 (Zhonghua shuju ed.), 7.671; tr. modified from Alain Arrault, "Les calendriers de Dunhuang," in *Divination et société dans la Chine médiévale: étude des manuscrits de Dunhuang de la Bibliothèque nationale de France et de la British Library*, ed. Marc Kalinowski (Paris: Bibliothèque nationale de France, 2003), 94–95.

lishing industry.[94] The Tang *Jixian zhuji*'s 集賢注記 account of the logistics of distribution is a case in point:

自置院之後，每年十一月内，即令書院寫新歷日一百二十本，頒賜親王公主及宰相公卿等，皆令朱墨分布，具注歷星，遞相傳寫，謂集賢院本。

Ever since the establishment of the [Jixian] Academy (A.D. 725), the academy has been ordered to make 120 copies of the new calendar to disseminate to the kings and princesses of royal blood as well as the Grand Councilor, Excellencies, Ministers, etc. within month XI of every year. All of these are ordered to be distributed in red and black ink with annotations concerning the sequence of stars (*li xing* 歷星) so that they may be passed around for copying. [The master copies] are referred to as the Jixian Academy edition.[95]

The Tiansheng Ordinances ("Tiansheng ling" 天聖令) of A.D. 976 confirm that this model persisted well into the printing age:

諸每年司天監預造來年曆日，三京、諸州各給一本。量程遠近，節級送。樞密院散頒，並令年前至所在。

Every year, the [Clerk's Office] is to fabricate in advance a calendar (*liri*) for the upcoming year, giving one copy each to the three capitals and the various prefectures. They are to be dispatched sequentially, based on the measured distance of the journey required. The Privy Council disseminates them and are furthermore ordered that they do so such that they arrive before the beginning of the civil year.[96]

---

94. On this point in the context of early European print culture, see Adrian Johns, *The Nature of the Book: Print and Knowledge in the Making* (Chicago: University of Chicago Press, 1998).

95. *Jixian zhuji*, cited in *Yuhai* 玉海 (Siku quanshu ed.), 55.43b.

96. Tianyige bowuguan 天一閣博物館 and Zhongguo shehui kexue yuan lishi yanjiusuo Tiansheng ling zhengli keti zu 中國社會科學院歷史研究所天聖令整理課題組 eds., *Tianyige cang Ming chaoben Tiansheng ling jiaozheng (fu Tang ling fuyuan yanjiu)* 天一閣藏明鈔本天聖令校證（附唐令復原研究）(Beijing: Zhonghua shuju, 2006), 734. On these edicts, their relation to almanacs excavated from Dunhuang and

Transmitted sources tell us very little about the logistics of civil time prior to the Tang. Here, we must rely instead on suppositions drawn from period calendars. First of all, we can assume that if the "pass around for copying" model of transmission was the norm for the print age, it was probably the norm for the pre-print age as well. Surprisingly, while production lay in the hands of the individual—be it those of the user or professional copyist—it was anything but lawless. As mentioned above, the coincidence of forms across space and time is evidence of the active acceptance, if not enforcement, of national standards. Copyists were disciplined. No matter how disciplined they were, they still made mistakes, of course: they mistransposed lines, miswrote *ganzhi*, and faithfully reproduced errors. They were disciplined, but they were not machines. In an age *before* machines, though, we might expect a different threshold of tolerance for human volatility in "mechanical" reproduction. It is my sense, therefore, that the sort of mistakes that we see in calendar copying have much more to do with *humanity* than, say, literacy. In my own anecdotal experience reproducing figures for Section 3.1, I found that I made *many more* of the *exact same* mistakes in Photoshop than my predecessors had on bamboo and wood, and it was not, I must insist, for want of literacy or *li* expertise.

The one thing that transmitted sources *do* reveal about this period is an apparent shift in terminology: the term *ban li* 頒曆 "disseminate the *li*" appears only in the mid- to late-Tang, whereas earlier sources persist in the classical idiom of "new moons."[97] The idiom of "new moons" is still very much the norm in the *Sui shu* 隋書 (A.D. 636), for example:

梁初因齊，用宋元嘉曆。天監三年下詔定曆... 至九年正月，用祖冲之所造甲子元曆頒朔。

At the beginning, the Liang 梁 (A.D. 502–557) followed the Qi 齊 (A.D. 479–502) in using the [Liu-]Song 劉宋 (A.D. 420–479) Epochal Excellence system (#22),

Turpan, and the "pass around for copying" model of transmission, see Chen Hao 陳昊, "Tulufan Taizangta xinchu Tangdai liri yanjiu" 吐魯番臺藏塔新出唐代曆日研究, *Dunhuang Tulufan yanjiu* 敦煌吐魯番研究 10 (2007): 207–220.

97. The locus classicus of *ban li* appears to be like Du You's 杜佑 *Tongdian* 通典 of A.D. 801 (*Tongdian* [Zhonghua shuju ed.], 186.5016).

but in Tianjian 3 (A.D. 504), an edict was issued ordering the fixing of the *li*... and in 9-I (A.D. 510) the *Jiazi*$_{01}$-origin system (#32) constructed by Zu Chongzhi 祖冲之 was used to promulgate the new moons (*ban shuo*).[98]

Given their relationship, it makes sense that actors might use "the new moons" as a synecdoche for "the calendar," but I suspect that it was more than just that. It is conceivable that "the promulgation of the new moons" might refer more concretely to the distribution of *shuo-run* tables. The terminology certainly fits—there is no talk of promulgating *zhiri*, *shiri*, or *liri* in this period—and, of all those surveyed in Section 3.1, the *shuo-run* table is certainly the most ideal form for relaying time-sensitive calendrical information, given its economy of contents, language, and dimensions. Less is more, and it is not just a matter of how many calendars one can load into a courier sack: a simple list of twelve *ganzhi* dates would at once take minimal time to "pass around for copying" and leave minimal room for textual corruption.

Scholars have been quick to point out breakdowns in distribution channels, especially as they affected the far-flung border outposts of the Northwest. For example, Loewe provides a list of nine Edsen-gol documents dated with obsolete reign-names (*nianhao* 年號), one explanation for which, he offers, is "the delay in the promulgation and receipt of the new order."[99] Chen Hao 陳昊 points to an even clearer instance of this problem evidenced in an administrative document from Turpan dated A.D. 754:

為正月二月歷日未到，准小月支，後歷日到，並大月，計兩日料。今載二月十三日牒送倉曹司充和糴訖。

Because the calendar (*liri*) for month II had not arrived by month I, [we took the liberty of] setting it on a [*gan*]*zhi* date befitting a small month. Later, when

---

98. *Sui shu*, 17.416.

99. "Some Notes on Han-time Documents from Chüyen," 316–319. A more comprehensive collection of obsolete reign-names appearing in excavated Han-time documents can be found in Yu Zhongxin, *Han jian kao li*. For the same phenomenon in later Dunhuang cave library almanacs, see Arrault, "Les calendriers de Dunhuang," 93.

the calendar arrived, we discovered that it was a double big month, and so we counted two days' feed. On II-13 of this year, the *die* 牒 invoice was dispatched to Director of the Granaries Section Chong He 充和 to purchase the full amount of grain.[100]

This is not particularly surprising, since it could take more than 50 days for important government documents such as the the Yuankang 5 (61 B.C.) edict on seasonal ordinances (below) to arrive at Edsen-gol from the capital.[101] What is surprising, rather, is that the majority of Northwestern documents and calendars *do* reflect timely transitions between reign-names, suggesting that, more often than not, the system worked as it was intended. Take for instance the rather confusing span of time surrounding Wang Mang's 王莽 (c. 45 B.C. – A.D. 23) ascension to the throne: in the autumn of A.D. 8 (months VII–IX, or 8 Aug 21 – Nov 16), Wang Mang ordered the year changed from Jushe 3 to Chushi 1; then, only a matter of weeks later on Chushi 1-XI-25 *wuchen*.05 (A.D. 9 Jan 10), Wang Mang took the throne and announced the founding of his Xin 新 "New" dynasty (A.D. 9–23), changing Chushi 1-XII to Shijianguo 1-I (a change from the "Xia" 夏 to "Yin" 殷 first month).[102] It is unclear whether Chushi began as early as month IX. The one administrative document extant from month IX of that year is dated Jushe: "Jushe 3-IX-*bingchen*.53" 居攝三年九月丙辰 (Edsen-gol, Mu-durbeljin T59 [101]). Either way, Chushi would have certainly been in effect by month XI, the last month of that year. Among Northwestern materials, we have found two documents dating to month XI of this year: one, from the Shule River 疏勒河

---

100. "Tang Tianbao shisan zai Jiaohe-jun Changxing-fang ju yi zhi jiuyue celiao poyong zhang qing chufen die" 唐天寶十三載交河郡長行坊具一至九月芻料破用帳請處分牒 (73TAM506: 4/32–10), published in Tang Changru 唐長孺 et al., eds., *Tulufan chutu wenshu* 吐魯番出土文書, 10 vols. (Beijing: Wenwu chubanshe, 1992), vol. 4, 487. See Chen Hao, "Tulufan Taizangta xinchu Tangdai liri yanjiu," 218.

101. Hsing I-t'ien 邢義田, "Yueling yu Xihan zhengzhi: cong Yinwan jibu zhong de 'yi chunling chenghu' shuoqi" 月令與西漢政治——從尹灣集簿中的「以春令成戶」說起, *Xin shixue* 新史學 9, no. 1 (1998): 25–27. Likewise, the "Shizhe Hezhong suo ducha zhaoshu sishi yueling wushi tiao" 使者和中所督察詔書四時月令五十條 (below) took some three and a half months to arrive at Xuanquanzhi 懸泉置, Dunhuang; see Charles Sanft, "Edict of Monthly Ordinances for the Four Seasons in Fifty Articles from 5 C.E.: Introduction to the Wall Inscription Discovered at Xuanquanzhi, with Annotated Translation," *Early China* 32 (2008–2009): 137 n. 16.

102. See *Han shu*, 99.4095, 99.4113. On the first month of the civil calendar, see Table 1.3 on p. 52.

(292) dated "Jushe 3-XI" 居攝三年十一月, maintains the old reign-name, while the other, from Edsen-gol (312.6), is dated "Chushi 1-XI-*renzi*.$_{49}$" 初始元年十一月壬子 (A.D. 8 Dec 25). Whatever delay in communications there may have been between the two sites at the end of A.D. 8, *both* sites were evidently informed about the change in dynasties, reign-names, and first months by the first half of the next year: we find a document dated "Shijianguo 1-V" 始建國元年五月 at Mu-durbeljin T17 (3), and *two* different documents dated "Shijianguo 1-XI-*xinhai*.$_{48}$" 始建國元年十月辛亥 (A.D. 9 Oct 20) from Mu-durbeljin T52 (263) and the Shule River (357).[103]

State ritual

The practical logistics of coordinating civil time over an empire stretching from P'yŏngyang to Kashgar was, it turns out, the easy part. On the matter of ceremony—the *symbolic* control of time and space—the court experienced centuries of deadlock punctuated by paroxysms of decisive action.

For all that they do chronicle, the dynastic histories' "Treatises on Ritual" (Li zhi 禮 志) leave no trace of "sighting," "hearing," or "announcing" ceremonies as ever having been performed by an imperial court. The only time that we *do* see early imperial actors mention them is in discussing how ritual worked in antiquity and, thus, in theory. Rites at

---

103. For the aforementioned documents, see Yu Zhongxin, *Han jian kao li*, 146. Lest we make too much of dates in Northwestern materials that either do or do not reflect changes in imperial reign-names, I offer Loewe's sound words of caution on the matter:

> These references are of little help in an attempt to estimate the interval that occurred between the promulgation of orders by the central government and their effective implementation in far flung parts of the empire. For, as will be seen, the dates in question are usually in the second half of the year, and are thus too late to be of value; and although the new *nien hao* were adopted for immediate use, it is not usually known at what precise time the adoption took place. It will be seen that in at least one instance the adoption did not precede the beginning of the year in question.

> There are several instances in which years are designated incorrectly on the strips, in so far as an obsolete *nien hao* is used. These cases can be explained by various reasons, e.g. the delay in the promulgation and receipt of the new order, the advance preparation of documents, or the adherence of a scribe to an old title to which he was accustomed ("Some Notes on Han-time Documents from Chüyen," 316).

the acknowledged core of classical ceremonial languished, but not for lack of cooperation or impetus among ritual scholars, who labored for centuries to make, remake, and enforce expansive state ritual canons. The problem, rather, seems to have been a recognized disconnect between ancient and contemporary practices. Examples of this attitude and the confusion surrounding classical new moon rites abound, but one sticks out as particularly illustrative: Director of Rites, Erudit Pilü Renxu's 辟閭仁諝 response to Wu Zetian 武則天 (r. A.D. 690–705) edict ordering that "the proclamation of the new moon ceremony be held at the Bright Hall on the first of every month" 每月一日於明堂行告朔之禮 in Shengli 1 (A.D. 698):

謹按經史正文，無天子每月告朔之事。惟禮記玉藻云：天子「聽朔於南門之外。」周禮天官太宰：「正月之吉，布政于邦國都鄙。」干寶注云：「周正建子之月，告朔日也。」此即玉藻之聽朔矣。

Careful examination of the text of the classics and histories reveals that there is no such thing as the Son of Heaven's monthly announcement of the new moon. The only thing is the *Record of Rites* [chapter] "Yu zao," which says that the Son of Heaven "hears the new moon outside the southern gate." The *Rites of Zhou*, "Celestial Offices," Great Steward [entry reads], "on the first day of the first month, policies are disseminated to the states, cities, and settlements." Gan Bao's 干寶 (d. A.D. 336) commentary [explains]: "the Zhou first month, which is established at $zi._{B01}$, is the day of the announcement of the new moon(s)." *This is the "hearing the new moon(s)" in the "Yu zao"*!

今每歲首元日，於通天宮受朝，讀時令，布政事，京官九品以上、諸州朝集使等咸列於庭，此則聽朔之禮畢，而合于周禮、玉藻之文矣。而鄭玄注玉藻「聽朔」，以秦制月令有五帝五官之事，遂云：「凡聽朔，必特牲告其時帝及其神，配以文王、武王。」此鄭注之誤也。故漢魏至今莫之用。

Nowadays, on the New Year's Day of every year, court is held, the seasonal

ordinances are read, and policies are disseminated at the Tongtian Palace 通
天宮, while capital officials of grade nine and above, territorial representatives
from the prefectures, etc. all line up in tiers in the courtyard—it is at this that
the ceremony of hearing the new moon(s) is finished, and this accords with the
wen (language/cultural patterns) of the *Rites of Zhou* and "Yu zao." Zheng
Xuan's 鄭玄 (A.D. 126–200) commentary to the "Yu zao," however, posits the
Qin-instituted monthly ordinances with sacrifices to the Five Thearchs and Five
Officials and then says: "the hearing of the new moon necessitates the sacrifice
of a single ox, so that one may announce oneself to the thearch and spirit of that
season as well as mate oneself with King Wen 文王 (r. 1099–1050 B.C.) and King
Wu 武王 (r. 1049–1043 B.C.) [of the Zhou]." This is where the Zheng commentary
is wrong, and that is why, from the Han and [Cao-]Wei 曹魏 (A.D. 220–265) all
the way to today, no one has ever done this.

按月令云「其帝太昊，其神勾芒」者，謂宣布時令，告示下人，其令詞云其帝
其神耳。所以為敬授之文，欲使人奉其時而務其業。每月有令，故謂之月令，
非謂天子月朔日以祖配帝而祭告之。其每月告朔者，諸侯之禮也。故春秋左氏
傳曰：「公既視朔，遂登觀臺。」又鄭注論語云：「禮，人君每月告朔於廟，有祭
謂之朝享。魯自文公始不視朔。」是諸侯之禮明矣。今王者行之，非所聞也。

Note: the monthly ordinance's "[Spring:] its Thearch is Taihao, its spirit is
Goumang" refers to the proclamation of seasonal ordinances—announcements
made to [the Son of Heaven's] subordinates and concerning "its Thearch" and
"its spirit" in language only. This is the cultural pattern (*wen*) for "reverently
granting [the people the seasons]," the desire being to make people respect the
seasons and devote themselves to their patrimonies. There are ordinances for
every month, which is why we refer to them as "monthly ordinances"—this does
not refer to the Son of Heaven performing a sacrificial announcement to mate
his ancestors with the Thearchs on the new moon day of every month. The

monthly announcement of the new moon is a ceremony for marquises. Thus does the *Zuo Tradition* of the *Spring and Autumn Annals* say, "upon sighting the new moon, the duke ascended the observation terrace." Furthermore, Zheng [Xuan]'s commentary to the *Analects* says, "according to the rites, the lord of men announces the new moon at temple every month, and, if there be sacrifice, it is called "audience offering"; Lu stopped sighting the new moon from the time of Duke Wen 文公 (r. 626–609 B.C.)." This is clear evidence that it is a ceremony for marquises. Nowadays, I have never heard of a king (the imperial-era equivalent of marquis) performing it.[104]

The disconnect here, as Pilü Renxu alludes to, is that ritual scholars had long since rolled "sighting," "hearing," and "announcing" into the Bright Hall (*mingtang* 明堂) and monthly ordinance (*yue ling* 月令) complex. In his commentary to the *Record of Rites*, for example, Zheng Xuan interprets the second half of the "Yu zao" passage on "hearing the new moon" (see p. 244) as taking place in the Bright Hall:

| 天子之廟及路寢，皆如明堂制。明堂在國之陽，每月就其時之堂而聽朔焉。卒事，反宿路寢亦如之。閏月非常月，聽其朔於明堂門下，還處路寢門終月也。|

COMMENTARY: |The Son of Heaven's ancestral temple and road chamber (central hall) are all as per the specifications of the Bright Hall. The Bright Hall is on the sunny (south) side of the [city walls], and is where [the Son of Heaven] each month goes to the hall appropriate to the season to hear the new moon. When finished, he returns to lodge in his road chamber, where he does the same. Intercalary months are not normal (*chang* 常) months, [so] he hears their new moons beneath the gate of the Bright Hall and then returns to dwell in the road chamber until the end of the month.|[105]

---

104. *Jiu Tang shu*, 22.868–869.

105. *Liji zhushu*, 29.1b (commentary).

Neither the "Yu zao" nor any of the other classical precedents enumerated in Section 3.3.1 explicitly connect new moon rites with the Bright Hall. Once the connection had been made in Han scholarship, however, it was perpetuated by subsequent commentators like Kong Yingda 孔穎達 (A.D. 574–648) and Fang Que 方愨 (fl. A.D. 1118).[106]

According to legend, the Bright Hall was the cornerstone of the Western Zhou's 西周 (1045–771 B.C.) cosmic legitimacy—a ritual edifice, integrated with the Circular Moat (*biyong* 璧雍) and Numinous Terrace (*lingtai* 靈台) south of the Zhou capital, where the Son of Heaven performed the most august of his ritual duties. Described in the "Yue ling" 月令 and "Mingtang wei" 明堂位 chapters of the *Record of Rites* and the "Sheng de" 盛德 and "Mingtang" 明堂 chapters of *Dai the Elder's Record of Rites*, classical sources disagree on whether the Bright Hall was a temple to King Wen—the dynastic founder and prototypical sage king—or an architectural complex modeled upon the very cosmos, a juxtaposition of round (: HEAVEN) and square (: EARTH) elements divided into nine rooms (: NINE DIRECTIONS) and twelve halls (: TWELVE MONTHS).[107] Either way, it was there, the

---

106. For Kong Yingda, see *Liji zhushu*, 29.3a–b (subcommentary). Fang Que's *Liji jieyi* 禮記解義 is cited in Wei Shi's 衛湜 *Liji jishuo* 禮記集說 (A.D. 1205–1224), *Liji jishuo* (Siku quanshu ed.), 73.9a (commentary). Summaries of this position can be found in the following commentaries as well: Wu Cheng's 吳澄 (A.D. 1249–1333) *Liji zuanyan* 禮記纂言 (*Liji zuanyan* [Siku quanshu ed.], 4.1b [commentary]), Chen Hao's 陳澔 (A.D. 1260–1341) *Chen-shi Liji jishuo* 陳氏禮記集説 (*Chen-shi Liji jishuo* [Siku quanshu ed.], 13.1b [commentary]), Hu Guang's 胡廣 (A.D. 1369–1418) *Liji daquan* 禮記大全 (*Liji daquan* [Siku quanshu ed.], 13.2a–b [commentary]), Li Guangpo's 李光坡 (A.D. 1651–1723) *Liji shuzhu* 禮記述註 (*Liji shuzhu* [Siku quanshu ed.], 13.2a–b [commentary]), and the collaborative works commissioned by the Qing 清 court (A.D. 1644–1911), *Qinding Liji yishu* 欽定禮記義疏 (*Qinding Liji yishu* [Siku quanshu ed.], 41.5b–10a [commentary]) and *Rijiang Liji jieyi* 日講禮記解義 (*Rijiang Liji jieyi* [Siku quanshu ed.], 33.2a [commentary]).

107. The "Mingtang" chapter of *Dai the Elder's Record of Rites* itself notes this distinction:

明堂者，所以明諸侯尊卑。外水曰辟雍，南蠻、東夷、北狄、西戎。明堂月令，赤綴戶也，白綴牖也。… 上圓下方。九室十二堂，室四戶，戶二牖。其宮方三百步。在近郊，近郊三十里。

The Bright Hall is that by which one illustrates (*ming* 明) the hierarchy among marquises. The water outside is called the Circular Moat [and delineates] the Southern Man 南蠻, Eastern Yi 東夷, Northern Di 北狄, and Western Rong 西戎 [border peoples]. The Bright Hall is [where] the monthly ordinances [are promulgated], it has red ornamental doors and white ornamental windows. ... It is round on top and square at the bottom. It has nine rooms and twelve halls, each room having four windows, and each window having two shutters. The palace is a square three-hundred (double) paces a side. It is located in the nearby suburbs, within 30 *li* 里 [of the capital].

或以為明堂者，文王之廟也。朱草日生一葉，至十五日生十五葉；十六日一葉落，終而復始也。周時德澤洽和，蒿茂大以為宮柱，名蒿宮也。此天子之路寢也。

Some think that the Bright Hall was the temple of King Wen. There, the vermilion grass grew

classics tell us, that the Zhou kings offered cult to King Wu, held ceremonial audience with the marquises (to keep them in rank), and maintained Heavenly order via seasonal progression through its chambers. The latter we find detailed in monthly ordinance literature, e.g. the *Record of Rites*' "Yue ling," which catalog the sidereal, climatological, natural, agricultural, and ritual events that occur over the course of the (ideal) year. In his monthly progression through the Bright Hall, by his ceremonial garb, ritual gestures, and reading of monthly ordinances and prohibitions, the Son of Heaven ensured the continued harmony between these cycles and the renewal of Heaven's blessings.

The history of the Bright Hall was a tortuous affair—a point made abundantly clear in Henri Maspero and Lillian Tseng's seminal studies on the topic.[108] Whatever ritual complex the Zhou kings may have patronized, it had vanished into dust and legend long before the rise of the Qin and Han empires. There was a strong incentive to reclaim this hallowed symbol, but, yet again, the devil was in the details.

The history of the Bright Hall is the story of three prominent men. The first was Han Wudi. At the beginning of his reign in 140 B.C., Wudi encouraged the debate and planning of a Bright Hall in the southern suburbs of the Han capital; amid allegations of corruption and the protestations of the Empress' clique, however, he withdrew his support from the project as quickly as he had given it. A generation later, in 110 B.C., Wudi reconsidered and commissioned a Bright Hall on the supposed site of the Yellow Emperor's former ritual complex at the foot of Mount Tai 泰山. Some 800 km east of Chang'an, the first Bright Hall of the historical period was built as a support structure for Qin Shihuang's newfangled *feng-shan* 封禪 ceremony, whereby the emperor was to travel to Mount Tai every five years

one blade per day, arriving at fifteen blades by the fifteenth day, all of which would fall off on the sixteenth day, whereupon the cycle would repeat. In the time of the Zhou, all was blessed and harmonious, and so [the grass] luxuriantly flourished, [its stems] growing large enough to serve as palace columns, and so it was called the Luxuriant Palace. This was the Son of Heaven's road chamber (*Da Dai Liji* 大戴禮記 [Siku quanshu ed.], 8.22a–24a).

108. Henri Maspero, "Le *ming-t'ang* et la crise religieuse chinoise avant les Han," *Mélanges chinois et bouddhiques* 9 (1951): 1–71; Lillian Lan-ying Tseng, *Picturing Heaven in Early China* (Cambridge: Harvard University Asia Center, 2011), 17–88.

to offer sacrifice to Heaven and Earth and renew his mandate to govern the subcelestial realm on their behalf. Wudi kept this up for the rest of his reign, making a total of eight treks to Mount Tai, but the practice was abandoned upon his death in 87 B.C. with the exception, that is, of three desultory Eastern Han expeditions in A.D. 56 by Guangwudi 光武帝 (r. A.D. 27–57), A.D. 85 by Zhangdi 章帝 (r. A.D. 76–88), and A.D. 124 by Andi 安帝 (r. A.D. 106–125).

The first Bright Hall built along classical lines in the capital's southern suburbs was that commissioned by Wang Mang and finished in A.D. 4. Debated in the millenarian atmosphere of the late Western Han 西漢 (206 B.C. – A.D. 9), presided over by the regent in his meteoric rise to power, and finished the year before one feckless child emperor was poisoned and replaced with another, the circumstances of its construction could not be more different—"the second Bright Hall was built not to ensure Han legitimacy, but to prepare for the concession of the Han mandate."[109] Upon his promotion to Regenting Emperor (*she huangdi* 攝皇帝) in A.D. 6, Wang Mang took it upon himself to hold ceremonial audience with his vassals at the Bright Hall, becoming the first man to reenact this classic royal rite in the imperial era. Then, upon accepting the child emperor's abdication and declaring himself emperor of the Xin dynasty in A.D. 9, Wang Mang repurposed the Bright Hall as a temple to Sage King Shun 舜 to establish an ancient and symbolically potent pedigree for himself (Shun accepted the throne from Sake King Yao, the purported ancestor of the Han ruling family). Like Wang Mang's fledgling empire and most of the city from which he ruled it, the Chang'an Bright Hall was destroyed in A.D. 23, when rebel armies sacked the capital.

In A.D. 56, a generation after reconsolidating the Han Empire, Guangwudi commissioned a third Bright Hall in the southern suburbs of the new capital at Luoyang 洛陽. There, like Wang Mang before them, the Eastern Han emperors held ceremonies modeled upon those of the Zhou kings, holding audience with their vassals and sacrifices to their dynastic founders until the Bright Hall was once again destroyed in A.D. 189, when Dong Zhuo's 董卓 (d.

---

109. Tseng, *Picturing Heaven in Early China*, 28.

A.D. 192) forces sacked the new capital. From then on the pattern stuck. Subsequent courts operating from Luoyang restored and modified the Bright Hall there from time to time: Wei Wendi 魏文帝 (r. A.D. 220–226), for example, held sacrifice to Heaven and Earth there in A.D. 221, as did Jin Wudi 晉武帝 (r. A.D. 265–290) in A.D. 266, then, two centuries after fall of Luoyang in A.D. 311, the Northern Wei court rebuilt it once again.

In addition to the Son of Heaven's annual audience held with his vassals on New Year's Day and his sacrifices to the Five Thearchs—the latter, Pilü Renxu reminds us, being a Qin innovation—the one time-control ceremony that we do consistently see performed at the Bright Hall is "the reading of seasonal ordinances" (*du shi ling* 讀時令). From what we can gather from the dynastic histories and compendia like Du You's 杜佑 *Tongdian* 通典 (A.D. 801), this practice seems to have come about in the Eastern Han, around the time that the Luoyang Bright Hall began to see regular use.

> 後漢制，太史每歲上其年曆。先立春、立夏、大暑、立秋、立冬，常讀五時令。皇帝所服，各隨五時之色。帝升御座，尚書令以下就席位。尚書三公郎中以令置案上，奉以先入，就席伏讀訖，賜酒一巵。

According to the stipulations of the Later Han, the Grand Clerk memorializes the annual *li* every year, [after which] it is customary to read the ordinances of the five seasons just prior to Enthronement of Spring.[Q01], Enthronement of Summer.[Q07], Greater Heat.[Q12], Enthronement of Autumn.[Q13], and Enthronement of Winter.[Q19]. The [vestments] worn by the emperor [on these occasions] should be of a color appropriate to each of the five seasons. When the emperor ascends to his throne, the Prefect of the Masters of Writing descends to take his mat (seat). The Masters of Writing, Three Excellencies, and Gentlemen-of-the-Palace then place the ordinances upon a desk, which is carried in and presented with both hands. They then proceed to their mats, where they genuflect until the reading is finished, at which point they are bestowed a goblet of wine.[110]

---

110. *Tongdian*, 70.1922. Note that this is the first entry under the heading "The Reading of Seasonal

As a matter of state economic policy, by contrast, evidence for the promulgation and enforcement of monthly/seasonal ordinances goes back to the third century B.C. From his (as of 1998) exhaustive catalog of transmitted and excavated testimony, Hsing I-t'ien 邢義田 has concluded that these practices came together organically over the first three centuries of the imperial age: "the monthly ordinances implemented in the Han dynasty were not in strict accordance with any one Ruist classic or system, they were instead the [product] of Han experts formed from an admixture of exigency and 'ancestral precedent' through a process of eclectic cobbling and ceaseless revision and adjustment."[111] We begin to see courts actively imposing seasonal injunctions at a local level in legal texts such as the Qin royal ordinance of 309 B.C. found at Qingchuan 清川 M50, Sichuan, the "Tian lü" 田律 (Statutes on Agriculture) of the *Qin lü shiba zhong* 秦律十八種 from Shuihudi 睡虎地 M11 (c. 217 B.C.), Hubei, as well as the "Tian lü" section of the *Ernian lüling* 二年律令 (186 B.C.) from Zhangjiashan M247, which variously dictate the appropriate seasons/months for pastoral activities such as forestry, fishing, hunting, and repairing field boundaries, dykes, and roads.[112] There are traces of the *throne's* personal engagement with monthly/seasonal ordinances quite early on—e.g. Han Gaozu's 漢高祖 (r. 206–195 B.C.) edict concerning the seasonal change of regalia and Wendi's 漢文帝 (r. 179–157 B.C.) springtime philanthropy— but it is not until Xuandi's 宣帝 (r. 73–49 B.C.) reign, Hsing I-t'ien argues, that powerful ministers like Wei Xiang 魏相 (d. 59 B.C.) and Bing Ji 丙吉 (d. 55 B.C.) effected the codi-

---

Ordinances" (Du shi ling 讀時令).

111. "Yueling yu Xihan zhengzhi," 51. On Han implementation of monthly ordinances, see also Wang Meng'ou 王夢鷗, "Du 'Yueling' " 讀「月令」, *Guoli zhengzhi daxue xuebao* 國立政治大學學報 21 (1970): 1–14.

112. See Yu Haoliang 于豪亮, "Shi Qingchuan Qin mu mudu" 釋清川秦墓木牘, *Wenwu* 文物 1982.1: 22–23; Shuihudi Qin mu zhujian zhengli xiaozu 睡虎地秦墓竹簡整理小組, ed., *Shuihudi Qin mu zhujian* 睡虎地秦墓竹簡, 2d ed. (Beijing: Wenwu chubanshe, 1990), 19–20; Zhangjiashan ersiqi hao Han mu zhujian zhengli xiaozu 張家山二四七號漢墓整理小組, *Zhangjiashan Han mu zhujian (ersiqi hao mu)* 張家山漢墓竹簡（二四七號墓）(Beijing: Wenwu chubanshe, 2001), 41–44. For translations of these materials, see Sanft, "Edict of Monthly Ordinances for the Four Seasons in Fifty Articles from 5 C.E.," 171–172; A. F. P. Hulsewé, *Remnants of Ch'in Law : an Annotated Translation of the Ch'in Legal and Administrative Rules of the 3rd Century B.C., Discovered in Yün-meng Prefecture, Hu-pei Province, in 1975* (Leiden: E.J. Brill, 1985), esp. 21–26.

fication of these practices. Furthermore, it is not until the reigns of Yuandi 元帝 (r. 48–33 B.C.) and Chengdi 成帝 (r. 32–7 B.C.) that we begin to see actors placing these policies under a single theoretical rubric, as in the following edict from the spring of 23 B.C.:

昔在帝堯立羲、和之官，命以四時之事，令不失其序。故『書』云「黎民於蕃時雍」，明以陰陽為本也。今公卿大夫或不信陰陽，薄而小之，所奏請多違時政。傳以不知，周行天下，而欲望陰陽和調，豈不謬哉！其務順四時月令。

In the past, when Thearch Yao established the offices of Xi and He, he commanded them to adhere to the matters of the four seasons such that they not get out of order. Thus it was, the *Book of Documents* tells us, that "the numerous people were amply nourished and prosperous and then became concordant"—a clear indication of the foundational importance of yin & yang.[113] Today, there are Excellencies, Ministers, and Grandees who do not believe in yin & yang but dissemble and belittle it, and many of the petitions that they have memorialized violate seasonal policies. Passed around out of ignorance, they circulate the subcelestial realm, but if the desire is to harmonize yin & yang, then is this not absurd?! May that *the monthly ordinances of the four seasons* be duteously observed.[114]

We begin to get a clear picture of what this looked like on the ground in the time of Wang Mang, who in A.D. 15, Ban Gu's 班固 *Han shu* 漢書 (A.D. 111) tells us, had "eleven Grandees of the First Order spread out [across the countryside] to exhort agriculture and sericulture and promulgate seasonal ordinances" 十一公士分布勸農桑，班時令.[115] Unequivocal evidence of this (building) campaign is found in the "Shizhe Hezhong suo ducha zhaoshu sishi yueling wushi tiao" 使者和中所督察詔書四時月令五十條 (Edict on the Fifty Monthly

---

113. *Shangshu zhushu,* 1.6b–7a; tr. Bernhard Karlgren, "The Book of Documents," *Bulletin of the Museum of Far Eastern Antiquities* 22 (1950): 1–81.

114. *Han shu,* 10.312.

115. Ibid., 99.4140.

Ordinances for the Four Seasons, Supervised and Inspected by Emissary Hezhong), an edict dating to Yuanshi 5-V-*dingchou*.[14] (A.D. 4 Jun 14) discovered on the wall of a government office in Xuanquanzhi 懸泉置, Dunhuang.[116] Distilled largely from the *Lüshi chunqiu* 呂氏春秋 and the *Record of Rites*' "Yue ling" chapter, the "Shizhe Hezhong suo ducha zhaoshu sishi yueling wushi tiao" is a list of simple prohibitions on construction and agricultural activities provided item-by-item vernacular explanation. Omitting all reference to the grand sidereal, climatological, natural, agricultural, and ritual cycles that (in theory) give these prohibitions meaning, this instantiation of the seasonal ordinance genre is, Charles Sanft argues, aimed at a peasantry who "may have had a more active role in their own governance than has sometimes been recognized."[117] These plebeian prohibitions are, however, framed within a dialogue between Wang Mang and the empress dowager (his maternal aunt) that is pregnant with classical language and allusions to the legend of *li*:

大皇大后曰：「往者陰陽不調，風雨不時，降農自安，不堇作【勞】，是以數被菑害，惻然傷之。惟 □ 帝明王，靡不躬天之曆（曆）數，信執厥中，欽順陰陽，敬授民時，□ 勸耕種，以豐年 □，蓋重百姓之命也。故建羲和，立四子，... 時以成歲，致憙... 其宜 □ 歲分行所部各郡。」

The Empress Dowager said: "In the past, yin & yang were not in accord, and wind & rain were not in time; indolent farmers were self-satisfied, and did not diligently rise to their labors—this is why they endured numerous disasters and suffered grievously therefrom. It is the sagacious emperor and enlightened king who never fails to embody the *li* numbers of Heaven, faithfully upholding the balance between them, respectfully obeying yin & yang, reverently granting the people the seasons, and ...ingly exhorting plowing and seeding to ensure a bounteous

---

116. See Zhongguo wenwu yanjiusuo 中國文物研究所 and Gansu sheng wenwu kaogu yanjiusuo 甘肅省文物考古研究所, eds., *Dunhuang Xuanquan yueling zhaotiao* 敦煌懸泉月令詔條 (Beijing: Zhonghua shuju, 2001). For an overview and translation of the "Shizhe Hezhong suo ducha zhaoshu sishi yueling wushi tiao," see Sanft, "Edict of Monthly Ordinances for the Four Seasons in Fifty Articles from 5 C.E."

117. Ibid., 141.

harvest...—all of this is out of weighty consideration of the hundred surnames'
fate. Thus have We created [the offices of] Xi-He 羲和 and established [the offices
of] the four masters (for the four corners of the earth) [to fix the four] seasons
to complete the year (*sui* 歲) and deliver happiness unto... may that every
year they split up and travel through each commandery under their respective
jurisdictions" (lines 1–4).[118]

... (prohibitions) ...

安漢公、【宰衡、】大傅、大司馬【莽】昧死言：「臣聞帝...【之治天下也。】...
曆（曆）象日月... 以百工允釐...【大】皇大后聖德高明，... 遭古... 序元氣以成
歲事，將趨... 今義和中叔之官初置，監御史、州牧、閭士...【大】農、農部丞
脩 □□ 復重。臣謹... 義和四子所部京師、郡國、州縣，至... 歲竟行所不到者，
文對... 牒 □。臣昧死請。」

His Excellency Pacifier of the Han, Steward-regulator of the State, Grand Tutor,
and Commander-in-Chief [Wang Mang] dares risk his life to say: "Your servant
has heard that emperor...'s rule over the subcelestial realm... 'to *li* 曆 and *xiang*
象 the sun and moon'... thereby 'regulate' the 'hundred artisans'...[119] Empress
Dowager is sagacious and wise... encounter ancient... order the primal *qi* so as
to complete the affairs of the year, about to hasten... Today, the offices of second
and third Xi-He brothers have been appointed for the very first time, and the

---

118. On the office of Xi-He, see p. 65 n. 78.

119. Wang Mang is alluding here to the following passage from the "Yao dian" 堯典 chapter of the *Book of
Documents*:

乃命羲和，欽若昊天，歷象日月星辰，敬授人時。... 帝曰：「咨！汝羲暨和。朞三百有六旬有六
日，以閏月定四時，成歲。允釐百工，庶績咸熙。」

And then he charged Xi and He, in reverent accordance with august Heaven, to *li* and *xiang*
the sun, moon, and stars and respectfully grant the people the seasons. ... The Thearch said:
"Oh, you Xi and He, the year has three hundred, sixty, and six days, by means of an intercalary
month do you fix the four seasons and complete the agricultural year. If you earnestly control all
the functionaries, the achievements will all be resplendent (*Shangshu zhushu*, 1.8b; tr. modified
from Karlgren, "The Book of Documents," 3).

266

Inspecting Secretaries, Shepherds of the Provinces, Gentlemen of the Villages....
Divisional Assistant to the Grand Minister of Agriculture Xiu 脩... reiterate.
Your servant cautiously.... the capitals, commanderies, kingdoms, provinces, and
counties over which the four Xi-He children exercise jurisdiction to... those not
arrived by the end of the year to respond in writing... invoice... Your servant
risks death to entreat you."

皇大后【制曰】: 可。

The Empress Dowager decreed: "that is acceptable" (lines 83–91).[120]

Seven centuries later, when Wu Zetian ordered the revival of the proclamation of the new
moon ceremony, it was in the context of a thriving (albeit changed) Bright Hall-monthly
ordinance ceremonial complex.[121] So, of all the time-control rites mentioned in the classics,
why was it that *this* was the one that early imperial courts (eventually) latched onto? Lillian
Tseng argues that it was because the Bright Hall-monthly ordinance complex met the exigencies of the day better than any other. Han and Xin dynasts were consumed with the issue
of legitimacy: they were, to their knowledge, the first ruling houses in history to have risen
from anonymity and wrested the throne from ancient bloodlines, and this left them plagued
with insecurity. The Bright Hall-monthly ordinance complex addressed this insecurity on no
less than three levels. First, it allowed ambitious dynasts like Han Wudi and Wang Mang
to bolster their pedigrees—they followed in the footsteps of the Zhou kings, on the hallowed
ritual grounds of the Yellow Emperor, and in service to ancestors adopted from among the
Sage Kings of old. Second, it tapped into the five-virtues correlative philosophy upon which
theories of the transfer of Heaven's Mandate had recently come to rest; more importantly,
the correlative totality of this complex spoke elegantly to the broader cultural and intellec-

120. Cf. Sanft's translation in "Edict of Monthly Ordinances for the Four Seasons in Fifty Articles from 5
C.E.," 178–188.

121. On the innovations of Wu Zetian's Bright Hall, see Antonino Forte, *Mingtang and Buddhist Utopias
in the History of the Astronomical Clock: the Tower, Statue and Armillary Sphere Constructed by Empress
Wu*, Serie Orientale Roma, v. 59 (Roma ; Paris: Istituto italiano per il Medio ed Estremo Oriente; Ecole
française d'Extrême-Orient, 1988).

tual atmosphere of the Han cosmological synthesis, which, in the eyes of its contemporaries, would have surely placed it at the cutting edge of ritual science. Third, classical precedence provided the perfect cover for continuing extant imperial rites (e.g. sacrifices to the Five Thearchs), putting a Zhou cap on real-world practices inherited from the Qin.[122]

The appeal of the Bright Hall-monthly ordinance complex makes perfect sense in theory; in practice, however, it is hard to imagine that its inherent preposterousness was lost on the average man. To begin with, the court's ritual/symbolic control over time languished decades behind its administrative/logistical control thereof—the system worked, but no one could agree on how to justify it. Then, when charismatic leaders like Wudi and Wang Mang finally pushed through the construction of the appropriate facilities, they did so in a manner that conspicuously contravened the precedence from which they were working— Wudi built his Bright Hall at Mount Tai, and Wang Mang presided over royal rites as regent. Furthermore, taken as evidence of how the court went about "reverently granting the people the seasons" on the ground, the "Shizhe Hezhong suo ducha zhaoshu sishi yueling wushi tiao" is a fascinatingly bizarre document. Written on the mud wall of a lowly office surrounded by the sand-swept landscape of what today still seems like the ends of the earth, Wang Mang's aunt reaches out from it to speak directly to the common man. From her home amid the cool tree-lined boulevards of Chang'an and the luxuriant gardens of Weiyang Palace 未央宫, what she communicates to him is a patronizing lecture on hard work and proper farm life pulled from the pages of an idealized almanac written for the Yellow River Valley. If the peasants of Dunhuang could read, one can only imagine what they would have made of this document. The irony of their situation was, unfortunately, compounded by strict enforcement, mass arrests, and the resettlement of thousands of recalcitrant commoners to the godforsaken mountains of Xihai 西海 (modern Qinghai).[123]

---

122. Tseng makes the first two points in *Picturing Heaven in Early China*, 21–36.

123. Zhongguo wenwu yanjiusuo and Gansu sheng wenwu kaogu yanjiusuo, eds., *Dunhuang Xuanquan yueling zhaotiao*, 45.

3.4 Conclusion: Time and Imperial/Individual Space

Calendars may not make for good reading, but they do have a story to tell. In this chapter, I have drawn together this scattered, fragmentary, and lifeless corpus of materials and put it in dialogue with transmitted sources in an attempt to tease that story out. Of all the sources examined in this dissertation, theirs is perhaps the most valuable, since it is a story of everyday life told from the perspective of the early imperial everyman. This perspective is valuable not simply because we are so often denied it in the court-centered tradition of elite literature that mostly survives from the period, but because it allows us to reflect upon an entire network of knowledge and textual production running from the emperor down to the lowly clerk, and from the imperial center out to the ends of the earth. This, legend tells us, is what *li* is all about—community and the quotidian. At the same time, the perspective of extant calendars also shows us that so much of what *li* had become by the time of the Han had nothing whatsoever to do with this vision, leaving us to ponder the disparity between the its public and private faces, and what *li* was even about anymore.

Calendars took on a life of their own. To the copyist and average consumer, a calendar was but a functional expansion of a *shuo-run* table, which was, itself, but a list of 12 or 13 *ganzhi*. Both followed the simplest of rules: *shuo-run ganzhi* came in pairs, each binome 6 *zhi* apart, and each pair one *ganzhi* back; and daily calendars came in registers, each sequence moving one *ganzhi* left as the user moved one line down. Simple as they were, however, they were more than just numerical tables: they were extensions of imperial power, frameworks for lives lived, and gateways to the spiritual/correlative hypostases governing man's fate. Individual (if not personal) productions, calendars got away from their masters and fast, changing, adapting, and devolving as the proliferated the world of their own momentum every year. Like with the hatching of sea turtles, clever men might collude to intervene or redirect this annual dispersion of fragile forms, but there is only so much that one can do.

If there is one thing that I hope to have impressed upon the reader in this chapter it is that there is no such thing as "the calendar." We often speak of it as if "the calendar" were *regalia*—a staff wielded by the king—or an emanation—a specter enveloping the land—but *calendars* is all there ever were. In an age before print, no two calendars were the same; there were standards, for sure, but calendars took myriad forms and titles, each a localized production of imperial knowledge and a hybrid of public and private space. Unlike ham-handed edicts we might find on public display at government offices, the imperial voice was curiously absent from functional *li*. In fact, the first intrusion of that voice that we see comes only in the *Jiayin nian liri* 甲寅年曆日 (P. 2765) of A.D. 834, the first lines of which read:

夫爲曆者，	The practice of *li*
自古常規：	has been governed by convention since antiquity:
諸州班下行用，	the prefectures disseminate it down and carry it out
尅定四時，	so that they might fix the four seasons;
並用八節，	they go by all the eight nodes
若論種蒔，	so as to select [times] for seeding and transplanting;
約 □ 行用，	be frugal... implementation
修造亦然。	and much the same with repairs and construction.
恐凡神祇，	Fearing the spirits of Heaven & Earth,
一一審自詳察，	one-by-one, they meticulously check
看五姓行下。	to see that the five surnames carry it out below.
沙州水總一流，	At Shazhou, the waters converge into a single flow,
不同 □ 川，	different... rivers;
惟湏各各相勸，	gently rolling, each and every one urging on the others,
早農即得善熟。	early farming gets you good ripening.
不怕霜冷，	Fearing neither frost nor cold,
免有失所，	spared of losing house and home,
即得豐熟，	a bounteous harvest is obtained,
百姓安寧。	and the hundred surnames know security and calm.

By contrast, a thousand years earlier we find that more than half of the calendars extant from the Qin persist in using the term *zheng* 正 (for month I) despite the then decades-old taboo on Shihuang's given name—a startling omission given the semi-official nature of these documents.[124] The state may have exercised some control over their calculation, dissemination, and standardization, but calendars were in the end a shared space and community effort. If anything, it was the absence of ideological meddling that afforded their usefulness as canvasses upon which to record the past and ciphers through which to plan the future.

---

124. Those that use the term *zheng yue* 正月 "correct (first) month" are as as follows: (1) the Yuelu Academy *Sasi nian zhiri* Shihuang 34 (213 B.C.) daily calendar (fig. 3.1), (2) the untitled Zhoujiatai M30 Shihuang 34 (213 B.C.) daily calendar (fig. 3.2), (3) the Yuelu Academy *Sawu nian si zhiri* Shihuang 35 (212 B.C.) "private" daily calendar, and (4) the Zhoujiatai M30 *Saliu nian ri* Shihuang 36–37 (211–210 B.C.) calendar round (fig. 3.8). Those that replace *zheng yue* with *duan yue* 端月 are as follows: (1) the Yuelu Academy *X-qi nian zhiri* Shihuang 27 (220 B.C.) daily calendar and (2) the Zhoujiatai M30 Ershi 1 (209 B.C.) *shuo-run* table (fig. 3.11).

CHAPTER 4

TESTING, DEBATE, AND THE INSTITUTIONAL

FRAMEWORK FOR ASTRONOMY

In this chapter, we move from the diffuse world of manuscripts and popular astronomy to the circles of lettered experts at the epicenter of it all. As a case study in the logistics of progress, this chapter takes up in detail the *yi* 議 debate on calendro-astronomy held by the Cao-Wei 曹魏 court (220–265) circa 226—"the Yellow Inception debate." The subject matter is, in some sense, a continuation of Christopher Cullen's substantial work on such debates held in the Western 西漢 (206 B.C. – A.D. 9) and Eastern Han 東漢 (25–220).[1] Preserved in the *Jin shu* 晉書 "Lü li zhi" 律曆志 (Harmonics and *Li* Treatise), a compilation of the early Tang 唐 (618–907), what the transcript of this debate may lack in proximity to events (vis-à-vis Cullen's sources, that is) it makes up for in the richness and peculiarity of its details. First, where well-documented Han debates tend to pit experts against cranks, the Yellow Inception debate features intellectual peers with similar commitments hashing out details of methodology, accuracy, and precedence. Second, the surrounding events provide an interesting contrast to the bureaucratic dysfunction that many scholars point to in the history of astronomy in China—here, for once, it is the capable staff of the state astronomical office who are at the forefront of innovation and policy debate. Third, we have here a detailed account of a *failed* reform, which offers us some balance against the successes that tend to preoccupy other histories of the field. Lastly, and most importantly, the *Jin shu* provides

---

1. In particular, see Cullen's "Motivations for Scientific Change in Ancient China: Emperor Wu and the Grand Inception Astronomical Reforms of 104 B.C.," *Journal for the History of Astronomy* 24, no. 3 (1991): 185–203; "Actors, Networks, and 'Disturbing Spectacles' in Institutional Science: 2nd Century Chinese Debates on Astronomy," *Antiqvorvm Philosophia* 1 (2007): 237–267; "Huo Rong's Observation Programme of AD 102 and the *Han Li* Solar Table," *Journal for the History of Astronomy* 38, no. 1 (2007): 75–98.

us with the earliest extant example of the sort of test results that we know to have been at the center of *li* 曆 policy decisions. Parts of the text read like an oral back-and-forth, but the fact that lists of data are inserted between statements (one of which comes unintroduced and goes unexplained) is evidence that it has undergone at least some degree of editing. We cannot be certain about what may have been omitted or how closely the speeches reflect what was actually said, but technical features of their contents and parallel descriptions in third and fifth century sources do at least confirm its historicity.[2]

In Section 4.1, I introduce the origins, authorship, and hermeneutical issues surrounding our source. Then, in conjunction with other sources, I use the chronicle within which the debate is embedded to lay out the larger historical context of the debate, explain the technical issues at its center, and ruminate upon the historical outlook of the treatise itself. This leads us to a translation and discussion of the Yellow Inception debate in Section 4.2, wherein I attempt to elucidate the meaning of participants' jargon-laden opinions and plot their rhetorical moves. Section 4.3 is devoted to the two epistemic strategies at the heart of the debate: numbers and precedence. In the first half, I analyze the aforementioned test results, reconstructing, to the best of my ability, the technical features of the *li* systems from which they were derived and the process of competitive testing to which they were subjected. In the second half, I then examine the nature and function of astronomical legend as it is recounted in both the debate and the "Harmonics and *Li* Treatise" genre itself. The object of this case study is something of a departure from previous chapters—transmitted court literature looking *back* on the period through which we have been working our way forward— as such, it offers valuable perspective on the questions at the center of this study thus far: the incongruities between products and normative accounts of practice, and ancient actors'

---

2. First, matching, though abbreviated, descriptions of this debate occur in Wang Yin's 王隱 (fl. 249–260) now lost *Wei shu* 魏書, as cited in Pei Songzhi's 裴松之 (372–451) commentary to the *Sanguo zhi* 三國志 (*Sanguo zhi* [Zhonghua shuju ed.], 3.108) and Shen Yue's 沈約 (441–513) *Song shu* 宋書 (*Song shu* [Zhonghua shuju ed.], 12.231–232). Second, the five eclipse observations listed in the debate match observable phenomena and do not appear to be retrodicted. Third, the hour system used in the eclipse observations is peculiar to the third century. On the last two points, see Section 4.3.1.

ideas about empiricism and progress in the astral sciences.

4.1   Introduction to the *Jin shu* Materials

4.1.1   Provenance and hermeneutics

The *Jin shu* was compiled at the order of Tang Taizong 唐太宗 (r. 627–649) between the spring of 646 and the autumn of 648 by more than a dozen scholars under the direction of Linghu Defen 令狐德棻 (582–666) and Fang Xuanling 房玄齡 (579–648). The project directors delegated the "Harmonics and *Li* Treatise" to then Assistant to the Grand Clerk (and future Prefect Grand Clerk) Li Chunfeng 李淳風 (602–670), whom Fang Xuanling's biography describes as "deeply enlightened in planetary astronomy and adept at composition" 深明星曆，善於著述.[3] Though the Tang compilers were at a significant remove from Jin-dynasty events, the historiographic outpour of the intervening centuries left them with a lot to work from: eighteen of thirty-four chronicles and histories, half of which were written by contemporaries. Of these, their primary source and contender was Zang Rongxu's 臧 榮緒 (415–488) *Jin shu* in 110 *juan* 卷, a Southern Qi 南齊 (479–502) synthesis of state histories written in the Western and Eastern Jin. We cannot establish a chain of custody for information pertaining to calendrics, but we do know that Zang Rongxu's work included a standard array of "treatises" (*zhi* 志), as did several of its forerunners.[4]

---

3. *Jiu Tang shu* 舊唐書 (Zhonghua shuju ed.), 66.2463. In all, three treatises compiled by Li Chunfeng— "Harmonics and *Li*," "*Tianwen*" (Tianwen zhi 天文志), and "Five Agents" (Wuxing zhi 五行志)—found their way into *Jin shu* project. For Li's role, see also ibid., 79.2718.

4. On the composition and forerunners of the seventh century *Jin shu*, see Ran Zhaode 冉昭德, "Guanyu Jin shi de zhuanshu yu Tang xiu *Jin shu* zhuanren wenti" 關於晉史的撰述與唐修『晉書』撰人問題, in Jin shu, *"Ba shu," "Er shi" yanjiu* 『晉書』、「八書」、「二史」研究, ed. Zhou Wenjiu 周文玖, 20 shiji Ershisi shi yanjiu congshu 6 (1957; rpt. Beijing: Zhongguo da baikequanshu chubanshe, 2009), 14–27; Li Peidong 李培棟, "*Jin shu* yanjiu" 『晉書』研究, in Jin shu, *"Ba shu," "Er shi" yanjiu*, ed. Zhou Wenjiu 周文玖, 20 shiji Ershisi shi yanjiu congshu 6 (1982; rpt. Beijing: Zhongguo da baikequanshu chubanshe, 2009), 44–76. According to the *Nan Qi shu* 南齊書, Zang Rongxu "combined the Eastern and Western Jin into one book with annals, records, treatises, and biographies in 110 *juan*" 括東西晉為一書，紀、錄、志、傳百一十卷 (*Nan Qi shu* 南齊書 [Zhonghua shuju ed.], 54.936). Later encyclopedias cite the "records" (*ji* 記) of Wang Yin's 王隱 (fl. 317) *Jin shu* in 93 *juan* and the "discourses" (*shuo* 說) of He Fasheng's 何法盛 (fl. 5th cent.) *Jin zhongxing shu* 晉中興書 in 78 *juan* that are analogous in content to "treatises" with which we are familiar; see *Jiu jia jiu Jin shu jiben* 九家舊晉書輯本 (Qi Lu shushe ed.), 14–35, 223–234, 399–410. According to the

The seventh century *Jin shu* "Harmonics and *Li* Treatise," like other histories up to that time, inherits its organizational structure from Ban Gu's 班固 *Han Shu* 漢書 (111): harmonics and calendrics, despite their supposed relation, are segregated into different *juan* and distinct discourses; the calendro-astronomy *juan* are essentially annals of events for the dynasty in question, the skeleton of which is fleshed out with citations of memorials, edicts, and debates derived, presumably, from court records; the continuity of the chronicle is interrupted by the insertion of the prefaces, numbers and/or complete manuals of definitive astronomical systems; and the chronicle is prefaced with a brief history of the field from the time of the Sages through to the end of the preceding dynasty. The *Jin shu* calendro-astronomy *juan* cover the period from 172 to 384 but focus on the third century, amid the transition from the Eastern Han to the Cao-Wei to the Western Jin 西晉 (265–317).

The dynastic histories are not unbiased sources; they are "written for officials by officials" and thus require careful reading.[5] They meticulously document the astral sciences as they intersect with the state and the statesmen of the capitol region but omit or caricature the process and substance of practice. Furthermore, they are also ideological creations—mirrors, the metaphor goes, to reflect upon the exigencies of the present—that subsume people and events into totalizing moral visions and teleologies of legitimacy. From Taizong's commission and personal participation in the *Jin shu* project, for example, it is particularly evident that the history of the Jin was written as an answer to the sobering questions of his reign: how a fledgling dynasty was to survive succession struggles and the fracture of officialdom, and how history was to judge their efforts.[6] Meeting the moral and political imperatives of

---

Jin shu, the Western Jin scholar Shu Xi 束晳 (d. 300) also "composed emperor annals and ten treatises for a *Jin shu*" 撰晉書帝紀、十志 (*Jin shu* 晉書 [Zhonghua shuju ed.], 51.1432, 1434). Given the precedent of the *Shiji* 史記 and *Han shu* 漢書, we might also expect the large and purportedly complete histories of Shen Yue 沈約 (441-513)—*Jin shu* in 110 *juan*—and Xiao Ziyun 蕭子雲 (487-549)—*Jin shu* in 102 *juan*—to have possessed treatises.

5. Herbert Franke, "Some Remarks on the Interpretation of Chinese Dynastic Histories," *Oriens* 3, no. 1 (1950): 8. For an overview of historiography in the Tang, see Denis Twitchett, *The Writing of Official History Under the T'ang* (Cambridge: Cambridge University Press, 2002).

6. On Taizong's motivations and participation in the *Jin shu* project, see Li Peidong, "*Jin shu* yanjiu," 46–56.

historiography involved, to different degrees, a selectivity and flexibility with records, and the *Jin shu* was no exception.[7]

That said, the "Harmonics and *Li* Treatise" requires a more precise set of caveats than those we broadly level at dynastic histories. These treatises are themselves never the focus of state history projects. They are tangential and dispensable to these projects—the sort of thing for which the historian usually turns to extant accounts or outside help.[8] They do not feature "judgments" (*ping* 評) or "praise" (*zan* 贊) of the sort we see in annals or biographies. They say nothing of the virtue of men or the legitimacy of ruling houses, nor a single word about the *meaning* of celestial phenomena. This is not to say that they are ideology-free but that they inhabit *a different ideological space.* Fitting with the traditional historiographic model of "praise and blame" (*bao bian* 褒貶), the imperative to judge is every bit as strong in this space, but it is expressed in terms reminiscent of Whig histories of science: to determine who was "accurate" and "inaccurate," to condemn charlatans, and to identify and praise the discoverers of correct contemporary knowledge. Judgment is "internalist"—internal to the field of calendrics—and recognizes the context of ideas only as it is perceived to be a hindrance to correct understanding. Joseph Agassi identifies modern instantiations of such history as performing a ritualistic function that, less its tone of derision, applies equally well to early imperial ones:

> The function of [these] histories is to stress that the field of study is important and that big marks must be given, at least as a token of gratitude, to some past scientists. The inductivist histories of science are, briefly, *scientific ancestor-*

---

7. For examples of historical revisionism evident in the *Jin shu*, see Michael C. Rogers, "The Myth of the Battle of the Fei River (AD 383)," *T'oung Pao* 54, no. 1/3, Second Series (1968): 50–72; Glen Dudbridge, *Lost Books of Medieval China* (London: British Library, 2000).

8. Eight of the "Twenty-five Histories" do not possess treatises on calendrics: *Sanguo zhi* 三國志, *Nan Qi shu, Liang shu* 梁書, *Chen shu* 陳書, *Bei Qi shu* 北齊書, *Zhou shu* 周書, *Nan shi* 南史, and *Bei shi* 北史. Those that *do* tend to have appropriated them from the extant writings of experts, e.g. the *Han shu* from Liu Xin 劉歆 (c. 50 B.C. – A.D. 23), the *Hou Han shu* 後漢書 from Cai Yong 蔡邕 and Liu Hong 劉洪 (below), and the *Song shu* 宋書 from He Chengtian 何承天 (c. 370-447).

worship in pseudo-scholarly guise.[9]

The *Hou Han shu* 後漢書 is a case in point. Sima Biao 司馬彪 (243–306) compiled a "Harmonics and *Li* Treatise" for his *Xu Han shu* 續漢書 (later incorporated into the *Hou Han shu*) from one written by renowned experts Cai Yong 蔡邕 (133–192) and Liu Hong 劉洪 (c. 135–210) near the end of the Eastern Han.[10] The treatise presents us with an account of *li* policy that may be somewhat normative: problems with the official system are identified and reported; solutions are proposed; these are submitted for official testing at the Clerk's Office and tried; results are debated; the optimal solution is agreed upon and implemented; and responsible parties are rewarded or demerited accordingly. Furthermore, where wrong or outmoded knowledge—e.g. the weft text *li* that "scholars studied in the backwaters, laboring under the belief that it was correct" 學士修之於草澤，信向以為得正 —seeks conflict with right knowledge, the latter emerges victorious through a display of reasoning, demonstration, and a superior grasp of the matters at hand.[11] Christopher Cullen opines that:

> Given that Cai Yong and Liu Hong both appear as successful contenders in the debates they are recording, it is surely probable that their editorial selection of the views of others in the same collection will tell us something about their wider views of what constitutes good astronomy, and what constitutes a valid astronomical argument.[12]

If anything, the *Jin shu* propounds these self-same views, but its tone is somewhat less triumphant. Somebody *wrote* this treatise; every word and every ellipse was the conscious choice of editorial hands—hands operating at multiple layers of the text, no less—as they

---

9. *Science and Its History* (Dordrecht: Springer, 2008), 129 (emphasis added).

10. On the composition of the *Hou Han shu* treatises, see B. J. Mansvelt Beck, *The Treatises of Later Han: Their Author, Sources, Contents, and Place in Chinese Historiography* (Leiden: E.J. Brill, 1990), esp. 56–63.

11. *Hou Han shu* 後漢書 (Zhonghua shuju ed.), *zhi* 2, 3033.

12. "Actors, Networks, and 'Disturbing Spectacles' in Institutional Science," 264. Note that Cullen's statement is in response to Mansvelt Beck, *The Treatises of Later Han*, 61–62.

worked to shape the way that later generations would remember these episodes. We might suspect, for example, that the treatise unnecessarily foregrounds the breakdown of institutions as concomitants to the breakdown of imperial order with which Taizong and his historians were fixated. Of course, so long as we read with a critical mind and a careful eye to parallel accounts, there is no need to throw the baby out with the bath water.

4.1.2 A Chronicle of Wei-Jin calendro-astronomy

The *Jin shu* calendro-astronomy *juan* begin with a history of the field from the time of the Sages to the second century A.D. his is a typical sequence of great men and achievements reiterating that introduced in Chapter 1. What is less typical is the space that the treatise devotes to the Jin dynasty's predecessors and rivals. The compiler's stated goal is to contribute to the historiographic continuity of a field rather than parcel people and events between regimes:

> 及光和中，乃命劉洪、蔡邕共修律曆，其後司馬彪因之，以繼班史。今采魏文
> 黃初已後言曆數行事者，以續司馬彪云。

> During the Glorious Harmony reign (178–184) it was ordered that Liu Hong and Cai Yong work together on [a treatise on] harmonics and *li*, upon which Sima Biao later relied to pick up where [the treatise in] Ban [Gu]'s history left off. [Likewise,] my current decision to start from the Wei's Yellow Inception reign (220–226) in discussing past matters of *li* numbers is to follow up on Sima Biao's account.[13]

Due to its origin in Liu Hong's writings, Sima's "Harmonics and *Li* Treatise" does not linger on his contributions, nor does it continue past 179, when Liu was transferred from the capital. The *Jin shu* picks up where Sima leaves off, eulogizing Liu's accomplishments (see

---

13. *Jin shu*, 17.498.

Section 1.2.2), then turning to developments at the Cao-Wei court. The annals—the skeletal framework of the treatise—then chronicles the following sequence of events:

魏文帝黃初中，太史令高堂隆復詳議曆數，更有改革。太史丞韓翊以為乾象減斗分太過，後當先天，造黃初曆，以四千八百八十三為紀法，千二百五為斗分。

During the Yellow Inception reign of Wei Wendi, Prefect Grand Clerk Gaotang Long made another detailed *yi*-debate on *li* numbers that there may be reform. Assistant to the Grand Clerk Han Yi thought that the Supernal Emblem system (#10) went too far in reducing the DIPPER PARTS and that in time it would slip ahead of Heaven, so he constructed (*zao* 造) the Yellow Inception system (#11), using an ERA FACTOR of 4883 and a DIPPER PARTS of 1205.

其後尚書令陳羣奏，以為：「曆數難明，前代通儒多共紛爭。黃初之元以四分曆久遠疏闊，大魏受命，宜改曆明時，韓翊首建，猶恐不審，故以乾象互相參校。其所校日月行度，弦望朔晦，歷三年，更相是非，無時而決。案三公議皆綜盡典理，殊塗同歸，欲使效之璿璣，各盡其法，一年之間，得失足定。」奏可。

Later, Prefect of the Masters of Writing Chen Qun 陳羣 submitted a petition of the opinion that:

> *Li* numbers are difficult to comprehend and have been a point of much contention among the expert scholars of the previous age. At the inauguration of the Yellow Inception reign, the Quarter Remainder system (#9) had long been far-off, loose, and wide (inaccurate). The Great Wei has received the Mandate, and it is time to change the astronomical system to illuminate the seasons. Han Yi was the first to establish one; however, still afraid that it was untried, he collated it with the Supernal Emblem system (#10). What he collated was the motion degrees of the sun and moon as well as the quarter, full, new, and dark

moon (i.e. lunar phases).[14] Over the course of three years, there was dispute back and forth, which was at no point resolved. According to the *yi*-debate of the Three Excellencies, they gathered everything together and put it to a hearing, arriving by different paths to the same conclusion: that they wished to have [the two] proven at the *xuanji* (armillary sphere)—each to the utmost of their methods—such that in one year's time there should be sufficient grounds to determine their respective success/failure.[15]

---

14. In the vocabulary of calendrics treatises, "motion degrees" (*xingdu* 行度) refers to a moving object's position as calculated between synodic phenomena and can thus refer more broadly to its "motions." "Quarter, full, new, and dark moon" (*xian-wang-shuo-hui* 弦望朔晦) is a synecdoche for "lunar phases." Roughly speaking, syzygy—when the moon is in conjunction with the sun and totally dark—is followed in 7-8 days by first or "ascending quarter" (*shang xian* 上弦), which is followed in 7-8 days by full moon, which is followed in 7-8 days by third or "descending quarter" (*xia xian* 下弦). "New moon" (*shuo* 朔) refers both to syzygy and the first day of the month, which coincide. "Dark moon" (*hui* 晦) is a more specifically calendrical term, referring to the last day of the month—the day in which the moon was to go totally dark preceding the appearance of the new crescent moon of the next month. Chen Qun seems to describe Han Yi as having compared lunisolar data predicted by both systems—e.g. the longitude and instant of full and quarter moons—to observational data. His use of the word "collate" (*jiao* 校) draws attention to the final *textual* phase of this testing—the comparison of inscriptions—rather than the processes by which these inscriptions were produced—calculation, observation, tabulation, etc.—leaving the latter to the reader's imagination.

15. *Xuanji* 璿璣 is a term with archaic and mysterious connotations. The term first appears in the "Yao dian" 堯典 chapter of the *Book of Documents*—a fifth- or fourth-century B.C. text that purports to originate from high antiquity. The "Yao dian" tells us that, upon his ascension to the throne, the sage king Shun 舜 "attended to the *xuanji* and jade transverse so as to order the seven matters of government" 在璿璣玉衡以齊七政 (*Shangshu zhushu* 尚書注疏 [Siku quanshu 四庫全書 ed.], 2.6a). In his second-century B.C. commentary, Fu Sheng 伏生 glosses *xuanji* as "rotational subtlety" (*xuan wei* 還微), referring to the pole star, based on the homophony (and possibly etymological relationship) between *xuan* 璿 (*zwjen*; some type of precious stone or stone implement?) and *xuan* 還/旋 (*zjon*; "rotate") as well as that between *ji* 璣 (*kjəj*; some type of precious stone or stone implement?) and *ji* 幾 (*krjij*; "incipience," and by extension *wei* "subtlety") (*Taiping yulan* 太平禦覽 [Siku quanshu ed.], 29.4b–5a). In the second century A.D., Ma Rong 馬融 (79–166) and Zheng Xuan 鄭玄 (127–200) expanded on the theme of rotation and identified the *xuanji* as a *huntianyi* 渾天儀 (armillary sphere) (*Shiji* 史記 [Zhonghua shuju ed.], 1.24 [commentary]; 27.1292 [commentary]). The idea of positing the ancient Sage Kings with the invention of an astronomical instrument that Han-era texts suggest went into use no earlier than the first century B.C. is anachronistic and was recognized as such by many later scholars. Even so, the identification stuck, if either for the sake of conviction or literary allusion. Therefore, the call here to have "[the two] proven at the *xuanji*" refers to testing involving observational instruments. On *xuanji* and the "jade transverse," see Donald Harper, "The Han Cosmic Board: a Response to Christopher Cullen," *Early China* 6 (1980–81): 50–52; Christopher Cullen and Anne S. L. Farrer, "On the Term *Hsuan Chi* and the Three-lobed Jade Discs," *Bulletin of the School of Oriental and African Studies* 46, no. 1 (1983): 53–76. All phonetic reconstructions are according to William Baxter's Old Chinese in *A Handbook of Old Chinese Phonology* (Berlin: Mouton de Gruyter, 1992).

The petition was approved.[16]

A debate concerning Han Yi's 韓翊 Yellow Inception system (#11)—"the Yellow Inception debate" (Section 4.2)—was then convened sometime between the spring of 223 and the summer of 226. However, "before testing and deliberation had been settled, the emperor died and was laid to rest" 校議未定，會帝崩而寢.[17]

The annals continue:

至明帝景初元年，尚書郎楊偉造景初曆，表上。帝遂改正朔，施行偉曆，以建丑之月為正，改其年三月為孟夏，其孟、仲、季月雖與夏正不同，至於郊祀蒐狩，班宣時令，皆以建寅為正。三年正月帝崩，復用夏正.

In the inaugural year of the Luminous Inception reign (237) of Mingdi 明帝 (r. 226–239), Gentleman of the Masters of Writing Yang Wei 楊偉 constructed (*zao*) the Luminous Inception system (#13) and submitted it to the throne. The emperor thereupon changed the first month of the civil year and implemented [Yang] Wei's astronomical system. He took the month established at *chou*.$_{B02}$ (the month after that containing the winter solstice) as the first month, changing month III of that year to the first month of summer (month IV). Though the first, middle, and last months of the seasons were different from those according to the Xia first month (calendar), when it came to the suburban sacrifices, the spring and winter hunts, and the proclamation of seasonal ordinances, all of these were done according to a first month established at *yin*.$_{B03}$ (the Xia calendar). In year 3 (239) the emperor died, and the state reverted to the Xia first month.

其劉氏在蜀，仍漢四分曆。吳中書令闞澤受劉洪乾象法於東萊徐岳，又加解注。

---

16. *Jin shu*, 17.498–499. An abbreviated version of these events is found also in *Song shu*, 11.231.

17. *Jin shu*, 17.503. Wei Shou 魏收 (506–572) tells us that "in the Glorious Harmony reign (178–184) there was a change to the Supernal Emblem [system] (#10), and in the time of Wei Wen[di] they used the one set down by Han Yi" 光和中易以乾象，魏文時用韓翊所定 (*Wei shu* 魏書 [Zhonghua shuju ed.], 107A.2659). His obvious confusion on the first point (see Section 1.2.2), however, casts doubt on the otherwise uncorroborated claim that Han Yi's work won official recognition.

中常侍王蕃以洪術精妙，用推渾天之理，以制儀象及論，故孫氏用乾象曆，至
吳亡。

The House of Liu 劉 were in [the state of] Shu 蜀 (221–263), where they kept the
Han Quarter-remainder system (#9). Prefect of the Palace Writers for the state
of Wu, Kan Ze 闞澤, received Liu Hong's Supernal Emblem method from Xu Yue
徐岳 of Donglai 東萊 and added exegesis and commentary to it. Regular Palace
Attendant Wang Fan 王蕃 considered [Liu] Hong's technique marvelous, and he
used it to extrapolate the principles of Spherical Heaven [world-model cosmology]
to formulate an instrument and discourse. Thus it was that the House of Sun 孫
used the Supernal Emblem system (#10) until the demise of the Wu 吳 [state]
(222–280).

武帝踐阼，泰始元年，因魏之景初曆，改名泰始曆。楊偉推五星尤疏闊，故元
帝渡江左以後，更以乾象五星法代偉曆。

When [Jin] Wudi 武帝 (r. 265–290) ascended the throne in the inaugural year of
the Grand Beginning reign (265), he inherited the Luminous Inception system
(#13) of the Wei but changed its name to the Grand Beginning system (#13).
Yang Wei's calculations for the Five Stars (planets) were particularly loose and
wide (inaccurate), so these were swapped out for the Supernal Emblem system's
(#10) [planetary] method after Yuandi 元帝 (r. 317–322) crossed to the left bank
of the Yangtze (in 317).[18]

4.1.3 Issues

In the words of the treatise, there are two issues at play here: there is the *zheng* 正 (first
month of the civil calendar), and there are the *li shu* 曆數 (numbers of the *li* [astronomical
system]). Both lay equal claim to the rubric *li,* but the distinction could not be clearer: in

---

18. *Jin shu,* 17.503.

modern terms, one is a matter of the calendar, and the other, astronomy. Throughout this dissertation I have reiterated the importance of acknowledging the semantic breadth and contextual polysemy of categories like *li* as well as the unique contours that they occasion upon actors' sociocultural landscapes. Equally essential, however, is that we are able to extricate ourselves from certain of their ambiguities when the need arises. To this end, I have chosen to frame our analysis of *li shu* and *zheng* around "astronomy" and "the calendar," respectively.[19]

Astronomy

The issue of *li shu* concerns the predictive accuracy of mathematical constructs vis-à-vis observations of the phenomena that they are intended to model. To this end, the compiler frames the first calendro-astronomy *juan* around Liu Hong and the precedent for accuracy that he set for the field. Liu Hong is the central theme of the Yellow Inception debate as well, and the annals begin and end with his praise. Then, after the concession to Liu's planetary astronomy, the authorial voice of the treatise emerges to declare that "Hong's methods became an exemplar for the calculations of the subsequent age" 洪術為後代推步之師表, before reproducing the Supernal Emblem system (#10) it in its entirety.[20] The element of Liu Hong's legend that most concerns us here is his reduction of the DIPPER PARTS (*Dou fen* 斗分), the meaning of which may not be self-evident.

In the terminology of the Supernal Emblem system (#10), the DIPPER PARTS is the dividend of the fractional part of the circumference of Heaven as expressed in *du* 度. Liu Hong derives the circumference of Heaven from the ratio of CIRCUITS OF HEAVEN (*zhou tian*

---

19. In the same vein, Wolfram Eberhard distinguishes within the history of Han *li* reform two "changes" of "differing character": "the date of the New Year" and "the basic astronomical data"; see Eberhard, "The Political Function of Astronomy and Astronomers in Han China," in *Chinese Thought and Institutions*, ed. John Fairbank, Comparative Studies of Cultures and Civilizations (Chicago: University of Chicago Press, 1957), 64–66.

20. *Jin shu*, 17.503

周天) 215130 to the ERA FACTOR (*ji fa* 紀法) 589:

$$215130/589 = 365\frac{145^{\circ\circ}}{589} \approx 365.2462^{\circ\circ}$$

Of this, 145 is the DIPPER PARTS. The reason that this is called "DIPPER PARTS" is that this fraction—which has to go somewhere between the otherwise integral equatorial widths of the twenty-eight lodges—is appended to Southern Dipper.08 (Nan dou 南斗; Sagittarius), the lodge of the winter solstice.

Of course, the DIPPER PARTS has less to do with lodge-widths than the length of the solar year. Because the *du* is defined as the distance traveled by the mean sun in one day, the circumference of Heaven in *du* equals the length of the solar year in days (365.2462 days). Thus, the DIPPER PARTS is *also* the fractional part of a day at the end of one year. This "solar year" is a conflation of the tropical and sidereal years, which were as yet undifferentiated. Compared to modern mean values adjusted for an epoch of 225 (Table 4.1), ours is at once 5^m35^s longer than the tropical year and 14^m40^s shorter than the sidereal year. Over time, these errors would produce undesirable effects, but the problem was neither evident nor solvable in the third century.[21]

The real problem with the DIPPER PARTS—at least, the one with which Liu Hong and Han Yi grappled—is its relation to the length of the mean lunation. Until the fifth century, the year and month were locked together in the RULE (*zhang* 章) ratio of 235 months : 19 years for the sake of intercalation. As such, any adjustment to the DIPPER PARTS affects the length of the mean lunation, and vice versa. Unlike the sun, the moon is fast-moving and directly observable; this means that the effects of any such adjustment would first manifest in

---

21. Namely, the winter solstice would occur progressively earlier than predicted, and the sun would fall progressively behind its predicted position. The result is that a systematic error of several minutes would not be easily detectable given the indirect means of measuring the sun's progress available in this period. Even if it were detected, the fact that third century actors had not yet distinguished the tropical and sidereal years (i.e. had no concept of the precession of the equinoxes) meant that they were consigned to choose a value for the "solar year" that could manage for both. On precession, see He Miaofu 何妙福, "Suicha zai zhongguo de faxian jiqi fenxi" 歲差在中國的發現及其分析, *Keji shi wenji* 科技史文集 1 (1978): 22–30.

Table 4.1: Values for mean solar years and mean lunations Han to Cao-Wei

System	Sui-length		Error		Mean Lunation		Error
	ratio	decimal	trop.	sid.	ratio	decimal	
Triple Concordance	562120 : 1539	365.2502^د	+11^{m}20^s	−8^{m}56^s	2392 : 81	29.530864^d	+24.1^s
Quarter-remainder	1461 : 4	365.2500^d	+11^{m}06^s	−9^{m}10^s	27759 : 940	29.530851^d	+23^s
Supernal Emblem	215130 : 589	365.2462^d	+5^{m}35^s	−14^{m}40^s	43026 : 1457	29.530542^d	-3.7^s
Yellow Inception	[1783500] : 4883	365.2468^d	+6^{m}27^s	−13^{m}48^s	[356700 : 12079]	[29.530590^d]	+0.5^s
Luminous Inception	673150 : 1843	365.2469^d	+6^{m}36^s	−13^{m}39^s	134630 : 4559	29.530599^d	+1.2^s
MODERN MEAN VALUES							
Tropical year		365.2423^d					
Sidereal year		365.2564^d					
Mean lunation						29.530585^d	

lunar phenomena. In fact, evidence suggests that it was the exact values of solar parameters like the DIPPER PARTS that were derived from lunar ones rather than vice versa.[22]

By the late second century, the Han Quarter-remainder system (#9) was running "behind Heaven." First, Liu Hong addressed the Quarter-remainder's inherent lag by reducing the DIPPER PARTS. Worried that he had gone too far, Han Yi then increased it, lest things slip "ahead of Heaven." Despite his protestations against Han Yi, Yang Wei later made a similar increase. According to the *Jin shu*, these adjustments were based on the observation of primarily lunar phenomena—phases and eclipses—thus the problem appears to be the predicted mean moon falling "ahead" or "behind" the observed moon. On Table 4.1, we can how consecutive adjustments to the DIPPER PARTS affect values for the mean lunation in this sense (short values tending to get "ahead" and vice versa). Errors are on the order of 0.5^s to 24.1^s per lunation, but these can accumulate over time. Of course, mean values are only part of the story and, as we will see below, do not by themselves guarantee the perceived accuracy of an astronomical system.

The calendar

The *zheng* ("first month") is a matter of the beginning of the civil calendar and the naming of months. Mingdi's change of the first month to *chou*.$_{B02}$ or the "Yin first month" (*Yin zheng* 殷正) is the equivalent of calling December January, January February, and so on (see Table 1.3 on p. 52). This is a symbolic act that bears no relation to the workings of astronomical systems—one which left no mark on the Luminous Inception system (#13) itself, for example, as it is preserved in the *Jin shu*.[23] This decision was informed by the "three first months" (*san zheng* 三正) or "three concordances" (*san tong* 三統) scheme of dynastic succession first popularized by Dong Zhongshu 董仲舒 (179–104 B.C.). This scheme

---

22. Chen Meidong 陳美東, *Gu li xin tan* 古曆新探 (Shenyang: Liaoning jiaoyu chubanshe, 1995), 211–277.

23. As I note below, the Luminous Inception system (#13) seems to have been presented to the throne after Mingdi's change of the first month (note 47). It is thus curious that it has the user "count from the celestial first month (that containing the winter solstice) as month XI" 數從天正十一月起 and names the Enthronement of Spring.$_{Q01}$ as the nodal *qi* of month I—both features of the Xia calendar (*Jin shu*, 18.541).

posits a ternary cycle of dynasties, each of which is defined by qualities of rule, the order of its calendar, the color of its clothing, regalia, and sacrificial animals, and a host of other correlates.[24]

As discussed in Section 1.1.2, the difference between first months is expressed in terms of their "establishment" (*jian* 建) in one of twelve directions—enumerated in earthly branches—corresponding to the ideal direction of the handle of the Northern Dipper (Bei dou 北斗; Ursa Major) at dusk on the day of the medial-*qi* seasonal juncture contained therein. Thus the "Zhou first month" contains Winter Solstice.$_{Q22}$, when the Dipper points to *zi*.$_{B01}$ (north); the following month—the "Yin first month"—contains Greater Cold.$_{Q24}$, when the Dipper points to *chou*.$_{B02}$ (north-northeast); and the following month—the "Xia first month"—contains contains Rainwater.$_{Q02}$, when the Dipper points to *yin*.$_{B03}$ (east-northeast).[25] Furthermore, since the "first" (*meng* 孟), "middle" (*zhong* 仲), and "last" (*ji* 季) month of the seasons are counted from the beginning of the civil calendar, a change from a Xia to an Yin calendar, as ordered by Mingdi in 237, also has the effect of sliding the civil seasons one month forward.

It is important to note that, like most of Chinese correlative philosophy, differing versions of the three concordances scheme's correlative matrix coexisted in the Han and early medieval period. Furthermore, these coexisted in an ambiguous relationship with variations on a quinary scheme for dynastic succession based on the "five virtues" (*wu de* 五德) or "five agents" (*wu xing* 五行).[26]

---

24. On the "three concordance" theory in the history of astronomy in China, see Chen Meidong, *Zhongguo gudai tianwenxue sixiang* 中國古代天文學思想 (Beijing: Zhongguo kexue jishu chubanshe, 2007), 600–604.

25. See Chen Jiujin 陳久金, "Beidouxing doubing zhixiang kao" 北斗星斗柄指向考, *Ziran kexue shi yanjiu* 自然科學史研究 13, no. 3 (1994): 209–214.

26. Howard L. Goodman stresses these points in *Ts'ao P'i Transcendent: The Political Culture of Dynasty-founding in China at the End of the Han* (Seattle: Scripta Serica, 1998), 177–181. On the five agents and Chinese correlative philosophy, see A. C. Graham, *Yin-yang and the Nature of Correlative Thinking* (Singapore: The Institute of East Asian Philosophies, National University of Singapore, 1986). For a general treatment of the place of "five virtues" theories of dynastic succession and symbolism in the history of astronomy in China, see Chen Meidong, *Zhongguo gudai tianwenxue sixiang*, 604–611. Gopal Sukhu details the complexity of the discourse concerning the "three concordances" and "five virtues" theories in Han politics in "Yao, Shun, and Prefiguration: The Origins and Ideology of the Han Imperial Genealogy," *Early*

Table 4.2: "Three concordances" correspondences

no.	Dynasty				Domain	Color	First Month
	a	b	c	*thus*			branch Xia cal.
1	夏 Xia	堯 Yao	高辛 Gaoxin	漢 Han	Earth	black	*yin.*B03 I
2	殷 Yin	舜 Shun	堯 Yao	魏 Wei	Heaven	white	*chou.*B02 XII
3	周 Zhou	虞 Yu	舜 Shun		Man	red	*zi.*B01 XI

Table 4.3: Five agents (production sequence) correspondences

no.	Virtue	Color	Season	Dynasty
1	metal	white	autumn	
2	water	black	winter	
3	wood	green	spring	
4	fire	red	summer	Han
5	earth	yellow	middle	Wei

4.1.4   Historical context

The sparse annals of the *Jin shu* "Harmonics and *Li* Treatise" divest *li*-related events of any greater context. For this context, we must turn instead to sources such as Chen Shou's 陳壽 (233–297) *Wei zhi* 魏志, Pei Songzhi's 裴松之 (372–451) commentary to the *Wei zhi*, the "Li zhi" 禮志 (Treatise on Ritual) of Shen Yue's 沈約 (441–513) *Song shu* 宋書, and the biographies, where they exist, of the actors in question. Modern scholarship has reconstructed this context in considerable detail, particularly Howard Goodman's monograph-length study of the people, politics, and rhetoric of the Cao-Wei transition and Hasebe Eiichi's 長谷部英一 work on Six Dynasties ritual/astronomical reform.[27]

In the decades that Liu Hong spent contemplating Heaven in the late second century, the world below tore itself apart. His earliest appointment took place amid a succession of young emperors and powerful empresses; in the capital, contention and purges raged between the cliques of empresses, palace eunuchs, and officialdom, while the provinces saw revolts,

China 30 (2005–2006): 91–151.

27. Goodman, *Ts'ao P'i Transcendent*; Hasebe, "Gi Shin Nanbokuchō no rekiron" 魏晉南北朝の曆論, *Chūgoku tetsugaku kenkyū* 中國哲學研究 3 (1991): 1–43.

rival claimants to the throne, millenarian religious uprisings, and population movements that were staggering in both scale and succession. The government found itself increasingly unable to staff the offices of the capital or bring stability to (and revenue from) the regions beyond its walls, and so it turned to desperate measures: the sale of high office and noble titles, the hurried packing of lower offices with unlikely candidates, and the divestment of centralized power onto regional commanders and private armies. In 189 Liu was recalled to discuss *li* reform in what was surely an eleventh-hour measure to stop the hemorrhaging; in the time that it took to make the 1000 km journey to the capital, however, the 34-year-old emperor succumbed to illness and Dong Zhuo's 董卓 (d. 192) forces, interceding on behalf of the officials against the eunuchs, sacked the capital and burnt the palace to the ground. Turning back half-way to the relative safety of the provinces, one imagines that the felicity of returning home at all must have offset any disappointment that Liu felt. Whatever safety that the provinces afforded was short-lived, however, as the empire quickly devolved into a theater of rivaling warlords.

In the north there arose a military leader with the intelligence, connections, and resources necessary to begin turning the tide: Cao Cao 曹操 (155–220). Cao Cao was a major player in the campaign against Dong Zhuo that helped reclaim the capital and free the new boy emperor Xiandi 獻帝 (r. 189–220), who he moved to a new capital at Xu 許. As the new real power behind the throne, Cao Cao spent the next two decades in a prodigious drive to reconsolidate territory from rival warlords in the north. It was in the north, some three-quarters of the way through this campaign, that Liu Hong passed away, having known neither peace nor recognition in his last days. On 220 March 15, Cao Cao too died, passing his new and unprecedented title of King of Wei to his son Cao Pi 曹丕 (187–226).

Off and on for three centuries, intellectuals, politicians, diviners, and religious leaders had prophesied the end of Han rule as revealed in omens of Heaven and Earth, the auguries of *chen wei* 讖緯 prophecy literature inevitable cycles of cosmic powers, and the mantic arithmetic of *li shu* "calendar numbers." At the frighteningly real dissolution of Han authority, however, these claims reached a fevered pitch. On December 11 of that year, Xiandi abdicated to Cao Pi, that he rule the new Wei Empire as Wendi 文帝 (r. 220–226). The memorials and edicts from this period—as preserved in Pei Songzhi's commentary to the Wei zhi—frame the immanence and legitimacy of this succession around ethical philosophy, classical precedents for abdication, and, importantly, a growing lore of prophecies and signs. The Mandate of Heaven had transferred to the Wei, the embodiment of the ascendant virtue of earth (HAN : FIRE :: WEI : EARTH, and fire produces earth) and Shun (Table 4.2, seq. b), who had himself taken the throne through abdication.

Goodman's study reveals the five-week process culminating in Cao Pi's ascension to have been a complex project of consensus-building, mediated through classical precedence and correlative symbolism, between parties of scholars, diviners, and civil and military officials. Of these, three reappear as central actors in the Yellow Inception debate.

The first is Chen Qun, who Goodman identifies as one of a group of eight "legitimation experts" at the core of the transition. Chen hailed from an Yingchuan 潁川 family that was well-established at court and among intellectual circles. Conversant in seals and the classics, Chen was a learned polymath who actively memorialized the throne on issues of spending and ritual. Among his more noteworthy accomplishments are his revision of the Wei criminal code in 230 and his proposal of the famous *jiu pin* 九品 system of bureaucratic recruitment. Like Liu Hong, Chen had begun his career in the military. By the time of Cao Cao's death, however, he had been transferred to the post of Palace Attendant and, earlier that year, been ennobled by Cao Pi as the Neighborhood Marquis of Changwu 昌武. In the years covered by the annals of the *Jin shu*'s first calendro-astronomy juan, he would go on to serve Cao-Wei as Master of Writing, Prefect of the Masters of Writing, and then Minister of Works.[28]

The second is Xu Zhi 許芝, a lower-ranking Assistant to the Grand Clerk learned in the

---

28. For Chen Qun's biography, see *Sanguo zhi*, 22.633–638. See also Goodman, *Ts'ao P'i Transcendent*, 92–95.

classics, weft and prophecy texts, and all manners of the divinatory arts. Xu's memorial of November 21 is by far the most masterfully mysterious assertion of Wei legitimacy of any of those preserved in Pei Songzhi's commentary. It runs the full gamut from the *Book of Changes*, hemerology, prophecy texts, mantic wordplay, numerology, five agents correlations and "calendar numbers" to stars, comets, and field allocation astrology. Little is known about Xu beyond this except that he was promoted within the Clerk's Office to lead it as Prefect Grand Clerk during at least the Yellow Inception (220–226) and Grand Harmony (227–233) reigns.[29]

The third is Dong Ba 董巴, then Serving within the Palace, Erudit and apparent expert on court ritual, regalia, and omenology. Dong coauthored a memorial on November 22 with several members of the core group affirming the significance of Xu Zhi's memorial of the previous day. Likewise, we know little about Dong except that he authored an "Yu fu zhi" 輿服志 (Treatise on Carriages and Robes) and coauthored an "Wuxing zhi" 五行志 (Treatise on the Five Agents, i.e. prodigies and omens) for the Eastern Han, both of which were incorporated into Sima Biao's *Xu Han shu*, and thus the *Hou Han shu*.[30]

Upon his ascension, Wei Wendi declared the beginning of the Yellow Inception reign—an unequivocal claim that this new dynasty was to legitimately succeed the Han (: FIRE : RED) with the virtue earth (: YELLOW)—and set the Three Excellencies to begin deliberations on changing regalia such as the first month of the calendar, court robes, sacrificial animals, and appellations.[31] Then, at the advice of Palace Attendant Xin Pi 辛毗, he ordered that all regalia be changed to that appropriate the new dynasty's virtue and concordance—all, that is, except the first month. Whatever practical considerations may have been at play,

---

29. Ibid., 100–105. Xu Zhi appears in 220 as Assistant to the Grand Clerk then, beginning with the Yellow Inception debate (c. 223/226) below, and again in the Green Dragon reign (227–233), as Prefect Grand Clerk (*Sanguo zhi*, 2.62 [commentary]; *Song shu*, 34.1011; *Jin shu*, 12.338, 17.499). On the problem of multiple Prefect Grand Clerks, see note 44.

30. Goodman, *Ts'ao P'i Transcendent*, 108–109; Mansvelt Beck, *The Treatises of Later Han*, 147–149, 242–246.

31. *Xiandi zhuan* 獻帝傳 as quoted by Pei Songzhi in *Sanguo zhi*, 2.75 (commentary).

Wendi and Xin Pi justified this decision with classical precedents drawn from the *Analects* and the *Zuo Tradition*:[32]

行夏之時，乘殷之輅，服周之冕，樂則韶舞。

Follow the calendar of the Hsia, ride in the carriage of the Yin, and wear the ceremonial cap of the Chou, but, for music, adopt the *shao* and *wu* (*Analects* XV.11).[33]

夏數得天

The Xia numbers get Heaven (*Zuo zhuan* 左傳, Shao 17).

Prefect of the Masters of Writing Huan Jie 桓階 et al. petitioned the emperor to reconsider, given that the use of a Xia first month with Yin sacrificial animals would violate the correlative scheme of the three concordances. Unconvinced, Wendi went ahead with his reforms.[34] The divisiveness of the issue is understandable. As eager as scholar-types were to theorize about such things, a radical change to the civil calendar might, in practice, generate a significant amount of confusion. Furthermore, scholar-types were just as eager to forget that the only ruler to have actually presided over such a change was Wang Mang 王莽 (c. 45 B.C. – A.D. 23)—who adopted the same set of dynastic emblems, no less—and everyone knew how that turned out.[35]

It was after all of this that Gaotang Long 高堂隆 (d. c. 240) "made another detailed *yi*-debate on *li* numbers that there may be reform" and Han Yi produced his Yellow Inception system (#11) (see (p. 279). Nothing is known about Han Yi beyond his title: Assistant

---

32. For Wendi's edict, see *Song shu*, 14.328. For Xin Pi's opinion, see *Sanguo zhi*, 25.696.

33. Tr. modified from D. C. Lau, *Confucius: The Analects* (Hong Kong: The Chinese University Press, 2000), 151.

34. *Song shu*, 14.328.

35. It is true that states used different calendars in the period of disunion between the eighth to third centuries B.C., but the Qin and Han empires had only ever used the Xia first month. The only difference between them was that the Qin began the year on month X, which the Han changed to month I in 104 B.C. Thus, the only emperor to Cao Pi's day to have actually renamed the months *for the sake of five-agent/three-concordance symbolism* was Wang Mang. On this point, see Section 1.2.1.

to the Grand Clerk. We know that Gaotang Long was a man of Taishan 泰山, where Liu Hong was born, enfeoffed, and spent much of his career, though there is no evidence that the two knew each other. Gaotang started his career as a local official and began his rise in 213, when Cao Cao appointed him instructor of his son Cao Hui 曹徽 (d. 243), then mentor to Cao Rui 曹叡 (204–239), the future emperor Mingdi. Under Wendi, Gaotang served in the relatively low rank of Prefect Grand Clerk before being awarded under the rule of his former pupil with progressively higher positions within the bureaucracy and a marquisate. Mingdi described him as deeply learned and skilled at *tianwen* 天文 uranomancy, and he appears to have known enough about calendro-astronomy to have participated on that front, though his biographers conclude that "his intentions exceeded his expertise" 意過其通; the bibliographic treatise of the *Sui shu* 隋書 also attributes him with works on law, calendar divination, prodigies, and bovine physiognomy.[36] However, it it was his ritual scholarship of the Zheng Xuan 鄭玄 (127–200) school for which he was primarily known and for which he was chosen to compile the dynasty's *feng shan* 封禪 rites. He was so respected for his ritual scholarship, in fact, that in the late 230s Mingdi assigned thirty students to preserve his and two other eminent Ruists' teachings lest classical knowledge pass away with their generation.[37]

There are two potentially important issues of timing upon which the *Jin shu* "Harmonics and *Li* Treatise" is silent. The first is that the Yellow Inception system (#11) was created, considered, tested, and debated *after* the order to leave the first month as it was. Nor did Gaotang Long use astronomy reform as a platform to push calendar reform, his ardent interest in which he waited until Mingdi's reign to publicize. This is yet another example of how matters of astronomy and the calendar could be quite independent of one another within the rubric "calendro-astronomy."

---

36. *Sanguo zhi*, 25.708 (commentary), 25.719; *Sui shu* 隋書 (Zhonghua shuju ed.), 33.973, 34.1035, 34.1038–1039.

37. For Gaotang Long's biography, see *Sanguo zhi*, 25.708–719. For a chart of Gaotang's career path, see Table 1.6 on p. 80.

The second issue of timing involves concurrent developments in the south. In 220, Governor of Kuaiji, Sun Quan 孫權 (182–252), sent an envoy to Wendi's accession ceremony to recognize the dynastic transition, but relations quickly broke down. In 222, he declared himself King of Wu 吳 and inaugurated the Yellow Martial reign (222–229)—an equally unequivocal claim to the virtue earth and the legitimate succession of the Han, though Sun Quan only declared himself emperor in 229. Then, in February or March of 223, the state of Wu adopted Liu Hong's Supernal Emblem system (#10).[38] This timing may explain the Wei court's sudden interest in *astronomical* reform and why the Supernal Emblem system (#10), for all of its perceived merits, never presented itself as an option. The Yellow Inception debate took place sometime in the next few years, but Wendi's death on 226 June 29 brought matters to a halt.

Upon taking the throne in 226, Mingdi and issued an impassioned call to reconsider *calendar* reform:

黃初以來，諸儒共論正朔，或以改之為宜，或以不改為是，意取駁異，于今未決。朕在東宮時聞之，意常以為夫子作春秋，通三統，為後王法。正朔各從色，不同因襲。自五帝、三王以下，或父子相繼，同體異德；或納大麓，受終文祖；或尋干戈，從天行誅。雖遭遇異時，步驟不同，然未有不改正朔，用服色，表明文物，以章受命之符也。由此言之，何必以不改為是邪。

Since the [beginning of the] Yellow Inception, Ruists have discoursed upon the first month, some considering it apt to change it, and others considering it correct not to. Wishing to choose from dissenting opinions, the matter has gone unresolved to our day. In Our time at the Eastern Palace (as heir-apparent), We heard about it but had always been of the opinion that the Master (Confucius) had created (*zuo* 作) the *Spring and Autumn Annals* and circulated the three concordances as a model for later kings. [And this states that] the first month should each be according to [dynastic] color not that it it should be the

<hr>

38. *Sanguo zhi*, 47.1129.

same through inheritance. Since the time of the Five Thearchs and Three Kings, some were succession of father to son, who were of the same form but different virtues; some (referring to Shun) were "sent to the great plains at the foot of the mountains" and "received [the former ruler's] retirement in the temple of the Cultured Ancestor;" and some took up shields and dagger-axes to administer punishment at the bidding of Heaven. Though they met with different times and took different steps, there has never been a case of not changing the first month, using robe-color, or elucidating of cultured (ritual) objects to display the tallies of having received the Mandate. If we speak about it from this [perspective], why must not changing [the first month] be correct?[39]

At this, the Excellencies, Ministers, and their subordinates engaged in a "broad debate." There, Palace Attendant Gaotang Long issued an *yi*-opinion forcefully arguing for change based on precedents in the *Book of Changes*, the *Book of Documents*, the *Odes*, the *Record of Rites*, the *Spring and Autumn Annals*, and their respective weft texts. By the end of debate, however, opinions were still divided.[40]

The third-century *Wei lüe* 魏略 tells us that it was also in Mingdi's Grand Harmony reign (227–233) that the Grand Clerk presented the throne with an eponymous *li* to address inaccuracies in the Han Quarter-remainder system (#9). Mingdi ordered Gaotang Long, by reason of his deep learning and talent with *tianwen*, to work together with Master of Writing Yang Wei and Expectant Appointee to the Grand Clerk Luo Lu 駱祿 to perform comparative testing. The result was several years of quarreling and mutual incrimination. According to Yang Wei, the problem was that "Lu got the solar eclipses but put them before the dark moon had finished (the day prior to conjunction), while Long did not get the solar eclipses but put [conjunction correctly] at the finish of the dark moon" 祿得日蝕而月晦不盡，隆不得日蝕而月晦盡. In the end, they were ordered to "follow the Grand Clerk" 從太

---

39. *Song shu*, 14.328–329; cf. Hasebe, "Gi Shin Nanbokuchō no rekiron," 9. On Shun, Mingdi is quoting the "Shun dian" 舜典 chapter of the *Book of Documents*.

40. *Song shu*, 14.329–330.

Table 4.4: Opinions for and against changing the first month at the debate of 227

for	(Palace Attendant Gaotang Long 高堂隆) Grand Commandant Sima Yi 司馬懿 Supervisor of the Masters of Writing Wei Zhen 衞臻 Master of Writing Xue Ti 薛悌 Supervisor of the Palace Writers Liu Fang 劉放 Gentleman-in-attendance of the Palace Writers Diao Gan 刁幹 Erudit Qin Jing 秦靜 [Erudit] Zhao Yi 趙怡 Capital of the Central Capital Region by direct appointment Ji Qi 季岐
against	Palace Attendant Miao Xi 繆襲 Regular Cavalier Attendant Wang Su 王肅 Gentleman of the Masters of Writing Wei Heng 魏衡 Member of the Suite of the Heir-apparent Huang Shisi 黃史嗣

SOURCE: *Song shu*, 14.330.

史.[41]

The Grand Harmony system (#12) is a matter of some ambiguity in the historical record. The *Wei lüe* attributes it only to "the/a Grand Clerk," which scholars have understood to imply Gaotang Long.[42] However, he, Xu Zhi, Yang Wei, and Luo Lu are all identified as Prefect Grand Clerks in this period. To make matters worse, the third-century *Wei zhi* tells us that "Grand Harmony" was the former name of Yang Wei's Luminous Inception system (#13).[43] Given what we know about the latter, the equation of these systems seems forced; Chen Shou's implication that they were both Yang Wei's creations is, however, a distinct

---

41. The *Wei lüe*, now lost, was a private work of history written by Yu Huan 魚豢 in or after Wei Mingdi's reign (*Shi tong* 史通 [Siku quanshu ed.], 12.9b–10a). This passage is cited in *Sanguo zhi*, 25.708; cf. Hasebe, "Gi Shin Nanbokuchō no rekiron," 10–11. It is possible that the solar eclipse(s) to which Yang Wei refers are those that occurred on 232 January 9 (max. 23% at Luoyang) and 233 June 25 (max. 15%).

42. Zhu Wenxin 朱文鑫, *Lifa tongzhi* 曆法通志 (Shanghai: Shangwu yinshuguan, 1934), 2; Chen Zungui 陳遵嬀, *Zhongguo tianwenxue shi* 中國天文學史, 2d ed. (Shanghai: Shanghai renmin chubanshe, 2006), 1006, Table 50; Chen Meidong, *Gu li xin tan*, 125, Table 8–1; Chen Xiaozhong 陳曉中 and Zhang Shuli 張淑莉, *Zhongguo gudai tianwen jigou yu tianwen jiaoyu* 中國古代天文機構與天文教育, Zhongguo tianwenxueshi daxi (Beijing: Zhongguo kexue jishu chubanshe, 2008), 48; Nathan Sivin, *Granting the Seasons: The Chinese Astronomical Reform of 1280, with a Study of Its Many Dimensions and a Translation of Its Records* (New York: Springer, 2009), 43, Table 2.1.

43. *Sanguo zhi*, 3.108.

possibility.[44]

Deliberations on both astronomy and the calendar appear to have gone nowhere during the Grand Harmony (227–233) and Green Dragon (233–237) reigns. On Green Dragon 7-II-*renchen*.29 (237 April 7), Renchi 山荏 County reported the appearance of a yellow dragon—a monumental reaffirmation of Wei legitimacy and replay of events prophesied of their founding.[45] This and another memorial from the Clerk's Office spurred Mingdi back into action. He ordered another broad debate among the Three Excellencies, Specially Advanced, Nine Ministers, the General of the Gentlemen-of-the-Household, Grandees, Erudits, Gentleman Consultants, and officers of 1,000- and 600-*shi* 石 rank.[46] The next month, when they failed to arrive at a consensus, Mingdi issued an edict ordering the change to go into effect, declaring the beginning of the Luminous Inception reign (237–239), and leaving additional matters of regalia to further deliberation. However, because this change would effectively shift the seasons one month forward, he ordered that the state ritual calendar—which aimed to promote cosmic harmony through precisely timed seasonal rituals—continue to run on the Xia calendar. At this point or soon after, he also ordered the official adoption of Yang Wei's Luminous Inception system (#13), which had only just been submitted to the throne.[47]

---

44. On the Office of the Grand Clerk, see Section 1.3.1. Gaotang Long appears as Prefect Grand Clerk during the Yellow Inception reign (220–226) in the *Jin shu* "Harmonics and *Li* Treatise," as does Xu Zhi (*Jin shu*, 17.498–499). By around the Green Dragon reign (233–237), Gaotang Long was later "transferred to Palace Attendant while being kept on as Prefect Grand Clerk" 遷侍中，猶領太史令 (*Sanguo zhi*, 25.709). However, Xu Zhi was also Prefect Grand Clerk in the Green Dragon reign; on Xu Zhi, see note 29. According to the *Wei lüe*, furthermore, "Wei and Lu were Grand Clerks" 偉、祿是太史 during this same period (ibid., 25.708 [commentary]). The mess of Grand Clerks in the Green Dragon reign seems to suggest that multiple actors held this post concurrently, even though there is no precedence whatsoever for this in administrative literature like the *Hou Han shu* "Baiguan zhi" 百官志, *Han guan yi* 漢官儀, or *Tang liu dian* 唐六典. I would like to thank Yin Shoufu 殷守甫 for drawing my attention to another example of concurrent Grand Clerks from the *Zizhi tongjian* 資治通鑒: in 427, the Northern Wei "obtained the Xia Prefect Grand Clerks Zhang Yuan and Xu Bian and reinstated them as Prefect Grand Clerks" 得夏太史令張淵、徐辯，復以為太史令 (*Zizhi tongjian* [Siku quanshu ed.], 120.36a).

45. *Sanguo zhi*, 3.108. Earlier, the Wei zhi tells us that a yellow dragon appeared in 176 and was prophesied to return again in less than fifty years' time to mark the ascendancy of the virtue earth, which it did forty-five years later in 220 (ibid, 2.58).

46. Wang Yin's *Wei shu*, as cited in *Sanguo zhi*, 3.108 (commentary).

47. The fullest account of these events is that of the *Song shu* "Li zhi," which records a series of edicts and memorials between the emperor and his advisers on the matter (*Song shu*, 14.330–332; cf. Hasebe, "Gi Shin Nanbokuchō no rekiron," 11–12). Wang Yin's *Wei shu* also quotes an edict to the same effect, but its

Mingdi died on New Year's Day, Luminous Inception 3-I-1 *dinghai*.24 (239 January 22). The *Jin shu* "Harmonics and *Li* Treatise" tells us that "the state reverted to the Xia first month" but does not explain why. Whatever the contentions at court or the effects, real or perceived, of running separate civil and ritual calendars, by the winter of 239 it was clear that the timing of Mingdi's death had created an impossible dilemma for the new calendar: Cao Fang 曹芳 (r. 239–254) could not possibly hold the upcoming New Year's audience with his ministers, which would feature feasting and music, on the one-year anniversary of his father's death. A number of solutions were proposed, such as moving the ceremony back one or five days, but the emperor decided to go with Master of Writing Lu Yu's 盧毓 suggestion to return to the Xia first month, resurrecting Wendi's prior justification for the choice. His edict reads:

省奏事，五內斷絕，奈何奈何！烈祖明皇帝以正日棄天下，每與皇太后念此日至，心有剝裂。不可以此日朝羣辟，受慶賀也。月二日會，又非故也。聽當還夏正月。雖違先帝通三統之義，斯亦子孫哀慘永懷。又夏正朔得天數者，其以建寅之月為歲首。

Upon looking into the matter of your memorials, [We feel as if] Our five organs are severed. What to do, oh what to do? Our meritorious ancestor Emperor Mingdi abandoned the world on New Year's Day, and every time We think about the approach of this day with the Empress Dowager [We feel as if] our heart is being peeled and ripped open. We cannot hold court for the mass of lords on this day and receive their congratulations. Meeting on the second is, furthermore, unprecedented. We have heard that it is right to return to the Xia first month. Though We violate the former emperor's understanding of the three concordances, this is [an expression of] His descendants' grievous misery and eternal

language is different from that of the *Song shu* (*Sanguo zhi*, 3.108 [commentary]). The *Wei zhi* and *Jin shu* suggest that the adoption of Yang Wei's Luminous Inception system (#13) was ordered together with these changes (ibid., 3.108; *Jin shu*, 17.503). However, in the preface to his system, Yang Wei says that, "now that the era has been changed to Luminous Inception, it is apt that this be called the Luminous Inception system (#13)" 今改元為景初，宜曰景初曆, which suggests that it submitted only afterward (ibid., 18.536).

remembrance. Furthermore, since the Xia first month "attains the numbers of Heaven," may that the month established at *yin*.B03 be made the beginning of the year.[48]

In 265, Sima Yan 司馬炎 (r. 265–290 as Wudi) officially deposed the last Cao-Wei emperor to establish the Jin Dynasty (265–420). The history of calendrics in the Jin is beyond the scope of this chapter, but one point merits mention. The Jin court claimed to legitimately succeed Cao-Wei in the sequence of three concordances and five virtues, making the obligatory changes to regalia that that entailed—e.g. renaming Yang Wei's astronomical system after their opening reign—*but it left the calendar as it was.* Calendar (*zheng*) reform, in contrast to astronomy (*li shu*) reform, was a once in a millennium venture that never really stuck. In fact, besides Wang Mang and Cao Rui, the only other ruler to have changed the first month was Empress Wu Zetian 武則天 (r. 690–705).[49]

4.1.5 Conclusion: features of ancient historiographies of astronomy

If there is one thing that we may glean from these events it is the distinction between the objects of reform. It is a distinction that nebulous and context-sensitive actors' categories like *li* and *li shu* can sometimes obscure. It is a distinction, however, inherent in the very questions being asked: "what are we to name things as a demonstration of the rightness of our rule?" and "which are the best numbers and mathematical models to predict the next eclipse or appearance of Jupiter?" The two types of reform can coincide—as the momentum of the one seems to have led to the other in 237, for example—but mostly they do not. In a way, they occupy different worlds.

---

48. *Song shu*, 14.332–333; cf. Hasebe, "Gi Shin Nanbokuchō no rekiron," 13.

49. Jean-Claude Martzloff catalogs the few instances of "les années irrégulières" resulting from such reforms in *Le calendrier chinois: structure et calculs, 104 av. JC-1644: indétermination céleste et réforme permanente: la construction chinoise officielle du temps quotidien discret à partir d'un temps mathématique caché, linéaire et continu*, Sciences, techniques et civilisations du Moyen Âge à l'aube des Lumières 11 (Paris: Champion, 2009), 101–106.

By separating contents from context in Sections 4.1.2 and 4.1.4, I also hoped to highlight how ancient "historians of science" and conventions of genre create such divides. A "Harmonics and *Li* Treatise" tends to tell only one side of the story, as does a "Treatise on Ritual." If we were to read only one or the other we may come away with radically different ideas about "*li* reform." It is our job as twenty-first century historians to undo their work and supply context to contents—and rightly so, considering how factors such as cultural values, court politics, institutions, social ties, and international competition help explain participants' actions in this case. However, we should also stop to ask why the authors of this literature only tell the parts of the story that they do.

Any apparent lack of context in a work like the "Harmonics and *Li* Treatise" is, we must remember, *intentional*. Of course, the educated reader was probably expected to supply his own; but let us consider the possibility that the author *is* providing us with all the context that he deems relevant: that *li* is the work of sages and men clear of sight and clear of mind, who observe the mysterious patterns of the cosmos and capture them in numbers; that the model of the age was Liu Hong, whose lunar, solar, and planetary models were acclaimed by all but matched by none; that the one thing to make or break a man's name was the verified accuracy of his predictions; and that to convince the throne to adopt new and better knowledge was tough but necessary business.

When presented out of context, other matters that creep into the picture appear absurd. The *Jin shu*'s account of 237 is basically that "Mingdi [irrationally] changed the seasons around but kept state rituals running on the old calendar, then he died and things went back to normal." This episode is plainly a matter of "*li* reform" and merits mention in the treatise; however, it is introduced without a word about the history of resistance against it, the politics and personal ties compelling its implementation, or the undeniable ritual and emotional logic of its abolition. To "Treatise" authors like Cai Yong, Liu Hong, and Li Chunfeng, apparently, *these were the sort of thing that had no place in the history of calendro-astronomy*. Indeed, the only difference between their accounts is that where Cai and Liu's derisive comments give us direct insight into what they considered ludicrous (see Chapter 1), the *Jin shu*'s compiler(s) have left us to guess where their silence masks similar judgment.

Finally, this is not a question of historiography alone but of the way that calendro-astronomers understood the meaning of their own endeavor. Of course, not everyone wrote a "Harmonics and *Li* Treatise" like Cai, Liu, and Li. The centrality of legend to the rhetoric of practice, however, made every calendro-astronomer a historian of science in his own right. Across centuries and cultural sea changes, we see the reiteration of a remarkably stable worldview within this discourse. This is a worldview that—absent categories like magic, religion, and science—is not unlike Agassi's "inductivism" (i.e. positivism/Whiggism). These are now bad words in the history and philosophy of science. Of course, our postmodern taboo on "pseudo-scholarly" practices of "scientific ancestor-worship"—a taboo with its own fascinating sociology—should not compel us to disallow our pre-modern colleagues their fetishes. Lest we implicate ourselves in our own Whig history, we must take seriously their rites of "scientific ancestor-worship" and actors' discernments of what is and is not relevant to the astral sciences.

4.2   The Yellow Inception Debate

The dynastic histories preserve a rich and continuous corpus of court debates on calendar and astronomy policy that is without rival in the pre-modern world. For decades, historians of Chinese astronomy have mined this corpus for information on astronomical systems but have rarely made the policy debate itself the focus of detailed textual or sociological analysis. In his work on the Han dynasty, Christopher Cullen has begun to utilize these materials to their full potential. Particularly noteworthy in this regard is his "Actors, Networks, and 'Disturbing Spectacles' in Institutional Science," in which he applies a Latourian analysis to the institution of the Eastern Han *yi*-debate, examining the goals, strategies, rhetoric, and etiquette of debate, the range of professions and expertise spanned by their participants, and the clashes between methods and worldviews.[50] What follows is my attempt to extend similar analysis to the *Jin shu* record of the Yellow Inception debate of circa 226.

The debate opens with Grand Clerk Xu Zhi, who, in one sentence, establishes the central issues of the ensuing exchange: the legacy of Liu Hong and the predictive accuracy of lunar models. Like Han Yi, he expresses concern about the sustainability of Liu's Supernal Emblem system (#10):

劉洪月行術用以來且四十餘年，以復覺失一辰有奇。

Liu Hong's method for lunar motion has been in use for more than 40 years now, and it has been repeatedly perceived to miss the mark by one double-hour and a fraction.[51]

With this begins an outpouring of support for the late Liu Hong. The first to his defense is Sun Qin 孫欽. Little is known about Sun other than that he participated in a number of debates on imperial ritual upon Cao Pi's accession in the official capacity of Libationer of the Erudits.[52] Here, Sun interjects with a history lesson to remind the audience of Liu Hong's accomplishments and credibility. He compensates for the triteness of his message by couching Liu's accomplishments in rhyme and the mysterious language of prophecy literature:

史遷造太初，其後劉歆以為疏，復為三統。章和中，改為四分，以儀天度，考合符應，時有差跌，日蝕覺過半日。至熹平中，劉洪改為乾象，推天七曜之符，與天地合其敘。

[Grand] Clerk [Sima] Qian 司馬遷 (145/135–86 B.C.) constructed (*zao*) the Grand Inception.[53] Afterward, Liu Xin 劉歆 (c. 50 B.C. – A.D. 23) considered it loose and thus made the Triple Concordance. In the Manifest Harmony reign (87–88),

---

50. See also Cullen, "Motivations for Scientific Change in Ancient China."

51. *Jin shu*, 17.499.

52. *Tongdian* 通典 [Zhonghua shuju ed.], 72.1970.

53. This is not actually true, see p. 352.

this was changed to the Quarter-remainder. Using the celestial *du* of instruments to test the match between foretoken and answer (i.e. prediction and observation), [we find that] this has slipped out of time and have become aware that it overshoots solar eclipses by half a day. By the Illustrious Tranquility period (172–178), Liu Hong had changed to the Supernal Emblem, and

> the foretokens for the Seven Luminaries of Heaven it predicts (侯 *buo[B])
>
> match the order that between Heaven and Earth exists (魚 *zi [B]).[54]

Next, Dong Ba responds, describing the way that sages supposedly went about the business of mathematical astronomy:

> 聖人迹太陽於晷景，效太陰於弦望，明五星於見伏，正是非於晦朔。弦望伏見者，曆數之綱紀，檢驗之明者也。

Sages tracked the Great Yang (sun) from gnomon shadows, verified the Great Yin (moon) via quarter and full moons, elucidated the Five Stars (planets) via appearances and concealments and settled right and wrong via the first and last day of the month. Quarter moons, full moons, concealments and appearances are the guiding order of *li* numbers and are brilliant for inspection and verification.[55]

Dong Ba's response to Sun Qin is somewhat indirect. In contrast to the "tokens," "luminaries," and grandiose language of prophecy literature, Dong favors dry technical description—although nothing any more complex than the formulaic language of the classics. He brings

---

54. *Jin shu*, 17.499. I would like to thank Jeff Tharsen for pointing me to W. South Coblin's work on Eastern Han phonology to confirm my hunch that the last two lines of Sun Qin's statement do indeed rhyme. For evidence of the interrime of *yu* 魚 and *hou* 侯 finals at this time, see Coblin, *A Handbook of Eastern Han Sound Glosses* (Hong Kong: Chinese University Press, 1983), 100–105. For their parts, Ting Panghsin 丁邦新 and Luo Changpei 羅常培 & Zhou Zumo 周祖謨 place both *fu* 符 and *xu* 敘 under the rime category *yu* 魚 in the Eastern Han and Wei-Jin period; see Ting, *Chinese Phonology of the Wei-Chin Period: Reconstruction of the Finals as Reflected in Poetry*, Special Publications (Institute of History and Philology, Academia Sinica) 65 (Taipei: Institute of History and Philology, Academia Sinica, 1975), 76; Luo and Zhou, *Han, Wei, Jin, Nanbeichao yunbu yanbian yanjiu* 漢魏晉南北朝韻部演變研究 (Beijing: Zhonghua shuju, 2007), 142–143. The phonetic reconstructions here are Axel Schuessler's Later Han Chinese, see his *ABC Etymological Dictionary of Old Chinese* (Honolulu: University of Hawai'i Press, 2007).

55. *Jin shu*, 17.499.

astronomy back down to earth, so to speak, emphasizing the roots of astronomical knowledge in empirical method as opposed to revelation or spontaneous insight. The attribution of a method to the Sages is, of course, no less than the most ardent expression of how something should be. Like Sun Qin, he makes an argument from authority, but it is one to a very different effect: where Sun urges us to trust the man, Dong urges us to trust the method.

From here, Liu Hong's disciple Xu Yue (see p. 282) redirects Dong Ba's affirmation of empirical ideals to support Sun Qin's argument from authority: it is precisely because Liu Hong toiled for decades on the empirical method of the Sages that his astronomical system is unimpeachable.

劉洪以曆後天，潛精內思二十餘載，參校漢家太初、三統、四分曆術。

Liu Hong absorbed himself in inner contemplation for more than twenty years about why the calendar was behind Heaven and checked the *li* methods of the Han experts: the Grand Inception (#7), Triple Concordance (#8), and Quarter-remainder [systems] (#9).

課弦望於兩儀郭間，而月行九歲一終，謂之九道；九章，百七十一歲，九道小終；九九八十一章，五百六十七分而九終，進退牛前四度五分。學者務追合四分，但減一道六十三分，分不下通，是以疏闊，皆由斗分多故也。課弦望當以昏明度月所在，則知加時先後之意，不宜用兩儀郭間。

If you test the quarter and full moons from the two-instrument perimeter interval (?), you would find that lunar motion is complete in nine years.[56] This was called

---

56. The meaning of *liang yi guo jian* 兩儀郭間 is obscure. *Guo* is interchangeable with *kuo* 廓, both of which can denote "rim" or "outline," as in the outline of moon or the raised perimeter of a round copper coin. I have found one instance where the term is used in an identical context to mean something like "trace around the perimeter of the instrument," i.e. measure in angle. That instance is the *Hou Han shu*'s description of the "Grand Clerk Yellow Road bronze instrument" (commissioned in A.D. 92):

史官以郭日月行，參弦望，雖密近而不為注日。儀，黃道與度轉運，難以候，是以少循其事。

The Clerk's office uses it to *guo* solar and lunar motion and inspect quarter and full moons, and though it is TIGHT and CLOSE it is not used for noting the sun. As for the apparatus (*yi*), the Yellow Road and *du* rotate, it is difficult to use for observation, which is why it the matter (the order to use it) is rarely heeded (*Hou Han shu, zhi* 2, 3030).

the "Nine Roads." Nine rules (19y)—171 years—is a LESSER TERMINATION of the Nine Roads. In nine nines—81 rules—there are 567 parts and nine [LESSER] TERMINATIONS. It advances and retreats around 4 *du* and 5 parts before Ox.$_{09}$.[57]

Scholars duteously strained to match this with the Quarter-remainder by simply subtracting the 63 parts of one road such that the parts would not carry forward.[58] This is why it was loose and wide; it was all due to the fact that the DIPPER PARTS was too large. To test quarter and full moons it is best to measure the degree of the moon at dusk and dawn, by which you will know if the hour is ahead or behind; it is inadvisable to use the two-instrument perimeter

---

If I am right, Xu Yue's *liang yi guo jian* could refer to determining the moment of lunar quadrature and opposition (when the moon is 90° and 180° from the sun, respectively) by measuring the angle between the two bodies between two apparatus on an observational instrument. Whatever *liang yi guo jian* means, Xu does not explain his disapproval of this practice.

57. The Nine Roads is a 9-year scheme for the inequality of lunar motion based on the 8.85-year cycle of precession for the moon's perigee. On the Nine Roads, see Section 1.2.2. Here, Xu is repeating almost word-for-word the description in Liu Xin's Triple Concordance system (#8):

九章歲為百七十一歲，而九道小終。九終千五百三十九歲而大終。三終而與元終。進退於牽牛之前四度五分。

Nine rules in years makes 171 years, in which the Nine Roads experience LESSER TERMINATION. Nine [LESSER] TERMINATIONS is 1539 years, in which they experience GREATER TERMINATION. In three [GREATER] TERMINATIONS (3 × 1539 = 4617) they terminate with the origin. They advance and retreat 4 *du* and 5 parts before Led Ox.9 (*Han shu* 漢書 [Zhonghua shuju ed.], 22.1007).

58. In the systems of the time, the length of the year and synodic month was bound into a ratio of 235m : 19y by the RULE intercalation scheme. As described above, the LESSER TERMINATION is the coincidence of the cycle of the "Nine Roads" with the RULE (9y × 19y = 171y). One LESSER TERMINATION, however, is not an integral number of days: in the Grand Inception/Triple Concordance system, which assigns the synodic month a length of $29\frac{43}{81}$ days, one lesser remainder amounts to $62457\frac{63}{81}$ days (= 171y × $\frac{235m}{19y}$ × $29\frac{43}{81}$ d/m). In one GREATER TERMINATION (nine LESSER TERMINATIONS, or 1539y; also the Triple Concordance system's (#8) CONCORDANCE FACTOR [*tongfa* 統法]), the remainder accumulates to the "567 parts" mentioned above and, thus, an integral number of days (9 × $62457\frac{63}{81}$d = 562120d), at which time Winter Solstice.$_{Q22}$, new moon, and beginning of the "Nine Roads" coincide at midnight. In the early Eastern Han, a growing lag was perceived between the Grand Inception/Triple Concordance system and observed lunar phenomena. In Xu Yue's third-century terms, this was a problem caused by the Triple Concordance system's (#8) large "DIPPER PARTS" (385/1539 ≈ 0.2502) and addressed by the Quarter-remainder system's (#9) smaller "DIPPER PARTS" (1/4 = 0.25). The *Hou Han shu* describes how advocates of the Triple Concordance system (#8) proposed to ameliorate this lag by dropping the 63-part (i.e. $\frac{63}{81}$-day) remainder at the end of the 171-year LESSER TERMINATION (one of which elapsed unmolested in A.D. 68), essentially restarting the solar and lunar cycles three quarters of a day early—a stop-gap that proved historically unsuccessful (*Hou Han shu, zhi* 2, 3033, 3035–3036; cf. Ōhashi Yukio 大橋由紀夫, "Kōkan Sibunreki no seiritsu katei" 後漢四分曆の成立過程, *Sūgakushi kenkyū* 數學史研究 93 [1982]: 12–14).

interval.

洪加太初元十二紀，減十斗下分，元起己丑，又為月行遲疾交會及黃道去極度、
五星術，理實粹密，信可長行。

Hong added 12 eras to the origin of the Grand Inception System (#7), reduced
10 from the fraction at the end of Dipper.$_{08}$, and started his origin from year
jichou.$_{26}$.[59] In addition, he worked on the speed and nodes of lunar motion as
well as Yellow Road north polar distance and a method for the Five Stars. He
worked out their truths in a way that was PURE and TIGHT, and I believe that
it can operate for a long time to come.

今韓翊所造，皆用洪法，小益斗下分，所錯無幾。翊所增減，致亦留思，然十
術新立，猶未就悉，至於日蝕，有不盡效。

Now, what Han Yi has constructed (*zao*) is completely based on Hong's method.
It slightly increases the fraction at the end of Dipper.8, but the difference does
not amount to much. As for Yi's emendations, though he was thoughtful in
rendering them, ten methods (?) are new and are as yet imperfect, and they are
sometimes not completely effective in regard to solar eclipses.

效曆之要，要在日蝕。熹平之際，時洪為郎，欲改四分，先上驗日蝕：日蝕在
晏，加時在辰，蝕從下上，三分侵二，事御之後如洪言，海內識真，莫不聞見，
劉歆以來，未有洪比。

The key to testing a *li* lies in solar eclipses. In the Illustrious Tranquility period
(172–178), Hong was, at the time, a Court Gentleman and wished to reform the
Quarter-remainder. Previously, he had sent up a solar eclipse prediction. The

---

59. According to the Supernal Emblem system (#10), "from high origin in year jichou.26 to Establishment
of Peace year 11, *bingxu*.$_{23}$, the ACCUMULATED YEAR is year 7378" 上元己丑以來，至建安十一年丙戌，歲積
七千三百七十八年 (*Jin shu*, 17.504). Establishment of Peace 11 (A.D. 206) is 309 years after Grand Inception
1 (104 B.C.), which places high origin 12 eras (589y) prior ($12 \times 589y + 309y = 7377y$, Establishment of Peace
11 being the 7378th year from high origin). Liu Hong employs a DIPPER PARTS of $\frac{145}{589} = 0.2462$. Xu Yue
appears to claim that he reduced the Dipper dividend of the Grand Inception/Triple Concordance system
by 10 ($\frac{385-10}{1539} = 0.2437$), the difference, in actuality, being a little over 6 parts.

eclipse was on a clear day at the double-hour *chen*.B05 (08:00–10:00), and the eclipse went from bottom to top, intruding two thirds (over the disk of the sun). After the matter had been inspected, it was found to have happened just as Hong said. Everyone within the oceans recognized the truth of it, and there was no one who did not hear of it. Since Liu Xin, there has been no match for Hong.[60]

At this point in the text is inserted a list of five carefully-timed eclipse observations between 221 and 223—three solar and two lunar—to which are compared predicted times of syzygy calculated by the Yellow Inception, Supernal Emblem, as well as a Supernal Emblem *xiaoxi* 消息 ("waxing and waning") method. The details of this list are presented in Tables 4.5 & 4.6 and provided detailed analysis in Section 4.3.1.

Some five centuries later, Yixing 一行 (673–727) comments that among Liu Hong's innovations "it was, however, originally the *xiaoxi* that was the most astonishing, but the method was not passed down" 然本以消息為奇，而術不傳.[61] Indeed, there is no mention of *xiaoxi* in the Supernal Emblem system (#10) manual as it is preserved in the *Jin shu* or *Song shu*, and as we will see below, there was disagreement about its details within even living memory of its creator. As Chen Jiujin 陳九金 has argued and my analysis in Section 4.3.1 confirms, what is indeed astonishing about the *xiaoxi* is that it appears to be an adjustment for the solar equation of center, whose invention in China is otherwise attributed to Zhang Zixin 張子信 in the sixth century.

Suffice it to say for now that the list is clearly Xu Yue's production, the *xiaoxi* consistently outperforms the other methods, and the list concludes with the following score:

凡課日月蝕五事，乾象四（遠）【近】，黃初一近。

Out of a total of five tests of solar and lunar eclipses, the Supernal Emblem was

---

60. *Jin shu*, 17.499–500.

61. *Xin Tang shu* 新唐書 (Zhonghua shuju ed.), 17B.622. Note that Yixing is repeating Xu Yue's description below.

(farthest) [closest] four times, and the Yellow inception was closest once.[62]

Now let us return to Xu's speech. Amidst the wealth of technical details Xu makes the following points:

1. Before Liu's time (in the late first and early second century), there was a real DIPPER PARTS-related lunar lag for which scholars proposed a misguided stop-gap based upon an inferior observational technique.

2. Through hard work and genius, Liu created an innovative and peerless astronomical system.

3. Han Yi's improvements are a failure: his adjustment of the DIPPER PARTS—the project's raison d'être—is inconsequential, and his work is derivative, immature and ineffective at predicting solar eclipses.

4. Solar eclipse prediction is the key, and Liu once made an awesome and universally recognized prediction of every detail of an eclipse.

5. Furthermore, here is a list of recent eclipses whose time Liu's system predicts with a greater accuracy than Han's.

Employing details of expert knowledge, Xu Yue mystifies Liu Hong's status well beyond what Sun Qin is able to achieve with rhyme and prophecy. By elevating the conversational idiom and by introducing data analysis he establishes his own credibility as an expert, dramatically raising the bar for further participation. Xu's eclipse list is the perfect example of a Latourian "black box": it is the product of years of observation and calculation, the nitty-gritty of which is effaced; it is an inscription, in which a complex question like the overall quality of competing products is reduced to neat, commensurable quantities; it is complete and self-contained, its data pointing to one inexorable conclusion; and, most importantly, it is so

---

62. *Jin shu*, 17.500. The text here mistakenly reads "far" for "close" in the case of the Supernal Emblem system (#10), which is emended on the basis of each individual score as can be found on Tables 4.5 & 4.6 below.

complex and well-manufactured that it is impossible to deconstruct and contest without a considerable investment of time and resources, let alone on the spot in a debate.[63] Perhaps Xu is being biased or dishonest in defense of his own academic lineage, but what matters is that he is acting the part of the consummate expert: he comes to the debate prepared, and appeals to a common interest in predictive accuracy as verified through testing and tabulation. For now, let us allow the force of his data to wash over us unexplained as it would have his audience.

Of course, Xu Yue is every bit as adept with rhetoric as he is with numbers. To drive home Liu Hong's unparalleled virtuosity, he ends on an impressive anecdote reminiscent of that by which Hank Morgan reduced king, sorcerer, and peasantry to awe in *A Connecticut Yankee in King Arthur's Court*. And Liu's accurate prediction of the hour, magnitude, and angle of a solar eclipse would have been every bit as sensational since this was well beyond the technical capabilities of his age. Methods for predicting the latter two details appear only in the Luminous Inception system (#13) of 237 and are nowhere near this level of accuracy.[64] The fact that there were no eclipses matching his description in this period casts further doubt on Xu's story.[65] If this is the bar he is setting for Han Yi, he has set it impossibly high. From the eclipse list, however, it is clear that what is intended by "the key to testing a *li* lies in solar eclipses" (p. 306) is something much more predictably mundane: the accurate prediction of the time of maximum eclipse as an indicator of the instant of syzygy rather than how or whether an eclipse will occur.

---

63. See Bruno Latour, *Science in Action: How to Follow Scientists and Engineers Through Society* (Cambridge: Harvard University Press, 1987), 2–3.

64. On the methods and accuracy of Chinese solar eclipse prediction, see John M. Steele, *Observations and Predictions of Eclipse Times by Early Astronomers*, Archimedes: New Studies in the History and Philosophy of Science and Technology (Dordrecht: Kluwer Academic Publishers, 2000), 161–216.

65. Liu Hong served in the capital as a Gentleman in the Prolongation of Brightness period (158–167) and between 174/177 to 179. The only solar eclipse in Illustrious Tranquility-period (172–178) Luoyang that overlapped with his time as Gentleman was that of 178 November 27, which began at 08:38 local apparent time (LAT) and reached maximum eclipse at 09:42 LAT. While this falls within the pre-Tang double-hour *chen*.B05 (08:00-10:00, see p. 320), the lunar disk obscured only about a quarter of the area of the solar disk (vs. two thirds) and went from top to bottom (vs. "bottom to top"). Neither is there any solar eclipse through to the end of Liu's life that matches this description.

Some of the rest of what Xu has to say about his teacher seems to amount to obfuscation. Point (1) really has nothing to do with the rest of the debate; and when Xu goes off topic, he does so to trudge out the obscure and arcane.[66] *Liang yi guo jian* 兩儀郭間 is jargon that was probably just as obscure to the average third-century intellectual as it is to us today. It seems to invoke the *liang yi* of the "Xi ci zhuan" 繫辭傳 (Appended Statements Commentary) to the *Book of Changes*—a thoroughly untranslatable word implying a binary division of an inchoate cosmos into either Heaven and Earth or yin and yang in the mysterious cosmogony of numerological categories.[67] However, *yi* can also simply mean "apparatus," and it turns out that *guo* (lit. "city wall" or "perimeter") is a rare technical term for use with observational instruments. Whatever it is, Xu speaks authoritatively against it.[68]

Xu also quotes (without identifying it as such) Liu Xin on the Nine Roads—another numerology-laden topic that no one seems to agree upon or understand. The Nine Roads is a model for lunar inequality, which, more than any other factor, is what makes or breaks the systems Xu has submitted to comparison. He invokes the Nine Roads not to discuss lunar inequality, however, but to allude to a failed and forgotten early second-century stop-gap to solve a tangentially related problem in the Triple Concordance system (#8)—systematic lunar lag. The only relationship between these things is that the misguided proponents of the latter arbitrarily chose the beginning of a Nine Roads LESSER TERMINATION as the place to lop off a fractional excess. Xu offers all of this as a flattering foil to Liu Hong's elegant solution—reducing the DIPPER PARTS. One would think that for Xu to have so belabored this point the DIPPER PARTS must be vitally important to predictive accuracy,

---

66. It could be that what I identify as unnecessary erudition is indirect criticism, the nuance of which is simply lost on us. That said, it seems unlikely that the Triple Concordance stop-gap discussed in the next paragraph is deployed as a critical allegory of Han Yi's modification of Liu Hong's DIPPER PARTS given the technical dissimilarity between the two cases.

67. "Therefore, there is in the *Changes* the Great Culmen (the cosmos in its primordial undifferentiated state); this spawns the *liang yi*; the *liang yi* spawn the Four Images (*xiang*); the Four Images spawn the Eight Trigrams; the eight trigrams fix auspice and bane; and auspice and bane spawn the Great Patrimony" 是故，易有太極，是生兩儀，兩儀生四象，四象生八卦，八卦定吉凶，吉凶生大業 (*Zhouyi zhushu* 周易注疏 [Siku quanshu ed.], 11.43a).

68. See note 56

but it is not—at least not immediately, not by itself, and not compared to models for lunar inequality—and Xu himself says as much in the very next breath to disparage Han Yi. In the end, one gets the sense that this tortuous journey has been little more than a scenic route through Xu Yue's erudition.

Han Yi immediately contests Xu's results, and the two go back and forth debating the proper method of applying *xiaoxi*:

翊於課難徐岳：「乾象消息但可減，不可加。加之無可說，不可用。」

[Han] Yi raised difficulty with Xu Yue over the test results: "The Supernal Emblem's *xiaoxi* can only be subtracted, it cannot be added. If you add it, there is no justification, it cannot be used!"

岳云：「本術自有消息，受師法，以消息為奇，辭不能改，故列之正法消息。」

[Xu] Yue said, "The original method itself has *xiaoxi*; I have received the master method, and it is the *xiaoxi* that make it astonishing. I am afraid that there is nothing that I could do to improve upon this, thus I have arranged here the proper method of *xiaoxi*."

翊術自疏。

[Han] Yi backed down.[69]

Han Yi obviously worked from some version of Liu Hong's system as he developed and tested his own. Furthermore, as Assistant to the Grand Clerk it is safe to assume that he would have worked from the same version available to the Clerk's Office. With this in mind, it is noteworthy that the initial round of testing entrusted to that office proved inconclusive. The fact that the Clerk's Office staff did not unequivocally validate their supervisor's work suggests that they were able to perform their duties with a certain degree of professional objectivity. The same inconclusiveness also suggests that Han Yi gave said version of the

---

69. *Jin shu*, 17.500.

Supernal Emblem system (#10) a good run for its money. After several years of development and political consensus-building, however, Xu Yue suddenly produces a new secret version of that system that purports to excel both Han and his office hands down. The fact that this revelation is presented in the context of a public debate, furthermore, leaves Han Yi no choice but to concede on account of Xu's affiliation with the source and the apparently self-evident results of his calculations.

Inserted here into the text is more data analysis: a list of the observed dates of fourteen first and last planetary visibilities, to which are compared the dates predicted for the Supernal Emblem (#10) and Yellow Inception systems (#11). The details of this list can be found in Table 4.10, and is the subject of detailed analysis in Section 4.3.1. Suffice it to say for now that we are missing one item, there is no mention of either Mars or *xiaoxi*, and the list concludes with the following score:

凡四星見伏十五；│乾象七近二中，黃初五近一中。│

Out of a total of fifteen appearances and hidings of four stars (planets), COMMENTARY: |the Supernal Emblem was closest seven times and on twice, while the Yellow Inception was closest five times and on once.|[70]

Without any mention of the planets or the damning results of the Yellow Inception system's (#11) second ordeal, discussion of the moon continues. Gentleman of the Interior Li En 李恩, about whom we know nothing, takes a pragmatic stance and turns the conversation away from the question of Liu Hong's greatness to the more immediate problem at hand:

以太史天度與相覆校，二年七月、三年十一月望與天度日皆差異，月蝕加時乃後天六時半，非從三度之謂，定為後天過半日也。

If you reexamine it with the Grand Clerk's Heavenly Degrees (ephemeris), you will find that for the full moons of 2-VII (221 August 21) and 3-XI (223 January

---

70. Ibid., 17.501. Note that the Zhonghua shuju edition of the text applies a very different formatting to this list than to the last: it does not start each entry on a new line; and it records the predicted dates and scores in double-line commentary form.

5), they are not even on the same date as the Heavenly Degrees—the hour of lunar eclipse was six and a half double-hours (13 hours) behind heaven. This is not what we call "following the three measures" (?). Thus is it determined that [the state astronomical system] is behind heaven by more than half a day.[71]

Li En reminds us that, however many fractions of an hour Liu and Han are off the mark, the century-and-a-half-old Quarter-remainder system (#9) inherited by the state was behind by as much as one calendar day. By this point, *anything* would have been a welcome improvement. Li En too justifies his point with data analysis, though nothing nearly so sophisticated as that that Xu Yue has produced. To give the reader a commensurate sense of the its performance, I have included calculated predictions for the Quarter-remainder system (#9) in Table 4.5 & 4.6. The difference is striking; of course, one look at Table 4.6 will alert the reader to the fact that Li's assessment is somewhat exaggerated: the predicted syzygies fall $9^{\mathrm{h}}10^{\mathrm{m}}$ ($4\frac{7}{12}$ double-hours) and $7^{\mathrm{h}}45^{\mathrm{m}}$ ($3\frac{10}{12}$ double-hours) behind the observed time of eclipse maximum, and the only reason for the difference in date is the convention that, for lunar phenomena alone, the calendar day begins at dawn.[72]

Out of nowhere, Dong Ba then begins to pontificate on the selection of the first month of the civil calendar, giving us another history lesson on the Sages:

昔伏羲始造八卦，作三畫，以象二十四氣。黃帝因之，初作調曆。歷代十一，更年五千，凡有七曆。

In the past, Fuxi first created (*zao*) the eight trigrams and invented (*zuo*) the three lines of the trigrams in order to symbolize the 24 *qi*. The Yellow Emperor followed suit and first invented (*zuo*) the Adjusted system (#1). Over eleven

---

71. Ibid., 17.502. *Tiandu* 天度 ("heavenly degrees") is a term that occurs with a variety of referents in *li* texts. Judging from context, *tiandu* seems to refer here to some sort of official calculated results of the state astronomical system produced by the Clerk's Office—an "ephemeris"—though we have no idea how formal or public a production this may have been.

72. The figure of a $6\frac{1}{2}$-double-hour (13-hour) lag is probably derived from the consensus that the Quarter-remainder system (#9) was generally half a day behind heaven: see for example Sun Qin's comments on p. 303. On the counting of civil days for lunar phenomena, see p. 320.

dynasties, five thousand successive years, there was a total of seven astronomical systems.

顓頊以今之孟春正月為元，其時正月朔旦立春，五星會于天廟，營室也，冰凍始泮融解，蟄蟲始發，雞始三號，天曰作時，地曰作昌，人曰作樂，鳥獸萬物莫不應和，故顓頊聖人為曆宗也。

Zhuanxu made the current first month of spring, month I, his origin. At the time, on the first day of the first month, on the Enthronement of Spring, the Five Stars congregated at Heaven's Temple—that is, Hall.13—as the ice first began to melt, the hibernating bugs first came out, and the cocks first began to cry three times. In Heaven, it was the rise (*zuo*) of seasons, on Earth, it was the rise (*zuo*) of prosperity, and with man, it was the rise (*zuo*) of music/joy, and none of the birds, beasts or myriad creatures did not respond to one another. Thus Sage Zhuanxu is the progenitor of *li*.

湯作殷曆，弗復以正月朔旦立春為節也，更以十一月朔旦冬至為元首，下至周魯及漢，皆從其節，據正四時。夏為得天，以承堯舜，從顓頊故也。禮記大戴曰「虞夏之曆，建正於孟春」，此之謂也。

Tang invented (*zuo*) the Yin system (#4), which no longer took as its node the Enthronement of Spring.Q01 on the first day of the first month but changed to an origin head of winter solstice on the first day of the eleventh month. Down to Zhou, Lu, and Han, everyone followed this node, by which they based their corrections of the four seasons (regulated intercalation). The Xia won the support of Heaven by inheriting from Yao and Shun—that is, because they followed Zhuanxu. The *Da Dai li ji* says "The *li* of Yu-Xia established its first month on the first month of spring," that is what this refers to.[73]

The intention behind this statement is unclear. The first month of the civil calendar is not

---

73. *Jin shu*, 17.502–503; citation to *Da Dai li ji* 大戴禮記 (Siku quanshu ed.), 9.14a.

the topic of the debate at hand, nor had it been a topic of debate since Wendi's decree of 220; neither, for that matter, is Dong Ba doing anything more than simply restating its premises.

Finally, paying no heed to Dong's interjection, Yang Wei closes the debate on a sour tone, forcefully inveighing against the participants of the debate thus far:

六十日中疏密可知，不待十年。若不從法，是校方員棄規矩，考輕重背權衡，課長短廢尺寸，論是非違分理。若不先定校曆之本法，而懸聽棄法之末爭，則孟軻所謂「方寸之基，可使高於岑樓」者也。

In sixty days LOOSENESS and TIGHTNESS can be known, you need not wait ten years. If you do not follow the/a method, this is like abandoning the compass and T-square when checking squareness and roundness; it is like forsaking a scale when investigating light and heavy; it is like abandoning the ruler when testing long and short; and it is like turning away from distinctions and principles when analyzing right and wrong. If you do not first fix a "root" method for checking astronomical systems, but baselessly entertain "branch" disputes that abandon method, then this is what Meng Ke 孟軻 (Mencius) refers to as "you can make a piece of foundation an inch long reach a greater height than a tall building."[74]

今韓翊據劉洪術者，知貴其術，珍其法。而棄其論，背其術，廢其言，違其事，是非必使洪奇妙之式不傳來世。若知而違之，是挾故而背師也；若不知而據之，是為挾不知而罔知也。

Now, the fact that Han Yi bases himself on Liu Hong's techniques means that he knows to esteem his techniques and treasure his methods. And yet he dismisses

---

74. *Mencius* VIB.1; tr. D. C. Lau, *Mencius* (Harmondsworth: Penguin, 1970), 171. Note that the received *Mencius* actually reads "wood" 木 instead of "foundation" 基. In the *Mencius*, a man of Ren 任 asks Wuluzi 屋廬子 about the importance of *li* 禮 ("ritual appropriateness") compared to eating and sex. To make his point that determinations of priority must be made according to the situation rather than as blanket statements, Wuluzi adduces this and a second, more famous, metaphor to the effect that "in saying that gold is heavier than feathers, surely one is not referring to the amount of gold in a clasp and a whole cartload of feathers?" Ironically, Yang Wei is making the opposite point: that "you can make a piece of foundation an inch long reach a greater height than a tall building" is precisely the sort of epistemic chaos that ensues without a single standard methodology for comparison.

his discourse, forsakes his techniques, abandons his words, and strays from his endeavor. The inevitable result of this will be to make Hong's marvelous model cease to transmit to future ages. If he strays from it knowingly, then has intentionally forsaken his master; if he bases himself upon it unknowingly, then he has ignorantly arrived at a confused understanding.[75]

Yang first upbraids the process of competitive testing as needlessly long and methodologically incoherent. Though his rhetoric is much more about style and cadence than it is about details, he does makes a particularly trenchant point: without a standard methodology, one can craft data to substantiate any conclusion one likes, no matter how bizarre. In this case, each party has presented a version of the Supernal Emblem system (#10) that tips the scales in his own favor. And if there was one thing that contemporary experts could not abide by it was unproven claims of astounding predictive abilities based on secret knowledge.[76] It is no doubt to avoid these types of situations and to provide an informed and impartial perspective on competing claims that the Clerk's Office so often played the role of testing agency in Chinese history.

Yang's ire then turns more specifically towards Han Yi. Yang accuses him of having at the same time imitated and ruined Liu Hong's work out of either ignorance or deceit. Based as it was on the metaphor of family, it is often said that the early Chinese model of education

---

75. *Jin shu*, 17.503.

76. For example, see Jia Kui's 賈逵 (30–101) assessment of Zhang Long's 張隆 *Changes*-based approach to eclipse prediction on p. 93. See also Cullen's case study of Feng Guang 馮光 and Chen Huang's 陳晃 prophecy-based reform proposal of 175 in "Actors, Networks, and 'Disturbing Spectacles' in Institutional Science," 250–263. One of the more explicit statements to this effect is found in the *Hou Han shu*:

以是言之，則術不差不改，不驗不用。天道精微，度數難定，術法多端，曆紀非一，未驗無以知其是，未差無以知其失。失然後改之，是然後用之，此謂允執其中。

If a technique isn't off then don't fix it, and if it isn't verified then don't use it. The way of Heaven is perfect and subtle, and its degrees and numbers are hard to fix; techniques and models are multifarious, and there is no singular program for calendro-astronomy. If something has not been proven, then there is no way to know if it is correct, and if it has not [been shown to] err then there is no way to know if it is amiss. If it is amiss, then you fix it; if it is correct, then you use it. This is called "holding truly to the middle way" (*Hou Han shu*, *zhi* 2, 3041 citing *Analects* XX.1).

was marked by a collectivist spirit, the commitment to orthodoxy, and an unswerving loyalty to intellectual commitments of one's master and his master before him.[77] On the surface, Yang Wei's indignation and Xu Yue's piety seem to support this characterization, but let us not forget that it is Liu Hong's own rupture with tradition that is the object of this piety. If there is one thing that I hope to have to highlighted in this section it is the centrality of legend to actors' engagement with the field of their day, and the nature of that legend as a sequence of personality-driven innovations.

Yang Wei's ire is best understood in the context of his actions. Several years after his attack on Han Yi's character, culminating in his Luminous Inception system (#13) of 237, Yang himself set upon improving the Supernal Emblem system (#10), making many of the exact same changes (e.g. increasing the DIPPER PARTS) and many of the the exact same blunders (e.g. the omission of *xiaoxi* and concessions in planetary elements). The major difference between them, from what we can determine, is the relative success with which they were pitched at court; and how much of this success came down to simple timing is an open question. So how are we to read Yang's criticism? If we predicate our reading on the principle of charity—positing the speaker a rational and philosophically consistent position—we might suppose him to be accusing Han of hubris: it is not his *claim* to outdo his master that offends but his failure to live up to that claim. If, on the other hand, we assume only the principle of humanity—"that the imputed pattern of relations among beliefs, desires, and the world be as similar to our own as possible"—we might be justified in invoking terms like hypocrisy, rhetoric, or even cynicism to explain his tirade.[78] Unfortunately, the consistency/sincerity of Yang Wei's criticism is not something that we can ever really know.

---

77. For the case of "science," see G. E. R. Lloyd and Nathan Sivin, *The Way and the Word: Science and Medicine in Early China and Greece* (New Haven: Yale University Press, 2002), 42–61. On education in the early imperial astral sciences, see Section 1.3.1.

78. On the principles of charity and humanity in the theory of translation, see Richard Grandy, "Reference, Meaning, and Belief," *The Journal of Philosophy* 70, no. 14 (1973): 439–452.

4.3   Epistemic Strategies

In Section 1.3.3 I stated that innovation in calendro-astronomical policy is typically judged by four criteria: (1) trial-verified accuracy; (2) authoritative precedence—scriptural or professional—; (3) numerological/correlative elegance; and (4) symbolism of political legitimacy. Furthermore, when the matter at hand is *astronomy* reform, as it was in the Yellow Inception debate, criterion (1) takes the lead, and criterion (4) is directly informed by criteria (1)–(3).

While they may disagree over methodology, the participants in the Yellow Inception debate all affirm the primacy of (1) trial-verified accuracy—indeed, it is the one criterion mentioned in almost every single opinion. As we might expect, the participants tend to take for granted what this means. Our analysis of the conceptual vocabulary of accuracy in Section 1.3.3 is a helpful point of entry, but it is equally important to examine the cultural mechanisms for *knowing* LOOSENESS/TIGHTNESS. The *Jin shu* "Harmonics and *Li* Treatise" is the earliest source with sufficient data from which we might explore those mechanisms.[79] In the process of analyzing the numbers of the Yellow Inception debate in this section, therefore, I make a point of assessing the assessment. My goal is to display the messy, human quality of these mechanisms: how they were at once cultural constructs with obvious limitations and, no less, the realization of an empiricist ideal that acted to ensure (actors' idea of) progress.

Other than Dong Ba, who wants to rehash the matter of the first month (see p. 313), the debate participants are largely silent on the criteria of (3) numerological/correlative elegance and (4) symbolism of political legitimacy per se. Accuracy's only real competition is (2)

---

79. The next such example is Prefect Grand Clerk Qian Lezhi's 錢樂之 443 report to Song Wendi 文帝 (r. 424–453), which compares lunar eclipse and winter solstice predictions made by the Luminous Inception (#13) and Epochal Excellence systems (#22) (*Song shu*, 12.262–264). For a translation and study of the rather more sophisticated Season-Granting system "evaluation" of 1280 (as preserved in the *Yuan shi* 元史), see Sivin, *Granting the Seasons*, 254–388. Of course, Liu Xin and Du Yu's 杜預 archaeoastronomical work with the *Zuo Tradition* in the first and third centuries, respectively, do leave us with certain parallels. On this, see Christopher Cullen, "The Birthday of the Old Man of Jiang County and Other Puzzles: Work in Progress on Liu Xin's *Canon of the Ages*," *Asia Major* 14, no. 2 (2001): 27–60; Zhang Peiyu 張培瑜 et al., *Zhongguo gudai lifa* 中國古代曆法 (Beijing: Zhongguo kexue jishu chubanshe, 2008), 267–289.

precedence. Participants frame many of their opinions around relevant precedents, since episodes from the (perceived) history of calendro-astronomy provide a crucial framework for the interpretation of current data and events. The stock of shared examples that they draw upon range from sage kings to recently departed contemporaries, but, be it myth or human history, their vision of the past smacks of legend. After discussing the data in Section 4.3.1, I proceed in Section 4.3.2 to examine the the nature and historical outlook of this legend as well as its function vis-à-vis the community of practitioners.

4.3.1 The numbers

In "*Li* Treatise" history, "testing" (Section 1.3) is the first resort and final solution for actors attempting to gauge the merits of competing claims and arrive at informed decisions on state practice. While their preoccupation with testing is nothing less than incessant, they tend to tell us very little about the process itself. The Yellow Inception debate provides us with artifacts of that process: lists of the the very sort of "facts" (*shi* 實, *zhen* 真) to which actors resorted to settle disputes. Like the *Wuxing zhan* 五星占 tables discussed in Chapter 2, these lists are also artifacts of astronomical practice for which we might suspect *li* manual literature of providing a more-or-less normative account. As in previous chapters, I examine here products of calculation to reveal features of lost knowledge and incongruities between technical literature and practice. What is unique about the inscriptions examined in this chapter, however, is that they collate calculation with observation, which allows us to discuss actors' expectations, emphases, accuracy, and even integrity as concerns the practice of *li*.

Modern knowledge of celestial mechanics allows us in the history of astronomy to comment upon the phenomena that actors saw, and the effectiveness of their attempts to model them, with a certitude that is otherwise rare in the study of ancient history. Lest we implicate ourselves in Whig history, of course, it is important that we not judge ancient "science" on the basis of our own, nor assume the infallibility of the latter. A more meaningful assessment might instead be framed around the specific goals that actors set for themselves and the success with which they understood one another to have achieved them. Used carefully to this end, modern scientific knowledge—like the fruits of sociology, literary criticism, etc.—can help us develop a nuanced picture of ancient practices as serious and coherent entities in themselves.

The eclipse list

The first list is found at the end of Xu Yue's speech (see p. 307). The *Jin shu* offers no explanation for this list, but its context and the fact that it features a method—*xiaoxi*—with which only Xu is familiar suggest that it is his creation. The list is comprised of three solar and two lunar eclipses, the details of which I have divided between Tables 4.5 & 4.6.

In his study of medieval hour-systems, Qu Anjing 曲安京 points out that this list exhibits two noteworthy conventions. The first is that the dates of lunar phenomena are counted from dawn rather than midnight, as is common of early observational records and computational procedure. For example, the observation of the lunar eclipse that culminated at approximately two hours after midnight, local apparent time, on 223 January 5 (otherwise day $bingwu._{27}$), is recorded as Yellow Inception 3-XI-15 $yisi._{26}$ (223 January 4). For the sake of consistency, however, I count the dates in Tables 4.5 & 4.6 from midnight, as per the Julian calendar. The second noteworthy convention is that the list employs a short-lived 24-hour scheme first described in Yang Wei's Luminous Inception system (#13). This scheme, depicted in fig. 4.1, is different from the post-Tang 12-double-hour system with which we are familiar in that the hour $zi._{B01}$ begins at 00:00 rather than 23:00 (and so on for the other earthly branches), and that the eight outside heavenly stems and the four corner trigrams are staggered between the twelve branches. Each hour is further divided into six fractions of ten minutes each.[80]

---

80. Qu Anjing, "Zhongguo gudai lifa zhong de jishi zhidu" 中國古代曆法中的計時制度, *Hanxue yanjiu* 漢學研究 12, no. 2 (1994): 157–172.

Table 4.5: Xu Yue's solar eclipse list

1	2	3	4	5	6	7
Item	Local Apparent Time		Error	Assessment		Error
(1) 221 AUGUST 5 (MAG. 0.151)						
Xiaoxi	Aug 05 14:00	未	–(0)	"close"	與天近	0
OBSERVED	14:00	未				
CALCULATED	14:07	未				
Supernal Emblem	17:07	庚				+18
Supernal Emblem	17:10	申半強	+19	"close"	後天一辰半強為近	+19
Yellow Inception	19:10	辛強	+30(31)	"far"	二辰半為遠	+31
Quarter-remainder	Aug 06 14:48	未少強				+148
(2) 222 JANUARY 30 (MAG. 0.054)						
Supernal Emblem	Jan 30 12:30	午少	–26(22)	"far"	先天二辰少弱... 為遠天	–21
Supernal Emblem	12:36	午少				
Xiaoxi	14:00	未	–13	–	先天一辰強	–12
CALCULATED	16:04	申				
OBSERVED	16:10	申北 *				
Yellow Inception	17:50	酉弱	+6(10)	"close"	後天半辰，近	+11
Quarter-remainder	18:03	酉				+12
(3) 223 JANUARY 19 (MAG. 0.915)						
Supernal Emblem	Jan 19 13:46	丁少強				–7
Supernal Emblem	14:00	未初	–12(6)	"far"	先天一辰遠	–5
Yellow Inception	14:10	未強	–6(5)	"close"	先天半辰近	–4
CALCULATED	14:58	坤弱				
OBSERVED	15:00	西南維 *				+1
Xiaoxi	16:00	申	–(+6)	"close/on"	近中天	+7
Quarter-remainder	Jan 20 04:08	寅				+79

NOTE: Column ① identifies each item. To the constituents of the Xu Yue's original list I have added my own calculations for the Supernal Emblem and Quarter-remainder systems (in gray) as well as the local apparent time of maximum eclipse at Luoyang (34°45′ N, 112°28′ E, +144 meters) based on the Besselian elements and values for ΔT provided for Fred Espenak and Jean Meeus' *Five Millennium Canon of Solar Eclipses* on the "NASA Eclipse Web Site" (http://eclipse.gsfc.nasa.gov/eclipse.html). Column ② gives the Julian date of the event as counted from midnight. Column ③ gives the time in both the modern and third-century 24-hour notation. Column ④ gives Xu Yue's quantitative assessment of the each prediction's accuracy in terms of 10-minute fractions. Corrected values are provided in parentheses where these are omitted or inconsistent with other values. Column ⑤ gives Xu's qualitative analysis. Column ⑥ gives the analysis in the original language of the text. Column ⑦ gives each item's error from the modern calculated time of maximum eclipse, also in 10-minute fractions.   * See p. 324.

Table 4.6: Xu Yue's lunar eclipse list

1	2	3	4	5	6	7
Item	Local Apparent Time		Error	Assessment		Error
(4) 221 AUGUST 21 (UMBRAL MAG. 0.920)						
OBSERVED	Aug 21 00:00	子・午 †				
CALCULATED	00:09	子・午				
Xiaoxi	02:00	丑・未	+12	"close" 後一辰為近		+12
Supernal Emblem	04:00	寅・申	+24	– 後天二辰		+24
Supernal Emblem	04:43	寅少強・申少強				+28
Quarter-remainder	09:10	巽・乾				+55
Yellow Inception	12:00	午強・子強	+72	"far" 後天六辰遠		+72
(5) 223 JANUARY 5 (UMBRAL MAG. 0.291)						
Supernal Emblem	Jan 04 23:00	亥半・巳半	−24(18)	"close" 先天二辰近		−21
Supernal Emblem	23:00	壬・丙				
Xiaoxi	Jan 05 00:00	子・午	−12	先一辰		−15
CALCULATED	02:00	丑・未				−3
OBSERVED	02:31	丑少・未少				
Yellow Inception	06:10	卯強・酉強	+25	"far" 後天二辰強為遠		+22
Quarter-remainder	09:45	巽少強・乾少強				+43

NOTE: The format of this table is identical to the previous except that Column ③ gives the "hour" of the sun (left) and moon (right).   † The text records that the eclipse was observed with the sun at *ren*.$_{S09}$ (23:00) and the moon at *bing*.$_{S03}$ (11:00), but the calculated time of maximum eclipse and the reported errors of all three systems' predicted times suggests that this this is some sort of textual error for *zi*.$_{B01}$ (00:00) and *wu*.$_{B07}$ (12:00), respectively. The alternative is that all three predicted times are missing a 半 ("and a half") and there was a more than one-hour error in the time of observation.

Figure 4.1: The early third-century 24-hour scheme

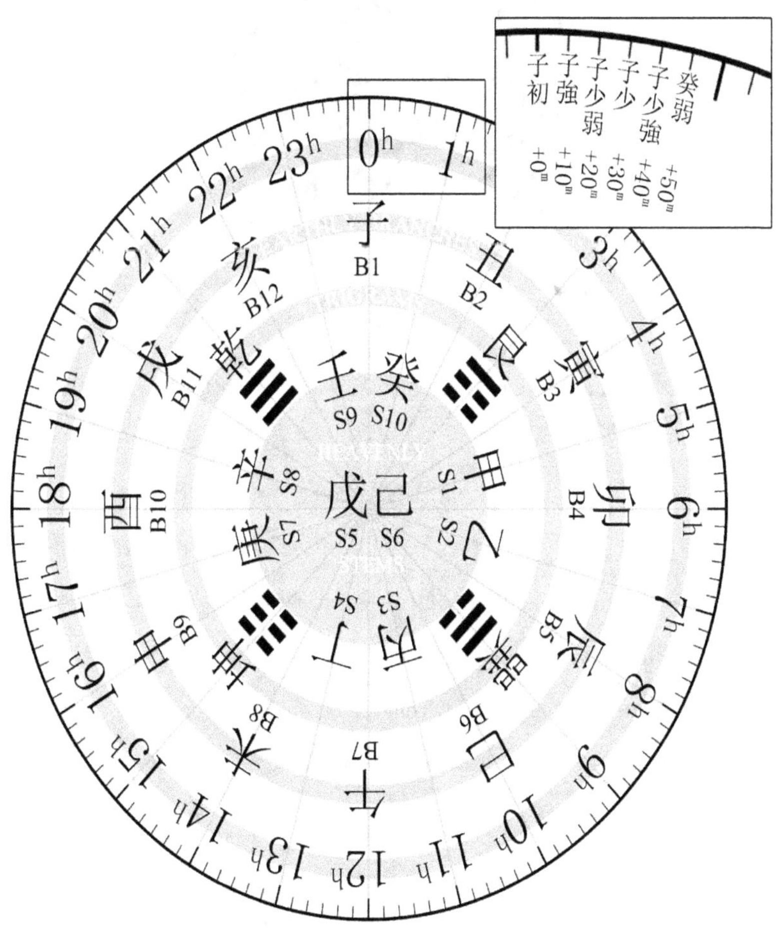

Figure 4.2: Six Dynasties bronze *liu ren*-style diviner's board

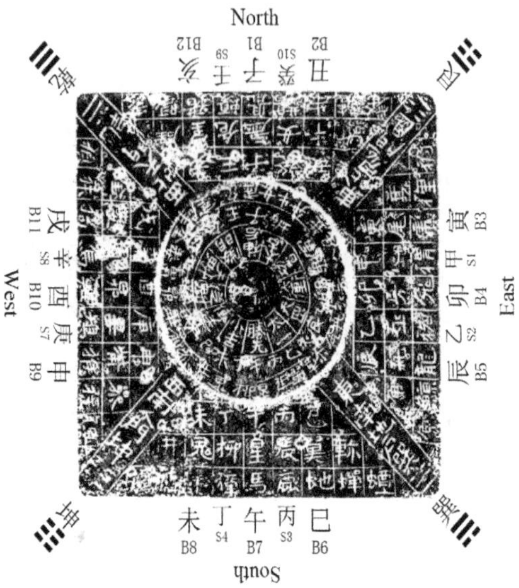

Source: Shanghai Museum; image modified from Yan Dunjie 嚴敦傑, "Ba liuren shipan" 跋六壬式盤, *Wenwu cankao ziliao* 文物參考資料 1985.7: 20.

This scheme is clearly borrowed from the symbology of mantic diagrams like the *shipan* 式盤 (Figure 4.2).[81] This is yet another example of the sort of conceptual borrowing that occurred between calendar divination and mathematical astronomy (see Chapter 2). Each point on this diagram marks a position in time *and* space. In fact, this very arrangement—the "Twenty-four Mountains"—would later become the horizontal coordinate grid for geomantic and navigational compasses. In the context of *li*, this scheme is likewise just as much about space as it is about time: for the solar eclipses of 222 January 30 and 223 January 19, the "hour" (*jia shi* 加時) of observation is given as "north of *shen*.B09" (16:10) and "the southwest corner" (15:00), respectively; and for lunar eclipses we are given the "hour" of

---

81. On the *shipan* and similar mantic diagrams employed in calendar divination, see Marc Kalinowski, "Les instruments astro-calendriques des Han et la méthode *liu ren*," *Bulletin de l'Ecole française d'Extrême-Orient* 72, no. 1 (1983): 309–419; Li Ling 李零, "Shi yu Zhongguo gudai de yuzhou moshi" 式與中國古代的宇宙模式, in *Zhongguo fangshu zheng kao* 中國方術正考 (Beijing: Zhonghua shuju, 2006), 69–140; Ho Peng Yoke, *Chinese Mathematical Astrology: Reaching Out to the Stars*, Needham Research Institute Series (London: RoutledgeCurzon, 2003).

the sun—the time of observation—and the "hour" of the moon—the position opposite the sun.[82]

This so-called "hour" is clearly a measure of both hour and angle analogous to the Greek hour angle. For example, the text tells us that a lunar eclipse occurred on 223 January 5 with the sun's "hour" at $chou._{B02}$ (02:00) and the moon's "hour" at $wei._{B08}$ (14:00). From this we know that:

- The eclipse was observed at 02:00;

- Hence the sun's last meridian transit (at noon) occurred 14 hours previous;

- Hence the sun is 14/24 of the sky—i.e. 14 hours of right ascension—west of the meridian;

- And since eclipse occurs at full moon—i.e. opposition—the moon is thus 2/24 of the sky west of the meridian at eclipse.

Introduced at around the time of the Yellow Inception debate, our "Chinese hour angle" fell completely out of use by the fifth century. Its appearance in Xu Yue's list is thus noteworthy in two regards: it is a solid indicator of the historicity of the list itself; and it is yet another example of how innovations in state system manuals—the Luminous Inception system (#13) of 237, in this case—tend to follow, rather than lead, popular practice.

---

82. "North of $shen._{B09}$" and "the southwest corner" are not standard terminology in the Luminous Inception system (#13) hour-scheme. In the case of the solar eclipse of 222 Jan 30 (mag. 0.054), Qu Anjing suggests that 北 "north" might be a corruption of 半 "half past," placing the observation at 17:00, since, in the contemporary double-hour scheme, "half past" is one (single-)hour past the mark ("Zhongguo gudai lifa zhong de jishi zhidu," 165). Xu Yue's assessments of the Supernal Emblem (#10) and Yellow Inception systems (#11) both imply an observation at 16:50 (260 minutes after 12:30 and 60 minutes prior to 17:50). On the other hand, three considerations point to 16:10 as an equally likely candidate: (1) "half past" is standard terminology for the 12-double-hour scheme and occurs only twice in these lists; (2) 16:10 is the hour of observation implied by the $xiaoxi$'s reported error (it is 130 minutes after 14:00); (3) 16:10 accords with the narrow window between 15:39 and 16:28 LAT during which this diminutive eclipse would have occurred at Luoyang. Therefore, we might understand "north of $shen._{B09}$" to mean one fraction (10 min) "north"—that is, towards $zi._{B01}$ (00:00)—of $shen._{B09}$. For the solar eclipse of 223 Jan 19 (mag. 0.915), Kun 坤 ☷ clearly occupies the southwest corner of the diagram, and the corresponding time of 15:00 matches the calculated eclipse maximum of 14:58 as well as, by a margin of 10 minutes, the Yellow Inception's reported error. At the same time, however, the reported errors for the Supernal Emblem with and without $xiaoxi$ imply an observation at 16:00, when the eclipse would have been at a magnitude of only 0.251.

Lastly, let us note that this random coincidence of Chinese and Mediterranean conventions highlights a contradiction inherent in two axioms of sinology: (1) the "calendrical nature" of Chinese astronomy (GREECE : SPACE :: CHINA : TIME) and (2) the inseparability of space/time in ancient Chinese thought.[83] Whatever the actual implications of (2) for cultural studies, the commutability of time and space in the astral sciences is neither philosophically profound nor characteristically Chinese; it is simply the way that things work. Up until 1961, time had always been a function of position (i.e. our position relative to the sun), and units traversing categories of time/space are common to every ancient astronomical tradition.[84] The division of the celestial equator into one *du* for each day of the year in China is thus no stranger than its division into 24 "hours" in the Mediterranean world; nor is it any stranger than the division of the year and day into the 360 units of a circle (*tithi* and UŠ) in India and Mesopotamia, respectively. Astronomy cannot be limited to hour or angle any more than architecture can be practiced in one dimension; if we are to have a meaningful discussion about the defining features of a tradition, therefore, we must

---

83. Western-language scholarship has discussed *li* in terms of "calendrics," "calendrical science," "calendrical astronomy," etc. since at least the early works of Wolfram Eberhard in the 1930s. For axiom (1), the primacy of calendrics/time over space in Chinese astronomy, see Joseph Needham, *Science and Civilisation in China, Vol.3: Mathematics and the Sciences of the Heavens and the Earth* (Cambridge: Cambridge University Press, 1959), 390–391; Nakayama Shigeru 中山茂, "Characteristics of Chinese Calendrical Science," *Japanese Studies in the History of Science* no. 4 (1965): 124–131; cf. *A History of Japanese Astronomy: Chinese Background and Western Impact* (Cambridge: Harvard University Press, 1969), 68–69; Nathan Sivin, "Cosmos and Computation in Early Chinese Mathematical Astronomy," *T'oung Pao* 2d ser., 55, no. 1/3 (1969): 3–4; Marc Kalinowski, "Le calcul du rayon céleste dans la cosmographie chinoise," *Revue d'histoire des sciences* 43, no. 1 (1990): 8–9; "Astrologie calendaire et calcul de position dans la Chine ancienne: les mutations de l'hémérologie sexagésimale entre le IVe et le IIe siècles avant notre ère," *Extrême-orient, Extrême-occident* 18 (1996): 71; "Fonctionnalité calendaire dans les cosmogonies anciennes de la Chine," *Études chinoises* XXIII (2004): 8–89; Christopher Cullen, *Astronomy and Mathematics in Ancient China: The Zhou Bi Suan Jing* (Cambridge: Cambridge University Press, 1996), 39–40. For axiom (2), "spacetime" and the unity of time and space in Chinese thought, see for example Marcel Granet, *La pensée chinoise* (Paris: La Renaissance du livre, 1934), 77–99; Kalinowski, "Astrologie calendaire et calcul de position dans la Chine ancienne," esp. 74–78; Wang Aihe, *Cosmology and Political Culture in Early China* (Cambridge: Cambridge University Press, 2000), esp. 48–54, 107–109; Mark Edward Lewis, *The Construction of Space in Early China* (New York: State University of New York, 2005), 277, passim.

84. 1961 marks the introduction of Coordinated Universal Time (UTC), later International Atomic Time (TAI), a time scale based on the electromagnetic properties of the cesium atom. For seminal works on the ancient and modern histories of time, see Anthony F. Aveni, *Empires of Time: Calendars, Clocks, and Cultures* (New York: Basic Books, 1989); Dennis D. McCarthy and P. Kenneth Seidelmann, *Time: From Earth Rotation to Atomic Physics* (Weinheim: Wiley-VCH, 2009).

be careful to avoid too simple a juxtaposition of "East" vs. "West."

Of the three methods that Xu Yue puts to the test, the Supernal Emblem (without *xiaoxi*) is the only one that is still extant. The extant manual (*Jin shu, juan* 17) allows us to recalculate the predicted instant of fixed new/full moon (given in grey on Tables 4.5 & 4.6) for each of the dates in question to, if you will, see how Xu did. The two correspond exactly (to the nearest 10-minute fraction) in three out of five cases. Another is off by only two 10-minute fractions due, it seems, to special circumstances. All in all, it seems like Xu was following the same instructions available to us.[85]

The *xiaoxi* method has not survived. Luckily, Xu's numbers do afford us a window into what it was, if not how exactly it worked. Chen Jiujin notes that the direction (positive or negative) of the difference between the predictions of the Supernal Emblem system (#10) with and without *xiaoxi* reflects a correction appropriate to the solar equation of center: in the northern hemisphere, the summer is several days longer than the winter, thus the true sun travels slower than the mean sun in August, entailing a negative adjustment to the moment of true conjunction; and the situation is reversed in winter.[86] Furthermore, if we compare their *size* to values of solar equation of center calculated by modern methods, we find that these too correspond reasonably well (Table 4.7). In fact, the name "*xiaoxi*" itself is suggestive of this reading: fitting the theme of Liu Hong's work, *xiaoxi* is the concept of seasonal (solar) waxing and waning of yin and yang described in the *Book of Changes*.[87]

---

85. The 14-minute (two-fraction) discrepancy for the predicted time of new moon on 223 January 19 is perhaps negligible, but it is interesting from a technical perspective for the fact that it may be the product of the distinct and convoluted set of procedures that the Supernal Emblem system (#10) employs for the fractional last day of the anomalistic cycle (within which said instant fell). For the procedure, see Liu Hongtao 劉洪濤, *Gudai lifa jisuanfa* 古代曆法計算法 (Tianjin: Nankai daxue chubanshe, 2003), 129–132; Christopher Cullen, "The First Complete Chinese Theory of the Moon: The Innovations of Liu Hong c. A.D. 200," *Journal for the History of Astronomy* 33 (2002): 27. The 43-minute discrepancy for the lunar eclipse of 221 August 21 is more conspicuous and difficult to explain. For comparison, Qu Anjing's recalculations in "Zhongguo gudai lifa zhong de jishi zhidu," 165.

86. *Zhongguo gudai tianwenxuejia* 中國古代天文學家, Zhongguo tianwenxueshi daxi (Beijing: Zhongguo kexue jishu chubanshe, 2008), 112–115.

87. The Tuan 彖 commentary to "Feng" 豐 [55] ䷶ states: "When the sun stands at midday, it begins to set; when the moon is full, it begins to wane. The fullness and emptiness of heaven and earth wane and wax in the course of time. How much truer is this of men, or of spirits and gods!" 日中則昃，月盈則食，天地盈虛，

What is more, the compiler(s) of the *Jin shu* unambiguously lists a solar equation of center among Liu's accomplishments:

其為之也，依易立數，遁行相號，潛處相求，名為乾象曆。又創制日行遲速，兼考月行，陰陽交錯於黃道表裏，日行黃道，於赤道宿度復有進退。方於前法，轉為精密矣。

What he did was set up his numbers according with the *Changes*, such that fleeting motions called out to one another, and hidden places sought one another out, and he called it the Supernal Emblem system (#10). *Furthermore, he instituted the acceleration/retardation of solar motion while at the same time investigating lunar motion*: that yin and yang cross at the insides and outside of the Yellow Road (ecliptic), that the Sun travels on the Yellow Road, and that there is, furthermore, advancing and retreating in Red Road (equator) lodge degrees. Only then was there a turn towards the FINE and TIGHT (accuracy) relative to the previous method.[88]

The first Chinese model for solar inequality is traditionally attributed to the sixth-century figure Zhang Zixin, whose work is also lost.[89] The *Jin shu* suggests a (perhaps preposterously) more complicated story: that Liu Hong actually invented such a model some four centuries prior, which was transmitted to his disciples; and yet, despite its recognized excellence, not a single expert incorporated it into his own *li* system, allowing it to disappear from the world within living memory of its hallowed creator, only to be be independently

---

與時消息，而況人於人乎？況於鬼神乎？ (*Zhouyi zhushu*, 9.22b; tr. Richard Wilhelm, *The I Ching or, Book of Changes*, trans. Cary F. Baynes, 3d ed., Bollingen Series XIX [Princeton: Princeton University Press, 1967], 670). A more concrete expression of *xiaoxi* develops in Han *Changes* exegesis and exerts a pervasive influence on subsequent cosmology and divination, i.e. the 12 *xiaoxi* hexagrams—hexagrams assigned to each of the 12 months such that the rising and falling levels of Yin and Yang in each hexagram reflects the seasonal cycle of celestial, climatic, and agricultural phenomena; see Bent Nielsen, *A Companion to Yi Jing Numerology and Cosmology: Chinese Studies of Images and Numbers from Han (202 BCE - 220 CE) to Song (960-1279 CE)* (London: RoutledgeCurzon, 2003), 274–276.

88. *Jin shu*, 17.498; see also the abbreviated version in *Song shu*, 12.231.

89. On Zhang Zixin, see p. 159 ff.

Table 4.7: Supernal Emblem *xiaoxi* and the solar equation of center

1	2	3	4	5	6	7
Date	Type	Hour		Solar Equation of center		
221 Aug 05	solar	17:07	14:00	-187^m	-186.8^m	0.4^m
221 Aug 21	lunar	04:43	02:00	-163^m	-211.2^m	48.2^m
222 Jan 30	solar	12:36	14:00	$+84^m$	$+192.8^m$	108.8^m
223 Jan 04	lunar	23:00	00:00	$+60^m$	$+106.2^m$	46.2^m
223 Jan 19	solar	13:46	16:00	$+134^m$	$+172.6^m$	38.6^m

NOTE: Column ① gives the date of the eclipse from Xu Yue's list. Column ② gives the type: solar/lunar. Column ③ gives the predicted hour of new/full moon for the Supernal Emblem system (#10) as calculated by its system manual (without *xiaoxi*). Column ④ gives the predicted hour according to the *xiaoxi* method, as reported in Xu's list. Column ⑤ gives the difference between Columns ③ and ④, and thus the magnitude of the *xiaoxi* adjustment in minutes. Column ⑥ gives the expected magnitude of the solar equation of center for that day. In this column, I have calculated the solar equation of center in *du* for the date in question according to the methods in Meeus, *Astronomical Algorithms* (Richmond: Willmann-Bell, 1998), which I have converted into a correction for the hour of syzygy by the Supernal Emblem system's instructions. Column ⑦ gives the difference between *xiaoxi* and the solar equation of center.

rediscovered four centuries later. It is difficult to know what to make of this.

Han Yi's Yellow Inception system (#11) has also faded into obscurity. Fortunately, the *Jin shu* provides us with enough clues to reconstruct an approximate picture of its features. First, we are repeatedly reminded that, like Yang Wei's Luminous Inception system (#13) of the following decade, Han was working within the framework and vocabulary of the Supernal Emblem system (#10). We are also provided with two numbers: an ERA FACTOR of 4883 and a DIPPER PARTS of 1205.[90] If we recall, these are divided to produce the fractional part of the *sui* 歲 solar year, whose length is thus:

$$365 + 1205/4883 = 1783500/4883 = 365.2468 \text{ days}$$

In the Supernal Emblem framework, an ERA FACTOR is the number of years required for new moon and winter solstice to coincide at midnight. In other words, it amounts to an integral

---

90. *Jin shu*, 17.498.

number of years, days, and months. The number of days in an ERA is the CIRCUITS OF HEAVEN, which amounts to 1783500 days in this case. The number of months in an ERA—ERA MONTHS (*jiyue* 紀月)—depends here upon the RULE ratio (235 months : 19 years), and thus amounts to 60395 months ($= 4883 \times 235/19$) in this case. In the Supernal Emblem framework, the month is not expressed as ERA MONTHS : CIRCUITS OF HEAVEN but as the ratio between the more elegantly factored COMMENSURATION FACTOR (*tongfa* 通法) 356700 and DAY FACTOR (*rifa* 日法) 12079. From here, we may derived for the Yellow Inception system (#11) a mean synodic month of:

$$\frac{1783500}{4883} \times \frac{19}{235} = \frac{5}{19} \times \frac{356700}{257} \times \frac{19}{5} \times \frac{1}{47} = \frac{356700}{12079} = 29.530590 \text{ days}$$

Having determined its mean lunisolar elements, we may turn to Xu Yue's list for additional clues about the Yellow Inception system (#11). On Table 4.8 we see that the time elapsed between predicted syzygies does not correspond to a neat number of mean lunar phases. The difference is listed in Columns 4 and 8. What is more, this difference is itself the difference of subsequent equations of center in Columns 5 and 9. Nonzero numbers in Column 8 indicate that Yellow Inception system (#11) too features some sort of model for lunar inequality, and parallels in magnitude with Column 4 suggest an affinity of parameters. In fact, given the purportedly derivative nature of Han Yi's work, we might expect him to stick fairly closely to the components of Liu Hong's lunar model: a speed sequence (*chiji li* 遲疾曆) anomalistic month of 27.5534 days (modern value $= 27.5546$ days) and a table for computing the instantaneous equation of center, which ranges between $+10.60^{\text{h}}$ on day 9 and -7.25^{h} on day 22.

Without knowing where the Yellow Inception system (#11) places mean syzygies, we can only speculate about how to divide the differences in Column 8 into a sequence of equations of center in Column 9. However, if we assume hypothetical values for its lunar model that are identical with Liu Hong's, we find that a first mean syzygy approximately 3.8^{h} behind that

Table 4.8: Lunar equation of center in the Yellow Inception (#11) and Supernal Emblem systems (#10)

1	2	3	4	5	6	7	8	9	10
Event	Supernal Emblem (calc.)				Yellow inception				Dif.
SE 1	1801 995.20	–	–	$+9.90^{\mathrm{h}}$	1801 995.29	–	–	$\mathbf{+11.15^{\mathrm{h}}}$	$+1.25^{\mathrm{h}}$
LE 4	1802 010.69	15.48^{d}	$+17.25^{\mathrm{h}}$	-7.34^{h}	1802 010.99	15.70^{d}	$+22.47^{\mathrm{h}}$	$\mathbf{-11.31^{\mathrm{h}}}$	-3.97^{h}
SE 2	1802 173.02	163.33^{d}	-2.18^{h}	-5.17^{h}	1802 173.23	162.24^{d}	-4.20^{h}	-7.11^{h}	-1.94^{h}
LE 5	1802 512.45	339.43^{d}	-4.00^{h}	-1.17^{h}	1802 512.75	339.51^{d}	-2.11^{h}	-5.00^{h}	-3.83^{h}
SE 3	1802 527.06	14.62^{d}	-3.63^{h}	$+2.46^{\mathrm{h}}$	1802 527.08	14.33^{d}	-10.37^{h}	$+5.37^{\mathrm{h}}$	$+2.91^{\mathrm{h}}$

NOTE: Column ① gives the number and type of the eclipse from Xu Yue's list in order of chronology rather than typology—solar (SE) or lunar eclipse (LE). Columns ② and ⑥ give the predicted Julian Day of syzygy. Columns ③ and ⑦ give the time elapsed between successive phenomena in days. Columns ④ and ⑧ give the difference between the time elapsed between predictions and the time elapsed by the nearest number of mean lunar phases (according to each system's values for the mean synodic month). Columns ⑤ and ⑨ give the lunar equation of center (*jiashi yingsuo* 加時盈縮) to be subtracted from the hour of mean syzygy. Column ⑤ is calculated from the Supernal Emblem system manual while Column ⑨ is a hypothetical value for the sake of demonstration that is derived from a sequence of mean lunations beginning 3.8 hours after that of the Supernal Emblem system on 221 August 6, 03:02. The two numbers in bold exceed the Supernal Emblem system's maximum values for the equation of center: +10.60 and – 7.25 hours. Column 10 is the difference between the two equations of center.

of the Supernal Emblem system's (#10) produces an optimal spread of values in Column 9. Still, the spread is imperfect in two regards. No matter where one moves the time of mean syzygy, or whether or not one applies *xiaoxi*, one value consistently exceeds the its expected range by a matter of several hours: LE 4, the full moon of 221 August 21. Furthermore, there does not appear to be a simple systematic deviation from the Supernal Emblem system's (#10) values.

In sum, though Han Yi's mean lunisolar elements are a conscientious improvement upon his predecessor, the computed times of fixed syzygy in Xu Yue's list reflect a model for lunar inequality that appears to differ from it somewhat erratically. This impression is no doubt due in part to our ignorance about how exactly their lunar models differed. At the same time, our ignorance on the matter also makes it more difficult to eliminate external factors such as dishonesty or textual corruption that may explain, for example, the disproportionately large 12-hour lag resulting from the disproportionately large equation of center for the full moon of 221 August 21.

Xu Yue's list of eclipse observations are precise to 1/12 double-hour (10 minutes). Other carefully-timed eclipse records that have come down to us (all from the sixth century onward) tend to include information such as position and the time of first and last contact.[91] The focus here, however, is not the eclipse per se but the time of maximum eclipse as an indication of the time of syzygy. All told, these records appear reliable and accord quite well with the results of modern calculation.

In Tables 4.5 & 4.6, we see that four out of five instants of maximum eclipse calculated for local conditions at Luoyang fall in or within 2 minutes of the reported 10-minute span; the one outlier—the lunar eclipse of 223 January 5—is 21–31 minutes off. These discrepancies could be due to any number of factors. There are human factors like eyesight, the inexactness/subjectivity of determinations of the exact moment of maximum eclipse, and the

---

91. These are collected, translated, and studied in F. Richard Stephenson, *Historical Eclipses and Earth's Rotation* (Cambridge: Cambridge University Press, 1997), 284–307.

obscurity and corruption of written records. There are also factors relating to the technology and practice of time-keeping. For example, Hua Tongxu 華同旭 finds from laboratory experiments that the high-end clepsydra design of the period produces a standard deviation of up to 10 seconds per *ke* 刻 (0.14%; 1 *ke* = 1/100 day = 14.4 minutes); on the other hand, John Steele concludes from his study of timed eclipse observations that, in pre-modern China, the mean error of solar and lunar eclipse timings was 0.41 hours and 0.52 hours, respectively.[92] Last but not least is the Earth's rotational clock error (ΔT), which is the product of long-term and short-term fluctuations in the Earth's rate of rotation caused by forces like tidal friction. F. R. Stephenson and L. V. Morrison have gone a long way to resolve this issue through the analysis and curve-fitting of an exhaustive corpus of pretelescopic eclipse records; however, there remains a degree of uncertainty concerning eclipse geometry that may amount to as much as 3.5 minutes and several percentage points of magnitude in third-century Luoyang.[93]

Far more remarkable than the precision with which our astral scientists timed these eclipses, however, is the fact that they saw them at all: the solar eclipses of 221 August 5 (mag. 0.151) and 222 January 30 (mag. 0.054) would have been so small in Luoyang as

---

92. Hua Tongxu, *Zhongguo louke* 中國漏刻 (Hefei: Anhui kexue jishu chubanshe, 1991), esp. 157–169; John M. Steele, *Observations and Predictions of Eclipse Times by Early Astronomers*, 210. The results cited are for Hua's experiments with a two-tier polyvascular inflow clepsydra—the design, he argues, that would have represented the cutting-edge of third century time-keeping technology (pp. 61–62). The regularity of a water-clock depends, in addition to design, on factors like the viscosity and purity of the water that passes through it—a fact which ancient actors describe themselves as being keenly aware of and taking careful measures to counteract. Hua's experiments show the effectiveness of these techniques in a laboratory setting (198–214), and Steele concludes from the absence of a seasonal systematic error that "evidently the Chinese astronomers were successful in their attempts to regulate the flow of water throughout the year" (212–213). Steele's conclusions about the accuracy of time-keeping in practice differ considerably from Hua's conclusions about the technological potential for accuracy, which is an important distinction to make. At the same time, however, I offer Steele's numbers with the caveat that they are for the entire pre-modern period and that they cannot claim complete independence of the contributing factors listed above.

93. On ΔT, see F. R. Stephenson and L. V. Morrison, "Long-term Fluctuations in the Earth's Rotation: 700 BC to AD 1990," *Philosophical Transactions: Physical Sciences and Engineering* 351, no. 1695 (1995): 165–202; Stephenson, *Historical Eclipses and Earth's Rotation*; L. V. Morrison and F. R. Stephenson, "Historical Values of the Earth's Clock Error ΔT and the Calculation of Eclipses," *Journal for the History of Astronomy* xxxv (2004): 327–336. My estimation of the effects of the uncertainty concerning ΔT on third century Luoyang are based the century-by-century standard deviation of their curve as published in ibid., 332, Table 1.

Figure 4.3: Small magnitude solar eclipses

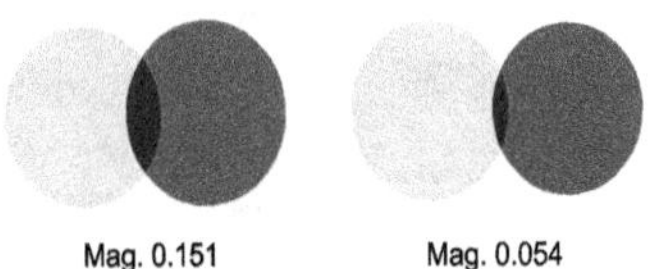

to have been practically invisible to the unaided eye (Figure 4.3). The accuracy of these observations vouch for their authenticity.[94] They also vouch for the the skill with which third-century observers could detect minute changes to the solar disk. Of course, this should not come as a total surprise: observers in the Eastern Han had begun observing sunspots and had managed to report six of eight minute solar eclipses ($<$ mag. 0.2) that occurred at Luoyang in the two centuries prior (Table 4.9).[95] There is also the question of whether eclipse reports necessarily issue from the capital, but Stephenson and Steele present a convincing case to this end.[96]

The planetary visibility list

The second collation is found after the altercation between Han Yi and Xu Yue (see p. 311). This list is composed of 14 dates of observed first and last visibilities for Jupiter, Saturn, Venus, and Mercury, to which are compared predictions made by the Supernal Emblem (#10) and Yellow Inception (#11) systems (Table 4.10). Compared to the previous list, it is much less clear how this fits into the context of the debate or to whom we should attribute

94. On the predictive accuracy of period knowledge, see Steele, *Observations and Predictions of Eclipse Times by Early Astronomers*, 235. Note that laconic records of the three solar eclipses on Xu Yue's list appear elsewhere in the dynastic histories as well: *Sanguo zhi*, 2.78, 79, 82; *Song shu*, 34.1011; *Jin shu*, 12.337.

95. On sunspot observation, see Chen Zungui, *Zhongguo tianwenxue shi*, 768–786.

96. Their case rests on two points: the centralized nature of the Chinese state; and the fact that the *Hou Han shu* explicitly comments upon reports originating from outside the Clerk's Office. See Stephenson, *Historical Eclipses and Earth's Rotation*, 230–231; Steele, *Observations and Predictions of Eclipse Times by Early Astronomers*, 191–192. Carefully-timed eclipse observations lend further credence to this assumption, since early imperial actors had no concept of geographic longitude or its effects on local apparent time, let alone how to compensate for it so as to convert from one locality to another.

Table 4.9: Solar eclipses of magnitude < 0.2 observed in Eastern Han Luoyang (25–190)

no.	Date	Mag.	Record	Note
1	40 Apr 30	0.175	HHS 1.66; 18.3359	
2	46 Jul 22	0.171	HHS 1.74; 18.3359	
3	54 Jul 23	0.009	–	
4	61 Oct 02	0.017	–	
5	90 Mar 20	0.101	HHS 4.170; 18.3362	史官不見，涿郡以聞 "Not seen by Clerk's Office but reported from Zhuo Commandery"
6	168 Jun 23	0.002	HHS 8.329; 18.3369	
7	169 Dec 6	0.069	HHS 8.331; 18.3369	
8	171 Apr 23	0.193	HHS 8.332; 18.3369	

NOTE: Records are taken from *Zhongguo gudai tianxiang jilu zongji* 中國古代天象記錄總集 (Nanjing: Jiangsu kexue jishu chubanshe, 1988). Magnitude is calculated according to the Besselian elements and values for ΔT provided for Fred Espenak and Jean Meeus' *Five Millennium Canon of Solar Eclipses* on the "NASA Eclipse Web Site."

it.[97]

There is nothing evidently suspicious about this list, but we are admittedly in a far weaker position to assess its contents. Once again, the list's predictions for the Supernal Emblem system (#10) accord more or less exactly with recalculations performed according to the received system manual. Unfortunately, received sources are silent on the planetary side of Han Yi's work. As discussed at length in Chapter 2, furthermore, the question of when a planet is or is not visible is so subjective and so dependent on unpredictable atmospheric factors that it is beyond our ability to retrodict within any meaningful margin of error. All that we can say here is that none of the data suggest themselves as bizarre or implausible, and that Han Yi's predictions are all much closer to Liu Hong's than either is to the dates of observed phenomena.

---

97. The eclipse list featured the Supernal Emblem *xiaoxi* method with which only Xu Yue seems to have been familiar. The fact that *xiaoxi* is absent from the planetary list, however, is probably to be expected, since the solar equation of center would have more negligible effect on the predicted dates of the phenomena here.

Table 4.10: Yellow Inception debate list of planetary visibility dates

1 no.	2 Phenomena	3 Observed	4 Supernal Emblem predict.	5 error	6 Yellow Inception predict.	7 error	8 Dif.
JUPITER							
1	FMR	222 Jun 20	Jun 13	–9$^\text{d}$	Jun 11	–7$^\text{d}$	2$^\text{d}$
			Jun 11	–7$^\text{d}$			
MARS							
–	–	–	–	–	–	–	–
SATURN							
2	FMR	221 Dec 27	Dec 22	–5$^\text{d}$	Dec 19	–8$^\text{d}$	3$^\text{d}$
3	LES	222 Dec 02	Dec 02	+0$^\text{d}$	Nov 28	–4$^\text{d}$	4$^\text{d}$
4	FMR	223 Jan 11	Jan 04	–7$^\text{d}$	Jan 01	–10$^\text{d}$	3$^\text{d}$
VENUS							
5	LMR	222 Aug 09	Jul 21	–19$^\text{d}$	Jul 18	–23$^\text{d}$	2$^\text{d}$
6	FES	222 Nov 02	Oct 11	–23$^\text{d}$	Oct 08	–25$^\text{d}$	2$^\text{d}$
MERCURY							
7	FMR	221 Dec 18	Dec 14	–4$^\text{d}$	Dec 13	–5$^\text{d}$	1$^\text{d}$
8	LMR	222 Jan 13	Jan 15	+2$^\text{d}$	Jan 14	+1$^\text{d}$	1$^\text{d}$
9	FES	222 Jun 14	Jun 14	+0$^\text{d}$	Jun 13	–1$^\text{d}$	1$^\text{d}$
10	LES	222 Jul 09	Jul 16	+7$^\text{d}$	Jul 15	+6$^\text{d}$	1$^\text{d}$
11	FMR	222 Aug 19	Aug 03	–16$^\text{d}$	Aug 02	–17$^\text{d}$	1$^\text{d}$
12	LMR	222 Aug 31	Sep 04	+4$^\text{d}$	Sep 03	+3$^\text{d}$	1$^\text{d}$
13	LMR	223 Jan 03	Dec 29	–5$^\text{d}$	Dec 28	–6$^\text{d}$	1$^\text{d}$
14	FES	223 Feb 16	Jan 31	–16$^\text{d}$	Jan 31	–16$^\text{d}$	–
			Feb 01	–15$^\text{d}$			

NOTE: Column ① gives the number of each phenomenon; note that number 15 is missing. Column ② gives the type of phenomena: FMR for "morning appearance" 晨見 (first morning rising), LES for "hiding" 伏 (last evening setting), and for the inferior planets, LMR for "morning hiding" 晨伏 (last morning rising), and FES for "evening appearance" 夕見 (first evening setting). On planetary visibility phenomena, see Chapter 2. Column ③ gives the reported date of observation, converted to Julian Dates. Columns ④ and ⑥ give the reported predictions of the Supernal Emblem (#10) and Yellow Inception (#11) systems. Calculated predictions for the former are provided in gray where they conflict with the date reported. Columns ⑤ and ⑦ give the reported error from the observational results in Column 3. Column 8 gives the difference between Supernal Emblem and Yellow Inception system predictions.

Implications

What do these lists have to tell us about the sociology of *li*? Given the abruptness with which they are inserted into the dialog of the debate, it is hard to know what exactly they are doing there. All that we know for certain is that the eclipse list is a product of Xu Yue's calculation and collation. However, even if these are representative of nothing more than a single actor's personal style, they still speak to the central themes of this study and help complicate our bigger picture. They remind us, for example, that the reality of the field was more complex than the archetype of state monopoly asserted in the classics (and twentieth-century histories of science): Office-outsiders were at the forefront of the field and were respected as such, and knowledge could travel freely from professional to expert (observation records) and from expert to professional (theoretical advances). They also remind us that the absolute reverse—a totally open information society and passive Clerk's Office—is equally absurd: fed as it was from outside talent, the Clerk's Office could also be at or near that forefront (the Yellow Inception system [#11]); and *li* could very well involve esoteric transmission (e.g. *xiaoxi*).

In the "*Li* Treatise" genre, actors present collations such as these as *facts* that may effectively arbitrate matters of uncertainty. There is nothing particularly suspicious about the *Jin shu* lists in this regard: their time notation is specific to the third century, their calculations accord more-or-less exactly with what we know of contemporary *li*, and their observations accord with what we know about celestial mechanics. All of this seems to point to the realist conclusion that there *is* some sort of timeless astronomical reality, that humans have some reliable sensory access thereto, and that the third-century astral scientist was, for his part, capable of some degree of professional integrity.[98] This is not to deny

---

98. I offer this in supplement to the realist position expressed on p. 97 and p. 319. The lunisolar data points of the *Jin shu* list are not included in Stephenson's studies of the Earth's clock error ΔT. It happens that the observed instants of eclipse maxima that the first list records are completely consistent with his curve of historic values for ΔT (note 93). To repurpose Hillary Putnam's "miracle argument," it seems that realism "is the only philosophy that doesn't make the success of science a miracle" in this situation (*Mathematics, Matter, and Method* [London: Cambridge University Press, 1975], 73).

the theory-ladenness of observation or the social construction of facts. In the end, lists are textual creations whose data is the product of selection and whose meaning is subject to interpretation. My point, rather, is that it is because actors conspired to produce these facts (and because we can, at the same time, say with relative confidence what they were looking at as they did so) that they can be made to tell us about the questions on actors' minds and their approaches thereto.

The identification of *li* with "calendrics" has traditionally led scholars to focus on the calendrical (lunisolar) elements of *li*. Nakayama Shigeru 中山茂 and Nathan Sivin have gone so far as to attribute the Chinese with a "lack of concern with planetary motions."[99] This, they argue, was due to an exclusive mystification with eclipses.

> Systems rarely stood or fell on their planetary techniques alone. It is not hard
> to see why. China's earliest written documents, in the second millennium B.C.,
> recorded eclipses of the sun and moon as baleful omens. From at least the second
> century B.C. on, as astronomers learned how to predict eclipses, the state came
> to be intensely concerned with unpredicted ones as highly visible omens—threats
> to the dynasty's mandate. That kept the solar and lunar techniques at the center
> of attention until, by A.D. 500, bureaucrats were predicting a large proportion
> of visible eclipses.

> The political priority of eclipses kept planetary phenomena peripheral, no matter
> how technically interesting they were. Astronomers recognized that the motions
> of the five classical planets were very different from each other, but coming to
> grips with those differences would have required sustained, precise measurement
> over a number of years. That would have entailed new government priorities,
> additional time, and more money. Precisely because planetary prediction tech-
> niques were a weak point, challengers fairly often attacked a current system for
> predictions of planetary phenomena that had failed. By the end of the tenth

---

99. Nakayama, "Characteristics of Chinese Calendrical Science," 127.

century, one system was comparing its computations of planetary events with those of important predecessors, but even 300 years later that had not become the norm.[100]

The fact that the Yellow Inception debate presents us with test results concerning both eclipses and planetary motions suggests the latter *were* a matter of concern, at least in the third century. This is not particularly surprising. Alongside the calendar and lunar/eclipse theory, planetary astronomy was one of three constituent elements of the *li* system manual (see p. 34, Table 1.2). Also, anyone familiar with the *tianwen* side of the astral sciences knows how (if not how much more) important planets were to that field.[101] Lastly, the early imperial period provides us with numerous examples wherein the effectiveness of planetary models were a criterion of *li* policy decisions, e.g. the scrapping of Yang Wei's planetary methods circa 317 and the dispute between Li Yexing 李業興 and Xindu Fang 信都芳 in 540.[102]

On the topic of eclipses, Xu Yue's first list is a good indicator of how demystified experts had become of even solar eclipses: data divorced of awe and politics, eclipses were, in Xu's words, "the key to testing a *li*" (see p. 306). There was nothing new about this attitude. Experts had used eclipses as data points for appraising lunisolar *li* in this manner for centuries.[103] Of course, for this practice to make any sense at all it would have had to have been predicated on the understanding that eclipses were, in Sima Qian's words, inherently

---

100. Sivin, *Granting the Seasons*, 32–33; cf. Nakayama, *A History of Japanese Astronomy*, 150–151.

101. For example, Gautama Siddhārtha's 瞿曇悉達 *Kaiyuan zhanjing* 開元占經 (729) devotes 3 *juan* to eclipse omens (2 solar, 1 lunar) and 41 *juan* to planetary omens. Likewise, the historical records portion of the Zhonghua shuju edition of the *Jin shu* "*Tianwen* Treatise" devotes less than 8 pages to solar eclipses and more than 40 to planetary phenomena (for a table of contents, see p. 26, Table 1.1). For a typological study of Chinese astral omen series, see Jiang Xiaoyuan 江曉原, *Zhongguo xingzhanxue leixing fenxi* 中國星占學類型分析 (Shanghai: Shanghai shudian chubanshe, 2009).

102. For the official scrapping of Yang Wei's planetary astronomy, see *Jin shu*, 17.503; *Song shu*, 12.260. For Li Yexing and Xindu Fang's debate about planetary *li*, see Section 2.5 and *Wei shu*, 107B.2695–2699. Similarly, in 462 Zu Chongzhi 祖沖之 lists the failure to predict of planetary visibility phenomena among three problems afflicting the state system of the time; see *Song shu*, 13.289 ff.; *Nan Qi shu*, 52.904–905.

103. For Han examples, see *Hou Han shu*, *zhi* 2, 3034, 3036. A clear parallel with Xu's approach here can also be found in the tests run on the Epochal Excellence system (#22) in 443; see *Song shu*, 12.262–264.

"periodic" (*you shi* 有時) rather than "ominous" (*zhan* 占) phenomena.[104] So confident were *li* experts in the regularity of eclipse cycles, in fact, that they expected them to be reducible to mathematical models and knowable in advance.[105] It is not my intent to question the sincerity with which ancient actors theorized, memorialized, or performed ritual action concerning eclipses—their *belief*—but to simply emphasize that, in all their complexity, they were also able to recognize in eclipses something mundane and knowable and could treat them in kind.

Xu Yue's list uses eclipses to mark the instant of syzygy (the alignment of sun, moon, and earth) to determine the error, "ahead" or "behind Heaven," of the predicted "hour" (*jia shi*) of eclipse. In other words, like the planetary list, the focus is here is *time*. Time, it will be recalled, is commutable with and inseparable from position in astronomy. In previous chapters, we have seen the *Wuxing zhan* tables, *li* system manuals, and the Li Yexing-Xindu Fang debate place equal emphasis on both, and, in the following century, we begin to see experts use eclipses to mark the *position* of syzygy.[106] So why do Xu Yue's lists focus on time? It stands to reason that our lists' focus has less to do with the nature of Chinese astronomy per se than that of the specific questions posed to it in this case. There is a strong precedent, going back to at least the Han, for the state to emphasize the timing of lunisolar phenomena in the assessment of *li*. Cullen argues that, more than anything, it was

---

104. *Shiji*, 27.1349–1350.

105. Of course, actors realized these expectations with varying degrees of success. What I want to emphasize here, however, is simply the *expectation* of regularity, which, as the case of Mars should remind us (below), is not always a safe assumption on our part. For the history of eclipse prediction in the Han, see *Hou Han shu, zhi* 2, 3040–3043. For a thorough critique of the limitations of early Chinese methods of eclipse prediction, see Sivin, "Cosmos and Computation in Early Chinese Mathematical Astronomy."

106. In 443 Qian Lezhi's Clerk's Office ran tests resulting in an eclipse list identical to Xu Yue's in form, except that it also marks the position of the eclipsed sun/moon, showing that such a test *could* be performed and that someone, albeit more than a century later, had the mind to perform it (*Song shu*, 12.262–264). The first mention of the idea of using eclipses to determine the position of the sun and moon is in the 384 preface to Jiang Ji's 姜岌 *Jiazi*.01-origin system (#18); see *Jin shu*, 18.567; *Song shu*, 13.289. In fact, over the early imperial period, observation and testing programs took an increasingly active interest in the lodge/degree of eclipses, as is readily apparent in the records studied in Stephenson, *Historical Eclipses and Earth's Rotation*, 213–333 and Steele, *Observations and Predictions of Eclipse Times by Early Astronomers*, 161–215. Note also that position plays a more important role in *tianwen* omenology than timing.

the court's interest in the rigorous synchronization of celestial, agricultural, and ritual events that informed this emphasis.[107] This may not explain the planetary visibility list, but it is probably better that we eschew old generalizations about the "official" and "calendrical nature" of Chinese astronomy here in favor of more precise formulations, e.g. the calendrical emphasis of official astronomy in China.

Lastly, it is interesting to note what questions actors identify as meaningful and solvable. As in the *Wuxing zhan*, we see in the *Jin shu*'s planetary list a preoccupation with first and last visibilities. Theoretically, the choice is understandable: within the paradigm of the motion-degree model (*xingdu* 行度), with its unitary vision of the synodic period, first and last visibilities are understood to occur at fixed intervals in time and space from conjunction, and are, thus, reliable indicators of the time and place of conjunction, which serve to anchor the entire model. In the words of Li Yexing, "even if a [planet's] *du* between conjunctions is not verified, it invariably returns upon terminating at conjunction" 但一合之裏星度 不驗者，至若合終必還.[108] As discussed in Section 2.5.2, however, visibility phenomena are subjective and beyond period actors' (and our own) technical ability to predict with any certainty. The spread of planets is also interesting. First, the list omits any reference to Mars. The proximity of Mars' orbit to our own makes its luminosity and retrograde behavior particularly variable—variable in a way that the traditional motion-degree model is particularly ill-equipped to handle. One would never know it from looking at a *li* system manual, where motion-degree models are presented side-by-side without qualification, but early imperial experts were quite self-aware of their limitations here. The second-century B.C. *Wuxing zhan* offers only that Mars' "[advancing and retreating] are without constancy (*wu heng*) and cannot be taken as a [standard]" 【進退】無恒，不可為【極】; and in the sixth century A.D., Li Yexing still bemoans that "The planet Mars does sometimes fail

---

107. "Actors, Networks, and 'Disturbing Spectacles' in Institutional Science," 241; cf. Cullen, "People and Numbers in Early Imperial China," 597–598. See also Section 1.3.2 of this dissertation.

108. *Wei shu*, 107B.2698. The system that Le Yexing is defending still assumes first and last visibilities to occur at a fixed interval in time and space from conjunction (see p. 111 ff.). Therefore, the date and *du* of first and last visibilities are functions of the date and *du* of conjunction.

to accord with its [predicted] *du* since the phenomenon of its appearance/disappearance is inherently inconstant (*wu chang*)" 熒惑一星，伏見體自無常，或不應度.[109] It seems reasonable, therefore, that the Supernal Emblem (#10) and Yellow Inception (#11) systems are not judged on account of their models for "The Sparkling Deluder" (Yinghuo 熒惑). Less reasonable, we might say, is the confidence expressed towards Mercury's behavior, whose orbit is very eccentric and close to the sun, and which extremely difficult to even see, let alone model.[110]

Let us now turn from questions to approach. The lists adduced in the Yellow Inception debate cover five eclipses (3 solar, 2 lunar) and fourteen first/last planetary visibilities from a 544-day period between 221 August 21 and 223 February 16. For each phenomenon, the compiler collates (*jiao*) the results of calculation and observation: he computes each system's error, determines which is *zhong* 中 "on the mark," which is *jin* 近 "close," and which is *yuan* 遠 "off," then scores each system based on the number of *zhong*, *jin*, and *yuan*.

凡課日月蝕五事，乾象四（遠）【近】，黃初一近。

Out of a total of five tests of solar and lunar eclipses, the Supernal Emblem was (farthest) [closest] four times, and the Yellow inception was closest once.[111]

凡四星見伏十五；| 乾象七近二中，黃初五近一中。|

Out of a total of fifteen appearances and hidings of four stars (planets), COM-MENTARY: |the Supernal Emblem was closest seven times and on twice, while the Yellow Inception was closest five times and on once.|[112]

---

109. *Wuxing zhan*, line 45, in Liu Lexian 劉樂賢, *Mawangdui tianwen shu kaoshi* 馬王堆天文書考釋 (Guangzhou: Zhongshan daxue chubanshe, 2004); *Wei shu*, 107B.2698

110. On the complexities of Mercury's behavior and early attempts to deal with them in China, see Jiang Xiaoyuan and Niu Weixing 鈕衛星, "Zhang Zixin zhi Shuixing 'ying xian bu xian' shu jiqi keneng laiyuan" 張子信之水星「應見不見」術及其可能來源, in *Ouzhou tianwenxue dongjian fawei* 歐洲天文學東漸發微 (Shanghai: Shanghai shudian chubanshe, 2009), 223–239.

111. *Jin shu*, 17.500. See note 62

112. *Jin shu*, 17.501.

Presumably, the relative number of *zhong* and *jin* are then taken as a reliable metric for each system's overall TIGHTNESS (*mi* 密).[113]

The procedure of *jiao* "collation/testing" here is not particularly sophisticated. First, the sample size is quite small, covering only the time that the Yellow Inception system (#11) was under review at the Clerk's Office (see p. 280). Logic dictates that the Clerk's Office need not have run tests in real time—that comparison with past records would have sufficed. Sometimes actors did just that, but other times they expressed a preference for real-time trials.[114]

The advantages of the real-time trial are never explicitly enumerated, but they merit speculation. First, prior to the fifth-century integration of *suicha* 歲差 (precession) into *li*, historical records would have been of limited help to the appraisal of contemporary TIGHT-NESS. In 176, for example, Cai Yong tells us that:

且三光之行，遲速進退，不必若一。術家以筭追而求之，取合於當時而已。故有古今之術。今〔術〕之不能上通於古，亦猶古術之不能下通於今也。

Moreover, the motions of the Three Luminaries, in their slowings and acceler-ations and their advances and retardations are not necessarily as one. When experts try to chase after them through calculation, all they can do is to seek a fit at the corresponding time. So there are ancient methods, and also mod-ern ones. The inability of modern methods to be extended back to antiquity is the same as the inability of ancient methods to be extended forward to modern

---

113. On the rhetoric of accuracy, see Section 1.3.3.

114. The Han provides examples of both approaches. For example, in 92 Jia Kui compares results retrodicted with the Grand Inception (#7) and Quarter-remainder systems (#9) to records covering the period 206 B.C. – A.D. 24 to make the point that each outperforms the other in their respective centuries (*Hou Han shu, zhi* 2, 3028). In 123, Zhang Heng 張衡 (87–140) and Zhou Xing 周興 compare the Grand Inception (#7) and Yin system (#4) to *yi zhu* 儀注 "instrument records" to determine that neither outperforms the Nine Roads lunar model (ibid., *zhi* 2, 3034). In 143, Yu Gong 虞恭 and Zong Xin 宗訢 perform a similar collation covering 48 eclipses (20 solar, 28 lunar) from A.D. 87 to 143 to defend the Quarter-remainder system (#9) against its detractors (ibid., *zhi* 2, 3036–3037). Between 78 and 74 B.C., however, Zhang Shouwang's 張壽王 Yellow Emperor Adjusted system (#1) was put to a real-time trial against the official Grand Inception system (#7) (*Han shu*, 21A.978). Zong Gan 宗紺, Feng Xun 馮恂, Liu Hong, and Zong Cheng's 宗誠 methods for eclipse prediction were put to a similar trial from 179 to 181 (*Hou Han shu, zhi* 2, 3040).

times.[115]

Second, in 226 adequate records may not have been available. The capital had recently been sacked and relocated, and it is conceivable that observatory records may have become lost or disarrayed. What is more, because lunar models had only just become accurate to the hour, it is possible that collation required new observational records of commensurate accuracy.[116]

Third, actors may have held that, in Karl Popper's words, "apart from explaining all the *explicanda* which the new theory was designed to explain, it must have new and testable consequences (preferably consequences of a new kind); it must lead to the prediction of phenomena which have not so far been observed."[117] This is to say that the verification (*yan* 驗) of novel predictions may have outweighed accordance (*he* 合, *tong* 通) with available facts. The *Hou Han shu* tells us that:

未驗無以知其是，未差無以知其失。失然後改之，是然後用之。

If something has not been verified (*yan*), then there is no way to know if it is correct, and if it has not [been shown to] err then there is no way to know if it is amiss. If it is amiss, then you fix it; if it is correct, then you use it.[118]

Late twentieth-century scholarship has adequately problematized this claim as it applies to the justification of scientific theories.[119] Though the context is obviously different, there are meaningful parallels to be drawn here with the exemplar case from modern science—general relativity and the prediction of light bending. Stephen Brush argues that this prediction

---

115. *Hou Han shu, zhi* 2, 3038; tr. Cullen, "Actors, Networks, and 'Disturbing Spectacles' in Institutional Science," 260.

116. If the observational records in the dynastic histories' "Tianwen zhi" are any indication, it is possible that the Han observatory produced records of only the *date* of eclipses. Furthermore, the first few centuries A.D. also saw the sort of improvements in clepsydra design necessary for the level of timekeeping accuracy on display in Xu Yue's eclipse list; see Hua Tongxu, *Zhongguo louke*, 45, passim.

117. *Conjectures and Refutations: The Growth of Scientific Knowledge* (New York: Basic Books, 1962), 241.

118. *Hou Han shu, zhi* 2, 3041.

119. For an overview of this topic, see Stephen Brush, "Dynamics of Theory Change: The Role of Predictions," *PSA: Proceedings of the Biennial Meeting of the Philosophy of Science Association* (1994): 133–145.

made a far greater impact on the (subsequent) popular imagination than Einstein's own work or the contemporary community of physicists; "so the main value of a successful forecast (as compared to successful deduction of a known fact) is favorable publicity."[120] Likewise, the result of Liu Hong's eclipse prediction, Xu Yue claims, was that "everyone within the oceans recognized the truth of it, and there was no one who did not hear of it" (p. 306). This, it seems, might explain the preference for prediction in *yi*-debate. In a debate held before a general audience and decided by imperial fiat, a feat of showmanship may speak louder than data analysis and, by induction, convince us that a repeat performance might lie in store.[121]

In that sense, the Clerk's Office's real-time trial had every feature of a game. It was a game, in Roger Caillois' terms, of *agôn* and *alea*—"a free act of will stemming from the satisfaction felt in overcoming an arbitrarily conceived and voluntarily accepted obstacle."[122] Two or more contestants entered their *li* systems onto the bounded playing field of the observation program. This playing field was equalizing and rule-governed, subjecting each contestant to the same challenges and the same criteria of success. That the contents of the challenge were unknown in advance, and that a *li* runs independent of its maker, made this something of a game of chance—a surrender to destiny—though the author of that destiny was ultimately the (predictive) superiority of his creation (as defined by the rules of the game). Good sportsmanship dictated that all involved voluntarily submit to the judgments of a fair referee and that the spheres of play and real life be contained from spilling into one another—e.g. by punishing the losing party "for real."

This was the ideal, at least, but the Yellow Inception debate broke embarrassingly from it: Xu Yue and the Clerk's Office held Han Yi's system up to different versions of the Supernal

---

120. "Prediction and Theory Evaluation: The Case of Light Bending," *Science* 246, no. 4934, New Series (1989): 1127.

121. Cullen discusses the nature and political impact of the *yi* in "Actors, Networks, and 'Disturbing Spectacles' in Institutional Science," 250–253. Whatever instances there may be of voting or the publicly recognized outcomes of *yi* swaying the will of the emperor (or his secretariat) in history, one should note that matters of *li* policy are inevitably decided by imperial decree.

122. *Man, Play, and Games*, trans. Meyer Barash (Urbana: University of Illinois Press, 2001), 75.

Table 4.11: Yellow Inception vs. Supernal Emblem without *xiaoxi* on eclipses

Phen.	Date	Y.I.	S.E.	Winner	Margin
SE 1	221 Aug 05	+31	0	Supernal Emblem	31
LE 4	221 Aug 21	+72	+12	Supernal Emblem	60
SE 2	222 Jan 30	+11	−21	Yellow Inception	10
LE 5	223 Jan 05	+22	−21	Supernal Emblem	1
SE 3	223 Jan 19	−4	−7	Yellow Inception	3

NOTE: The errors for the Yellow Inception system (Y.I.), Supernal Emblem system (S.E.), and the margin of victory are given in the 10-minute fractions used throughout. The Supernal Emblem system error is given according to Han Yi's understanding of *xiaoxi*: "the Supernal Emblem's *xiaoxi* can only be subtracted, it cannot be added" (see p. 311).

Emblem system (#10). By the methodology evident in the list scores, the Supernal Emblem (with *xiaoxi*) wins the eclipse collation hands down. But how did Han Yi do against the version of the Supernal Emblem system (#10) that he (and his Office) thought he was competing against—one where only negative *xiaoxi* applies? He loses the planetary contest, but, then again, so too does Yang Wei some ten years later. The result of the eclipse contest is less evident (see Table 4.11). The score is 3:2, with the Supernal Emblem system (#10) squeaking by by a single 10-minute margin. As noted above, furthermore, the errors and implied equations of center for the first two dates are, for the Yellow Inception system (#11), so extreme as to look suspicious. Who knows what the outcome may have been had the collation selected a different brief window of events. When we look at the results in this way it seems much easier to understand the confidence with which Han Yi and Gaotang Long touted the Yellow Inception system (#11) at court, as well as how the three-year real-time trial held at the Clerk's Office had originally proved so inconclusive.

4.3.2 Legend

Second only to predictive accuracy in the Yellow Inception debate is the participants' preoccupation with historical precedent. In the nine *yi* statements comprising the debate as we have it, we see no less than four appeals to precedent—two to sagetime events and two to the events of recent history. Our calendro-astronomers on the ground, we might say, seem every bit as invested in their past as the one(s) writing their history in subsequent centuries. Above, I have discussed this preoccupation in terms of history and historiography, but I would like to transition here to "legend," reflecting upon Philip Kitcher's use of the term. This is not to place a spotlight on historicity—the stories were true enough for contemporary actors to deploy them for rhetorical purposes, and that is all that matters here—but on outlook and function.

> Once, in those dear dead days, almost, but not quite beyond recall, there was a view of science that commanded widespread popular and academic assent. That view deserves a name. I shall call it "Legend." Legend celebrated science. Depicting the sciences as directed at noble goals, it maintained that those goals have been ever more successfully realized. For explanations of the successes, we need look no further than the exemplary intellectual and moral qualities of the heroes of Legend, the great contributors to the great advances. Legend celebrated scientists, as well as science.[123]

Some of the contents of the legend of the astral sciences are clearly mythological. Echoing the compiler of the *Jin shu* "Harmonics and *Li* Treatise" and the sources surveyed in Chapter 1, Dong Ba recounts the origin and development of *li* over the Three Dynasties and the sagetimes prior (see p. 313). The sequential invention (*zuo*) of the elements of human culture by the Sages (and their ministers) is a common trope in early texts. According to the *Hanfeizi* 韓非子, for example:

> 上古之世，人民少而禽獸眾，人民不勝禽獸蟲蛇，有聖人作，搆木為巢以避群
> 害，而民悅之，使王天下，號曰有巢氏。民食果蓏蜯蛤，腥臊惡臭而傷害腹胃，
> 民多疾病，有聖人作，鑽燧取火以化腥臊，而民說之，使王天下，號之曰燧人
> 氏。中古之世，天下大水，而鯀、禹決瀆。近古之世，桀、紂暴亂，而湯、武

---

123. Philip Kitcher, *The Advancement of Science: Science Without Legend, Objectivity Without Illusions* (New York: Oxford University Press, 1993), 3.

征伐。今有構木鑽燧於夏后氏之世者，必為鯀、禹笑矣。有決瀆於殷、周之世者，必為湯、武笑矣。然則今有美堯、舜、湯、武、禹之道於當今之世者，必為新聖笑矣。是以聖人不期脩古，不法常可。

In the earliest times, when the people were few and the birds and beasts numerous, the people could not overcome the birds, beasts, insects, and snakes. Then there appeared a sage who created (*zuo*) the building up of wood to make nests so as to hide the masses from harm. The people were pleased with him and made him king of all under Heaven, calling him the "One Having Nests." The people ate fruits, berries, mussels, and clams; they were so rank, rancid, bad, and foul-smelling that they hurt their stomachs, and many of the people became sick. Then there appeared a sage who created (*zuo*) the boring of wood to get fire so as to transform the rank and rancid food. The people were pleased with him and made him king of all under Heaven, calling him the "Fire Man." In the time of middle antiquity, all under Heaven was greatly flooded, and Gun and Yu opened channels (for the water). In the most recent period of antiquity, Jie and Zhou were oppressive and chaotic, and Tang and Wu campaigned against them. Now, to have the building up of wood and the boring of wood in the time of the Xia would certainly have made Gun and Yu laugh, and to have the opening of channels in the time of the Yin and Zhou would certainly have made Tang and Wu laugh. As such, to exalt the way of Yao, Shun, Tang, Wu, and Yu in the present age would certainly make the new sages laugh. This is why sages do not try to cultivate the ancient ways and do not model themselves on constancy.[124]

In the philosophical tradition, as Michael Puett has shown, such inventories were at the center of a centuries-long debate concerning progress, legitimacy, and the relationship between

---

124. *Hanfeizi jishi* 韓非子集釋 (Zhonghua shuju ed.), 19.1040; tr. Michael Puett, "Nature and Artifice: Debates in Late Warring States China Concerning the Creation of Culture," *Harvard Journal of Asiatic Studies* 57, no. 2 (1997): 499.

man and nature.[125] In technical literature, similar inventories often preface contemporary statements, providing a genealogy of the field and/or precedence for specific practices therein.

The astral sciences have their sage-genealogies, which I have discussed in Section 1.1.2, but so too do harmonics, music, law, commerce, sacrifice, five-agents omenology, geography, water management, standards, medicine, warfare, and so on.[126] In the context of technical literature, what is at stake is not the value of innovation, per se, but the legitimacy of a tradition, in terms of the Sages' civilizing project, and the specifics of the Sages' "scientific method." The former takes on a grand soteriological tone typical of other literature on the topic: when Zhuanxu set his SYSTEM ORIGIN (*li yuan* 曆元), Dong Ba tells us, "in Heaven it is called creating seasons, on Earth it is called creating prosperity, and with man it is called making joy, and none of the birds, beasts or myriad creatures did not respond to one another" (see p. 314).[127] In contrast, the latter—method—is more specific to the particular

---

125. Ibid.

126. On "culture bearer" myths, see Anne Birrell, *Chinese Mythology: An Introduction* (Baltimore: Johns Hopkins University Press, 1993), 40–66. Like the "Harmonics and *Li* Treatise" genre, dynastic history treatises on other technical topics are frequently prefaced with the sage-origins of that field. For example, on harmonics, see *Shiji*, 25.1240–1241; on music, see *Han shu*, 22.1036–1042; on law, see *Han shu*, 23.1081–1086; on commerce, see *Han shu*, 24A.1117–1118; on sacrifice, see *Shiji*, 28.1355–1360 and *Han shu*, 25A.1190–1194; on five-agents omenology, see *Han shu*, 27A.1315–1316; on geography, see *Han shu*, 28A.1523–1524; on water management, see *Shiji*, 29.1405–1408 and *Han shu*, 29A.1675–1677; on standards, see *Shiji*, 30.1442–01443.

127. Compare this to the utopian vision of the Sages' pursuit of the "Grand Way" (*da dao* 大道) presented in the "Li yun" 禮運 chapter of the *Record of Rites*:

大道之行也，天下為公。選賢與能，講信脩睦，故人不獨親其親，不獨子其子，使老有所終，壯有所用，幼有所長，矜寡孤獨廢疾者，皆有所養。男有分，女有歸。貨惡其弃於地也，不必藏於己，力惡其不出於身也，不必為己。是故謀閉而不興，盜竊亂賊而不作，故外户而不閉，是謂大同。

When the Grand Course was pursued, a public and common spirit ruled all under the sky; they chose men of talents, virtue, and ability; their words were sincere, and what they cultivated was harmony. Thus men did not love their parents only, nor treat as children only their own sons. A competent provision was secured for the aged till their death, employment for the able-bodied, and the means of growing up to the young. They showed kindness and compassion to widows, orphans, childless men, and those who were disabled by disease, so that they were all sufficiently maintained. Males had their proper work, and females had their homes. (They accumulated) articles (of value), disliking that they should be thrown away upon the ground, but not wishing to keep them for their own gratification. (They laboured) with their strength, disliking that it should not be exerted, but not exerting it (only) with a view to their own advantage. In this way (selfish) schemings were repressed and found no development. Robbers, filchers, and rebellious traitors did not show themselves, and hence the outer doors remained open, and were not shut. This was (the period of) what we call the Grand Union (*Liji zhushu* 禮記注疏 [Siku quanshu ed.], 21.3b–4a; tr. James Legge, *Li Chi: Book of Rites. An Encyclopedia*

field: "Sages tracked the Great Yang (sun) from gnomon shadows, verified the Great Yin (moon) from quarter and full moons, elucidated the Five Stars (planets) from appearances and concealments and settled right and wrong from the first and last day of the month" (see p. 303). Be it method or results, the details of sagecraft were invariably the product of later imagination; the Sages that the calendro-astronomer strove to emulate were sages he made in his own image.

As the first major entrée into the topic, Leonid Zhmud's study of the historiography of science in Greek antiquity provides us with a helpful framework to reflect upon the Chinese case. Zhmud traces the origin of this historical genre to the inventories of *prōtoi heuretai* found in the earliest works of Greek literature—lists of "first inventors" addressing the question "who discovered what?" Like its Chinese analog, the *prōtoi heuretai* genre focused on *technē* and its benefits to mankind, attributing discoveries to gods and mythical figures. After Plato's (429/423–347 B.C.) elevation of the exact sciences to the status of *epistēmē*—knowledge-as-such—writers began to turn from the *prōtoi heuretai* model, with its emphasis on utility, to the model of doxography then prevalent in philosophy. This transition was particularly evident in the first generation of Aristotle's (384–322 B.C.) students at the Lyceum, who launched an unprecedented historiographical project "concerned exclusively with scientific discoveries, with the development of new theories and methods carried out within the framework of the professional community" (16). Zhmud notes that the products of this movement witness a marked secularization of the history of science. Driven by a sharpened interest in priority as such—part and parcel of the period's agonistic intellectual culture—works like Eudemus' (c. 370 – c. 300 B.C.) *History of Astronomy* tended to critically reassess ancient claims, shifting the priority of invention from gods to either semi-divine/heroic figures, and then men, or to Greece's ancient Near Eastern neighbors. Thus, for example, is the credit for originating astronomy transferred from Atlas and Uranus to Thales (c. 624

of Ancient Ceremonial Usages, Religious Creeds, and Social Institutions, ed. Ch'u Chai and Winberg Chai, 1885; 2nd ed. [New Hyde Park, N.Y.: University Books, 1967], 364–366).

– c. 546 B.C.), Anaximander (c. 610 – c. 546 B.C.) and, later, to the priests of Egypt and Babylon, from whom Pythagoras (c. 570 – c. 495 B.C.) and Hipparchus (c. 190 – c. 120 B.C.) were said to have learned their respective sciences.[128]

The historiography of astronomy underwent its own process of secularization in pre-modern China as well. Needless to say, the product looked somewhat different. First, astronomers by and large took for granted the Chinese origin of their science and its priority (if not superiority) over foreign traditions.[129] Second, by delimiting each to their own respective epochs, the mythical and the secular were allowed to coexist: separating sagetimes from human history is, if you will, the Fall, i.e. the centuries of political chaos ensuing from the collapse of the Western Zhou 西周 (1045–771 B.C.) and leading to political unification under the Qin and Han empires in the late third century B.C. Behind this vision of history, it should be noted, was probably the perceived gap between the ample historical records of

---

128. Zhmud, *The Origin of the History of Science in Classical Antiquity,* Peripatoi 19 (Berlin: de Gruyter, 2006); cf. Nicholas Jardine, *The Birth of History and Philosophy of Science: Kepler's A Defence of Tycho Against Ursus, with Essays on Its Provenance and Significance* (Cambridge: Cambridge University Press, 1984). On the pre-modern historiography of science in China, see John B. Henderson, "Premodern Chinese Notions of Astronomical History and Calendrical Time," in *Notions of Time in Chinese Historical Thinking,* ed. Chun-chieh Huang and John B. Henderson (Hong Kong: Chinese University Press, 2006), 97–113.

129. The topic of considerable debate in previous centuries, the question of the West or South Asian origin of Chinese astronomy has not progressed much beyond the identification of a handful of parallels between constellations and coordinate systems, the meaning of which, given the paucity of early source materials, is less than certain. For a review of this debate, see Needham, *Science and Civilisation in China, Vol.3,* 171–177; Jiang Xiaoyuan, *Tianxue zhen yuan* 天學真原, 2d ed. (Shenyang: Liaoning jiaoyu chubanshe, 2007), 227–315. As Zhmud astutely notes:

> The history of science becomes really necessary for scientists only when, for whatever reason, the scientific or, in a more general sense, the cultural tradition, which normally ensures the transmission of knowledge from generation to generation, is disrupted. It is when foreign science is being assimilated that the main question of the history of science—'who discovered what?'— arises in the process of scientific investigation itself (*The Origin of the History of Science in Classical Antiquity,* 3).

Indians and Arabs began to take over the Clerk's Office in the Tang and Yuan dynasties, respectively, but there was relatively little intercourse between traditions and Chinese contemporaries did not view them as much of a threat. It was not until the Jesuit transmission of Renaissance European astronomy that figures like Mei Wending 梅文鼎 (1633–1721) launched themselves into a historical justification for Chinese priority vis-à-vis another tradition. On Mei Wending and the "Chinese origins of Western learning" movement, see Benjamin A. Elman, *On Their Own Terms: Science in China, 1550–1900* (Cambridge: Harvard University Press, 2005), 63–189; Jiang Xiaoyuan, "Shilun Qingdai 'Xixue zhongyuan' shuo" 試論清代「西學中源」說, *Ziran kexue shi yanjiu* 7, no. 2 (1988): 101–108.

the imperial period and origin myths purporting to antedate the Fall.[130]

The history of men was, in its own right, no less legendary than that of the Sages. Chinese astronomers canonized their predecessors in a long list of *prōtoi heuretai* stretching back to sagetimes and the very origins of human civilization. Part of this process is reminiscent of the sort of positivism decried by modern historians of science like Agassi. Actors' associations with ideas, technologies, and/or systems were described in increasingly simple and formulaic terms, effacing the processes by which they were created. Discovery was often described in terms of sage-like spontaneous gnosis through interaction with the cosmos. In addition to blurring the lines between observation and invention, nature and artifice, this epistemological ideal seems to have effected certain tautologies in the recounting of history. On the one hand, implied in at least one sage-like act, discoverers tended to take on other larger-than-life qualities in later anecdotes of scientific performance, e.g. Liu Hong's (and Thales') dubious solar eclipse prediction. On the other hand, the fact of discovery itself seemed to call for a larger-than-life discoverer, resulting in something like Robert Merton's Mathew effect— "the accruing of greater increments of recognition for particular scientific contributions to scientists of considerable repute and the withholding of such recognition from scientists who have not yet made their mark."[131] Be it in the case of collaborative work or independent multiple discoveries, lead authors and established figures tend to get all the credit. Sun Qin, for example, misattributes the Grand Inception system (#7) to Grand Clerk Sima Qian rather than its no-name lead author, Deng Ping 鄧平, or its more than two dozen actual contributors.[132]

---

130. Later actors place only two events in this 550-year gap. One is Confucius' "subtle words" (*wei yan* 微言) criticism of post-Western Zhou *li* practices in his *Spring and Autumn Annals* (below). The other is the supposed line of "transmitters of Heaven's numbers" (*chuan tianshu zhe* 傳天數者) that Sima Qian places between sagetimes and the Warring states (*Shiji*, 27.1343). Of these, all that is extant is fragments of tianwen literature attributed to three of them—Wuxian 巫咸 (Shang), Shi Shen 石申 (Warring States), and Gan De 甘德 (Warring States)—in much later literature. Sun Xiaochun 孫小淳 and Jacob Kistemaker present the case that the their respective star catalog fragments were either composed or modified in the Han in *The Chinese Sky During the Han: Constellating Stars and Society* (Leiden: Brill, 1997).

131. "The Matthew Effect in Science," *Science* 159, no. 3810 (1968): 58.

132. For Sun Qin's misattribution, see p. 302. On the Grand Inception system (#7) project, see p. 62 ff.

Another part of the process of canonization was more closely linked with the early imperial state and state-centered historiographic tradition. Innovative approaches and models were duly noted, but the primary object of invention (and thus historical interest) was still the state astronomical system, what Jean-Claude Martzloff calls "les canons astronomiques officiels."[133] One of the results of this focus was the neglect of unofficial knowledge and the processes by which it fed into official knowledge, e.g. the tortuous history of the lunar equation of center prior to the Supernal Emblem system (Chapter 1). We might attribute this focus to the mission of the dynastic history vis-à-vis the astral sciences—recording for posterity how expert knowledge intersected with state interests—but there is probably more to it than just that.

The state was deeply embedded in the field's reward structure. The court provided an (ideally) impartial apparatus for testing and accreditation via the Clerk's Office, and it awarded honor and recognition via periodic competitions for system reform. Whatever the practical and political motivations behind reform may have been, the affair must have looked something like a scientific prize from the perspective of *li* experts, and a once-in-a-lifetime one at that. Historians of modern science have identified economies of credit as the driving force behind various scientific communities, detailing, for example, how credit is produced, translated into access, and reinvested into the production of more knowledge.[134] Early imperial sources are insufficient for us to map such economies, but they do suggest that credit was likewise the currency of reward in calendro-astronomy. True, winning official status for one's *li* system could result in transfer to, or promotion within, the Clerk's Office,

---

133. *Le calendrier chinois*, passim. Judging from the bibliographic treatises of the dynastic histories, there were various genres of *li* literature besides the system manual that circulated in the early imperial period, e.g. general titles like Zhen Luan's 甄鸞 (A.D. 535–536) *Li shu* 曆術 (*Li* Methods; *Jiu Tang shu*, 47.2038) and treatises dedicated to gnomonics and timekeeping. However, these neither survived nor merited the level of historical attention in transmitted *li* literature as the system manual genre.

134. See, for example, Bruno Latour and Steve Woolgar, *Laboratory Life: The Social Construction of Scientific Facts*, 2d ed. (Princeton: Princeton University Press, 1986), 187–234; Steven Shapin, *A Social History of Truth: Civility and Science in Seventeenth-century England* (Chicago: University of Chicago Press, 1994).

but for most it did not.[135] More importantly, time reveals how the credit associated with system reform tended to win actors (and their works) a hallowed place in the ancestral temple of history. This is particularly evident in the "Harmonics and *Li* Treatise" genre, which preserves official system manuals and privileges actors who directly contributed to state policy. However, it is also apparent in actors' contemporary petitions and speeches and the way that official systems tended to circulate and accumulate commentary over the centuries.[136]

The legend of the astral sciences, as mentioned earlier, was also enmeshed with the "praise and blame" model of historiography. Indeed, classicists and *li* experts alike identified the *Spring and Autumn Annals* itself—the putative origin of this model—as the first such history of science. As part of his larger mission, the *Song shu* tells us, "Confucius [edited] the Spring and Autumn Annals to elucidate the mistakes of the *li* officials" 孔子正春秋以明司曆之過.[137] In the *Zuo Tradition,* Confucius often drops the "subtle words" (*wei yan* 微言) approach to offer open historical criticism such as this:

冬十二月：螽。季孫問諸仲尼。仲尼曰：「丘聞之，火伏而後蟄者畢。今火猶西流司曆過也。」

Winter, month XII: katydids. Jisun 季孫 asked Zhongni 仲尼 (Confucius) about it. Zhongni said, "what [I], [Kong] Qiu 孔丘, have heard is that hibernation

---

135. On tangible career advancement resulting from proficiency in *li,* see Chapter 1, note 109. By and large, however, the successful petition of one's *li* system before the court did not appear to affect the expert's career trajectory, particularly for those, like Yang Wei, who held a position higher than the Prefect Grand Clerk.

136. For example, *Sui shu* "Jingji zhi" 經籍志 records a *Qianxiang li* 乾象曆 (Supernal Emblem system) by Kan Ze in 3 *juan* and, from the lost Liang 梁 (502–557) dynasty collection, a *Qianxiang li* annotated by Liu Hong et al. in 5 *juan,* a *Qianxiang li* annotated by Kan Ze in 5 *juan* an an anonymous *Qianxiang wuxing huanshu* 乾象五星幻術 (Supernal Emblem Planetary Magic) in 1 *juan* (*Sui shu,* 34.1022); to these the *Jiu Tang shu* and *Xin Tang shu* add a *Qianxiang lishu* 乾象曆術 (Supernal Emblem System Technique) by Liu Hong in 3 *juan* (*Jiu Tang shu,* 47.2037; *Xin Tang shu,* 59.1546). Also, the *Sui shu* "Jingji zhi" records a *Jingchu li* 景初曆 (Luminous Inception system) by Yang Wei in 3 *juan,* a *Jingchu renchen yuan li* 景初壬辰元曆 (Luminous Inception *Renchen*.26-origin system) by Yang Chong 楊沖 (?) in 1 *juan* and, in the lost Liang dynasty collection, a *Jingchu lifa* 景初曆法 (Luminous Inception System Method) by Yang Wei in both 3 and 5 *juan* and a *Jingchu lishu* 景初曆術 (Luminous Inception System Technique) by Yang Wei in 2 *juan* (*Sui shu,* 34.1022).

137. *Song shu,* 12.227.

354

is only over after Fire (Antares) has [set], but as of today Fire is still flowing westward [above the horizon]—this is the mistake of the *li* officials."[138]

Not surprisingly, the standards of praise and blame tend to be observational hindsight and contemporary knowledge. Earlier, we saw Gautama Siddhārtha dismiss centuries-old tian-wen planetary models as "absurd" (*miu* 謬); we also saw the author of the *Han shu* "Harmonics and *Li* Treatise" frame Zhang Shouwang's argument for reform with adverbs like "obscenely" (*wei* 猥) and "preposterously" (*wang* 妄).[139] The problem with hindsight is that it, and the historical *telos* that it entails, are constantly evolving. Participants in the Yellow Inception debate display unwavering confidence in the veracity of the Supernal Emblem system (#10)—in Xu Yue's words, it "worked out their truths in a way that was PURE and TIGHT, and I believe that it can operate for a long time to come"—and the fallacy of the Nine Roads and the "two-instrument perimeter interval" (see pp. 306, 305). Li Chunfeng, the compiler of the *Jin shu* "Harmonics and *Li* Treatise," is equally sanguine, but for him the events surrounding the Yellow Inception debate are less about veracity than the historical vindication of Liu Hong's methods vis-à-vis his contemporaries'. Compare this to Yixing's more critical summary of events several decades later:

漢會稽東部尉劉洪以四分疏闊，由斗分多。更以五百八十九為紀法，百四十五為斗分，減餘太甚，是以不及四十年而加時漸覺先天。韓翊、楊偉、劉智等皆稍損益，更造新術，而皆依讖緯「三百歲改憲」之文，考經之合朔多中，較傳之南至則否。玄始曆以為十九年七閏，皆有餘分，是以中氣漸差。據渾天，二分為東西之中，而晷景不等；二至為南北之極，而進退不齊。此古人所未達也。更因劉洪紀法，增十一年以為章歲，而減閏餘十九分之一。春秋後五十四年，歲在甲寅，直應鍾章首，與景初曆閏餘皆盡。雖減章閏，然中氣加時尚差，故未合于春秋。其斗分幾得中矣。

[Eastern] Han Chief Commandant of the Kuaiji Eastern Regiment, Liu Hong,

---

138. *Chunqiu Zuo zhuan zhushu* 春秋左傳注疏 (Siku quanshu ed.), Ai 12. See also Xiang 26, month XI.

139. For Gautama's statement, see p. 175. On Zhang Shouwang, see p. 64 and *Han shu*, 21A.978.

thought that the Quarter-remainder [system] (#9) was loose and wide because its DIPPER PARTS was too large. He replaced this with a ERA FACTOR of 589 and a DIPPER PARTS of 145, which reduced the remainder far too much, and this is why the [predicted] hour [of phenomena] (*jia shi*) were gradually perceived to [have slipped] ahead of Heaven in less than 40 years' time. Han Yi, Yang Wei, Liu Zhi 劉智, et al. all made slight adjustments [to this] and constructed (*zao*) new techniques; however, they all went by the line from the prophecy texts that "there be a change of the [Dipper] constitution (*li* reform) every three-hundred years," [so] they were mostly on the mark when examined against the classic's (*Spring and Autumn Annals*) syzygies, but not so much when compared to the traditions' [winter] solstices. In the Epochal Beginning system (#22), [Zhao Fei 趙歐] understood the 19-year : 7-intercalation [RULE] to have a fractional remainder, which [would explain why] the MEDIAL-QI gradually err. According to the Spherical Heaven (*huntian*) [theory/device], the two equinoxes are the center of east and west, and yet their gnomon shadows are unequal; the two solstices are the extremes of north and south, and yet their ADVANCE/RETREAT (reduction to the equator) is uneven. *This is something that the ancients did not yet understand.*[140]

The human history of calendro-astronomy, as recounted by early imperial actors, had all the features of legend: it canonized human creators in a glorified line of *prōtoi heuretai* stretching back to prehistory, conjoining myth and human events; it subsumed the lives and work of individuals to the history of empires; and it was continuously rewritten from the evolving perspective of current knowledge. Again, I emphasize this point not to draw a distinction with early historiography—for the same things could be said of it—but to point to experts' historical vision as a rich repository of their values and notions of identity. Before moving to the next section, therefore, let us reopen the divide and note where the

---

140. *Xin Tang shu*, 27A.593.

substance of myth and legend diverge. Unlike sages, human creators are only seriously judged by the standard of predictive accuracy, be it relative or absolute, *not* their ability to return society to a paradise wherein "none of the birds, beasts or myriad creatures did not respond to one another" (p. 314). Furthermore, whatever distortion historical events and personalities may have undergone, early imperial histories of *li* paid meticulous attention to authorship, credit, and even the contents of obsolete knowledge. Unlike the Mediterranean world, where Ptolemy's (c. 90 – c. 168) *Almagest* seems to have swept away its predecessors, Chinese calendro-astronomers continued to read, annotate, transmit, and compare historical contributions to the field.

Progress and the function of legend

If we are to discuss the function of the legend vis-à-vis the practice of *li* in early imperial China, we cannot overemphasize the rationale at this legend's core: that the (human) history of *li* is a history of progress driven by empirical inquiry. Of course, as I have emphasized throughout, we should expect ancient concepts of scientific progress to differ from our own. In addition to the relative limitations of scope, for example, Zhmud notes that in the exact sciences of ancient Greece, "the more striking the progress that had already been made, the more natural it seemed to believe that the efforts of contemporaries, including their own, would soon reach a perfection not, or unlikely, to be surpassed in the future."[141] The same might be said of Chinese *li* literature, which, more often than not, expresses exuberant confidence in current knowledge. As I have already commented upon in Section 1.4, it is impossible to know whether the sort of triumphalism expressed by actors like Xu Yue or Sun Qin is *genuine*, especially when we see it coupled with pessimism directed at others. That said, one wonders if, like Eudemus, Li Chunfeng and Yixing might not have seen themselves as perched near the apex of human knowledge.

If so, why look back? In the Greek case, Zhmud offers three reasons: for traditions to

---

141. *The Origin of the History of Science in Classical Antiquity*, 79.

settle "who discovered what?" upon interruption or the assimilation of foreign traditions; to determine fruitful avenues of future research; and to establish the antiquity of a science.[142] None of these are out of place in the Chinese context, though one might want to reverse their order. Another reason may have been to address, in John Henderson's words, the "disquieting historical possibility" of human progress beyond sage-knowledge, since "astronomy was one of the few fields of knowledge in pre-modern China in which progress was so evident as to override the more deeply ingrained regressive and cyclical models of time.[143] On the pragmatic side, we might also attribute actors' penchant for historical precedence to the latter's rhetorical effectiveness in the context of, according to Sivin and Lloyd's characterization, a classicist intellectual culture stressing deference to authority.[144] Instead of beginning here, however, let us proceed from the uses of legend evident in the *Jin shu* and the arguments of its historical subjects.

Above all, actors set up the sages and great men of the past as exemplars for contemporary practice. Li Chunfeng, like most writers in the genre, begins with an account of how the Sages founded the institutions of *li* and then handed their operation over to capable ministers.[145] Not stopping at that, Dong Ba goes on to describe how they also founded the core empirical method of the field, being the first to observe gnomon shadows, track lunar phases, record planetary visibility phenomena, and, most importantly, subject their knowledge to testing (see p. 303). Likewise, Xu Yue acclaims the latter-day *prōtos heuretēs*, Liu Hong, for his use of eclipses to assess lunisolar models (see p. 306). Of course, Sun Qin reminds us that legends are not forged out of sound methods and good ideas alone but triumphs of will that push the field ever forward and ever closer to "the order that between Heaven and Earth

---

142. *The Origin of the History of Science in Classical Antiquity*, 1–10, passim.

143. "Premodern Chinese Notions of Astronomical History and Calendrical Time," 100–101. Of course, as Puett shows, the early Chinese concept of historical progress was by no means limited to calendro-astronomy, see his "Humans, Spirits, and Sages in Chinese Late Antiquity: Ge Hong's 葛洪 *Master Who Embraces Simplicity (Baopuzi)* 抱朴子," *Extrême-Orient, Extrême-Occident* 29, no. 29 (2007): 95–119.

144. *The Way and the Word*, esp. 42–79.

145. *Jin shu*, 17.497–498. Li's historical precis is too long to translate here, but it reads much the same as those surveyed in Section 1.1.2.

exists" (see p. 303). Finally, like the Sage Kings before him, it is the wise emperor that accommodates and fosters this progress.

On a superficial level, we might liken the function of such lore to Thomas Kuhn's discussion of "exemplars" in the 1969 postscript to *Structure*:

> Because the term ("paradigm") has assumed a life of its own, however, I shall here substitute "exemplars." By it I mean, initially, the concrete problem-solutions that students encounter from the start of their scientific education, whether in laboratories, on examinations, or at the ends of chapters in science texts. To these shared examples should, however, be added at least some of the technical problem-solutions found in the periodical literature that scientists encounter during their post-educational research careers and that also show them by example how their job is to be done. More than other sorts of components of the disciplinary matrix, differences between sets of exemplars provide the community fine-structure of science.[146]

The difference is that exemplars, as we see them deployed in transmitted *li* literature, tend to blur the lines between technical and institutional matters, and problem-solutions are rarely described in significant detail—empiricism, vaguely defined, is always the solution.

How this repertoire of shared examples apply to any given case is, of course, a problem of perspective. The participants in the Yellow Inception debate are divided on one fundamental issue: some hold that the Supernal Emblem system (#10) can be improved upon (Han Yi, Gaotang Long and Xu Zhi), while others are, to varying degrees, indignant at the thought (Sun Qin, Xu Yue, and Yang Wei). Both sides deploy shared examples to make their case, couching current affairs in the language of legend. From this perspective, the debate unfolds like this:

1. Xu Zhi: the Supernal Emblem system (#10) is more than one double-hour in error.

---

146. *The Structure of Scientific Revolutions*, 3d ed. (Chicago: University of Chicago Press, 1996), 187.

2. Sun Qin: in the Han, Sima Qian, Liu Xin, and Liu Hong addressed such problems through reform (*gai* 改), but, [whatever the precedent for reform], Liu Hong has already proven himself insuperable.

3. Dong Ba: the Sages settled such matters through empirical testing.

4. Xu Yue: Liu Hong devoted himself to *decades* of empirical testing, solved an intractable problem, and proved himself by spectacle before the entire world. Also, [my] tests show that Han Yi quantitatively underperforms him.

5. Han Yi: you have his numbers wrong.

6. Xu Yue: I studied with him, I should know.

7. Li En: [anyways], the state Quarter-remainder system (#9) is off by more than *six* double-hours.

8. Dong Ba: the Sages brought about cosmo-social harmony by changing the first month of the civil calendar, [and so too should we].

9. Yang Wei: there are methods for getting around the need for prolonged testing, but if you go about things the wrong way, as Mencius warns us, you can produce any result you want. The fact that Han Yi bases himself upon [but underperforms] Liu Hong's work implicates him in either treachery or idiocy.

Philosophically, the difference seems to come down to the sanctity of *knowledge* over *method*—method that leads to the production of ever newer knowledge—and vice versa. Either way, there is no "ambivalence of creation" here—at least not of the sort that gripped the imagination of philosophers in the preceding centuries.[147] Human calendro-astronomers were expected to *zuo*, *zao*, and *gai* their way into ever better techniques, the question is whether Han Yi was up to the task.

---

147. Michael Puett, *The Ambivalence of Creation: Debates Concerning Innovation and Artifice in Early China* (Stanford: Stanford University Press, 2001).

In as much as individuals (and institutions) shared consensus practices and values, legend—the repository of exemplars—bound them into a community across office, station, and space. It also bound them into a community across time. As we have witnessed throughout, the astral sciences were a profoundly retrospective affair: predictive models relied upon centuries of observational data; current issues were debated in terms of past examples; and obsolete knowledge was preserved and studied into posterity. Most importantly, actors formed their own identities out of the stuff of legend, emulating Liu Hong, the "exemplar" (*shibiao* 師表), and cultivating Ban Gu's "six virtues of the Sages" (see p. 53). Actors' ties to their (imagined) past are clear, but what about their ties to the future?

It was certainly one of their virtues, as Ban Gu suggests, that the calendro-astronomer "know the future" (*zhi lai* 知來), be it of celestial or human events. However, actors also express anxiety concerning the future of the field as such. With regard to the Supernal Emblem system (#10), Han Yi is concerned that "in time it would slip ahead of Heaven" (though Xu Yue believes that "it can operate for a long time to come"), and Yang Wei worries that "Hong's marvelous model cease to transmit to future ages" (see pp. 279, 306, 316). History shows that these anxieties were well founded. The 710-year period covered in Table 2 (p. 20 ff.) shows actors producing new *li* systems at a rate of at least one every 13 years, and none that were denied official status managed to pass the test of time. This brings us to one final conclusion: in a field operating on a credit economy, and with a long view of history, actors may have been motivated to innovate for the sake of securing *themselves* a place in that history as it would continue to unravel into the future.

4.4   Conclusion

In this case study, I have attempted to build upon the work of scholars like Christopher Cullen and Hasebe Eiichi on early *li* debates to add to the sociological and epistemological picture laid out in Chapter 1. The Cao-Wei Yellow Inception debate not only presents a unique perspective on the Han, and the continuity of technical traditions through its collapse, it has a number of features that stand out from Han-era records: it is a debate *between* experts, one party of which actually hails from the Clerk's Office, and it is one of the most detailed records of a failed reform project. Most importantly, like the *Wuxing zhan*, the *Jin shu* "Harmonics and *Li* Treatise" leaves us with data that are products of mathematical astronomy. As products of practice, these data allow us to reflect upon further incongruities between actual practices and the normative accounts of *li* manual literature: they reveal evidence of concepts that had not yet found their way into state *li* manuals, e.g. the system of 24 stem-branch hours and a model for solar inequality; they show the use of something similar to the hour angle, further affirming the commutability of time and space in our "calendrical sciences"; and they provide additional evidence about the accuracy of early eclipse observation. What is more, these data are the products of another practice about which we know considerably less—competitive astronomical testing. As important as we know this practice to have been in shaping the history of astronomy in pre-modern China, the *Jin shu* presents us with the first extant example of test results, which allow us to examine the assumptions, strategies, and limitations of their methods. In addition, these test results evidence the use of eclipses as mundane data points devoid of omenological meaning, and reaffirm the (oft-questioned) importance of planetary astronomy in the politics of system reform.

As important as it is to reconstruct historical details as such, this chapter has attempted to go one step further and explore how early imperial astronomers constructed their own histories—both the "Harmonics and *Li* Treatise" itself and the histories that its subjects recount of their own. The field's vision of its history, I argue, is remarkable for its consistency across time and space as well as its insulation from more familiar forms of Chinese historiography (and their political and ethical bent). This history, I have attempted to show, was an extension of the sage-inventor mythos, to which historical figures are sequentially strung after having been canonized in sage-like terms. A product of their own creation, this history—this *legend*—was a repository of values and exemplars from which actors drew to contextualize and negotiate current issues. Finally, this history—and the potential to contribute to it—seems to have had an important place in the reward structure of their science, ensuring that worthy men receive "scientific ancestor-worship."

At the center of the legend of *li* calendro-astronomy lie the two themes addressed in this study: empiricism and progress. The Sages laid the playing field, establishing the necessary institutions and methods, but it took generations of men working within those structures to achieve the knowledge of today. True, the act of innovation could be considered impious, but only when performed ineffectively or deceitfully. Looking back on their history, as they were so wont to do, we can see astronomers vying to leave names for themselves with the discovery of "something that the ancients did not yet understand."

CONCLUSION

In Chapter 3, the reader was introduced to the ceremony of "sighting the new moon" (*shi shuo* 視朔) as it appears in the classics and the early imperial discourse on state ritual purportedly derived therefrom. As we will remember, the *Zuo Tradition* of the *Spring and Autumn Annals* offers the following description:

五年，春，王正月，辛亥朔，日南至，公既視朔，遂登觀臺以望，而書，禮也。凡分，至，啟，閉，必書雲物，為備故也。

Year 5, spring, royal month I, [day] *xinhai.*$_{48}$, new moon, the sun reached its southern limit (winter solstice): upon sighting the new moon, the duke ascended the observation terrace to look upon it and write it down—this is what is ritually appropriate. At every equinox, solstice, opening (Enthronement of Spring.$_{Q01}$ & Enthronement of Summer.$_{Q07}$), and closing (Enthronement of Autumn.$_{Q31}$ & Enthronement of Winter.$_{Q19}$), one must take note of clouds and (prodigious) things for the sake of preparedness (Xi 5 [655 B.C.]).[1]

A nexus through which we may descry the interconnectedness of all things, this remembered rite (and the ritual science that later scholars constructed around it) is a felicitous microcosm of the themes at the core of this study. Sighting typifies the degree to which the astral sciences were embedded in the sciences of ceremony and statecraft. This was particularly in so theory: the avowed purpose of *li* 曆 "calendro-astronomy" was to maintain an (astronomically) empirical calendar that would ensure a mutually-sustaining harmony between nature and society; working from the opposite direction, that of *tianwen* 天文 "celestial patterns" omenology was to decode the book of nature for clues concerning the throne's success or

---

1. *Chunqiu Zuo zhuan zhushu* 春秋左傳注疏 (Siku quanshu 四庫全書 ed.), 11.27a–b.

failure in this regard. Sighting, as ritual is want to do, collapsed time and space. It was at once a localized emanation of royal authority modeled upon and synchronized to the ceremonies of the capital and a reenactment of the *wen* 文 "cultural patterns" upheld by the long line of dukes that had come before (as well as, perhaps more importantly, the very cosmogonic gestures by which the sage kings had brought the civilized world into being). It is a testament to the dependence of technical knowledge on writing—both the explicit need for data-collection via inscription and the implicit guidance of observation via calendar or *shuo-run* 朔閏 table—as much as it is of its dependence on performance and spectacle. It is, furthermore, an example of the convergence *in practice* that we might expect between discrete genres of written knowledge—*li* and *tianwen*. But most important of all is that it is *illusory*, a reminder of the vast gulf that often exists between classical precedent—theory— and later practice, for as ritual scholars like Pilü Renxu 辟閭仁諝 (fl. A.D. 698) sometimes jarringly admit of such rites, "nowadays, I have never heard of a king performing it" 今王者 行之, 非所聞也.[2]

That said, this classical rite is more than an illusion—an element of the "imagined orthodoxy" towards which G. E. R. Lloyd and Nathan Sivin identify our natural philosophers as aspiring—it is a *paradox*.[3] The term *shuo* 朔 "new moon" refers unambiguously to the moment of syzygy, when earth, moon, and sun fall in a straight-line configuration on the plane—in actors' own astronomical terms, "the sun and moon exist in flux, the sun languid and the moon rapid; when they are co-located it is called 'conjunction-new moon' " 日月相 推, 日舒月速, 當其同所, 謂之合朔.[4] To be specific, alignment or "co-location" occurs on the plane of one of the imaginary great circles that we project onto the sky—the equator or the ecliptic—when the moon, now totally dark to us on Earth, ensconces itself well

---

2. *Jiu Tang shu* 舊唐書 (Zhonghua shuju 中華書局 ed.), 22.868–869. On Pilü Renxu's *yi* 議 opinion, see Section 3.3.2.

3. *The Way and the Word: Science and Medicine in Early China and Greece* (New Haven: Yale University Press, 2002), 44.

4. *Hou Han shu* 後漢書 (Zhonghua shuju ed.), *zhi* 3, 3055.

within the fiery skirt tails of the sun. *Shuo* is, in other words, a theoretical construct, an unobservable. How then is our duke to go about observing the unobservable? Failing some spontaneous gnosis instilled by sagacious bloodline or *dao* 道, he must do so indirectly via, if you will, falsification—sighting a visible crescent on the (calendar-appointed) day of new moon—or induction—extrapolating the halfway point between last and first crescent or, in the rare case of an eclipse, that between first and last contact. Whatever his certitude in the calendar—in *li*—he is on ground little surer than Mencius (c. 372–289 B.C.) when the latter declared that "whatever the heights of the heavens and the distance of the stars, if one seeks out former instances, one can calculate the solstices of a thousand years hence without stirring from one's seat" 天之高也，星辰之遠也，苟求其故，千歲之日至，可坐而致也 (*Mencius* IVB.26; see Introduction).

Unobservables are part and parcel of the scientific endeavor, or, we may say of pre-modern times, man's quest to master the workings of Heaven. Philosophers of science go back and forth on the accessibility of such entities and, for example, distinctions of "seeing," "seeing as," and "seeing that"—our Duke of Lu, Norwood R. Hanson would say, is not *seeing* the new moon but *seeing that it is* the new moon—for the good reason that history so often uproots the ontologies that constitute our world.[5] As it was with phlogiston so too may it have been with *shuo*, for the nature of lunar phenomena was as yet unsettled conjecture in the early

---

5. For Hanson's treatment of "seeing" and the theory-ladenness and language-embeddedness of observation, see his *Patterns of Discovery: An Inquiry into the Conceptual Foundations of Science* (Cambridge: Cambridge University Press, 1965), esp. 4–30. In a nutshell, Hanson's point is this:

> The gap between pictures and language locates the logical function of 'seeing that'. For vision is essentially pictorial, knowledge fundamentally linguistic. Both vision and knowledge are indispensable elements in seeing; but differences between pictorial and linguistic representation may mark differences between the optical and conceptual features of seeing. ... There is a 'linguistic' factor in seeing, although there is nothing linguistic about what forms in the eye, or in the mind's eye. Unless there were this linguistic element, nothing we ever observed could have relevance for our knowledge. We could not speak of significant observations: nothing seen would make sense, and microscopy would only be a kind of kaleidoscopy. For what is it for things to make sense other than for descriptions of them to be composed of meaningful sentences? (ibid., 25).

imperial period.[6] Some, like Zhang Heng 張衡 (A.D. 87–140), held that celestial bodies are spherical—"the three luminaries are the same shape, one akin to pearl-jades (marbles)" 夫三光同形，有似珠玉 —and that "moonlight is engendered by sun shines, and moondark, by its obstruction" 月光生於日之所照，魄生於日之所蔽.[7] Others, like Wang Chong's 王充 (A.D. 27 – c. 100), insisted that "the sun and moon are not round but only appear so at a distance" 夫日月不圓，視若圓者，去人遠也, and that, manifestations as they were of yin & yang, phenomena such as eclipses occurred due to "spontaneous diminishment of light" 光自損.[8] The safest gambit—that, indeed, which is played throughout extant *li* literature—is to content oneself with an instrumentalist approach: to hone models to effectively predict observable phenomena regardless of their underlying cause or ontology. What lends credence to our adoption here of a realist approach, however, is the mutability of the boundaries that we draw between observables and unobservables. Having begun in the last century to send eyes up into the heavens to see the moon both up close and in all its aspects, we can now speak with unwavering certainty about what occurs at *shuo*. Ian Hacking introduced the

---

6. In the history and philosophy of science, phlogiston is the go-to example for debating the ontology of unobservable theoretical entities. Phlogiston was a substance that eighteenth-century chemists posited to be a substance contained in inflammable substances that was released into the air upon combustion and identified with the effects of what we would now call oxidation. Joseph Priestley (1733–1804) famously claimed to have produced *dephlogosticated air* by heating the red calx of mercury to draw the phlogiston out of the surrounding air; later, however, Antoine Lavoisier's (1743–1794) experiments successfully reframed the process in terms of oxygen, which combustion and oxidation were *drawing from* rather than *releasing into* the air. In short, phlogiston was a theoretical entity that "fails to refer"—that is, that was shown not to correspond with something existing in reality. On the phlogiston debate, see James Bryant Conant, *The Overthrow of the Phlogiston Theory; the Chemical Revolution of 1775–1789*, Harvard Case Histories in Experimental Science 2 (Cambridge: Harvard University Press, 1950); Thomas S. Kuhn, *The Structure of Scientific Revolutions*, 3d ed. (Chicago: University of Chicago Press, 1996), passim; Maria Caamaño, "A Structural Analysis of the Phlogiston Case," *Erkenntnis* 70, no. 3 (2009): 331–364.

7. *Ling xian* 靈憲, cited in *Kaiyuan zhanjing* 開元占經 (Siku quanshu ed.), 1.3b, 1.4b. Note that the *Ling xian*'s classic explanation of lunar phenomena follows those of Jing Fang 京房 (77–37 B.C.)—"the moon and stars are the epitome of yin; they have shape but no luminescence, they have luminescence only when shined upon by the sun" 月與星至陰也，有形無光，日照之乃有光 (*Yi shuo* 易説, cited in *Taiping yulan* 太平御覽 [Siku quanshu ed.], 4.16b)—and the *Zhoubi suanjing* 周髀算經 —"thus, moonlight only emerges when the sun shines upon the moon, and thus do we have 'the luminous moon' " 故日兆月，月光乃出，故成明月 (*Zhoubi suanjing* [Zhonghua shuju ed.], B1.54–55).

8. *Lunheng jiaoshi* 論衡校釋 (Zhonghua shuju ed.), 11.507, 11.505. On Zhang Heng and Wang Chong's respective cosmologies, see Christopher Cullen, "Cosmographical Discussions in China from Early Times up the T'ang Dynasty" (Ph.D. diss., University of London, 1977), 165–205.

criterion "if you can spray them, then they are real"; "how much more so," we might ask, "if you can land men and machines upon them?"[9]

As historians of science in the ancient world, we too labor to circumscribe and reveal unobservables. One sense in which we go about this is by stepping out of the perspective of transmitted historical sources—in this case, the hegemonic perspective of policy, statecraft, and classical learning. Dynastic histories, omen compendia, and philosophical treatises too often present the history of astronomy in China as a unilinear succession of policy reforms driven by emperors, great men, and eureka moments. It is a vision of history that is sadly reducible to a table of names, dynasties, dates, and mean values.[10] Modern scholarship that would perpetuate this (pre-modern) mode of historiography is, we all agree, insipid; for we are no longer content with counting milestones if it means losing sight of the full spectrum of agency entailed in and indeed the very *contents* of, to borrow Latour's term, "science in action."[11] This is admittedly something of a straw man. The last half century has seen a wealth of scholarship willing to work against the grain, so to speak, to flesh out the political history of astronomy in China with details of agency, society, setting, institutional apparatus, epistemological contentions, and the interconnection of astral, political, and ritual sciences—context that, modern and pre-modern alike, outmoded historians of science often act to efface. The meticulous scholarship of Yabuuti Kiyosi 藪內清, Ōhashi Yukio 大橋 由紀夫, Chen Meidong 陳美東, Christopher Cullen, Hasebe Eiichi 長谷部英一, Nathan

---

9. *Representing and Intervening: Introductory Topics in the Philosophy of Natural Science* (Cambridge: Cambridge University Press, 1983), 22–24. Hacking, in this now famous phrase, is referring to an experiment to detect fractional charges indicative of quarks by spraying matter with positrons and electrons—things that were once themselves theoretical entities but are now so well within our grasp as to provide reliable means to get at new theoretical entities. For the realist approach to the perceptual accessibility and ontological certainty of unobservables, see Grover Maxwell, "The Ontological Status of Theoretical Entities," in *Scientific Explanation, Space, and Time*, ed. Herbert Feigl and Grover Maxwell, Minnesota Studies in the Philosophy of Science, v. 3 (Minneapolis: University of Minnesota Press, 1962), 3–15; Philip Kitcher, "Real Realism: The Galilean Strategy," *Philosophical Review* 110, no. 2 (2001): 151–197. My approach is explained briefly in Section 1.4.

10. For examples of such tables, see p. 225, n. 50 and, of course, my own Table 2 on p. 20 ff.

11. Bruno Latour, *Science in Action: How to Follow Scientists and Engineers through Society* (Cambridge: Harvard University Press, 1987).

Sivin, and the many others to whom this study is deeply indebted have come a long way in reconstructing from available sources a political history of astronomy in China that is at once more believably and satisfyingly human.

Needless to say, the first step is the careful reading of primary sources. Even when recounted as a sequence of policy reforms, experts' accounts of the history of their own science reveal a complexity of circumstances reducible to neither timeline nor table (the compilation of Table 2, I must admit, stood out from the rest of this project as a particularly time-consuming misadventure). Take for instance this brief synopsis of Han-era astronomical policy provided in the *Hou Han shu* 後漢書 (A.D. 445):

昔太初曆之興也，發謀於元封，啟定於【元】鳳，積（百）三十年，是非乃審。及用四分，亦【始】於建武，施於元和，訖於永元，七十餘年，然后儀式備立，司候有準。天事幽微，若此其難也。中興以來，圖讖漏泄，而『考靈曜』、『命曆序』皆有甲寅元。其所起在四分庚申元後百一十四歲，朔差却二日。學士修之於草澤，信向以為得正。及太初曆以後【天】為疾，而修之者云「百四十四歲而太歲超一【辰】，百七十一歲當棄朔餘六十三，中餘千一百九十七，乃可常行」。自太初元年至永平十一年，百七十一，當去分而不去，故令益有疏闊。此二家常挾其術，庶幾施行，每有訟者，百寮會議，羣儒騁思，論之有方，益於多聞識之，故詳錄焉。

As to the rise of the Grand Inception system (#7) way back when, it was dreamt up in Epochal Enfeoffment (110–105 B.C.) and first settled [only] in Epochal Phoenix (80–75 B.C.)—it was only after thirty years that its veracity (*shifei* 是非) was finally tried. Now, the Quarter-remainder [system] (#9) was, for its part, [dreamt up] in Establishment of Militarism (A.D. 25–56) and implemented [decades later] in Epochal Harmony (A.D. 84–87), and it was not until Perpetual Epoch (A.D. 89–105)—some seventy years later—that the [Clerk's Office] was fully provided with instrument model(s) and that the directors of observation possessed a standard. Celestial matters are recondite and subtle and are plagued

369

with difficulties such as these. Since the resurgence [of the Han], diagrams and prophecies have been revealed, and the *Kaolingyao* 考靈曜 and *Minglixu* 命曆序 both posit a *jiayin.*51 ORIGIN. Their start point falls 114 years after the Quarter-remainder's *gengshen.*57 ORIGIN, and syzygy is off by two days. Scholars studied this in the backwaters, laboring under the belief that it was correct. Now, as to the Grand Inception system's lag behind Heaven, its students said, "Taisui exceeds one chronogram every 144 years, so every 171 years we should drop 63 [parts] from the NEW MOON REMAINDER and 1197 from the MEDIAL-QI REMAINDER—then it can function perpetually (*chang* 常)." From Grand Inception 1 (104 B.C.) to Perpetual Tranquility 11 (A.D. 68) is 171 [years], but the parts have not been dropped as they should be, which thus exacerbates [the Grand Inception system's] LOOSENESS and WIDENESS (inaccuracy). These two schools (*Jiayin.*51-origin and Grand Inception system) often jerry-rig their methods in the hope that they may see implementation. And every time there is a dispute, the Hundred Officials convene an *yi* 議 debate, and, in a stampede of ideas, the herd of *Ru*-scholars discuss the matter methodically, contributing their erudition to the understanding of it. Thus do we record it in detail here.[12]

What progression is this? Where are we to erect our milestones? To whom should we to attribute them—to patrons of policy, to nature, to the quorum, to the inventors, to the technicians charged with their renewal and upkeep, or to the outside forces clamoring for their periodic reassessment? And how are we to understand the criteria by which such accounts assess and rank the quality of astronomical systems?

The answer is that there is no good answer. Astronomical systems succeeded one another in state service, but they did so in an openly agonistic environment, coexisting, adapting, and, more often than not, capitulating to outside knowledge. To erect milestones at the point of institution—in this case, 104 B.C. and A.D. 85—is to collapse the motley lifespan of a policy

---

12. *Hou Han shu, zhi* 2, 3033.

into a single point when it is so often their trials and evolutions that impress themselves on the historical imagination, e.g. Liu Xin's 劉歆 (c. 50 B.C. – A.D. 23) development of the Grand Inception system (#7) or the solar table incorporated into the Quarter-remainder system (#9) in A.D. 173. In Chapter 4 (pp. 302, 352), I call out Sun Qin 孫欽 (fl. A.D. 226) for misattributing the Grand Inception system (#7) to Sima Qian 司馬遷 (145/135–86 B.C.), but how fair is my own blithe attribution of it to "Deng Ping 鄧平" in Table 2? True, the *Han shu* 漢書 names Deng as its lead author, but "an idea, even an idea of genius, even an idea that is to save millions of people, never moves of its own accord. It requires a force to fetch it, seize upon it for its own motives, move it, and often transform it."[13] If we are to be fair, then, we must acknowledge the whole cast of actors: the 20+ technicians working under him; then Prefect Grand Clerk, Sima Qian, who had a hand in implementation and the initial and final stages of policy review; Han Wudi 漢武帝 (r. 140–87 B.C.), who for his own reasons set the ball rolling; Xianyu Wangren 鮮于妄人 and the 20+ people under him who ran the tests of 78–74 B.C. to determine stellar positions and the accuracy of the Grand Inception system's (#7) lunisolar elements; Zhang Shouwang 張壽王, the incompetent Prefect Grand Clerk who called it into question; the 17 and 11 experts (*jia* 家) against which it faced off in its respective trials; Liu Xin, of course, who modified it into the Triple Concordance system (#8); Wang Mang 王莽 (c. 45 B.C. – A.D. 23) and his clan, who provided the ideological setting for Liu Xin's work; subsequent enthusiasts who continued to modify it well into the Han; astronomers and historians of astronomy who actively determined its place in history; and, let us not forget, the peaceful empire of consumers who copied, passed on, and made daily use of its products. But let us neither limit ourselves to human actors, for were it not for the (observed) behavior of the sun and moon the Grand Inception system (#7) would not have stood out from its competition and secured its place in history. Lastly, it is nowhere explained why actors consistently preferred the institution of new methods over

---

13. Bruno Latour, *The Pasteurization of France*, trans. Alan Sheridan and John Law (Cambridge: Harvard University Press, 1988).

"jerry-rigging" (*xie* 挾) old ones, though the two may produce comparable results.[14]

This is only the beginning, of course, because underneath, within, alongside, and, more importantly, *prior to* astronomical policy lies astronomical practice. Policy, in the end, is but a catalyst for the rare irruption of technical practice into politics and the quotidian. As much as the well-meaning among us may wish to place practice at the forefront of our histories of astronomy, like the instant of syzygy, practice is observable to us only infrequently, indirectly, and indistinctly. It is safe to say that we know frighteningly little about it. We have texts—and how!—some of which prescribe it, some of which describe it, and some of which were even tools and products thereof, but no combination of texts amounts to a *performance*—to the concomitance of textual, verbal, and unverbalized "patterns of doing things and of organizing men to practical ends" or, in Wittgenstein's terms, "forms of life."[15] Most of what we know we must extract from *li* manuals preserved in the dynastic histories. The pitfall of manuals, as I hope to have convinced the reader via the Supernal Emblem system (#10), is that they offer us no guarantee as to textual integrity, technical currency, or the fidelity of real-world practice to their instructions, nor do they give us any great insight into the sometimes decades of observation and experimentation—the "scientific process"—of which they are the final product. From literary and historical accounts, we are also able to tease out clues about actors' education, career paths, textual production and transmission, instrumentation, and experimental/testing culture. These provide an invaluable counterpoint to the raw *shu* 數 "numbers" and *shu* 術 "techniques" of manual literature, but they are, more often than not, spotty and frustratingly vague—a consequence, one suspects, of the intended audience of extant works, namely the deciders of state policy and the readers of state history. Time and again we see matters handed off to the Clerk's Office for competitive testing, for example,

---

14. The period covered in this synopsis is narrated at greater length in Section 1.2. See also Christopher Cullen, "Motivations for Scientific Change in Ancient China: Emperor Wu and the Grand Inception Astronomical Reforms of 104 BC," *Journal for the History of Astronomy* 24, no. 3 (1991): 185–203.

15. Here I am cite Steven Shapin and Simon Schaffer's adaptation of Wittgenstein's "forms of life" to the end of explaining experimental culture in *Leviathan and the Air-pump: Hobbes, Boyle, and the Experimental Life* (Princeton: Princeton University Press, 1985), 15.

but are told next to nothing about the actual procedure in which actors all around seem to universally bank their trust.

What method, what apparatus, may we deploy to lay bare and vulnerable our historical unobservables as if bacilli under a microscope? One is data analysis, specifically the analysis of *products of practice* (tables) against that which manual literature explicitly instructs the user to produce. This is a dry and laborious ordeal, but it is one that is well worth it, for numbers speak with a satisfying certainty that is preciously rare for the historian of the ancient world, and, to continue the metaphor, one frequently finds oneself staring out onto a crescent moon on new moon day. In Chapter 2, we analyzed the planetary tables of the second-century B.C. silk manuscript *Wuxing zhan* 五星占 from Mawangdui 馬王堆 tomb 3, showing how their compiler had cobbled together incommensurable genres of planetary model, plotting visibility phenomena upon a solar time frame distinct from the lunisolar one assumed, without exception, to frame civil and technical culture alike. We also followed the course of mathematical and omenological planetary models as they diverged and reconverged over a thousand-year span, examining the the pressures that advances in the former exerted upon the more conservative theories of the latter and the concomitant waning of particular forms of omenological practice in the court record. In Chapter 3, we assayed a variety of early imperial calendars to probe their overlap with the science nominally and ideologically devoted thereto, *li* "calendro-astronomy." Fanning the two circles of the Venn diagram apart, our analysis attempted to show just how little of the latter went into the former and narrate the life of its own that "the calendar" took on once out of the hands of the Clerk's Office. Then, in Chapter 4, we analyzed a set of competitive test results introduced into the Yellow Inception debate of circa A.D. 226 to assess how assessment was performed. The results not only reveal evidence for practices thought to have entered circulation at a later date—24-hour timekeeping and solar equation of center—they provide an invaluable window into the focus, scope, certainty, and methods of accounting that may have governed this otherwise opaque process.

Our second entrée, inseparable as it is from the first in this case, is to read transmitted and excavated testimony in dialogue—a platitude that we in sinology often attribute to Wang Guowei 王國維 and his "dual evidence method" 二重證據法.[16] Much as we began in the last century to set out into the heavens in exploration of the boundless Empyrean above us, so too have we begun in earnest to trowel through the earth, exploring the chthonic realm of caves and tombs, wells and dumps, for remnants of the boundless past before us. The wealth of materials thus far uncovered, and which continues to grow every day, affords us a vantage no less precious than a portal looking down upon the earth (or askance at a moon entering syzygy), for it is not simply that they are numerous and new but that they objectify a, to us, radical perspective. They are *realia*—actual tangible and imperfect actants in the scientific and quotidian lives of our historical subjects—and they are, for the most part, unfiltered and unadulterated by considerations of posterity. The *Wuxing zhan* in Chapter 2, for example, provides clues about a culture of connoisseurship for specialist knowledge hinted at in transmitted texts and the potential mutability of genre and corruptibility of text inherent to the transmission of knowledge via manuscript therein. In other words, it gives us a sense of the concrete material and textual form in which astral knowledge may have circulated in those days, the real-world uses to which it may have been put, and the potential complexity of any one text's history. Calendars in Chapter 3, moreover, allow us to reflect upon the selfsame issues but from the opposite end of the spectrum of expertise, calendars being the workaday medium through which *li* (and the throne's putative mastery thereof) insinuated itself into the lives of the citizenry.

This, as I see it, is but half of the problem, and the obvious half at that. Infinitely more vexing than unobservables that, like the instant of *shuo*, fall outside the reach of our unaided senses are those that lie hiding in plain sight. Woven brazenly throughout the fabric of our sources are coherent ontologies and ideas that simply no longer register with

---

16. See his "Zuijin er sanshi nian zhong Zhongguo xin fajian zhi xuewen" 最近二三十年中中國新發見之學問, *Xue heng* 學衡 45 (1925): 1–13.

us. And why should we expect otherwise? We historians of science, like our early imperial predecessors, are not conduits of unmediated fact, it is just that we bring a different set of interests and entailments to the table, the (perhaps) unfortunate result of which is that some of what our subjects have to say simply doesn't take. Observation, to borrow another term from science studies, is theory-laden: "research starts with a problem. The problem is the result of a conflict between an expectation and an observation which is constituted by the expectation."[17] Does this mean, as Paul K. Feyerabend and Thomas S. Kuhn would have suggested a half century ago, that our worlds are incommensurable—that we will never be able to make sense of our historical actors except as caricatures, projections of our own anxieties? No, not by a long shot.[18] It simply means that we must train ourselves—or *untrain* ourselves, as the case may be—to hear our subjects' cogent expositions through the din of expectation. This is easier than it sounds, for if there is anything that I hope to have achieved by juxtaposing Mencius and Moritz Schlick (1882–1936) (Introduction), or the historiography of astronomy in pre-modern China and Greece (Chapter 4), it is the congruity of certain naturalistic ideals across time and culture.

The one unobservable in particular that I have labored throughout this study to lay bare is our historical subjects' investment in their own ideas of empiricism and progress. Be they neck-deep in the action or narrating it at some historical remove, our subjects couch *everything* in terms drawn from a common pool of precedence and procedure—a cross between Kuhn's "exemplars" and Philip Kitcher's "Legend" (see Section 4.3.2). Legend tells us that it was the ancient sage kings who first intuited the importance of the astral sciences in harmonizing human civilization with the rhythms and signs of Heaven. This,

---

17. Paul K. Feyerabend offers this as a summary of Popperian doctrine in *Against Method*, 3d ed. (London: Verso, 1993), 152.

18. Feyerabend, "Explanation, Reduction, and Empiricism," in *Scientific Explanation, Space, and Time*, ed. Herbert Feigl and Grover Maxwell, Minnesota Studies in the Philosophy of Science, v. 3 (Minneapolis: University of Minnesota Press, 1962), 28–97; Kuhn, *The Structure of Scientific Revolutions*, esp. 150. In the last half century, the incommensurability thesis has been thoroughly explored, reduced, and problematized in the history and philosophy of science. For criticism, see Jerry A. Fodor and Ernest LePore, *Holism: a Shopper's Guide* (Cambridge: Blackwell, 1992); Philip Kitcher, *The Advancement of Science: Science Without Legend, Objectivity Without Illusions* (New York: Oxford University Press, 1993), esp. 90–126.

their most sacred duty, they tasked to capable ministers, setting a cultural pattern (*wen*) for subsequent eras to emulate. In brief, their purpose was "reverently granting the people the seasons" 敬授人時; their method, maintaining "reverent accordance with august Heaven" 欽若昊天.[19] From the blank pages of the early historical period, in which the sagecraft of science suffered numerous setbacks, a line of men begin to enter into view. Linked neither by filiation nor academic lineage, popping up adventitiously across time and space, our subjects weave these men's lives through the common warp of the field of knowledge to which they bequeathed some contribution, whatever their broader moral, political, or cultural standing. It is, more or less, a procession of winners, winners who passed rigorous third-party trials to secure a place for their *li* in the canons of state policy. In a way, this history is cyclic, for even the best of systems find themselves erring and overturned within a matter of decades, inspiring experts to deliberate on the limits of empirical knowledge; but so too, on the other hand, do the selfsame experts promote their own work as insuperable pinnacles of human achievement. When we cut through the rhetoric of salesmanship to see how subjects narrate the history of their field, however, what we find is a consistently linear vision of quantitative and conceptual progress. Looking back, our subjects are often struck by, in Yixing's 一行 (A.D. 673–727) words, "what the ancients did not yet understand" 古人所未達.[20]

To this end, in Chapter 1, I lay out the legend of the astral sciences as culled from classical sources and its subsequent iterations in the early imperial period, discussing how the motivations and actions of our motley cast of characters were framed in terms of remembered sagecraft. Drawing our attention back to the human history of astronomy, I then present a synopsis of the development of *li* in and around the Han from the perspective of both policy and ideas, providing a framework of reference for subsequent chapters. In Chapter 2, I proceed to examine the quantitative and qualitative changes that occurred in planetary models over the entire thousand-year period, giving special consideration to historical actors'

---

19. *Shangshu zhushu* 尚書注疏 (Siku quanshu ed.), 1.8b.

20. *Xin Tang shu* 新唐書 (Zhonghua shuju ed.), 27A.593.

identification and discussion of these changes and their attitudes towards more conservative models preserved in omen literature. What we find is that these changes accord with both modern and ancient concepts of progress and that, in the wake of progress made in *li*, we see experts turn a critical eye to both the models of the past and those that would project non-mathematical norms upon planetary phenomena. In Chapter 3, I then turn to a matter of convention where other civilizations have proven change to be essentially meaningless— the civil calendar—to discuss how Chinese actors persisted in extending the rhetoric of empiricism and progress thereto. Driven by the ideal of "granting the seasons," I discuss experts' fervor for foisting astronomical innovations upon the calendar and the rationale of yet others who saw fit to oppose them. Most importantly, in Chapter 4 I explore how third-century A.D. debaters and their seventh-century historiographer frame and deploy the history of the field to rhetorical ends, paying particular attention to what they circumscribe as legitimate and illegitimate topics in the history of science. Rather than some singular and rigid model, I attempt to show how actors used the common pool of legend as an interpretive resource for advancing a plurality of positions and epistemologies to disparate ends.

Be it in the third or seventh century, our historical subjects profess a history and phi-losophy of science that, were it uttered by our twentieth-century predecessors, we would denounce as scandalously misinformed. Were it not an anachronism, and if this tired word had any meaning left in it, we may well indict them of "positivism." It is bad enough to watch them reduce the history of astronomy to teleologies culminating in their respective days, but we must countenance also the smugness of hindsight with which they look down from their perch to assign praise and blame to those who came before them. In the twentieth century, Joseph Agassi has upbraided this mode of historiography as "scientific ancestor-worship"— an image that I enthusiastically adopt in Chapter 4, albeit working at cross purposes.[21] If we historians of the ancient world are to take seriously our subjects' (religious) ancestor-worship, dare I ask, then what reason do we have to deny them scientific ancestor-worship? Maybe

---

21. *Science and Its History* (Dordrecht: Springer, 2008), 129.

they were misinformed; maybe their beliefs were just so much phlogiston. This, however, does not change the fact that such beliefs still (mis)informed the way that they conceived, practiced, and wrote about their craft. Thus, if there is one argument that I hope to have impressed upon the reader in so many pages it is that, as we have with cultures, and as we have with objects, so too must we reserve a place in any sophisticated history of science for unsophisticated histories and philosophies of science professed by our historical subjects.